MODERN CATHOLICISM

MODERN CATHOLICISM

Vatican II and After

Edited by
ADRIAN HASTINGS

SPCK
London

Oxford University Press
New York

First published in Great Britain 1991
SPCK
Holy Trinity Church
Marylebone Road
London NW1 4DU

First published in the USA 1991
Oxford University Press
200 Madison Avenue
New York 10016

British Library Cataloguing in Publication Data
Modern catholicism: Vatican II and after.
1. Catholic Church. Christian doctrine
I. Hastings, Adrian
230.2
ISBN 0-281-04470-8

Library of Congress Cataloging in Publication Data
Modern Catholicism: Vatican II and after/edited by Adrian Hastings.
p.   cm.   ISBN 0-19-520657-6
1. Catholic Church—History—1965–
2. Vatican Council (2nd: 1962–1965)
3. Catholic Church—Doctrines—History—20th century.
I. Hastings, Adrian.   BX1390.M63 1990   282′.09′045—dc20   90-40624

Printed in the United States of America

CONTENTS

PREFACE

This book has been planned and written to provide an authoritative one-volume guide to the Catholic Church and its developing life in the quarter-century since the close of the Second Vatican Council in December 1965. The Council was so immensely influential upon every side of the life of the Church that a history of the Church in this period can be little other than an account of the way the Council has been understood, implemented, built upon or resisted. But a detailed knowledge of what the Council itself did and said cannot be presumed twenty-five years later, and in consequence the first third of the book contains a compact commentary on its documents as viewed in the light of hindsight.

The writers of this book (with the exception of a single outsider) are committed Catholics, experts in their own areas. Our aim has been to combine objectivity with some degree of informed personal comment. Viewpoints vary somewhat, as is inevitable, but we have avoided extremes and aimed above all at an informative reliability and clarity, the production of a handbook of modern Catholicism which will, we hope, remain of use for many years.

Chapter 12 contains nine regional surveys. It was hoped in this way to cover the entire world, but effectively this did not prove possible in the space available. I much regret, for instance, that Japan, China, Korea and Vietnam are omitted, and also the Middle East. Nevertheless, the pattern of regional diversity in post-conciliar Catholic history is shown clearly enough. For a more detailed nation-by-nation survey, the reader can be referred to Thomas Gannon sj, ed. (1988) *World Catholicism in Transition* (New York, Macmillan; London, Collier Macmillan).

While the total plan of the book has remained my responsibility throughout, its achievement depends upon a very wide range of contributors. I want to thank them all most warmly for their excellent collaboration. Most of all, I must acknowledge how much the book owes to Peter Hebblethwaite, not only for writing seven different sections in it, but still more for much good advice, for sharing his great knowledge of the Vatican so generously, and for working with me in the revision of the complete text. Without the ever competent help of Mrs Ingrid Lawrie, my secretary, throughout the whole process of editing the book would have been in a shambles again and again, both to her and to Chris Maunder who constructed the index at very short notice, my warmest thanks.

Adrian Hastings
Leeds

CONTRIBUTORS

BENNY M. AGUIAR

Benny Aguiar is editor of the Bombay Catholic weekly, *The Examiner,* and Indian correspondent of the London *Tablet.* The author of *A Pope for the World,* a biography of Pope John Paul II, he has been president of the Indian Catholic Press Association and the South Asia Catholic Press Association.

JAMES TUNSTEAD BURTCHAELL csc

James Burtchaell, professor of theology at the University of Notre Dame, Indiana, directs his research principally to issues of systematic theology and Christian ethics. Recent books include *Rachel Weeping and Other Essays on Abortion* and *The Giving and Taking of Life: Essays Ethical.* Forthcoming is his *Leitourgia: Public Services and Offices in the Earliest Christian Communities.*

THEODORE DAVEY cp

Theodore Davey is head of the department of pastoral theology, Heythrop College, University of London, a position he has held for fifteen years. During this time he has been involved in the care of marriage, particularly in the Church's marriage tribunals, and he has latterly been concerned with the pastoral care of people with AIDS.

ENRIQUE DUSSEL

Enrique Dussel is an Argentinian living in Mexico. He has doctorates from Madrid (philosophy), the Sorbonne (history) and Freiburg (theology). He is the author of *A History of the Church in Latin America* (1981) and co-ordinator of the Working Commission for Church History in the Third World.

GERALD P. FOGARTY sj

Gerald Fogarty has been professor of religious studies in the University of Virginia since 1975. He previously taught at Woodstock College and Fordham University. His books include *The Vatican and the American Hierarchy from 1870 to 1965* and *American Catholic Biblical Scholarship: A History from the Early Republic to Vatican II.*

MICHAEL GAINE

Michael Gaine was ordained priest in 1954. He served as secretary/chaplain to two Archbishops of Westminster, Godfrey and Heenan. Head of the sociology department in Christ's College (now part of the Liverpool Institute of Higher Education) for twenty-four years, he is now back in parish life. He is chairperson of the Movement for the Ordination of Married Men, and director of the Liverpool Institute of Socio-Religious Studies (LISS).

JOSEPH GREMILLION

Joseph Gremillion was executive secretary of the Vatican's Justice and Peace Council, 1967–74. He is director of the Institute for Pastoral and Social Ministry, Notre Dame University, where he is now scholar-in-residence. Among his books are *The Gospel of Peace and Justice* (1976) and its sequel, *The Catholic World Church Becoming* (1990).

ADRIAN HASTINGS

Adrian Hastings has been professor of theology in the University of Leeds, England, since 1985, having previously been professor of religious studies in the University of Zimbabwe. Among his books are *A Concise Guide to the Documents of the Second Vatican Council* (2 volumes, 1968), *A History of English Christianity, 1920–1985* (1986), and *African Catholicism* (1989).

MARGARET HEBBLETHWAITE

Margaret Hebblethwaite is author of *The Theology of Penance, Motherhood and God* and *Finding God in All Things – Praying with St Ignatius*. She has been giving retreats in daily life since 1981, and has experience of prison chaplaincy and parish work. She lives in Oxford with her husband, Peter.

PETER HEBBLETHWAITE

Peter Hebblethwaite has been Vatican affairs reporter for *The National Catholic Reporter* since 1979. He reported the final session of the Council for the British Jesuit magazine, *The Month*, which he edited 1967–74. His books include *The Year of the Three Popes, John XXIII: Pope of the Council* (in the US *John XXIII: Shepherd of the Modern World*) and *In the Vatican*. He is completing a biography of Pope Paul VI.

DENIS E. HURLEY OMI

Denis Hurley joined the Oblates of Mary Immaculate in 1932, trained in Ireland and Rome, and was ordained priest in 1939. He was ordained bishop as vicar apostolic of Natal in 1947 and became archbishop of Durban in 1951. He attended all sessions of the Second Vatican Council and served as a member of the Commission on Seminaries, Studies and Christian Education.

ELIZABETH ISICHEI

Elizabeth Isichei has been reader in world religions at Victoria University, New Zealand, since 1985. Her first two books dealt with the early Church and Victorian Quakerism. She obtained an Oxford doctorate, held a postdoctorate fellowship at Oxford, and then taught in African universities for sixteen years. Her books include *A History of the Igbo People, A History of Nigeria* and *Entirely for God, a life of Michael Iwene Tansi*.

PATRICK A. KALILOMBE M AFR

Patrick Kalilombe is the former Catholic bishop of Lilongwe, Malawi. He has been lecturing in Third World Theologies at Selly Oak Colleges, Birmingham, England, since 1982 and is presently co-director of the Centre for Black and White Christian Partnership there. He was educated in Malawi, Tunisia, Rome and Berkeley. He was delegate to the Synod of Bishops in Rome in 1974. His publications include *Christ's Church in Lilongwe Today and Tomorrow* (1973) and *From Outstations to Small Christian Communities* (1984).

AIDAN KAVANAGH OSB

Aidan Kavanagh is a monk of the Benedictine Archabbey of St Meinrad. He teaches liturgics at the Divinity School, Yale University, where he was appointed dean in 1989. His books include *The Concept of Eucharistic Memorial in Thomas Cranmer, Elements of Rite, The Shape of Baptism, On Liturgical Theology* and *Confirmation: Origins and Reform*.

DERMOT KEOGH

Dermot Keogh is a lecturer in the department of modern history, University College, Cork, Ireland. He is the author of *The Vatican, The Bishops and Irish Politics, 1919–1939* (1985), *Ireland and Europe 1919–1948* (1988), and editor of *Church and Politics in Latin America* (1989) and *Central America: Human Rights and United States Foreign Policy* (1985).

JAN KERKHOFS SJ

Jan Kerkhofs entered the Society of Jesus in 1942. He was professor of pastoral theology in the Catholic University of Louvain, Belgium, from 1959 to 1989, and is now emeritus professor there. From 1963 to 1981 he was director of Pro Mundi Vita (Brussels). He was initiator and first chairman of the European Value Systems Study Group. He has published widely.

F.J. LAISHLEY

Joseph Laishley has taught systematic theology at Heythrop College in the University of London since 1969 and is currently head of the department of Christian doctrine. Most recently he has contributed three articles on repression and liberation in the Church to the *Heythrop Journal*.

MARY JOHN MANANZAN OSB

Mary John Mananzan is dean of college and academic vice-president of St Scholastica's College, Manila, Philippines. She is also founder and present director of the Institute of Women's Studies. She is national chairperson of GABRIELA (a national federation of women's organizations), is on the executive board of the International Association of Mission Studies, and on the board of editorial directors of *Concilium*. Her postgraduate studies were undertaken at Münster, Germany, and the Gregorian University, Rome (PhD in linguistic philosophy).

C.J. MAUNDER

C.J. Maunder is currently working on a PhD thesis at Leeds University, on Marian apparitions. He is also a part-time teacher in theology and religious studies and lives in an ecumenical community at All Hallows, Leeds.

RICHARD P. McBRIEN

Richard McBrien is Crowley-O'Brien-Walter professor of theology and chairman of the department of theology, University of Notre Dame, USA. He is past president of the Catholic Theological Society of America and winner of its John Courtney Murray award (1976). He is the author of *Catholicism* (1980), *Caesar's Coin: Religion and Politics in America* (1987) and *Ministry: A Theological, Pastoral Handbook* (1987). He is priest of the archdiocese of Hartford, Connecticut.

V. ALAN McCLELLAND

Alan McClelland is dean of the school of education in the University of Hull, England. He has written extensively on nineteenth-century ecclesiastical and educational themes, including major studies of Manning and Roman Catholic higher education. He is currently researching the history of Roman Catholicism in England and Wales, 1935–75.

JOHN McDADE SJ

John McDade lectures in systematic theology at Heythrop College, University of London, and is editor of *The Month*.

ENDA McDONAGH

Enda McDonagh is professor of moral theology at St Patrick's College, Maynooth, Ireland. His most recent publications include *The Gracing of Society* (1989), *The Small Hours of Belief* (1989) and *Between Chaos and New Creation* (1987).

ROBERT MURRAY SJ

Robert Murray was ordained in 1959. He has been teaching at Heythrop College, University of London, from 1963 (since 1970 in the University of London). He has written *Symbols of Church and Kingdom: A Study in Early Syriac Tradition* (1975) and many articles on ecclesiology, Bible, Syriac and Jewish literature.

DONALD NICHOLL

Donald Nicholl was educated at Balliol College, Oxford. He taught history at Keele University, 1953–74, was professor of history and religious studies, University of California, 1974–80, rector of the Ecumenical Institute for Theological Research, Jerusalem, 1981–5 and senior research fellow, Multi-Faith Unit, Selly Oak, Birmingham, 1985–8. His publications include *Recent Thought in Focus* (1951), *Holiness* (1981) and *Testing of Hearts* (1989).

EDWARD NORMAN

Edward Norman is a historian and Anglican priest who, after thirty years in Cambridge as a university lecturer and dean of Peterhouse, left in 1987 to become chaplain at a Church of England college of education. He has written historical works in a number of areas, among them his recent *Roman Catholicism in England* (1986), and has been a frequent broadcaster in Britain and the United States.

LADISLAS ÖRSY SJ

Ladislas Örsy studied at Louvain (theology), at Oxford (civil law) and in Rome (canon law). He taught at the Gregorian University in Rome, at Fordham University in New York City, and at present he is professor of canon law in the Catholic University of America, Washington DC. His most recent publications include *Marriage in Canon Law* and *The Church: Learning and Teaching*.

TIMOTHY C. POTTS

Timothy Potts was educated at Liverpool University, Ushaw and Oscott Colleges, St Benet's Hall and Balliol College, Oxford. He has been a lecturer in philosophy in the University of Leeds since 1962 and is the author of *Conscience in Medieval Philosophy* (1980).

WALTER H. PRINCIPE csb

Walter Principe CSB, MSD, FRSC is professor at the Pontifical Institute of Mediaeval Studies and the University of Toronto. He was formerly a member of the International Theological Commission, is President of the Catholic Theological Society of America, and an official member of the Lutheran Catholic Dialogue in the United States.

ROSEMARY RADFORD RUETHER

Rosemary Radford Ruether is the Georgia Harkness professor of applied theology at the Garrett Theological Seminary in Evanston, Illinois. She has also taught at Harvard Divinity School and been guest lecturer in the Universities of Lund, Sweden and Cape Town, South Africa. She is author or editor of twenty-one books, the most recent of which are *Contemporary Roman Catholicism: Crises and Challenges* and *The Wrath of Jonah: Religious Nationalism and the Israeli–Palestinian Conflict*.

SANDRA M. SCHNEIDERS ihm

Sandra Schneiders, a member of the Sisters, Servants of the Immaculate Heart of Mary since 1955, is professor of New Testament studies and spirituality at the Jesuit School of Theology and the Graduate Theological Union in Berkeley, California. She is author of *New Wineskins: Re-imagining Religious Life Today* (1986) and *Women and the Word: the Gender of God in the New Testament and the Spirituality of Women* (1986).

AYLWARD SHORTER

Aylward Shorter is an anthropologist and missiologist who has taught in Catholic seminaries and institutes in East Africa. He has been a consultant of the council for Interreligious Dialogue and is now president of the Missionary Institute, London. Among his books are *Theology of Mission* (1972) and *Towards a Theology of Inculturation* (1988).

GRAZYNA SIKORSKA

Grazyna Sikorska was born in Katowice in Polish Silesia. After being awarded an M.Sc. at the University of Katowice, she came to England in 1974 to continue her scientific research. In 1979 she joined the staff at Keston College, the centre for the study of religion in communist lands, researching all aspects of religious life in her native country. She is the author of *A Martyr for the Truth* and *Light and Life Renewal in Poland*.

TOM STRANSKY, Paulist

Tom Stransky is a former member of the Vatican Secretariat for Promoting Christian Unity and president, Paulist Fathers. At present he is rector of the Tantur Ecumenical Institute for Theological Studies, Jerusalem, and a member of the wcc/rcc Joint Working Group.

ROBERT F. TAFT sj

Robert Taft is professor of Eastern liturgy at the Pontifical Oriental Institute, Rome, visiting professor at the University of Notre Dame, editor of *Orientalia Christiana Analecta*, and consultor for liturgy of the Vatican Congregation for the Oriental Churches. He has written numerous scholarly publications, including *The Great Entrance* (1978), *Beyond East and West* (1984) and *The Liturgy of the Hours in East and West* (1986).

GEORGE H. TAVARD

George Tavard is professor emeritus at the Methodist Theological School in Ohio, resides at Assumption Center, Brighton, Massachusetts, and is the author of more than forty books, notably *Holy Writ or Holy Church: The Crisis of the Protestant Reformation* (1959), *The Quest for Catholicity: The Development of High Church Anglicanism* (1963), *Poetry and Contemplation in St John of the Cross* (1988), and *A Review of Anglican Orders: The Problem – and the Solution* (1990).

KATHLEEN WALSH

Kathleen Walsh is adult education officer, East London Pastoral Area, Diocese of Westminster, and part-time lecturer in religious and women's studies, Centre for Extra-Mural Studies, University of London. Her writings include contributions to Catholic and ecumenical publications on child and adult religious education, laity (especially women in the Church) and feminist theology.

MICHAEL J. WALSH

Michael Walsh is librarian of Heythrop College, University of London, and formerly editor of *The Month*. He is the author of a number of books on the history of the Church, including *The Vatican City State* (1983), *Roots of Christianity* (1986; in the United States, *The Triumph of the Meek*) and *The Secret World of Opus Dei* (1989).

BRIAN WICKER

Brian Wicker was formerly principal of Fircroft College of Adult Education, Birmingham, and is currently vice-chair of Pax Christi (British section) and sits on the Pax Christi International Commission of Security and Disarmament. He holds degrees in literature, philosophy and war studies. His publications include *Culture and Liturgy* (1963), *The Story-Shaped World* (1975) and *Nuclear Deterrence: What Does the Church Teach?* (1985).

MICHAEL E. WILLIAMS

Michael Williams was ordained priest for the Archdiocese of Birmingham in 1947. He taught theology at the English College, Lisbon, from 1953 to 1967 and was head of studies in theology at Trinity and All Saints' College, Leeds, from 1967 until retirement in 1987. He was a member of the Bishops' Conference's Theological Commission, 1974–83, and has been UK representative on OCIC since 1978. He is the author of histories of the English College, Rome and St Alban's College, Valladolid.

BASIC BIBLIOGRAPHY AND ABBREVIATIONS

Most sections of this book include their own select bibliographies, provided as a list for further reading in particular areas. Over and above these we list here some major works relating to the Council and fairly easily available.

There are a number of English translations of the documents of the Council. We have here mostly used the edition produced by Austin Flannery OP, *Vatican Council II: The Conciliar and Post-conciliar Documents* (New York, Costello Publishing Company; Dublin, Dominican Publications, 1975) as this includes many post-conciliar documents up to 1974, and there is a second volume, *Vatican Council II: More Post-conciliar Documents* (1983), including some as late as 1982. We refer to these as Flannery 1 and 2. The volume edited by Walter M. Abbott SJ, *The Documents of Vatican II* (London, Geoffrey Chapman, 1966) has also been used; we refer to this as Abbott.

A new edition in English of the decrees of all the ecumenical councils up to and including Vatican II, a translation of the standard *Conciliorum Oecumenicorum Decreta*, ed. G. Alberigo and others (3rd edition, Bologna) has just been published (too late for our own use) as *Decrees of the Ecumenical Councils*, ed. Norman P. Tanner SJ (London, Sheed and Ward; Georgetown University Press, 1989).

We refer to *Enchiridion Vaticanum* (Edizione Dehoniane, Bologna) as EV (plus number of volume), to G. Caprile, *Il Concilio Vaticano* as Caprile (and volume), the *Osservatore Romano* as OS, and the four volumes of Xavier Rynne's *Letters from Vatican City* (London, Faber and Faber, New York, Farrar, Straus & Co, 1963–6) as XR (and volume).

The standard commentary on the documents of the Council written in the later 1960s is the five-volume work edited by Herbert Vorgrimler, *Commentary on the Documents of Vatican II* (English edition, Herder and Herder, New York; Burns and Oates, London, 1967–9). We refer to it as Vorgrimler (plus volume).

Other major recent works in English include: Peter Hebblethwaite, *John XXIII: Pope of the Council* (London, Geoffrey Chapman, 1984; published in the United States as *John XXIII: Shepherd of the Modern World*, New York, Doubleday); eds Guiseppe Alberigo, Jean-Pierre Jossua and others, *The Reception of Vatican II* (The Catholic University of America Press, Washington; Burns and Oates, England, 1987), which we refer to as Alberigo and Jossua; Rene Latourelle, *Vatican II: Assessments and Perspectives* (New York, Paulist Press, 1988); ed. Alberic Stacpoole, *Vatican II by those who were there* (London, Geoffrey Chapman, 1986), which we refer to as Stacpoole; ed. Thomas Gannon SJ *World Catholicism in Transition* (New York, Macmillan; London, Collier Macmillan, 1988).

1

CATHOLIC HISTORY FROM VATICAN I TO JOHN PAUL II

ADRIAN HASTINGS

In 1989 much of the world was celebrating the 200th anniversary of the start of the French Revolution. The modern history of the Catholic Church has been immensely affected by that chain of events. Institutionally it was shaken almost to pieces, and certainly out of the torpor that had descended upon it in the long aftermath of the Counter Reformation and the seventeenth-century wars of religion, by the reverberations of the Revolution with their deeply anti-religious and anti-traditional note. For years the pope was in exile from Rome, most religious orders and seminaries were closed in the Mediterranean heartlands of the Church, and missionary work overseas was effectively suspended.

All the more striking was the subsequent nineteenth-century Catholic revival centred upon the reign of Pius IX and the First Vatican Council of 1870. It was an extraordinarily effective revival, in pastoral, missionary and institutional terms, equally effective in such varied situations as northern France, Ireland, the United States and Africa. The old religious orders were reinvigorated and hundreds of new ones – especially orders of teaching and nursing sisters – founded. In intellectual terms the predominant note of the revival was undoubtedly counter-revolutionary, despite the quite influential presence of Catholic 'liberals' and modernizers in many lands. But the more the revival got under way, the more it responded to Rome's own ethos, the less accommodating it was in regard to the values of either Protestantism or modern secular, liberal society.

Modern Roman Catholicism was shaped in the age of Pius IX in terms of the highest of papal doctrines, Marian devotions and a steadily growing organizational centralization upon Rome. From Pius IX on, every pope became the centre of a considerable personality cult made possible by the railway and, later on, the modern media. Thomist theology and philosophy were laid down in a rather ossified form as the normative Catholic intellectual system, drawn from the Middle Ages and therefore free of any taint of modern influence. Regional variations – Gallican or otherwise – were disapproved, whether liturgical, theological or pastoral. The definition of papal infallibility (even in its rather restrained terms) and of papal supremacy over the Church by the Council of 1870 merely formalized the pinnacle of a far larger system, theoretical and institutional, of monarchy.

The anti-modernist campaign of Pius X and his Secretary of State, Cardinal

Merry del Val, pushed further the theological and intellectual implications of this radical otherness of the Church in regard to the whole process of Western society's post-revolutionary modernization. Although society as a whole was very far from accepting the extremes of revolutionary order and, of course, most of Europe, Britain above all, had fought for years to suppress it, the painfulness of the Church's early experience of the Revolution helped to keep it profoundly opposed even to the Revolution's more moderate implications, ones increasingly accepted by European society as a whole.

At the same time it must be stressed that the ecclesiastical character of 'ultramontanism' (the dominant, Rome-centred, theory and practice of Catholicism in this period) was not a mere post-Revolution reaction: it was the direct heir of medieval papalist and Counter-Reformation Catholicism. The centralizing and autocratic nature of papal monarchy as it had developed after the Gregorian Reform of the eleventh century was probably the principal underlying problem behind the sixteenth-century Reformation. While the subsequent Council of Trent greatly strengthened the moral, pastoral and even intellectual life of the Church, it was reluctant to accept any part of the Protestant doctrinal and institutional critique. On the contrary, the lines of division were hardened between the two Western Christian camps, even on the more pastoral issues. To name but three: Protestants everywhere insisted upon the necessity of allowing the laity to worship in the vernacular, giving them the cup in communion, and allowing the clergy to marry. Rome steadily rejected any compromise upon all three and continued to do so into the twentieth century. It was very probably that rejection – over essentially non-doctrinal, but pastorally central, issues – rather than fundamental theological disagreements which rendered the sixteenth-century schism truly and practically irresolvable. The outcome in the wider area of Church organization was that while Protestantism surrendered more and more to nationalism, Erastianism and/or fragmentation, Catholicism held these forces in check through clericalism, centralization and an enhanced uniformity.

The nineteenth-century Catholic revival reinforced these, and other, medieval and anti-Protestant characteristics. The ultramontanist Church of the post-Vatican I era grew immensely strong in the conviction, loyalty and discipline of its members, especially the spirituality, unquestioned obedience and hard work of its religious orders. The renewal, after the dreary state of the early years of the century, seemed a miracle in itself and was felt to be one. Freed, furthermore, after 1870 from the embarrassment of the papal states and continually reinforced by its growing missionary societies, the Church was manifestly expanding in number and influence all through the first half of the twentieth century, when other large Churches were only too clearly declining rather than advancing. All this was a miracle which was deeply and self-consciously anti-accommodationist, anti-*aggiornamento* one might well say. One must never forget this long, almost glorious, background to the discontents, 'conservative' and 'progressive', of the post-Vatican II years. The final climax of the old regime may be seen in the twenty-year reign of Pius XII (1939–58), a pope at the time most profoundly revered. The model had been increasingly internationalized as the churches of Latin America, Asia and

Africa were given a more active role within it – but then in principle it always had been internationalist, and even in class terms egalitarian, the greatest of all ultramontanes being the socially radical English Cardinal Manning. Beneath the surface, the model in Pius XII's time had not greatly changed even if communism had, understandably enough, replaced either Protestantism or liberalism as the chief immediate foe. The Church remained a supernatural fortress set against the world, its walls manned night and day by the committed, its lonely leader almost an oracle of heavenly wisdom.

Yet beneath the surface many other things had been happening too. In an age in which the Church was living and functioning largely within more or less liberal, democratic societies and in which defence mechanisms such as the *Index* of forbidden books had ceased effectively to function, it was no longer possible to insulate Catholic society mentally from the world around it. Nor did Catholics for the most part wish to be so insulated. The crisis of modernism had arisen at the beginning of the century as a consequence of the profound, perhaps too rapid, infiltration of Catholic institutions and consciousness by the scholarly methods and intellectual attitudes and presuppositions which had developed earlier in predominantly Protestant and liberal milieus. While the anti-modernist purge put this process back a generation, it could not stop it re-emerging, especially in the most advanced areas of Catholic culture in northern Europe.

The growth of the liturgical movement, the lay apostolate, biblical scholarship, the need for Catholics to participate in democratic politics at least in order to protect Catholic rights, the urgency of collaborating locally with non-Catholics in opposition to Nazism: all this and much else had produced a profoundly altered consciousness within the more wide-awake parts of the Church by the later years of Pius XII's reign. The post-medieval, ultramontane model was simply not proving workable in either intellectual or social terms. The French Dominican, Yves Congar, perhaps the Church's greatest prophet of the age, demonstrated with learning, vigour and clarity that Catholicism had much to learn from Protestantism and much to reform in itself. The paradox of Pius XII's reign was the acceptance of chunks of a new model – the encouragement of modern biblical scholarship in the encyclical *Divino Afflante Spiritu*, of participant liturgical reform in *Mediator Dei*, of an increasingly multi-faceted lay apostolate – together with slightly ineffectual but still painful attempts to silence Congar and many others (the Jesuit Teilhard de Chardin most of all), the signing of highly reactionary concordats with Spain and Portugal, and an even greater stress on Marian devotion (culminating not only in the definition of the Assumption in 1950 but in the 'Marian Year' of 1954). All in all, an ever-growing institutional centralization was matched by a burgeoning theological pluralization. Congar had in point of fact expressed himself cautiously enough, yet several of his books were proscribed. In retrospect, one can see far better than even he could see at the time how deeply the logic of the 'New Theology', biblical and historical rather than scholastic, was bound to challenge the whole shape of the contemporary Church and the way it perceived orthodoxy. The denunciations of dangerous new ideas in the 1950 encyclical *Humani Generis* are intelligible enough, but by now they were

3

almost bound to be ineffective, and as the intellectual viability of ultramontanism crumbled, the now unprotected power structure surrounding the papal monarchy came more and more into open and criticizable view.

Whether Pope John quite saw the inevitable implications of his great *démarche* when, in 1959, he announced the calling of a general Council, does not matter very much. Once he had called it, appealed to *aggiornamento*, banned anathemas, included observers of other Churches within its deliberations, and allowed it to have its head against the warnings of the guardians of the old order such as Ottaviani and Ruffini, the consequences were inevitable: the foundations of many hundred years were going to be rocked upon every side. This volume is an attempt to review both the achievements of the Council and its impact upon the next quarter-century. The underlying cause of the achievement was not really Pope John, the bishops or even the theologians themselves. It was much more the sheer vitality and range of committed ability, lay and clerical, present in the Church at that time and just waiting for a new lead. The Catholic Church in the age of Mother Teresa and Barbara Ward, of Julius Nyerere and Lech Walesa, of Oscar Romero and Pedro Arrupe was a Church at the height of its confidence and its ability to relate to the world in a mood of inspiring solidarity. This was a great age of Catholic history and the importance of the Council can only be appreciated if the strength of the Church it triggered into a spiral of reform – a strength that had steadily grown beneath the surface in the pontificate of Pius XII – is well appreciated.

What is at once important to stress about the Council is the lasting caution, indeed conservatism, of the majority of its members and of their consultants, as much as of the curia and the popes. It is customary to divide the Council into a 'conservative' minority and a 'progressive' majority, but such a description can be profoundly misleading. Almost all were conservatives if compared with their contemporaries in most other Western Churches, in secular society or even with their own younger clergy. The division might more accurately be described as one between 'reactionary conservatives' and 'liberal conservatives' with hardly half-a-dozen genuine radicals in the Council chamber (Archbishop Roberts was never once permitted to speak!). It was for this reason that the Council's final documents remained so ambivalent. Nevertheless, the dynamic of four sessions did have a remarkable effect not unassisted by the fact that when Cardinal Montini became Paul VI, this meant that one of the most thoughtful and determined of the moderately progressive conservatives was now pope. Certainly the third and fourth sessions approved of texts and ideas that it would be hard to imagine would have appealed to many of the bishops before the Council began.

This dynamic could not indeed have developed as it did without the very considerable influence behind the scenes, particularly in the preparation of documents between sessions, of leading consultants whose theology was indeed far beyond that of any but a handful of bishops: Congar, Rahner, Philips, Chenu, Courtney Murray among others. The Council became a genuinely learning process, and once the name of the game had been defined as *aggiornamento*, once ecumenical understanding and co-operation with other Christians had been moved from the presupposition of 'dangerous' to that of

'Christian' and 'highly desirable', there developed for a while a new logic which could not easily be denied. Cautious as the Council's immediate formulations almost always were, the outcome was that the Latin liturgy was replaced by the vernacular, the cup was offered to the laity, married men would at least be ordained to the diaconate, Protestant Bible societies were to be worked with, the modern world was to be sympathized with rather than condemned. To an old and faithful servant of the ultramontane papacy such as Ottaviani, it was all the most absolute madness. Indeed, if the Bible was to be taken so very seriously, separated brethren listened to attentively, the world served and precisely in its contemporaneous form, all sorts of other things were bound to start falling into new places too, places extremely different from those provided by ultramontanism.

The ecclesiastically most delicate application of this lay in the area of collegiality. Vatican I immensely strengthened the theoretical authority of the papacy, and this had now passed into the common mind of Catholics lay and clerical alike. It said nothing whatsoever of any correlative power of the episcopate. Bishop Goss of Liverpool at the time declared disgustedly that 'bishops who went to Rome as princes of the household to confer with their august Father will return like satraps dispatched to their provinces'. Perhaps that seems a little severe, but in practice bishops were subjected henceforth to an ever-closer Roman control and appointment system, while being offered no theology to ground any distinct authority. It had been intended at Vatican I to complement the papal definitions with something much wider, but pressure from Franco-Prussian conflict combined, maybe, with a lack of Roman interest in a larger agenda, prevented anything further from being said.

The assertion of a doctrine of episcopal 'collegiality' as expressive of the Church's ministerial leadership, in continuity with the first group of twelve apostles, was far removed from a theology of papal 'monarchy' such as had long dominated Roman ecclesiology. A collegial model looked both more scriptural and more ecumenical – as well as being more suited to a post-monarchical world – even if bolstered up by a not-too-sound and rather fundamentalist interpretation of a selection of New Testament and patristic texts. It horrified the Council's more conservative wing for, despite all protestations that it was complementary to and not contradictory of Vatican I's teaching on papal primacy, it did inevitably suggest a remarkably different overall understanding of how the Church should be governed. Chapter 3 of the Constitution on the Church, spelling out the doctrine of collegiality, was theologically and dogmatically at the very heart of Vatican II's debate and contribution to Catholic self-understanding. Indeed its formulation provided the theological undergirding for having a Council at all and not leaving everything to the pope to decide alone. But while collegiality was undoubtedly accepted in theory (subject to the circumscribing commentary of the *nota praevia*), it was provided with no effective form of implementation outside a full Council, even if Paul VI's establishment of an advisory episcopal synod to be called regularly was in practice an attempt to provide some ongoing form for collegial responsibility.

The Council allowed a much increased use of the vernacular in the liturgy. It

5

never, however, approved the celebration of the Mass wholly in the vernacular, Eucharistic prayer and all. This was Pope Paul's decision two years after the Council was over. The Council permitted the laity to communicate with the cup on a very few occasions. It was the post-conciliar Church that came increasingly to recognize this as the norm, at least for smaller congregations. The point is that the Council took decisions that appeared revolutionary enough in the context of Catholic life as it had hitherto been, but that, only a few years later, seemed instead as rather cautious half-measures requiring very considerable extension.

A theoretical stress upon biblical study, an active laity, the reunion of Christians, and a positive commitment to the service of the world in its cultural, social and economic needs, coupled with an absence of guidance as to how all this was to be done and how far one could go in these various directions, led both to a state of real popular enthusiasm but also, almost inevitably, to tension and conflict. In some areas, most notably the liturgical and the ecumenical, Rome did get off to a good start in providing directives of a sort that would carry confidence at least temporarily; even here, however, there was the inherent problem that a body of directives implied the establishment of a stable state (e.g. in ecumenical relations), while the reality was in fact necessarily more fluid. Once one set of directives, however good, had been implemented, a new set of possibilities necessarily unfolded. In the immediate post-conciliar phase (1966–7), Rome remained not far off the *avant-garde* of progress, but once the first round of directives was complete and the curia firmly back in control, the conservative tendency regained the upper hand in the centre while progressive tendencies were still growing stronger in many a periphery. In general, people not actually involved in it saw the Council as the beginning of a new ecclesial era rather than a way of concluding some long-standing issues and leaving it at that, yet the Council's documents remain for nearly all Catholics the most authoritative Church teaching of this century, beside which even papal encyclicals have comparatively slight standing. They stand above and beyond any particular attempt, papal or otherwise, definitively to interpret them.

In this situation three recognizable approaches to interpretation can nevertheless be distinguished. The first is that of many Catholics who already thought the Council a strange and almost unnecessary development. They have, so far as is possible, wished to interpret the texts within a context of earlier teaching and pre-conciliar practice, against which the Council was, to a considerable extent, deliberately reacting; yet, as the texts even as finally formulated remain to a considerable extent a jumble deriving from different hands and including material composed substantially before the Council began, there is much in them to countenance such a viewpoint. The second is that of people, and they included Pope Paul himself and most of the Council fathers, who greatly welcomed what had been done and desired its effective implementation, but saw it as all in all a daring and radical reform which had gone beyond anything they sought when the Council began and which did not require significant further development. They found it hard to cope with the implications of the objective open-endedness of the Council's vast range of teaching. Once the phase of immediate implementation was passed, this group came little by little to realign itself with many in the first group against whom they had in the conciliar years themselves taken quite a clear stand: a new *status quo* must be achieved if the Church was not to be upset by ceaseless change and debate. A third approach was adopted by a small minority of bishops but an ever-larger circle of theologians, young priests ordained round about the time of the Council and lay activists, all far more aware of the objective inadequacy of the conciliar documents as they stood: inadequate precisely because their composers had been over-anxious not to make any sharp break with pre-conciliar practice. They now seemed too cautious, too reluctant to admit to the most defective aspects of the post-medieval Catholic tradition, too little aware of the real situation in the Church of the southern hemisphere (whose voice was heard remarkably little in the Council's debates).

On two crucial issues in particular the Council had, anyway, been prevented by the pope from deliberating: the morality of artificial contraception and the obligation of celibacy for all priests of the Western rite. It was these two issues that would remain as seemingly irremovable areas of tension across the next twenty years. The pre-conciliar Church was, publicly at least, remarkably homogeneous in opinion. The conciliar debate of the early 1960s was essentially a debate not only within the walls of St Peter's, but throughout the Church. When the Council ended in Rome, the wider debate did not, though the pope, the curia and, indeed, many of the bishops, found this hard to comprehend. It obviously could not end, at least until a coherent new form of Catholicism had gelled in practice. After twenty-five years this has still not happened.

The Catholic Church can be, and is, now seen by its members in extraordinarily different ways. For some, the Council was no more than a prudent but much misunderstood attempt to update a few relatively minor matters. Confidence in an infallible papacy remains here undiminished. The Church's inner spirit, organization and theology need be little different in the 1990s from how they were under Pius XII in the 1950s. For others, that is quite impossible. For them, the shift required, and in part even achieved, was theological rather than administrative: the Council represented a decisive, if still partial, move away from a one-sided theology which had prevailed in the Roman communion across the Middle Ages, the Counter Reformation and ultramontanism. The role of the papacy itself now requires basic reinterpretation. The Council effectively recognized that in a number of important matters Protestants had been right and Catholics wrong. The theological implications of such a recognition were profound, and required far more than a change in regulations. Furthermore, in this view, the world of the twentieth century again necessitated a quite extraordinarily different Church and theology from that appropriate in the past. In this context, issues dividing Catholics and Protestants themselves became almost trivial. If the Council did a good deal to catch up with the agenda of the Council of Trent, it did rather little to face the real agenda confronting the whole human and Christian community in the last decades of this century.

While in 1990 it is clear which of these views is currently favoured in Rome, it is far from clear which will finally prevail. It is, however, now possible, historiographically, to divide the twenty-five years following the Council into two distinctly different eras – that of Paul VI and that of John Paul II. The central event of the former's pontificate can hardly fail to be seen as *Humanae Vitae* in 1968, central because its publication marked a watershed separating the first years of enthusiasm, of an optimistic post-conciliar implementation in which Rome and leading Catholic theologians were still working more or less hand in hand (as they had done in the latter years of the Council) from the far more contestatory and unsure later period. Paul VI was from then on unable to identify himself with the 'progressives' in a way he had managed hitherto. Over contraception, but on much else too, his underlying Roman curial temper proved finally decisive. Yet he could never identify himself with a counter-attack either. He remained too personally committed to the values of the Council and to a certain vaguely liberal spirit. Hence he satisfied neither side within an increasingly polarized Church. He never penned another encyclical and his final decade remained one of conservative indecision rather than of reaction. But as he aged, the curia showed itelf once again to be more in control than the pope, the very curia which he had himself attempted, if with all possible politeness, to reform.

If today we can see better than we could at the time the agonized grandeur of the figure of Pope Paul, the one almost 'liberal' pope of modern times, we can also see how deeply uncertain was the Church he left behind him and – after twelve years – we begin too to be able to assess in its very different character the pontificate of John Paul II. Karol Wojtyla was not a 'liberal' in any Western sense, though he too may briefly have thought of himself in such terms in student days. A man of immense physical vigour, intellectual confidence and moral force, as naturally extrovert as was Paul painfully introvert, his decisive experience was not that of the Council (which he did attend), nor of the Western Christian's attempt to reshape the gospel when faced with the blandishments of agnostic affluence, still less was it any deep experience of the struggles of the third world; instead, it was that of the Church's singularly successful, no-nonsense resistance to communism in Poland: a combination of old-fashioned pieties, unquestioned doctrinal certainties, down-to-earth preoccupation with basic human rights, and a dose of sheer populism. He had little time for the confusion that the Council had appeared to generate in many parts of the Church. Despite his many languages, he also had little sense of cultures other than his own. Many aspects of the post-conciliar debate seemed simply, and not surprisingly, to have passed him by – they seemed to him but the fashionable irrelevancies of a West that had had it rather too good, yet dangerous temptations too. His was a world in which sacred and secular, clergy and laity, men and women, were all to be sharply separated in a way that neither modern secular society, nor those in the West attempting to rethink Christianity in relation to that society, could possibly accept. It would be gravely mistaken to understate the depth of difference between John Paul II and the general viewpoint of what one may call the Western Catholic *avant-garde*, the post-conciliar network of theologians, religious and committed laity. The pope came nearest to a characteristic post-conciliar viewpoint over social justice; here indeed his major encyclicals could be regarded as constituting a high-water mark in 'progressive' concern, even adopting elements of a Marxist analysis beyond any of his predecessors; he was also, very moderately, ecumenical, though he showed little interest in the theological implications of an ecumenical agenda. However, in his central theology and sense of the nature of religion in general and Catholicism in particular, he remained extraordinarily faithful to the papacy of Pius XII during which he had been trained and ordained.

Elected in 1978, it is hardly surprising that John Paul should see his task as the re-establishment of order and confidence on pretty traditional lines, though his charismatic personality shown forth throughout the world in an unending series of exciting international tours for a time almost concealed what was going on. Different as his experience was from that of the curia, he found in it an ally far more than had Paul with his long curial background. But he found other allies as well, everyone in fact who had been uneasy with the extent to which traditional Catholicism had been of late put into question. Even the extreme, and already almost schismatic, group of neo-traditionalists led by Archbishop Lefebvre from Ecône was very nearly reconciled. If the Jesuits had been the greatest implementers of post-conciliar renewal in the Pauline era, Opus Dei would shortly become John Paul's most reliable institutional arm. While the papacy of Pope Paul had remained uncomfortably unidentified with either 'progressive' or 'conservative', that of John Paul became increasingly closely tied to the latter, and at times in a state of not much less than guerrilla war with the 'magisterium' of the Church's principal theologians: a truly strange position for a pope to be in. In one way all this undoubtedly strengthened the papal role – people knew far more clearly what was now wanted – but on the other hand, it weakened it by narrowing the base of loyalty. While *Humanae Vitae* began the detachment of large segments of the Catholic community, particularly more vocal segments, from the near unanimous and unquestioned following of papal authority characteristic of the pre-Vatican II era, it was left to John Paul and Cardinal Ratzinger, prefect from November 1981 of the Congregation for the Doctrine of the Faith, to harden that detachment into a consistent attitude of distrust as the pope seemed to distance himself more and more from many of the central values of the Council, and of the most apparently positive and welcomed developments of Catholicism in the subsequent years. Collegiality seemed now once more a forgotten word.

It would all the same be gravely mistaken to interpret post-conciliar Church history almost wholly in terms of the personalities and persuasions of two outstanding popes. Despite an undoubted attempt to enlarge rather than curtail the sphere of effective papal control – an attempt that on the surface at least succeeded again and again in particular areas from Holland to Brazil – the wider agenda was seldom set in Rome. It was set a great deal more by the massive alteration in the balance of the Catholic community – the decline of France, Italy and Spain, the rise of Brazil, the United States, the Philippines, even Zaire, the revival of Catholic Eastern Europe, the larger shift from both west to east (especially in Europe) and from north to south. The geography of

9

the Catholic Church in 1990 has become remarkably different from that of 1960. Where, for instance, there was then a mere handful of African bishops, there are now many hundreds. This is not as such an effect of the Council, but the geographical shift has coincided with, been stimulated by and itself has greatly affected, post-conciliar change. If in the age of Paul VI the major challenges to Roman policy still came from Western Europe, by the age of John Paul II they were coming from other continents. In retrospect, the ending at this point of the long preponderance of Western Europe (that is to say, Italy, France, southern Germany, Belgium and Spain) – a preponderance common to the pre-conciliar Church, the Council and even the pontificate of Paul VI – in the affairs of Catholicism and its replacement by a far wider range of geographical influences, may appear as far more significant than any shift from the mildly liberal to the neo-conservative.

At the end of our period, developments in Soviet-dominated Europe still further altered the ecclesiastical map quite decisively, though the longer-term consequence of the sudden collapse of forty years of communist domination is, in 1990, impossible to predict. The Church's Eastern European resurgence, centred upon its long recognized strength in Poland – a country led from mid-1989 by a devout Catholic prime minister – but now including almost every country from Czechoslovakia to Lithuania, as well as what previously seemed the almost unimaginable resurrection of Uniate Catholicism in the Ukraine, has ensured that Catholic history and geography in the 1990s are likely to look very different from that of the 1980s. This liberation of what had been, since the end of the Second World War, 'a Church of silence', may do much to transform an atmosphere of widespread ecclesial decline, noticeable particularly in Western Europe, into one of confident revival. It cannot but contribute to the impression of providential suitability of an Eastern European pope.

To understand the internal dynamic of debate, change and tension within Catholic history in this period, it may be helpful to divide it into three parts. The first phase, that of the theologians of the 1950s and the central issues of the Council itself, might be characterized as ultramontanism versus what we may call (using an old term, now largely abandoned) Cisalpinism. The latter, represented by people like Yves Congar, Henri de Lubac and Louis Bouyer, appealed away from the post-medieval neo-scholastic synthesis of contemporary official Catholic theology to a far more creative use of biblical and patristic sources; it accepted the rightness of part of the classical Protestant critique of Roman Catholicism; it fully adhered to the highest standards of modern scholarship, but in a really quite traditional way. It had adopted some of the theology of sixteenth-century Reformers and some of the learning of nineteenth-century Protestant scholars, but very little of it was genuinely very modern in terms of the second half of the twentieth century, and hardly anything in it challenged in the slightest the more basic dogmas of Catholic theology, Trinitarian, incarnational and sacramental. While the Council did not fully accept this viewpoint by any means, it owed a very great deal to it in its most influential formulations. Unfortunately, the institutional implications of this agenda in terms of the partial dismantling of Roman monarchy and a

10

particular style of clerical ministry seemed more revolutionary than did the theology itself, and neither Council nor curia was anxious to consider them, beyond the encouragement of national or regional episcopal conferences, the establishment of a consultative synod of bishops and the ordination of married men as deacons.

By the middle and later 1960s, however, this 'Cisalpine' theological agenda was being overtaken by a more evidently twentieth-century one: modern biblical scholarship turned out not to have stopped with Westcott and Lightfoot nor even with Dodd, but seemed much more a matter of swallowing Bultmann and Nineham; ecumenical theology now led one less to Luther and Calvin or even Barth than to the vapid profundities of Tillich, Bishop Robinson's *Honest to God* and beyond. Once young Catholic theologians began to think for themselves, the excitements of modernity in the wider cultural mood of the 1960s carried them far beyond Congar. De Lubac, von Balthasar, Bouyer and Jacques Maritain could cry 'treason', but Marxism, structuralism and post-structuralism collectively devastated the French School of Theology until it almost ceased significantly to exist. If Rome pulled further and further back from a willingness to tolerate new theologies, it was due to a not-unfounded belief that by 1970 'new theology' meant a very different thing from what it had meant before 1960. Ratzinger had himself been a seemingly progressive young conciliar *peritus*. His road back to traditionalism could appear the only way to escape a theological disintegration which threatened not just Vatican I, but Chalcedon and Nicaea as well.

By the 1980s the prevailing agenda had shifted yet again as Latin America, Africa and Asia came increasingly to the centre of Catholic concern with liberation theology upon the one side, inculturation upon the other. In point of fact, in terms of Catholic tradition, the challenges here might be less awkward than those of phase 2 (and to some extent John Paul II was able to recognize this), but the crucial ecclesiastical issue once more (as in phase 1) had become the acceptability of diversity, and the curial mind had never escaped from the conviction that unity requires uniformity. Moreover, while the 'Marxist' note of liberation theology, though played up by old-fashioned conservatives, did not frighten the pope, the 'basic community' implications of liberation theology for the structuring of the Church and the ministry posed once more a considerable challenge to the structures of celibate clericalism.

Whether pope and curia can or should win such battles is not for us to say. It is certainly much easier for them to win a great many individual battles than to win the war. There seem three conceivable different outcomes in the middle term. The first is that with another ten years of John Paul's rule, the silencing of awkward bishops and theologians, the appointment to the episcopate of a most carefully selected team of neo-conservatives, a rather traditionalist form of Catholicism will, in fact, harden and remain for a long time effectively unchangeable. The new episcopate, the troops of Opus Dei, Comunione e Liberazione and the like, reinforcements maybe from Poland and some parts of the third world, will have made the more liberal vistas of Vatican II and its immediate aftermath just another brief aberration within Catholic history comparable to the conciliar movement of the fifteenth century. While various

11

precise Vatican II reforms (such as the use of the vernacular) will, of course, be retained, its chief significance will have been reduced from the theological to the administrative, and John Paul II will appear in retrospect as the true successor and vindicator of Pius XII and of papal authority as proclaimed by Vatican I.

A second scenario is that this cannot happen. The pluralist forces within both the Western and the third-world Church are simply too strong and too lively to be tamed by a papacy with really quite limited weapons at its command. Resistance, grounded on a far deeper sense of the rights of conscience, the role of the laity and the fallibility of ecclesiastical authority than existed in pre-conciliar days, will not be overcome at the level of the clergy, the religious orders, the thinking laity or – above all – the theologians. It is relatively easy for Rome to control the bishops, exceedingly hard for it to control anyone else. The pendulum will swing back with a pope of another complexion and a new phase of more radical reform will curb the structures of ultramontanism in a way Vatican II almost wholly failed to do. John Paul's pontificate may then appear as, in part, aberration, while a pluralist Catholic Christianity will be revealed as not only heir to the central religious tradition of the West, but as able to respond without losing its core identity to the needs both of a truly world Church and of the ongoing transformation of human consciousness and intellectual understanding.

The third possibility is that neither of the others can work. The first will neither be abandoned nor genuinely prevail, and will merely sap the vitality of area after area of real ecclesial strength, thus preventing the second from getting under way. The Church cannot be reclericalized, but any alternative model of ministry or communion can be blocked from the top. The intellectual strength of Catholicism will fade under the pressure of a rather fundamentalist theology imposed upon seminaries and Catholic institutions of all sorts. The Church will then inevitably decline in an increasingly irreversible way, as in some parts of the world it may already be doing. Manifestly so vast a body does not collapse overnight and much of the decline can be masked for decades. It will retain its strength more in some places than in others. It will continue to win some local battles. But its overall role as a credible world community of faith and love, a body that can be ignored by no one, a living tradition that combines humanity and the most sophisticated rational understanding with divinity and mystical insight, will simply dwindle away in the twenty-first century, leaving the Church as a narrowing fellowship upon the margins of history. Perhaps even that future may be judged providential, but in such a story Vatican II will appear as the final occasion when Christianity was at the centre of significance for human and religious history, and John Paul II will be judged not the healer of a divided Church, but the gravedigger of Pope John's *aggiornamento*.

It is, of course, impossible to foresee the future, but the effective demise of the Catholic Church has been prophesied so often that it seems wiser to conclude that the vast movement of transformation begun by Vatican II will not be easily ended either internally or externally. It may well be that, for the Church historian of the middle of the twenty-first century, the tensions of the period of John Paul II through which we are now passing will themselves appear as but an interlude in the process initiated by the Council, and ending in a form of Catholicism still unimaginable today.

2

COUNCILS IN CHRISTIAN HISTORY

MICHAEL J. WALSH

When Vatican II met, the 1917 *Code of Canon Law* determined who had the right to attend. This code included cardinals, patriarchs, archbishops and bishops, heads of (male) religious orders, and any other prelate with jurisdiction over a district of his own. Decisions taken, said the *Code*, require papal confirmation, but a Council exercises supreme jurisdiction over the Church.

It wasn't always so. Which Councils – more often than not called synods during the first thousand years – were ecumenical was determined not by the pope, but by their reception in the Church at large. Theory now has it that Councils are convoked by popes: the early ones certainly were not. At Nicaea in 325 the bishops and priests (from the Western part of the empire, only priests attended) were called together by the emperor because theological disputes were putting too much of a strain on the unity he was striving to achieve. The imperial presence was manifest: those who attended had the advantage of travelling on the imperial transport system; the structure of the Council mirrored that of senatorial procedure, the 318 fathers (a traditional number – actual attendance was more likely to have been about 250) gathered in a hall of the imperial palace; Constantine spoke asking them to restore concord, and then left them to themselves.

That they were left to themselves is evident, for Eusebius of Nicomedia, who was close to Constantine, found himself on the losing side in the debate about the relationship between Father and Son, defeated by a group led by a mere deacon (though soon to be a bishop), Athanasius of Alexandria. It was another Eusebius, of Caesarea, who was the moving force behind the formula around which the Council eventually gathered, known now, with a number of amendments introduced at the Council of Constantinople, as the Nicene Creed. In the approved sequence, Constantinople (AD381) comes next, even though it was attended by fewer bishops (about 150) than the non-approved Rimini of 359 (about 400). What is more, the Council was wholly Eastern. Pope Damasus was not only not present, he was not even represented.

After Constantinople the debate about the nature of Christ polarized between two patriarchs, Nestorius of Constantinople and Cyril of Alexandria. Nestorius believed it heretical to describe Mary as *Theotokos*, or God-bearer, on the basis that Mary gave birth to a man, Jesus, in whom God dwelt. This view was rejected by Cyril, who had the Bishop of Rome, Celestine I, on his side. Nestorius was supported by John, Patriarch of Antioch. Theodosius, the Eastern emperor, summoned a Council to meet at Ephesus. Cyril opened it on 22 June 431, before the supporters of Nestorius had arrived. Nestorius himself refused to attend and had to be given protection by imperial troops. When the dispute was eventually resolved in Cyril's favour, it was not by the Council but by a decision of the Emperor Theodosius.

While Nestorians went their own way, the orthodox were again split over the manner in which divine and human natures were united in the person of Christ. Eutyches, archimandrite (or abbot) of a monastery in Constantinople, believed that in effect there was only one nature. This theory (monophysitism) was rejected at a Council held at Chalcedon in October 451. Again the number of Western representatives was small: there were only five papal legates, three bishops and two priests, but they were given the presidency partly at least because this council, though formally convoked by the emperor, had been called for by Pope Leo. And in the end it was Leo's formulation of the faith that was accepted by the Council fathers. Both the Emperor Marcian and his wife Pulcheria played an active part in the meetings: Marcian and Leo found themselves at loggerheads not so much over the dogmatic formulation as over the disciplinary canons that were appended.

Debates on the relation of divine and human in Christ were still not entirely over. In different forms they were pursued at the second and third Councils of Constantinople (553 and 680–1). In 692 a fourth Council of Constantinople, almost wholly taken up with disciplinary matters, marked a watershed in relations between East and West. The pope of the day refused to approve its conclusions, and the gathering is omitted from the Councils recognized in the West. The disagreement is significant. Hitherto, the ecumenical gatherings had chiefly been concerned with theological issues, even if matters of discipline such as the manner of determining the date of Easter had crept in. The important meetings had taken place in the East, and though very few representatives of the Western Churches had attended, the canons had been accepted as binding upon the whole Christian world.

It is sometimes asserted that Eastern bishops displayed greater theological learning than those in the West, which is why most Councils took place in the East. It is possibly true, and though the challenges presented to the Western bishops on the nature of the Church (Donatism) and about grace and free will (Pelagianism) were serious enough, theological debate rarely seems to have aroused the same passions in the West as it did in the East. There was little in the West to compare with the fanaticism shown by Eastern monks or lay people as well as bishops over the minutiae of dogma. It burst out again over iconoclasm.

In 730 Leo III the Isaurian issued an edict forbidding the veneration of images, icons. After much destruction of icons the conflict in the East was resolved in 787 by the second Council of Nicaea. Though there were two papal legates, the Council was an Eastern affair, to solve an Eastern problem. It was called not by a pope, nor even a patriarch, but by the Empress Irene. Just under a century later, in 869–70, the Emperor Basil II, though he had turned for help to Pope Hadrian II, was responsible for summoning the fourth Council of Constantinople. Some of its canons were concerned with the veneration of images, but the chief problem was the position of Photius as patriarch of Constantinople. He was deposed by what the Western Church regards as the 8th Ecumenical Council. It has not been recognized in the East.

The eleventh century saw the formal rupture between East and West, and also a determined effort by the papacy to reform the Church. Plans of reform were worked out at a succession of Councils or synods attended only by Western bishops. These were distinctly papal Councils, called by popes and used by them both to make their reforms better known throughout the Church and to involve other ecclesiastical dignitaries in the reform movement: it suited the papacy to extend the range of people invited. Invitees were not only bishops, but heads of monastic orders, theologians representing the academic magisterium, even lay people.

The first of such Councils to be recognized as ecumenical by the Western Church took place in the Lateran basilica, Rome, in 1123. It did little more than endorse reforms already introduced: the second ecumenical Council of the Lateran (1139) did likewise. Though exact figures are lacking, as indeed they are for the previous Councils, Lateran II seems to have been better attended than most, if not all, others hitherto. It has remained of particular interest because its canon seven was the first to declare the marriage of clerics not only unlawful but invalid. The third Lateran Council (1179) was the result of an imperially inspired schism. Again the number attending was large, and again the canons of the Council, after dealing with the problems occasioned by anti-popes, covered a range of reforming issues.

Lateran Councils I to III were a prelude to one of Christianity's greatest of all assemblies, Lateran IV, summoned by Innocent III to meet in November 1215. Eastern bishops were invited – though those in communion with Constantinople did not turn up – as well as abbots and lay representatives not only of princes, but of some city-states as well. It was remarkably brief, but encompassed a great deal and was consciously planned and carried through as an ecumenical Council, the first of its kind. Its impact upon the Church was considerable – especially perhaps in England; its conclusions were chiefly to do with discipline, and its provision requiring annual confession and Communion, remains today.

With the 13th general Council, the chief subject was the conflict between the pope and the emperor. It was held at Lyons in June and July 1245, and ended with a sentence of deposition being passed against Frederick II, though a number of other canons concerned chiefly with structural matters within the Church were also given the force of law. Lyons I was poorly attended: Lyons II (May and July 1274), though not up to the numbers of Lateran IV, had a wide spread of members. There were places for kings or their representatives and, more particularly, for Greeks. They approved an act of union between the Churches, acknowledging the primacy of the popes. This patently political act was rejected by the vast majority of the Greek hierarchy.

The next Council, that of Vienne, south of Lyons, took place from October 1311 to May the following year, and was unusual in that only a selection – though a geographically fairly wide selection – of bishops were invited. It took place under the shadow of the French king, Philip the Fair. He already had all the Knights Templar in France arrested on trumped-up charges of immorality: now he wanted conciliar approval. The fathers failed to give Philip the satisfaction of a full-scale condemnation: the Order was suppressed by an administrative act of the pope's and not by the Council.

Vienne marked the beginning of the papacy's long exile in Avignon. Its return to Rome towards the end of the fourteenth century resulted in a schism with two, and for a time three, rivals for the papacy. The obvious way to resolve the dispute was to call a Council to decide among them – though such a course of action might be taken to imply the supremacy of a Council over a pope. It was the German King Sigismund who summoned the 16th Ecumenical Council, though invitations were later also sent by Pope John XXIII. It met at Constance in November 1414 and Pope John was deposed. Expecting this, he had first tried to flee the city, and in the aftermath of John's flight the Council passed a decree (*Sacrosancta*) proclaiming the supremacy of the Council over the pope. One of John's rivals, Gregory XII, resigned his claim and returned to the ranks of the cardinals. The other, Benedict XIII, fled to the castle of Peñiscola in north-east Spain, where he spent the remainder of his days: the Council deposed him in July 1417. In November the cardinals, together with representatives of the different national groupings, elected a new pope for the whole Church, Martin V. Before doing so, however, they had ensured through the decree *Frequens* that Councils were to be called at regular intervals of ten years.

Martin complied with *Frequens*. After five years he held a Council first at Pavia then at Siena, but it was so poorly attended it has not been counted as ecumenical. Seven years after that he summoned another, this time to meet in Basle. By the time it began, in July 1431, there was a new pope, Eugenius IV. The weariness with Councils that Martin had experienced at Pavia and Siena was apparent: the Council was opened by the papal legate without a single bishop present. Eugenius then tried to dissolve the Council he had not wanted in the first place. The few conciliar fathers who had finally gathered refused to accept his decision. He was forced to withdraw his dissolution, though only after more than two years of controversy, during which time the Council had gone about its business and drafted a number of decrees that restrained the power of the papacy, and laid down reforms throughout the Church.

But the chief issue turned out to be reunion with the Greeks, required by Emperor John VIII Palaeologus for political reasons. The emperor wanted to meet pope and Council. The majority at Basle wanted the emperor to go there or to Avignon: the pope proposed Ferrara, which suited the Greeks better. In September 1437 Eugenius transferred the Council to Ferrara: the majority refused to go and, after proclaiming conciliar superiority to the pope, deposed Eugenius and elected an anti-pope. Meanwhile, after the Greeks had reached Ferrara, Eugenius was forced to transfer the meeting to Florence. It was therefore at Florence that agreement between Greeks and Latins was reached – though again it was to be of short duration. The Council, the longest so far, moved to Rome in 1442 and came to an end, while the rump of the Basle gathering gradually faded away.

It is scarcely surprising that popes did not like calling Councils. It is also not surprising that there continued to be those who believed the papacy on its own incapable of reforming the Church, and that a Council was needed. When a pope next called a Council it was only because the French king, then at war with the papacy, had called one of his own. But the popes of this Council,

Julius II and Leo X, bore out the fears of the conciliarists. Reforms for the Church were proposed, but on the eve of the Reformation, Lateran V (1512–17), under the presidency of the popes, achieved little or nothing.

Perhaps Trent has been the most important of all Councils in the history of the Roman Catholic Church but, like Lateran V before it, it was forced upon an unwilling papacy. It might possibly have been convoked earlier had not Luther urged that a general Council, to which the pope would be compelled to submit, should decide for or against his Ninety-Five Theses, thus reviving the spectre of conciliarism. The sack of Rome in 1527 by the troops of the Emperor Charles V finally forced Clement VII to agree to a Council, though it was left to Paul III to summon it in 1544. Charles feared for the unity of his dominions under the threat of Protestantism, and it seemed he might call a national synod in Germany which would not only undermine the authority of the papacy, but in the interests of political unity approve theological positions Rome could never accept. Trent (Triento in northern Italy) was within the imperial territory, but sufficiently close to Rome for the papacy to influence events.

Trent lasted, on and off, from December 1545 to December 1563, Pius IV giving his approval to its final conclusions in January 1564. For a time it was held at Bologna, in the papal states, but the imperial representatives protested and the pope moved it back to Trent. Numbers were small at first, but by the end some 250 bishops were present. For a time Protestants attended, but hopes that the Council might reunify the Western Church – the Eastern was scarcely considered – were dashed. The Council fathers decisively rejected Protestant doctrines on central issues such as justification, the presence of Christ in the Eucharist and sacramental efficacy, and promulgated a series of decrees on purgatory, the veneration of relics, images and saints, and indulgences – almost, it seems, as an act of defiance to the reformers who had denied them.

Alongside doctrinal debates, it was decided early in the Council that the fathers were to legislate for widespread reform in the Roman Church. The whole package, doctrinal decrees and disciplinary reforms, has shaped Catholicism down to the present. 'Tridentine', rather unfairly, has become a term of abuse: Trent was a great reforming Council. But its very success was its undoing. Nobody for a very long time afterwards felt the need to change things. The Church ossified. There was not another Council for over 300 years.

When the next one met, attracting three-quarters of all the world's 1,050 or so Catholic bishops, it was in the basilica of St Peter's for the first Vatican Council. They gathered in December 1869: they rapidly dispersed the following July at the outbreak of the Franco-German War. In between, the bishops had debated a number of issues both doctrinal and pastoral, though only the doctrinal ones reached definitive form and were approved. Chief among these were the definitions of papal primacy and infallibility. So lofty were these papal prerogatives, that no further Council would ever be needed, or so it seemed to many. Though the definition of infallibility was a good deal more circumscribed than often presented, Vatican I did what its promoters had asked of it. It elevated the papacy to a new level of authority within the

Church, compensating for the steady erosion of its political role during the nineteenth century. Pius IX had attempted to make it ecumenical by summoning representatives of the Eastern Churches not in communion with Rome. They did not come. Protestants were another matter: they were not invited as such, but urged instead to return to the fold of Roman Catholicism. Anglican bishops were not asked to attend or to send observers. There were no representatives of governments. It counts as the 20th Ecumenical Council.

The 20th, that is, in Roman Catholic lists. East and West went their own ways after Constantinople IV, ecumenical in the West though not in the East. Since Trent, even the West has been divided. One can debate whether gatherings after Constantinople or after Trent have been ecumenical, but it is a sterile argument. What emerges from the history of the Councils is that it is impossible to determine a pattern. Some have been called by popes, but others called by rulers against papal wishes. Some have been purely doctrinal, others purely pastoral, a good many have been both. The number of bishops attending, at least until Vatican I, has been a small proportion of the total, and membership has not always been restricted to bishops, or even to clergy. The synods regularly meeting in Rome since Vatican II could claim to be more representative of the Church than the majority of Councils.

Not by history alone, in other words, would one come to the firm description of a Council, and its relationship to the Roman Pontiff, that is contained in the 1983 *Code of Canon Law*. The facts are much more messy. As the foregoing brief chronology has demonstrated, which Councils have been recognized as ecumenical is far more arbitrary than is acknowledged by the bland words of the current *Code*. What has mattered is their ultimate reception as ecumenical by the Church at large. And by that criterion Vatican II has greater claim to be ecumenical than many of its predecessors.

2 Councils in Christian History: Bibliography

Bogolepou, A. A. (1963) 'Which Councils are Recognized as Ecumenical', *St Vladimir's Seminary Quarterly*, vol. 7, no. 2, pp. 54–72.

Davis, L. D. (1987) *The First Seven Ecumenical Councils (325–787): Their History and Theology*. Wilmington, Delaware, Michael Glazier.

Franzen, A. (1969) *A Concise History of the Church*. London, Burns & Oates.

Jedin, H. (1960) *Ecumenical Councils of the Catholic Church: An Historical Outline*. Edinburgh, Nelson.

Margull, H. J., ed. (1966) *The Councils of the Church: History and Analysis*. Philadelphia, Fortress Press.

Sieben, H. J. (1979) *Die Konzilsidee der Alten Kirche*. Paderborn, Ferdinand Schöningh.

Sieben, H. J. (1984) *Die Konzilsidee des lateinischen Mittelaler (847–1378)*. Paderborn, Ferdinand Schöningh.

Watkin, E. I. (1960) *The Church in Council*. London, Darton, Longman & Todd.

3

PIUS XII

MICHAEL J. WALSH

For many within the Roman Catholic Church the remote, emaciated, ascetical figure of Pius XII remains the paradigm of what a pope should be. Though after the Lateran Pact of 1929, which settled the conflict between the Holy See and Italy, the Bishop of Rome was no longer a (self-imposed) 'prisoner in the Vatican', the papacy's isolation remained, heightened in popular consciousness by the war years. His readiness to speak on almost any topic, and especially on medical ethics, was remarkable: his speeches averaged out over the pontificate at almost one a day. Though (except for the definition of the bodily Assumption of Mary in November 1950) none of these declarations fell into the formal category of infallible as defined at Vatican I, none the less Catholics came to expect authoritative guidance from Rome on all manner of issues – a strong tendency within the Church down to the present day. Much of the conflict over the nature of authority since Vatican II derives from the manner in which it was exercised by Rome in the first half of the twentieth century, and particularly during the pontificate of Pius XII.

Eugenio Maria Pacelli was born on 2 March 1876. His Pacelli grandfather had served Pius IX in the administration of the papal states: his father Filippo was a lawyer practising in the papal courts – he became an adviser to the commission for the codification of canon law set up by Pius X in 1904. After his ordination to the priesthood by the Cardinal Vicar for Rome (May 1899), Eugenio himself studied law and then entered the Congregation for Extraordinary Ecclesiastical Affairs (now the Council for the Public Affairs of the Church), which handled relations between the Holy See and civil governments. He was, however, chosen by the Congregation's secretary, Cardinal de Gasparri, to assist the codification commission. From 1909 to 1914, when he became secretary to the Congregation, he lectured on ecclesiastical diplomacy at the Academia dei Nobili.

In 1917 he was consecrated archbishop and sent to Munich as nuncio, or papal ambassador, where he was considerably shaken by first-hand experience of a Bolshevik revolution. In 1920 he was made nuncio to the German Republic, although he did not move to Berlin until 1925. This period was a particularly happy one for him. He became a fluent German speaker and Germanophil. In 1929 he was recalled to Rome to take part – with his lawyer brother – in the final negotiations over the Lateran Treaty. In December he became a cardinal; and the following February he followed his old master de Gasparri as Secretary of State. On 2 March 1939 Pacelli was elected pope in succession to Pius XI in the shortest conclave there had been since 1623.

As pope, his affection for Germany reasserted itself. He surrounded himself with anti-Nazi German Jesuits, among them his secretary and his confessor, Augustine Bea. In 1933, as Secretary of State, he negotiated a concordat with Hitler – on paper, a triumph for the Church; in practice, totally ignored by the German leader. Pacelli sent off formal notes of protest at violations of the terms of the agreement: these, too, were ignored. Four years later, in March 1937, at the instigation of Pacelli and with the assistance of a number of German bishops, Pius XI issued an encyclical, *Mit Brennender Sorge*, in bitter condemnation of Nazism.

Yet that clear vision of Pius XI's last years seems to have been lost when his Secretary of State succeeded him as pope. Pacelli's relationship with Germany during the Second World War, and his apparent failure to act sufficiently vigorously in defence of the Jews, remains the great enigma of his pontificate. It seems likely that the Vatican was much better informed than the official collection of documents, *Actes et Documents du Saint Siége*, would have the world believe. Pius XII was trained as a diplomat, and retained his faith in diplomacy despite its obvious failure in the case of Germany. After Cardinal Maglione's death in 1944 Pius acted as his own Secretary of State and increasingly reserved decision-making to himself.

Any assessment of Pius XII's long pontificate – he died at Castel Gandolfo, the papal summer residence, on 9 October 1958 – must take account of his early career. Although he engaged in some pastoral work in the years after his ordination, preaching and hearing confessions, his time was spent almost entirely in the papal civil service and, until the appointment to Germany for just over a decade, almost entirely in Rome. He travelled a little as papal legate, and made a private visit to the United States and Latin America, but his experience of countries other than Germany (which he loved) and Italy was practically non-existent. Perhaps conscious of this disadvantage, one of his first acts after the war was to internationalize the college of cardinals. In February 1946 he appointed thirty-two cardinals from all parts of the world, and twenty-four more in 1953. There were still more Italians in the sacred college than any other national group, but they now numbered only one-third of the total.

Pius's motives were not perhaps as straightforward as it might seem. In the aftermath of the war, an international Church had to dilute – at least – the influence of Italian prelates. And it also seems likely that Pius XII wanted the cardinals to act as papal legates, representatives of the pope in their different territories, ensuring through the bishops under their charge that true doctrine was taught to the laity. That true doctrine was to be handed down by Pius XII through his speeches and writings. He had spent his early years as a priest in the papal service under Pius X, whom he canonized. Holy though he may have been, Pius X, abetted by the English-born Cardinal Rafael Merry del Val, waged a vigorous and not always clean campaign against the dangers of modernism. His successor was determined to be no less a guardian of the strictest orthodoxy.

Given his vision of the Church, it is easy to categorize Pius XII as a theological conservative. The truth, however, is not so straightforward. During the modernist crisis, no area of scholarly research had been subjected to as much intellectual oppression as the study of the Scriptures. The Biblical Commission, originally established to foster biblical scholarship, had been used by Pius X to repress it. Its declarations required Catholic scholars to believe, for example, that Moses had written the Pentateuch, and that St Matthew's Gospel was the first Gospel to be composed. More remarkable still, in 1907 Pius X instructed Catholics to give assent not only to what the Biblical Commission had already decided, but to all decisions that it might make in the future.

Despite these difficulties, Catholic biblical scholarship had advanced, albeit cautiously, particularly as far as the Old Testament was concerned. Oddly, much credit for this advance has also to be given to Pius X who, in 1909, founded the Biblical Institute (the Biblicum) in Rome and handed it over to the charge of the Jesuits, the Dominicans having earlier founded the Ecole Biblique in Jerusalem. The violently anti-modernist spirit lived on, however, and just before the Second World War found expression in a thirteen volume, wholly uncritical commentary on the Old Testament by an Italian priest, Dolindo Ruotolo. This commentary was put on the *Index* of forbidden books for its errors. Ruotolo apparently submitted, but then published a pamphlet attacking current exegesis, especially as it was taught at the Biblicum. The Biblical Commission responded with a letter which came to serve as the first part of an encyclical, *Divino Afflante Spiritu*, published by Pius XII on 30 September 1943. Though it naturally carries the pope's name, credit for writing this most liberalizing document belongs to the pope's confessor, the German Jesuit Father (later Cardinal) Augustine Bea, who was then rector of the Biblicum.

Though the immediate effects of the encyclical were muted – in 1943, as one commentator noted, 'the excitement was elsewhere' – the long-term effects were dramatic. Not only had a pope approved the scholarship of Catholic exegetes, but he had encouraged their endeavours and removed the threat of condemnation by the Church because of their use of modern exegetical method. Its whole tenor was positive, with particular stress being put upon the need to return to the original languages in which the sacred texts had been composed. While it did not mark the end of the conflict – though the early decrees of the Biblical Commission were quietly withdrawn in 1955, the Biblicum was to come under attack on the eve of the Council – it was the most important milestone in the history of Catholic scriptural scholarship. It freed scholars to pursue their researches without having to look over their shoulders at the Holy Office. It prepared the way for the men who were to prepare the way for the Council. Though the Constitution on Revelation at Vatican II has often been regarded as the major landmark in Catholic biblical studies, the real turning point had occurred with *Divino Afflante Spiritu* two decades earlier.

The implications of the papal encyclical reached further than the study of Scripture. The principles of historical criticism could be applied to religious disciplines other than biblical ones, most notably to the development of doctrine. Theology began to take a direction that Pius XII found uncomfortable. The outcome was another encyclical, *Humani Generis*, published on 12 August 1950. 'Evolutionism' and 'historicism', together with existentialism, were among the non-Christian philosophies listed by the pope as contributing to the spread of 'error' in Catholic theology. No theologian was censured, nor even mentioned by name. None the less, a number of distinguished theologians, French Jesuits and Dominicans in particular, were dismissed from their teaching posts soon afterwards. They included Henri de Lubac, later to be raised to the rank of cardinal, though only after he had retreated from the more extreme position on the relationship between nature and grace he had adopted in 1946 in his book *Surnaturel*; Marie-Dominique Chenu, one of whose books was placed on the *Index* in 1942 for daring to suggest that Thomas Aquinas ought to be studied against the history of his times; and Yves Congar, who survived to become one of the leading theologians of Vatican II.

The publication of *Humani Generis* came as an especial shock to the Catholic world because the theological developments it criticized had passed largely unnoticed. The writings of one of the great visionaries of the period, the Jesuit Pierre Teilhard de Chardin, were not allowed to be published and he remained little more than a name, if even that, to all but a few scholars. Those who had read his mimeographed books and articles, however, were among those who were removed from their posts in the aftermath of the encyclical.

But quite apart from this degree of thought control, still in operation in the theological sciences despite the freedom granted to biblical studies by *Divino Afflante Spiritu*, Pius XII had succeeded in focusing Catholic attention upon issues other than theological ones. It was a period of increasing devotion to Mary, with the establishment of Marian institutes and journals to foster it. Between 1948 and 1957 a thousand titles a year appeared in praise of Mary. This was actively encouraged by Pius XII, who himself was particularly attracted to Our Lady of Fatima – perhaps he found the message of doom congenial. There were also stories circulating that he had been the beneficiary of Marian apparitions. On 1 November 1950 he declared that Mary had been assumed bodily into heaven – the doctrine of the Assumption, which had no scriptural, or other early Church, warrant, but which had been celebrated liturgically at least from the fourth century and certainly from the fifth.

Marian fervour was also encouraged by the declaration of a 'Marian Year' in 1954, and celebrations for the centenary of the Lourdes apparitions four years later: the 1950s was probably its highest point. Sober theologians warned against the excesses of the devotion, attempting to root devotion to Mary in the Scriptures, and pointing to the difficulties that were occasioned in relations with other Churches. This reaction, in its turn, peaked during Vatican II: no separate document on Mary was produced, and her role, when it was treated, was linked to that of the Church in *Lumen Gentium*. In 1950, however, many saw in the Dogma of the Assumption a test of the loyalty of those theologians who had been criticized, if not condemned, by *Humani Generis*.

The issue of papal authority was central to the encyclical. Although Pius conceded that popes were not exercising their full authority in these letters, if a view was expressed it was 'no longer [to] be a matter of free debate among theologians'. The pope applied to himself the words of Christ, 'He that heareth you heareth me'.

Just over a decade later, as the papal curia prepared for the Vatican Council,

23

Cardinal Ottaviani proposed a profession of faith for the Council fathers which would repeat the anti-modernist oath (no remarkable thing in itself: the anti-modernist oath was required to be taken by all those teaching in seminaries, and all priests before ordination) and once again to repudiate the errors that had been condemned by *Humani Generis*.

A number of those 'errors' were directly concerned with Scripture, but there was also a particular problem associated with the origins of the human race. Pius, it was clear, was not happy with the theory of evolution: more problematic still was the whole question of original sin. It was far from clear to the pope how this could have been transmitted to the whole human race unless there had been an historical Adam and Eve, that is, a single set of parents. Even as distinguished a scholar as Karl Rahner loyally attempted to fall in line with papal doctrine, but only at considerable cost to his credibility.

The general tenor of *Humani Generis* was a reaffirmation of a whole string of Catholic doctrines that Pius or his advisers believed to be under attack, including the existence of angels, transubstantiation, the value of Thomism as the Church's philosophy, and the centrality of tradition. Among these doctrines was one that Pius had made particularly his own, the notion of the mystical body of Christ.

His encyclical *Mystici Corporis* had been published on 29 June 1943; in other words, only three months before *Divino Afflante Spiritu*. It did not display, perhaps could not have done so, the depth of biblical scholarship that the later encyclical did so much to encourage. It was striking for its insistence on the role of the Holy Spirit, but equally remarkable for its firmly identifying the Roman Catholic Church with the body of Christ. It served in consequence to reinforce in Catholics their already strong, triumphalistic, sense of their own distinctiveness from other Christians.

While clearly it is unhistorical to judge Pius XII in the light of the later developments at the Council, it is equally wrong to deny him, and to attribute to the Council, credit for many of the liturgical changes in the Church. This is not to diminish *Sacrosanctum Concilium*, which ranks with the Constitutions on the Church, on Scripture and the Pastoral Mission of the Church as one of the major documents of Vatican II, but at least as much as they – and perhaps more so – it had been prepared for during the pontificate of Pius XII. His encyclical *Mediator Dei*, published on 20 December 1947, was the first one in the history of such documents to be devoted exclusively to the liturgy.

This encyclical was, of course, theological rather than practical in its purpose, and though it undoubtedly helped to quicken the pace of liturgical reform in the Church, the driving force of change lay elsewhere – most particularly perhaps in Germany. At a conference organized in June 1950 by the Liturgical Institute of Trier, a lecture by Romano Guardini led to a resolution calling upon the German bishops to request Rome to move the long Holy Saturday service from the early morning to the late evening, thus again making it the vigil service it once had been. The request was granted – in the first instance for a year. A second conference – though the first international gathering for it was co-sponsored by the Centre de Pastorale Liturgique of Paris – was held in July 1951. This time the subject was the rubrics of the

Roman missal and the form of the Holy Saturday vigil. Again reforms were introduced.

Numerous changes followed, either by way of decree from the Sacred Congregation of Rites, or through direct papal intervention. Rules that had once obliged Catholics to fast from midnight before receiving Communion were eased. Evening Mass was permitted. More changes were made to the Holy Week liturgy. The question of music in the liturgy was addressed. A little of the vernacular (the proclamation of the Epistle and Gospel) was allowed into the Mass.

In September 1956 liturgical leaders, including six cardinals and 800 bishops, came together in Assisi to express their gratitude to the pope for all the changes that had been brought about in the liturgy during his pontificate. But by that time Pius had become alarmed at the pace of change. There had already been warnings issued to clergy not to take the law into their own hands, and in his allocution to the participants the 80-year-old pontiff gave expression to his fears.

Apart perhaps from the revision of the Holy Week liturgy, the changes brought about in the Church's worship under Pius XII now seem relatively modest. But they were a good deal more important at a symbolic level. The unchanging nature of the Latin, Roman liturgy was something upon which many Roman Catholics set – and some still set – great store. That changes were possible at all even in this most sacred area of ritual meant that changes were possible elsewhere. This was of immense psychological importance. And in encouraging the biblical movement, Pius XII had made an indirect contribution to liturgical renewal of equal significance. For that, too, Pius deserves much credit.

There is a great deal in Pius's character that seems contradictory. The liturgical reforms, the encouragement he gave to biblical scholarship, the beginning he made, for whatever reason, at internationalizing the college of cardinals, his call to bishops to send their clergy as missionaries to Latin America and, more particularly, to Africa, these all suggest a pope who was far from conservative in outlook. And if the doctrine of collegiality is to be seen as one of the major contributions of Vatican II to the life of the Church, even that can be found in the pontificate of Pius XII, for it was he who set up CELAM, the Conference of Bishops of Latin America.

And there had even been an abortive project for a Council. This proposal, which has only fairly recently come to light, was made by Archbishop Ruffini of Palermo and Monsignor Ottaviani, then an official of the Holy Office. They had wanted an updating of canon law, a reassertion of control over Church organizations, the declaration of Mary's Assumption (perhaps as a sop to the pope), and a firm condemnation of nascent ecumenism and what they saw as a new outbreak of modernism. The plan was for a short gathering, possibly not more than a month long, which would reassert the unity of the Church and its authority in matters of the faith.

Preparatory commissions were set up, bishops were consulted. And then the idea was dropped. Pius took it upon himself to proclaim the Dogma of the Assumption. Without recourse to the world-wide episcopate, he issued

Humani Generis to condemn the string of 'false philosophies' that had been identified by the commission on speculative theology. It is unclear why he so suddenly dropped the idea that he first pushed forward with some vigour. If it is true that he saw the Church in the form of a pyramid, as many people did, with authority flowing down from himself to cardinals, bishops and then to priests, then a Council had no place in any such scheme of things: it only confused the pattern of authority. But it also appears that the bishops who were consulted replied with considerable enthusiasm, proposing a much wider agenda than that originally intended. It may have become obvious to Pius and his advisers that a Council would not be as easy to manipulate as they had imagined. Vatican II was to prove them correct.

3 Pius XII: Bibliography

Aubert, R., ed. (1978) *The Christian Centuries, Volume Five: The Church in a Secularised Society*. London, Darton, Longman and Todd.

Blet, P. *et al.*, eds (1965–81) *Actes et Documents du Saint Siège pendant la seconde guerre mondiale*. Vatican Polyglot Press.

Chadwick, O. (1977) 'Weizsäcker, the Vatican and the Jews of Rome', *Journal of Ecclesiastical History*, vol. 28, no. 2, April, pp. 179 ff.

Chadwick, O. (1986) *Britain and the Vatican During the Second World War*. Cambridge, Cambridge University Press.

Falconi, C. (1970) *The Silence of Pius XII*. London, Faber.

Holmes, J. D. (1981) *The Papacy in the Modern World*. London, Burns & Oates.

Jedin, H., ed. (1981) *History of the Church, Volume X: The Church in the Modern Age*. London, Burns & Oates.

Purdy, W. A. (1965) *The Church on the Move*. London, Hollis & Carter.

Rhodes, A. (1973) *The Vatican in the Age of the Dictators*. London, Hodder & Stoughton.

Schambeck, H., ed. (1977) *Pius XII. zum Gedächtnis*. Berlin, Duncker und Humblot.

4

JOHN XXIII

PETER HEBBLETHWAITE

John XXIII was elected pope in October 1958. Barely three months later he announced his Ecumenical Council (together with a synod for the diocese of Rome and the reform of the Code of Canon Law) on 25 January 1959, the last day of the Octave of Prayer for Christian Unity. He was speaking in private in the chapter house of the abbey of St Paul's-without-the-walls. Seventeen Roman cardinals were present. He had known most of them for half a lifetime. They did not react. Instead of the enthusiasm Pope John had hoped for, there was what he was reduced to calling 'a devout and impressive silence' (Hebblethwaite, 1984, p. 196).

Yet we now know that the silence was not total. Cardinal Nicola Canali, responsible for Vatican finances, enquired whether 'once again the preparation of the Council would be entrusted to the Holy Office'. Canali was referring to the project for a short, sharp Council conceived in 1948–9, which would have reasserted Catholic unity around the Holy Father after a murderous war, condemned contemporary errors and defined the Assumption by acclamation. That project had been abandoned.

So Canali's question assumed that Pope John had *the same kind* of Council in mind as Pius XII. Yet this was not so. Cardinal Carlo Confalonieri, who is our source for this story, goes on: 'Pope John paused for a moment, as though surprised at this question and then said, with a calm but decisive voice: "The Pope presides over the Council (*Presidente del concilio è il papa*)"' (Riccardi, 1987, p. 153).

The implications of this remark were not immediately obvious. But with hindsight it is possible to say that Pope John had already rejected the defensive-minded, judgemental, negative Council projected in 1948–9. He had thought about conciliar history and knew what sort of Council he wanted.

It is very striking to note the way Pope John always claimed paternity of the idea of the Council. 'The summoning of the Ecumenical Council', wrote the editor of his diary, 'was entirely his own initiative and *in capite* under his own jurisdiction' (Roncalli, 1965, p. 345). He allowed that others had proposed the Roman synod and the revision of the Code of Canon Law. But he always insisted that the Council was his responsibility. In his farewell letter to Capovilla, he defined himself as 'Pope of the Council' (Hebblethwaite, 1984, p. 474). In all this we should see not personal vanity – Pope John was too old for that – but an act of primatial responsibility. *Presidente del concilio è il papa*.

It has often been said that he did not really have any very clear idea of what he wanted from his Council; and as far as *content* goes, that may be true. He did not have a blueprint for the Council. But he had a very clear idea of the *manner* in which his Council should be conducted. In his address opening the Council he expressed it by saying that the Council would be 'pastoral' rather than dogmatic, and talking about *aggiornamento* and *rinnovimento* – terms that harked back to his youth when both were slightly suspect. (Abbott, p. 716).

But it was not such language that captured the imagination of the world. John thought in images. On the death of Pope Pius XII he wrote: 'One of my favourite phrases brings me great comfort: we are not on earth as museum-keepers, but to cultivate a flourishing garden of life and to prepare a glorious future ' (Capovilla, 1978a, p. 481).

John expressed this sense of burgeoning new life in the Church by calling the Council 'a new Pentecost'. It is highly significant that he had used this expression in a letter written from the conclave to a friend, Giuseppe Piazza, the Bishop of Bergamo: 'My soul finds comfort in the thought that a new Pentecost can blow through the Church, renewing its head, leading to a new ordering of the ecclesiastical body and bringing fresh vigour in the journey towards truth, goodness and peace' (Capovilla, 1978b, p. 47). Within a few days of his election he already *knew* that the way to realize this 'new Pentecost' was an Ecumenical Council.

He chose his first Whitsunday as pope to announce details of how the Ante-preparatory Commission would be organized. He noted how Pius IX had used the Feast of the Immaculate Conception, 8 December, to advance the various stages of Vatican I. He used Pentecost in this way because, as he said, 'It is from the spirit and doctrine of Pentecost that the great event of the Ecumenical Council draws its substance and its life' (*Acta Apostolica Sedis* 52, p. 517). This implied far more than the juridical observation that the Holy Spirit would 'assist' the Ecumenical Council. It meant that in John's mind the Council was an event of the Holy Spirit in which the whole Church was involved. Everyone was urged to say his 'prayer for the Council': 'Renew thy wonders in this day, as by a New Pentecost.'

This, though it aroused enthusiasm, could not set the agenda of the Council. Some 2,150 replies had been received from the prelates and Catholic institutions consulted. They were not particularly inspiring, though Michael van der Plas has shown that neither were they nugatory. Cardinal Bernard Alfrink, for example, launched the theme of the local Church, talked of 'unity in diversity' and invented collegiality before there was a word for it. (Van der Plas, 1984; for Alfrink, see pp. 55–6).

John's next decision was at first blush disconcerting. On Whitsun eve, 1960, the Central Theological Commission was set up to prepare the Council; subject to it were ten sub-commissions presided over by the heads of the corresponding Roman dicasteries. Thus Gaetano Cigognani, of the Congregation of Rites, was responsible for liturgy. This meant that the preparation of the Council would be in the hands of the 'museum-keepers' of the Roman curia. But John had not taken leave of his senses. He knew that he had to coax the curia along. A Council prepared *against* the curia would be doomed to fail. In any case, by involving the curia in the preparations for the Council, he hoped to 'convert' it to his own sense of the priority of the pastoral.

On 20 June 1961 Pope John addressed the first meeting of the central commission. Here for the first time the actual shape of the Council was outlined. Pope John dealt with practical aspects: choice of theologians and canonists to act as experts; rules of debate; voting procedures; working-language (Latin); relations with the press.

More important was Pope John's statement that the purpose of the Council was the *aggiornamento* of the Catholic Church. This would of itself set off ecumenical vibrations such that, although it could not be called a 'Council of reunion' like Florence, it could be a Council leading towards what he called 'the recomposition of the whole mystical flock of Christ'. He admitted that this would involve 'a change in mentalities, ways of thinking and prejudices, all of which have a long history'. Finally, he hinted at a principle of crucial importance: 'The language we use in the Council should be serene and tranquil; it should shed light on and remove misunderstandings; and it should *dissipate error by the force of truth*' (*Discorsi, messagi, colloqui del Santo Padre Giovanni XXIII*, vol. 3, p. 575).

Cardinal Alfredo Ottaviani, Pro-prefect of the Holy Office and President of the Central Theological Commission, appeared to think that this was mis-guided or purely formal. The question of how to deal with errors was at the heart of the debates in the central commission in the twelve months that preceded the Council. Ottaviani continued to believe that 'error has no rights' and argued for repression; Cardinal Augustin Bea, President of the newly created Secretariat for Christian Unity, shared Pope John's judgement that 'condemning errors' was not the best way to open up a conversation (or dialogue) with other Christians or the modern world. These meetings were a dress-rehearsal for the first session of the Council. But since they were held in secret, few knew this.

Another great advance in precision about the goals of the Council came on Christmas Day, 1961, with the solemn apostolic constitution, *Humanae Salutis*, the official convocation of the Council. In a single sentence, Pope John provided the Council with a method and commentators with material that could last a lifetime. He spoke of the need to 'discern the signs of the times': 'We should make our own Jesus' advice that we should know how to discern "the signs of the times" (Matthew 16.4), and we seem to see now, in the midst of so much darkness, a few hints which augur well for the fate of the Church and humanity' (Abbott, p. 704). Pope John's 'optimism' was later criticized – why should he ignore apocalyptic signs of disaster to concentrate on those that gave grounds for hope? – but hope was in such short supply in 1961 that his words were eagerly seized upon (Moltmann, 1977, p. 368, n. 64; The Extraordinary Synod of 1985 likewise gave a more 'pessimistic' reading of the 'signs of the times').

The *motu proprio Consilium Dei Nostrum* in February 1962 fixed the date for the start of the Council: 11 October 1962. Astonishing to relate, it was still widely believed at this time that a single session would suffice, and indeed the Council actually started under this illusion. Yet the *schemata* or draft texts were piling up. Pope John did not seem worried. In April he told the fifth session of the central commission that 'the consent of the Bishops will not be difficult to obtain and their approval will be unanimous' (Rouquette, 1968, p. 114).

This raises the most difficult problem of all for the historian of the Council. Does this remark mean that Pope John approved of the curially prepared texts, and hoped that they would win unanimous acceptance? This view has been put forward by Joseph Ratzinger in his interviews with Vittorio Messori. Pope John, it is said, 'had not envisaged the possibility of rejection and expected a rapid and painless vote in favour of projects that he had read through and welcomed with full approval' (*Ratzinger Report*, 1985, p. 41). The implication is that Pope John sided with the minority at the first session and was 'upset' (as the minority often asserted) at the rejection of such excellent drafts.

But this view is, as Giuseppe Alberigo remarks 'unfounded and therefore unreliable' (Riccardi, 1987, p. 238, n. 69). There is evidence on the contrary that Pope John was less than happy about certain *schemata*. On 27 July 1962, he told Roberto Tucci, editor of *Civiltà Cattolica*, that he 'did not like the technical and harsh tone' of some of the drafts (ibid.). On 24 July he had criticized the first version of the ecumenical decree, *Ut Omnes Unum Sint:*

> This is a very valuable study, but the mosaic of biblical texts with which it begins does not seem in very good taste. In general this piling up of biblical texts in the exposition of elementary notions and principles, with the biblical quotations buttressing each other up and introducing ideas foreign to the main theme, creates confusion in the minds of simple average souls who are the majority among good Christians (Capovilla, 1978a, p. 546).

So although it is no doubt true to say that Pope John approved in general of the prepared texts, he was not deeply attached to them and was prepared to see them dropped without any deep sense of personal loss. They would do – until something better came along. In any case, the Council was sovereign. If it wanted to reject the preliminary drafts, so be it. That was sad, maybe, but not tragic. The preparatory work for the Council was neither definitive nor sacrosanct. It could be discarded.

On 11 September 1962, Pope John broadcast to the world in Latin. His opening words were *Lumen Christi Ecclesia Christi* (The Church of Christ is the Light of Christ). This was his indirect comment on the seventy *schemata*. 'Has there ever been an ecumenical Council', he asks, 'which was not a way of self-renewal through an encounter with the Risen Jesus, the glorious and immortal King, whose light illumines the whole Church for the salvation, joy and glory of all peoples?' The question was rhetorical. It was another way of saying there would be no condemnations. But there was also a new note. It will be illuminating and helpful to present the Church 'in the under-developed countries as the Church of all, and *especially of the poor*'.[1] This provided the impetus for the opening sentence of *Gaudium et Spes*.

One last idea was slotted into place in this 11 September broadcast. From Cardinal Suenens, Pope John had learned to distinguish between the Church *ad intra* and the Church *ad extra*. Though this distinction could be abused, at this precise moment it helped to clarify two sets of problems the Council would have to deal with: internal questions (nature of the Church, worship, ecumenism, etc.), and external questions (war, peace, birth control, hunger, etc.). Just over a week later, on 23 September 1962, X-ray examinations revealed that Pope John was suffering from cancer. Nothing was said publicly, but from now on he realized that if the Council lasted more than one session, he would not be present to see it through. As he told Cardinal Gabriel-Marie Garrone, Archbishop of Toulouse: 'At least I have launched this big ship – others will have to bring it into port.'

He launched his big ship with his opening address to the Council at the end of an exhausting morning on 11 October 1962 (For complete text, see Abbott, pp. 710–19). 'Launch' is an apt term: it was never his intention to control or manipulate the Council, for it was a sovereign body under his presidency; his duty was to see that it was heading in the right direction. After calling it, this was his most important and abiding contribution to the Council. He stressed four points.

First, the Council was to be a *celebration* of Christian faith. That was why it began with rejoicing, and one can regret that it did not become known by its opening words: *Gaudet Mater Ecclesia* (Mother Church rejoices). The Church rejoiced in its 'unity in diversity' manifested in the various rites that witnessed to the richness of 'catholicity' (so often reduced to bland uniformity). This would have to be remembered in the rough and tumble of debate.

Second, John wanted the Council to share in his optimism about the presence of the Holy Spirit in the modern world. He denounced the 'prophets of misfortune' who see in the modern world 'nothing but betrayal and ruination. They claim that this age is far worse than previous ages, and they go on as though they had learned nothing at all from history – and yet history is the great teacher of life *(magistra vitae).'* John made it clear enough that he was thinking of the Roman curia: 'In our everyday ministry we often have to listen, greatly to our sorrow, to those . . . who do not have much discretion or balance'.

So, third, the purpose of the Council was not just to restate and defend past doctrines – for that a Council was not necessary – but to 'make a leap forward in doctrinal insight and the education of consciences in ever greater fidelity to authentic teaching. But this authentic doctrine has to be studied in the light of the research methods and the literary forms of modern thought. For the substance of the ancient deposit of faith is one thing, and the way it is presented is another,' (my translation). The last sentence of this immensely significant passage was the only text from this address quoted by the Council (in *Gaudium et Spes* 62).

Finally, John repeated that he wanted a positive not a negative Council. He did not deny that errors abounded in the contemporary world, but in a characteristic image said that 'they often vanish as swiftly as they arise, like mist before the sun'. Nor did he deny – how could he? – that the Church in the past had been preoccupied, not to say obsessed, with rooting out errors. 'Today', he blithely continued, 'the Spouse of Christ prefers to use the medicine of mercy rather than severity. She considers that she meets the needs of the modern age by showing the validity of her teachings rather than by condemnations.'

In this way Pope John circumvented the nineteenth-century thesis, still defended by Cardinal Ottaviani at the Holy Office, that 'error has no rights'.

The abandonment of this thesis was a precondition of the Council's treatment of ecumenism, religious liberty and non-Christian religions.

This was the issue that dominated the first session of the Council, the only one Pope John knew. He intervened rarely, but always decisively, to ensure joint commissions so that the minority (mostly from the curia) would be able to accept the Council's verdict without being humiliated.

But during this autumn of 1962 there were other things on his mind. The Cuban missile crisis brought the United States and the Soviet Union close to war. Pope John's message to heads of state – broadcast on Vatican Radio on 25 October – made the front page of *Pravda* the next day under the banner headline: 'We beg all rulers not to be deaf to the cry of humanity'. This was unheard of. John's appeal enabled Khrushchev to step down without losing face. It encouraged Pope John to think of an encyclical on peace and *Pacem in Terris* became his testament.

It was now clear that the Council could not be concluded in a single session. The announcement was made on 12 November that the second (and final) session would take place from 12 May to 29 June 1963 – an indication that Pope John, despite his mortal illness, still hoped to be present at it. The first session was in danger of ending in chaos and frustration when a series of planned interventions, approved by Pope John, rescued it. First, Suenens proposed a *plan d'ensemble*, an overall plan, to reduce the number of topics and give some direction to their work. Cardinal Giacomo Lercaro was assigned 'the Church of the poor', and he developed the text of Acts quoted by Pope John on 11 October: 'Silver and gold I have not, but what I have I give you.'

Then Montini dealt with the order of questions the Council had to answer (he had already developed this in a letter to Pope John only a week after the Council began). They should start with the *mystery* of the Church, its self-understanding as the sacrament of Christ in the world; this would lead to a consideration of 'roles' in the Church – bishop, priest, layperson, religious, etc. Next would come the *mission* of the Church, what the Church does in liturgy and apostolic work. This redefinition would make it possible to discuss the *relationships* of the Church with separated brethren, civil society, non-Christian religions, the world of work, economics and 'the Church's enemies'. Pope John used to say, 'The Church may have many enemies, but she is no one's enemy' (p. 207). He accepted this programme, and half knew that Montini would have to carry it through.

The news that Metropolitan Josef Slipyi, Major Archbishop of the Ukrainian Catholic Church, had been released from his Soviet labour camp and was on his way to Rome, helped Pope John in the final stages of the preparation of *Pacem in Terris*. It strengthened his conviction that 'there exists in man's nature an undying capacity to break through the barriers of error, and to seek the road to truth' (*Pacem in Terris* 158). This leads to the distinction between the error (always to be rejected) and the one who errs (always to be respected), and the idea that even 'erroneous' systems can have 'good and commendable elements' (159). This is why *Pacem in Terris* was the first papal encyclical that was addressed to 'all men of good will'.

It had other novel features. While nineteenth-century Catholic teaching had been suspicious of 'human rights' discourse, John embraced it eagerly and made it a central theme, greatly extending the range and number of 'rights', including those of minorities (95–7) and refugees (103–8).

Pacem in Terris was also original in noting three features of the modern world in which John believed the influence of the Holy Spirit could be discerned: 'the progressive improvement in the social conditions of working people who insist on being treated as human beings' (40); the part played by women in political life and the fact that 'women are gaining an increasing awareness of their natural dignity' (41); and the ending of imperialism.

There was also an implicit condemnation of atomic weapons: 'In this age which boasts of its atomic power, it no longer makes sense (*alienum a ratione est*) to maintain that war is a fit instrument with which to repair the violation of justice.'

Pacem in Terris summed up Pope John's magisterium, and gave the age-old term a new meaning. He spoke about universal human concerns, and articulated the aspirations of ordinary people towards peace and a better life. Whatever authority it had, came not from the power of the speaker – he had none in the conventional sense – but from the cogency and relevance of what he said and the hope it inspired. Pope John was not a 'liberal' in most senses of that term, but he wanted to close the gap between the gospel and life. In *Pacem in Terris* he nudged the Council firmly in that direction.

Note

[1] Gustavo Gutierrez has stressed the importance of this remark for Latin America, adding: 'The preference, the predeliction (not exclusive, let's be clear) for the poor is not opposed in the mind of the Pope to his universal mission; on the contrary it makes his universal mission quite concrete' (Alberigo and Jossua, pp. 239, 240).

4 John XXIII: Bibliography

Bonnot, B. R. (1979) *Pope John XXIII, an Astute Pastoral Leader*. New York, Alba House.

Capovilla, L. F. (ed.) (1978a) *Giovanni XXIII, Lettere 1958–1963*. Rome, Storia e Letteratura.

Capovilla, L. F. (ed.) (1978b) *Vent' Anni dalla Elezione di Giovanni XXIII*. Rome, Storia e Letteratura.

Capovilla, L. F. (1983) *Ite Missa Est*. Padua/Bergamo, Messagero/Grafica e Arte.

Discorsi, massagi, colloqui del Santo Padre Giovanni XXIII, 1958–1963 (1960–7), five volumes plus index, Vatican Polyglot Press.

Hales, E. E. Y. (1965) *Pope John and his Revolution*. London, Eyre and Spottiswoode.

Hebblethwaite, P. (1984) *John XXIII: Pope of the Council;* in the United States, *John XXIII: Shepherd of the Modern World*. London, Geoffrey Chapman; New York, Doubleday.

Moltmann, J. (1977) *The Church in the Power of the Spirit*. London, SCM.

Ratzinger, J. and Messori, V. (1985) *Ratzinger Report: an exclusive interview on the state of the Catholic Church*. Leominster, Fowler Wright; San Francisco, Ignatius Press.

Riccardi, A. (1987) 'Dalla Chiesa di Pio XII alla Chiesa Giovannea', in G. Alberigo, ed., *Papa Giovanni*.Rome-Bari, Laterza.

Rouquette, R. (1968) *Vatican II, la fin d'une Chrétienté*, 2 vols. Paris, Cerf.

Roncalli, A. G. (1965) *Journal of a Soul, Pope John XXIII*, trans. D. White. London, Geoffrey Chapman.

Roncalli, A. G. (1966) *Mission to France 1944–1953*, trans. D. White. London, Geoffrey Chapman.

Trevor, M. (1967) *Pope John*. London, Macmillan.

Van der Plas, M. (1984) *Brieven aan Paus Joannes*. Weesp, The Netherlands, Villa Publishing.

5

THE HISTORY OF THE COUNCIL

MICHAEL J. WALSH

THE YEARS 1959–61

It was the best-prepared Council ever. Some 800 theologians and other experts prepared the agenda. The Church's 2,500 bishops and prelates, heads of men's religious orders (though not of women's!), and faculties of some thirty-seven Catholic universities were asked what they thought were the major problems facing the Church. Some 2,000 replies were received.

Preparatory commissions were set up: the central one included the pope. There were eleven more, together with three secretariats (press, unity and administration), created on 5 June 1960, the feast of Pentecost. At solemn vespers in St Peter's that day, Pope John said, 'The preparation of the Council, however, will not be the task of the Roman curia but, together with the illustrious prelates and consultors of the Roman Curia, bishops and scholars from all over the world will offer their contribution.'

The central commission approved seventy schemata, of which seven went to bishops the July before the Council: on the sources of revelation, moral order, the deposit of faith, family and chastity, liturgy, media and unity. Pope John talked of unity being achieved through the Council. More frequently, however, he spoke of it as a means to modernize the Church so that unity might become possible.

The curia was worried by talk of modernization – especially perhaps by the thought that 2,500 bishops in Rome might make them change their procedures in unwelcome ways. They were even more alarmed by hostility to the papal diplomatic service. They countered the threat by inviting only safe theologians – largely Rome-based – to sit on the preparatory commissions. When pressure was put on them for more radical appointments, invitations were mostly too late to make any significant impact.

THE YEAR 1962: THE FIRST SESSION

In the summer of 1962, in *Appropinquante Concilio*, Pope John promulgated rules of procedure for the Council (confirmed with some additional points the following year by Paul VI's *Ordo Concilii Oecumenici Vaticani Secundi*). This made it clear that *periti* might not all be theologians ('canonists and other experts' were also mentioned), and that there was a distinction between conciliar *periti* and private advisers to bishops. The former, summoned by the

35

pope, could attend discussions in the Council (though normally not speak) and be brought into conciliar committees with the approval of the chairman and members. In practice, chairmen seldom called those whose ideas they found unacceptable. Some two hundred *periti* were summoned to the first session, but by April 1963 the number had reached 348. The final count was 480, though not all were there together. In the event, 281 took part in the whole Council, 95 in only three sessions, 63 at two, and 41 at one.

Of the observers whom Pope John had decided to invite, there were some forty present when the Council began. They represented the spectrum of Christian conviction, East and West – though there was no one from the Eastern Orthodox Churches when it opened, and two Russian Orthodox clergy came shortly after the Council had got under way. By the time it ended, however, the number had swollen to eighty. Most were delegated by their Churches, a few were especially invited – 'as motley a group of "non-Catholics" as ever had been assembled', as Dr Albert Outler, one of their number, described them in 'Strangers within the Gates' (see Outler, 1986, p. 173).

They were placed in the tribune of St Longinus, close to the moderators' table, both for the conciliar proceedings and other events, which gave them an excellent view. Once a week they met together to discuss, with one of the *periti*, matters then under debate in the Basilica. Occasionally they appear to have had some direct influence on the formulation of the documents – the particular mention of the Anglican communion in the decree on ecumenism for example, as of the 'hierarchy of truths' – and their advice was sought, at least by the Unity Secretariat (whose guest they were) on religious freedom. They could also seek to express their views by searching out a friendly bishop to speak for them in the debates. But it was perhaps their indirect influence which, ultimately, was more significant. Not only could they see, they could clearly be seen: every speaker could not but be aware of their non-Catholic auditors, and trim his words to cause as little upset as possible. And they talked regularly to, and presumably influenced, conciliar fathers they met socially.

The observers found the proceedings difficult to follow, and had to be supplied with interpreters, for both pope and curia had insisted on Latin as the language of the debates. The Council, it was claimed, might thus better formulate precise statements. Perhaps it was also expected to put non-Italians at a disadvantage. Curial officials ensured conservative cardinals led discussions in the central commission, and that reports of commissions in the *L'Osservatore Romano* reflected conservative views. Not all members of commissions could be stifled, however, and debates were at times acrimonious.

The opening was on 11 October 1962. John's address stressed that the Council was to be pastoral rather than dogmatic, thus distancing himself from his advisers, and endorsing the view, condemned by Cardinal Ruffini, that the task of the Council was not to proclaim new dogmas but to find new ways of expressing the old (see Abbott, p. 710–19).

Over the next few days Pope John talked with groups such as the press and the observers. The latter were treated with especial courtesy, being provided with the best seats and a translation service. The press, about 1,000 at the opening, were not so lucky. Reporters could not attend meetings, press releases were couched in generalities and favoured the conservative line. The London *Tablet* protested that one press release contained fifteen 'condemns' in twenty-four pages despite the tenor of Pope John's opening address. The secrecy of the Council at first proved a problem for journalists, though gradually language groups of bishops and experts emerged to brief reporters after each congregation. By the fifth week, *La Croix* was linking names of bishops with the general gist of what they had said in the debates: its editor had the good fortune himself to be a *peritus*.

Each day began with Mass celebrated in as many different rites as were represented in the Council Hall inside St Peter's. It was claimed there were twenty-six.

The first general congregation, or working session, was on Saturday, 13 October. The agenda specified the election of sixteen members to each of the ten Conciliar Commissions – the successors of the preparatory ones. Eight members were then to be added by the pope. The commissions were to present the schemata already prepared, and consider amendments. Cardinal Liénart of Lille proposed an alternative plan. Instead of voting immediately, he suggested, regional groups should meet to choose the best qualified candidates. This intervention was backed by Cardinal Frings of Cologne. The two cardinals were so loudly applauded that it was clear they represented the wishes of the majority.

Not only did this process of consultation demonstrate that the Council was in charge of its own proceedings, but it brought the bishops together and helped them to get to know one another. It also allowed the commissions to be representative of the whole Church.

The first conciliar text to be considered, on 22 October at the 4th general congregation, was that on liturgy. It promptly divided the Council into 'traditionalists' and 'progressives'. The former, while rejecting any change, insisted in particular on the retention of Latin. The 'progressives' were alarmed by the fact that the document produced by the preparatory commission on the liturgy had been altered between approval by the central commission (over which the pope himself presided) and reaching the Council itself. It now carried the warning that the Holy See had to approve changes before they could be implemented locally – effectively putting the curia back in charge.

Much of the debate of the first few days concerned the use of Latin in the liturgy, but the debate itself of course took place in Latin. When Cardinal Spellman was presiding, he had such difficulty making himself understood that he had to have someone speak for him. When Maximos IV Saigh, Melchite Patriarch of Antioch, closed the 5th congregation on 23 October, he spoke in French – to the great relief of many.

On 24 October Archbishop Parente, an assessor of the Holy Office, complained of the criticism of the curia implied in the speeches, and wanted the whole schema sent to the Theology Commission to be reworked. He argued that the Holy Office had already yielded a great deal. Further changes required the greatest prudence. A few days later Cardinal Ottaviani asked whether the fathers were planning a revolution. To introduce too many changes, he argued, would cause scandal among the faithful. Ottaviani overran his time, but at first refused to be stopped. When forced to do so, the president's action was greeted by applause: the fact that the president was Alfrink of Utrecht added piquancy to the event. Ottaviani stayed away for a fortnight. Debate continued until 13 November. An attempt was made to stop applause, which brought considerable opposition, and another to put Joseph in the canon of Mass – which the pope himself did in a decree of 13 November.

The liturgy schema was an important opening. It was something about which people felt deeply and divisions among the Council fathers became clear. On the other hand, it did not touch dogma. Revelation was another matter. This followed next, the debate opening on 14 November with a speech from Ottaviani, followed by a presentation of the text which suggested that it was a dogmatic decree concerned with the defence of Catholic doctrine: the existence of 'two sources' of revelation, Scripture and tradition. The schema was promptly attacked by Liénart on the basic ground that there are not two sources of revelation, but only one: the Word of God. He was supported by Cardinal Bea. Debate on 16 November was enlivened by a passionate defence of the schema from the Bishop of Faenza who attacked the Jesuit-run Biblical Institute, of which Bea had been rector. The following day Cardinal Döpfner claimed that the commission responsible for producing the schema had been too much under the influence of the Lateran University – then at odds with the Jesuits, and that the commission had refused to collaborate with the Secretariat for Promoting Unity. The schema therefore reflected only one particular outlook, he argued, and should be rejected. This upset conservatives who insisted, inaccurately, that schemata could only be accepted or amended, not rejected. None the less, an attempt on 20 November to reject the schema failed, though narrowly – possibly because of the way the proposal was framed. The following day the pope ordered its withdrawal. It could not be sent back to the original commission which was dominated by Lateran supporters, so a neatly balanced new one had to be constituted with Ottaviani and Bea as joint chairmen.

During this time the bishops were not only rubbing shoulders with the experts in the coffee shop (known as the Bar-Jonah), but they were also attending lectures by the *periti*. Ottaviani, feeling that the authority of the Holy Office was threatened, tried to persuade the pope to forbid lectures by the Jesuits of the Biblicum – and even have Karl Rahner banned from Rome. Pope John flatly refused. During the third week of the Council, Archbishop Parente appealed to African bishops for support, criticizing them for turning against their old masters (many had been trained at Propaganda Fide) and siding with the northern Europeans. They appeared to ignore him – and organized themselves with a secretariat of their own. Similar evidence of unity emerged from the numerous (about 600) Latin American bishops.

Debate on the all-important, but heavily traditionalist, schema on the Church began at the 31st general congregation on 1 December. It was introduced by Ottaviani, who again stressed that the document before the fathers had been prepared by learned theologians and had the pope's approval.

The previous evening *L'Osservatore Romano* had carried an article critical of news coverage of the Council and commiserating with the curia because it was constantly under attack. The Council, said the author, should not be reported as if it was divided along party lines. The piece tended to blame left-wing publications, whereas in fact the most virulent opposition to the Council had come from the Italian – and to some extent the French – ultra-right. *Osservatore's* view was not shared by Council members. Cardinal Montini, in one of his weekly newsletters for his diocese, directly blamed the slowness of the Council on the curia which had prevented the various commissions co-operating during the preparatory period. When, on 4 December, Suenens called for a complete redrafting of the schema on the Church, he was greeted with prolonged applause and backed by Montini.

Two days later the secretary general, Archbishop Felici, responded to this by announcing that all schemata would be reworked while the Council was in recess. There were to be mixed commissions whose deliberations would be sent to bishops and experts for comment, while a new committee would oversee collaboration between the commissions. It was within these commissions, which now included some of the leading theologians of Germany, France, Belgium and America, that much of the Council's most delicate work of redrafting texts would be done.

Pope John was present at the general congregation on 7 December. Rumours of his ill-health had cast gloom over the previous weeks, and his presence – on foot – brought great applause. Though he was more like his old self, many suspected they were seeing him for the last time. He admitted the Council had begun slowly, but said that was inevitable, and that bishops would work better now they had come to understand different points of view. He asked them to do their homework with the schemata to be sent them, for the Church had no time to lose. Although not a single document had yet been approved, he hoped all would be over by Christmas 1963, the 400th anniversary of the Council of Trent.

THE YEAR 1963: THE SECOND SESSION

In June 1963 Pope John XXIII died. Ironically it fell to Cardinal Ottaviani, most conservative of cardinals, to announce the election of the Cardinal Archbishop of Milan to the papacy as Paul VI. And one of the first acts of Pope Paul was to determine an early date for the opening of the new session – 29 September. The Co-ordinating Commission was summoned to meet on 3 July, just twelve days after Paul's election. The choice of Montini as pope was an enormous encouragement to those working for change in and through the Council. It was known he believed conciliar mechanisms clumsy and its secrecy too strict. He also wanted the schema on the Church debated as soon as possible: it was put first on the new session's agenda. And just a week before the Council opened he warned the papal curia that it must not be an obstacle in the way of reform.

In his opening address on 29 September the pope rejected the notion, common since Vatican I, that the authority of the pontiff alone was sufficient to govern the Church, and listed the four aims of the Council: that the Church should have a clearer idea of its own nature; that there was need for renewal; that Christians of all denominations be brought closer together (he apologized for the Catholic Church's own failings in its relations with non-Catholics); and finally, the need for dialogue between Church and world.

At the beginning of the 37th general congregation Archbishop Felici announced an alteration in the rules governing secrecy: from now on it was permissible to reveal what was said in debates in the Council, though discussion in commissions was still to be kept from journalists. It was also announced that the number of conciliar *periti* was not to be increased – a decision not strictly adhered to. Then debate began on the document on the Church.

The most contentious issue in the early days of the second session was the collegiality of bishops. There was also a skirmish around the question of married deacons, an idea broached in chapter II of the document on the Church, *Lumen Gentium* (officially, *De Ecclesia*). After the Council had moved on from chapter II, Cardinal Ottaviani, without protest from any of those presiding, returned to it in defiance of the rules. His objection was specifically against the idea of a married diaconate, and he accused three *periti* (unnamed but thought to be Rahner, Martelet and Ratzinger) of distributing pamphlets to the fathers soliciting support for such a project. Yet the document referred to by the cardinal did not mention a married diaconate and, somewhat oddly, one of Ottaviani's own advisers, Carlo Balic OFM, promptly did what Ottaviani condemned, distributing pamphlets in favour of a separate schema on Mary in the Council Hall in clear contravention of the rules.

Debate on the Church went on through half the time available for discussion in the entire session, and revisions still had to be brought back for approval. The commission responsible for undertaking this revision was convoked only once a week by its president, Ottaviani. Suspicion began to be voiced that the minority was attempting to control the Council by a delaying tactic which would render it ineffectual and, as the number of bishops attending declined, unrepresentative of the Church at large. Cardinal Suenens's attempt to call a vote to test attitudes in the hall occcasioned a crisis between the moderators (chairmen), the four presidents, and the secretary general, Archbishop Felici, who threatened to resign. The fundamental issue was that of speeding the Council by giving clear directives to the Theological Commission of the collective mind of the fathers. This crisis was not so much averted as won by the progressives, but only after Pope Paul had taken a hand and, on the issues that Suenens had wished to put to the vote, the progressives won a clear majority on 30 October. Ottaviani let it be known, however, that his Theological Commission would regard such votes as guidelines only, not directives.

It was in this atmosphere of crisis that debate began on the pastoral office of bishops on 5 November. It swiftly transpired that the document handed to the fathers for discussion was not that drawn up by the Preparatory Commission, but one revised by members of the Commission who were also members of the curia. None the less, there was a substantial majority in favour of accepting it as a basis for discussion, largely because there was much to be said about the interrelationship of pope, bishops and curia, and the draft provided this opportunity. It was made use of on 8 November by Cardinal Frings of Cologne precisely to call the Theological Commission into line, reminding it that it was there to carry out the wishes of the Council, not to determine what the Council should decide. He went on to criticize the Holy Office for acting as judge and jury when it condemned theologians without giving them an opportunity to know what they were accused of, or of responding. He ended by calling for reform of the curia to include many more qualified lay people.

Cardinal Ottaviani seized the first possible opportunity to reply to Frings's attack, to reassert the authority of the Theological Commission as he understood it, and to claim that an attack on the Holy Office was an attack on the pope himself as its prefect. But that afternoon (8 November) Pope Paul phoned Frings to express his approval of what had been said. He also saw Ottaviani – effectively refusing him support. Indeed, the day before he had received Karl Rahner to thank him for his work for the Council. Not only had Rahner been attacked by Ottaviani a little while before, but he had long suffered at the hands of the Holy Office and his public rehabilitation could be seen as a snub for Ottaviani.

This was soon followed by a further defeat for the conservative faction in the Theological Commission. They had been delaying a statement of the Secretariat for Unity on religious liberty, which, at this stage, was intended to form part of the schema on ecumenism. The American bishops in particular were eager to have the issue debated, and petitioned the pope. Ottaviani first tried to prevent any discussion in the Commission and, when that failed, to delay referring the text to the Council. On 12 November he was out-voted in his own Commission and the document was sent to the printer.

On 15 November Pope Paul presided over a gathering of those in charge of running the Council. Cardinal Lercaro, one of the moderators, stressed the need for greater speed on the part of the commissions, reminding them – an indirect but clear reference to the Theological Commission – that it was not their task to decide disputed issues by presenting for discussion one straightforward text, but to evaluate and organize amendments so that they could be more easily decided in the Council Hall. Though these were the words of Lercaro, there was no doubt he spoke for the pope. On 21 November it was announced that the pope had decided to increase the size of commissions to thirty, and to allow the Council direct election of most of the new members. When the votes were announced it became clear that by far the greater number of the new members were on the 'progressive' wing of the Church.

It was encouraging news, but the second session drew to a close with the vexed issues of religious freedom and the Jews, which were dealt with in the final two chapters of the document on ecumenism, still undecided – though Cardinal Bea insisted they would be discussed in due course. Some were cheered, however, by the news that thanks to lobbying by a group concerned with problems of underdevelopment, 'Schema 17', which treated of the

Church and poverty, would be placed at the beginning of session three, to be introduced as soon as the debate on the Church had been completed.

On 4 December the session came to a formal close, presided over by Pope Paul. In the course of Mass the fathers were asked to vote first upon the Constitution on the Liturgy, and then upon the Decree on Social Communications. Both achieved massive majorities, only four fathers voting against the liturgy document, but a significant number voted against that on communications – which hardly anyone rated highly and some thought an inappropriate subject for the Council. After the votes, the two documents were solemnly promulgated, but the bishops travelled back to their dioceses with a sense that too little had been achieved. It was a poor end to a session begun with high hopes.

THE YEAR 1964: THE THIRD SESSION

Between sessions the Co-ordinating Commission drafted new rules of procedure to speed matters up. There were also new rules for the *periti*, who henceforth might give advice only when asked. Should they attempt to influence the bishops, Archbishop Felici warned them on the first day of the new session, they would lose their privileges, a threat that caused considerable resentment as much among the fathers as among their advisers. The debate on chapter VII on the document on the Church then got underway. It was 15 September 1964, and the 80th general congregation.

The pace certainly quickened – too much so for some fathers who believed the conservative minority was trying to hurry them towards a close, leaving some business unfinished. Chapter II of the Constitution on the Church was finally approved, as was much of Chapter III, article by article, and discussion was begun on the pastoral office of bishops. Then, on 23 September, the 86th general congregation began debate on what had now become a Declaration on Religious Liberty, promptly attacked by Cardinal Ruffini who insisted the title should be 'Religious Tolerance' rather than Liberty, for the latter could not be justified theologically. He was just as promptly rebutted by a string of North American cardinals. Another staunch supporter of liberty was Cardinal Heenan, explicitly drawing upon the experience of English Catholics.

On 28 September, debate was reopened on a Declaration on the Jews, a topic postponed at the end of the second session and, between times, distinctly watered down by the Theological Commission. In the Council Hall the new draft was subjected to such criticism that it was returned to the Commission to be revised into its earlier form.

On 7 October the Council launched into debate about the Apostolate of the Laity. Though the document was about the laity, it had failed to take account of the views of the laity – at least until the previous spring, by which time it was too late for them to have much influence upon its formulation. It was no surprise, therefore, that this schema was decisively rejected by the majority, in part at least because of the emphasis on 'Catholic Action', an ambiguous term which in Italy, Spain and other Latin countries referred to an organization of the laity dependent upon the bishops, while elsewhere it was synonymous with the lay apostolate in any form. At the end of the discussion Pat Keegan, a lay auditor, was invited to speak, the first occasion in modern times that a layman had addressed an ordinary session of an Ecumenical Council. What he chose to say, however, struck the fathers as unexceptional, almost clerical in tone. It was 13 October 1964 and the 100th general congregation.

On 20 October the debate on 'Schema 13' began, what had now become the 'Church in the Modern World'. Though no document had been so thoroughly prepared, there was a last-minute suggestion that it should be dropped, for it was clear that, if this schema was presented, the Council would not be able to finish with the third session. However, as the pope himself had been so committed to it before his election, such an outcome was unthinkable.

The reception of the schema was at first fairly favourable, but gradually became more and more hostile, with Cardinal Heenan of Westminster emerging as perhaps the harshest critic. On 23 October, however, a rather unexpected mid-morning vote (which left some 200 bishops absent from the hall) declared it acceptable as a basis for further discussion. For the next fortnight it was examined section by section. The debates encompassed a vast range of subjects, racial justice, discrimination against women, the *Index* of forbidden books, even tourism, but the most delicate was the discussion on marriage. Between the sessions, Pope Paul had called for restraint on this topic, and on 28 October Cardinal Agagianian announced that some matters would not be brought to the Council floor in a move widely interpreted as favourable to the conservative forces in the curia. In practice, this prohibition did not work – the 'two ends' of marriage and birth control being addressed directly, the latter most outspokenly by Patriarch Maximos IV Saigh. Cardinal Agagianian brought the debate to a sudden close on 30 October to forestall further public discussion outside the Council. By then, however, it was clear no matter how much the fact was denied by the conservative group that the schema would demonstrate a considerable development in the Church's teaching on marriage.

After marriage it was the turn of 'culture' (the Bishop of Strasbourg called for the rehabilitation of Galileo) and of economics. Article 24 was devoted to world solidarity. The suggestion had been made that the topic should be introduced by a lay expert. The name of Barbara Ward was canvassed, and appeared to be accepted until the secretary general intimated it was 'premature' for a woman to address the bishops. Instead, James Norris, an American and the person who had put forward Barbara Ward's name in the first instance, found himself having to deliver a special address, and in Latin, at six hours' notice. It was 5 November 1964, and the 115th general congregation. Norris made a much greater impact than Keegan had done earlier, and his speech was followed by an appeal by Cardinal Frings for a concerted effort on the Church's part to support projects in relief of poverty. There was a brief look at war and peace before debate on 'Schema 13' closed on 10 November, the 119th general congregation.

The debate on 'Schema 13' had been interrupted on 6 November to allow Pope Paul to make an appearance in the Council Hall. Popes had rarely attended Councils, but Paul may have wanted to demonstrate the unity between himself and the bishops. It was imperative, however, to ensure he would be present at the table of Council presidents when debate was reasonably tranquil. The document on missionary activity seemed a likely occasion. Paul introduced the document briefly, and then handed over to Agagianian. He listened to what the cardinal had to say, then left the hall. In the event, the document proved so unacceptable that after two days' debate it was sent back for thorough revision.

The end of the debate on 'Schema 13' was followed by two days of discussion on that on religious life. It was judged acceptable, yet aroused considerable criticism, not least because no women religious had been consulted in its drafting. The formation of priests was next considered. Discussion lasted from 12 to 17 November, apart from 13 November when the pope made a ceremonial offering of his tiara for the benefit of the poor. This document won praise from the liberal majority at the Council, and was readily accepted, subject to a few amendments. Similar, though slightly more muted, approval was given to the propositions on Christian education, discussed from 17 to 19 November, and on the latter date the Council turned its attention briefly to recommendations to simplify marriage legislation and end discrimination against non-Catholic partners in mixed marriages. The proposals were largely welcomed, though Cardinal Heenan objected to removal of the promise by the non-Catholic parent to allow children to be brought up as Catholics, and there was no time to conclude this debate.

These final days of the third session were taking place in increasing gloom. Several documents gave rise to concern as they were wrestled with in the appropriate commissions, none more so than the all-important Dogmatic Constitution on the Church. The minority had proposed a number of important changes: would the Theological Commission accept or reject them? The section mainly at issue was that on collegiality. On 14 November a booklet was distributed outlining the amendments together with the Commission's comments. The text of *Lumen Gentium* had been more or less left alone, but it was now prefixed by an 'Explanatory Note' (*Nota praevia*) which, it was clear when Archbishop Felici communicated it formally to the Council two days later, had come from Pope Paul himself.

The pope's purpose was evident enough. He had been under pressure to water down the doctrine of collegiality. He had not given in – nor had the Commission – as far as the text itself was concerned, but the 'Explanatory Note' interpreted the text in favour of papal authority. In the light of this document, conservative opposition to the constitution all but disappeared. The vote on the constitution as a whole occurred on 19 November, and only ten of the Council fathers voted against it. The text as it now stood was a compromise. The alternative, many of the fathers believed, would have been no text at all.

That same Thursday the majority received another setback. Cardinal Tisserant suddenly announced that further voting on religious liberty would be postponed until the next session, claiming the document now before the Council was so different from what had gone before it needed to be debated all over again. There was an immediate outcry. A petition was organized to the pope, but Pope Paul refused to change Tisserant's decision – made, he said, in accordance with the Council's rules of procedure.

The conservatives had a third victory the following day when the fathers were to vote on the Decree on Ecumenism. Felici said the document had not yet been printed, and some emendations had been made to the text. There was no doubt these eleventh-hour changes were made at the wish of Pope Paul, acting to retain the support of the minority. They had the effect of diminishing the force of the decree, to the distress of non-Catholic observers.

Next the minority requested another postponement, this time of the Unity Secretariat's Declaration on non-Christian religions. The Council's presidents this time would not hear of it, no doubt after the consternation which had been caused the day before, and it received a favourable vote. The Decree on Ecumenism was likewise approved, and so was the schema on the Oriental Churches.

At the closing public session on Saturday, 21 November, there was no applause as a grim-faced pope was carried into St Peter's. The Constitution on the Church, the Decree on Ecumenism and the Decree on Oriental Churches were formally voted upon, and solemnly promulgated. It should have been an occasion for rejoicing. Instead, Paul, in his closing address, implicitly rebuked the Theological Commission for having refused to confer upon the Virgin Mary the title of 'Mother of the Church' in the chapter devoted to her in *De Ecclesia*. The pope now did so himself. There was a noticeable lack of warmth from the assembled bishops.

THE YEAR 1965: THE FOURTH SESSION

At the beginning of the final session, 14 September 1965, Pope Paul entered the basilica with little of the pomp that hitherto had surrounded the papacy. He did not comment upon the subjects the fathers were to discuss. Instead, he announced that he was going to the United Nations in New York to appeal for peace, and that in accordance with the Council's wishes he would establish the long-awaited synod of bishops. Much to the surprise of the bishops, he did this by a *motu proprio* on 15 September, *Apostolica Sollicitudo*.

It was the Council's first full working day, the 128th general congregation, devoted to the vexed topic of religious liberty or, rather, civil liberty in religious affairs. Debate lasted until 20 September, opposition being voiced by a number of Italian and Spanish prelates. Pope Paul was to speak to the United Nations on 4 October and this document was one he very much needed approved, at least in principle, before then. The Council fathers were asked simply to decide whether the text before them was an appropriate basis for a definitive document. By a vote of nearly 2,000 in favour to just over 200 against, it was agreed, amid applause, to be so.

Immediately after this vote, the Council turned its attention once more to 'Schema 13', now denominated by the Co-ordinating Commission, a 'Pastoral Constitution'. It was a long document (as one speaker remarked, there was a danger it would grow so long that no one would read it), but after only two days of discussion the fathers voted overwhelmingly to accept the draft as the basis for the final document and went on to debate it section by section.

On 7 October there began the debate on the revised version of the document on the missionary activity of the Church, and on 11 October votes were taken on the schemas on religious life and priestly formation in the seminaries. The latter document dealt, among other topics, with the obligation to celibacy, but, before it could be voted on, Archbishop Felici read a letter from the pope effectively banning discussion of celibacy, and insisting upon the observance of celibacy throughout the Latin Church. Paul thus neatly avoided a vote expressly on this issue, which might have revealed the Council fathers to have been more or less evenly divided. Cardinal Bea had later to point out firmly that it did not apply in the East.

Discussion on the schema on priestly life and ministry began on 13 October. It was voted upon as a whole on 16 October, and taken up again after a week's break on 25–27 October. The debate was unremarkable save, perhaps, for a paean on the virtues of golf for the clergy from Cardinal Heenan. On 23 October, however, the pope re-established the 'priest-worker' movement in France, suppressed in 1954 at the instigation of the Holy Office. This somewhat unexpected decision gave ammunition to those who felt the schema on priestly life was too spiritual in tone.

On 14 and 15 October – the latter date was the 150th general congregation – there was a touch of drama over the document on the Jews, or, more correctly, the Declaration on Non-Christian Religions, of which the earlier declaration on the Jews now formed a part. The final vote was due on 16 October. It was suddenly realized, however, that many of the bishops would be absent, some on pilgrimage to the Holy Land. Too small a number of affirmative votes could seem an insult to the Jews; the vote was taken immediately. The numbers against it were still high (250), but it passed with a respectable majority and was ready for promulgation.

There was a feeling, after the week's break, that the Council was all but over. At a public session on 28 October, five documents (on the Pastoral Office of Bishops, on Priestly Formation, on Religious Life, on Christian Education and on Non-Christian Religions) were formally voted upon, and promulgated, as were the documents on Divine Revelation and the Apostolate of the Laity on 18 November. On 30 November the Decree on Missionary Activity was voted through chapter by chapter, and then approved in its entirety.

The Pastoral Constitution on the Church in the Modern World, however, provided the bulk of the work of the fourth session. Section by section it was being revised in the commissions and then approved during the general congregations – despite last-minute attempts to modify it to contain an explicit condemnation of communism. A more serious challenge to the text, however, came from a 'higher authority' – which could only mean the pope – on 24 November when the Secretary of State asked that explicit mention be made of Pius XI's and Pius XII's doctrine on marriage, which would not only condemn all forms of artificial contraception (at this point, before *Humanae Vitae*, such a ban was not a foregone conclusion), but would also subordinate conjugal love to the procreation of children as the purpose of marriage. The pope's request was all the odder because there was already in existence a special papal commission discussing birth control and related issues. Eventually the commission managed to produce a text which cited Pius XI in footnotes, generally disapproved of birth control without being too specific, and recognized the importance of children to a marriage without limiting marriage to that purpose.

Monday, 6 December, was a dramatic day in the history of the Council. The Constitution on the Church in the Modern World was resoundingly approved, a special jubilee was proclaimed to celebrate the Council, and a major reform of the Roman curia was announced which, in particular, seemed to curtail the power of the Holy Office – its name being changed to the 'Congregation for the Doctrine of the Faith'.

As the Council drew to a close, Pope Paul said formal goodbyes to different groups. On 4 December he took his leave of the observers from other Churches in a prayer service which scandalized a number of the bishops because it breached the old rules against *communicatio in sacris*. The final public session took place on 7 December, in the course of which Pope Paul removed the excommunication of 1054 against the patriarch of Constantinople. In Istanbul the patriarch himself reciprocated. The final four documents were voted upon, and promulgated. That evening the *periti* were thanked for their help, and urged to go on talking to bishops now that they had learned to do so. The following day, the feast of the immaculate conception, there was a closing ceremony in St Peter's Square. Two days earlier, at the 168th and last general congregation, 2,392 Council fathers had been present.

5 The History of the Council: Bibliography

Hebblethwaite, P. (1984) *John XXIII: Pope of the Council.* London, Geoffrey Chapman.

Moorman, J. R. H. (1986) 'Observers and Guests of the Council', in Stacpoole, pp. 155–69.

Neufeld, K. H. (1988) 'In the Service of the Council: Bishops and Theologians at the Second Vatican Council', R. Latourelle, ed., *Vatican II, Assessments and Perspectives, Vol. I.* New York, Paulist Press, pp. 74–105.

Outler, A. C. (1986) 'Strangers within the Gates', in Stacpoole, pp. 170–83.

Suenens, Cardinal L. J. (1986) 'A Plan for the Whole Council', in Stacpoole, pp. 88–105.

6

PAUL VI

PETER HEBBLETHWAITE

At some point in 1975, when he was seventy-eight and beginning to feel weary, Pope Paul VI made the following note:

> What is my state of mind? Am I Hamlet or Don Quixote? On the left? On the right? I don't feel I have been properly understood. My feelings are: '*Superabundo gaudio*. I am full of consolation, overcome with joy, throughout every tribulation' (2 Cor. 7.4) (*Notizario*, 1, p. 50).

The whole of Giovanni Battista Montini is contained in these lines. He certainly underwent many 'tribulations' and was often misunderstood. He knew that he was accused of indecisiveness and vacillation (that is what Hamlet means to Italians) and seems to have felt he may have broken his lance on windmills (that is what Don Quixote means). He thought he was a moderate. Neither left nor right, he believed he occupied that 'extreme-centre' briefly claimed by Cardinal Léon-Joseph Suenens in the post-conciliar period. Did he not suspend Archbishop Marcel Lefebvre to the right as intrepidly as the 'liberal' ex-Abbot of St Paul's-without-the-walls, Giovanni Franzoni? He did. Case proven.

But this passage reveals other features of Montini's nature. He was lucid about himself and knew perfectly well what was being said behind his back. With his keen sense of the complexity of situations, he refused to see the world or the Church in black-and-white terms. By professional training he had the diplomat's sense of nuances. He listened to critics as well as to flatterers (no court is complete without them), and was able to learn from them.

Second, his spirituality was based on the Epistles of St Paul. Though not a Scripture scholar in the strict sense, he knew the Pauline Epistles well and a selection of his lectures on St Paul from the 1930s were published after his death (*Colloqui Religiosi*, Brescia, 1981). This interest also helps explain his unexpected choice of name when elected pope. One can also add that St Paul, who plumbs the depths of desolation but also knows the heights of consolation and joy, provided Montini with a practical spirituality that kept him going throughout his long 'hidden life' in the Secretariat of State (1925–54), his pastoral ministry in Milan (1955–63) and finally, his Petrine ministry. He quotes frequently Seneca's maxim, '*Quotidie morimur*' (We die daily), but transforms it by St Paul's gloss: '*Quotidie morior per vestram gloriam, fratres*' (Brethren, for you I die every day: 1 Cor. 15.31) (*Lettere ai Familiari*, I, p. 351, and II, p. 371).

In a word-association test, joy, *gioa*, *Gaudium et Spes*, are not terms that readily spring to mind in his connection. Those who saw Paul VI from a distance heard only his increasingly strangulated voice and apparently complaining tone. Yet people almost invariably felt better for meeting him privately. His last question to bishops on their *ad limina* visits was always the courteous: 'And now, is there anything I can do for *you*?' The sense of sustaining joy was not incompatible with feeling that the papal office was like being crucified. He had served directly under two popes, Pius XI and Pius XII, and knew the stresses and strains he would have to face.

After his election, he went to the 'Milanese' church of San Carlo Borromeo and quite openly wept (why not? we used to pray for the 'gift of tears') as he quoted the words of Jesus to Peter: 'When you were young, you girded yourself and walked where you would; but when you are old, you will stretch out your hands, and another will gird you and carry you where you do not wish to go' (John 21.18). He was already sixty-seven. Was that too old? One might argue that Montini, who had more 'on-the-job' training for the office of pope and was intellectually better prepared for it than anyone since Benedict XIV in the eighteenth century, became pope too late to give of his best.

In th 1950s Montini was the man everyone wanted to meet. Frank Giles, then Rome correspondent for *The Times*, says that though technically below Monsignor Domenico Tardini in rank,

> Most people credited him with having more influence, especially with the Pope. That belief must have accounted for the number of those wanting to see him and the fevered state of his waiting-room. He had the enviable but potentially inconvenient gift of making each visitor feel that he was the person Montini had been waiting all his life to talk to. The result was that his daily arrangements became hopelessly dislocated. It was not unknown for people with appointments to wait several hours before they were ushered in (Giles, 1986, pp. 106–7).

Giles was advised to take sandwiches.

But it was worth waiting, for 'Montini was a great talker of great subtlety, the very opposite of the earthy and outspoken Tardini'. Giles recalls one remark when Montini was criticizing the De Gasperi Christian Democratic government for inaction while denying that he was doing anything of the kind (a typical Montini ploy): 'In political questions the Church has to be general, just as in religious matters she cannot afford not to be particular' (ibid., p. 109).

But if Montini was so indispensable in the later stages of the pontificate of Pius XII, why was he suddenly packed off to Milan *without* the cardinal's hat that routinely went with the office? That the archbishop of the prestigious see of Milan, graced by St Ambrose and St Charles Borromeo, should not be made a cardinal looked like a deliberate snub. Montini's very popularity meant that he had enemies. He knew French lay intellectuals like Jacques Maritain (ambassador to the Holy See, 1945–8) and Jean Guitton, who spent 8 September with him every year from 1950 to the end of his life. He was believed to be pro-French, and therefore 'liberal'. In 1953 the young Monsignor Derek Worlock was taken aside by Cardinal Giuseppe Pizzardo and warned that 'Montini is the most dangerous man in Rome'.

The particular incident that led to his removal was apparently as follows. Montini attended a 'secret' meeting of the Catholic youth movement (GIAC), whose president, Marco Rossi, was nominated by the pope. Their purpose was to put a stop to the alliance of the Christian Democrats and the Neo-Fascists being promoted by Luigi Gedda, head of Catholic Action. Montini agreed with the students that such an alliance could only prove disastrous for the Church, and Rossi resigned as a protest. It was unheard of to resign from posts nominated by the pope. Montini kept the letter on his desk, wondering what to do. He was accused of 'withholding information from the Holy Father' and so relegated to Milan.

This story has an added interest. Rossi went on to become a psychiatrist. In a book published in 1975, he praises Montini for the courage he had displayed in supporting him twenty years earlier, but adds this comment:

> This was when I began to understand his drama, though never to accept it. There was a conflict between the role and the man, between the priest who wanted to lead a hidden life and the public *persona* who worked within a regime of absolute power which he faithfully served while understanding the need to revolt against it. This led to a deep conflict within himself which carried with it the handicap that he did not really understand the ordinary world, was remote from everyday life, and so lacked balance. He was always tempted by abstraction and idealism (Rossi, 1975, p. 117).

One does not have to accept all of that to recognize that the assessment is shrewd. What happens when the man who for decades faithfully served the absolute regime while at the same time understanding the need to revolt against it, becomes the head of it? He will seek to reform it (see Chapter 9(A) curial reform) and make it less absolute (see Chapter 9(F) synods), but he will hardly revolutionize it.

The tension that every honest office-holder in the Church must feel between 'the system' and his (male language appropriate here) Christian pastoral impulses is most acute for the Bishop of Rome. For there is no one to blame above him. Everything Rossi says is illustrated by the story of *Humanae Vitae*, which proved to be the central crisis of his pontificate. Once the Papal Commission had been disbanded in June 1966, Paul VI was on his own.

'How easy it is to study, to study,' he said, 'how hard to conclude?' But what on earth was he studying? Rossi's remarks about 'abstraction and idealization' come in here. A celibate cannot possibly *imagine* without sin (in which there is no *parvitas materiae*) what sexual intercourse is like, and is therefore hardly well placed to judge the psychological effects of artificial contraception.

Did Paul VI, for example, ever wonder how it was that his parents, belonging to the prosperous and cultivated Lombardy semi-aristocracy, contrived to have only three children, while the share-cropping peasants, the Roncallis, had no less than twelve? Such questions are distasteful for a fastidious cleric who thinks of sexuality as a loss of self-control.

His letter written to congratulate his elder brother Lodovico when his engagement was announced, is typical of the sermons he preached at the marriages of so many friends. Here is a sample:

> Looking at it selfishly, I can say that the happiness of the family now depends on you, for it is in you that the family is renewed and starts again. We who stand on the touchline are glad that you are happy. You know that being happy is a difficult business. But the Lord has made it easier for you by giving us the lesson taught so

50

simply and sublimely by our parents – the joy of love, that is of understanding and being understood, of giving and receiving, of sacrificing oneself to be recreated, of pouring out the treasures of one's own heart only to find them multiplied endlessly. You have the privilege of having found a lovely woman, privileged and – you know this better than I do – unique. Having found your precious pearl, see to it that your soul is clad in a new personality (*Notizario*,12, pp. 99–100).

Lodovico treasured this letter and published it only in 1986. More than a period piece – it dates from 1924 – it may throw light on the view of marriage that led to *Humanae Vitae*.

Thus the 'study' on which he embarked was, one suspects, confined to one aspect of the question: was the Church's authority so committed by *Casti Connubii* of 1931 that any change now would discredit that authority? Once the four moralists of the minority took over, and the question reverted back to the Holy Office (still presided over at this date by Cardinal Alfredo Ottaviani), there could be no doubt about the answer: consistency required a continued ban on contraception. Paul VI tried to modify the harshness of the early drafts by injecting a tone of patient pastoral compassion, but by then the damage to the Church's credibility was done.

Yet *Humanae Vitae* was 'prophetic' in two senses at least. The feminist movement has combined with ecology to make many women feel that stuffing themselves with pills is not what Mother Nature wants, and that learning to understand their bodies by the rhythm method is superior. Second, how liberal Catholics pooh-poohed when Paul VI said that the widespread use of contraceptives 'could open the way to marital infidelity and a general lowering of standards' (*Humanae Vitae* 17). No, they said, we are talking only about the responsible use of contraceptives by those who have already had several children. Here not much study was needed (a few David Lodge novels would do) to show that the pope was right and the liberal Catholics wrong. Yet one cannot escape the feeling that if *Humanae Vitae* had been essentially a reasoned condemnation of abortion, the witness of the Church would have been all the more powerful.

Another way of expressing the 'tension' that racked Paul VI is to consider him as the heir of Pius XII and John XXIII. He could emulate neither the austere aristocracy of Pius XII, whom he revered and always defended, nor the comfortable geniality of John XXIII for whom he felt great affection (dating back to 1925).

An Italian scholar has tried to trace their influence on Paul VI by noting how many times he quoted them. We get the following result in the first five years (Pius first): 1963, 28–63; 1964, 53–36; 1965, 30–43; 1966, 31–34; 1967, 22–35. In the year of *Humanae Vitae*, Pius wins 26 to 17 and in 1969 by 34 to 28. I will pursue this arithmetic no longer except to say that John's only winning year subsequently was 1971, and that the last two years were 3–3 and 2–2 draws (Melloni, 1984, p. 173). Melloni uses these data to argue that the influence of Pius prevailed as the pontificate wore on. There is something in that. But such statistics can be used to prove almost anything. Yet there is, of course, what Melloni calls a 'double continuity'.

If Montini had immediately succeeded Pius XII, it is unlikely that he would have called a Council. We know this from the fact that on the evening of the day Pope John announced *his* Council, Cardinal Montini rang his old mentor, the Oratorian Giulio Bevilacqua, and said: 'This holy old boy doesn't realize what a hornet's nest he's stirring up.' To which Bevilacqua replied: 'Don't worry, the Holy Spirit is still awake in the Church' (Fappani and Molinari, 1979, p. 171).

But he soon became the keenest and most enlightened Italian expounder of the Council, and wrote a pastoral letter for Lent 1962, *Pensiamo al Concilio* (Let's think about the Council), that learnedly explains to the Milanese what is going to happen. It is fair to say that it has the sweep and scope of an encyclical. Some saw it as a policy platform for the conclave that could not long be delayed. It also implied that the Roman curia would have to change as a result of the Council:

> The Church throughout the world received orders and instructions which it obeyed willingly enough, though sometimes it regretted that there were no arrangements for dialogue and that it had not been invited to collaborate; the result was that unity had to be lived out in passive acceptance rather than celebrated in fraternity (*Pensiamo al Concilio* 9; see Hebblethwaite, 1984, p. 409).

There he defined, but in his customary idealistic way, his own pontificate. Fraternity would become something to celebrate joyfully, and unity would no longer be glum uniformity.

In an hitherto untranslated note probably dating from the summer of 1963, just after his election, Paul VI reflects on the 'difficult succession'. It would be naïve and vain to try to emulate Pope John, who was unique and unrepeatable. Paul can't hope to equal John but, he adds wistfully, he can't even be *like* him. His attempts to dangle babies on his knee had proved disastrous. So he stopped trying. However, he then says that he has continued the work of John XXIII with such fidelity that, 'if anything, the criticism that I lack initiatives of my own would be nearer the mark' (*Notizario*, 13, pp. 15–16).

He then remarks on the 'myth' that had grown up around John XXIII:

> Harm, and serious harm is done to the memory of Pope John when one attributes to him attitudes he did not have . A good man? yes. An indifferent man? no. How firmly he clung to doctrine, and much he feared certain dangers . . . Pope John was not weak, was not a compromiser, was not indulgent towards erroneous opinions or towards the so-called inevitability of history etc. His dialogue was not merely goodness leading to cowardly renunciation (ibid.)

This is an important statement. It means that Paul VI saw himself as the true heir of Pope John – but of a very different Pope John from the version usually presented to the public. He laboured throughout his pontificate from (what he considered) the false expectations aroused by Pope John. He could do nothing to change that.

In the same note he claims that, in some sense, he was 'more modern' than good Pope John (he mentions his appearances at the Milan Fair as evidence); and says 'perhaps our life is marked by love of our own time, of our world more clearly than by anything else' (ibid.) When he said much the same thing at the end of the Council, Archbishop Marcel Lefebvre and the right-wing were up in arms at this 'humanism'. Paul VI did love the 'modern world' and saw it reflected through the painters and writers he admired. But there was always what he calls in this note 'the loyal conviction that Christ is both necessary and true'.

There has been much unprofitable speculation about whether John XXIII *could* have concluded the Council successfully. What is absolutely sure is that Montini, even during the first session when Pope John was alive, provided the plan that saved the Council from chaos and then, on becoming pope, saw it patiently through to the end despite formidable difficulties.

The plan was put forward in a letter to Cardinal Amleto Cicognani, Secretary of State, dated 18 October 1962, when the Council was barely a week old (*L'Osservatore Romano*, 26 January 1984, or Hebblethwaite, 1984 pp. 442–4). No one has so far questioned the judgement that 'Montini's letter is the single most important document for understanding not only the first session but the whole Vatican Council'.

Montini was more far-sighted than anyone else present, certainly more than the many 'progressives' who could see no further ahead than the next vote (perhaps that was the influence of the press). But even so, it was far easier to set out a project for the Council than to implement it.

Let us consider one 'test-case' for Paul VI's handling of the Council. The second and third sessions were dominated by the question of 'collegiality'. That episcopal ordination made one a member of the episcopal college was accepted in principle by the second session. But there was still a long way to go, for the intransigent opposition not only refused to give way but put intense private pressure on Paul to reject this pernicious doctrine of collegiality. A private note, signed by twenty cardinals and ten major religious superiors, reached Paul VI on the eve of the third session (see Hebblethwaite, 1988, pp. 598–601 and p. 614).

The leader in this initiative was the Spanish canonist Cardinal Arcadio Larraona, patron of Opus Dei, and Archbishop Marcel Lefebvre was among the signatories. The letter said that collegiality was novel, unfounded, unscriptural, 'not even solidly probable', and hinted at the powerful influence of 'non-doctrinal forces, whose aims and methods are not beyond reproach' (by which they meant that the press was distorting the event by presenting it in terms of heroes and villains). Paul would be going against his papal oath if he accepted collegiality. The matter should not be put to the vote. Recommended action: suspend the session, and submit the matter to a new mixed commission that would report when the question had 'matured'. That might take a long time, they intimated.

Paul VI was very sensitive to this minority position. He admitted he felt somewhat bitter, though only in Latin: *Quadam amaritudine affectus sum*, and resolved to stress henceforward the positive aspects of collegiality. So he held firm and, after the decisive vote on paragraph 21 of chapter 3 of *Lumen Gentium*, noted late at night:

> We are satisfied because: this is not a new doctrine, except for the good it allows us to foresee; it is not *immatura* (not yet ripe): the yes vote is attributable to Vatican I, to the two previous sessions, to the really profound studies of the Theological

Commission, to the general development of theological studies in the Church, to the Church's self-awareness, to ecumenism; it is not contrary to the primacy (reaffirmed at least 20 times).

The Church is both monarchical and hierarchical; having collaborators is not a limitation; what would happen if this doctrine were not approved? Feudalism? Ecclesiastical irresponsibility? etc.

Instead: solidarity, charity, unity; intrinsic and constitutional bonds with the primacy; overcoming of Gallicanism, nationalism (cf. local episcopal conferences) and fears of papal aggression; obedience derived from within; authority without jealousy or exclusiveness (*Non rapinam arbitratus est* – He did not think it plunder, (Phil. 2.6). (Caprile, 1986, pp. 351–2).

These rather scrappy notes, jotted down late at night on 22 September 1964 take us to the heart of Paul VI, and illustrate how he saw his Petrine ministry in relation to the ministry of other bishops. They show that he was thoroughly sincere in his acceptance of collegiality.

But – in Montini's case there was always a but – he still felt he should try to enable the minority to vote *placet* on collegiality. He did not want to see them simply crushed, not only because he respected their opinion, but because he would have to go on working with them after the Council. Hence the formula: after the Council he wanted there to be *des convaincus, pas de vaincus*.

This, it is now clear, was the motive behind the *nota praevia* which accompanies *Lumen Gentium* (Abbott, pp. 97–101). It was not designed to contradict chapter 3 on collegiality, still less subtly to undermine it; it was to enable the die-hard conservative minority to vote for chapter 3 with a clear conscience. The other 'disappointments' during the final week of the third session (known as *la settimana nera*), such as the last-minute papally imposed amendments to the decree 'on Ecumenism', had a similar function: to make the text more acceptable to the minority.

But little of this was clearly known at the time, and so some observers concluded that Paul VI secretly connived with the minority. On the conscious level, this was almost certainly not so, though deep down there may have been a certain complicity. But Paul's 'solution' to the problem was a typically 'diplomatic' one that appears to achieve something valuable but may satisfy neither side in the long run. The majority went on feeling unsure about his real convictions, while the minority were not assuaged. Paul's penchant for 'diplomatic' solutions of this kind also meant that many Council texts remained ambivalent.

Whatever the theory, Paul VI's pontificate acted out dramatically the tensions between primacy and collegiality – but this came about only because he took collegiality seriously. Cardinal Suenens pointed out to him that although no one could say he had *no right* to produce *Humanae Vitae* on his own, it would have had more credibility had it been collegially prepared. Is that why he wrote no more encyclicals after *Humanae Vitae*?

Octogesima Adveniens (1971) on the 80th anniversary of *Rerum Novarum* was not an encyclical but a letter to Cardinal Maurice Roy, then president of International Justice and Peace. Yet it represented a great advance on *Populorum Progressio* (1967), which showed that he was still listening and learning. It assigns to the local churches the task of discerning the signs of the times, for 'in view of the varied situations in the world, it is difficult to give one teaching to cover them all, or to offer a solution that has universal value' (no. 4). Such is not our intention or our mission, he modestly concedes. His last major document, *Evangelii Nuntiandi* (1975), was even more 'collegial' in that it represented his resolution of the impasse of the 1974 Synod on Evangelization. Here one sees the function of the primacy as holding in balance the different tendencies which always threaten to tear the Church apart. He was still trying to govern the Church from what he took to be the 'centre'.

In 1930, while making a retreat at Monte Cassino, Montini meditated on 'authority as service' and wrote:

> When one has an office, one should carry it out with courage and firmness; without being depressed or crawling, one should not merely do what is possible, but should try, dare and risk making the office as beneficent as possible. All dodging of problems – whether out of laziness or exhaustion – goes against the Holy Spirit. One should therefore learn how to give orders, and how to put up with the unsuccessful results of one's efforts (*Notizario*, 11, 1985, p. 21).

Not a bad epitaph.

6 Paul VI: Bibliography

Caprile, S.J. (1986) *Paolo VI, Discorsi e Documenti sul Concilio*. Brescia, Istituto Paulo VI.

Fappani, A. and Molinari, F. (1979) *Montini Giovane*. Turin, Marietti.

Giles, F. (1986) *Sundry Times, An Autobiography*. London, John Murray.

Hebblethwaite, P. (1984) *John XXIII, Pope of the Council*. London, Geoffrey Chapman.

Hebblethwaite, P. (1988) 'From G. B. Montini to Pope Paul VI', *Journal of Ecclesiastical History*, April, pp. 309–20.

Hebblethwaite, P. (1988) 'A Private Note and What It Wrought', *America*, 18 June, pp. 598–601.

Hebblethwaite, P. (1989) 'An Anglican Visit to Milan', *Theology*, September, pp. 374–83.

Magregor-Hastie, R. (1964) *Pope Paul VI*. London, Frederick Muller.

Melloni, A. (1984) '*Paulo VI e l' imaggine dei suoi predecessori*', in *Paul VI, Modernité dans l'Eglise*. Rome, Ecole Française.

Notizario. The Istituto Paolo Sesto in Brescia has held conferences on the work of Paul VI and publishes a *Notizario* of its many activities (available from Istituto Paolo Sesto, via Gesio Calini 30, 25121 Brescia, Italy).

Paul VI et la Modernité dans l'Eglise, Acta of a conference organized and published by L'Ecole Française de Rome, Palazzo Farnese, 1984.

Rossi, M. V. (1975) *Il Giorni della Onnipotenza*. Rome, Coines.

7

THE KEY TEXTS

ADRIAN HASTINGS

The documents of the Second Vatican Council have provided the Catholic Church with what is undoubtedly the weightiest body of official teaching in the twentieth century. However, although the Council said an awful lot, much of it was rather long-winded; moreover, it avoided solemn definitions and almost avoided direct condemnations. Its teaching is not – at least for the most part – either definitive or exclusive of error. Nevertheless, the authority of an ecumenical Council, more representative of the whole world than any previous Council, working responsibly and prayerfully across four years with all the support it could get from the ablest theologians, is clearly in human and ecclesial terms as considerable as can be. While the Council was in general described as having a 'pastoral' rather than a 'dogmatic' purpose, it went out of its way to name two of its principal documents 'Dogmatic Constitutions'. So its teaching may in theory be ranged along a spectrum from the 'dogmatic' to the 'pastoral'. In reality, however, it is not so easy to separate the two. The more dogmatic statements were surely ventured upon chiefly for pastoral purposes, while the more pastoral initiatives invariably contain within them very considerable theological presuppositions.

In practice – and even in theory – there is also a spectrum of the more and the less significant. In theory, the 'Constitutions' were clearly intended to be more authoritative than the 'decrees'; and, all in all, they were. But while some things in one document may be manifestly weighty, other parts of the same document appear platitudinous, verbose or banal, a stringing together of old-fashioned clichés gilded with a little rhetoric drawn from the often superficial optimism of the early 1960s. Cardinal Heenan declared both the decree on the mass media and the Declaration on Christian Education 'not of conciliar calibre'. It is hard to disagree. There is indeed in all a welter of words; and while some sections of the final documents had been intensely discussed, formulated and reformulated across several sessions, much else – quite inevitably – was barely discussed at all. In these circumstances, it is crucial for the reader twenty-five years later, faced with these sixteen documents, to be able to apply principles of evaluation; but these principles should not be drawn extraneously from some private viewpoint or ideology, but instead drawn intrinsically from the Council's own experience and the immediate aftermath of implementation.

What mattered most? To answer that question it is possible to make use of a number of criteria:

1 Things matter if, as themes, they can be seen to be frequently returned to

in the documents and, moreover, to be responding to the stated purposes of Pope John in calling the Council.

2 Things matter to the extent that they are significantly new in terms of official Catholic teaching; that is to say, in comparison with papal teaching or the major textbooks of approved theology of the first half of the twentieth century. It is, of course, important to remind ourselves that the Council went out of its way, for instance, to reiterate that it was in no way contradicting Vatican I and instances of contradiction should not be lightly proposed. It would seldom, anyway, be a matter of contradiction, more – as the Council itself would have stressed – of complementarity. But you do not call an ecumenical Council and keep it going for four years at vast expense in order principally to repeat what is already well known to be the teaching of the Church. That would be absurd. Common sense requires one to recognize that the most significant things were what was being said for the first time, at least in that form, in modern Catholic history and with such authority.

3 Things matter to the extent that they were discussed at considerable length and drafted with particular care. We know which those passages were from detailed accounts of the Council events. Passages on collegiality, religious liberty and the Jews, for instance, matter greatly because they were at the centre of lengthy conciliar debate as many other passages were not.

4 Things matter because the precise form of words in which they are expressed indicates that the Council intended this particular passage to have an especially authoritative character.

5 Things matter because they directly lead to specific and major changes in the life of the Church, its worship and institutional structures. Such passages (at least outside the Constitution on the Liturgy) are remarkably rare, but there are a few which called for and obtained almost immediate implementation in a way that introduced significant new dimensions into Church life.

Applying these five criteria to the documents it is possible to distinguish reasonably enough between three types of significance which can best be considered separately. The first type is that of new general orientations of a very wide sort, basic themes that keep coming back across the documents and hence can be said to characterize the Council's mind and achievement as a whole. The second type is that of rather specific passages which contain a recognizable shift on pre-conciliar teaching. The third type is that of major practical decisions requiring some sort of new institution or the adoption of specific behaviour of a sort hitherto either forbidden or, at least, not encouraged.

As regards new and wide-ranging orientations in Church life – our vaguest category – we will note six, while recognizing that these might well be grouped in different ways.

(a) 'The People of God'. At the time of the Council this was surely the characteristically conciliar expression which mattered most to the majority of people throughout the Church. Previously, the Church had been usually defined as a 'society' (even a juridically 'perfect society'), a term taken to imply the primary need for authority, and frequently used in relation to the state. It was almost never described as the 'People of God'. This highly biblical term, though basic to the New Testament and frequently used in early liturgical prayers, had almost completely disappeared from pre-conciliar ecclesiology. Its evocative power derived not only from its biblical roots, but also from the fact that it did not evoke clergy or hierarchy but rather the basic equality of all the baptized. The decision to accord a full chapter to it in the Constitution on the Church, and prior to that on the hierarchy, was symbolically one of the most important the Council ever took. While the whole theological context of that chapter was important, we may note here especially the stress on the priesthood of all the faithful – a theme that Luther made much of, but which Catholic tradition had downgraded ever since.

The active role of the laity in the Church was very much a theme of the pontificates of Pius XI and Pius XII. The conciliar stress upon it was not new and the Decree on the Lay Apostolate is one of the less advanced texts the Council produced. Nevertheless, even here the shift is noticeably away from a hierarchically controlled model of 'Catholic Action', as it had come to be called, to a far more diversified one. But still more important for the laity in the Church than either the decree or chapter 4 of *Lumen Gentium* (precisely on the laity), remains chapter 2, 'The People of God', which located the basic roles of all Christians in aspects of the nature of the Church deeper than the hierarchical. Nothing has been more ominous in the doctrinal shift of the 1980s than the actual hostility to this term which can now be found in Roman teaching.

(b) Next comes the extremely widespread stress upon the Eucharist as the centre of the Church and its unity. Again and again in different documents it is emphasized that 'in the sacrament of the eucharistic bread the unity of all believers is both expressed and brought about' (*Lumen Gentium* 3), the Eucharistic celebration is 'the centre and culmination of the whole life of the Christian community' (*Christus Dominus* 30). While Pius XII's encyclical *Mystici Corporis* brought back the concept of the Church as the body of Christ to the centre of Catholic teaching, it most remarkably avoided the slightest reference in this to the relationship between the Eucharistic body and the ecclesial body, and omitted the slightest notice of the basic Pauline text for that relationship, 1 Corinthians 10.17. The Council, on the contrary, when speaking about the Church as body of Christ, insisted that it is the Eucharistic body which forms the ecclesial body and twice quoted 1 Corinthians 10.17. Again the Council stressed that the Church itself in consequence of all this has a sacramental character: it too is the 'sacrament of salvation'. Further, the word 'communion', a term again involving a verbal identification of Church and Eucharist, was so much used by the Council that it has subsequently been seen to express the Council's ecclesiology most profoundly and has been made great use of in such documents as those of ARCIC. Finally, it is the Council's stress upon the Eucharist–Church relationship that provides the root for its theology of local churches; wherever the Eucharist is celebrated, there is the

Church present: *Ubi Eucharistia, ibi Ecclesia*. Nothing of this was to be found in mainstream pre-conciliar Roman ecclesiology (though it is to be found in 1950s books representative of the 'new theology' by scholars like de Lubac and Congar, writers under much official suspicion at the time). Where post-conciliar theology will say that the Eucharist gives the Church its unity, pre-conciliar theology would undoubtedly have been most likely to declare that it was the papacy that did so.

(c) The third decisive orientation is the widespread insistence upon the primacy of Scripture in theory and in practice. The 'Teaching Office is not above the word of God, but serves it' (*Dei Verbum* 10), 'Easy access to Sacred Scripture should be provided for all the Christian faithful' (*Dei Verbum* 22). While the preparatory drafts, drawn up in Rome before the Council opened and very largely rejected by the fathers, had made heavy use of scholastic terminology and not much of Scripture – as was generally characteristic of pre-conciliar theology – the Council almost systematically reversed this, eliminating scholastic terms again and again and falling back on biblical ones. This scriptural insistence is naturally to be found set out most clearly in the Dogmatic Constitution on Revelation, but it is in fact present in all the important documents. It was probably this scriptural revolution more than anything else which made the ecumenical one possible, and one of its earliest post-conciliar consequences was the beginning of active co-operation with the Bible translation societies, whose work had hitherto been boycotted by Catholics.

(d) Pluralism. A repeated stress upon the benefits brought by diversity is a recurrent theme of the Council documents. This returns again and again in a variety of contexts, but the theological heart of it is to be found in the development of a theology of the Church as a communion of 'churches'. Use of the word in the plural is utterly uncharacteristic of pre-conciliar Roman theology, stress being always upon the unity and singleness of the Catholic and Roman Church. Even in the Constitution on the Liturgy, approved in the second session, where a theology of liturgical pluralism is to some extent accepted, there is no use of the word 'church' in the plural nor of the phrase 'ecclesia particularis' (particular church), though the thought of the constitution would have benefited from such use. It is only in the third- and fourth-session documents that this is to be found, and increasingly frequently, as, for instance, in chapter 13 of *Lumen Gentium* or in chapter 3 of the Decree on Missionary Activity, entitled 'Particular Churches' – a chapter written largely in the fourth session and one of the Council's most mature texts.

Besides ecclesial and liturgical pluralism, theological pluralism is also commended – a genuine diversity 'even in the theological elaborations of revealed truth' (*Unitatis Redintegratio* 4), the natural consequence of the 'lawful freedom of theological enquiry to which laity and clergy alike have a right' (*Gaudium et Spes* 62). Differing theological formulations, we are assured, are 'often to be considered as complementary rather than conflicting' (*Orientalium Ecclesiarum* 17). It would be quite impossible to find a comparable commendation of theological, or indeed ecclesiastical, pluralism coming from pre-conciliar Rome. It should be linked with the equally remarkable assertion

59

that there exists within doctrine 'a hierarchy of truths' (*Unitatis Redintegratio* 11).

(e) All this helped to make possible, and is again included within, the constant ecumenical note. Theologically separated Christians are no longer seen as simply 'outside' the Church, (except by some internal desire on their part) but, on the contrary, recognized as being united visibly with the Church even if in a state of 'imperfect' communion. Communion becomes a matter of degree. In practice, prayer in common, above all within a non-Catholic church, theological dialogue and practical co-operation were all either forbidden or highly restricted until the Council. From then on they have developed as an almost necessary part of Church life. While the principles for a Catholic ecumenism were formulated principally in the decree specifically devoted to this, all the other main documents of the Council – most notably the two dogmatic constitutions and the Declaration on Religious Freedom – were profoundly affected by this concern.

(f) The final wide-ranging orientation, as obvious as any, and especially of course in *Gaudium et Spes* (the Council's final major document and by far the longest), is the concern with secular human values, with justice and peace. This is obviously not new, and is in part an expansion of the teaching of a long line of papal encyclicals on social justice beginning with Leo XIII's *Rerum Novarum* and extending up to Pope John's *Mater et Magistra* and *Pacem in Terris*, but there is no possible doubt that the Council, following in this the footsteps of Pope John, gave both a wider range and a new urgency to concerns of this kind as properly constitutive of a very large part of Christian living. Indeed here more than anywhere we may detect the Council's most characteristic of orientations in comparison with all other Councils: a concern with 'the signs of the time' (*Gaudium et Spes* 4 and cf. 44), things outside the Church's own life, the major problems cultural, economic and political of the contemporary world. For an understanding of the Council's orientation this remains absolutely pivotal: the Church's life and career cannot be self-sufficient. It is a strength, not a weakness, that it responds precisely to the 'signs of the time' presented by secular society. However, this was not a merely secular orientation. It remained a profoundly Christological one, though this has too seldom been recognized. The first part of *Gaudium et Spes* returns again and again to the theme of Christ, the New Adam who 'fully reveals man to man', himself making man's vocation clear, and in whom is to be found the key and focal point for human history and civilization.

These wide orientations underpin and make sense of our second series – certain rather specific texts that represent in more precise manner the Council at its most authoritative. While the list could undoubtedly be extended, the eight chosen here all have great weight, and not one of them is really imaginable as appearing in a pre-conciliar Roman document.

The first to be noted must surely be that relating to collegiality – a long text including most of *Lumen Gentium* 22. Any doctrine of collegiality at all was bitterly resisted by a small minority. As the majority (and Pope Paul too) was most anxious both to carry the minority with it and not to seem to be in any way undermining the Roman primacy, there was such a lot of qualifying done in the course of the final formulation of the text that, as it stands, it reads a little weakly. Nevertheless, it still asserts that the episcopal college as such is empowered with 'supreme authority . . . over the whole Church, exercised in a solemn way through an ecumenical council'. That this was significantly new is demonstrated by the bitter resistance to it from people who had been near the heart of the Church, yet it was finally approved overwhelmingly and constitutes the most precise dogmatic statement within this 'dogmatic constitution'. While not intended as a dogmatic definition, it was in fact little less.

The second text, coming again from *Lumen Gentium*, is the statement in article 8 that the unique Church of Christ 'subsists in' the Roman Catholic Church. Taken by itself such a statement may not suggest any great alteration from previous doctrine, but it was intended to be and it was. *Mystici Corporis* and all other recent official teaching had simply identified the Roman Catholic Communion with the Church, and the Council's text, as first written, did the same with the simple verb 'is'. The very deliberate rejection of 'is' and its replacement by 'subsists in' opened the door to acceptance of the, at least, partial ecclesial status of other Christians and other ecclesiastical bodies. The Council declared that the Church of Christ is to be found here, but it no longer says that it is not to be found anywhere else as well. This brief statement is fundamental for all subsequent Catholic involvement in the ecumenical movement and provides the foundation stone for the Decree on Ecumenism.

The third text is an equally remarkable but less well known one. It is remarkable first because it is found in two places in almost identical form (*Orientalium Ecclesiarum* 5, and *Unitatis Redintegratio* 16); secondly, because in each case, and only here, did the Council use the word 'solemnly': it solemnly declares. The word is one traditionally used for definitions or other dogmatic statements of exceptional weight. The complete statement (*Orientalium Ecclesiarum* 5) is as follows: The Council 'solemnly declares that the Churches of the East, as much as those of the West, fully enjoy the right, and are in duty bound, to rule themselves'. This text provides the dogmatic core for the theology of a 'particular church'. Theologically, the Churches of the East cannot finally be different from Churches anywhere else. If Eastern Churches have such rights and duties, then American, African and Asian Churches have also. The Council is, then, here solemnly declaring that throughout the world local churches, or groups of linked churches, have the right and duty, not to be ruled from Rome, but to govern themselves with their own traditions and pastoral needs just as the decree implies the Oriental Churches should do. The Decree on Ecumenism recognizes that, unfortunately, this principle 'has not always been honoured' (rather an understatement). It rightly adds that the exercise of such a right must be done 'while keeping in mind the necessary unity of the whole Church', but also that a 'strict observance of this traditional principle is among the prerequisites for any restoration of unity'. It had, of course, once more the Eastern Orthodox Churches in mind at that point, but again the principle is no less valid in regard to all other Christian Churches.

The fourth text, in the Decree on the Ministry of Priests (16), is a brief recognition and commendation of the Ministry of married priests in Eastern

Churches. While this as such simply acknowledges the situation as it is and is followed by a far longer passage relating to the benefits of celibacy for the Western rite, it remains a highly important text because it is the first time a Roman Council or any major Roman document has explicitly accepted and recommended the uniting of priesthood and marriage in a single life. Once more, it is theologically impossible to separate East from West. What is theologically and pastorally appropriate in the eastern Mediterranean and the Ukraine cannot be theologically wrong and pastorally unsuitable anywhere else. Here, as in the previous item, conciliar recognition of the rightness of the Oriental tradition in principle undermines the Latin system as legally enforced elsewhere.

The fifth text is the central thesis of the Declaration on Religious Freedom: 'This Vatican Synod declares that the human person has a right to religious freedom. This freedom means that all men are to be immune from coercion on the part of individuals or of social groups and of any human power' (*Dignitatis Humanae* 2). This statement and the Declaration as a whole has been claimed on good authority as 'the most controversial document of the whole Council' (J. Courtney Murray: Abbott, p. 673). It explicitly reversed the accepted Catholic teaching which related freedom only to truth and not to persons, claiming that error had no rights. It is certainly irreconcilable with various nineteenth-century Roman statements and does, of course, implicitly condemn the practice of the Inquisition and much else. The Declaration was fiercely resisted by the minority. Ecumenically it is as important as anything. Doctrinally it demonstrates that 'development' may have to proceed at times more by reversal than by an extension of what has hitherto been taught.

The sixth text is the condemnation of anti-semitism: the Council 'deplores the hatred, persecutions, and displays of anti-Semitism directed against the Jews at any time and from any source' (*Nostra Aetate* 4). Such condemnation was not, of course, new. Pius XI, for instance, repeatedly condemned anti-Semitism during the 1930s, as did Pius XII subsequently; but this was – all in all – a stronger, more public, more obviously unqualified condemnation. It was still not much to say after the Holocaust and so many long centuries of discrimination by Christians, and often by Church authorities, against the Jews. It was, however, of great importance that it was said as clearly as it was by the Council.

The seventh text is a further condemnation, this time relating to war: 'any act of war aimed indiscriminately at the destruction of entire cities or of extensive areas along with their population is a crime against God and man himself. It merits unequivocal and unhesitating condemnation' (*Gaudium et Spes* 80). This is the unique text in which the Council formally used the word 'condemn' (it had, perhaps regrettably, been persuaded in the case of anti-Semitism to substitute 'deplores' for 'condemns'). It is already significant for that reason: the Council's resolve to condemn mass destruction in modern war is shown to be all the more strong. The test certainly covers, and therefore condemns unequivocally, the American dropping of nuclear bombs on Hiroshima and Nagasaki; it does, however, not deal as absolutely as did Pope John in *Pacem in Terris* with all possible aspects of modern war or even with every possible use of nuclear weapons. It remains significant – perhaps all the more significant – for what it does say.

The final text concerns the responsibility of the married in deciding to have or not to have a child. The Council did not discuss the morality of methods of contraception because Pope Paul asked it to leave the matter to his own special commission. It did, nevertheless, develop a theology of marriage in which procreation was no longer seen as its sole purpose, but conjugal love was recognized as of equal importance, and this inevitably placed the issue of contraception in a somewhat different light. Still further, it explicitly commended the concept of family planning. Whereas in the past Catholic teaching had implied that all such matters should be left to God, however large a family one already had, the Council affirmed that 'parents themselves should ultimately make the judgement' (*Gaudium et Spes* 50) as to whether or not they should have further children. They might rightly decide that 'at least temporarily the size of their families should not be increased' (*Gaudium et Spes* 51). Conciliar recognition that the practice of family planning, and not simply the acceptance of as many children as came was the morally responsible and best form of behaviour for a Catholic, represented a very considerable change in attitudes. While the issue of means was left unresolved, clear teaching in regard to the issue of ends was in the long run probably more important.

We have now to turn to a survey of the third area of significance: the main points that had a specific and almost immediate practical effect upon the life of the Church. The list is restricted to seven but, again, there are others with a claim to inclusion. The first, deriving also from the Council's first major text, and with little doubt the most decisive for the life of most Catholics, was that to make far greater use of the vernacular in the liturgy (*Sacrosanctum Concilium* 36 and 54). This did not at first include the canon of the Mass, but the momentum of change was such in the early post-conciliar period – moreover, the absurdity of retaining an isolated island of Latin was so obvious – that this quickly followed. More than anything else it has changed the public lifestyle of Catholicism for the ordinary churchgoer so that it is hard for the young actually to realize that thirty years ago Mass said wholly in Latin, including even a first reading of Epistle and Gospel, was simply taken for granted by most people. Even in countries like England where there was initially a relatively strong movement to retain Latin, it is clear twenty-five years later that interest in any return to its regular use is minimal.

The second, and closely related, change is the permission in the Constitution on the Liturgy (55) for Communion under both kinds to be given to religious and laity in certain circumstances. The Council indicated a few limited examples of such circumstances (e.g. to the newly baptized in a Mass following their baptism), but here again, once admitted, the essential rightness of Communion under both kinds became more and more widely recognized so that communion is now so given at all Masses in many churches and dioceses throughout the world. It is becoming difficult to imagine that for centuries even a nun receiving daily Communion was never once in her life permitted to receive the cup. Here, as with the vernacular, the Council for the sake of strengthening the 'active participation' which it correctly laid down as a vital principle of liturgy, overthrew a deformation which had become customary in the Middle Ages and against which the Reformation had vigorously protested. In making the change, the Church effectively admitted that on these points the Reformers had been in the right.

The third matter is again liturgical and again related – that of concelebration (*Sacrosanctum Concilium* 57 and 58). From about the twelfth century and until the Council, every priest was expected to say Mass separately each day. This involved the multiplication of side altars (in some seminaries and religious houses literally dozens of small altars were still being constructed in crypts even in the 1950s) for the celebration of 'private' Masses. In religious communities and seminaries most priests never received Communion (except on Maundy Thursday) in a community mass, but removed themselves to celebrate on their own with a single server. The profound symbolism of the sacrament of unity was thus gravely impaired. The Council's permission for many priests to share in a single concelebration was again, initially, limited to a very few occasions, but before the end of the 1960s the absurdity of the former practice had become rather obvious and concelebration was rapidly becoming the norm for all circumstances where the number of priests exceeded the number of community Masses needed for a pastoral purpose. Side altars and crypt altars survived, if at all, only as an unused oddity whose purpose would require considerable explanation for the young. This proved in itself a major revolution, not only for the liturgy, but also for clerical life, even if the initial rather clumsy practice of massive concelebration by all priests present at any Mass itself expressed over-forcibly a clergy–laity divide and has later tended to give way – except for certain symbolic occasions (e.g. of a bishop meeting with his diocesan clergy) – to a pattern in which most supernumerary priests at a given Mass simply join with the lay congregation.

Our fourth point is the restoration of the diaconate as a permanent order in the Church to which the married could be ordained (*Lumen Gentium* 29). There are now several thousand married deacons in the Church, mostly in North America. The duties of the deacon were specified as 'to administer baptism solemnly, to be custodian and dispenser of the Eucharist, to assist at and bless marriages in the name of the Church, to bring viaticum to the dying, to read the Sacred Scriptures to the faithful, to instruct and exhort the people, to preside at the worship and prayer of the faithful, to administer Sacramentals, and to officiate at funeral and burial services'. It cannot escape notice that almost without exception these duties were performed, and in most countries – at least of the West – *only* performed, by priests until the Council. It noted that 'these duties so very necessary for the life of the Church can in many areas be fulfilled only with difficulty according to the prevailing discipline of the Latin Church'. That is to say, with a law of clerical celibacy and a consequent inadequate number of priests, there was often no one available to do them. Hence the revival of the very ancient order of the diaconate (in the pre-conciliar Church the diaconate was indeed conferred, but only on people who were almost immediately afterwards going to be ordained priests). The decision to include married people in this was both practically and theoretically crucial. It was crucial in practice, because otherwise few would have been available and no significant increase in manpower for the fulfilment of these duties would have been forthcoming. But theoretically, the significance was still greater: the traditional Western bar on the ordination of the married had always applied to the diaconate as much as to the priesthood (and for the same initial reason: marriage involving the practice of sex was regarded as causing pollution). The Council's decision to scrap the tradition in regard to the diaconate suggested that the same tradition in regard to the priesthood could equally well be abandoned if it was pastorally desirable.

The fifth point is rather more ambiguous in its conclusions and present degree of applicability (*Unitatis Redintegratio* 8; *Orientalium Ecclesiarum* 26 and 27). Prior to the Council, *communicatio in sacris* – that is to say, sharing in the formal worship of a Church other than one's own, and especially in communion – was completely condemned. The term was never used in regard to anything acceptable. The Council's use of the term is therefore revolutionary. It does not condemn the practice. On the contrary, it sees it as in some circumstances actually commendable, but restricts this by declaring that (1) it should not be used 'indiscriminately' for the restoration of unity, (2) the fact that communion should 'signify unity' means that it is 'generally' to be excluded, at least if somehow it 'would damage the unity of the Church', (3) it must never involve 'formal acceptance of falsehood or the danger of deviation in the faith, scandal or indifferentism'. These are major restrictions but the balance has decisively changed from a simple 'No' to a nuanced 'Yes and No'. The conclusion would seem to be that where there seems no danger of damaging the unity of the Church and no danger of scandal or deviation from the faith, admission to communion may be used discriminately.

In fact, the Council went on at once to put this principle into practice and agree that admission to communion (that is to say, in common parlance, partial intercommunion) may be accepted 'in order to promote closer union' (*Orientalium Ecclesiarum* 26). 'To promote closer union' means that it is, in the Council's judgement, an acceptable means towards fuller unity in some circumstances, and not only to be seen as an expression of full unity already achieved. The decree goes on to allow Eastern Christians, separated from the Catholic Church, to receive Catholic sacraments in some circumstances. Catholics are permitted to receive valid sacraments in other churches in similar circumstances of pastoral need. While these clauses as such refer to the East only, the same theological principles apply elsewhere, and were subsequently explicitly applied in the Secretariat of Unity's first Directory.

The principles here are clear, fully Catholic and yet in terms of pre-conciliar Roman theory revolutionary (not so revolutionary in practice: some sacramental sharing had always continued in parts of the East where ecclesiastical reality had never quite caught up with the theory of ultramontanism). They have increasingly been applied by ordinary church members in the years following the Council. However, official teaching has gone the other way, becoming increasingly restrictive in its emphasis on the grounds that the sharing of communion is acceptable only as an expression, and not as a cause of unity. This is, of course, poor sacramental theology which makes of every sacrament a cause of what it signifies. It is also explicitly opposed to the conciliar text. There is, undoubtedly, a tension between cause and consequence, but no acceptable way in which significance can be confined to the realm of an expression and consequence of unity institutionally achieved. Sacraments go deeper and by nature precede, not follow. The element of causality in the sacrament of unity is undoubtedly the primary one, from 1 Corinthians 10 onward. Sharing the Eucharist is a major part of a Christian's basic baptismal rights, only to be denied in principle on account of grave sin.

The sixth point is the instruction (*Christus Dominus* 37–8) to establish Episcopal Conferences with considerable authority and well-defined responsibilities in all nations or pastoral areas. In many places, such conferences had already come into existence, but their authority has been greatly enhanced by the Council. This undoubtedly developed a practice of regional collegiality which has been characteristic of the post-conciliar Church. While it has greatly strengthened individual bishops, hitherto left very much to cope on their own, it has also decreased the scope for unilateral action on the part of an independent-minded bishop.

Last but by no means least must be noted the recommendation in *Gaudium et Spes* (90) to establish 'some agency of the universal Church' in order to 'stimulate the Catholic community to foster progress in needy regions and social justice on the international scene'. From this has come the immense development of Justice and Peace Commissions, both in Rome and throughout the Catholic world, which have greatly helped bring to fruition a whole new dimension of church life, a social activism concerned with the service of the poor, of economic justice and of genuine peace (Paul VI later declared that 'Development is the new name for Peace'). This in turn has helped generate, and been refuelled by, theologies of liberation which have become central to much Catholic thinking in the latter part of our period.

This list could certainly be extended, but it is sufficient to indicate the deep and wide-ranging impact that the Council had, or should have had, on both theology and practice. Still today genuine fidelity to the Council needs to be measured by a living commitment both to these specific matters and to further organic developments implicit within their logic. It is fairly clear that no one would now seriously seek to impose a return to the regular liturgical use of Latin or the celebration of private masses or decree an actual dissolution of episcopal conferences, but full acceptance of many of them is still far from clear even in Rome. Thus the implications of the Eucharistic nature of the Church have never been recognized by Church authority in areas of an acute shortage of priests; and when, in some of them, episcopal conferences have requested permission to ordain married men to ensure the maintenance of a minimum of regular Eucharistic celebration in local communities, they have been rebuffed by Rome.

Genuine acceptance of the spirit and implications of Vatican II can probably best be seen in the use of a 'people of God' ecclesiology, in a stress upon both a working collegiality and the genuine centrality of the Eucharist within the Church, especially the local church, in the warm recognition of the values of pluralism and freedom within and between 'particular churches' as within human society generally, and in a commitment to work and find Christian holiness within the struggle for justice and peace in solidarity with the poor. That list may provide the five most authentic hallmarks of a Vatican II spirit present and active in the Catholic Church twenty-five years later.

8

THE CONCILIAR DOCUMENTS

8A Liturgy (*Sacrosanctum Concilium*)

AIDAN KAVANAGH osb

The Constitution on the Liturgy, *Sacrosanctum Concilium* promulgated on 4 December 1963, was the first document issued by the Second Vatican Council. This was not because the Council fathers assigned *a priori* most importance to this subject, but because *Sacrosanctum Concilium*'s pre-conciliar preparation proved far more satisfactory than that of other comparably important texts. But coming first as it did, *Sacrosanctum Concilium* set the atmosphere for subsequent debates and documents.

Its ecclesiology of the Church as a diversified people of faith gathered in unity around its bishop influenced the Dogmatic Constitution on the Church, *Lumen Gentium* (1964), the Decree on Ecumenism, *Unitatis Redintegratio* (1964), the Pastoral Constitution on the Church in the Modern World, *Gaudium et Spes* (1965), and the Decree on Missions, *Ad Gentes* (1965). Certain of these later documents, moreover, such as *Lumen Gentium* 3–14 and *Ad Gentes* 13, develop certain aspects of *Sacrosanctum Concilium* beyond its own preliminary content; for example, the priority of faith and baptism and on the catechumenate (*SC* 64–71).

It would not be unfair to characterize *Sacrosanctum Concilium* as a 'Liturgical Movement' document. This does not mean that it represents only late and narrow enthusiasms of liturgical advocates. It means, rather, that it rests on a massive tradition both legislative and scholarly extending back some four centuries and culminating in this century in the movement of pastoral liturgy.

Basic is the historical research that strove from the sixteenth century to recover a clearer picture of what was truly traditional in the welter of Western worship materials. This began even before the Council of Trent (1545–63), the liturgical reforms of which were not completed until 1614.

Next comes the large body of liturgical legislation issued by the Holy See, estimated as some 6,000 entries during the first three centuries after Trent, and around 300 during the present century (Megivern, 1978, pp. xiv–xvi).

Third was a second and more sophisticated wave of scholarly research into liturgical origins extending from the seventeenth century to now, represented by scholars of great stature: from Bona and Mabillon in the seventeenth century to Edmund Bishop and J.A. Jungmann in the twentieth.

This long and patient recovery of liturgical sources made possible the fourth body of literature on which *Sacrosanctum Concilium* rests, namely, that of the pastoral and parish-oriented phase, the modern Liturgical Movement, dating from an address by L. Beauduin at the Louvain Conference of 1909, and followed by a half-century of sensitive reflections by thinkers such as Beauduin himself (who died on the eve of the Council), R. Guardini, V. Michel, G. Diekmann, C. Howell, P. Parsch, H.A. Reinhold and others.

At the same time and under comparable influences, the other fundamental modern theological disciplines were evolved – biblical exegesis and theology, historical theology, the history of doctrine, and patristics and finally, the Ecumenical Movement was born. All this influenced liturgics. In addition, the modern social action and liturgical movements were conceived in the same egg, so to speak: *actuosa participatio*, as papal documents on both liturgy and social reform from Leo XIII onward would name it, and the two movements have lived in symbiosis ever since, at least until recently. Particularly during the pontificate of Pius XII, this pastoral phase was enhanced by the encyclical *Mediator Dei* (1947), and affected Catholic worship markedly in the growing use of the vernacular, the practice of the 'dialogue Mass', and most strikingly in the 1951 restoration of the Easter Vigil and the 1955 reform of Holy Week (Megivern, 1978, pp. 128 and 128–40).

The 130 paragraphs of *Sacrosanctum Concilium* are a distillation of this long development into remarkably brief and intense form. The first words of this Constitution were also the first words the Council addressed to the world, and are, in consequence, in a special way programmatic:

> The sacred Council has set out to impart an ever-increasing vigor to the Christian life of the faithful; to adapt more closely to the needs of our age those institutions which are subject to change; to foster whatever can promote union among all who believe in Christ; to strengthen whatever can help to call all mankind into the Church's fold. Accordingly it sees particularly cogent reasons for undertaking the reform and promotion of the liturgy (*SC* 1).

Remarkable though it may now seem, the Council's primary self-understanding was not framed in terms of peace or social activism, but in terms of 'the reform and promotion of the liturgy'. Indeed, in one of the Council's most categorical statements, the liturgy is the summit toward which the activity of the Church is directed; it is also the fount from which all her power flows (*SC* 10). This is even more remarkable when one recalls that the vast majority of bishops who voted for the document had not before the Council in their own dioceses been involved in, much less in the forefront of, the Liturgical Movement. With few exceptions they had been enforcers of official liturgical practices and rather cautious followers of papal encyclicals such as Pius XII's *Mediator Dei* (1947). Standard fare in the majority of parishes worldwide was low Mass in Latin, sometimes followed by Benediction of the Blessed Sacrament or, as in some places in Germany and Austria, accompanied by fairly indiscriminate hymn-singing in the vernacular.

While the Mass was greatly revered, much popular piety was just as much shaped and influenced by a spread of para- and non-liturgical devotions to the Sacred Heart, the Mother of God, and the saints. The Breviary (containing the

Liturgy of the Hours) was obliged to be read daily by all clerics in major orders; outside religious houses it was rarely celebrated in public, even in part, and almost never in parishes. Although one might hear some choral music in larger churches, the restoration of 'Gregorian' chant and the polyphonic tradition based on it, commended by Pius IX, Pius X and Pius XII, never really caught on in parishes, despite the labour of love expended on it by many devoted and talented people.

These matters are recalled to illustrate what a contrast *Sacrosanctum Concilium* afforded when it stated the Council's intent to impart new vigour to Christian life, to adapt more closely to the needs of the age, to promote union among all believers in Christ, and to strengthen the call of all mankind into the Church's fold by undertaking the reform and promotion of the liturgy. This move put worship squarely at the heart and front of Christian endeavour because worship presumes the presence of God in Christ by the Holy Spirit, from whom the whole of creation, revelation and redemption flow. The most appropriate response to this active presence is not analysis or speculation, but worship in thanksgiving for all that has been gratuitously given our race.

While Christians obviously do more than worship (*SC* 9), all they do is finally directed towards, and flows forth from, this crucial activity (*SC* 10–13). So 'Mother Church earnestly desires that all the faithful should be led to that full, conscious, and active participation in liturgical celebrations which is demanded by the very nature of the liturgy, and to which the Christian people, "a chosen race, a royal priesthood, a holy nation, a redeemed people" (1 Pet. 2:9, 4–5) have a right and obligation by reason of their baptism' (*SC* 14).

The document draws many cogent inferences from this (*SC* 15–46), among which is the basic practical reform policy, revision of the liturgical books as soon as possible (*SC* 25). Conciliar liturgical reform for the past quarter-century has turned on revision of the Roman Rite's library of liturgical books as on a hinge; the final revision of some is still under way, while some already reformed are being fine-tuned even yet. General norms for this process are given in chapter I (1–46). Specific norms follow for the Eucharist in chapter II (47–58), for the other sacraments and sacramentals in chapter III (59–82), for the Divine Office or Liturgy of the Hours in chapter IV (83–101), for the liturgical year in chapter V (102–11), for sacred music in chapter VI (112–21), and for sacred art and sacred furnishings in chapter VII (122–30). To initiate, oversee and write the reforms for actual use, a special commission, later named 'The *Consilium* for the Implementation of the Constitution on the Sacred Liturgy', was established in 1962 by John XXIII's *motu proprio Sacram Liturgiam* (Flannery 1, pp. 41–4); this body was absorbed in 1969 by the newly reconstituted Sacred Congregation for Divine Worship, which remains the main curial body governing implementation of the reform. Its first secretary, A. Bugnini, had been secretary of Pius XII's Commission for Liturgical Reform and represents the sole example of curial continuity of a reformist kind from the time of Pius to the middle years of Paul VI.

The revision of liturgical books was at its most intense during the reign of Paul VI between the years 1963–73 (Megivern, 1978, pp. xvii–xxi). The pope in 1977 looked back on the course of the reform with basic confidence, but mixed feelings about those who would run too fast and those who would not run at all (Megivern, 1978, pp. 453–7). Left unmentioned were problems caused by the quantity and rapidity in the reforms themselves, problems that reflect perhaps the greatest of all the reform's weaknesses, namely, the almost total absence of any anthropological dimension in the approach to revision of so massive and long-standing a ritual system. For ritual patterns, which have much to do with sustaining identity and the social bond, are for these reasons essentially conservative and normally need to change slowly.

SC 23 cautions that before revisions are made, a careful investigation – theological, historical, and pastoral – should always be made into 'each part of the liturgy which is to be revised'; the anthropological dimension seems never to have crossed anyone's mind. Thus the naivety of *SC* 31: 'The [revised] rites should be distinguished by a noble simplicity. They should be short, clear, and free from useless repetitions. They should be within the people's powers of comprehension, and normally should not require much explanation'. This is an educationalist outlook, certainly not that of anyone knowing anything about ritual behaviour, which is rarely short, clear, free of repetition and usually transcends the comprehension of the whole congregation, including its officiants. Yet it is this simplistic educationalist sense of rite that has tended to be given prominence in the revisions of the liturgical books, and to have taken root in people's minds, to the detriment of traditional sacred polyphony (repetitions) and to that perhaps greatest of liturgical arts, ceremony. Hence the untranscendental blandness felt by many in their attempts to use the reformed rites, and the rites' often aggressive educationalism when used imprudently.

Anthropological studies by Mary Douglas, Victor Turner and many others could have been helpful here, from Van Gennep's 1909 work on *Rites of Passage* onwards, but recent manuals in liturgics contain little bibliography on the anthropology of ritual behaviour, and the category 'Ritual' does not even appear in their indexes (cf. Jones, Wainwright and Yarnold; Wegman; Cattaneo; Marsili). This is the more unfortunate since the recent upsurge in calls for inculturation of Christianity, and in particular, liturgy in Africa and the Far East, carries with it anthropological issues not covered by the more usual theological, historical and pastoral approaches. One may anticipate fearsome mistakes being made without some well-learned anthropological lessons being attended to as inculturation proceeds.

Reception of *Sacrosanctum Concilium* and its reforms has been generous and positive. The reforms themselves are mostly of high quality, far more richly traditional in the best sense than those of Trent, given its times, ever could have been. They include several (all of them in fact restorations) that have profoundly changed the way in which the Church thinks of itself and is perceived by others.

Chief among these is surely the move from Latin, the sacred language of the clergy and 'their' liturgy, to the vernaculars of the modern world. Pius XII had already grudgingly noted in 1947 that 'the use of the mother tongue in connection with several of the rites may be of much advantage to the people' (*Mediator Dei* 60). Few could then have imagined that the entire liturgy would be vernacular within thirty years, making both worship and ministry more accessible to non-clergy, thus reflecting deep ecclesiological shifts even yet not wholly assimilated. Abetting this was the restoration of Catholic initiatory practice (*SC* 66–71), culminating in the reformation of the baptismal rites for infants (1969) and adults (1972), and of confirmation (1971), by which the catechumenate was restored as a permanent structure (*SC* 64) and evangelization emphasized. Shifts in language and initiation signalled recovery of a less clerical and more egalitarian view of the Church as the baptized people of God, which all but demanded three other restorations: Communion under both kinds for all (*SC* 55), Eucharistic concelebration by bishops and presbyters (*SC* 57), and the permanent diaconate (*Lumen Gentium* 29). These restorations of practice and reforms in ritual procedure have left no group – lay, clerical or monastic – unaffected in the deepest manner.

Paul VI was assiduous in implementing these reforms (indeed, he carried them even to translating the Eucharistic prayer into the vernacular, something which few if any Council fathers had contemplated or wished to authorize); John Paul II perhaps less so, in his concern to appeal to Lefebvreists by spreading permissions for celebrating the 'Tridentine Mass' and commending celebration of the conciliar reforms in Latin. Although the use of Latin for the post-conciliar rite has always been an option, many view the maintenance of the 'Tridentine Mass' as a mistake that compromises the quality, not to say the deeply traditional Catholicity, of the conciliar reforms themselves. Some would see this as an unwarranted use of the liturgy for short-term ends meant to overcome a minor schism, which could finally not succeed. History will no doubt show Paul VI to have been the pope most intelligently committed to liturgical restoration and reform over the long haul; his instincts and courage were both deep and correct. Despite the problems reform always presents, he knew that once this was embarked on one must persevere and see it through.

But if the liturgical reforms have been qualitatively good on the whole, especially in the area of Christian initiation, the use to which the reforms have been put in many places remains uneven. Their lack of preparation for the reform called for by *Sacrosanctum Concilium* has hampered English-speaking congregations, especially, from grasping and then enacting much more than the letter of the reform. The symbolic minimalism that afflicted the liturgy of such groups prior to the Council is still often in evidence, as is a certain clericalism which has now spread idiosyncrasies to new ranks of lay ministers and liturgy committee members. Perhaps more serious is the increasing speed with which parish liturgy may become a celebration of middle-class values, creating a narrow new elitism which tends to exclude the lower classes and alien ethnic groups (cf. Archer; Douglas; Flanagan). As this happens, not only is the Church splintered, but the organic sacramentality of the Church as redeemed humanity standing worshipfully and in unity before God in Christ by the Holy Spirit falls away. Individualism flourishes, and the liturgy may almost become the plaything of its celebrants, in which case it ceases to be a bulwark against individualism and becomes instead a casualty to it. Such a liturgy, understandably, no longer appears to have any connection with social *actuosa participatio* by which both Church and world might be built up by a community of faith, the very given of baptism in Christ Jesus.

This situation is general enough in some parts of the Western world to contribute to a noticeable decline in Sunday liturgical attendance, which may be as much as 30 per cent in the United States over the past twenty years. What is needed now is a new phase of the Liturgical Movement to re-expound in post-conciliar terms what it is truly all about: in particular (1) the fundamental purpose of liturgy (*SC* 2, 106); (2) the concept of participation in its theological and ascetical aspects, linking it to the sacrificial character of the liturgy, especially in the Eucharist, as the basic articulation point for a liturgical 'spirituality' (*SC* 47–48); (3) the concept of sacrament embracing both act and the Church that acts (*SC* 5–8); (4) the intimate relationship between liturgy and the edification of the social order in the modern world (*SC* 9–12; *Gaudium et Spes*); (5) the objective normativeness of the liturgical act itself, in all the details of its ceremony and iconography, as the Church's primary theological and contemplative endeavour.

What is called for is a new and richer 'mystagogy' that expounds the liturgy in its own terms from within, and a theology more sensitive to the nature of the liturgical assembly as a theological corporation in its own right, speaking a theological language of symbol and ceremony soaked in the gospel of Jesus Christ for the life of the world.

8A Liturgy (*Sacrosanctum Concilium*): Bibliography

Archer, A. (1986) *The Two Catholic Churches: A Study in Oppression*. London, SCM.

Cattaneo, E. (1984) *Il culto Cristiano in occidente*. Rome, C.L.V. Editizioni Liturgiche.

Chupungco, A. (1982) *Cultural Adaptation of the Liturgy*. New York, Paulist Press.

Douglas, M. (1970) *Natural Symbols: Explorations in Cosmology*. New York, Pantheon.

Flanagan, K. (1987) 'Resacralizing the Liturgy', *New Blackfriars*, vol. 68, pp. 64–75.

Grimes, R. (1982) *Beginnings in Ritual Studies*. Washington, University Press of America.

Jones, C., Wainwright, G., and Yarnold, E. (1978) *The Study of Liturgy*. London, SPCK; New York, OUP.

Koenker, E. (1954) *The Liturgical Renaissance in the Roman Catholic Church*. Chicago, University of Chicago Press.

Lévi-Strauss, C. (1963) *Structural Anthropology*. New York, Basic Books.

Megivern, J. (1978) *Worship and Liturgy: Official Catholic Teachings*. Wilmington, N.C., McGrath.

Turner, V. (1969) *The Ritual Process: Structure and Antistructure*. Chicago, Aldine.

Van Gennep, A. (1909, ET 1960) *The Rites of Passage*. Chicago, University of Chicago Press.

Wegman, H. (1985) *Christian Worship*. New York, Pueblo.

8B Revelation (*Dei Verbum*)

ROBERT MURRAY sj

Dei Verbum is theologically the most fundamental of the documents of Vatican II. Of the four Constitutions, only it and *Lumen Gentium* are called 'Dogmatic', indicating a more formal doctrinal authority. There are many important links between them, as also with the Constitution on the Liturgy. These three correspond most to the expectations and hopes previously voiced by bishops and theological faculties. The nature of the Church and its tradition were central to the unfinished business from Vatican I; Modernism and the Roman reaction to it had left serious questions about the inspiration and inerrancy of the Bible and about the development of doctrine; the Liturgical Movement was already revealing both the need for major pastoral renewal and a vision of what its fruits could be, not merely inside the Catholic Church but also in its ecumenical relations.

Of the four Constitutions, *Dei Verbum* is the most theologically concentrated; but in its wider relevance it both undergirds and touches most of the Council documents – obviously those on the Church and the liturgy, but also all those with a mainly pastoral thrust. This wider outreach makes the opening words, 'The Word of God', perhaps more arresting than the more technical title 'On Divine Revelation'. But if *Dei Verbum* is so important, has its influence been proportionately great? A number of factors make it a complex task to estimate the degree of success in twenty-five years. Before we can try, it will be helpful to recall the issues that were at stake, the aims of the Council in this document, and the main emphases in its teachings and recommendations.

The history of *Dei Verbum*, (abbreviated to *DV* throughout this chapter), as one of the focal points of tension and conflict between theological viewpoints at the Council, is well known. (See, for example, XR 1, pp. 140–73; XR 3, pp. 35–48; and XR 4, pp. 184–96.) It was when the draft for a document on revelation was presented in November 1962 that the Council really began to experience the creative polarization that was to shape its whole history. No other theme was more suited to bring this about. On one side were found churchmen set on defending truth (seen in a mainly static and propositional way), on condemning error, and on protecting Catholics against ideas of development and change. The draft on revelation (and a companion, 'On preserving the deposit of faith in its purity', also rejected) were prepared mainly by theologians of this tendency, who had been brought up to think of modernism as the most fundamental, comprehensive and insidious of all heresies.

On the other side were many who voiced optimism and trust in the Holy Spirit rather than defensiveness, saw more need for encouragement than for condemnations, and were convinced that there was a new opportunity for liturgical and pastoral use of the Bible which must not be missed. Here there were probably more pastors than scholars, especially from the third world, but there was a significant number of biblical scholars and theologians who looked back on decades in which loyal Catholic scholars had been harassed and impeded by an obsessive witch hunt against Modernism. They were convinced that the Catholic Church needed a credible account of how God's word acts in history, from the first formulation in human language through the gradual process of understanding, under changing historical conditions and as the Holy Spirit gives new insights. After three years of redrafting and hard debate, a large majority in the Council was able to welcome a text reflecting both the ideas and the spirit of the more 'pastoral' tendency.

THE MAIN FEATURES AND EMPHASES OF *DEI VERBUM*

The Prologue (*DV* 1) sets the tone for the whole document. In the Latin, 'the Word of God' stands first, as object of the Church's *listening* and then proclamation. The order is important. Only subordinate to this order are references to Trent and Vatican I tucked in, with the promise of doctrinal guidance on revelation and its transmission. This order of values in the Prologue is reflected in the whole Constitution.

Chapter 1, 'Divine Revelation Itself' (*DV* 2–6), maintains the note of proclamation in mainly biblical language, and only towards its end does it reaffirm teachings of Vatican I on the human response to God's self-revelation. Before this, however, important new emphases have appeared. The pregnant sentence 'The economy of Revelation is realized by deeds and words, which are intrinsically bound up with each other' (*DV* 2) challenges two basic 'conservative' positions: the fear of allowing historical development in our understanding of divine truth, and the theory of separate sources of revelation. History is not merely the theatre in which God's self-revelation becomes known, but is itself a mode of revelation. All understanding is guided by the Holy Spirit, whose manifold activity is emphasized (whereas the first draft had practically restricted it to biblical inspiration).

In chapter 2, 'The Transmission of Divine Revelation' (*DV* 7–10), the sense of historical revelation continues, with repeated emphasis on the Holy Spirit, in relation not only to the apostles but also to the Church as a whole. The teaching role of the bishops, as successors to the apostles, is described as a service to the whole Church. The faith is a living Tradition (in a comprehensive sense, made clearer by capital T). It grows and develops: all members play their part in this, as they feed their understanding of the revealed message by their 'contemplation and study' and by experience of 'spiritual realities' (*DV* 8; cf. *Lumen Gentium* 12 on the 'prophetic function' in the whole people of God). It is by this living and developing Tradition that the canon of Scripture is recognized and its inner power made actual for believers, guided by the Holy Spirit. This passage, the tone of which reminds one of Newman, goes far beyond the timid language of the first draft and its companion with its static view of the 'deposit'.

In this way the dispute about Scripture and Tradition as distinct sources of revelation can be resolved (*DV* 9). The insistence on separate sources had been an ill-judged reaction to the Reformation *Scriptura sola*; now, by viewing both Scripture and Tradition as dynamic realities, they can be seen as intimately connected, gifts of the one Spirit, in a way that satisfied not only almost all the Council's members, but even the Reformed observers (Schutz and Thurian, 1968, ch. 2). A final section (*DV* 10) describes how the Church holds, and is helped to interpret rightly, this single deposit of God's Word which is formed by Scripture and Tradition together. The ideal (expressed in words again reminiscent of Newman) is a harmonious consensus of the faithful and the bishops; but authority in interpretation of the Word of God is vested in the 'living teaching office' entrusted to the bishops. However, this is no autonomous authority; it 'is not superior to the Word of God, but is its servant', bound to listen to it and expound it faithfully (*DV* 10). This was well symbolized by the enthronement of the gospel book at the Council, though more could have been made of it (de Maio, 1963, p. 21; Bianchi, 1987, p. 117). The responsibilities of *magisterium* remain an issue to which we shall return.

Chapters 3–5 deal in turn with the inspiration and interpretation of Scripture and with the two Testaments. These chapters are comparatively less weighty, and are perhaps most valuable for what they do not say, if we remember the pressure for definitions and anathemas. Chapter 3 (*DV* 11–13) deals quietly with two ancient *questions mal posées* that were still causing storms: the question of 'inspiration' (or how human authors wrote 'God's Word') and that of 'inerrancy' (or how far everything they wrote must be God's truth). There is a touch of 'learned ignorance' about the disarmingly simple solutions proposed, but they succeeded in breaking the impasse. The treatment of the principles of interpretation (*DV* 12) reaffirms the teaching of Pius XII's encyclical *Divino Afflante Spiritu* (1943) – very necessarily, since it was still being attacked, even by an Italian cardinal, as late as 1961 (XR 1, pp. 54–5). *Dei Verbum* 12 may seem very elementary today, but it gave needed encouragement to long-suffering Catholic exegetes.

Chapter 4, on the Old Testament (*DV* 14–16), is the least substantial part of *Dei Verbum;* it mainly repeats traditional Christian formulas, with no sensitivity towards Judaism as is called for in *Nostra Aetate* 4. Chapter 5, on the New Testament (*DV* 17–20), likewise partly consists of rather conventional summaries; but it does deal, firmly yet flexibly, with questions of the historicity of the Gospels, and agrees that the development of the Gospel tradition was influenced by oral transmission and preaching (for allowing which, responsible scholars had been accused of heresy). The tone is reassuring to conservative piety yet far from fundamentalism, and it pronounces neither censures nor warnings to inhibit scholarly research. Today this chapter may seem almost too anodyne to be significant, but it gave much-needed relief and encouragement to Catholic New Testament scholars (see Fitzmyer, 1982, pp. 97–142).

Chapter 6, on Scripture in the life of the Church (*DV* 21–6), develops the main intention expressed in the Prologue and outlines a pastoral policy for liturgy (21; cf. *Sacrosanctum Concilium* 7, 24, 35, 51–2, 92), and for provision of Bible translations (22, including by co-operation with other Christian Bible Societies) with encouragement to reading, study and meditation by every section of the Church (23–5). Watchfulness and guidance by the 'magisterium' are mentioned several times, but the condescending and protective tone of the first draft has happily gone.

AFTER TWENTY-FIVE YEARS

The question was posed above: If *Dei Verbum* is so important, has its influence been proportionately great? In terms of continuing public notice and practical effectiveness, the truthful answer has to be 'no'. Perhaps too much of it is a text for skilled professionals. And yet, if we look for signs of the biblical revival that the Council wanted to awaken, in many ways and in many parts of the Catholic world the answer is indeed 'yes', and all the more so if we remember how much leeway there was to be made up in knowledge and use of the Bible by Catholics. It is not easy to survey the many areas in which there has been not only response to *Dei Verbum*, but also developments traceable to its influence, yet going far beyond what most of the Council's members could have foreseen. After looking at first reactions I shall sketch the main lines of theological comment and response, and then liturgical, practical and ecumenical developments; then some 'growing points' and problems in areas both of praxis and of theological reflection.

The promulgation of *Dei Verbum*, in November 1965, was welcomed with widespread enthusiasm by Catholics and other Christians alike. Catholic biblical scholars, theologians and many active lay groups had good reasons to be grateful. Among the 'observers', the Orthodox now had something more like their own teaching on Tradition than from any previous Western Council. Anglicans and Protestants now not only heard the first systematic teaching on the word of God in the Church ever formulated by a Catholic Council (for Trent had only dealt with particular points at issue with the Reformers), but also admired it. Most remarkable of all, Karl Barth, having been unable to serve as an observer, later published his reflections (1967, 1969), asking himself such questions as 'How would things look if Rome (without ceasing to be Rome) were one day simply to overtake us and place us in the shadows, so far as the renewing of the church through the Word and Spirit of the gospel is concerned?' (Barth, 1969, p. 75).

Dei Verbum invited Catholics to see God's revelation and human response to it less in merely propositional terms, but more as dynamic operations guided by the Holy Spirit. For many seminary-trained churchmen this was a radical change in both direction and spirit after some eighty years of official censures and directives, which too often saw a danger of heresy whenever the human part in the dialogue of revelation and the development of doctrine were explored. (To appreciate the reorientation that was called for after this period, see Latourelle, 1968, pp. 207–309; on Tradition, see Congar, 1966, especially pp. 196–221; on the trials of biblical scholars, see Levie, 1961.) As the Council proceeded, theologians had a fair idea of what kind of text was coming, and were prepared to explain its teaching and its practical implications. Among the commentaries that appeared, several were by participants in the Council as members, *periti* or observers. Perhaps the most distinguished and rich in content is that edited by Alonso Schökel (1969). Though this is in Spanish, the contributors were international, reflecting the work of the Pontifical Biblical Institute in Rome. This volume goes far beyond mere commentary, but ranks with more systematic works on the theological areas dealt with in *Dei Verbum* which appeared in the 1960s. Theologians were constantly in demand to speak and write for a wide public which was eager to understand the Council's message and importance. (The scene was surveyed regularly in *Concilium*: during the years 1965–72, when its issues were arranged in volumes, the successive parts of volume 1 (Dogma) and volume 10 (Scripture) contain many valuable articles.)

What Karl Rahner achieved in those years can hardly be summarized (but see his *Foundations of Christian Faith*, 1978, ch. V). However, his former colleague, Hans Urs von Balthasar, though a comparable (but contrasting) giant in the theology of revelation, hardly took any part in the Council or in the subsequent work of exposition and discussion. Not that he was remote from the Council's concerns; his long-standing dialogue with Karl Barth makes him no exception to the keen and growing ecumenical awareness that characterizes almost all Catholic theological writing since the 1960s.

Out of many systematic works from this period we may select for mention two, both titled *Theology of Revelation:* that by Latourelle (1968), which is more historically based, and that by Moran (1967), which focuses more on the experience of revelation as personal communion. The various possible emphases in thinking about revelation are illuminatingly analysed by Dulles (1983), using the method of 'models' which he had previously applied to ecclesiology. On the other main themes of *Dei Verbum*, Congar's monumental *Tradition and Traditions* (1966), though finished before the end of the Council, remains unsurpassed. On the Bible as the word of God, the balance achieved by *Dei Verbum* is worked out in comprehensive works such as those by Grelot (1968) and L. Alonso Schökel (1967). Since the study by Vawter (1972), the old problems of inspiration and inerrancy have largely been given a rest by Catholic theologians; perhaps for sheer weariness and relief, but perhaps also because from the late 1960s many of them were theologizing in exciting new university contexts and learning the arcane language of philosophical hermeneutics.

The most fundamental aspects of the liturgical renewal for which the Council called are all related to the biblical element in liturgy and to making it more accessible to all in the vernacular: the enormous enrichment of the lectionary, the emphasis on preaching the Word that has been read, the revelation of how biblically based the Eucharistic prayers and other sacramental actions are, and the restoration of the 'divine office' as the 'prayer of the Church'. (On the broader context of all this, see Chapter 8A.) Huge tasks had to be undertaken, and much has been achieved. The readings and psalms in the vernacular (often helped by clearer new versions, on which see below) and the call for more biblical sermons have already brought appreciable changes in Catholic worship and attitudes. But there are continuing blockages and problems, many of them practical. In many large churches, built to enable the greatest possible numbers to attend Sunday Mass, the circumstances of worship too often hinder an effective liturgy of the Word. In contrast, in smaller and more informal gatherings such as house Masses, the power this can release has often been experienced so impressively that one wonders whether the new liturgy was not given to the Church prophetically, with a view to new circumstances which were to come, but which till now have been realized only unevenly.

The reform of the lectionary, despite experiment and evaluation before the contents were fixed, has also left serious problems. One arises from the increase in the sheer quantity of texts to be read, heard and (ideally) expounded, some of them very difficult both for preachers and for their congregations. Too often, public readers are not trained, either in technique or in appreciation of their role, for this important ministry of mediating the power of the word.

The problem of unrenewed attitudes is most acute among older clergy trained before the Council. Besides insecurity, there is a theological cause due to an unbalanced view of the relationship of Word and sacrament. *Sacrosanctum Concilium* speaks of the presence of Christ both in the sacraments and in the liturgical reading of the Word (*SC* 7); *Dei Verbum* likewise speaks of 'the one table of the Word of God and the Body of Christ' (*DV* 21). Though this doctrine is patristic, some 'conservatives' at the Council saw a threat to faith in the Eucharistic real presence. This reveals a mentality for which the Word is metaphorical and therefore less 'real'. The truth is that *all* sacramental thinking and language are symbolic, and precisely thereby, they work in a way not weaker but actually stronger than the way the naïve realist calls 'real'. The Council was clearly implying that (as Newman saw) Scripture itself works *sacramentally*, especially when it is made actual by effective reading and preaching in the liturgy. Whenever the liturgy of the Word remains formal and lifeless, it shows that these fundamental sacramental and liturgical principles have yet to be learnt (see Bianchi, 1987, pp. 120–2).

While training for preaching has happily improved since the Council, other factors have sadly hampered and slowed down the work of theological re-education. A tragic number of those best equipped to explain the Council's teaching retired from the clergy in the later 1960s and the 1970s, and thereafter were disqualified from teaching as a ministry in the Church, though there is no moral justification for a general judgement that such persons become unworthy to teach. The right to preach within the Mass is jealously reserved to the clergy, whereas members of the laity often prove to be endowed with this charism. To see the biblical renewal of liturgy successful in Europe, one still has to seek out certain churches. The greatest renewal is elsewhere.

The Council's encouragement in the field of Bible translation and interconfessional co-operation (*DV* 22) has borne abundant fruit. The key figure here was Cardinal A. Bea, the veteran biblical scholar whose experience and contacts fitted him uniquely to head the Secretariat for Christian Unity, to develop sensitive relations with both Christians and Jews, to bring all this manifold competence to the redrafting of *Dei Verbum* and the production of *Nostra Aetate*, and to foster the desired biblical renewal both pastorally within the Church and by ecumenical co-operation. The World Catholic Federation for the Biblical Apostolate (WCFBA) was formed in 1969, both to co-ordinate Catholic projects and to be the appropriate organ to work in partnership with the United Bible Societies. This world-wide structure and partnership has developed remarkably. In many countries the Bible really has proved, as the

Latin American bishops said at Puebla in 1979, 'the soul of evangelization' and of religious education. Ecumenical pooling of resources for translation work is now normal; in 1984, out of 590 translation projects in progress, 390 were inter-confessional involving Catholics. There is equally fruitful ecumenical co-operation in activities such as the production of aids to daily Bible reading.

The encouragement to Bible study in *Dei Verbum* (23–5) speaks in turn of scholarly work, of the training and spiritual formation of the clergy, and of reading by the laity. Though there has been good response in the first two areas, it is in the third that the brief hints in the text have been totally transcended through the amazing growth of lay groups meeting for prayer or study, representing various degrees of organization or none, some purely Catholic but most of them ecumenically open. The best-known developments of this kind are the 'basic ecclesial communities' in Latin America, but comparable movements have appeared in all continents, varying according to social structure and tradition. In these new communities Christians have developed their own way of listening to the Word and responding to it from their own situation. Typical methods are described by Mesters (1980, 1989) and discussed by Rowland (1988, pp. 130–5). The members may be without education, or able to use handbooks such as those of Abesamis in the Philippines (1988) or of Tamez in Costa Rica (1982). These communities were discussed by Pope Paul VI in *Evangelii Nuntiandi* 58 (1975; Flannery 2, pp. 738–40), appreciatively though with some warnings: there is a danger of manipulation of the Word through ideological pressure and too selective reading (cf. Bianchi, 1987, pp. 132–6); but the vitality of this movement surely surpasses all other responses to *Dei Verbum*.

The Council's message to those engaged in biblical and theological research was encouraging and trustful. In this atmosphere Catholic scholarship has flourished, increasingly in an ecumenical setting and moving in directions not yet envisaged by *Dei Verbum*. Its chapter (4) on the Old Testament reflected the 'biblical theology' of the 1950s and the patristic viewpoint as enshrined in the liturgy. Catholic teachers turned with new confidence to biblical criticism, but by the 1980s many of its presuppositions were being questioned and its power to generate real understanding doubted. The ideal of 'listening to the text' and allowing different possible 'readings' has come to the fore, helped by a new appreciation of Jewish exegesis, often through joint study with Jews (as was recommended in *Nostra Aetate* 4), and by refreshing contributions from students of other literatures. This 'new look' need not, of course, exclude older interpretations; but it may well rejuvenate preaching.

New Testament studies have flowered to an extent too rich to summarize; let one work stand for all: Brown's magisterial commentary on the Fourth Gospel (1971). The relationship of Christology to New Testament study has remained a crucial area of study and debate. A useful contribution to this, entitled *Scripture and Christology*, appeared in 1984 from the Pontifical Biblical Commission in its new character since its reconstitution in 1971. This text, without carrying official papal authority, truly maintains the spirit of *Dei Verbum*. It surveys eleven contemporary approaches, evaluating them fairly and positively sketching the *desiderata* for an integral Christology (see Fitzmyer, 1986).

This document is significant not only for New Testament studies. In the ecclesiological context of *Dei Verbum* 10, it represents an exemplary exercise of magisterium as the ministry of teaching in the Church. This term always had this broader sense until, in the mid-nineteenth century, it began to have a capital M and a personified sense restricted to the episcopate, or more often just the papacy, as holders of teaching authority (see Congar, 1976; Hill, 1988, pp. 75–88). *Dei Verbum* 10 describes the magisterium as subordinate to the Word, but follows this with a problematic image of Scripture, Tradition and the Magisterium as a kind of trinity. The propriety of this depends on how inclusively or exclusively magisterium is being used. The third member is only commensurate with the two modes of revelation if it means a charism, constantly in action throughout the Church, guiding true understanding and teaching it. It is always to be hoped that this charism will be active in popes and bishops, but it is not, nor can it be, reduced solely to their authority. The more inclusive, 'small m' sense of magisterium has the main weight both of history and of Tradition behind it, and it is in this direction that the most vital movements in the Church – especially the increasing witness of women – are developing (cf. Metz and Schillebeeckx, 1985).

In the open intellectual milieu where Catholic exegetes and theologians now move among colleagues of other traditions of faith or of none, the traditional term 'hermeneutics' (the art and the principles of interpretation) has been taken over for a mode of philosophical discussion so technical that its products are usually baffling even to a well-educated reader. This is a tragedy, for biblical hermeneutics concerns the problems facing any ordinary person who wants to find meaning in texts coming from a remote past, and to understand in what sense they can be 'the Word of God'. The traditional doctrines of 'inspiration' and 'inerrancy' were posed in terms that actually added to the problems. Yet they were attempts to answer real questions, and not simply for fundamentalists. There is a ministry here that theologians and biblical scholars owe to the Church, to develop a hermeneutics more widely accessible to ordinary intelligent people today. This is done outstandingly by Mesters (1989).

One other critical feature of the present situation for maintaining the ministry of the word should be mentioned: it concerns the study of the biblical languages (Hebrew, Aramaic and Greek) and those of the classical ancient versions, at a level sufficient to assure that there will be enough scholars able to serve as fully competent exegetes and, therefore, as active tradents of Tradition. The primacy of classical studies in their chief base (Europe) came to an end about the middle of this century. What was a broadly based culture has become a field of specialization. This must be a matter of serious concern for the Church. Training scholars will not physically feed the hungry, but failing to train enough of them will mean clogging the springs from which we drink.

After twenty-five years we can indeed see much response to *Dei Verbum*, but it is still limited. Bishops at the Synod of 1985 and Pope John Paul II himself in 1986 complained that the message has not yet been heard. In 1984 the WCFBA Plenary Assembly asked for a Synod entirely on the biblical apostolate in the Church. The desired agenda would include the relation between the Word and

Modern Catholicism

the Eucharist; the liberating power of the Word of God; the Bible and the laity: the various ministries of the Word and their relation to exegesis; the danger of fundamentalism; the Bible and ecumenism; inculturation of the Word of God; the Bible and other sacred scriptures. This summary list indicates the amount of work still to be done.

Note

In 1989 the WCFBA was renamed more simply the Catholic Biblical Federation (CBF).

8B Revelation (*Dei Verbum*): Bibliography

Abesamis, C. H. (1988) *A Third Look at Jesus*. Quezon City, Philippines, Claretian Publications.

Barth, K. (1969) *Ad Limina Apostolorum* (1967). Edinburgh, St Andrew Press.

Bianchi, E. (1987) 'The Centrality of the Word of God', in Alberigo and Jossua, pp. 115–36.

Brown, R. E. (1971) *The Gospel According to John*. Garden City, NY, Doubleday, 1966; London, Geoffrey Chapman.

Congar, Y. (1966) *Tradition and Traditions*. London, Burns & Oates.

Congar, Y. (1976) 'Pour une histoire sémantique du terme magisterium', RSPT, vol. 60, pp. 85–98.

de Maio, R. (1963) *The Book of the Gospels at the Oecumenical Councils*. Vatican City.

Dodd, C. (1989) *Making Scripture Work: a practical guide to using Scripture in the local Church*. London, Geoffrey Chapman.

Dulles, A. (1983) *Models of Revelation*. Dublin, Gill & Macmillan.

Fitzmyer, J. A. (1982) *A Christological Catechism*. New York, Paulist Press.

Fitzmyer, J. A. (1986) *Scripture and Christology*. New York, Paulist Press; London, Geoffrey Chapman.

Grelot, P. (1968) *The Bible, Word of God* (1965). New York, Desclee.

Hill, E. (1988) *Ministry and Authority in the Catholic Church*. London, Geoffrey Chapman.

Latourelle, R. (1968) *Theology of Revelation*. Cork, Mercier.

Levie, J. (1961) *The Bible, Word of God in Words of Men* (1958). London, Geoffrey Chapman.

Mesters, C. (1980) 'How the Bible Is Interpreted in Some Basic Christian Communities in Brazil', *Concilium*, no. 138. pp. 41–6.

Mesters, C. (1989) *Defenseless Flower: A New Reading of the Bible* (1983) Maryknoll, NY, Orbis Books; London, CIIR.

Metz, J. B., and Schillebeeckx, E., eds (1985) *The Teaching Authority of Believers*, *Concilium*, no. 180.

Moran, G. (1967) *Theology and Revelation*. London, Burns & Oates.

Rahner, K. (1978) *Foundations of Christian Faith*. London, Darton, Longman and Todd.

Rowland, C. (1988) *Radical Christianity*. Cambridge, Polity Press.

Schökel, L. Alonso (1967) *The Inspired Word*. London, Burns & Oates.

Schökel, L. Alonso, ed. (1969) *Concilio Vaticano II: Comentarios a la Constitución Dei Verbum*. Madrid, BAC.

Schutz, R. and Thurian, M. (1968) *Revelation: A Protestant View (La parole vivante au Concile*, 1966). Philadelphia, Westminster.

Tamez, E. (1982) *Bible of the Oppressed* (1979). Maryknoll, New York, Orbis Books.

Vawter, B. (1972) *Biblical Inspiration*. Philadelphia, Westminster; London, Hutchinson.

8C The Church (*Lumen Gentium*)

RICHARD P. McBRIEN

HISTORY AND CONTENT

The Second Vatican Council was concerned primarily with the nature and mission of the Church. Its explicit theological focus, therefore, was ecclesiological rather than Christological, eschatological, or anthropological. Two of the Council's sixteen documents served as the twin pillars of its ecclesiology: the Dogmatic Constitution on the Church (*Lumen Gentium*) and the Pastoral Constitution on the Church in the Modern World (*Gaudium et Spes*). This essay is concerned exclusively with the former document, although in the beginning both were intended to be part of a single document on the Church (*De Ecclesia*).

The first draft of *Lumen Gentium* (more precisely: *De Ecclesia*) was prepared by the Council's Theological Commission (*De Doctrina fidei et morum*), headed by Cardinal Alfredo Ottaviani, Prefect of the Holy Office (now the Sacred Congregation for the Doctrine of the Faith). The Commission's secretary was Father Sebastian Tromp sj, formerly professor of ecclesiology at the Pontifical Gregorian University in Rome and the principal author of Pope Pius XII's encyclical *Mystici Corporis* (1943), on the Church as the Mystical Body of Christ.

The first draft of what was to become *Lumen Gentium* consisted of eleven chapters and an appendix:

1 The nature of the Church militant.

2 The members of the Church and the necessity of the Church for salvation.

3 The episcopate as the highest grade of the sacrament of orders; the priesthood.

4 Residential bishops.

5 The State of evangelical perfection.

6 The laity.

7 The teaching office of the Church.

8 Authority and obedience in the Church.

9 Relationships between Church and state and religious tolerance.

10 The necessity of proclaiming the gospel to all peoples and in the whole world.

11 Ecumenism.

Appendix: Virgin Mary, Mother of God and Mother of Men.

This initial draft was discussed in six separate meetings during the final week of the Council's first session (1–7 December 1962). Although there was some praise for the Theological Commission's work, the most significant comments called attention to the deficiencies of the first draft. Several bishops found the draft 'too juridical' in tone and too little concerned with the Church as mystery, faulted its lack of structural coherence (a point raised explicitly by Milan's Cardinal Montini), complained that it portrayed the laity too much as mere appendages of the hierarchy, expressed concern that the document was insufficiently sensitive to the legitimate role of the state alongside that of the Church, deplored the absence of any genuine ecumenical dimension, and criticized its lack of attention to the works of the Eastern fathers of the Church and to various biblical images of the Church, especially that of people of God. Bishop Emile de Smedt of Bruges (Belgium) synthesized these criticisms in a ringing, three-pronged attack on the first draft. He challenged its 'triumphalism', its 'clericalism', and it 'juridicism'.

Cardinal Suenens insisted that this central conciliar text should speak first of the Church's inner life (*Ecclesia ad intra*) and then of its outward life in the world (*Ecclesia ad extra*). The second part was later separated off from the first in a document known as 'Schema 13' (still later as *Gaudium et Spes*). Cardinal Suenens also suggested the title *Lumen Gentium*, noting, however, that Christ alone is the real 'Light of the Gentiles'.

A central commission was appointed to direct and co-ordinate the work of the various conciliar commissions (including that of the Theological Commission) during the nine-months' recess beteen the first and second sessions. Six norms were laid down by the Council secretariat to guide the work of the central commission. The second norm is of particular interest, given the kind of criticisms directed against the first draft of *Lumen Gentium:* 'The stress is on the pastoral, rather than doctrinal or juridical, nature of the council.' The norms explicitly referred to Pope John XXIII's speech on the Council's opening day (11 October 1962), in which he insisted that this Council had not been called for doctrinal but for pastoral purposes.

A second draft was prepared by the Theological Commission and presented to the Council fathers at the beginning of the second session in September 1963. It contained only four chapters:

1 The Mystery of the Church.
2 The hierarchical constitution of the Church and the episcopate in particular.
3 The People of God and the laity in particular.
4 The call to holiness in the Church.

This revised draft elicited a more positive reception, although the discussion still revealed a basic (but far from equal) division between the bishops on their approach to the document as a whole. In the first chapter the Church was no longer spoken of as the Church militant but as a mystery, a community still on pilgrimage rather than already finished and perfected. Nevertheless, Cardinal Raul Silva Henriquez of Santiago (Chile) felt it necessary to suggest an additional chapter on the People of God.

Chapter II caused the greatest controversy: it was concerned with the question of collegiality. Conservative Italian and Spanish bishops expressed grave caution about this concept, preferring a more juridical understanding of the episcopate – one in which each individual bishop is related vertically and subordinately to the pope, without horizontal relationships with the other bishops. Opposition to collegiality was rooted in the concern that collegiality might compromise the primacy of the pope (and perhaps also the 'sovereignty' of the bishop in his own diocese). The overwhelming majority of the Council fathers, however, including Pope Paul VI, did not regard this as a serious danger, and so the discussion and the voting moved inexorably forward in support of the doctrine of collegiality, based on appeals to the New Testament, the liturgy of episcopal consecration, and the theology and practice of the East.

As the discussion moved to the third chapter of the second draft, it was clear that the fathers wanted the chapter divided and the material on the people of God moved to a position immediately following chapter I, and before the chapter on the hierarchy. It was also clear that, in spite of some residual clericialism in the text, the bishops were generally enthusiastic about the portrayal of the laity as full partners in the life and mission of the Church. Most of the pastoral application, however, would be reserved for a separate document: the Pastoral Constitution on the Church in the Modern World (*Gaudium et Spes*).

The discussion of the second draft focused finally on Mary, about whom a separate schema had been prepared, 'The Blessed Virgin, Mother of the Church'. Again, there was division within the Council. One side favoured the idea of a separate schema, while the other wanted it made a part of the constitution itself. On 25 October 1963 the Council moderators asked the Council fathers to come to a decision, one way or the other. A debate was arranged, for and against the incorporation of the chapter on Mary into the general schema on the Church. Cardinal Franz König of Vienna spoke on behalf of incorporation, and Cardinal Rufino Santos of Manila spoke on behalf of separation. Cardinal Santos insisted that Mary's role in our redemption transcended her place and function within the Church. But Cardinal König's argument prevailed, if only by a slim margin (1,114 to 1,074); namely, that Mary is a type of the Church and is herself its pre-eminent member. For theological, pastoral and ecumenical reasons alike, she should not be isolated from the unity of the economy of salvation nor from the central ecclesiological focus of the Council itself.

Between the second and third sessions of the Council the Theological Commission tried to bring the text into line with various criticisms and suggestions. Pope Paul VI, in his turn, worked tirelessly to win the widest possible support for the emerging document. In his opening address to the third session (14 September 1964), he linked the work of the Second Vatican Council with that of the First Vatican Council (1869–70). Vatican I had provided formal declarations concerning the primacy and infallibility of the pope, but it did not have time to complete its teaching on the hierarchical structure of the Church. Specifically, Vatican I left no doctrine of the episcopate. For Pope Paul VI this constituted 'the weightiest and most delicate' subject still facing Vatican II. This Council would have 'as its principal objective the task of describing and honouring the prerogatives of the episcopate'. Otherwise, the pope feared, the false impression would persist that Vatican I had 'limited the authority of bishops' and had 'rendered superfluous . . . the convocation of a subsequent ecumenical council'.

The four chapters of the document on the Church were expanded to six, and two new chapters were added to bring the total number to eight: one on eschatology and another on Mary. A section was added in chapter I to show the subordination of the Church to the Kingdom of God (*LG* 5); the relationship between the Church of Christ and the Roman Church was carefully nuanced to leave room in the Body of Christ for the non-Catholic Churches (*LG* 8 and 13); a separate chapter was added on the people of God to bring out the historical nature of the Church and the fundamental equality of its members (chapter II); another chapter was added on the laity, underscoring their participation in the prophetic, priestly, and kingly ministries of Jesus (chapter IV); a separate chapter on religious was approved (chapter VI), and so, too, was the new chapter on the eschatological nature of the Church (chapter VII); and, after much discussion, the Council fathers approved the new chapter on Mary, carefully formulated to avoid both Marian maximalism and Marian minimalism (chapter VIII).

The major debate over this penultimate draft, however, had to do with the doctrine of the episcopate in chapter III. The drafters were caught between two forces: the one jealous of papal prerogatives and fearful of any undermining of papal primacy, the other suspicious of papal absolutism and supportive of collegiality. The text bent over backwards to reassure the former group. If it succeeded in satisfying some of the more conservative Western bishops, it weakened the text in the eyes of the Easterners, who insisted on the divine institution of the episcopacy. When the final votes were taken, however, more than two-thirds approved, even though about 500 voted *placet juxta modum* (yes, with reservations). Accordingly, a *nota explicativa* ('explanatory note', also known as a *nota praevia* because it 'came before' the Theological Commission's comments on various last-minute *modi*) was hastily added as an appendix to the constitution to meet the minority's persistent concerns about papal primacy (16 November 1964). The *nota* insisted that the word 'college' was not to be taken in a juridical sense, that the college does not even exist without its head whose function as 'Vicar of Christ and pastor of the universal Church' is left 'intact', and that the pope, 'as supreme pastor of the Church, may exercise his power at any time, as he sees fit, by reason of the demands of his office'. Not surprisingly, the Council majority was exceedingly displeased, and the third session ended in an atmosphere marked by considerable tension. Nevertheless, the entire document was approved with near unanimity on 19 November 1964, followed by a final solemn vote on 21 November.

The final version of *Lumen Gentium* thus has eight chapters (with their principal teachings given in parentheses):

I The Mystery of the Church: the Church's sacramental nature, the Trinitarian framework for the mystery of the Church; various biblical images of the Church, especially that of body of Christ.

II The People of God: the Church as on pilgrimage through history; the Church and Christ's threefold mission as prophet, priest and king; the Church and the sacraments; the Church and non-Catholic Christians and non-Christians.

III The Hierarchical Structure of the Church, with Special Reference to the Episcopate: the New Testament basis for the episcopate; the relationship between the episcopate and the papacy; collegiality; the local church; priests and deacons.

IV The Laity: the fundamental equality of the laity with clergy and religious; the place of the laity in both the Church and the temporal world.

V The Call of the Whole Church to Holiness: the holiness of groupings within the Church: bishops, clergy, religious, laity; the holiness of the Church itself.

VI Religious: the nature and import of consecration and religious profession and of the observance of the evangelical counsels.

VII The Eschatological Nature of the Pilgrim Church and her Union with the Heavenly Church: the Church and the kingdom of God; death and the resurrection of the body; the communion of saints.

VIII The Role of the Blessed Virgin Mary, Mother of God, in the Mystery of Christ and the Church: The role of the Blessed Virgin in the economy of salvation; the Blessed Virgin and the Church; devotion to the Blessed Virgin in the Church; Mary as a sign of sure hope and of solace for God's people on pilgrimage.

Prefatory Note of Explanation (*nota praevia*, or *nota explicativa*): a 'theological qualification' of the doctrine of collegiality adopted in chapter III, to safeguard the primacy and pastoral independence of the pope.

IMPLEMENTATION AND SIGNIFICANCE

The authority of an official teaching of the Church is not determined solely by its source, in this case an ecumenical Council, but also by the way in which the teaching has actually transformed the self-understanding and pastoral practice of the Church as a whole. This is what is meant by 'reception'. The principle of reception also guides and shapes what follows in this second major section of the entry.

(a) Methodological principles

1 The first and methodologically most significant point to be made about *Lumen Gentium* is that it begins with a chapter on the 'mystery' of the Church, unlike the traditional textbooks and catechisms which began with the Church as 'hierarchical' institution. The Church is indeed, first and foremost, a mystery, that is to say, 'a reality imbued with the hidden presence of God' (Pope Paul VI, 29 September 1963). This is more than an editorial move. It reflects a fundamental shift in the way we understand the reality of the Church. Thus, when we confess that 'we believe in the Church', the act of faith is centred on the presence of God who is *in* the Church, and not on the hierarchy or on the Church simply as a religious institution or ecclesiastical organization.

2 The mystery of the Church in *Lumen Gentium* is also placed in a 'trinitarian' framework (*LG* 2–4), thereby situating the Church in the context of salvation history (elected and called by the Father) and also underscoring its communitarian dimension (enlivened by the Holy Spirit). The Church is no longer conceived in Christomonistic terms, as if it were related only to Christ as the 'prolongation of the Incarnation'.

3 *Lumen Gentium*, furthermore, portrays the Church according to many different biblical images, not just as the Mystical Body of Christ, which had been interpreted in the past in a highly juridical manner. If there is, for the constitution, a single dominant biblical image of the Church, it is indeed that of people of God, to which an entire chapter is devoted.

4 The sacraments are also presented in *Lumen Gentium* as an integral part of the mystery of the Church rather than as a kind of appendage to Christology (*LG* 10–11). Indeed, the Church itself is presented as a fundamental sacrament of Christ, just as Christ is the fundamental, or primordial, sacrament of God (article 1).

5 The fact that the chapter on the hierarchical structure of the Church follows the chapter on the People of God is also highly significant. This reverses the priorities and modifies the perspective of pre-Vatican II Catholic ecclesiology. The Church is primarily a people in whom God is present and through whom God acts on behalf of all humanity. The Church is not primarily a hierarchical institution, nor can it speak and act as if it were.

6 A final methodological principle concerns the place of Mary in the document. Like the sacraments, Mary is no longer considered separately from the mystery of the Church and the economy of salvation. Neither is Mariology any longer an appendage to Christology. Mary is instead a type or model of the Church. Thus, the Church is a community seen, like Mary, as ever open to the Word of God, obedient to the Word in faith, and serving always the mission of Jesus Christ.

(b) General ecclesiological principles

1 *Lumen Gentium* presents the Church as itself a sacrament, 'a sign and instrument, that is, of communion with God and of unity among all men' (*LG* 1). This is clearly one of the most significant emphases in the entire constitution, and indeed in the whole of the Council itself. The sacramental character of the Church has extremely important practical consequences; specifically, it means that the Church must signify what it is. If the Church *is* the Body of Christ, it must look and act like the Body of Christ. If the Church *is* the People of God, it must look and act like the people of God. If the Church *is* the temple of the Holy Spirit, it must look and act like the temple of the Holy Spirit. Church renewal and reform are a direct theological consequence of the sacramentality of the Church, and the strong emphasis on both since Vatican II is a direct result of this teaching.

2 The Church is not only a sacrament of our union with God and with one another; it is also 'for each and everyone the visible sacrament of this saving

unity' (*LG* 9). This principle must be seen in the context of one of the most important developments in contemporary Catholic theology, linked especially with the work of the late Karl Rahner sj; namely, the shift away from an Augustinian pessimism about salvation to a more hopeful, universalistic outlook, as reflected in this and other documents of the Council. The human race is no longer seen as a *massa damnata* from whom a few are saved to manifest the glory and mercy of God, but as an essentially saved community from whom a few may, by the exercise of their own free will, be lost.

3 The Church of *Lumen Gentium* is also an eschatological reality, which means that we cannot understand the nature and mission of the Church except in relationship to the Kingdom of God. The Church and the Kingdom of God are inseparable and yet not the same. To identify the Church and the Kingdom of God, as was done so often in the years before Vatican II, is equivalent to ecclesiastical triumphalism (to which Bishop de Smedt had referred). *LG* 5 makes it clear that the Church is 'the seed and the beginning of that kingdom' rather than the Kingdom of God itself.

4 In a principle that is reminiscent of the Reformation itself, *Lumen Gentium* acknowledges that, since the Church is not yet the Kingdom of God, it is at the same time holy and sinful (*LG* 8). Therefore, although the Church is the very Body of Christ and the temple of the Holy Spirit, it 'follows constantly the path of penance and renewal'.

5 Without prejudice to the universality of the Church, particular and local churches retain their own importance and dignity in *Lumen Gentium* (*LG* 13, 23, and 26). *LG* 23 is especially important because it acknowledges that the unity of faith and the divine constitution of the universal Church are not undermined by diversity in discipline, liturgy, theology and spirituality. On the contrary, 'This multiplicity of local Churches, unified in a common effort, shows all the more resplendently the catholicity of the undivided Church.' This assurance was borne out in the immediate post-conciliar period. *LG* 26 is also exceedingly important because it expresses very succinctly the principle of local church that underlies this diversity:

> This Church of Christ is really present in all legitimately organized local groups of the faithful, which, in so far as they are united to their pastors, are also quite appropriately called Churches, in the New Testament. For these are in fact, in their own localities, the new people called by God, in the power of the Holy Spirit and as the result of full conviction (cf. 1 Thess. 1:5). In them the faithful are gathered together through the preaching of the Gospel of Christ, and the mystery of the Lord's Supper is celebrated.

This renewed emphasis on the doctrine of the local church has also reinforced the Council's positive estimation of pastoral diversity and led to a new appreciation for the pastoral practicality of the principle of subsidiarity, heretofore found only in the Church's social teachings. If the local church is a true expression of the Body of Christ in a particular place, its own unique experience and pastoral wisdom must not be suppressed in an effort to impose uniformity on the universal Church. The development of national episcopal conferences since Vatican II has been one ecclesiological implication of this.

6 Indeed, the interaction of the universal Church and the network of local

churches that constitutes the universal Church is at the core of the doctrine of collegiality. It should allow the Catholic Church, in its self-understanding and pastoral practice, to transcend its former attachment to papal absolutism. This is one of the major areas of Vatican II ecclesiology which poses great pastoral challenges to the Church in our own time. Unfortunately, the principle of collegiality has encountered stubborn resistance as it is being assimilated into the life, structure and mission of the Church. Many of the Church's present pastoral leaders continue to prefer a more centralized structure of authority and jurisdiction and make every effort to circumvent the pastoral prerogatives of bishops and faithful at the level of the local church.

7 This tendency to administer the Church as if it were in fact a monarchical institution also ignores the crucial principle articulated at the beginning of chapter IV: 'Everything that has been said of the People of God [in chapter II] is addressed equally to laity, religious and clergy.' All have 'a common dignity . . . deriving from their rebirth in Christ' (article 32). This principle of communal equality applies especially to the threefold mission of the Church, which is, in turn, participation in the threefold mission of Jesus Christ, as prophet, priest and king. The principle has been embodied since Vatican II in such pastoral developments as parish and diocesan councils and in the increasing involvement of the laity in theology, religious education, liturgy, spiritual direction, and even parochial and diocesan administration.

8 The whole Church, therefore, is also called to holiness, and not just the ordained and religiously professed (chapter V). This emphasis on the universal call to holiness is at least partially responsible for the 'democratization' of Catholic spirituality since the Council. It is no longer a matter of concern for priests, nuns and brothers alone.

9 *Lumen Gentium* also significantly recast our understanding, and eventually our practice, concerning the relationship between the Catholic Church and the various other Christian Churches and non-Christian religions. 'This Church, constituted and organized as a society in the present world, subsists in the Catholic Church, which is governed by the successor of Peter and by the bishops in communion with him' (*LG* 8). The Council explicitly avoided making the kind of identification of Body of Christ and Catholic Church that we find in Pope Pius XII's encyclical, *Humani Generis* (1950). On the contrary, we have a fundamental Christian bond with all other Christians. We honour and are nourished by the same sacred scriptures; we believe in the Trinity; we are consecrated by the same baptism; and we recognize and receive many of the same sacraments. We are even united with some other Christians in the place we accord to the episcopate, the Eucharist, and the Blessed Virgin Mary. We also share with our non-Catholic brothers and sisters a common experience of prayer and other spiritual benefits (*LG* 15). Furthermore, because we all come from the same creative hand of the one God, we are spiritually related as well to non-Christians, especially Jews and Moslems (*LG* 16).

10 Although the Church of *Lumen Gentium* is clearly a Church that offers the salvation of God in Christ, *Lumen Gentium* recognizes that salvation is possible even apart from explicit faith in Christ, or even apart from any religious faith at all: 'Nor shall divine providence deny the assistance necessary for salvation to

those who, without any fault of theirs, have not yet arrived at an explicit knowledge of God, and who, not without grace, strive to lead a good life' (*LG* 16).

(c) Ecclesiological corollaries

1 The Church must be a Church of poverty, following 'the same path' as Christ who 'carried out the work of redemption in poverty and oppression' (*LG* 8). This is a corollary of the fundamental principle concerning the sacramentality of the Church. As *Lumen Gentium* declares: 'Likewise, the Church, although she needs human resources to carry out her mission, is not set up to seek earthly glory, but to proclaim, and this by her own example, humility and self-denial' (*LG* 8).

2 By way of a corollary of the principle that the Church is the whole people of God, *Lumen Gentium* teaches that all the faithful share in the one priesthood of Christ: 'the common priesthood of the faithful and the ministerial or hierarchical priesthood are none the less ordered one to another; each in its own proper way shares in the one priesthood of Christ' (*LG* 10). The ordained priesthood ministers to this general, or common, priesthood of the whole Church, recognizing the latter's 'contributions and charisms' and moving the faithful 'with one mind [to] co-operate in the common task' (*LG* 30).

3 These charisms are available to all the faithful 'of every rank' (*LG* 12). This is a corollary of the principle that the whole Church is called to holiness, and not just the ordained or the religiously professed minority.

4 Membership in the Catholic Church is not sufficient to guarantee salvation, nor is it something we merit and, therefore, can take pride in. 'Even though incorporated into the Church, one who does not however persevere in charity is not saved . . .. All children of the Church should nevertheless remember that their exalted condition results, not from their own merits, but from the grace of Christ' (*LG* 14). *Lumen Gentium* tilts consistently against triumphalism. This is a corollary of the principle that the Church is not itself the Kingdom of God, but that salvation is available to the many, not just to the few.

5 The episcopal office of sanctifying, teaching and governing is transmitted by ordination, not by the granting of jurisdiction (*LG* 21). *Lumen Gentium* explicitly rejects the popular, but misguided, view that bishops are simply 'vicars of the Roman Pontiff'. On the contrary, they are 'vicars and legates of Christ' and their pastoral power, which 'they exercise personally in the name of Christ', is 'proper, ordinary and immediate' (*LG* 27). This is a corollary of the wider principle of collegiality.

6 There is no inequality in the Church based on race, nationality, social or economic condition, or sex (*LG* 32). This, too, is a corollary of a larger principle which understands the Church as the People of God wherein all are equal in dignity: laity, religious and clergy alike. This corollary also raises some controversial questions about access to ministry and to pastoral influence in the Church.

7 As another obvious corollary of the principle that the Church is the whole people of God, *Lumen Gentium* teaches that the lay apostolate is a direct participation in the mission of the Church, and is not simply a participation in the mission of the hierarchy: 'The apostolate of the laity is a sharing in the salvific mission of the Church. Through Baptism and Confirmation all are appointed to this apostolate by the Lord himself' (*LG* 33). Therefore, the laity has something also to contribute to the life of the Church and not simply to the transformation of the world in the so-called temporal order: 'By reason of the knowledge, competence or pre-eminence which they have the laity are empowered – indeed sometimes obliged – to manifest their opinion on those things which pertain to the good of the Church' (*LG* 37). The traditional division of labour – clergy in the 'sacristy' and laity in the world – is artificial and even false.

8 Holiness is a principal sign of the credibility of the Church: 'God shows to men, in a vivid way, his presence and his face in the lives of those companions of ours in the human condition who are more perfectly transformed into the image of Christ' (*LG* 50). This stands as a corollary of other principles; namely, that the whole Church is called to holiness, and that the Church is itself a sacrament, called to practise what it preaches. The witness and example of the Church as a community is always a matter of highest missionary significance. Renewed attention to church reform since Vatican II is a direct consequence of this ecclesiological insight.

(d) Deficiencies

Although one of the great achievements of the Second Vatican Council, *Lumen Gentium* is not without deficiencies. Two are offered here by way of example.

1 To be sure, Vatican II was an ecclesiological Council, but ecclesiology itself presupposes Christology, among other fundamental theological areas. Unfortunately, the Council's Christology remains always implicit, and it is not a Christology that reflects the rich biblical and theological developments of the last twenty-five years. 'While this may be understandable from a historical point of view, theologically it is not the healthiest of situations,' Edward Schillebeeckx OP has written. 'However, a church which proclaims more of Jesus as the Christ and less of itself would delight a great many Christians' (Schillebeeckx, 1981, p. 103).

2 In general, chapter III of *Lumen Gentium* is unaffected by even the main lines of New Testament scholarship regarding the early Church. The chapter assumes, for example, that Jesus gave the company of his original disciples a kind of ecclesiastical blueprint from which they were to build an entire structure. Thus, the chapter assumes that the apostles and the Twelve were one and the same group and that each local church was governed by a bishop from the beginning. Furthermore, there is a constant preoccupation with papal authority, but without the nuancing we find in such ecumenical studies as *Peter and the New Testament*, a 'collaborative assessment by Protestant and Roman Catholic scholars' in the United States (Brown *et al.*, eds, 1973). The

prefatory note of explanation for chapter III (*nota praevia*, or *nota explicativa*) only accentuates this stress on the papal office and its prerogatives, at the expense of a genuinely collegial understanding of the Church.

CONCLUSION

On balance, *Lumen Gentium* has stimulated an extraordinarily rich and fruitful change in Catholic self-understanding and pastoral practice (what we mean by 'reception'). One can only reflect on the document, some twenty-five years later, with a full measure of admiration and gratitude. The achievement of Vatican II should call us, however, not to some new form of progressive triumphalism (a counterpart perhaps to the triumphalism generated by the Council of Trent), but to a higher sense of our own responsibility, individually and corporately, to live up to the ideals of the Church that *Lumen Gentium* so compellingly articulated.

8C The Church (*Lumen Gentium*): Bibliography

Baraúna, G., ed. (1966) *L'Eglise de Vatican II*, 3 vols. *Unam Sanctam*, no. 51a,b,c. Paris, Cerf.

Brown, R. *et al.*, eds (1973) *Peter and the New Testament*. New York, Paulist Press.

Dulles, A. R. (1982) *A Church to Believe In*. New York, Crossroad.

Dulles, A. R. (1985) *The Catholicity of the Church*. Oxford, Clarendon Press.

Fagin, G. M., ed. (1984) *Vatican II: Open Questions and New Horizons*. Wilmington, Delaware, Michael Glazier.

Grootaers, J. (1986) *Primauté et Collégialité*. Le dossier de Gérard Philips sur la Nota Explicativa Praevia (*Lumen Gentium* ch. III). Leuven, Leuven University Press.

Holstein, H. (1970) *Hiérarchie et Peuple de Dieu d'après 'Lumen Gentium'*. Paris, Beauchesne.

Kloppenburg, B. (1974) *The Ecclesiology of Vatican II*, trans. M. J. O'Connell. Chicago, Franciscan Herald Press.

Lindbeck, G. (1970) *The Future of Roman Catholic Theology*. Philadelphia, Fortress Press.

McBrien, R. P. (1980) *Catholicism*. Minneapolis, Winston, chs. 17–24.

Miller, J. H., ed. (1966) *Vatican II: An Interfaith Appraisal*. Notre Dame, Indiana, University of Notre Dame.

O'Donaghue, N.D. (1983) 'Vatican II: The Hidden Questions', *Doctrine and Life*, vol. 33pp. 41–7.

Rahner, K. (1963, 1966, 1969, 1973, 1974, 1976, 1981) *Theological Investigations*, vols. 2, 5, 6, 10, 12, 14, 17, and 20. New York, Crossroad; London, Darton, Longman and Todd.

Rahner, K. (1974) *The Church after the Council*. New York, Seabury Press.

Richard, L., Harrington, D.J., and O'Malley, J.W. (1987) *Vatican II: The Unfinished Agenda. A Look to the Future*. New York, Paulist Press.

Rikhof, H. (1981) *The Concept of the Church*. London, Sheed & Ward.

Schillebeeckx, E. (1981) *Interim Report on the Books Jesus and Christ*. New York, Crossroad.

Tillard, J. M. R. (1981) 'The Church of God is a Communion: The Ecclesiological Perspective of Vatican II', *One in Christ*, vol. 17, pp. 117–31.

Van Eijk, A. H. C. (1987) 'The Church as Sacrament. A Contribution to Ecumenical Understanding', *Bijdragen*, vol. 48, pp. 234–58.

Vorgrimler, H., ed. (1967) *Commentary on the Documents of Vatican II*, vol. I. New York, Herder & Herder.

Willebrands, J. (1987) 'Vatican II's Ecclesiology of Communion', *One in Christ*, vol. 23, pp. 179–91.

8D The Church in the Modern World (*Gaudium et Spes*)

ENDA McDONAGH

When the Pastoral Constitution, *The Church in the Modern World (De Ecclesia in Mundo Hujus Temporis*; but better known by its opening words, '*Gaudium et spes . . .*' ('The joys and the hopes . . .')), was approved overwhelmingly by the fathers of Vatican II and Paul VI added his signature, the Council endorsed a document unprecedented in conciliar history and quite radical in Church history. Its unprecedented character derived from the pastoral concerns of the Council as originally conceived by John XXIII. Its openness to the world of its time built on social and other encyclicals, various episcopal and lay initiatives and on the pioneering theological work of Chenu, Congar, Rahner and many others. In face of the flat rejection of the 'modern world' by Pius IX in the Syllabus of Errors just a century before and its continuing influence to the very eve of the Council, the Council's shift in perspective may well be described as revolutionary. It was certainly profoundly liberating.

Nevertheless, such adjectival evaluation offers little direct insight into the document and may easily become a source of futile controversy. Radical or conservative in a document is as radical or conservative interprets. More significant may be the document's sense of incompleteness. This is obviously true in the discussion on marriage and the family (*GS* 50) in regard to the means of family planning. It is also clearly true in regard to some of the other 'urgent questions' as pastoral reflection and teaching continue to develop through papal documents like *Populorum Progressio, Laborem Exercens* and *Sollicitudo Rei Socialis*; through documents of the Synods of Bishops and through pastoral statements by particular conferences of bishops such as those of the American bishops on peace and war and on the economy. Subsequent theological movements such as Latin American liberation theology, feminist theology, the beginnings of African and Asian theologies and of theologies of the environment reveal the limitations of history and geography in this and other conciliar documents. Church and world continue to change. Vatican II was well aware of this fact and of its inability to stop the world in order to get off (a tendency evident in much of the previous century). In this Constitution (and in other documents) it saw the Church as a dynamic, pilgrim people within the historically developing human community. The openness that became so quickly characteristic of the Council found its fullest expression in Schema 13, as this Constitution was known for so long, but so did the incomplete, unfinished nature of the Council's business. *The Church in the Modern World* is not a tidy, closed statement of principle, requiring no more than dutiful application to new circumstances.

ORIGINS AND HISTORY

The remoter origins of this Constitution in Church teaching, theology and practice may be found, as indicated above, in the development of the Church's social teaching from Leo XIII. No less important were the recovery of confidence in biblical studies with Pius XII's encyclical *Divino Afflante Spiritu*, the renewal in patristic studies, the emergence of '*la nouvelle théologie*' despite the setback associated with *Humani Generis*, and a host of practical missionary and pastoral initiatives in the first half of the century. John XXIII's convocation of the Council (25 January 1959), and particularly his opening address, emphasized the pastoral thrust of his intentions. Yet there was no hint of any major pastoral document in the preparatory documents. After Cardinal Suenens's intervention on 4 December 1962 outlining a programme for the Council both *ad intra* and *ad extra*, endorsed the following day by Cardinal Montini, proposals for such a document began to take shape, first as Schema 17 and later, and for most of the remaining period of the Council, as Schema 13.

Social issues had been considered by the Theological Commission and the Commission for the Lay Apostolate. From these commissions came the mixed commission that was to develop the schema. The consultations over almost three years (January 1963–December 1965) in Rome, Malines, Zürich, Ariccia and in-between times and places were complex and protracted. In method, structure and content the document changed course many times. How far it should be doctrinal or pastoral, general or particular, evangelical or philosophical exercised consultants and fathers of the Council right up to the end. The treatment of particular questions (part II of the final document), for example, remained for long a series of appendices to the earlier 'doctrinal' statement. And the particular questions themselves, especially those of marriage and the family and of peace and war, were in doubt and debate up to the very end.

Papal activities, independently of the Council, influenced the development of Schema 13 quite significantly. Pope John's encyclical *Pacem in Terris*, issued shortly before he died in 1963, seemed to some Council fathers to make the work on Schema 13 redundant. In fact, it headed them in the right direction and proved a valuable resource in method and content, although there was some modification in the Council's document of the encyclical's very strongly worded teaching on war. The establishment of a papal commission on birth regulation and Paul's explicit instructions precluded full treatment of this aspect of marriage in the Council document. His visit and address to the United Nations during the Council's final session, while it was debating this constitution, reinforced the value and validity of its subject for many fathers.

METHOD AND STYLE

As there was no proper precedent, questions of approach, method and style figured prominently in the discussions of commissions and in debates in the Aula. Encyclicals on social issues were perhaps the closest model in approach and concern. They had, prior to John XXIII, adopted a largely natural law approach to social, economic and political questions. In the background, and sometimes in the foreground, lay the conceptual analysis of two distinct 'perfect societies', Church and state. The power of this approach was still evident in manuals of public ecclesiastical law on which Cardinal Ottaviani, Prefect of the Holy Office, was a notable authority. However, its appeal was waning. As the Church recovered more biblical richness in self-understanding, natural law categories (for all their continuing validity in so many areas) seemed less appropriate to those charged with discussing the Church in the world.

'World' itself was a world away from state, particularly state as 'perfect society'. The ambiguity, indeed multiguity, of the word caused much difficulty for drafters and debaters. The biblical difficulty of a world that God so loved (John 3.16) and a world that Jesus' disciples must be in but not of (John 17.16) had been greatly exacerbated in the history of the Church and of theology. The world as created and viewed as good was inextricably entangled with the world as sinful and destructive. But this was also a world redeemed in Jesus Christ. Under the influence of his redeeming grace, the world of the whole human community could be approached as positive partner by the community of explicit believers in Christ. In adopting this approach, the Constitution sought release from the suspicion and fear which certainly characterized the Church in Europe for so much of the previous hundred years.

This approach was basically evangelical, founded in the biblical goodness of creation and new creation with their universal thrust. Difficulties about describing the world, about the categories and the language to be used, found their resolution within this evangelical evaluation. The two-tier nature and grace terminology, as well as the older dualism of sin (world) and grace (Church), yielded to a descriptive language about human achievements and failures (pp. 4–10) which could then be analysed in the light of the gospel of Jesus Christ. Technical theological language was as far as possible avoided in favour of a language shared by Christians and others. So the wider human audience which was also addressed could be engaged and perhaps opened up to the further Christian reflection central to the document. The 'signs of the times', a concept crucial both to this Constitution and to the Council as a whole, must of course be recognizable before they could be usefully scrutinized and analysed in Christian terms.

This approach and language were reinforced by the pastoral tone of the document. 'Pastoral', in the sense of loving care, first of all for Church members, but then for all Christians and all humanity, was a key word of the whole Council. It is sometimes contrasted with 'doctrinal' and 'juridical' in so far as they involve more explicit attention to exposition of truth and disciplinary regulation. Truth and discipline have their 'pastoral' loving-care dimensions. The Pastoral Constitution was very aware of this and doctrine, expressed in a caring mode of course, was central to its development. Indeed, for many at the Council and subsequent commentators, the main contribution of the document was seen to be a Christian doctrine of humanity or a Christian anthropology. Its emergence involved a pastoral sensitivity, a loving awareness of humanity in its actual condition and a loving sense of responsibility to it. Such care and commitment are also a source of understanding and knowledge, and not just derived from them.

The Constitution deliberately avoided condemnations. The one exception, on indiscriminate nuclear warfare (*GS* 80), maintained despite criticism, helped to prove the rule. Beyond that the language was one of encouragement rather than juridical imposition. The combination of evangelical approach, non-technical language and evident loving concern suggest that in the Constitution a new style of Church teaching was emerging, if not always successfully. Clarity occasionally was lost as the language or ideas were insufficiently developed. The chapter on culture (*GS* 53–62) is one illustration. The attempts to achieve clarity by sheer repetition throughout the document are seldom successful. These are the hazards of innovative work and of committee work. One must finally marvel at the achievement, given its scope, innovative character and the continuing pressures of time and diversity of personnel at Commission and Council levels.

STRUCTURE

The structure of a document like this is always closely related to method and style. As method and style were clarified for the Constitution, so was the structure. That of the final text responded quite faithfully to the original inspiration, although it had undergone several crises in the meantime. The integration of the particular questions and the addition of an introductory statement were the latest major changes which gave the text that unity, substance and relevance for which it received a final massive endorsement.

After a Preface signalling the basis and intent of the document, comes the Introductory Statement on 'The Situation of Humanity in the Modern World'. This is a general descriptive statement in language acceptable to Christians and others. The two main parts that follow are designated 'The Church and the Human Calling' (Part I) and 'Some Problems of Special Urgency' (Part II). It should be noted here that the translations from the 1960s, which are still in vogue, were not yet sensitive to risks of sexist language. So instead of 'Human Condition' one finds 'Man's Condition'; instead of 'Human Calling', 'Man's Calling', and so on. This commentary will endeavour as far as possible to avoid such language without, one hopes, offence to the original sense.

Part I, 'The Church and the Human Calling', is divided into four chapters; 1. The Dignity of the Human Person (*GS* 12–22); 2. The Community of Humankind (*GS* 23–32); 3. Human Activity Throughout the World (*GS* 33–9); 4. The Role of the Church in the Modern World (*GS* 40–5). Part II, 'Some Problems of Special Urgency', is divided into five chapters: 1. Fostering the Nobility of Marriage and the Family (*GS* 47–52); 2. The Proper Development of Culture (*GS* 53–62); 3. Socio-Economic Life (*GS* 63–72); 4. The Life of the Political Community (*GS* 73–6); 5. The Fostering of Peace and the Promotion of a Community of Nations (*GS* 77–90).

The logic of the overall structure is quite clear. The Introductory Statement sets the contemporary scene. Basic or general considerations in Part I on human person, community and activity in the context of the gospel are completed by examining the overall role of the Church in the modern world.

All this should provide the proper preparation for discussing the more specific issues of Part II. Yet, as frequently happens in such exercises, the discussion in Part II, while consistent with that in Part I, might well have gone on independently of the first part. This is no doubt partly due to the more developed state of discussion on many of these specific issues, with the exception of culture, and partly to the truly innovative aspects of Part I. They were not entirely ripe for integration into some of the more mature discussions in Part II.

With Part II itself there is a certain lack of coherent development. 'Some Urgent Problems' cannot be expected to form a neat logical package, so the chapter on 'Marriage and the Family', while overlapping with other problems, for example, demography and poverty, stays uneasily within a (healthy) tradition of personal values while the others are concerned with more social values. Here the order is not entirely clear, with some clear issues of economics appearing in the discussion of the international community in chapter 5 and so separated from the discussion in chapter 3. Similarly, with political issues in chapter 4 and chapter 5. The chapter on 'Culture', while in point of fact unsatisfactory and less mature than the other discussions, could well in theory have formed the overall matrix for Part II. Certainly it would have been a more coherent starting-point than 'Marriage and the Family'.

Bishops and experts alike were conscious of some of these deficiencies. However, they rightly decided that time was running out and it was better to have something than nothing, so they approved the present document as the best available in the circumstances and time available.

TITLE

The final official title, *De Ecclesia in Mundo Hujus Temporis*, literally, 'The Church in the World of this Time', aptly caught the intentions of its promoters. Despite earlier variations, it became a firm choice for the majority in the final debates. Difficulties about both major terms 'Church' and 'world' have already been noted and will arise again.

A different difficulty arises about the word 'modern' in English translation, which as indicated is not an absolutely literal translation of the Latin (*hujus temporis*, of this time). My preferred translation in Abbott, unfortunately uses 'The Church Today' as a running head, missing the great word 'world'. French and German translations, by contrast, are literal, such as *L'Eglise dans le monde de ce temps* and *Die Kirche in der Welt von Heute*. In cultural and political debates, with which this Constitution is directly concerned, 'modern' is often used to cover the last two centuries – history since the American and French revolutions. With this usage the Constitution and its authors could well feel comfortable. For many Catholics and others, Vatican II – and particularly this Constitution – meant the final acceptance of the democratic revolutions. Their rejection by popes and Church leaders in the nineteenth century had been definitively overcome.

In other respects too, 'modern' could be a useful term to those who accept

100

the Constitution. The Industrial Revolution, urbanization and the further implication of developing technology are addressed honestly and fairly. The achievements of science are no longer seen as a threat. Galileo has become an embarrassment. The hope is for dialogue and partnership between science and religion. The values of the Enlightenment, so long the bogey of Church authorities, are being critically integrated into Catholic thinking and teaching.

The Constitution is also regularly referred to by the first three Latin words of the text, *Gaudium et Spes*. This traditional form of reference for Church documents captures very well the spirit of the document as a whole.

Finally, it was termed a 'Pastoral' Constitution. While the title 'Constitution' adds weight to its teaching beyond that of 'decree' and places it beside the documents on the Church, Revelation and the Liturgy, 'Pastoral' sets it on its own against the 'Dogmatic' Constitutions on the Church and Revelation. The word may be interpreted diversely. On the one side, it might be used to diminish the weight of its teaching – it is *merely* pastoral. On the other, it can be said that Pope John declared his intention to call a *pastoral* Council so that *Gaudium et Spes* as its one and only *pastoral* Constitution represents the central purpose of Pope John better than anything else and thus has, in a way, the greatest authority. It may well be claimed that this document does express better than any other what was finally most characteristic of Vatican II.

PREFACE AND INTRODUCTORY STATEMENT

Gaudium et Spes are in fact the first words of the Preface. The distinction between Preface and the subsequent 'Introductory Statement' may be worth noting. The Preface (*GS* 1–3) stresses the intimate connection between Church and world as the Church makes its own the joys and hopes, the griefs and anxieties of all humanity. It addresses not only all Catholics and Christians but all of humanity in order to be of service. The engagement, openness and desire to be of service are far removed from the triumphalism and exclusivism that have characterized Church statements at other times.

Following this up, the Introductory Statement (*GS* 4–10) attempts to discern (that is, discover in difficult circumstances) 'the signs of the times' by surveying, fairly briefly at this point, the current human situation. The language and categories are accessible to people beyond the Church. The preliminary and selective nature of the description opens up the deeper and more detailed reflection without tying the substance of the Constitution's reflections to the necessarily limited and perhaps transient features mentioned here.

The profound and rapid changes evident in the contemporary world affect every dimension of human living. Many listed here receive fuller treatment in the main text. However, it is worth remarking on the further reference to 'socialization' and its relation to 'personalization'. Socialization first appeared in John XXIII's encyclical *Mater et Magistra* (1960) and met with some sharp criticism in the United States of America and elsewhere. Its reappearance here and the balance attempted later between person and community (*GS* 12–32) in human living and in the light of the gospel, offers an important contribution to human and Christian anthropology. Under the heading 'The Broader Desires of Humankind', reference is made to women's claims to 'equity with men before the law and in fact'. But there is no sign of foreseeing the immense impact the women's movement was about to make on society, Church or theology. A final section on 'Deeper Questions' arising from this sketch indicates the document's fuller strategy. Such questions may open one up to what Jesus Christ has to offer, to what God has achieved in Jesus Christ for humanity's self-understanding and fulfilment. We have here the beginnings of a Christology formulated precisely 'to illuminate the mystery of man'.

PART I: THE CHURCH AND THE HUMAN CALLING

The introduction and the four chapters of this part outline a Christian anthropology for our times. The first two chapters on 'The Dignity of the Human Person' and 'The Community of Humankind' seek to integrate the irreducible personal quality of each human being as created in the image of God with the equally constitutive social dimension of the human in relationship and structure. Despite the best efforts of these chapters and the document as a whole, the integration is not complete. The individual person remains dominant, with the social essential perhaps but subordinate. The influence of personalism was a dominant and in many ways a welcome influence at the Council. Its grounding in the image of God and final relation to Christ gave the person a power and role congenial to the Council fathers. That community was equally rooted in God's image and Christ's body did not have quite the same impact. 'Socialization' remained to some extent the poor relation of 'personalization', as the emphasis on the person as centre and goal of society and society's functions indicated.

A more complete Christian anthropology would have recognized that the person may only be person as person-in-relationships-in-structures, as person-in-community, and as in an immediate dialectic with a community-of-persons. Only by such hyphenated expressions may we hope to break the hold of a personalism that in practice readily becomes individualism, without falling victim to the collectivism against which the Council rightly warns.

In the discussion of a Christian anthropology, sin enters immediately after the paragraph on creation in God's image (*GS* 13). It is a brief reference and fits into the document's overall positive affirmation of humanity and world. Even with later references to human death and to the suffering and danger to which humanity is exposed in poverty, hunger and war, there seems to be insufficient awareness of the tragic dimensions of human life. This is surprising as the dominant theologians and fathers of the Council had experienced at first hand the awful tragedies of war in Europe and the horrors of the Holocaust. It is very much a reflection of the optimism of the 1960s, in which war and Holocaust seemed, temporarily, almost forgotten.

The paragraphs on Conscience and Freedom (*GS* 16–17), as essential aspects of human dignity, relate clearly to the Council's Declaration on

Religious Liberty (*Dignitatis Humanae*). The subsequent paragraphs on atheism (*GS* 19–21) embody a long and difficult discussion in Commission and Council. Relationship to God enters into human dignity. The Council makes this dimension very clear. Yet it displays considerable sensitivity in differentiating between the various forms of atheism, theoretical and practical, systematic and personal. It does not ignore possible personal culpability, but is also conscious of Christian responsibility for others' lack of belief. And it shows itself willing to work with all in the cause of human dignity. Despite strong pressure, explicit condemnations of Marxism, communism or other systems were avoided.

The return to Christology – Christ, the new human being, the final Adam – at the end of chapter 1 (*GS* 22) confirms the Council's strategy: Humanity can only be finally understood and explained in terms of Jesus Christ. In him we are revealed properly to ourselves.

The Community of Humankind in chapter 2 is presented as part of God's plan (*GS* 24). The 'Interdependence of Person and Society' (*GS* 25) and 'Promoting the Common Good' (*GS* 26) emphasize the further intimate connection of the personal and social. The primacy of the person reasserts itself in *GS* 27, although the attempt to maintain the intimate connection continues in *GS* 30 on the limitations of an individualistic ethic. Chapter 2 finds its inevitable completion in Christ, with 'The Incarnate Word and Human Solidarity' (*GS* 32).

'Human Activity Throughout the World', the concern of chapter 3 (*GS* 33–9), gives a positive and helpful account of human creativity and work. 'The Rightful Independence of Earthly Affairs' (*GS* 36) is another effort to recognize certain 'secular' implications of creation/incarnation and the demand that the Church be servant not Lord. The Christ-fulfilment of human work anticipated in the Eucharist (*GS* 38) reaches its completion in 'A New Earth and a New Heaven' (*GS* 39). The eschatological character of Christian faith, Church and world, strongly insisted on by one group of consultors and fathers, receives explicit if brief treatment here. The values of the 'Green Movement' are no more anticipated in chapter 3 than are those of feminism in earlier sections, yet some basis is offered for current environmental discussion. More apocalyptic views of eschatology are also largely ignored. The period 1963–5 was no doubt a happier and more optimistic time than 1989–90.

Chapter 4, 'The Role of the Church in the Modern World', moves from Christian anthropology to active ecclesiology or missiology, but the relationship between Church and world is seen to be a two-way one, of mutual interaction: 'The Church knows how richly she has profited by the history and development of humanity' (*GS* 44) – that may well be one of the Council's most significant admissions.

The bonds uniting Church and world (*GS* 40) prompt the Church to help individuals and society. The dignity and freedom of the individual, human rights, are given final foundation in the Church's teaching and – it is claimed – helped to effective implementation in the Church's practice. Again, although she has 'no proper mission in the political, economic or social order' (*GS* 42), the Church's religious mission supports society and recognizes the value of movements towards unity and socialization.

The paragraph on the Church's help to society is hesitant and tentative in comparison with later or even earlier Church documents. The Council is clearly feeling its way. The earlier paragraph on helping the individual is much stronger and clearer, confirming perhaps the stronger sense of the individual in this anthropology. Church help to human activity (*GS* 43) is mainly concerned with the duties of lay Christians. It forthrightly rejects any false opposition between worship and one's professional social activities. 'Secular duties and activities belong properly although not exclusively to lay people'. The duty of bishops and clergy is primarily to see that these activities of the laity 'are bathed in the light of the Gospel'. This general view of the Council may be insisting on too sharp a distinction between clergy and laity. However, it did help to cope with two traditional difficulties, the tendency of bishops and clergy to interfere improperly in political and social affairs and the tendency of the laity to separate sharply their Sunday worship and their work lives.

GS 44 endorses once again the mutual relationship sought by the Council. The help that the Church receives from the modern world includes the progress of the sciences and the wisdom of the philosophers, the leadership of politicians, even the actions of critics and persecutors. It is an exciting passage: 'With the help of the Spirit, it is the task of the entire People of God, especially pastors and theologians, to hear and interpret the many voices of our age . . . in this way revealed truth can be better understood.' The spirit, methodology and purpose of the Council were here exceptionally well expressed.

This chapter, like each of those in Part I, ends Christologically. If these four paragraphs (*GS* 22, 32, 39 and 45) are put together, they present a quite exciting doctrine of Christ and a partial response to the complaint that the Council concentrated too much on ecclesiology and too little on Christology.

PART II: SOME PROBLEMS OF SPECIAL URGENCY

Marriage and the Family

Chapter 1, 'On Fostering the Nobility of Marriage and the Family', was inevitably one of the most sharply debated chapters of the Constitution. After adverting to the state of marriage and the family in the modern world (*GS* 47), the Constitution develops a theology of marriage that is scriptural, sacramental and deeply human. A community of love open to life established in covenant between free and equal partners and founded in the covenant relationship between Christ and his Church might fairly summarize the Council's teaching. Juridical and contractual language is avoided. So too is the discussion of (or distinction between) primary and secondary ends. Children are the fruit of conjugal love and are to be welcomed accordingly. The loving family is life-giving beyond its own boundaries to society as a whole.

104

This is an excellent expression of a theology of marriage that had been developing in the Church since the 1940s. It has by and large stood the test of time since.

The discussion of responsible transmission of life (*GS* 50 and 51) is sensitive to the pressures on families to limit or postpone further children without violating the objective moral law. Indeed, here for the first time the Church positively stressed the concept and practice of 'responsible parenthood': that it is morally right for the married to decide when and how many children they should have: 'Parents themselves should ultimately make the judgment in the sight of God'. This constituted a major step forward in the field of Catholic marital teaching. The question as to which means can rightly be used must seem secondary in comparison. In practice, they were, of course, vital. The increasingly common use of the contraceptive pill and worldwide fears of the consequences of a population explosion, linked with a falling death-rate, made a reconsideration of the morality of artificial contraception urgent. Its earlier rejection by other Churches, including the Anglican Communion, had already been reversed and the pressure to reconsider the teaching of Pius XI and Pius XII in this area coming both from lay people and many pastors was immense. Conciliar discussion of contraception was, however, forbidden by the pope, who insisted that it be further investigated by a special papal commission and then left to him to decide. The Council accepted this and merely declared, without specifying which, that those methods of regulating procreation found wrong by the Church's teaching authority should not be practised by Catholics.

Footnote 14 of the Latin text, with its references to Pius XI's *Casti Connubii* and some allocutions of Pius XII at the direction of Paul VI, made the state of play clear but was not meant to foreclose further discussion. Reference to the Papal Commission was to explain why the Council could not complete the work itself. The footnote's terms have been claimed to be ambiguous depending, according to some commentators, on where you put a comma. After mentioning the work of the Commission, the footnote concludes: '*Sic stante doctrina Magisterii, S. synodus solutiones concretas immediate proponere non intendit*' ('With the doctrine of the magisterium in this state, this holy Synod does not intend to propose immediate concrete solutions'; Abbott, p. 256. Placing the comma after *sic* to make it read *Sic, stante doctrina magisterii* . . . could translate as: 'So, with the doctrine of the magisterium still intact, etc.', but this is a highly implausible interpretation which does not fit the context of the footnote.) The accepted punctuation and translation in fact suggest that the Church did not regard the issue as a closed one despite the teaching of earlier popes. The way was left open for a papal decision in either direction. The judgement of *Humanae Vitae* three years later was not necessarily implicit within what the Council was permitted to say.

Many people regretted then and since that the Council was not free to complete the discussion on birth control. There were, undoubtedly, great practical difficulties in the way, not least the pressure of time. If these could have been overcome and the Council had reached some conclusion, whatever it might have been, it would probably have received much more widespread support than *Humanae Vitae* did subsequently. A reaffirmation of the traditional position by the Council in 1965 would never have produced the crisis that it did when coming from the pope three years later.

The Proper Development of Culture

This, the subject of chapter 2, was by far the most novel of the special questions considered, and Cardinal Lercaro spoke of it as being at the heart of the Constitution.

The Introduction (*GS* 53) displays a proper openness to attempts to define, or rather describe, culture. It adverts to attempts by the more empirical sciences to categorize cultures as total ways of life of particular peoples at particular times, a series of human creations. Acceptance of a plurality of cultures and the categorization of religion with cultural schemes indicate the free spirit of the document. The freedom of spirit was, however, also a source of weakness owing to vagueness of language and concept, and it came in for some criticism both within and without the Aula. The lack of maturity, remarked on earlier, affects the chapter as a whole. Yet it breaks important new ground. There are some valuable insights and it must be regretted that so little theological attention has subsequently been paid to it.

Two crucial features of human culture for Christians emerge. It is in and through culture that divine as well as human creativity is revealed. To discern God's activity in the world, to read the divine signs of the times, the Church must be in dialogue with and so understand the language of particular cultures. This also applies to the Bible as expression of a particular culture. All divine communication is mediated through human culture. Moving in the other direction, the Church must seek to translate its message and liturgy from one culture to another. The Word of God must take flesh in cultures outside traditional Western ones (*GS* 58). The Constitution does not develop such points. The language and repetition tend to obscure them, and they still await more serious theological exploration and practical implementation.

The logic of creation and incarnation that has just been applied to faith and culture also involves respect for the autonomy of culture, of human creative activities, in science and the arts, in politics and economics. The Church's acceptance of scientific progress and its respect for scientific method is stressed once again. This is part of a wider respect for the search for truth, for artistic freedom and for the integrity and freedom of intellectual enquiry. All this must be understood, worked with and applied by Christians and theologians in the search for fuller truth and deeper harmony between gospel and culture.

Despite a certain vagueness in this chapter as a whole, its final article (*GS* 62) is precise enough, and one of the most important of any Council text, applying as it does the spirit of the Declaration on Religious Freedom to the Church's own intellectual life:

> Furthermore it is to be hoped that many lay people will receive an appropriate formation in the sacred sciences, and that some will develop and deepen these studies by their own labours. In order that such persons may fulfil their proper function, let

it be recognized that all the faithful, clerical and lay, possess a lawful freedom of enquiry and of thought, and the freedom to express their minds humbly and courageously (*in humilitate et fortitudine*) about those matters in which they enjoy competence.

Some of the bishops objected to 'courageously' (*in fortitudine*), but the Council accepted it. It is not a text to be forgotten.

Economics and Politics

Chapters 3 and 4, and chapter 5, section 2 (*GS* 83–90), deal with economic and political issues in ways that owe a good deal to the encyclicals of John XXIII and have been developed since by Paul VI, John Paul II, the Synod of Bishops and particular bishops' conferences. Again, brief commentary on the more important points must suffice.

Chapter 3, 'Socio-Economic Life', is a look at the current economic scene with its achievements and failures, leading to a series of important if conventional points about the primacy of human beings over economics, which is to be at the service and in the control of human beings. Reducing human beings to economic units in a collectivist or free-market economy offends against this basic human and Christian vision. So do the huge differences in people's share in economic power and in the goods of the world (*GS* 63–6). In seeking principles for proper economic development, the Constitution expresses the primacy of the human by the primacy of labour over profits as the person's way of providing a living for self and family. Freedom to organize as workers, to withdraw labour, to participate in its fruits and in decision-making about it are reaffirmed.

As for the goods of the earth and their ownership, the Constitution remains consistent with its entire understanding of humanity in creation. The goods of the earth belong first to the whole human community (*GS* 69). This reversal of the usual order in discussing ownership makes theological sense and recalls the reversal effected in the Constitution on the Church where the People of God are discussed prior to structures and hierarchy. Private ownership is subsequently justified as a safeguard of personal freedom, but it is subsequent and secondary. The obligation to provide everybody with a basic income, the social obligations of all private property, respect for communal ownership as it has traditionally existed, the rights of a person in extreme necessity – all these emphasize that the world's goods belong primarily to the whole human community. A just economic system must recognize this primacy. So must Christians in seeking first the Kingdom of God (*GS* 72). Some further international implications of this are taken up in chapter 5, section 2.

Chapter 4, 'The Life of the Political Community', opens with a description of modern political society stressing appreciatively the world-wide pursuit of personal rights, minority rights and civil liberties as ways to realizing the 'common good'. It is striking how a traditional Catholic political preoccupation with the primacy of the common good and natural law is here expressed and given concrete shape in modern liberal, democratic terms. It is on the basis of the organization of people to pursue 'a dynamically conceived common good' (*GS* 74) with respect for rights and the possibility of democratic participation that the Council endorses the 'evolution' of modern politics. While there is nothing new or surprising in all this, the Council's clear-cut and positive endorsement does finally bring to an end the century-old quarrel between Church authorities and democracy.

The role of the Church in political life is handled circumspectly but hardly brilliantly. Its witness to and protection 'of the transcendence of the human person' is primary. 'In their proper spheres, the political community and the Church are mutually independent and self-governing.' However, in promoting justice, charity and other social virtues, the Church contributes significantly to the common good.

Sentences like 'the Church herself employs the things of time to the degree that her own proper mission demands' make little sense, implying as they do that the Church is not only in part external to the state, but also basically outside time and society. Here as elsewhere an underlying inadequacy in a theology of the world and the Church in the world surfaced to produce a certain confusion.

To complete the discussion of economics and politics, it is helpful to consider the second section of chapter 5 before the discussion of peace and war in section 1. Chapter 5 as a whole is entitled 'The Fostering of Peace and the Promotion of the Community of Nations'; section 2 bears the title 'Building up the International Community' (*GS* 83–90).

As mentioned earlier, the final debates on this Constitution occurred during and after Pope Paul VI's visit to the United Nations in New York. There is a natural tendency within the Catholic Church to favour mechanisms for international co-operation and organization (the Hapsburg empire in the past, the United Nations today). John XXIII's *Pacem in Terris* had strongly taken up the need and met with world-wide acclaim: it was part of its appeal. The United Nations Declaration on Human Rights in 1948 has become increasingly integrated with Christian and Catholic social theology. Cardinal Roncalli's presence in Paris as Papal Nuncio during the years leading up to the Declaration has been claimed as significant both for the Declaration and for subsequent Church teaching. It is in this spirit that this section of the Constitution promotes the cause of international solidarity and unity.

There is a keen awareness of the social and personal reasons for disunity and discord, from economic and political oppression to personal jealousy and ambition. International political co-operation is essential, requiring effective organizations and a reformed international economic order. The obligations of developing and advanced nations and of the international community to create such a reformed economic order for the fulfilment of all is spelled out.

The difficult problem of high population growth is also faced (*GS* 87). The need for regulation, and the responsibilities of the political authorities are recognized within, however, the limits of the moral law and with final respect for the rights of parents in deciding on size of family. Consistency with the chapter on the family and with John XXIII's teaching in *Pacem in Terris* ensures that the matter was here ignored, and few of the Council fathers would have been willing to go as far as they did prior to Vatican II. The duties of Christians in all this is related to the international presence of the Church as support, guide and inspiration in the development of a truly just and peaceful political and economic order. As earnest of this commitment, it is proposed that an international Catholic Church agency be established 'for the world-wide promotion of justice for the poor' (*GS* 90). This practical suggestion, implemented in the Secretariat for Justice and Peace, was proposed by one of the few outsiders to address the Council, American lay Catholic, James J. Norris. That it should be Catholic rather than ecumenical was criticized, but defended on the grounds that for ecumenical co-operation there must first of all be a Catholic institution. It is certainly the outstanding institutional consequence of the Constitution.

Peace and War

Section 1 of chapter 5 bears the title 'The Avoidance of War' (*De Bello Vitando*). Its first significant discussion is of the nature of peace (*GS* 78). This paragraph refuses to accept peace as a mere absence of war or simply a balance of forces. Following again *Pacem in Terris*, it attempts a far more positive description of peace as an 'enterprise of justice' and as related to the gift and intention of the Divine Creator and founder of society.

The real concern of the section, however, does remain the avoidance of war. This is understandable enough in the light of the international tensions of the times and the possibilities of total nuclear destruction. These debates probably generated the most interest and certainly the most heat of any in the Constitution. While the final text emphatically condemned the indiscriminate destruction of cities or other extensive populated areas as 'a crime against God and man' (*GS* 81) – by far the strongest condemnation made anywhere by the Council – it drew back from Pope John's wider condemnation in his final legacy to the world, *Pacem in Terris*, of modern war in any circumstances, and also from one of the multiplications of weapons as a deterrent. While the resultant text remains strong in striking rhetorical phrases ('the arms race is an utterly treacherous trap for humanity') its teaching upon war remains ambiguous and open to a range of interpretations (see 11K).

The condemnation of total war and the arms race had not gone undisputed, especially by some United States bishops, and various stratagems were suggested to avoid what seemed to some a 'pacifist' bias. However, the wider condemnation of the consequent misuse of resources badly needed for the hungry and deprived could hardly be faulted, any more than could the urgency of the ultimate goal – the abolition of war (analogous it would seem to the abolition of slavery). For that, it was agreed, a new international authority is needed.

The condemnation of total war, the rejection of the arms race as a safe way to peace and the acceptance of the right to conscientious objection, were very considerable steps beyond the traditional just war theory and its understanding in the 1950s. The overall position of the Constitution did not, nevertheless, outlaw wars of defence or undermine the authority of those responsible for them. On paper, at least, some balance was struck.

If the Constitution made little, in the strategy for peace, of conscientious objection, it did not even advert to the power of peace movements like those of Gandhi and Martin Luther King as expressing the spirit of the gospel and of shalom. Again, a brief reference to opposition to injustice within the state (GS 74) is quite inadequate as a commentary upon gross oppression, and is seen by some as a failure to address the issue of revolution. Here, as in many other matters, Pope Paul was to advance in *Populorum Progressio* far beyond the viewpoint of *Gaudium et Spes*.

The concluding paragraphs of the Constitution constitute an appeal to everyone, whether or not one even explicitly believes in God, to help the vast programme the Council has tried to sketch in this document to 'fashion the world more to man's surpassing dignity, search for a brotherhood which is universal . . . meet the urgencies of our age . . .' Whether or not the Constitution in its many sections adequately spelt out the intricate problems of culture, marriage, politics and economics, the programme of this worldly renewal is in its extent an exciting and moving one. It might be hard to claim that the text of *Gaudium et Spes* has in many of its parts greatly influenced the subsequent life of the Church, but it seems undeniable that the overall emphasis of this vast document – so much longer than anything else the Council produced – has done so. Its influence has depended not on its precise analysis or formulations, but on the direction of concern it so clearly indicated.

AFFIRMATION AND RESERVATION

The text remains. Twenty-five years on it is still an inspiring and powerful document. Yet its splendid achievement should not obscure its limitations. A few will be discussed here, but not in any ungrateful or ungracious spirit.

The first, most obvious and perhaps most superficial limitation is the Constitution's European or first world character. This criticism might be applied to all the Council's documents, it is more obvious and more telling in a document purporting to deal with the world as it is in the light of the gospel. The attention to third-world or second-world situations is, apart from the chapter on economics, merely occasional.

The second limitation must be the absence of the cross from the gospel reflections: social sin, mass oppression, a sheer conspiracy of evil needed to explain so much of human history, all that is largely absent. The world it portrays is one needing development rather than liberation. It is one whose problems seem rather easily resolvable with a bit of goodwill and a renewal of Christian idealism. And this from a dominantly European–American gathering whose members had been through two world wars in this century and still had to live with the responsibility of the Holocaust. The sense of the tragic is largely missing from its world-view as the cross is from its theology.

There are limitations and confusions too in its understanding of the way

Christ related to the world, because it concentrates on the mediating symbol of the Church and largely ignores that of the Kingdom. Any attempt to discuss the Church in the world without spelling out the Church's role in discerning, promoting and realizing the Kingdom in the world is bound to be limited and frustrated. And the world proves very difficult to focus without a clearer vision of the relation between creation and new creation and the emergence of the Kingdom in myriad ways beyond but not unrelated to visible Church. Effectively, Christians looking for authoritative guidance in almost any field touched upon by *Gaudium et Spes* are likely to find it better in subsequent documents, from Paul VI's *Populorum Progressio* to John Paul II's *Sollicitudo Rei Socialis*, but to understand the emergence of the vast movement that has led to the Catholic pursuit throughout the world of justice and peace, liberation and brotherhood, the impact of *Gaudium et Spes* remains decisive.

8D The Church in the Modern World (*Gaudium et Spes*): Bibliography

Commentaries

Baum, G., and Campion, D. (1967) *Pastoral Constitution on the Church in the Modern World of Vatican II*. New York, Paulist Press.

Falconer, A., *et al.* (1985) *Freedom to Hope, Documents of Vatican II*. Dublin, Columba Press.

Rahner, K., *et al.* (1967) *Gaudium et Spes, l'Eglise dans le Monde de ce Temps*. Paris, du Cerf.

Theology since the Council

Rahner, Schillebeeckx, Congar *et al.* have in their personal writings and through such publications as *Concilium* taken the programme of Vatican II and particularly the first half of the Constitution on *The Church in the Modern World* on to further and fuller development. Their writings in the late 1960s and 1970s are very important.

Rahner, K. (1974) *Theological Investigations*, vol. XI. London, Darton, Longman and Todd.

Rahner, K. (1976) *Theological Investigations*, vol. XIV. London, Darton, Longman and Todd.

Schillebeeckx, E. (1968) *God and Man*. London, Sheed & Ward.

Schillebeeckx, E. (1971) *World and Church*. London, Sheed & Ward.

Schoonenberg, P. (1964) *God's World in the Making*. Dublin, Gill and Macmillan.

A somewhat different line has been opened up by J.B. Metz and others with the development of 'Political Theology'. Where the Constitution had sought to integrate critically so much of the liberal and secular tradition of the previous two centuries, Political Theology pursued more explicitly the dialogue with socialism. It also sought to take account of the interruption of the Holocaust as crucial to future Christian theology.

Metz, J.B. (1968) *The Church in the World*. London, SCM.

Metz, J.B. (1981) *The Emergent Church*. London, SCM.

With Latin American liberation theology, a more radical turn was taken.

Gutierrez, G. (1973) A Theology of Liberation, London, SCM, remains the classical work, but a great many other significant works have appeared including:

Boff, L. (1988) *Trinity and Society*. New York, Orbis.
Bonino, (1983) *Towards a Christian Political Ethics*. London, SCM.
Segundo, (1977) *The Liberation of Theology*. Maryknoll, NY, Orbis.
Sobrino, J. (1978) *Christology at the Crossroads*. London, SCM.

English language theologians in Britain and Ireland have been more eclectic, drawing on very different traditions, as they sought to develop some of the themes and the spirit of *The Church in the Modern World*. A short list is provided:

Davis, C. (1980) *Theology and Political Society*. Cambridge University Press.
Dorr, D. (1982) *Option for the Poor*. Dublin, Gill and Macmillan.
Lane, D. (1977) *Liberation Theology, An Irish Dialogue*. Dublin, Gill and Macmillan.
Lash, N. (1981) *A Matter of Hope*. London, Darton, Longman and Todd.
Mackey, J.P. (1987) *Modern Theology*. Oxford University Press.
McDonagh, E. (1980) *The Demands of Simple Justice*. Dublin, Gill and Macmillan.
McDonagh, E. (1989) *The Gracing of Society*. Dublin, Gill and Macmillan.

The United States and Canada have also supplied a rich if eclectic pattern, in addition to feminist and black theologies. The foundational work of David Tracy is pre-eminent here, but people like John Coleman and Gregory Baum have been combining social analysis with theological reflection in very illuminating ways.

Baum, G. (1982) *The Priority of Labour*. New York, Paulist Press.
Baum, G. (1988) *Theology and Society*. New York, Paulist Press. An outstanding review of twenty-five years of Catholic social teaching.
Coleman, J. (1982) *An American Strategic Theology*.
Lamb, M. (1982) *Solidarity with the Victims*. New York, Crossroad.
McCann, D. (1982) *Liberation Theology and Christian Realism*. New York, Orbis.
Tracy, D. (1981) *The Analogical Imagination*, London, SCM.
Tracy, D. (1987) *Plurality and Ambiguity*. London, SCM.

While a good deal of writing has occurred on special issues in marriage and sexuality, the overall vision of *Gaudium et Spes* is still valid and valuable. Among the more useful books are:

Cahill, L.S. (1985) *Between the Sexes*. Philadelphia, Fortress.
Dominian, J. (1981) *Marriage, Faith and Love*. London, Darton, Longman and Todd.
Genovesi, V.J. (1987) *In Pursuit of Love*. Wilmington, DE, Michael Glazier.
Guindon, A. (1976) *The Sexual Language: An Essay in Moral Theology*. Ottowa, University Press.
Keane, P.S. (1976) *Sexual Morality: A Catholic Perspective*. Dublin, Gill and Macmillan.

8E Ecumenism (*Unitatis Redintegratio*)

TOM STRANSKY, PAULIST

The Decree on Ecumenism is the most authoritative charter for the active participation of the Roman Catholic Church in that one ecumenical movement which many Protestants, soon joined by some Orthodox, initiated on a global scale in the first decades of this century.

The official pre-Vatican II attitude towards the Church unity movement was that of deliberate distance and prudent wait-and-see. The Catholic Church passed judgement on the movement without being a participant in it.

In 1927 Pius XI promulgated *Mortalium Animos*, on 'fostering true religious union' (1928). The encyclical letter was clear: Catholic 'participation in assemblies of non-Catholics' would falsely imply that one religion or church is as valid as another; that one could negotiate revealed truths through compromise; and that some prevalent Protestant ecclesiologies were acceptable. Hence the conclusion, if Catholics were to encourage or support such gatherings, 'they would be countenancing a false religion quite alien to the one true Church of Christ'.

The pope then stated what the Catholic Church judges should be the goals and methods of the 'outside' ecumenical movement: 'There is only one way in which the unity of Christians may be fostered, and that is by promoting the return to the one true Church of Christ of those who are separated from it; for from that one true Church they had unhappily fallen away.'

The basis for this judgement and policy was ecclesiological: the Roman Catholic Church understood itself to be co-extensive or identical with the one true Church of Christ. To be faithful, the ecumenical movement should move but one way. The reunion of divided Christians means the return of others to the Catholic Church.

A change to a more positive evaluation of the ecumenical movement began in the 1950s. The Holy Office Letter *Ecclesia Sancta* (20 December 1949) recognized that the ecumenical movement 'derives from the inspiration of the Holy Spirit' and is 'a source of holy joy in the Lord' for Catholics, who must take these efforts of other Christians seriously, in charity and in prayer. Under strict conditions Catholic experts can participate in discussions 'on faith and morals' with other Christians, but such Catholics must avoid religious indifferentism and stand firm in the ecclesiology of 'return'.

After John XXIII had established the Secretariat for Promoting Christian Unity to help other Christians 'follow the work of the Council' (5 June 1960), the secretariat drafted a document on Christian unity.

During the first session in 1962, the Council fathers were faced with three separate documents dealing explicitly with the unity of the Church: a chapter of the Theological Commission's *On the Church*; the Eastern Churches Commission's *That They May Be One*; and the yet unseen secretariat's draft. The Council voted for a single document which would fuse the contents of the former three. Eventually the secretariat became the principal author. After two sessions of debate and redrafting, the decree was almost unanimously approved (21 November 1964). The decree has three chapters:

Chapter I (*UR* 2–4) unfolds the Catholic understanding of the fundamental invisible and visible unity of the Lord's 'one Church and one Church only' as the expression of the undivided Trinity. This Church 'subsists in' the Roman Catholic Church but is not co-extensive with it, because 'outside its visible borders', that is, in other Christian communions, exist 'elements and endowments which together build up and give life to the Church itself'. (*UR 3*)

True, the division among Christians 'openly contradicts the will of Christ, scandalizes the world and damages . . . the proclamation of the gospel'. Nevertheless, there already is *real* communion between Christians because of what God has done and does to and through them, but an *imperfect* one because of what they have done and continue to do to each other – 'a real but imperfect fellowship' between all Christian communions (*UR 3*).

These ecclesiological positions shape the fundamental shift in Roman Catholic understanding of Christian relations and underlie the guidelines, methods and helps for Catholic participation in 'the restoration of unity'. The shift is from an ecclesiology of self-sufficiency and the unification model of 'return', to that of incompleteness and the mutual need for one another in the one but still divided household. Ecumenism deals not with foreign relations, but with domestic ones. It is not a return to the past but a common search for future reconciliation.

In the practice of ecumenism (chapter II, *UR* 5–12) the whole Church is involved, laity and clergy alike. Ecumenism demands both the 'continual reformation' of the pilgrim Church, as well as the continual conversion of each Catholic. In fact, 'the very soul of the ecumenical movement is the change of heart and holiness of life', along with private and public prayer for unity and with occasional joint-worship. A loving understanding of each other's Communion through dialogue, an ecumenically oriented formation in theological studies and a common search into the word of God will foster mutual understanding and esteem. And to express the bond that already unites Christians to the Servant-Lord and to one another, common witness is strongly encouraged through co-operative action, especially in social matters.

Chapter III (*UR* 13–24) describes the principal historical divisions in the Christian family – in East and West. With regard to the Eastern Churches, the Council here (and here alone) uses the word 'solemnly' to assert their right to govern themselves according to their own traditions and historical development. The Eastern liturgical and monastic traditions, Eastern spiritualities and Church disciplines, and 'complementary rather than conflicting' theological formulations should be respected, for they contribute to the comeliness of the one Church and to its mission. Prayer, dialogue and co-operation in pastoral work are the means for restoring full communion.

Among the Christian Communions in the West, the decree proposes a programme for the dialogue. The commitment to Christ as Lord and Saviour, the loving reverence for Holy Scripture, the baptismal liturgy and celebration of the Last Supper, the apostolic witness to the gospel in social action – all provide points of agreement still more than of disagreement among Catholics and their Anglican and Protestant brethren in Christ.

The decree ends with a plea for God's blessings on the ecumenical movement, born of God's Spirit and resting in hope on his continuing guidance.

In the post-Vatican II period, the general principles and pastoral directives for the decree were detailed in a series of documents from the Secretariat for Promoting Christian Unity, in papal statements, and in the 1983 *Code of Canon Law*. Most national episcopal conferences and local bishops have issued detailed guidelines. The range of ecumenical activities and structures, official and unofficial, on the parish, diocesan, national and world levels is astonishing in its variety. In all these ecumenical advances, despite the flaws, the Roman Catholic Church has been experiencing a series of surprises – issues and events unforeseen or unanticipated at Vatican II. Five of them are listed here:

1 Authentic ecumenical thinking, attitudes and practices have still entered the bloodstream of only a minority of Catholics, whether laity, clergy or bishops. This fact should not cause unease or anger. Twenty-five years ago the Decree on Ecumenism did not affirm an already developed, sanctioned ecclesiology and practice present in the pre-Vatican II scene. The decree began a new tradition. Bishops, priests and laity were suddenly expected to 'own' the decree and to carry out its theological, pastoral and missionary demands. Too much came too soon for too many. At stake was that secure Catholic identity which for so many was based on being over and against other Christians.

The surprise is not that a new ecumenical tradition is not yet pulsating through every committed Catholic and every Catholic institution or structure. The surprise is how strong and how irrevocable is the Church's commitment, even though it is so weakly and so inconsistently expressed in attitudes and practices at every level of church life, whether in Rome or in whatever nation, diocese or parish. Indeed, ecumenism is still a stumbling infant, perhaps an awkward adolescent, certainly not a prematurely aged gent with gasping last breaths.

2 Vatican II classified historically 'the two principal types of division that affect the seamless robe of Christ': the initial and gradual dissolving of ecclesiastical communion between the Patriarchates of the East and the Roman See in the West; and then within the West, four centuries later, between the Roman See and the national or confessional churches that issued from the Reformation. These divided Western churches later gave birth to almost all the Christian communities in Asia, Africa, Latin America and Oceania. Following this typology of Christian divisions and their Western offspring, the decree implies that theological dialogue and pastoral solicitude should concentrate on the healing at their source of the East–West and intra-West divisions.

What was not foreseen twenty-five years ago is the new and growing tension between this classical typology of Christian divisions (with its specific agenda of reconciliation) and the rapid emergence of the 'Third Church'. The traditional Christian heartland that embraces the local churches of the northern Atlantic/eastern European/Mediterranean areas is fading in its dominant influence over the centres of the southern hemisphere. The 1985 Synod is a symbol of the new factor. At Vatican II, no one anticipated that, twenty years later, 60 per cent of the bishops at a world synod would not be from Europe or North America.

These new centres do not accept without question the priorities of renewal, mission and unity that are based on the historical experience of the classical Christian divisions ('East or West, it's still North!'). Nor do they always accept the conclusions passed on for everybody's consumption.

The holy and unholy tensions between the East/West and the North/South centres have become a new factor in the struggle to incarnate mission, renewal and unity in all six continents. The tension has already borne good and ill effects in the debates about liberation theologies emerging in Latin America and elsewhere, about liturgical forms in Africa, and about the living dialogue with those of other world faiths, which dialogue is so pronounced in Asia.

3 The Vatican II ecumenism charter programmed dialogues by which each partner 'explains the teaching of one Communion in great depth and brings out clearly its distinctive features'. But more than compiling explanations, these continuing dialogues become a joint reflection on a shared faith, as each communion asks: 'Do we recognize here the faith of the Church through the ages?'

Not predicted at the Council's end was the extent and pace of such formal dialogues on the international and national levels between the Roman Catholic Church and almost every world confessional family: Orthodox, Old Catholics, Anglicans, Lutherans, Reformed, Methodist, Disciples of Christ, Pentecostals, and Baptists. Joined to these is the active Catholic participation in multilateral dialogues within the forum of the World Council of Churches.

The flood of results, with various degrees of consensus, convergence and agreements or disagreements, has done little more than trickle into the consciousness of local congregations. The printed results are often not easily available and, if so, they seem digestible only by the theological elite.

For some Catholics, formerly clear signposts of their identity over and against other Christian traditions are being stripped away 'from above', or so they fear. For other Catholics, it seems nothing prevents immediate full communion except the fearful stubbornness of 'the authorities' in not acknowledging that all fundamental theological obstacles have already collapsed.

Pastoral leadership in guiding Catholics who share either this fear or this optimism is handicapped, since so many of the leaders – episcopal, priestly and lay – have enough else to digest on their pastoral plates, apart from the heavy morsels of the dialogues still waiting to be served.

One should not dismiss the gradual entrance of the dialogue results into educational materials, seminary and adult education classes, and liturgical services. An assimilation is there. More local dialogues do take place, and often these are in healthy rivalry with the high-level ones. The latter can take off in strange, unrealistic directions if they do not reflect the objective concerns of the whole Christian community. For one thing, the actual meaning of Christian faith as expressed in the practical decisions of the laity and clergy may be quite different from the faith envisioned in systems of theology.

4 The Decree on Ecumenism reflected Catholic awareness of differences with many other churches 'in moral matters', and recommended that 'the ecumenical dialogue could start with the moral application of the Gospel'.

The bulk of the formal dialogues has been concentrating on everything but ethical issues. Two decades ago one had not foreseen the present quick reversal. Just as convergences appear on those doctrinal affirmations that helped to cause and perpetuate classical divisions between the churches, emerging are personal and social ethical issues that are more divisive in the public arena than they were in the 1960s. Most folk consider that they matter far more than what the dialogues are communicating about biblical doctrine and Church teaching on other subjects.

Abortion, the death penalty and euthanasia; active homosexuality and premarital sex; peace and economic policies and prudential decisions based on them; women's rights in society and in the churches – these form but the short list.

These ethical issues rise high like flags, and transdenominational coalitions are formed to wave a particular flag. They may take opposite sides, and each claims fidelity to the gospel. Sometimes there is no dialogue between them, only diatribe. Brothers and sisters in Christ become enemies – distorting witness, wounding communion.

5. As Catholics in the 1960s officially entered into the ecumenical arena, they found only mainline Protestants, Anglicans and Eastern Orthodox. Absent were conservative evangelicals, whether within the mainline communities or in their own, and most Holiness and Pentecostal churches. These were considered intentionally 'anti-ecumenical', as they envisaged the movement. Many had an anti-Catholic stance and were aggressively proselytizing among vulnerable Catholic flocks.

Not anticipated at Vatican II, and now catching Catholics off-guard, was the evangelicals 'coming out of the closet' in the 1970s.

Just as in the pre-Vatican II period the ecumenical movement was hampered by the absence of the Catholic Church, so now one realizes how sectarian the movement remains because of the absence of a large, vigorous, fast-growing segment of the Christian household. But alongside those evangelicals who rigidly remain aloof are those who regard former foes as common allies. They are bringing new energies to old agendas. They do not take kindly to being considered second-class participants in the movement because of their later entry (as Catholics did not want the same label when their Church entered in the mid-1960s).

8F Religious Freedom (*Dignitatis Humanae*)

JAMES TUNSTEAD BURTCHAELL csc

In reckoning the influence of Vatican II on religious liberty, one must enquire not merely into the doctrine of its Declaration on Religious Freedom, *Dignitatis Humanae*, and its precise after-effects. A Church Council is less an initiative than a sanction. Its enactments must be read as vindications of insights and arguments that had been elaborated earlier by scholars and pastors, and were sustained against vigorous opposition even from many of the bishops who in Council were eventually brought to accept them. The force of this new official consensus then gave these doctrines a fresh impetus that would inevitably propel the reflections and convictions of the Church towards further developments well beyond the formulations of the Council itself. Occasioned usually by stress, a Council is tempted to resolve a controversy by endorsing one or another competing partisan doctrine. Its authentic calling, by contrast, is to rise to a higher perspective that will honour the driving insights that gave stubborn vitality to each adversarial group, and then to frame a formula in communion with the past, yet more developed and more serviceable than any the normative past had yet provided. Vatican II, by design more pastoral than polemic (especially by contrast with its predecessor Councils, Trent and Vatican I), may be more enduringly influential as a guide to the large movements it punctuated, precisely because its enactments were generally more creative than reactive, and thus less bound to time and circumstance.

In the matter of religious freedom especially, Catholic doctrine had previously been reactive. In the eighteenth century the Enlightenment liberals had endorsed religious freedom because, as a private and individual undertaking, religious faith had no standing or value in the public order. The believer was free to believe as he or she wished, because private faith impinged on no one else. Regarding churches it was another matter: they were inappropriate participants in civil life since their assumptions were nothing the populace could discuss out in the open, or negotiate and resolve together, and since churches were public entities that could be disempowered by civil restraint. Catholic reaction to this threat was to reinforce the Church's position where possible, and, where that was no longer possible, to negotiate concordats to protect whatever privileges could be salvaged.

In the nineteenth century increasingly totalitarian regimes with their eye upon the Church's landed wealth, and republican regimes dominated by anticlericals, roughed up the Church badly in Europe. The Church's response was to rely upon the pope as a political sovereign; a policy that was to suffer humiliation and increasing irrelevance from the Congress of Vienna (1815) to the Treaty of Versailles (1919).

In the present century, totalitarian, atheistic ideologies and new populist nationalist movements repressed the Church as a rival, 'counter-revolutionary' force, menacing because it is a transnational agency and a rival of the state for primary loyalty. While the Vatican's response was still to salvage what it could through a concordat, that of Catholics, first in Europe and later in Latin

118

America, was often to resort instead to a Catholic political party. As these efforts waned or collapsed the papacy was gradually transformed from a political to a spiritual agency with a twofold strategy: wielding the leverage of international sympathy to protect beleaguered local churches, and yielding to local resourcefulness when national churches enjoyed freedom. Though this twentieth-century shift was as reactive as before, it constituted a bold departure in both the conception and the defence of religious freedom. Vatican II, of course, was a product of that shift, not its origin.

By the time the Council assembled, popes since Leo XIII (1878–1903) had become accustomed to serving as a moral voice appealing to national populations rather than as a political force leaning on their governments. Catholics in many lands were evidently enough patriots, rather than opponents of nationalism. Clergy had been disentangled from political patronage and the ownership of real estate. Also, in a pluralist society some Catholics realized that their Church had a common stake with other religious communities and they had begun to ground their claim to freedom, not on the divine warrants of their faith, but on the more neutral right of any believer to freedom of belief and worship.

Dignitatis Humanae followed this line in its arguments for religious freedom. The Declaration claims no recognition of Church authority by a believing state; it seeks freedom, not establishment (*DH* 6). This doctrine represents a sharp break with the tradition since Constantine, Justinian and Charlemagne. The people have now replaced the prince as sovereign, and the state is not only not called to acknowledge the true Church; now it is no longer even competent to believe.

Secondly, the ground for this inviolable constitutional right to freedom is the dignity of the human individual. Because the act of faith requires personal judgement and conscientious self-determination, it must proceed from the intrinsic cogency of the accepted truth, and not from extrinsic coercion. The freedom is thus argued from the dignity of the person, not from the authority of the Church. While the revealed truths of Christ's Church present binding claims on people's consciences, the Council asks no confessional acknowledgement from the civil powers, but only that men and women

> should fully exercise their own judgment and a responsible freedom in their actions and should not be subject to the pressure of coercion but be inspired by a sense of duty. . . . Truth can impose itself on the mind of man only in virtue of its own truth, which wins over the mind with both gentleness and power (*DH* 1).

Third, this right to freedom inheres in both the individual and the association of believers, and it comprises freedom of enquiry, association, communication, finance, public testimony, worship and (in so far as it does not conflict with the imperatives of the public peace) common moral endeavour (*DH* 4–7).

Has religious freedom been significantly augmented in the intervening years? Totalitarian powers continue to resent and repress religious belief. Former colonial lands, apprehensive of Christian churches established by missionaries from Europe or North America, restrict the entry of further church workers, as in India and the Sudan. Other countries such as Zaire, like

Mexico and China in previous years, have in one way or another harassed even indigenous churches. Muslim countries such as Iran, Egypt and Saudi Arabia repress not only non-Islamic religions, but also dissident Islamic sects. A similar imposition of religious law bears down on dissenting minorities in Israel. In Latin America violent oppression by rightist regimes in Chile and Haiti, or leftist regimes in Cuba and Nicaragua, have seen the churches, especially the Catholic Church, as their most formidable social critics. In the Soviet sphere the Church is enjoying a new freedom of movement largely through its role as a formidable expression of nationalism, as in Poland and Lithuania. Yet beyond that role, and even in Russia itself, Jewish, Protestant and Catholic communities are enjoying a thaw in official hostility towards them. In some areas, primarily ethnic or economic antagonisms coincide with religious identification: Northern Ireland, Lebanon, Yugoslavia, Vietnam.

Throughout this give-and-take of religious freedom and oppression, one can see little verifiable influence of the Declaration of Vatican II. By its lights Catholics should at least consider themselves better off as victims than as an established and oppressive majority. They are thus obliged to rely on persuasion, not coercion, and to forgo governmental subsidy and the dependence it so easily entails. Ironically, the Church may enjoy a deeper liberty in lands where it suffers stress than in those countries where its vigour comes at the price of cultural co-optation and secularization (one thinks of Poland on the one hand, West Germany and the United States on the other).

Vatican II has had little clear influence upon the freedom granted by the world's political powers to Catholics or other religious bodies. Ironically, though, the Council has had an unintentional yet striking effect upon another feature of religious liberty, one that it had not intentionally chosen to address: the intramural religious freedom of Catholics.

At the time the Council convened, Catholics were restricted in their freedom of belief, public testimony, communication, worship and moral endeavour by authoritative forces within the Church itself. Censorship restricted open communication. By the *Index* of forbidden books they were barred from reading religious publications of non-Catholics. By the requirement of an *imprimatur* for all publications by Catholics about religion or morality and by clerics or members of religious orders on any subject, most in-house discourse on matters of faith was put under episcopal censorship.

Virtually all policy-making positions in ecclesiastical institutions were held by clerics, who depended for their appointment and employment on their bishops. If they were in institutions controlled by religious orders, their obligation of obedience to the Holy See exposed all of their activities to intervention from above. This pervasive monopoly in institutional responsibility by clergy and members of religious orders enveloped them in the discipline and obedience of clerical and regular authority.

Theological enquiry and expression were also subject to control. Virtually all academics held their degrees from seminaries subject to papal or episcopal authority. Those who taught them held their positions by hierarchical appointment, after having sworn to oaths of rather explicit and detailed orthodoxy.

By other means as well, means more diffuse but none the less effective, the community of belief had its free initiatives curtailed. The prelates who exercised the power of control were commonly advised by consultors and by staffs of notable mediocrity, whose inability to contemplate innovation arose from the timidity of incompetence as much as from reactionary ideology. This was as true in Rome as it was in the typical diocese. Individuals with a grievance about the abuses of authority, be they lay or clerical, had little provision for corporate representation, and had to plead their cases as exposed individuals. The autonomy of each local diocese and the disparity of rules that prevailed from place to place left each local church to the sometimes idiosyncratic convictions of its bishop, free from open comparisons with other regimes. And the steady proclivity of the papacy to draw discretionary governance upwards away from local authority often put decisions in the hands of authorities far from the scene.

In the years since Vatican II this network of hierarchical control has been disrupted. The *Index* has been terminated and the *imprimatur* made optional. In the world of religious scholarship and publication, the footnotes of any serious work today testify to how thoroughly confessional frontiers have yielded to a common market of faith-enquiry. The vicissitudes of Church life have become a matter of regular surveillance and concern in the secular press, and the hierarchical exercise of authority, both in its use and its abuse, has been exposed to public accolade or criticism. This in turn has sponsored a more candid style of publication in the Church press. By a sort of reverse irony, the very persons who used to issue *imprimaturs* are subjected to more critical assessment than they whose work they previously censored.

Lay people have moved into almost every level of institutional responsibility in the Church, where they serve as university presidents, hospital administrators, diocesan chancellors, tribunal judges, financial officers, publishers, editors, press secretaries, theological and canonical experts, marriage counsellors and adoption agents, and pastoral associates in parishes. This laicization has interrupted the ability of episcopal or papal authority to direct Church life as before.

Catholic institutions have entered into professional alliance with their peer organizations in other religious communions and in secular society. Thus Catholic health-care enterprises, family-service agencies, schools, seminaries, colleges and universities, publishing houses, marriage and family-life ministries, religious educators, liturgists, public-information offices, financial and investment managers, even pastoral clergy, have in an abruptly brief period of transition been subjected to a professionalization whose norms and expectations have, if not actually extinguished autocratic control from within the Church, at least handicapped it by introducing rival standards and obediences.

Theology has migrated from the seminary to the university, and is now more subject to the academic guild than to the official teachers of the Church.

Collegial entities now offer more advocacy for the aggrieved individual. A bishop can seek protection within the episcopal conference and a priest within the presbyteral council. Lay persons have instant access to the media for their grievances. The whimsy of any local ordinary is subject to uncomplimentary

121

comparisons with other, more congenial, disciplines. And the geographical parish, at least in sizeable cities, no longer has exclusive jurisdiction over communicants living within its boundaries.

In sum, this onset of new religious freedom within the Church would appear to involve three new forces: open and free public discourse within the community, the establishment of professional norms in ministry and supervision, and restriction of the prerogative of hiring and firing as an instrument of religious discipline.

About all of this there was no prescription or presage in *Dignitatis Humanae*. Yet the principles that incited this onset of intramural liberty were articulated by the Council itself, albeit with other results in mind. And in many instances the new order was embodied or dramatically inaugurated by the very enactments of Vatican II.

The Declaration on Religious Freedom was the only one of the Council's sixteen major documents explicitly addressed, not simply to fellow communicants in the Catholic Church, but to the world at large, much as John XXIII had addressed his encyclical letter *Pacem in Terris*, not simply to his fellow bishops, but to 'All Persons of Good Will'. Having claimed the wide world's attention, the bishops proceeded to expatiate on the inviolable right of every human person, because of his or her inherent dignity, to profess and practise a religious faith publicly and privately without coercion or even psychological compulsion. The truth was to be offered, not enforced. This was a message intended for those in civil power, but its very eloquence caused it to reverberate back upon the pope and bishops, and to enjoin upon them a new respect for the need of their own faithful congregants to claim persuasive teaching, not disciplinary clout.

In various of its major documents, the Council spoke eloquently of initiative and responsibility from below. 'The People of God shares also in Christ's prophetic office', possessed of a penetrating understanding of the faith (*Lumen Gentium* 12; see 9–17). Their empowerment to serve the world is derived from the Lord, not from the clergy: 'From the fact of their union with Christ the head flows the laymen's right and duty to be apostles. Inserted as they are in the Mystical Body of Christ by baptism and strengthened by the power of the Holy Spirit in confirmation, it is by the Lord himself that they are assigned to the apostolate' (*Apostolicam Actuositatem* 3). In organic unity with the bishops and priests they share in formulating pastoral policy for the Church. Priests organized collegially carry the responsibility for the local church's ministry (*Christus Dominus* 27). Their organic relationship with the bishop is described in collaborative terms: 'On account of this common sharing in the same priesthood and ministry then, bishops are to regard their priests as brothers and friends' and are to consult them corporately through a senate (*Presbyterorum Ordinis* 7; see Paul VI's *motu proprio* Apostolic Letter, *Ecclesiae Sanctae* I 15). The bishops themselves as members of a college are directly responsible with the bishop of Rome for the service of the church world-wide (*Christus Dominus* 4–7). 'Together with their head, the Supreme Pontiff, and never apart from him, they have supreme and full authority over the universal Church . . .' The office of binding and loosing given to Peter was also assigned to the college of apostles (*Lumen Gentium* 22). The bishops are to band together within national boundaries into episcopal conferences to provide for the common good on-site (*Christus Dominus* 37–8; *Ecclesiae Sanctae* I ll).

It did not escape notice that each level – laity, priests, bishops, pope – was empowered through its initiatory consecration (baptism and ordination) by the Lord himself. Though no element in the Church could function authentically except in organic and peaceful unity with the others, this is typically spoken of as the condition, not the source, of their grace. The presidential role is characterized, not so much as one of initiative or command, but as one of orchestration.

Indeed a positive benefit is acknowledged in initiative arising close to the need rather than from the seat of superintendence. The principle of subsidiarity, which Pius XI and John XXIII had enjoined for the social order, held that a responsibility ought best be undertaken at the lowest practicable echelon of authority (*Lumen Gentium* 86; Pius XI, *Quadragesimo Anno* 79–80; John XXIII, *Mater et Magistra* 53, 117, 152). Vatican II adverted to this directly in acknowledging that the responsibility for Christian formation and education devolves upon parents, not the clergy (*Gravissimum Educationis* 3), and then gave it a more sweeping application in its depiction of Christian initiative as divinely, not hierarchically, inspired.

Here was a consistent reinterpretation of authority in the Church, one that was more organic than hierarchical, and implied that those who presided should in large part admire the ministry and service of their subordinates without imagining that it derived from their own superintendence. The implications for intramural religious freedom were immense.

They might have been given a more delayed and ambiguous interpretation had not the very events of the Council proceedings given such boisterous cues that a new ecclesial freedom was now in order. From the very first session the bishops rejected major drafts prepared by commissions dominated by the curial staffs, in a way the curia had certainly not anticipated. The Roman theologians, almost all from the professorate in the local seminaries, found themselves challenged and overridden in arguments by the university theologians brought in by individual bishops from around the world. The attempts of the papal establishment to retain control of proceedings were devastated by thorough exposure in the secular press, such as the dispatches to *Le Monde* by Henri Fesquet and coverage in *Time* by Robert Kaiser. On the floor there was a freedom of speech to bishops that most of them had never enjoyed before. National hierarchies asserted themselves and gave steady protection to the independent voices of their more articulate members.

In a word, the Council itself sanctioned an outburst of religious freedom in one echelon of the Church – the episcopate – that few would have imagined to have needed liberating. Even the bishops were somewhat surprised at the release of power that followed on the onset of freedom. If any of those bishops nourished the hope that this release of power would benefit their rank alone, it was a vain hope. The Council itself had indeed effectively liberated a second echelon, that of theologians. But at every level and in local churches in every continent, as venturesome and activist innovators claimed a wider ambit of liberty, initiative has been broadened. If a collegial sharing of responsibility and policy-making was proper to pope and bishops, why should that model not extend to bishop and priests, and then to priest and people?

The risks of this new religious freedom seem to be three: secularization, nationalism and lack of accountability. Religious liberty for Catholics has been won with the help of influential pressure from secular sources. Catholics are now more prone to be embarrassed by their autocratic past and the mediocrity of their leaders than suspicious of the materialism and ideological narrowness and prejudice of the public culture. A secularized Christianity is more likely to appreciate the gospel for its support of the present social agenda than to judge the latter by the former. And Catholics who welcomed the independence of professional status may yet find that the guilds and professions of this world have stiff dogmas and arbitrary fashions of their own.

Also, the newfound pride and autonomy of national churches makes them very touchy about outside criticism. More and more they doubt the competence of any outsiders, from sister or from mother churches, to call them to task.

Thirdly, the lightening of accountability to bishops and popes may simply expose a local community to the preferences of a local pastor, or to the cliques and conflicts within its own ranks. The dominant preference for populist freedom over official authorities seems ignorant of history's lesson that groups function dynamically only when they are enabled by strong yet deft officers.

It is such weaknesses that cautionary voices such as that of John Paul II are now endeavouring to counteract. The present papal strategy is to regain control of the episcopacy by using its emissaries to impose conservative and compliant bishops. Censorship and oaths of fidelity and hierarchical approbation are employed to tame theologians judged unreliable. 'Permissive' bishops are subjected to harsh discipline, but not their peers who are guilty of financial misappropriation, sexual scandal or homiletic boredom.

It may be timely for a compensatory swing of emphasis after Vatican II, in the matter of religious freedom within the Church. While resorting mostly to instrumentalities of command and compliance, however, the present papacy may not succeed in improving the quality or the persuasiveness of its public teaching and injunctions. This may prove to be a readjustment that moves backward instead of forward. It also reinforces the destructive assumption that authority and liberty are inveterate rivals rather than close and mutually protective allies.

John Courtney Murray sj, the theologian silenced by Pius XII who was brought to the Council as Cardinal Spellman's personal *peritus* and became the most influential drafter of *Dignitatis Humanae*, later described its genesis: 'Thus, the greatest argument on religious freedom in all history happily broke forth in the Church' (Abbott, p. 672). The truth in this is not that the bishops in Council conceived and provided for a wider scope of religious freedom in the Church, but that certain prophetic and loyal spirits like Murray himself took liberties, and at a certain point their superiors saw it was no longer wise to censor or censure them. If the inner wisdom about freedom in the community of belief is that, since the spontaneities of grace arise mostly in people of lesser station or none, the task of those in higher office is not to command but to preside: to lead the community in discerning those spirits and in orchestrating those initiatives. Freedom is almost always taken before it is given. Both during Vatican II and afterwards, it was the prophetic voices who have simply begun to act more freely and have thus led their leaders to appreciate that the spirit was being unstifled.

8F Religious Freedom (*Dignitatis Humanae*): Bibliography

Burghardt, W., ed. (1977) *Religious Freedom, 1965 and 1975: A Symposium on a Historic Document*. New York, Paulist Press.

Chadwick, O. (1978) *Catholicism and History: The Opening of the Vatican Archives*. Cambridge, Cambridge University Press.

Grelot, P. (1987) *Libres dans la foi: liberté civique et liberté spirituelle*. Paris, Desclée.

Janssens, L. (1964) *Freedom of Conscience and Religious Freedom*. Staten Island, NY, Alba.

John Paul II (1984) *John Paul II: Essays on Religious Freedom*. Milwaukee, Catholic League on Religious and Civil Rights.

Kasper, W. (1988) *The Christian Understanding of Freedom and the History of Freedom in the Modern Era*. Milwaukee, Marquette University Press.

Murray, J.C. (1960) *We Hold These Truths*. New York, Sheed & Ward.

Murray, J.C. (1965a) *The Problem of Religious Freedom*. Westminster (Maryland), Newman.

Murray, J.C., ed. (1965b) *Freedom and Man*. New York, P. J. Kenedy & Sons.

Murray, J.C., ed. (1966) *Religious Liberty: An End and a Beginning*. New York, Macmillan.

Novak, M. (1964) *The Open Church*. New York, Macmillan.

Roche, J.-B. (1967) *Eglise et liberté religieuse*. Paris, Desclée.

Stransky, T., ed. (1967) *Declaration on Religious Freedom of Vatican Council II*. New York, Paulist Press.

Swidler, L., ed. (1986) *Religious Liberty and Human Rights in Nations and in Religions*. Philadelphia, Ecumenical.

Zimmerman, M. (1981) *Structure sociale de l'église: doctrines et praxis des rapports église–état du XVIIIe siècle à Jean-Paul II*. Strasbourg, Centre de recherche et de documentation et des institutions chretiennes.

8G Other Religions (*Nostra Aetate*)

DONALD NICHOLL

The declaration made by the Church at the Second Vatican Council as a starting-point for innovatory relations with peoples of other faiths is found in the document entitled *Nostra Aetate*, a title taken from the opening sentence which runs, 'In this age of ours, when men are drawing more closely together, and the bonds of friendship between different peoples are being strengthened, the Church examines with greater care the relation she has to non-Christian religions.'

Yet it would be a mistake to imagine that one can grasp the significance of *Nostra Aetate* by reading it as though it was the first occasion upon which Catholics had addressed the matter of non-Christian religions, or as though a study of that document alone, without constant references to other decrees of Vatican II, would enable one to grasp its meaning.

Not only, for instance, do the efforts of de Nobili, Ricci and scores of other missionary thinkers in previous centuries witness to the Church's age-old confrontation with other great world religions, but so also do the researches of home-based theologians such as Thomas Aquinas and Nicholas de Cusa, to name but two. Nor should one ignore the immeasurable increase in recent years of contacts and friendships between representatives of all the world religions. One notable example is that of Rabbi Abraham Heschel, who was consulted by both Pope John XXIII and Pope Paul VI, and who undoubtedly influenced the Council's statements about the Jews. Similarly, the voice of Islam was heard in Rome through the contacts of Louis Massignon, the great French Arabist; and the breath of Hinduism was felt through the wide friendships of such pioneers as Swāmi Paramārūbyānanda (Abbé Jules Monchanin).

As regards the conciliar context of *Nostra Aetate*, it has to be recognized that many aspects of the document only reveal their full importance when seen in the light of the constitutions *Lumen Gentium* and *Gaudium et Spes*, to cite only two of the Council documents. *Gaudium et Spes*, for example, contains the sentence, 'All this holds true not for Christians only but also for all men of good will in whose hearts grace is active invisibly. For since Christ died for all, and since all men are in fact called to one and the same destiny, which is divine, we must hold that the Holy Spirit offers to all the possibility of being made partners, in a way known to God, in the paschal mystery.' *Nostra Aetate*, it may truly be said, was an early attempt by the Council to work out the implications of that statement.

Indeed one might well go on to observe that *Nostra Aetate* is peculiarly the work of the Council in that whereas it was not difficult – even before the opening of the Council – to predict at least the themes of the other documents, if not their development of those themes, the production of any document whatsoever on non-Christian religions was an unexpected outcome of the conciliar process itself. For in the early stages of the Council the only reference to non-Christian religions in general was to be found in the first draft of the

Decree on Ecumenism. In that draft almost all attention was focused on the relations of the Catholic Church with the Orthodox and Protestants; there followed, as a kind of appendix, a section on the Jewish people; and only then, almost as an afterthought, some attention was accorded to other world religions.

What took place in the five years preceding the Declaration on the Relation of the Church to non-Christian Religions (October 1965) was a process in which the Church fathers rapidly unlearned many prejudices and slowly realized a number of truths. That process may be conveniently outlined in the following chronological presentation:

June 1960. Pope John XXIII appointed Cardinal Bea as the president of the Secretariat for Promoting Christian Unity, at the same time entrusting to him the schema on the Jews.

June 1962. At a meeting of the Central Commission for preparing the Council, it was intended to discuss the schema on the Jews. But the discussion was abandoned, 'not because of the ideas or doctrine expressed in the schema but only because of certain unhappy political considerations at the time' (a reference to Arab/Jewish hostility).

November 1963. The schema on ecumenism was introduced for discussion during the eighth week of the second session of the Council. The first three chapters of the schema were devoted to the Christian Churches, the fourth was on the Jews, and the remaining chapter dealt with religious freedom.

In spite of the magisterial and eirenic presentation by Cardinal Bea, the discussion on both the Jews and religious freedom proved too tense for agreement to be reached. This was not only because Arab bishops feared that Bea's eirenic words about the Jews would endanger the position of Arab Christians living in Islamic countries. Nor was the tension simply a further manifestation of the anti-Semitism endemic in many Catholic circles. In fact, certain valid arguments for redrafting were made, such as that Jews could hardly feel happy at being placed under the umbrella of Christian ecumenism, any more than Muslims, for instance, would be pleased to see the Jews singularly acknowledged while they themselves seemed to be ignored. So it was decided to postpone further discussion of chapters IV and V to a later date.

May 1964. A sign of the increasing importance now being attached to relations with non-Christians was that a special Secretariat for the development of relations with non-Christian religions was set up by Pope Paul VI under the presidency of Cardinal Marella, although responsibility for drafting the Council statement on the subject still rested with the Unity Secretariat.

August 1964. Pope Paul VI issued the encyclical *Ecclesiam Suam*, probably the most profound statement in the official teaching of the Church concerning the spirituality of dialogue.

Throughout the whole of 1964 those responsible for preparing the statement on the Jews were subjected to fierce pressures from opposite sides. One result was that the text presented to the Council on 28 September was broadened to include mention of Muslims and other non-Christian religions.

November 1964. The declaration *Nostra Aetate* was approved on first vote.

127

October 1965. *Nostra Aetate* was officially promulgated.

It is well to have the story of *Nostra Aetate*'s passage through the Council in one's mind when trying to grasp its significance for the history of the Church, because that story is one of unexpected theological developments and ever-widening horizons. The same is true to an even greater degree of developments since the Council. Standing where we do now in 1990 it comes as something of a shock, when reading the text of *Nostra Aetate*, to notice how summary is its treatment of other religions apart from Judaism. The document, admittedly, does state that 'the Catholic Church rejects nothing of what is true and holy in these religions'; and it does specifically exhort Catholics to collaborate and conduct dialogue with their followers in promoting the values found in these religions. Moreover, the religions specified by name, Hinduism, Buddhism and Islam, are spoken of with unprecedented warmth. However, Hinduism and Buddhism are only accorded five lines each, and not many more are devoted to Islam (*NA* 2–3).

By contrast, the passage on the Jews (*NA* 4), possibly the most discussed of the whole Council, does contain a sustained attempt to determine the place of the Jewish people within the economy of salvation. It acknowledges, for instance, 'that the salvation of the Church is prefigured in the exodus of God's chosen people from the land of bondage' and that 'the Jews remain very dear to God for the sake of the patriarchs, since God does not take back the gifts he bestowed or the choice he made'. The document also disowns the notion that the Jewish people as a whole ever did bear responsibility for the crucifixion; and it deplores anti-Semitism 'at any time and from any source'.

The distinctive character of *Nostra Aetate* 4, therefore, indicates that the Council had come to recognize the need to distinguish between relations with the Jewish people and relations with other religions. For the same reason, Pope Paul VI, at the end of the Council, had already established a Vatican Office for Relations with Jews and Judaism which, on 23 October 1974, was given official status as the Vatican Commission on Religious Relations with Judaism. It was placed under the Secretariat for Christian Unity. This latter decision was meant to underline the Church's recognition of the special bond that links it to the people of the Bible, while making it clear that the Commission's task is limited to religious matters, thus leaving the issue of political relations between the Vatican State and Israel in the hands of the Vatican State Secretariat.

Some of the above considerations that motivated the Council to treat the Jews separately have led us to do the same in the present section. Hence relations with the Jews will be dealt with first, and then relations with other religions.

CATHOLIC–JEWISH RELATIONS SINCE VATICAN II

The fact that Catholics and Jews share a special relationship does not, of course, mean that their mutual relations are smooth and easy. Rather the contrary, since they behave towards one another in much the same way as do members of a very ancient extended family. When the members of such a family meet one another there is a special warmth, not to say heat, engendered, and a sense of participating in common traditions. Yet, as we all know, the joy of such an occasion can suddenly be shattered on account of some incident or remark which, in an instant, brings back memories of ancient family quarrels and opens up wounds long thought to have been healed. For some time afterwards everyone's nerves are taut as violin strings, ready to snap at the least maladroit gesture. In such an atmosphere even the most innocent remarks can arouse the darkest suspicions.

Granted the garrulity of the family in question and its extension over the whole face of the globe, there is no way of preventing something potentially disastrous being said or done virtually every day, whether that be a foolish article in a Vatican journal or a scathing comment on the pope by a Jewish journalist. And though the harm done by such incidents may usually be nullified fairly quickly by patience and good will, there are two issues over which reconciliation does not come so easily. They are the Holocaust and the State of Israel.

It is fair to say that the subject of the Holocaust (or *Shoah*,[1] as it is better named) has not come to occupy the place it should do in the consciousness either of Rome or of Catholic theologians, or amid the ranks of the faithful. This is true even of the generally excellent *Notes for Preaching and Teaching* issued in June 1985 by the Commission for Religious Relations with Judaism. Those *Notes* say, for instance, 'We must remember how much the balance of relations between Jews and Christians over two thousand years has been negative'; and 'catechesis should help in understanding the meaning for the Jews of the extermination during the years 1939–1945 and its consequences.' Both of those sentences are disturbingly evasive in the face of a thousand years of anti-Semitism and the slaughter of 6 million Jews. Equally disturbing is the seeming restriction of the 'meaning' or meaninglessness of the Holocaust to its 'meaning' for the Jews, as though the 'meaning' or meaninglessness of the Holocaust is not the most intractable matter for the faith of all believers in God.

Indeed most Catholic theologians have shrunk from proffering any clear meaning to the Holocaust, preferring instead to observe a reverent silence. Unfortunately a number of other Catholic authorities have proved less sensitive and have given grounds for the accusation that the Church is trying to 'exercise its imperial power to define the meaning of history' through 'Christianizing' the Holocaust (see Suchecky, 1989, pp. 98–114). In Cologne, for instance, on 1 May 1987, the pope officially beatified as a martyr the philosopher Edith Stein, a Jewess converted to Catholicism who became a Carmelite nun and was put to death in Auschwitz. Since Edith Stein herself, inevitably using pre-conciliar categories of thought and speech, had in 1939 described the offering of her life as 'expiation for the unbelief of the Jewish people', the process of beatification held the danger of at least two pitfalls. The first was to give the impression that this 'Jewish martyr' turned Christian was indeed an expiation for the unbelief of those other Jews who died in Auschwitz. Secondly, it countenanced the theory that *Nostra Aetate* had

129

repudiated: that God's covenant with the Jewish people had been displaced by the Christian covenant. The pope himself has not always avoided these pitfalls (see *Christian–Jewish Relations*, 1987, pp. 26–38; and *The Tablet*, 19 August 1989).

Misunderstandings generated by the above events have been compounded by the establishment of a Carmelite convent at Auschwitz which, to the Jewish community, seemed yet another instance of an attempt at a Christian takeover. This offence to the Jewish community appeared to have been removed in February 1987 when four cardinals, including the archbishop of Cracow in whose diocese Auschwitz is situated, made a formal agreement with Jewish representatives that the convent would be removed by February 1989. However, that agreement was not implemented by the date fixed and Catholic-Jewish relations once more neared flashpoint until wiser leaders in the Vatican, the International Council of Christians and Jews, and the Polish hierarchy in concert arranged for the convent to be transferred to a new Centre for Information, Education, Meeting and Prayer to be sited outside the Auschwitz camp. When that new Centre is completed the Carmelites will undoubtedly move there.

On the second contentious issue, that of the State of Israel, both the Vatican and the majority of Catholic theologians have steadily resisted the pressures exerted upon them to attach religious significance to the establishment of the State of Israel, although they do recognize the Jewish homeland of Israel. Their position has often been misinterpreted as ambiguous on account of their adherence to a principle which is nowadays generally recognized in dialogue between different religions. This principle is that no one in the dialogue should take it upon themselves to define the faith of the other religions: the Jews' definition of Judaism has to be accepted, for instance, by Christians, who have no right to tell a Jew what he is supposed to believe. But whereas certain Protestant theologians slide from rightly accepting Jewish self-definition as subjectively valid into accepting it as objectively true, Catholic theologians do not. Crucially and simply, this means that when a Jew states that ancient Judea and Samaria (almost entirely populated by Arabs) are for ever part of the State of Israel by virtue of God's gift recorded in the Bible, the Catholic denies that to be a consequence of accepting the principle of self-definition – if it were a necessary consequence then every subjective self-definition would have to be accepted as objectively true, which is absurd, since they often contradict each other.

Beneath this matter of Israel there lies a whole ganglion of nervous issues, such as the interpretation of God's promise to Abraham and the difference between Jewish and Christian notions of Church and state, to mention but two. Here, as elsewhere, the Vatican's time-honoured method of lowering the temperature is to adhere firmly to the diplomatic rules accepted by the international community. Consequently, the Vatican does not officially recognize the State of Israel since its sovereignty and frontiers are not recognized by its neighbours or by international authorities. At the same time, the Vatican in practice accords *de facto* recognition to the State, as witnessed, for instance, by the reception of Golda Meir at the Vatican as head of state (15 January 1973).

Not surprisingly, most Jews interpret the coolly diplomatic attitude of the Vatican towards the State of Israel as a sign of lack of warmth towards the people of Israel. Fortunately, however, there is no mistaking the warmth of the gestures made by Catholics at every level outside the conventions of diplomacy. Pope John Paul II, for instance, paid a visit to the Rome Synagogue in 1986 – the first visit ever of a pope to a synagogue – at which he spoke of Judaism as 'our elder brother' and of Jews as 'irrevocably the beloved of God'. Moreover, the French, German, Dutch, Brazilian, US and other episcopal conferences have all issued pastorals and directives urging the faithful to learn to treasure the inheritance they have received through the Jewish people and to root out all traces of anti-Semitism.

Most important of all are the numerous societies that have sprung up at grassroots level, particularly in Europe and North America, to nurture friendship between Jews and Christians, and in which Catholics play a full part. The amazing change in Catholic–Jewish relations is reflected in a statement made by Cardinal Etchegaray in 1983. The depth of that change is probably hard for anyone to measure who was not personally acquainted with the situation before the Second Vatican Council. The Cardinal said, 'as in the parable, neither of the two sons can gain possession of the entire inheritance; each one is for the other, without jealousy, a witness to the gratuity of the Father's mercy'.

CATHOLIC RELATIONS WITH FAITHS OTHER THAN JUDAISM

The speed with which the Church has moved beyond a fumbling rule-of-thumb relationship with other faiths is seen especially in seemingly small linguistic changes. In *Nostra Aetate*, for instance, it is said that Muslims 'associate themselves with the faith of Abraham', seeming to suggest that although Muslims consider themselves in the line of faith of Abraham, in fact Christians doubt it. Again, the Church is said to 'look with esteem' upon Muslims, yet gives no recognition to Islam itself as a way to God. Within a few years both of these deficiencies were remedied in a series of statements embodied in *Ecclesiam Suam, Evangelii Nuntiandi* (1975), *Redemptor Hominis* (the first encyclical of Pope John Paul II, 1978) and *The Attitude of the Church towards the Followers of other Religions* (issued in 1984 by the Secretariat for non-Christians). Here there is no longer any hesitation in acknowledging Islam as embracing 'spiritual descendants of Abraham'.

The impulse towards this ever-more open attitude towards other religions may already be detected in the refashioning at Vatican II of those schemata from *Lumen Gentium* and *Ad Gentes* that are devoted to other religions. The persons responsible for that refashioning were all outstanding theologians whose training led them beyond rules of thumb to the fundamental theological principles that were needed to introduce order into this uncharted area of the Church's concern. In *Lumen Gentium* 16, for instance, there is indicated a logic of the various degrees of intimacy with the Church enjoyed by different faiths. The list is headed by the Jews, to whom the covenants and promises were

131

given, followed by those who acknowledge the Creator, first of these being the Muslims who profess to hold the faith of Abraham; they are followed by those who seek the unknown God in shadows and images; and finally come those who have never heard of the gospel but try to live a good life according to their consciences.

However, the very inner logic of the Council's various statements has gradually crystallized the fundamental issue which now faces Catholic theologians concerning what is called 'the uniqueness of Christ'.

That issue can be stated quite simply: since the Church has expressed repentance (however muted) for its previous attitude towards other religions and now acknowledges 'seeds of the Word' in other religions and grants that adherents of these religions may come to salvation by way of their religions, does it not follow that there is now no need for evangelization? Pope John Paul II, for instance, on 1 February 1986, went to the site of Mahatma Gandhi's *samadhi* and laid a wreath there with the words, 'today as a pilgrim of peace I have come here to pay homage to Mahatma Gandhi, hero of humanity'. In doing so, was he not symbolically recognizing that a non-Christian, in this case a Hindu, may be sanctified by the practice of his own religion? And was the pope not also denying any exclusivist interpretation of the gospel sentence, 'I am the way, the truth and the life; no one comes to the Father except by me' (John 6.14) or of the text in Acts (4.12), 'there is no other name under heaven granted to men by which we may receive salvation'?

In facing this issue, the Catholic Church has exhibited a fund of the wisdom that is secreted within it to the surprise, very often, of both its supporters and its detractors. Above all, the Church's spokesmen have refused to be rushed into novel formulations which would not do justice to all the factors that need to be taken into account. The fact is that inter-faith experience for most human beings is something strange and almost entirely unprecedented. Consequently, we not only lack a language in which to express the experience; as yet we do not have the idiom or the grammar – scarcely even the alphabet – that we need. Moreover, almost every day new horizons are being disclosed to human awareness, whether in space research or bio-ethics or ecology or in nuclear apocalypse, that throw into quite different light everything in the past as well as in the present. Any attempt at the moment to produce a cut-and-dried formula regarding the uniqueness of Christ would therefore abort inter-faith experience and close off the widening horizons.

Such horizons often open up imperceptibly, as has happened lately within the Catholic Church itself. Until quite recently, for instance, the Church was accustomed to see itself as a perfect society and, therefore, a beleaguered fortress, and to have as its horizon the battlements over which it feared to see its enemies from 'the world' starting to pour at any moment. But now the Church admits that she herself 'will only attain perfection in the glory of heaven', when 'will come the time of the restoration of all things' (Acts 3.21). 'Then the human race, as well as the entire world, which is intimately related to man and achieves its purpose through him, will be perfectly re-established in Christ' (*Lumen Gentium* 48).

When that restoration of all things will take place no one knows, of course, 'for God alone knows those days, He to whom nothing is impossible, He whose mysterious and silent Spirit opens the paths of dialogue to individuals and peoples in order to overcome racial, social and religious differences and to bring mutual enrichment. We live therefore in the age of the patience of God, for the Church and every Christian community, for no one can oblige God to act more quickly than He has chosen to do.'[2]

It was surely a providential confirmation of this all-embracing vision of the Church when the World Wildlife Fund, on 29 September 1986, chose the home of St Francis, Assisi, as the location for its twenty-fifth Anniversary to be celebrated by an inter-faith ceremony at which Buddhists, Hindus, Christians, Jews and Muslims all made declarations affirming the sanctity of creation. And further confirmaton was given only a month later (27 October) when the pope, the Dalai Lama, an Orthodox patriarch, as well as Jewish, Muslim, Hindu, Buddhist, Sikh and Zoroastrian leaders and representatives of African traditional religions made pilgrimage together to Assisi for a day of prayer, fasting and silence in aid of world peace.

And although the Secretariat for non-Christians ensured that Assisi should not become an excuse for syncretism, there is no going back now behind the beautiful photograph of the pope and the Dalai Lama sitting peacefully side by side in the Basilica of St Mary of the Angels and flanked by the leaders of other faiths. There is no denying that each world faith has a unique contribution to make to the 'restoration of all things'.

Notes

1 The name *Shoah* is better, because 'holocaust' connotes sacrifice rising to heaven, whereas *shoah* rather connotes descent into the pit of dereliction.
2 This quotation comes from section 48 of *The Attitude of the Church towards the Followers of other Religions*, a most succinct examination of dialogue and mission, issued by the Secretariat for non-Christians. The theological penetration of this document is typical of the work of this highly gifted Secretariat.

8G Other Religions (*Nostra Aetate*): Bibliography

Barnes, M. (1989) *Religions in Conversation*, London, SPCK.
Buhlmann, W. (1982) *The Chosen Peoples*. Slough, St Paul Publications.
Bulletin of the Secretariat for Non-Christians (città del Vaticano) *passim*, esp. no. 56, 1984, pp. 126–41. *The Attitude of the Church towards the Followers of other Religions*.
Christian-Jewish Relations (1987) London, Catholic Truth Society.
D'Costa, G. (1986) *Theology and Religious Pluralism*. Oxford, Basil Blackwell.
Hick, J., and Knitter, P. (1987) *The Myth of Christian Uniqueness*. London, SCM.
Küng, H. (1987) *Christianity and the World Religions*. London, Collins.
Pieris, A. (1988) *Love meets Wisdom. A Christian Experience of Buddhism*. New York, Orbis Books.

Modern Catholicism

Pro Mundi Vita, Bulletin 95–96, *The Evolution of Relations between Christians and Jews from 1973 to 1983*. Brussels, 1983–4.

Suchecky, B. (1989) '*La christianization de la Shoah. Le carmel d'Auschwitz, les eglises de Birkenau et de Sobibor*', *Esprit*, Paris, May pp. 98–114.

Wigoder, G. (1988) *Jewish–Christian relations since the Second World War*. Manchester, Manchester University Press.

Willebroands, J. (1986) 'Christians and Jews: A New Vision', in Stacpoole, pp. 220–36.

8H Eastern Catholic Churches (*Orientalium Ecclesiarum*)

ROBERT F. TAFT SJ

Orientalium Ecclesiarum, the Decree on the Eastern Catholic Churches, is the third-shortest Vatican II document, after *Nostra Aetate* and *Inter Mirifica*.

HISTORY (SEE CAPRILE 4, PP. 218–39; EDELBY AND DICK (1970); DISTANTE AND MANNA (1986), PP. 7–16)

The initial documentation, *De Ecclesiis Orientalibus* ('On the Eastern Churches'), was prepared by the Preparatory Commission for the Eastern Churches, which included representatives of the Eastern Catholic Churches as well as specialists in Eastern Christianity. The questions they addressed, though largely disciplinary, were dominated by the twofold shadow that has darkened the history of these Eastern Catholic Churches: the rupture with their Orthodox mother Churches, and the cultural and administrative domination of the Roman Catholic Church they had joined. Differing perceptions of this twofold relationship were evident in the pre-conciliar work of the Commission (1960–2), whose Eastern members held opposed views depending on their degree of 'Latinization' or 'Orientalism'. This background also coloured the conciliar debate on the document (1962–4).

The original draft comprising eleven schemata would go through five redactions before an acceptable text was elaborated. Schema 11, on church unity, was ultimately assigned to the Decree on Ecumenism, *Unitatis Redintegratio*, and the rest reworked and abbreviated on the basis of the numerous *vota* and observations. The final redaction preserved the same structure as the fourth: 1. Particular Churches (*OE* 2–4); 2. Preservation of the Spiritual Heritage of the Eastern Churches (*OE* 5–6); 3. Eastern Patriarchs (*OE* 7–11); 4. Sacraments (*OE* 12–18); 5. Divine Worship (*OE* 19–23); 6. Relations with the Separated Brethren (*OE* 24–9). After eighteen emendations designed to strengthen the sections on the rights of patriarchs and on the canonical autonomy of the Eastern Churches, the text was presented in the Council Aula on 15 October 1964.

The conciliar debate from 15–20 October exposed the Latinizing tendencies still latent in the draft in spite of evident progress through the several redactions (XR 3, pp. 95–108). The text remained perforce a *Latin* document *about the East*, the document of a monolithic, basically Western Church with several minority satellite communities enjoying a special status and special rites, rather than a Catholic document about a single communion of several sister Churches, each one an equally 'particular' Church. Several Council fathers, Western and Eastern, spoke to defend an unambiguous affirmation of the autonomous patriarchal structure of the Eastern Catholic Churches and their right to rule their own affairs, and a more open approach to Orthodoxy as

135

the 'missing partner' in the entire Council. But the most electrifying interventions were those of the Melkite bishops, especially Patriarch Maximos IV, the only Eastern Catholic hierarchy that has shown intellectual leadership in the wider Church (Maximos IV, 1963, 1967). For the first time in the modern history of the Catholic Church, dissenting non-Latin voices were heard and heeded, to the enrichment of all.

CONTENTS

Despite traces of the defects already noted, as well as ominous silences on Eastern traditions threatening to entrenched Latin prejudices such as married clergy, the decree as finally amended and approved on 20 November 1964 is a notable document. Its scant thirty paragraphs contain several progressive elements remarkable for their openness and breadth of vision.

After a fully predictable reaffirmation of papal teaching on the equality of all rites (*OE* 3), of the Church's esteem for the Eastern traditions and desire to preserve and promote them (*OE* 1, 4, 5–6) as a sign of variety in unity (*OE* 2), of the need for all Catholics to be educated concerning these traditions (*OE* 4, 6), and of the need to recover them where they have been eroded by Latinization (*OE* 6), the decree goes on to treat of areas in which the Eastern Churches manifest special characteristics – especially the institution of the patriarchate (*OE* 7–11) and liturgical practice (*OE* 12–23) – and of relations with the non-Catholic Eastern Christians (*OE* 24–5), especially with respect to intercommunion (*OE* 26–29).

The decree can be understood only in the light of past Latin ecclesiastical and cultural imperialism *vis à vis* Eastern Catholics, especially in the Austro–Hungarian Empire, Poland, India, the Latin Patriarchate of Jerusalem, and North America. In this context the insistence on equality of rites, avoidance of Latinization, fostering and restoration of the Eastern heritage, loses its apparent banality. More remarkable is the admission of the provisional nature of the decree: it applies only to Eastern *Catholic* Churches (title and *OE* 30), thus effectively abandoning all pretence that Eastern Catholicism represents Eastern Christendom. The greater openness to the Orthodox regarding *communicatio in sacris*, seemingly remarkable from a 1960s Western perspective, actually just ratifies what had long been in practice in the Middle East. The true surprise, with implications that at the time were hardly appreciated, is the affirmation (*OE* 2) that Eastern Catholic communities are distinct *Churches* (not just 'rites') with the same rights and obligations, including the right and obligation to spread by preaching the gospel (*OE* 3). So Eastern hierarchies should be established where needed (*OE* 4), and these Churches have the right and duty 'to govern themselves' according to their own traditions (*OE* 5). Astonishingly, the decree specifies these norms thus: 'The rights and privileges are those which existed in the time of union between East and West' (*OE* 9). When these traditions include a patriarchal structure, the patriarch has jurisdiction over all bishops of his rite within the territory of the patriarchate, and a bishop of the rite outside patriarchal territory 'remains attached to the hierarchy of his rite' (*OE* 7) and, where necessary, new patriarchates should be erected (*OE* 11). Of course, all this is decreed in accordance with the norms of law, and without prejudice to the primacy of the Roman pontiff (*OE* 7).

Several statements on liturgy are also noteworthy. Not only is the Eastern liturgical heritage to be preserved and restored (read: purged of Latinisms) (*OE* 6, 12). It is also to be adapted to modern needs (*OE* 6), an invitaton that contained the seeds of future friction between local churches and Rome. There are unexpected advances here too: the explicit recognition of the Eastern practice that the Sunday or holy day precept can be fulfilled by attendance at the cathedral office, and not just by attending Mass (*OE* 15), of the fact that the Divine Office is not a prayer book but liturgy (*OE* 22), and of the age-old custom of vernacular liturgy (*OE* 23) under the control of the local church authorities.

IMPLEMENTATION

In the post-conciliar period, what some perceive as a failure to implement elements of this decree has been a major source of friction between Rome and, especially, the Ukrainian, Melkite and Syro-Malabar Catholic Churches. Most serious is the foot-dragging on the right of these communities to be individual Churches in the full sense, with the freedom to govern their own affairs everywhere as during the first Christian millennium, to live in accord with their own traditions, and to spread by their own missionary efforts unhampered by artificial restrictions imposed from without.

Three issues are especially contested: the 1971 Vatican refusal to validate the vote of the Ukrainian Catholic Synod that its Church be erected into a patriarchate, the demand of the Melkite patriarchate that its jurisdiction extend to Melkites in the diaspora, and the insistence of the Malabar and Malankara Churches that the containment policy exercised against them in their own homeland be ended.

In all three issues the problems are complex and responsibilities for solving (or not solving) them shared. So it is unfair to attribute Roman foot-dragging to ill-will. Sometimes, as in India, local Latin hierarchies hinder a quick and equitable solution. Sometimes patience is dictated by larger demands, such as political or ecumenical considerations. Sometimes the realities of Eastern Catholicism impede a satisfactory resolution of all issues. Eastern Catholic Churches do not always show themselves mature enough to shoulder the autonomy they claim. This is especially evident in matters liturgical where, contrary to popular myth, Latinized Eastern Catholics – not Rome – are the greatest threat to the integrity of the tradition. Such a situation hardly leads Rome to conclude that the local Churches are ready to assume unsupervised responsibility for their own liturgical life.

Of course it is unrealistic to expect that minority Churches, some with fewer than a million faithful, would acquire by conciliar fiat the ecclesial physiognomy of the autonomous patriarchates of the first millenium. Nevertheless, attempts to confine the effective exercise of their full autonomy to within their historic territories of origin remain a major irritant. The curial thesis holds that a sane ecclesiology limits patriarchal (or equivalent) jurisdiction territorially. Eastern Catholic dioceses in places like North America are, therefore, part of the local conference of bishops and not under the jurisdiction of the mother Church. Such dioceses can have their rights limited for the good of the whole Catholic Church in the area (read: if the Latin hierarchy so determines, as in the bitterly resented attempt to impose clerical celibacy on Eastern Catholic priests in North America).

But since the Latin patriarch also happens to be pope, without territorial limits to his sway, a double standard comes into play in the case of Latin hierarchies in the East. So the establishment of Eastern dioceses in areas where a Latin hierarchy is in place can be systematically impeded by Latin bishops regardless of the harm to souls, whereas in the East, Latin hierarchies are set up for infinitesimal minorities of faithful, often poached from the Eastern communities, without the Eastern bishops having anything to say about it. The classic instance is India. Unlike the Latin Church, which owes its existence to the missionary movement accompanying Portuguese exploration and colonialism, the native Malabar Church, which had flourished there for a millennium before the coming of the Latins in 1498, had been systematically confined to their corner of south-west India and prevented from having missions in other parts of India. The incredible vitality and missionary *élan* of this dynamic Church, combined with these restrictions, forced countless priests and sisters to abandon their native rite as the price of obeying the evangelical call to preach the gospel. This denial of what is a basic right of any Christian Church ended during the Council, when the first of several mission territories outside Kerala was assigned to the Syro-Malabar Church.

A more intractable problem was the adamant refusal of the Latin hierarchy of India to permit the Eastern hierarchy to provide pastoral care for their numerous *émigré* faithful in cities where the Latin rite was already in place. Here too, of course, a double standard was operative: there were no similar restrictions on the Latins in Kerala. These injustices were all the more galling to the Orientals because they were imposed not in the diaspora but in their own homeland where they, not the Latins, are the original historic – even apostolic – Church.

This too has finally met with some relief. In a letter of 28 May 1987 to the Catholic bishops of India (*Documentation Catholique* 1947, 4 October 1987, pp. 890–2), Pope John Paul II ordered that the pastoral needs of Eastern Catholics residing in Latin dioceses be attended to, and announced the erection of an eparchy (diocese) in Bombay-Pune for the Malabar Catholics resident there. He also decreed that the Eastern Catholic Churches of India have the right to their own hierarchical organization in accord with their own ecclesial and canonical traditions, and not just as minority members of the Indian Episcopal Conference.

Progress has been made, too in the purification and restoration of the Eastern liturgical heritage more or less eroded in the past by Latinization. On 8 February 1986, Pope John Paul II inaugurated at Kottayam the restored

Syro-Malabar *Raza* (solemn Eucharist), and recent efforts (1988) of the Oriental Congregation to reach a compromise solution on less solemn forms of the Eucharist for weekdays and ordinary Sundays that will be acceptable to the local hierarchy and clergy without doing violence to the essential genius of the rite, seem promising.

In addition, the recently restored Armenian *Patarag* (Eucharistic liturgy) was inaugurated as one of the Eastern liturgies celebrating the Marian Year on 21 November 1987 at Santa Maria in Trastevere, in the presence of the pope, by Armenian Catholic Patriarch Jean Pierre XVIII Cardinal Kasparian. The renewed text brings Armenian Catholic liturgy into line with Armenian Orthodox usage by restoring such ancient Armenian traditions as the unmixed chalice and the Creed without *filioque*. This ecumenical move received a favourable echo in the Armenian Orthodox press. This and other highly successful Eastern Marian Year liturgies, along with the pope's accompanying vigorous affirmations of the value and integrity of the Eastern heritage (*Documentation Catholique* 1954, 17 January 1988, pp. 55–7), gave further impetus to the renewed status of Eastern Catholic communities in the post-Vatican II Church, despite their sometimes dolorous past and numerous present problems, both pastoral and ecumenical.

In the area of education, renewed Vatican support for the work of the Pontifical Oriental Institute in Rome, and for the development, with the help of that institute, of the vigorous and highly successful St Thomas Apostolic Seminary and Pontifical Institute for Oriental Studies in Kottayam, has not been matched elsewhere. The dictates of the decree have been almost uniformly ignored in seminary education. To address this problem, on 6 January 1987 the Congregation for Catholic Education issued a *Circular Letter Concerning Studies of the Oriental Churches* stressing the need for education in the traditions of Eastern Christianity as a means of acquiring a balanced view of the Christian heritage.

One issue has been subjected to more critical discussion than all others: the preparation of the *Code of Oriental Canon Law* by a Commission established in 1972 to revise and complete the codification begun under Pius XI (Gallagher, 1987). Though the Commission was mandated to prepare a code faithful to Eastern tradition, the project has come under attack for not implementing satisfactorily the directives of Vatican II, especially regarding three issues: the canonical autonomy of the Eastern churches (*OE* 5); the desire to have the code promulgated not *by* Rome *for* the Eastern Churches but by the pope and the Eastern hierarchical authorities together; and the rights and privileges of patriarchs (*OE* 9). The latter is the main bone of contention, and proposed canon 77.2, which excludes the exercise of patriarchal jurisdiction over diaspora faithful living outside the territory of the patriarchate, has come in for extensive criticism.

In sum, progress has been made, though a few issues remain intractable, often because no solution that would not cause more problems than it solves is available. Thus the establishment of a Ukrainian hierarchy in Poland and the movement for a Ukrainian patriarchate are politically and ecumenically sensitive, and caution is understandable. But in several areas no legitimate ecumenical or political considerations impede acceding to Oriental demands. Among them are the question of imposed celibacy in North America, jurisdiction in the diaspora, the creation of a unified Eastern synodal or patriarchal structure for the Syro-Malabar Church, and the restoration of patriarchs to full status with precedence over all bishops and dignitaries except the first among them, the bishop of Rome. The issue is not one of personal honour, but of the dignity of peoples.

8H Eastern Catholic Churches (*Orientalium Ecclesiarum*): Bibliography

Distante G., and Manna, S. (1986) *Decreto sulle chiese orientali cattoliche 'orientalium ecclesiarum'*. Collana Concilio Vaticano II, no. 4.

Gallagher, C. (1987) 'The Revised Code of Eastern Canon Law and the Second Vatican Council'. *Seminarium*, vol. 28.3, pp. 222–39.

Edelby N., and Dick, I. (1970) *Vatican II: Les Églises orientales catholiques. Unam Sanctam* 76.

Maximos IV (Sayegh) (1963) *The Eastern Churches and Catholic Unity*.

Maximos IV (Sayegh) (1967) *L'Église grecque melkite au concile*.

8I Bishops, Presbyterate and the Training of Priests (*Christus Dominus; Presbyterorum Ordinis; Optatam Totius*)

DENIS E. HURLEY OMI

INTRODUCTION

These three interrelated themes are dealt with in four documents of Vatican II. In the third chapter of *Lumen Gentium* we find a theological treatment of the episcopate and the presbyterate. The other three documents are of a practical nature: the Decree on the Pastoral Office of Bishops in the Church, the Decree on the Ministry and Life of Priests and the Decree on the Training of Priests.

The presbyterate suffered from the poor emphasis it received in *Lumen Gentium*. It was a pity that it was not treated with more depth and in greater unity with episcopate, and that in fact the whole ordained ministry was not treated more comprehensively.

The history of all four documents reveals development from somewhat disjointed and legalistic beginnings to, generally speaking, greater unity, depth and coherence. Two of the documents, those on the ministry and life of priests and priestly training, were affected by the somewhat panicky situation that arose after the second period of the Council, when it was feared that the Council wuld be prolonged beyond all reasonable measure; it was then that the Co-ordinating Commission issued an instruction that drafts not yet debated should be drastically pruned, and in some cases reduced, to a series of propositions to be voted on without debate. The Council fathers reacted strongly against this decision and enough time had to be given for a restricted but reasonable debate and the proccss of amending. The contracting and expanding, slicing and splicing that materialized helped to give the two documents a lean and sinewy, but sufficiently substantial, shape. The documents also profited from the debates on the great central texts like *Lumen Gentium* and *Gaudium et Spes*.

HISTORY[1]

Pastoral Office of Bishops

Bishops commanded attention. Vatican I had left them hanging in the air after the intense treatment accorded to the papacy. Like many other topics treated in the preparatory commissions, bishops were dealt with in a largely legalistic manner. This was inevitable, given the preponderant influence of the Roman

141

curia in the preparatory work. Bishops figured in chapters II and III of the original draft on the Church, and were due for further treatment in another draft on bishops and the government of dioceses.

In the new agenda compiled by the Co-ordinating Commission, established after the first period of the Council, they received ample treatment in the new draft of the Constitution on the Church and in the draft of the decree on the pastoral office of bishops in the Church. The former was presented in the second session (1963) in four chapters, the second of which bore the title 'The Hierarchical Constitution of the Church and the Episcopate in particular'. Its discussion was one of the key debates of Vatican II, perhaps one should say *the* key debate, lasting from the 30 September to 31 October 1963, and for a few more days in September 1964. Chapter II (later III) on the hierarchy took up eight of these days. It was one of the longest drawn out and most contentious of the conciliar debates, dealing with the relationship between papal primacy and episcopal collegiality and attempting to do justice both to the 'traditionalist' stress upon the former, and the 'progressive' stress upon the latter.

The document that emerged from the Council as the Decree on the Pastoral Office of Bishops in the Church has to be read in the light of that debate. It began as two separate documents: Bishops and the Government of the Dioceses, and The Care of Souls. The first was debated between 5 and 15 November 1963, the second never came up for debate as a separate document. It was circulated to the Council fathers in April 1963 under the title of the Pastoral Office of Bishops and the Care of Souls, but in January 1964 the Co-ordinating Commission ordered that its basic principles be included in the draft on bishops and the government of dioceses, and that the new conflated document be entitled the Pastoral Office of Bishops in the Church. The new parts of this document were debated in September 1964, but only finally approved after further revisions in the final session, October 1965.

Ministry and Life of Priests

The Decree on the Ministry and Life of Priests began as three drafts prepared by the Preparatory Commission on the Discipline of the Clergy and the People of God. One dealt with the holiness of clerical life, another with ecclesiastical offices and benefices and the administration of Church goods, and the third with the distribution of clergy. At the end of 1962 the Conciliar Commission combined the three into one draft on clerics, and by November 1963 had produced a revised draft on priests.

Instructions were then received to reduce the text to mere propositions. Ten meagre propositions resulted. This did not go down well with the Council fathers. Their written criticisms led to another revision, which appeared under the title Priestly Life and Ministry. This was debated by the assembly from 13 to 15 October 1964 and, on being put to the vote, was rejected by 1,199 votes to 930. After a further revision, it was presented on 14 October 1965 and discussed for four days. It was voted acceptable, amended in places, and promulgated on 7 December 1965.

Training of priests

The Preparatory Commission on Studies and Seminaries submitted two drafts to the Central Preparatory Commission, one on the fostering of ecclesiastical vocations and the other on the formation of candidates to the priesthood. After debate in the Central Preparatory Commission, the two documents were combined into one with the treatment of vocations constituting the first chapter of the new document. This was published early in 1963 after the first period of the Council, and was entrusted for revision to the Conciliar Commission on Seminaries, Studies and Catholic Education with an instruction to submit the revised text to the Co-ordinating Commission by 10 March. The instruction was complied with, hurriedly, and the new draft was approved for debate by Pope John XXIII, a month before his death in June 1963.

It did not come up for debate in the second period, so the conciliar commission took the opportunity to effect further revisions in the hope that they would be accepted. They were. But before the new text could be published, new instructions were issued by the Co-ordinating Commission that the text should be reduced to a series of propositions for voting. The Conciliar Commission, like others similarly affected, was aghast, but obeyed the instructions; and had its propositions circulated to the Council fathers along with the full most recent text and a report on its history.

As has already been indicated, the Council fathers indicated by written criticisms that they were not willing to accept texts reduced to propositions, so the Commission was instructed during the course of the third period of the Council to put some flesh back on the bones.

The draft was well received when presented to the assembly. The final work on it was done in the spring of 1965, the final voting took place from 11 to 13 October, and the decree was promulgated on 28 October 1965.

SUMMARY OF TEXTS

All four documents dealt with here reveal a great concern for unity: unity in the nature of the episcopate, unity between episcopate and presbyterate, and unity in the training of candidates for presbyterate.

Concerning the episcopate, unity is emphasized:

1 in the relationship between the college of apostles and the bishops seen as their successors;

2 in the collegial unity and responsibility of bishops, which finds an echo in episcopal conferences;

3 in the structural coherence given to the body of bishops by the petrine office;

4 in the recognition of the episcopate as an essential element within the total sacramental nature of the Church;

5 in the connection between the sacrament of the episcopate and the offices flowing from it;

6 in the recognition that these offices are a particular expression of ministries in which all members of the Church share, inasmuch as they share in the prophetic, priestly and kingly roles of Jesus himself.

Unity between episcopate and presbyterate, while not sufficiently explored in *Lumen Gentium*, emerges from the understanding of the presbyterate as a share in the full priesthood of the episcopate and from the consequence that priests of a diocese should form a closely knit *presbyterium* around their bishop.

Unity in the training of candidates for the presbyterate was a dominant concern of the Conciliar Commission dealing with the topic, and was secured by insistence on the pastoral purpose of training for the priesthood and the need to have all aspects of training converge on this objective.

This work of unification owed much to the revival of the theology of the Mystical Body in the half-century that preceded the Council. This theology emphasizes the presence of Christ in the Church and the oneness of the Church with Christ in its life and activity. In the light of this theology, the Church is seen as the visible sacrament of the saving and sanctifying Christ, exercising through it his threefold role of prophet, priest and king. The whole Church and every member of it should be a sign of Christ, and bishops surrounded by their presbyters have a special importance in the sacramental totality.

This understanding led, as far as the theology of the episcopate was concerned, to an abandonment of the distinctions between residential, auxiliary and titular bishops, and of the disproportionate preoccupation with the difference between the power of order and the power of jurisdiction, in terms of which some empowerment comes from the order and some through delegation by a superior authority. The important thing is sacramental ordination, which carries with it incorporation into the episcopal college and participation in the threefold office of teaching, sanctifying and governing. Good order in the Church requires some practical co-ordination and subordination in the exercise of the offices, but the offices are essentially the same in all.

There was no great difficulty about this in the conciliar debate. The really intense debate arose around the concept of collegiality. Essentially it belongs to the tradition of the Church, but practically it had been long overshadowed by papal primacy. Vatican I had dealt with the primacy, but in the historical circumstances of 1870 had not had time to consider the episcopate as a whole. Collegiality came squarely before the Council in 1963. It deals with the apparent dilemma that the body of bishops as a collegial unit with the pope as its head, and therefore not without him, has full episcopal power in the universal Church, and yet the pope alone as primate has the same power which he can exercise without the participation of the whole body of bishops.

The problem for a certain number of Council fathers lay in the term 'college' with its juridical connotation of a body of equals that can elect its own president. The great fear was that the proclamation of collegiality would detract from the primacy. With patience and persistence and with special help from the new pope, Paul VI, the Council finally reached a not entirely enthusiastic consensus expressed in careful and caution-ridden formulas as exemplified in *Lumen Gentium* 22.

Decree on the Pastoral Office of Bishops in the Church (Christus Dominus)

This decree draws on the principles enunciated in chapter III of *Lumen Gentium* and deals with four major concerns of bishops: the universal Church, the Holy See, the diocese, and the common good of related dioceses.

Concerning the universal Church, there are three considerations: the first is the collegiate action of bishops exercised in an ecumenical Council or in other circumstances in which they act collegially at the call of the pope, or at least with his approval. No clear description is given of the second way of exercising collegiality (*CD* 4). Next the decree deals with the Synod of Bishops, an advisory body, announced by Pope Paul VI on 15 September 1965 in response to many calls for some form of regular consultation between the pope and the bishops. (*CD* 5). Finally, there is reference to how the bishops' concern for the universal Church must include interest in the evangelization of other areas, financial sharing, and fraternal support of brother bishops suffering harassment or detention or prevented in other ways from exercising their ministry (*CD* 6).

In regard to the Holy See, mention is made of the need to reorganize its departments, to have the role of papal legates more precisely determined, and to have officials of the Holy See drawn more widely from the universal Church (*CD* 8–10).

Concerning dioceses, the decree gives a fairly detailed description of episcopal responsibilities and of the bishop's relations with his fellow workers, coadjutor and auxiliary bishops, diocesan curia and council, the diocesan clergy and religious (*CD* 11–21, 25–7). The diocesan clergy have a very special relationship to their bishop. It is treated here as in the Decree on the Ministry and Life of Priests. As regards religious, the concern is once again that of unity. Religious play a very important role in evangelization, so their relations to the dioceses in which they live and work are to be governed by principles that respect their need for internal independence as religious families, their availability to the Holy See, and their filial dependence on the bishop in all that concerns their apostolic work (*CD* 33–5). Finally, in the treatment of related dioceses, the main theme is episcopal conferences, which are judged 'supremely opportune' (*CD* 37–8).

Decree on the Ministry and Life of Priests (Presbyterorum Ordinis)

The final form of the decree in the Latin text reveals a shift of emphasis not obviously discernible in other languages, the shift from the cultic term *sacerdos* to the more pastoral term *presbyter*. Italian continues to use *sacerdote* and English *priest*. The New Testament uses sacerdotal language of Jesus and of the Church (priestly people), but never of the Church's ministers. The Latin usage in the decree emphasizes the shift in theological thought from a ministry essentially connected with worship to one sharing in a wide sweep of the pastoral functions proper to bishops. It is also ecumenically of some significance.

145

The decree states that 'all priests together with their bishops so share in one and the same priesthood and ministry of Christ that the very unity of their consecration and mission requires their hierarchical communion with the order of bishops' (*PO* 7). Thus 'in their own measure priests participate in the office of the apostles' (*PO* 2). The decree indicates how priests share in the ministry of the word and of the sacraments, and how 'to the degree of their authority and in the name of their bishop priests exercise the office of Christ the Head and the Shepherd'(*PO* 6).

Inspired by these theological considerations, the decree paints a picture of what the relationship between bishop and priests should be. The bishop should regard priests as his brothers and friends, have at heart their material and especially their spiritual welfare. 'Upon the bishop rests the heavy responsibility for the sanctity of his priests.' He should be concerned about their ongoing formation and organize matters so that there can be regular consultation with them, especially about pastoral matters. For their part, priests must respect in their bishop the authority of Christ the chief Shepherd, and stand by him in sincere charity and obedience (*CD* 28, *PO* 7).

This close union between bishop and priests should be reflected in the union between priests themselves, in their fraternal spirit and mutual help, their common pursuit of priestly holiness and pastoral effectiveness, and the special assistance they should be ready to offer to brother priests in spiritual need, (*CD* 28, *PO* 8).

In regard to the laity, priests are fathers and teachers and yet at the same time brothers. Their leadership of the laity must be characterized by their willingness to listen and their respect for the dignity, freedom, expertise and experience of the laity (*PO* 9).

The Decree on the Training of Priests (Optatam Totius)

The Decree on the Training of Priests, echoing the Decree on Priestly Ministry and Life, opens with a directive on the promotion of vocation (*OT* 2–3). It then launches into the programme of major seminaries by clearly and forcefully enunciating the goal: the training of candidates for a pastoral ministry. To this end suitable staff must be provided and careful discernment made of seminarians (*OT* 4–7).

Spiritual formation must be closely linked with doctrinal and pastoral training. Training must be steeped in the mystery of Christ and his Church, and must prepare the candidates for the obligations that await them, with special reference to celibacy in those in whom it is required. Seminary discipline must be related to formation (*OT* 8–12).

The revision of ecclesiastical studies calls for a greater integration of philosophy and theology. The teaching of theology should explore the sources of theological knowledge in divine revelation and its development down the ages. However, in comparison with pre-conciliar seminary education, the stress is here upon the practical and the pastoral: the application of theology to present conditions and its communication in the pastoral ministry. Training in pastoral skills must go hand in hand with doctrinal education (*OT* 13–21), and provision should be made for ongoing post-ordination education (*OT* 22).

EVALUATION

Moving on to the evaluation of the implementation and significance of these documents twenty-five years later, the most that can be expected from an essay of this nature is a few personal reflections; genuine evaluation would require intensive world-wide research. The drawback of a few personal reflections is that they are severely limited by the experience and outlook of the writer.

A development that has had a profound effect on the implementation of the Council is the crisis in the priestly and religious life during the years immediately after the Council. There was a regular haemorrhage of priests and religious. Debates that had been overlooked or suppressed in the Council broke out in the post-conciliar Church. The one on the priesthood, the wider shape of its ministry, its decreasing numbers, its obligatory celibacy, even its stress and above all, the underlying rationale of its differentiation from the laity, moved it into the centre of the Church's *angst*. Celibacy looked less attractive within the context of the more explicit affirmation of human values, including the value of married love, in *Gaudium et Spes*: in the light also of the Council's own acceptance of a married diaconate (*LG* 29), as much an innovation in terms of Western tradition as would be the ordination of married men. Finally, taken in connection with all this, the extreme shortage of local priests in many parts of the third world, especially Latin America and Africa, came up for consideration in the Synod of 1971. Although a number of hierarchies, including that of South Africa, had asked to be allowed to ordain married men to the priesthood in circumstances of extreme pastoral need, this was rejected by a small Synod majority (107 to 87: in fact, a majority of *elected* members did vote in favour of the change; it was the papal nominees who ensured its defeat).

Apart from this major unresolved issue, let us try to answer the question: How have bishops, priests and the trainers of seminarians succeeded in making themselves effective promoters of the vision of Vatican II, fully expounded in many chapters of this book?

Within the over-all vision, two concepts stand out with particular clarity: community and evangelization. A vibrant, active Christian community, alive with the Spirit, is the most effective agent of evangelization. The apostles and their successors form an historical community, the bishops and their priests and deacons form a community of the ordained, the particular churches they serve form community with them, and the whole world-wide conglomeration of particular churches is a community of communities. And at every level of community there is responsibility for evangelization, for co-operating in the work of Jesus.

Starting with the bishops, the impression is that, by and large, since Vatican II there has been a great increase in their community relations through episcopal conferences, regional groupings, inter-conference contacts and so on. Renewal courses, study days, retreats and shared pastoral experiences have also helped. In this context episcopal conferences represent probably the most important organizational advance stimulated by the Council. They had previously existed in many parts of the world, but since the Council they have been established almost everywhere and have developed an immense importance in the collaborative working of bishops and in providing a positive regional lead in issues of evangelization, justice and inculturation. In some instances, particularly in the case of the United States and Brazil, they have shown that they can hold their own in dialogue with the Holy See.

The same is true of relations with the Holy See. Nevertheless, here problems do arise in such matters as the nomination of bishops in disregard of local preferences, curial action against theologians of a sort resented in their local churches and embarrassing to many bishops, and a criticism of episcopal conferences by the Cardinal Prefect of the Congregation for the Doctrine of the Faith that appeared unjustified to local hierarchies. Such developments indicate that the view from Rome does not always coincide with the local outlook. The Roman attitudes manifested in these occurrences are deeply disturbing to some people. They see them as contrary to the spirit of Vatican II, and as obstacles to its implementation. Other people obviously see them as welcome exercises in Church discipline.

The Synod of Bishops brings representatives of episcopal conferences along with others into consultation with the Holy Father and his curia every three years. Some good things have come out of the Synod particularly the apostolic exhortation of Pope Paul VI (*Evangelii Nuntiandi* Evangelization in the Modern World). However, there are shortcomings. Meetings of the Synod have little impact on the universal Church, and each pontifical document that comes out of a meeting of the Synod is seen as 'just one more document', with the exception, as already mentioned, of *Evangelii Nuntiandi* and, to be fair, also *Justice in the World*, which came out of the 1971 meeting.

So much for the community relations of bishops among themselves and with their head. What of their community relations with their priests, religious and laity? This varies enormously from place to place and person to person. In their community relations bishops exercise their threefold office of teaching, sanctifying and governing. They endeavour to organize matters so that the word of God is spread, the sacraments are celebrated and good order is promoted. The general impression is that dioceses operate well in terms of consulters, councils of priests and diocesan curial consultations. Diocesan and parochial pastoral councils have not always been so successful. In some places, they do not exist or are in recess while constitutions and methods of work are being revised. A major problem is the lack of training of council members.

Apart from these official or semi-official contacts between bishops and priests, how successful have bishops been in promoting the community relations with their priests advocated in the Decrees on the Pastoral Office of Bishops and the Ministry and Life of Priests?

Some bishops, gifted with the right kind of personality, have done well. Others among us have been less successful. Regretfully, concern for the priestly community, the *presbyterium*, has not been the priority it deserves to be. It remains a massive problem in big dioceses with hundred and even thousands of priests. Some bishops may never get to know all their priests. The division of dioceses into pastoral areas and deaneries becomes all important in the solution of the problem, but it is never a complete solution.

The aspect of the ministry of the word called catechesis calls for intense collaboration between bishops, priests and representatives, of religious and laity. At one time, the Catholic school was relied upon in many countries to be the main agent for the catechizing of children and young people. Where this is no longer the case, parishes struggle with an enormous problem of instructing the young. Since Vatican II a massive effort has been given to the development of catechetical instruction. By and large, we have not been too successful.

In the matter of liturgy again we have a variety of results. Generally speaking, the expectations of the pre-Vatican II liturgical reformers have not been realized. In many cases, possibly the majority of cases, the liturgy has not become the exciting, dynamic community experience that the reformers foresaw and hoped for. There are several reasons for this. One of them is the difficulty experienced by bishops and priests of entering into the attitudes required to transform the liturgy: a deep understanding of Church and worship and cultural needs; good community sense; good communication and dedication to educating the worshipping community along with oneself. It has happened in certain cases but not generally. There is still far too much of the mechanical and the routine in the leadership of the liturgy.

What of the community spirit of parishes and dioceses? In order that a particular church may truly reflect the vision of Vatican II, we need a method of promoting community as an indispensable element in all genuine Church life. We must not of course promote community just for the sake of community. There must be a goal for which community exists and operates. That goal must be evangelization, some form of evangelization, some participation in the spectrum that is laid before our eyes by *Evangelii Nuntiandi*, in its summing up what we are called by Vatican II to be and to do. This document has taught us that everything that the Church does is evangelization: preaching the gospel; cultivating prayer and celebrating the liturgy; providing a witness of living faith; promoting formation in the faith of children, teenagers, adults; of religious, deacons, priests and bishops; fostering education, Christian unity, culture and development, justice, reconciliation and peace; bringing the influence of Christ into every aspect of culture, which means humanizing and Christianizing both the personal and social dimensions of life.

This vision of an evangelizing community as indispensable to Church life is the inspiration behind the Basic Christian Communities and other initiatives like Renew, the process initiated in 1978 in the archdiocese of Newark New Jersey, in the United States, and now spread to over a 160 dioceses in several countries. Some such approach appears necessary to render the Church capable of coping with the problems of society in our time. It is a holistic approach to Christian formation.

The vision of Vatican II will never be fully realized. Perfection is not of this world, nor of the pilgrim stage of the Church and the kingdom; but the vision will be better realized when we manage to give a much fuller practical signficance to Christian community and evangelization.

Unity has been a recurring theme of this chapter. Working to make the Church a genuine evangelizing community should go a long way towards promoting unity: unity between clergy, religious and laity; unity between various forms of evangelization, including those very important ones of ecumenism and development, justice and peace; unity between personal holiness and social concern. At present, social concern tends to remain the preserve of specialized groups. Promoting an evangelizing community should make it common to all.

In so far as in most particular churches and the Church in its totality we are far from this preoccupation with community and evangelization, the evaluation of the implementation of Vatican II, particularly as it concerns bishops, priests and seminary staffs, must lead to the conclusion that we still have a long way to go, a lengthy process of education to pursue, before the spirit of Vatican II becomes characteristic of the Church.

Note

1 These historical notes are drawn from Vorgrimler, Caprile, and from personal records.

8I Bishops, Presbyterate and the Training of Priests (*Christus Dominus; Presbyterorum Ordinis; Optatam Totius*): Bibliography

Lash, N. and Rhymer, J. eds. (1970) *The Christian Priesthood*. London, Darton, Longman and Todd.

Rahner, K. (1968) *Servants of the Lord*. London, Burns & Oates.

Schillebeeckx, E. (1981) *Ministry: a case for change*. London, SCM.

Telfer, W. (1962) *The Office of a Bishop*, London, Darton, Longman and Todd.

Hastings, A (1976) *The Faces of God*, ch. 11, 'The reform of the ministry'. London, Geoffrey Chapman; New York, Orbis.

Hickey, R. (1980) *Africa: the case for an auxiliary priesthood*. London, Geoffrey Chapman.

John Paul II (1984) *A Priest Forever*. Slough, St Paul Publications.

Ratzinger, J. (1988) *Ministers of Your Joy*. Slough, St Paul Publications.

8J The Apostolate of the Laity (*Apostolicam Actuositatem*)

KATHLEEN WALSH

Apostolicam Actuositatem, the Decree on the Apostolate of the Laity, was approved by the fathers of the Second Vatican Council on 18 November 1965. The Preparatory Commission had begun its work in 1960, bringing developments in the Church's understanding of the apostolate of the laity in line with its developing understanding of the nature and mission of the Church as a whole. Most commentators point out that the Decree on the Laity must be read especially in conjunction with *Lumen Gentium* and *Gaudium et Spes*, and the enormous debt owed to the work of Scripture scholars and to the liturgical movement must not be underestimated.

The idea of organized lay apostolic action is usually traced back to Pius XI, under whose inspiration many lay organizations were started. It was described as 'Catholic Action', and in it the laity were intended to operate under strict episcopal direction. This reflected the belief that the hierarchy's was the true apostolate and the laity's derived from theirs. In its structured form, 'Catholic Action' never caught on in English-speaking countries. Part of *Apostolicam Actuositatem*'s function was to acknowledge a demand for and assumption of greater responsibility and autonomy of organization and action on the part of an increasingly better-educated laity, and to intensify and broaden this action. Further, it sought 'to describe the nature, character, and diversity of the lay apostolate, to state its basic principles, and to give pastoral directives for its more efficient exercise' (*AA* 1; Abbott translation). The descriptions and directives arrived at were then to be incorporated into the proposed revision of canon law.

The document is divided into six chapters, dealing with: 1. the call to the lay apostolate (*AA* 2–4); 2. the goals of the lay apostolate ((*AA* 5–8); 3. its various fields (*AA* 9–14); 4. its methods (*AA* 15–22); 5. the need for good order (*AA* 2–7); 6. the importance of adequate moral, theological and spiritual education and formation for the laity (*AA* 28–32).

It opens with the emphatic statement that the call to the apostolate comes to every Christian with baptism: 'For by its very nature the Christian vocation is also a vocation to the apostolate' (*AA* 2). The Church is the Body of Christ, founded to preach the good news of Christ for the salvation of all and the glory of God. It is the right and duty of all Christians to be active in the apostolate, though not all in the same way: '. . . there is diversity of service but unity of purpose' (*AA* 2). The document sees this diversity as fundamentally between the apostles and their successors, bishops and priests, upon whom Christ conferred 'the duty of teaching, sanctifying and ruling in his name and power', and the laity, the ones who are not ordained thus, but who nevertheless 'share in the priestly, prophetic and royal office of Christ' (*AA* 2).

The goals to be achieved by those participating in Christ's redemptive work include the salvation of individuals and, alongside other people of good will,

151

the laity have a special obligation to take direct and definitive action to perfect the intrinsic goodness of the temporal order. They must act in and on political, legal, scientific and cultural systems and institutions to correct those abuses that have crept in and direct them to their right ends for the good of all. Inspired by the Holy Spirit, their action must be taken in the light of the gospel and with the mind of the Church. They are to act in charity, but with respect for the freedom, dignity and eventual independence of those being helped.

In order to fulfil the mission of the Church, the laity have to exercise their apostolate in the Church as well as in the world, which, though distinct, are part of the one new creation that God is bringing about. Christ's message and grace is mainly communicated through the ministry of the Word and of the sacraments, which are entrusted in a special way to the clergy. The laity too, however, have an active part to play in the apostolic life of the Church itself where they are to evangelize, catechize and care for those in need, as well as provide financial assistance to the Church, and they are to support and collaborate with their pastors in reaching decisions that affect the Church and its mission. As women have an ever more active share in the whole life of society, they too must participate more widely in the various fields of the Church's apostolate (AA 9).

The individual form of apostolate is 'the origin and condition of the whole lay apostolate and admits of no substitute' (AA 16), and where the freedom of the Church is restricted this is especially important. But associations of laity are necessary too, not only to meet the social and spiritual needs of their members, but to sustain, form and organize laity to take effective united action to build up the Church and perfect the temporal order. Care must be taken to respect the different forms and functions of lay organizations, and to respect national differences while, in some cases, promoting international co-operation.

Good order is a primary consideration in the Church, and is best achieved by fostering a spirit of unity and harmony, developing mutual esteem and shared goals. Lay apostolic action must be incorporated into the apostolate of the whole Church, and be in 'union with those whom the Holy Spirit has assigned to rule God's Church' (AA 23). Although the laity must not be deprived of the possibility of acting on their own accord, no organization can claim the name 'Catholic' without permission of the hierarchy, and certain organizations, and individuals, engaged in educational and pastoral formation, can be called upon to work more closely under the direction of the hierarchy, whose right and duty it is to teach and interpret moral principles and values that are to be acted upon in the temporal sphere. Clergy and religious must learn to understand, co-operate with and support the apostolate of the laity. This collaboration can be achieved by establishing parish, deanery, diocesan and regional councils, and, at an international level, a special secretariat for the lay apostolate should be established at the Holy See.

Christian formation continues throughout life. Opportunities should be made available in parishes, in special centres of Christian education, in lay associations, through Scripture and theology study groups and retreats, for people to develop an awareness of being active members of the people of God, and to prepare themselves, as responsible adults, to make the Church present in the temporal order. The lay apostolate has a 'distinctively secular quality' (*AA* 29), and an appropriate spirituality must be developed which can help laity to see, judge and act in and on the world under the guidance of the Spirit. The closing exhortation stresses the urgency of the call to all the laity, especially young people, to be 'co-workers in the various forms and methods of the Church's one apostolate, which must be constantly adapted to the new needs of the times' (*AA* 33).

Twenty years after the Council, the new *Code of Canon Law* was issued and translated into the vernacular for the first time. One does indeed find here an attempt to incorporate the conciliar view of the laity. Thus Canon 208 declares: 'Flowing from their rebirth in Christ, there is a genuine equality of dignity and action among all Christ's faithful. Because of this equality they all contribute, each according to his or her own condition and office, to the building of the Body of Christ.' However, we detect a certain ambivalence towards the idea of equality when we read this in conjunction with the preceding canon: 'By divine institution, among Christ's faithful there are in the Church sacred ministers, who in law are also called clerics; the others are called lay people.' In other words, the laity are still 'other', their contribution to the building up of the Body of Christ, by implication is not of 'divine institution', nor is it 'sacred'. The laity are defined, not definers, and this seriously limits the concept (which admittedly marks a great change since the 1917 *Code*) of 'genuine equality of dignity and action'.

The Secretariat for the Laity that had been called for was established and formalized in 1977 as the Pontifical Council for the Laity, with an integral role in the curia. It has a presidency of three cardinals, and a permanent office in Rome with both clergy and lay officials, and a mainly lay, international membership of both women and men. It is divided into two departments, one of which 'deals with questions concerning the laity as Christians living in the world and as members of the ecclesial community', while the other deals with the Catholic international organizations. Although the Council acts as a place of meeting and dialogue in the Church, between different forms of lay activity and between the laity and the hierarchy, it is difficult to see how it affects the lives of most Catholics. And whereas some would argue that the Council is the voice of the laity in the Vatican, others would argue that as it consists mostly of those who work in a full-time, professional capacity for the Church, it is not a very representative voice.

Pastoral Councils have been attempted in many dioceses, deaneries and parishes. Sometimes these have been little more than a forum for issuing declarations of episcopal decision or clerical intent. In other cases, as the National Pastoral Congress for England and Wales held in Liverpool in 1980 demonstrates, an increased opportunity for participation has meant that the more educated, confident and articulate laity have found a new arena for exercising their skills as leaders. Unfortunately, little systematic attention has been given to ensuring that more active involvement is a real option for everyone in the Church, or to developing methods of handling the conflicts and

153

alienation that were bound to surface when new models of the Church opened up such new methods of participation and decision-making for conservatives and progressives alike.

The request for increased opportunities for higher theological education for the laity was realized to some degree, with many seminaries opening their doors to religious sisters and brothers, to lay men and also to women. For the theologically educated laity, one immediate question was that of employment and, after schools, colleges and universities, it was to the dioceses they turned. Until recently neither the will nor the salaries required to employ them were there, and the more general educational and pastoral enterprises demanded by a new ecclesiology, which these laity were often better qualified than many clergy to undertake, were very patchy. One of the consequences, as the consultations leading up to both the Extraordinary Synod and the Synod on the Laity showed only too clearly, is that Catholics continue to work and worship alongside each other with quite contradictory ideas and assumptions about both the nature and the purpose of the Church, and their own place and value within it.

At the end of January 1989 the document following the 1987 Synod on the Vocation and Mission of the Laity in the Church and in the World, *Christifideles Laici*, was finally published. On its own admission it adds little to the teaching on the laity found in Vatican II, which, it claims, 'has taken on a surprisingly contemporary character and at times has carried prophetic significance'. The Synod faced the challenge of indicating how the theory of Vatican II could be translated into authentic Church practice, acknowledging thereby that this had not yet happened. One difference about the document is that it is written in inclusive language, a fact adverted to in the text as evidence of the Synod fathers' sincerity in their desire that all the laity, and women especially, are to be positively encouraged to know about, be prepared for and take up the opportunities currently open to them in the Church. There is a far greater sensitivity to the call, from bishops, clergy and religious, as well as laity, for more widespread and genuine consultation and participation in the decision-making processes of the Church at all levels.

Nevertheless, this apparent encouragement of lay participation does not alter the fact that among the situations that can be regarded as post-conciliar concerns are the liturgical ministries of lay people within the Church, and especially the place and role of women. The very notion of lay 'ministries' is itself post-conciliar. *Apostolicam Actuositatem* spoke almost entirely in terms of 'apostolate', when speaking of the mission of the whole Church, and spoke only of ministry in relation to the ordained priesthood. There is one notable exception, when it refers to those full-time workers 'who devote themselves and their professional skill . . . to the service (ministry) of associations and other activities' (*AA* 22) in their home countries and especially in Catholic mission communities.

It seems clear that the notion of lay ministry developed because, in face of a shortage of priests, lay people have found themselves engaging increasingly in activities – proclaiming the Scriptures, moving in sacred space, handling sacred vessels, and even distributing the host itself – that had previously been reserved to the ordained clergy. One consequence has been a blurring of the sacred/secular and clergy/lay divide, a blurring that most Catholics seem to accept and indeed welcome. While the Holy Spirit can be seen to be at work here, there are, according to *Christifideles Laici*, certain difficulties, especially 'the temptation of being so strongly interested in Church services and tasks that some fail to become actively engaged in their responsibilities in the professional, social, cultural and political world'.

This expressed concern is unfounded, but is masking something much deeper. Where their ministry is respected and valued, lay people learn to respect and value themselves and each other. It is a common experience that the confidence and self-esteem generated by an enhanced role in the life of the parish actually leads many otherwise retiring people to become active in community and public life. The real concern behind the question of lay ministries is that in bridging the gap between the sacred and the secular, which Vatican II saw as being essential to making the Church relevant in the modern world; the very foundations upon which the authority structures of the Church are built are threatened. On the one hand, as lay people show themselves increasingly to be better equipped than many clergy with the kind of liturgical, pastoral and community-building qualities that are needed for the Church at the end of the twentieth century, the question of the nature and function of priestly ordination is raised, and with it the question of eligibility for ordination. On the other hand, by revaluing the secular, and in the face of negative experiences of out-of-touch or 'burnt out' clergy, some lay people have been led to question the very concept of sacred ministers or mediators, and therefore the need for a hierarchically organized Church at all. Either way, what has been constructed as the problem of the role and vocation of the laity can, more accurately, be seen as a problem of power and authority in the Church: who decides what, for whom, and on what does their claim to authority rest?

Traditionally, ecclesiastical control has rested on a clear distinction between the sacred and the secular and the identification, for all practical purposes, of the clergy with the sacred and the laity with the secular. There has been no question of the superiority of the former over the latter. The authority of the sacred ministers derived from their supposed ontological and moral superiority as celibate males, with roles and functions in the Church divinely ordained. Unfortunately, even this latest post-synodal document seeks to maintain the distinction and ordering (which inevitably involves a subordination of lay to ordained), yet at the same time it tries to promote a more elevated view of the laity without whom the Church can hope to exert no influence in the world.

There is a curious ambiguity in *Christifideles Laici*. It still sees the 'world' as being Spirit-filled, but believes much more than did Vatican II that it poses a strong threat to human dignity and fulfilment. What is most wrong with the world is what is described as its growing secularism, that is, its separation from the sacred, yet the significant thing about the laity is their 'secular character'. It is apparently because they are further removed from the sacred that the laity are more naturally suited to the secular as their proper and particular sphere of activity. Conversely, those furthest removed from the secular, males who are

155

not married, are considered the only ones fitted for the more sacred sphere of activity.

The language of an ordering of relationships in terms of superior and inferior sits uncomfortably beside the language of participation and equality. Not surprisingly, the ambiguities cause much confusion. New authority structures are needed which do not concentrate the final exercise of the powers of teaching, legislation and sacramental ministry in the hands of ordained celibate males on the assumption that this combination of attributes makes them better fitted for the task. It is perhaps a sign of our own times, a sign that the power of naming is shifting, that neither the laity nor the clergy alone can continue to be defined as 'the problem'. The whole question of ministry is undergoing a huge review in both theory and practice, by clergy and laity alike, on the assumption that both have a say in the matter. There is every reason to believe that the tensions caused will be creative, and that the Church will continue to exist as a positive force in the lives of its own members and through them in the wider society.

8J The Apostolate of the Laity
(*Apostolicam Actuositatem*): Bibliography

Coll, R. ed. (1982) *Women and Religion: A Reader for the Clergy*. New York, Paulist Press.

Congar, Y. (1965) *Lay People in the Church*. London, Geoffrey Chapman.

Cowan, M. A., ed. (1987) *Alternative Futures for Worship Vol. 6: Leadership Ministry in Community*. Minnesota, Liturgical Press.

Finn, V. S. (1986) *Pilgrim in the Parish*. Leominster, Fowler Wright.

Foley, N. (1983) *Preaching and the Non-Ordained*. Minnesota, Liturgical Press.

Guzie, T. (1981) *The Book of Sacramental Basics*. New York, Paulist Press.

Pontificium Consilium pro Laicis (1982) *The Pastoral Responsibility of Bishops vis-a-vis the Laity*. Vatican City, PCL.

Pro Vita Mundi Publications, especially:

De Looz, P. (1981) *Participation in the Catholic Church*, Bulletin no. 84. Brussels, PMV.

Grootaers, J. (1986) *The Laity within the Ecclesial Community*, Bulletin no. 106. Brussels, PMV.

Ruether, R. R. (1983) *Sexism and God-Talk*. London, SCM.

Schillebeeckx, E. (1985) *The Church with a Human Face*. London, SCM.

Thils, G. (1983) *Les Laics dans le nouveau code de doit canonique et au IIe Councile du Vatican*. Cahier de la Revue Theologique de Louvain, University of Louvain.

Whitehead, J.D. and E.E. (1986) *The Emerging Laity*. New York, Doubleday.

8K Religious Life (*Perfectae Caritatis*)

SANDRA M. SCHNEIDERS IHM

CONTEXT

The official renewal of religious life throughout the Church was inaugurated for modern times in the pontificate of Pius XII when, beginning in 1950, the Sacred Congregation of Religious (later SCRIS) held international convocations of the major superiors of monastic, contemplative and active congregations, in which they were urged to adapt their institutes to the modern world without sacrificing the essentials of their state of life in the Church. The pope issued a series of documents on religious life and its appropriate adaptation, notably *Sponsa Christi* (1950) and *Sacra Virginitas* (1954) (see Solesmes, 1967, for papal documents on religious life from Benedict XIV to John XXIII).

These Vatican initiatives were anticipated in the 1940s by such pioneers among American women religious as Bertrande Meyers DC and Madeleva Wolff CSC, who were already calling for the appropriate professional education of sisters in apostolic congregations. Their vision bore fruit in the 1950s and 1960s in the Sister Formation Conference, which undertook the development of a new kind of formation programme for sisters which would integrate their spiritual, psychological, intellectual and professional development. The work of the Conference helped prepare a generation of religious to respond enthusiastically and generously to the challenges of the Council in general, but especially in regard to religious life (for documentation on this period, see Kolmer, 1984, pp. 19–35).

The conciliar document on religious life began as a 1960 draft of nearly 200 articles entitled 'The States that Aim at Perfection', and was finally approved by the Council on 28 October 1965 as the Decree on the Appropriate Renewal of Religious Life (*Perfectae Caritatis*) a document of twenty-five articles which had undergone five revisions (see Vorgrimler 2, p. 301–32 for a history of the document).

The document represented an uneasy and rather full compromise between two polarized positions. The first, the Roman and traditional one, understood religious life in terms of a state of 'Perfection' according to the ascetical theology of Thomas Aquinas (see *Summa Theologica* II–II, Qq. 186–9) and the juridical provisions of the 1917 *Code of Canon Law*. The second was that of those bishops and leaders of religious congregations who were feeling their way towards a far more diversified view which stressed freedom, diversity and effective service to the contemporary world.

If the first position was theologically moribund, it at least had the advantage of being clearly articulated, widely practised, and traditionally justified. The second position contained the seeds of renewal, but was not yet mature. The document that resulted from the conciliar struggle is far from being the most visionary product of the Council. None the less, by finally concentrating not on the theology of religious life (which is somewhat better treated in *Lumen Gentium* 31 and esp. 43–7), but on the basic principles of appropriate renewal,

157

the decree provided an impetus towards a renewal that, in twenty-five years, has gone far beyond anything the Council fathers could have envisaged.

Perfectae Caritatis has been implemented by an extraordinarily large number of papal documents. The first of these continues to encourage innovations (Paul VI's *Ecclesiae Sanctae* II (1966) (Flannery 1, pp. 624–33) and *Renovationis Causam* (1969) (Flannery 1, pp. 634–55), an Instruction on formation). These documents authorized extensive experimentation, even contrary to common law, and thus launched the experience-based renewal of religious life, especially in North America, that resulted in the widespread revision of constitutions that is still underway.

Subsequent Vatican documents have, however, gone in a steadily contrary direction. *Venite Seorsum* (1969) (Flannery 1, pp. 656–75) on the enclosure of contemplative nuns, *Evangelica Testificatio* (1971) (Flannery 1, pp. 680–706) of Paul VI on renewal, *Mutuae Relationes* (1978) (Flannery 2, pp. 209–43) on relations between religious and bishops, and *Essential Elements in Church Teaching on Religious Life* (1983) (*Origins*, 1983, pp. 133–42), as well as the section on religious life of the 1983 *Code of Canon Law* (Part II, 573–746), have all witnessed to a gradual but steady retrenchment of even the moderate openness of the Council.

During the same period of time, roughly 1965–85, a drastic decline in numbers of religious occurred throughout the Western world, although some increase was occurring elsewhere. In the United States, which had experienced an unprecedented increase in religious vocations in the decade before the Council, the number of religious brothers declined from 12,271 to 7,429 and the number of sisters from 179,954 and 113,658. The decline was the result of far fewer entrances and a steep increase in departures, especially of younger religious. Congregations found themselves with depleted ranks and a rapidly rising median age, which has precipitated not only crises in the ministerial involvements of institutes, but serious financial problems as well.

THE MAJOR CONTRIBUTIONS OF *PERFECTAE CARITATIS*

Despite its very real limitations, *Perfectae Caritatis* did make significant contributions to a renewal of religious life already underway at the time of the Council. First, by defining renewal in terms of a 'return to the sources' (*PC* 2), namely, Scripture and Church tradition as well as the founding inspiration and sound traditions of the institute, the decree directed the attention of religious to resources that enjoyed both temporal and theological priority over the narrow ascetical–juridical understanding of religious life that had constrained it for centuries. At the same time by insisting that an 'adaptation to the changed conditions of our times' must complement a return to the sources, the decree opened the way for a genuine dialogue between religious life and the contemporary world.

Second, the decree articulated five principles that were to guide renewal:

1 The gospel is the ultimate norm of religious life.

2 The charismatic diversity of religious orders (greatly obscured by the *Code* of 1917) is to be enhanced by a return to the charism of the founder.

3 Institutes should be fully integrated into the Church's renewal and mission.

4 Religious must be equipped to interact prophetically with the contemporary world.

5 Religious life is primarily ordered to the following of Christ.

These principles have been so vigorously embraced by the more progressive orders that the Vatican has felt impelled to engage in increasingly repressive efforts at 'restoration', resulting in escalating tensions between religious and the Congregation for Religious and Secular Institutes in Rome.

Third, certain themes that could have appeared minor in the decree have become major focuses in the renewal efforts, especially of women. Subsequently, the essentially egalitarian and communitarian nature of religious life that had been obscured since the Middle Ages by the pan-hierarchicalism of society and Church re-emerged in the directives to abolish class distinctions among members (*PC* 15) and to involve all members of the community in the renewal process (*PC* 4), and in the significant omission by the Council of reference to the Tridentine teaching on the superiority of the religious state to marriage. The somewhat hesitant recognition that the apostolate of active orders is intrinsic to their form of religious life (*PC* 8), and that a cloistered lifestyle is incompatible with full dedication to apostolic work (*PC* 16), has galvanized a radical demonasticizing of these orders as well as a wide diversification in ministries. Finally, the encouragement given to conferences of major superiors has strengthened the leadership of religious in the local churches and facilitated co-operation among religious leaders of different nations (*PC* 23).

CHALLENGES FACING RELIGIOUS LIFE IN THE 1990S

The renewal of religious life that has taken place in the twenty-five years since Vatican II has been deep and authentic. However, as must now be clear, it has not been free of problems both theoretical and practical. Whether the Council fathers intended it or not, the decree signalled the beginning of a vast rethinking of the theology of religious life. The understanding of this life as an ascetical state constituted by the assumption of supererogatory obligations through the profession of juridically defined vows of poverty, chastity and obedience has given way to a predominantly theological and spiritual understanding of religious life as a particular (though not superior) way of actualizing one's baptismal commitment to follow Christ in his self-gift to God and to humanity. Consecrated celibacy, freely chosen for the sake of the reign of God and lived in community and mission, has emerged as the defining characteristic of this state. Poverty tends to be understood less as a collection of acts of personal self-denial and more as solidarity with and responsiveness to the poor of the world. Obedience is being reinterpreted in the context of gospel freedom as a commitment to discern and follow the will of God in a community

159

of equal disciples, rather than as a relation of subjection to superiors in a hierarchical power structure (Lozano, 1980, pp. 142–96, 221–53; Schneiders, 1986, pp. 87–190). The final point of religious life is seen especially in the freedom it engenders to be creatively marginal to normal society in order to challenge its defects and serve at the most critical points where truth and love are currently at stake, thus functioning as an eschatological sign of the Reign of God.

This radical reinterpretation of the religious life demands entirely new structures and procedures which have had to develop from courageous and sometimes ambiguous experimentation. These new understandings and their appropriate institutional embodiments have been articulated in revised constitutions, whose egalitarian and participative structures and procedures CRIS has been increasingly unwilling to approve – resulting in tension, growing frustration, and even hostility, on the part of many religious. In this area of Church life more than almost any other, a relatively radical attempt to implement conciliar insights has been, since the early 1970s, in continual struggle with a Roman resolve to limit, institutionalize and control all such implementation.

A potentially rich but challenging diversity in religious life has emerged in the context of the evolution of the world Church. Religious life is no longer a monolithic, basically European, cultural phenomenon. In Latin America, where vocations are numerous, religious life is being redefined in the context and categories of liberation theology (see Cussiánovich, 1979; Azevedo, 1988). In Soviet bloc countries, where religious have been driven underground by persecution or confined to those ministries viewed by the government as 'useless' to society, repression has led to both theological conservatism and practical heroism. In the young Churches of Africa and the Far East the challenge of inculturation is enormous. Local native congregations, usually founded by European-trained bishops, are often reincarnations of pre-conciliar continental religious life, while the more creative efforts at inculturation are being made by international orders whose governmental centres are elsewhere. Some international missionary societies may soon have a majority of their younger members from Asia and Africa. Meanwhile, the United States has assumed the leadership position in first world renewal, while European religious life has waned.

In short, diverse Churches in differing parts of the world are endeavouring to develop their own versions of religious life, even though the Vatican continues to try to define and control it in universally applicable categories.

Finally, mention must be made of the impact of the world-wide women's movement on religious life, which includes at least three times more women than men (approximately 700,000 women to 230,000 men, of whom the majority are clerics (*Statistical Yearbook of the Church*, 1985)). While the movement by women for liberation from all forms of discrimination and oppression and towards full equality in family, society and Church has affected different countries and cultures in varying degrees and diverse ways, women religious have been in the forefront of the movement in most countries, and especially in North America. Feminist analysis, which has led to a repudiation of patriarchal ideology and male domination, has made women religious particularly sensitive to the Vatican's claims to ultimate power over them and to its efforts to curtail their self-determination. Incidents of public confrontation have increased in number and seriousness, while private struggles over constitutions have been protracted and painful. Increasingly, congregations, especially those of women, are raising the question of whether they are willing to pay the price of subjection to male authority for the maintenance of canonical status as religious, while non-canonical communities of members with private vows are multiplying. The latter may well be the first representatives of a new form of religious life which will eventually be recognized as theologically, if not juridically, equivalent to current canonical forms.

Religious life at the end of the twentieth century is in crisis, that is to say, in a situation of ultimate risk and great opportunity. Outside the third world, orders are no longer receiving large numbers of candidates, but those who come tend to be more mature personally and motivationally and more stable in their commitments. Most congregations can no longer offer potential members instant identity, high social and ecclesiastical status, financial security, steady employment and freedom from personal responsibility. On the other hand, they can offer a challenging invitation to follow Christ in evangelical solidarity with the poor and in the company of companions who, in response to a personal call to consecrated celibacy, are committed to the evangelical transformation of the world through prophetic witness and action. Religious life itself is being transformed by the pressures of theological redefinition, radical spiritual renewal and cultural confrontation. As it has done in every new era of the Church's history, it will undoubtedly emerge from the challenges of the post-conciliar period alive and true to its deepest identity but probably very different in form.

8K Religious Life (*Perfectae Caritatis*): Bibliography

Azevedo, M. (1988) *Vocation for Mission: The Challenge of Religious Life Today*, trans. J. W. Diercksmeier. New York, Mahwah, Paulist Press.

Cussiánovich, A. (1979) *Religious Life and the Poor: Liberation Theology Perspectives*, trans J. Drury. Maryknoll, New York, Orbis Books. An attempt to rethink religious life in liberationist categories.

Kolmer, E. (1984) *Religious Women in the United States: A Survey of the Influential Literature from 1950–1983*. Wilmington, Michael Glazier.

Lozano, J. M. (1980) *Discipleship: Towards an Understanding of Religious Life*. Chicago, Claret Center for Resources in Spirituality.

Religious Institutes, Secular Institutes, Societies of the Apostolic Life: A Handbook on Canons 573–746 (1985) ed. J. Hite, S. Holland, D. Ward. Published under the auspices of the Canon Law Society of America, Collegeville, MN, Liturgical Press. The best commentary available on the new *Code*'s provisions.

Religious Life in the U.S. Church: The New Dialogue (1984) ed. R. J. Daly, M. J. Buckley, M. A. Donovan, C. E. Fitzgerald, J. W. Padberg. New York/Ramsey, New Jersey, Paulist Press. Collected papers of a conference in religious life responding to the pope's establishment in 1983 of a special commission, under the

161

leadership of Archbishop John Quinn as pontifical delegate, to study the decline of religious vocations in the United States.

Schneiders, S. M. (1986) *New Wineskins: Re-imagining Religious Life Today*. New York, Paulist Press.

Solesmes, (Benedictine Monks of) eds. (1967) *The State of Perfection*. Boston, St Paul Publications.

Solesmes, (Benedictine Monks of) (1983) 'Essential Elements in Church Teaching on Religious Life', *Origins*, Vol. 13, 7 July, pp. 133–42.

Who Are My Brothers? Cleric–Lay Relationships in Men's Religious Communities. (1988) ed. P. Armstrong. New York, Alba House. A study of the relationships experienced between clerical and lay religious in men's congregations in the United States, sponsored by the Conference of Major Superiors of Men. May be best resource on brothers available at present time.

8L Missionary Activity (*Ad Gentes*)

AYLWARD SHORTER

Ad Gentes is a practical document arising from the desire of the missionary bishops for a statement concerning the evangelization of the third world and the obligation of the dioceses of Europe and America to support it with finance and personnel. As such, the document is addressed to Western Christians in an effort to convince them that foreign missionary work is a vital function of the Church. The Preparatory Commission for the Missions was dominated by curialists and academics and had strong ties to the congregation of Propaganda Fide, the central organ for missionary co-ordination in the Church. The schemata produced by this commission were legalistic, and many were withdrawn and improved upon in other documents of the Council. What remained was assigned for redrafting to the Council's Missionary Commission, in which missionary and Latin American bishops, strongly critical of Propaganda Fide, had a powerful voice.

Opinions in this commision were so divergent that no satisfactory draft was forthcoming. During the third session of the Council it was announced that the draft would be reduced to thirteen propositions. These were subsequently put to the fathers in the presence of Paul VI, who gave the shortened proposals his support. In spite of the papal intervention, the propositions were flatly rejected in the subsequent debate, which included notable speeches by Cardinal Frings and Bishop Donal Lamont of Zimbabwe, who compared the meagre proposals to the dry bones of Ezekiel's prophecy (Stacpoole, 1985, pp. 270–82; Vorgrimler 4, pp. 88–98; O'Connell, 1986, pp, 180–3).

Joseph Schütte, superior general of the Society of the Divine Word, presided over a new editorial committee which strove to produce an acceptable document in the short time between the third and final sessions of the Council. The desires and suggestions of the fathers were taken into account, and the committee benefited from the discussion of other conciliar documents, notably the Dogmatic and Pastoral Constitutions on the Church, *Lumen Gentium* and *Gaudium et Spes*. The haste with which the new missionary decree was put together gave it a verbose, repetitious style of dubious Latinity, but the content was to the liking of the Council fathers, who accorded it the highest number of votes of all the Vatican II decrees in the last days of the final session (Vorgrimler 4, pp. 100–11; O'Connell, 1986, p. 184).

The decree comprises six chapters. The first contains doctrinal principles which trace the Church's missionary activity back to the Trinitarian processions, the incarnation and Pentecost. Missionary activity is an 'epiphany' of God (*AG* 8). It is also directed towards the fulfilment of human nature and its aspirations. The Church on earth is by its very nature missionary (*AG* 2), which is to say that an active and expansive evangelization is the essential mark of the Church. This is the Church's mission which contains nevertheless three specialist activities: pastoral work among the faithful, the missionary evangelization of the nations, and the fostering of ecumenism among separated Christians. Specialized missionary evangelization is directed towards foreign

163

missions, where its goal is to implant the Church among the different human groupings or cultures. The thinking seems to be that the de-christianized countries of the West are not analogous to missions, because the Church is already implanted among them. On this definition, their recovery belongs to the pastoral care of the (lapsed) faithful.

The second chapter deals with missionary work in detail. It accepts the empirical fact of cultural pluralism (*AG* 10) and, using the dynamic image of St Justin Martyr, 'seeds of the word', it expresses the belief that God is already secretly at work in these religions and traditions (*AG* 11). Missionary evangelization consists in a 'truly human dialogue' with the adepts of these cultures. Having said that, however, it appears that the newly implanted churches are to reproduce faithfully the model of the Church in the West. Having carried out primary evangelization or conversion work, the missionary must 'raise up communities of the faithful' (*AG* 15) and ensure that they are self-supporting. Priestly vocations must be fostered, and indigenous priests trained according to the general requirements of the Church. Catechists are singled out for special praise as auxiliaries of the priest and are recommended for ordination to the permanent diaconate (*AG* 16–17), but there is no mention of a celibate diaconate for the missions.

The third chapter is entirely devoted to the concept of the 'particular church' in mission areas, thereby showing that the decree has accepted the ecclesiological revolution of *Lumen Gentium* and *Gaudium et Spes*. The particular church is recognized as the basis for ecclesial diversity in unity, and this multiplicity is seen as being divinely willed. Most of the chapter, however, deals with the growth and position of what are somewhat invidiously called 'young churches'. These are churches recently implanted in the poorer parts of the world which still suffer from a lack of priests and material resources. Comparable to the young churches are those 'which, although long established, are in a state of decline or weakness'. This presumably refers to the churches of Latin America which still require the help of foreign missionaries. Although insufficient in number, the indigenous clergy of all these churches are exhorted to become missionaries themselves in abandoned areas of their own or other dioceses (*AG* 19–20).

The high point of the chapter, and indeed of the whole decree, is reached in the final paragraph (*AG* 22), where the picture is painted of a particular church as a local incarnation of Christianity carrying out a profound adaptation in every sphere of Christian life. These include theology, catechetics, liturgy and canonical legislation (*AG* 19–22). Episcopal conferences are to come together to form regional associations and to find common solutions.

The fourth chapter deals with the discernment of the missionary vocation as a life-long charism exercised under a mandate from the Church, and with the formation of the missionary. This training is directed principally towards primary evangelization and pioneer tasks, and must be given also to temporary missionaries. It is to include an acquaintance with the sciences of culture and religions. The last paragraph of the chapter (*AG* 27) deals with missionary societies and their changed situation after the demise of the *ius commissionis*, under which whole dioceses were placed in their charge. Now their members are to be inserted into the particular church under its own indigenous pastors.

The fifth chapter is concerned with missionary organization. Diocesan bishops have a duty to care for the evangelization of the whole world and not just their own dioceses. Propaganda Fide is to be reorganized in such a way that all missionary dioceses, without exception, are placed under its care, and there is a strong and active participation by missionary bishops in its workings. Agreements are to be drawn up between missionary societies and local ordinaries, and the former are to set up their own conferences to undertake common projects, in particular the setting up of missiological, pastoral and scientific institutes.

The final chapter of the decree deals with missionary collaboration. This is the duty of every Christian in virtue of the sacraments of baptism, confirmation and the Eucharist. Individuals, parishes and dioceses have an obligation to support the Church's missionary work. Bishops must help solve the shortage of priests in missionary countries, and episcopal conferences are to set up their own organs of collaboration. Even missionary dioceses are to make a contribution to the pontifical mission aid societies. The chapter contains one of the few mentions of lay missionaries in the entire decree. In its penultimate paragraph (*AG* 41) there is a call for foreign lay missionaries to promote the various forms of apostolate and to help in education, administration and development.

In the document known as *Ecclesiae Sanctae* issued by Paul VI in 1966, norms were laid down for the implementation of the missionary decree. These are contained in twenty-four paragraphs (*Ecclesiae Sanctae*, ch. 3; Flannery 1, pp. 857–62). Mission theology was to be an essential feature in the curriculum of all seminaries. Missionary vocations were to be promoted. Dioceses and parishes were to give material support to the missions and each episcopal conference was to set up its own missionary commission. Propaganda Fide was to be reorganized to allow twenty-four representatives, mainly from missionary dioceses and societies, to take part in its deliberations. This reform was also spelt out in *Regimini Ecclesiae Universae*, one of the documents reorganizing the Roman curia (see Flannery 1, pp. 1017–18 and *AAS* vol. 59 of 1967, pp. 885–928). Contracts were to be drawn up between missionary societies and the local ordinaries of missionary dioceses. The latter were required to set up pastoral Councils and eventually to hold a diocesan synod. Provision was also made for associations of missionary and religious superiors, for the setting up of scientific and pastoral institutes, and for the pastoral care of immigrants in Western countries.

The most important sections, however, dealt with the duties of regional associations of episcopal conferences. Their main task was to establish the Church's presence among the people of the region. They were to set up study groups to examine the local traditions, conduct a theological reflection on local culture, and discuss the adaptation of evangelization, worship, religious life and ecclesiastical legislation. This was also to be the work of higher pastoral institutes. Other duties included the reform of seminary studies and the redistribution of personnel.

A final paragraph of Chapter III of *Ecclesiae Sanctae* spoke of lay missionaries and the need to ensure their seriousness, security and support.

Although *Ad Gentes* is in may ways a positive and practical document, it contains internal conflicts and contradictions which are more clearly seen in the changed circumstances of the Church today. Theologically, its affirmation of the missionary character of the Church is important, but in other respects its theology is often deficient. Its Christology is firmly a 'Christology from above'. Much more emphasis is placed upon the incarnation than upon the paschal mystery as the source and model of missionary activity. The disadvantages of an incarnation model have led missiologists to adopt the theologically neutral concept of 'inculturation' (Shorter, 1988, ch. 6).

Although the fathers of Vatican II were sensitive to the growing critique of missionaries in an era of decolonization and presented the Church's missionary work as manifesting the fulfilment of human aspirations, they did not elaborate a concept of integral human development of the kind found in Paul VI's encyclical *Populorum Progressio* (14). In the aftermath of decolonization, socioeconomic development superseded missionary activity in the popular mind, but the missionary decree does not offer any profound explanation of the relationship between the two.

The document also contains a fundamental conflict between two opposing ideas of mission, one Christocentric and kerygmatic, the other ecclesiocentric and institutional. The first concept is ascribed chiefly to the whole Church as missionary. The second is applied to the specialized missionary activity of implanting the Church among the nations. This leads the authors of the decree into further difficulties. Having distinguished between missionary activity and pastoral activity (to say nothing of ecumenism), and having described missionary activity as being concerned with primary evangelization and pioneering tasks, the decree violates its own definition in chapter II by presenting a picture of missionary work that is almost entirely one of ordinary pastoral care. Later on, in chapter IV, missionary training is oriented towards the original definition. It is clear that the so-called specializations are not water-tight categories. Indeed, there is talk at the present time about 'the missionary second breath', in which missionaries help to deepen the faith of Christians and the spirituality of clergy and religious in recently founded churches through ordinary pastoral activity. Moreover, although the missionary vocation is identified as a distinct, lifelong charism, we find the document calling upon diocesan priests to become missionaries in their own country, or even to serve temporarily as missionaries abroad.

The dubious distinction between pastoral and missionary work is made to coincide with self-sustaining, mature churches on the one hand and non-self-sustaining or 'young' churches and churches 'in a state of decline or weakness' on the other. The young or declining churches are to be found in the 'poorer parts of the world'. It is clear that the picture conveyed by the decree is of a mature, sending-Church in Europe and America, with adequate structures and personnel, evangelizing the third world, where churches are lacking in structures, personnel and material resources.

At the end of the 1980s this picture of the Church is no longer true. The churches of the West would mostly qualify as churches in a state of decline or weakness. There has been a slump, not only in missionary vocations, but an acute shortage of diocesan personnel in Europe and America. Even if resignations have diminished and the number of vocations has begun again to rise in some places, the clergy are insufficient. It is also possible that assigning the recovery of dechristianized areas of the West to the sphere of pastoral care has retarded Western re-evangelization (see O'Connell, 1986, p. 185). The missionary decree spoke of the growing problem of immigrants in the West. This was the germ of a multiculturalism which today calls for the attention of missionary specialization.

In contrast to Europe and America, priestly and religious vocations are on the increase in many third world countries, especially in India and Africa. The idea of local diocesan priests carrying out missionary work in their own or neighbouring countries has been overtaken by the recruitment of third world members of the established missionary societies, a topic that was too controversial to be mentioned when *Ad Gentes* was written. Today there are missionaries from southern India, Mexico and Brazil in East Africa, East African missionaries in Colombia and Nigeria, and Vietnamese and Korean missionaries in Australia. There are even occasional assignments of third world missionaries to Europe and America. In most of the long-established missionary societies, the majority of students today come from the third world. Moreover, many churches in the third world now have their own national or regional missionary societies. If one thing is now clear, it is that the churches of the world cannot be divided into 'sending' and 'receiving' churches. They are not only conducting their own evangelization, but reaching out to others on every side.

This is not, of course, to say that the churches of the third world will ever have a sufficient clergy themselves. Vocations can never keep pace with the expansion of church membership. Ever since the introduction of the seminary system by the Council of Trent, no third world church has had, or is likely to have, sufficient priests. It is, in fact, the prevailing system of selection and training of priests that keeps the third world dependent on foreign missionaries. In spite of the decree's suggestion of ordaining some catechists to the diaconate, comparatively few third world churches have experimented with permanent deacons. Such a step was considered pastorally unnecessary and potentially subversive of the local clergy. It was unfortunate, to say the least, for the missionary decree to make priestly numbers a major criterion of ecclesial maturity, and therefore of missionary activity, to say nothing of wealth *vis à vis* poverty.

The ecclesiological and cultural aspects of the document are probably the ones that have best stood the test of time. The Synods on evangelization in 1974 and catechesis in 1977 built on the picture of the dialogue with culture presented by *Ad Gentes*. Paul VI, in *Evangelii Nuntiandi* and John Paul II, in *Catechesi Tradendae*, the post-Synodal documents, describe a communion of culturally diverse particular churches enriching one another and giving new expression to the gospel through 'inculturation' (*Evangelii Nuntiandi* 63; *Catechesi Tradendae* 53; see Flannery 2, pp. 711–61, 762–814). All of them, however, continue unrealistically to imply a distinction between faith and culture, and to ignore the massive obstacle to a truly multicultural Church posed by monoculturally biased structures of universal communion. It is a pity that the 1983 *Code of Canon Law* has precluded the cultural adaptation of canonical legislation envisaged by *Ad Gentes* (19) and *Ecclesiae Sanctae* (18).

The reform of Propaganda Fide, the setting up of national missionary commissions, the creation of associations of religious and missionary superiors, and the establishment of *consortia* for missionary training are all practical benefits today that derive from the missionary decree. Regional and even continental, episcopal associations have also been able to achieve a great deal, particularly through the scientific and pastoral institutes they have sponsored. However, the sustained study of traditional religion and culture, envisaged by *Ecclesiae Sanctae* (18), has not been achieved. Without it, and without freedom of experimentation, true inculturation is impossible.

Ad Gentes could not foresee many of the trends that are present in the Church today, the spread of urban culture, for example, or the popular movement for building basic Christian communities. It never defined the shape of the 'communities' of the faithful that were to be raised up by the missionary (*AG* 15). It is in these basic communities that the tension between a hierarchically and clerically defined mission on the one hand, and a dynamic, inculturated evangelization, on the other, is most acutely felt. It is with these communities, as much as with the current multi-directional missionary movement, that the realization of a multicultural Church must lie.

8L Missionary Activity (*Ad Gentes*): Bibliography

Burrows, W.R. (1986) 'Decree on the Church's Missionary Activity', in T.E. O'Connell, ed., *Vatican II and Its Documents*. Wilmington, Delaware, Michael Glazier, pp. 180–196.

Hickey, R. (1982) *Modern Missionary Documents and Africa*. Dublin, Dominican Publications.

Lamont, D. (1985) '*Ad Gentes*: A Missionary Bishop Remembers', Stacpoole, pp. 270–82.

Shorter, A. (1972) *Theology of Mission*. Cork, Mercier Press, and Notre Dame Indiana, Fides Press.

Shorter, A. (1988) *Toward a Theology of Inculturation*. London, Geoffrey Chapman; New York, Orbis Books.

8M The Media (*Inter Mirifica*)

MICHAEL E. WILLIAMS

The Decree on the Instruments of Social Communication (*Inter Mirifica*) was one of the first documents to be approved by the Council, but this was for reasons of convenience rather than urgency. Its discussion was tabled to fill a gap between other deliberations that were deemed to be of greater theological significance. The first chapter calls attention to the moral issues inherent in communications but has nothing very original to say, confining itself to the need to take into account the demands of truth, justice and charity in all information processes; the primacy of the objective moral order if there is conflict between morality and art; and the need for users of the media to be discriminating in their choice of reading, listening and viewing and to take note of judgements made by competent Church authority. Parents are reminded of their duty towards children in this regard. There is a special word to those who make and transmit information. They should be aware of their responsibilities towards the common good, while the civil authority is urged to strike a balance between the freedom of the press and the safeguarding of public morality.

The second and final chapter deals with pastoral activity and takes the form of an exhortation to faithful Church members to establish and support a Catholic press and to promote good films, radio and television. It acknowledges the need for priests, religious and laity to be trained in the skills and use of these new instruments. It recognizes the enormous financial expenditure involved in such activity and invites the wealthier members of the Church to give willingly of their resources and talents.

A large number of the Council fathers felt strongly that the document was inadequate in doctrine and excessively moralistic in tone, and that it was out of touch with those who work in the media since most of these are not acting as mandated or commissioned by the Church. Cardinal Heenan declared it 'unworthy of the Council'. The document's weakness was recognized to some extent in the decree itself, since paragraph 23 announced that a new Pontifical Commission for the Means of Social Communication would enlist the help of experts from different countries to prepare a Pastoral Instruction setting out basic doctrinal principles and general guidelines. This proved to be a much more difficult task than had been expected because of the rapid development in the media themselves and because of the varied circumstances under which they operate in different parts of the world.

The Pastoral Instruction *Communio et Progressio* was promulgated in 1971. It adopts a less narrow approach, taking into account other Council documents, especially *Gaudium et Spes*, *Ad Gentes*, *Unitatis Redintegratio* and *Dignitatis Humanae*. It makes some useful comments. It concedes that it is naïve to blame the media for declining moral standards. It recognizes that censorship should only be a last resort. It stresses the need for a two-way flow of information within the Church, from above and from below. But there is very little theological content, and until this is supplied its recommendations will not be taken to heart. Since 1971 there have been many occasions where leading churchmen have adopted a far from open attitude to the world press, and within the Church there has not always been that free flow of information that is desirable, and indeed necessary, from the nature of the Church itself. Fear and a craving for secrecy has impeded the desire for further consultation of the laity, and the lack of a communications policy during every single synod has had unfortunate consequences. There is room for a study of communications systems within the organization and their relationship to the exercise of power in the Church.

The implementation at the local level of the pastoral directives of the second chapter of *Inter Mirifica* has varied depending on the available resources. It is not possible to set up everywhere a Catholic daily press, an independent radio or television station, and it is by no means obvious that these are even desirable if they mean that the Catholic voice will be isolated, crying in the wilderness and not addressing the world from the world.

Diocesan and regional offices for the press, radio, television and cinema have been established in many places. These are not always a direct result of the Council, and are of varying strengths and influence. At the international level, before the Council there existed Catholic bodies concerned with radio and television (UNDA), cinema (OCIC) and press (UCIP). These have continued their work heartened by growing official awareness and approval.

Communication studies have developed rapidly since the 1960s and the Centre for the Study of Communications and Culture set up in London in 1977 has recorded and monitored recent research trends and made them available to the Church. There has been collaboration with the (Protestant) World Association of Christian Communications and, since the 1980s, the spread of video recording and satellite television has accentuated the problems raised at the Council. These developments have served to emphasize the increasing demands on the individual conscience, since these new means are not easily controllable by either Church or state. This underlines the need for media education to enable the public to discriminate and judge what values are consonant with those of the gospel, without having to rely solely on the pronouncements (not always well-informed) of those in authority.

For the Christian, media education will involve theology: a theology of creation and fall that does not think that human nature has been entirely corrupted by sin; a theology of the Church and revelation that is attentive to the word of God not only in the pulpit but in the presence of his Spirit in the world; a theology that is aware that the word of God in the Scriptures comes to us in a wealth of literary forms, similitudes and images, and that the message can only be discovered in and through the medium.

8M The Media (*Inter Mirifica*): Bibliography

'Audiovisuals and Evangelisation' (1977) *Lumen Vitae* (whole issue), vol. 33, no. 2.
Babin, P. (1973) *Catechesis in the Audio Visual Civilisation*. Rome, Multimedia International.

Consejo Episcopal Latinoamericano (CELAM) Departamento de Comunicacion Social (DECOS) (1979) *Evangelizacíon y Comunicacion Social en America Latina.* Bogota, Ediciones Paulinas.

McDonnell, J. M., (ed.) (1982) *Theology and Communication: A Bibliography.* London, Centre for the Study of Communication and Culture.

Pontifical Commission for the Means of Social Communication (1976) *Pastoral Instruction for the Application of the Decree of the Second Vatican Ecumenical Council on the Means of Social Communication (Communio et Progressio).* London, Catholic Truth Society.

8N   Education (*Gravissimum Educationis*)

V. ALAN McCLELLAND

Firmly based upon the encyclical *Divini Illius Magistri* of Pius XI (1929), the Council's Declaration on Christian Education (*Gravissimum Educationis*), contained no surprises. Concerned with establishing a broad philosophical and theological grounding for the Church's involvement in education, the document leaves the more specific issues to post-conciliar commissions and local episcopal conferences. Proceeding from the premiss that the Church's mission embraces a concern for the temporal as well as spiritual welfare of humanity, the document asserts the inalienable right to an education, the fundamental aim of which is the forming of persons in the light of their divine destiny.

The key concept identified by the Council as lying at the heart of the educative process is that of wholeness, coupled with a realization of human integrity and envigorated by a proper sense of community and mission. An education structured upon an appreciation of wholeness ensures that physical, spiritual, moral and intellectual advances take place within an understanding of harmony and relationship, a totality of human development resting securely upon the support provided by family, Church, school and society. Parents and teachers are co-operative agents in ensuring the vitality of the educative process and, to that end, parents must enjoy the fullest liberty in choice of school.

The Church's duty is to provide facilities for Christian education, whether in its confessional schools or by the witness of its teachers employed in a secular educational system. In the latter case, too, it must ensure adequate teaching in Christian doctrine is available for children unable to attend a Catholic school. The Catholic school itself must witness to a living community of faith and love in which the liberty and charity of the gospel is exemplified. *Gravissimum Educationis* makes brief reference to the need for the Church to be involved in the provision of further and higher education, including work for special educational needs, teacher training and university-level study. Joint episcopal action is urged in order that Catholic residences may be established, where appropriate, in non-Catholic universities.

This somewhat uninspiring and, in places, almost platitudinous document has been enriched over the ensuing twenty-five years by four major post-conciliar pronouncements, each expanding upon the themes of wholeness, community, and sense of mission. The themes are examined from the standpoints of catechesis, schools, teachers and, in 1988, the vitality of religious formation.

In 1971 the Sacred Congregation for the Clergy issued a *General Catechetical Directory* following consultation with a number of episcopal conferences and based upon the work of a commission made up of catechetical experts. Although specifically designed for the guidance of bishops and catechetical specialists, the Directory had a deep significance for Catholic schools. Starting from the somewhat jejune premiss that if the Christian faith was to take root in various cultures and changing social conditions it must devise new modes of expression, the Directory ensured the opening of a veritable Pandora's box of catechetical experimentation.

Unwittingly this led to a widening of the gulf between parents and schools, in that the religious education of the former had ill-prepared them for relating to the extensive new presentations of the faith that were to permeate the schools. In a certain sense this foreseeable development weakened the philosophical basis of *Gravissimum Educationis*. The widening divide found expression in England in the enforced closure of the national catechetical centre established in the aftermath of the Council at Corpus Christi College, London. In 1971 Cardinal Heenan informed Cardinal Wright of the Sacred Congregation of the Clergy that he shared the latter's feelings 'that some of our catechists are teaching a theology of their own' and that 'the great danger is that the faithful will be led to believe that there is no dogmatic theology left and that everything is a matter of free speculation' (Westminster Diocesan Archives, letter dated 13 December 1971).

Two important documents dealing with schools and teachers were issued in Rome in 1977 and 1982 respectively by the Sacred Congregation for Catholic Education. The first of these, *Catholic Schools*, defined the school as 'a privileged place in which, through a living encounter with a cultural inheritance, integral formation occurs' (Flannery 2, p. 26). The task of the school is to achieve a synthesis of culture and faith. This it does by helping the young to overcome selfish individualism, discover a sense of community, and effect principled interaction with the world at large. The weakness of the Catholic school, however, has often been its inability to establish a confident internal polity that eschews that element of divisiveness inherent in the attempt to develop practices operating in secular schools: aggressive competition, the premium placed upon worldly success; the use of selfish rewards and retaliatory punishments, the need for outward conformity in social attitudes. The prerequisite of the life of religion is liberation from self, and this can only be achieved within a *métier* of freedom and openness, one that does not entice suffocation by a Catholic school attempting in some essential aspects of its vision to conform to the secular practices of neighbouring schools. In the 1982 document, *Lay Catholics in Schools: Witnesses to Faith*, an attempt is made to teach this fundamental lesson by emphasizing the centrality of personal example and Christian dedication on the part of the Catholic teacher. The point is reinforced, too, in the fourth important post-conciliar document on education, *The Religious Dimension of Education in a Catholic School*, issued by the Sacred Congregation for Catholic Education in 1988, where the communitarian role is emphasized. The Catholic school cannot simply be an educational centre; it must be a place of authentic apostolate and pastoral action reaching out into the wider community, and adding essential Christian witness to the cultivation of traditional civic virtues. The catechetical directives of the post-conciliar period may find a temporarily definitive form in the 'Universal Catechism' due to be presented to the 1990 Synod of Bishops.

The main contribution of the Second Vatican Council to education was, perhaps, anticipated in a speech of the late Archbishop of Liverpool, George Andrew Beck, in 1963. He emphasized that the continuing role of Catholic involvement in education was not to support a sort of ghetto subculture, but to ensure that the full richness of faith was brought to bear upon the secularized and desacralized world it had perforce to encounter (see *The Catholic Herald*, 5 July 1963).

8N Education (*Gravissimum Educationis*): Bibliography

Brothers, J. B. (1964) *Church and School: A Study of the Impact of Education on Religion*. Liverpool, Liverpool University Press.

Greeley, A. M., McCready, W. C., and McCourt, K. (1976) *Catholic Schools in a Declining Church*. Kansas City, Sheed & Ward.

Jebb, P., ed. (1968) *Religious Education: Drift or Decision?* London, Darton, Longman and Todd.

McClelland, V. A., ed. (1988) *Christian Education in a Pluralist Society*. London, Routledge.

Nichols, K. F., ed. (1979) *Orientations: Six Essays on Theology and Education*. Slough, St Paul Publications.

Tucker, B., ed. (1968) *Catholic Education in a Secular Society*. London, Sheed & Ward.

9

INSTITUTIONAL RENEWAL

9A The Curia

PETER HEBBLETHWAITE

On the last day of the Council, 8 December 1965, an observer remarked: 'The end of the Council is its real beginning – the phase of documents is over, the era of implementation begins.' With the Council fathers back in their dioceses, however, much of this work of 'implementation' would fall on the Roman curia. How well did it cope?

The Roman curia has usually been considered as a kind of extension of the papal secretariat. It always acted 'in the name of higher authority'. Even if this did not give it the immunity from scrutiny and attack it frequently claimed, it meant that in practice its reform depended on the pope personally.

Since the pope in question was Paul VI, this was fortunate. Thirty years' work in the Secretariat of State meant that he knew the problems of the curia intimately; he had recognized the dangers of the 'Italianization' of the curia as long ago as 1943; in his 1960 *vota* he urged that patriarchs, metropolitans and bishops should be shown greater consideration by the curia (*Discorsi e scritti sul Concilio*, Brescia, 1983, p. 39). But, most of all, his speech as pope, on 21 September 1963, was a commitment to radical reform: 'People everywhere are watching Catholic Rome, the Roman Pontificate, the Roman Curia. The duty of being authentically Christian is especially binding here. We would not remind you of this duty if we did not remind ourselves of it everyday' (XR 2, p. 345). No modern pope had used such language before.

So *Christus Dominus* was modesty itself when it expressed 'a strong desire that these departments [i.e. of the Roman curia] . . . be reorganized and better adapted to the needs of the times, and of various regions and rites' (*CD* 9). This was remarkably unspecific. The next section, however, called for an 'internationalization' of the curia (and the Vatican diplomatic service), the involvement of diocesan bishops in the work of curial departments, and urged them to 'give a greater hearing to laymen who are outstanding for their knowledge, virtue and experience' (*CD* 11).

Christus Dominus was approved by massive majorities on 28 October 1965. The apostolic constitution *Regimini Ecclesiae Universae*, which responded to this part of it, was promulgated on 15 August 1967. This was a remarkably short time in which to accomplish so important a reform.

Even so, Paul VI could brook no delay. He had already anticipated some of the more urgent aspects of curial reform. The *motu proprio Integrae Servandae* of 7 December 1965, the crowded last-but-one day of the Council, changed the name of the Holy Office to the Congregation for the Doctrine of the Faith, and was intended to change its function. It abolished the *Index* of forbidden books, gave the accused the right to self-defence, and dropped the title 'general inquisitors' for cardinal members. Paul VI wanted to respond to the criticisms made by the Council, and give the 'progressives' some good news to take home at the end of the Council.

Reform of the Holy Office also provided the model for other reforms: 'modernizing' the curia would mean discarding outmoded defensive Counter Reformation attitudes and providing, it was hoped, a positive, relevant and helpful service for the collegial Church that emerged from the Council.

Pope John had founded the Secretariat for Christian Unity in 1960. In *Ecclesiam Suam* Paul VI described the 'concentric circles' that surrounded the Church of Rome, and devised Secretariats for Non-believers and Non-Christian Religions to deal with them. They formed the 'new curia' which, precisely because it had no traditions or precedents, was able to recruit more widely throughout the Catholic world. This put pressure – for the most part resisted – on the 'old curia'.

With the *motu proprio Catholicam Christi Ecclesiam* of 6 January 1967, Paul VI set up the Council of the Laity and the Pontifical Justice and Peace Commission. This was his response to *Christus Dominus*' desire to see competent laymen in the curia, and to proposals made by *Gaudium et Spes* for a body devoted to the problems of poverty in the world.

The *motu proprio Pro Comperto Sane*, of 6 August 1967, made diocesan bishops *de jure* members of all Roman dicasteries (departments). It is reasonable to deduce that this was done separately because the curia did not take kindly to it.

For Paul VI had laid down as a matter of principle that the reform of the curia should be largely self-reform. The result was that *Regimini Ecclesiae Universae* had a difficult gestation. The commission was made up of notably conservative cardinals: Francesco Roberti, André Jullien and Anselm Albareda, prefect of the Vatican Library since 1936. The last two died and were replaced by Oxford blue William Heard, and Efrem Forni. Possibly Paul VI chose such men on the grounds that if *they* could be induced to accept change, so too could the rest of the curia. There were arguments for a gradualist, department-by-department approach, but Paul VI presided in person over the later stages and insisted on a complete reform in a single document.

Regimini Ecclesiae Universae was an attempt to streamline and modernize the Roman curia. Tasks were reassigned to prevent rivalries, overlapping and demarcation disputes. Changes of name expressed new functions: thus Propaganda Fide became the Congregation for the Evangelization of Peoples. A severe blow was struck at the career structure that had made the old curia the refuge of entrenched and geriatric empire-builders: now appointments were for a five-year term; all prelates (including cardinals) had to tender their resignation at the age of 75; and all offices were to lapse on the death of a pope, thus leaving his successor a free hand. No one, in short, had the *right* to advancement in the curia. This, together with the introduction of the main modern languages, meant that there would be much more chance of 'internationalizing' the curia – a process that was already far advanced in the 'new' curia.

But the most decisive change in *Regimini Ecclesiae Universae* was contained in the innocent-seeming remark that all curial departments were juridically equal (no. 1, section 2). This meant a curbing of the power of the Holy Office, known for centuries as 'the *Supreme* Congregation'. Not only that, but in principle it placed the modern Secretariat for Christian Unity on an equal footing with the renamed Congregation for the Doctrine of the Faith.

More profoundly, it broke down false oppositions between the requirement of dialogue with other Christians and the legitimate concern for orthodoxy. The Congregation for the Doctrine of the Faith's declaration *Mysterium Ecclesiae* of 1973 illustrated the value of collaboration between the two departments, in that it recognized the time-conditioned nature of conciliar statements. Left to itself, the Congregation would have denounced Hans Küng's *Infallible?*. With the aid of the Secretariat, it was able to admit that the interpretation of conciliar statements involved a genuine question.

But none of this would have been possible were it not for another crucial provision of *Regimini Ecclesiae Universae*, which forms the centrepiece of Paul VI's reforms. All departments are juridically equal, but the Secretariat of State is assigned the task of overall co-ordination *'tum in cura universae ecclesiae, tum in rationibus cum Dicasteriis Romanis'* ('both in the pastoral care of the universal Church and in dealings with the Roman departments' 19, section 1). The Cardinal Secretary of State is made responsible for calling meetings of Prefects of dicasteries – a first embryo of 'cabinet' government (20, section 1). He is also responsible for seeing to it that the diocesan bishops who became full members of Roman Congregations should be involved 'in dealing with matters of greater importance, and matters of general principle' (2, section 2). This was intended to prevent the annual plenary sessions of the Congregations from being purely formal occasions when wool was pulled over the eyes of the visitors.

French theologian René Laurentin said of Paul VI's reform of the curia that it was 'the most surprising, boldest and most rigorously thought through achievement of his pontificate, his major historical decision, without which nothing else would have been possible' (Laurentin, 1984, pp. 569–70). By this reform Paul VI 'liberated the papacy' from the heavy downdrag of the curia. St Pius X's 1908 'restructuring' looked like timid tinkering by comparison. The Roman curia was largely the creation of the Franciscan pope, Sixtus V, in 1588, who needed an instrument to implement the Counter-Reformation. Paul VI earned the title of 'second founder of the curia' and forged an instrument to realize the implications of Vatican II.

But any bureaucracy – and the curia is a bureaucracy – is no better than the men (sexist language reflects the reality of the situation) who operate it. Paul VI waited until 1969 to replace 85-year-old Cardinal Amleto Cicognani as Secretary of State with a non-Italian, Jean Villot. The appointment of a Frenchman as Secretary of State sent shock-waves through the career-minded curia. Villot, who established a record by serving under three popes, was less 'political' than his predecessors, and made it his business to emphasize the links with episcopal conferences. Paul VI also put a non-Italian, the Croatian Franjo Seper, in charge of the Congregation for the Doctrine of the Faith (he had topped the poll in the 1967 elections for the Synod Theological Commission). A second Frenchman, Gabriel-Marie Garrone, presided over seminaries, while the American John J. Wright dealt with the clergy, and another American, Paul Casimir Marcinkus, presided disastrously (as it turned out) over Vatican finances.

The 'new curia' was even more in the hands of 'foreigners': Cardinal Franz König was president of the Secretariat for Non-believers without leaving Vienna, while Dutch Cardinal Johannes Willebrands for a time combined the Secretariat for Christian Unity with being archbishop of Utrecht. 'Internationalization' was making giant strides, and 'decentralization' was at least moving forward. In the long run this all helped to make a non-Italian pope thinkable.

None of this is contradicted – though it is qualified – by adding that in practice the reform of the curia and its day-by-day administration was in the hands of the *sostituto* (substitute), Giovanni Benelli. If the Secretariat of State's role was to co-ordinate all Vatican policies, then it needed a co-ordinator-in-chief. A man of great energy and dynamism, Benelli was in effect Paul VI's business manager and *chef de cabinet*. He had fingers in every pie, and he got things done. His critics accused him of turning 'co-ordination' into 'control'. Yet in terms of the organization of the Roman curia he was undoubtedly a 'reformer' – which is why his tyres were slashed more than once in the Vatican car park. When Paul VI reluctantly let him go to Florence as archbishop in 1977, it was a sign that he regarded his pontificate as over, and wanted to give Benelli a chance of the succession.

But the structure laid down in *Regimini Ecclesiae Universalis* in 1967 remained substantially intact for the next twenty-one years. Other specialized bodies were added: the Pontifical Commission for Migrations and Tourism in 1970, the umbrella charitable organization *Cor Unum* in 1971, and the Committee on the Family set up in January 1973 (largely as a sop thrown to those who were disappointed that the 1974 Synod would not be on marriage and the family). It became commonplace to observe that a problem was not admitted to exist in the Vatican unless there was a body to deal with it.

However, Paul VI never thought that *Regimini Ecclesiae Universalis*, so hastily composed, was beyond improvement. Reforming the curia was an ongoing process. In 1972 he appointed a commission headed by Cardinal Luigi Traglia to check that the goals of *Regimini Ecclesiae Universalis* were being achieved. Traglia died, there were changes of personnel, but nothing had been concluded by the death of Paul VI in 1978. The new pope, John Paul II, had no first-hand experience of the curia. His personal concerns were reflected in the setting up of two new specialist bodies: a Pontifical Commission for Culture in 1982 (which shared a joint president with the Secretariat for Non-believers) and one for health workers in 1984. Another innovation was to revive the college of cardinals as a kind of 'senate' of the Church, but they have so far had only three relatively brief meetings – in 1979, 1981 and 1985.

These gatherings of cardinals (for juridical reasons it was not done to call them 'consistories') were concerned with financial matters and curial reform from the outset. One result was the creation in 1981 of a Council of Cardinals – fifteen non-Roman cardinals reckoned experts in the field – to advise on fund-raising and other financial matters (though not the affairs of the Institute of Religious Works). The deficit continued to grow, partly because the curia itself had become more expensive to run.

The second major concern of the meetings of cardinals was the 'revision' of the Roman curia (talk of 'reform' was abandoned). Two more commissions were set to work, the first under Cardinal Aurelio Sabattini from 1983, and Cardinal Sebastiano Baggio from 1985. The work proceeded under conditions of great, though not impenetrable, secrecy. Finally, on 28 June 1988, there appeared the Apostolic Constitution *Pastor Bonus*, which took effect from 1 March 1989. Among other things this was designed to fill out the 1983 *Code of Canon Law*, which has only two canons devoted to the Roman curia (360–1).

There are more changes of nomenclature: for example, the ex-Congregation for Religious and Secular Institutes is now the Congregation for Institutes of Consecrated Life and Societies. There are changes of attribution: for example, priests seeking dispensation from their vows or laicization must now apply to the Congregation of the Clergy instead of the Congregation for the Doctrine of the Faith. But the most striking change is the way the three 'Secretariats' were transmuted into Councils for Christian Unity, for Non-believers and for Inter-religious Dialogue (formerly Non-Christian Religions).

Why this change? *Pastor Bonus* does not give any reasons. Cardinal Baggio offered two. A 'secretariat' had a provisional nature and was not a category that existed in the Roman curia (apart from the unique example of the Secretariat of State). Again, Baggio insisted on the clear, Cartesian distinction between curial bodies: congregations are organs of government, tribunals have a judicial function, while councils are seen as 'promotional agencies'. It was difficult not to conclude that the Council for Christian Unity has been downgraded, and that it is now strictly subordinate to the Congregation for the Doctrine of the Faith, which once more, in fact if not in name, is 'supreme'.

Pastor Bonus restores the Congregation for the Doctrine of the Faith to the dominant position it held before 1965. Its Prefect, Cardinal Joseph Ratzinger, has the last word on the entire output of the curia: 'Documents concerning faith and morals which are due to be published by other dicasteries of the Roman Curia must be submitted to the judgement of the Congregation' (56). This is spelled out in the case of the Council for Christian Unity: 'Since the material that this Council has to deal with frequently touches on matters of faith or morals, it is necessary that it should proceed in strict liaison (*collegamento*) with the Congregation for the Doctrine of the Faith, above all when it is a matter of producing public documents or declarations' (137). Clearly there can be no question any longer of a 'dialectic' between the Council and the Congregation. The implicit value-judgement is that concern for orthodoxy prevails over the search for Christian unity.

Nor can the Secretariat of State do much to ensure balance. It is still assigned a 'co-ordinating function' and exhorted to 'foster relations between the dicasteries', but 'without prejudice to their autonomy' (41, section 1). It remains responsible for the Vatican diplomatic service, *l'Osservatore Romano*, Vatican Radio and the new Television Centre (so far producing videos); but one of the principal tasks of a nuncio is to act on behalf of the Congregation for the Doctrine of the Faith in the pursuit of supposedly errant theologians, thus bypassing the local bishops. Nuncios also play a crucial role in the nomination of bishops, who are chosen above all for their soundness and orthodoxy. Once again, the trail leads back to the Congregation for the Doctrine of the the Faith *via* the Congregation of Bishops.

A telling example of the subordination of the Congregation of Bishops to the Congregation for the Doctrine of the Faith came with the position-paper issued in 1988 on episcopal conferences. It said they were merely practical arrangements without any theological reality or mandate to teach. Cardinal Bernardin Gantin, Prefect of the Congregation of Bishops, was not known to have any private opinions on this theological problem; but Cardinal Ratzinger had developed exactly the same ideas in *The Ratzinger Report* (1985) and *Church, Ecumenism and Politics* (1988).

The most novel feature of *Pastor Bonus* is the extraordinary emphasis it places on the *ad limina* visit to Rome – the five-yearly duty of going to '*videre Petrum*' ('to see Peter' – Gal.1.8 is the obligatory reference). They are mentioned in the long Introduction, in the body of the constitution (28–32), and Annex I is devoted to their 'pastoral significance'. It is made clear that going to Rome means submitting oneself to curial inspection, and long reports are called for on every aspect of diocesan work. Though the *ad limina* visits are said to be 'the centre of the supreme ministry' of the pope (10), the bishops see him only briefly and spend most of their time with the Congregation for the Doctrine of the Faith and the Congregation of Bishops. In this way they are said to share in 'the solicitude of all the Churches with Peter and under Peter' (*cum Petro et sub Petro*) (ibid.).

From all this one may conclude that the real function of *Pastor Bonus* is not to 'reform' the curia at all, but to strengthen its control over the life of the local churches. Pope John Paul already made this quite clear in an address to the curia on 28 June 1980:

> The prospect of the further putting into practice of the Second Vatican Council depends to a considerable extent upon the efficient functioning of the Roman Curia and of the well-organized co-operation with the corresponding structures within the local Churches and the Episcopal Conferences . . . . From the principle of Bishops' collegiality and their pastoral and teaching mission stems their shared co-responsibility . . . . They are called upon to collaborate closely with the competent departments of the Roman Curia, the centre of the ecclesial community. (9, 18, 23).

This appears as a very one-sided presentation of the case, and seems to deny any theological reality to local churches, reducing them to mere 'objects' of curial policies. Once again, the curia takes on the afterglow of the papal office itself. No predictions may be safely made for the future, except that the 'reform' of the curia will be an ongoing requirement. *Curia semper reformanda*: the curia is always in need of reform.

9A The Curia: Bibliography

Bull, G. (1982) *Inside the Vatican*. London, Hutchinson.
Cavallari, A. (1968) *The Changing Vatican*. London, Faber.
Hebblethwaite, P. (1987) *In the Vatican*. Oxford, Oxford University Press.
Laurentin, R. (1984) 'Paul VI et l'après-Concile', *Paul VI et la Modernité dans L'Eglise*, Ecole Française de Rome.
Nichols, P. (1981) *The Pope's Divisions*. London, Faber.

9B The Secretariat for Promoting Christian Unity

TOM STRANSKY, PAULIST

This originated as a preparatory organ of Vatican II, then functioned as a conciliar drafting body; it is now the office of the Roman curia which deals with the pastoral promotion of the Church's participation in the one Ecumenical Movement. Until 1989, it was called a Secretariat; thereafter, a Pontifical Council.

On 5 June 1960, John XXIII created the SPCU to enable 'those who bear the name of Christians but are separated from this Apostolic See to find more easily the path which they may arrive at that unity for which Christ prayed'. Catholics and other Christians immediately saw the new Secretariat as an active symbol of Pope John's loving concern for Christian unity. The general secretary of the World Council of Churches, W. Visser 't Hooft, exclaimed, 'We finally have a friendly address in Rome!'

John XXIII appointed Cardinal Augustine Bea SJ (1881–1968) to be the SPCU president; Monsignor Johannes Willebrands (1909–) to be its secretary (and its president from Bea's death until December 1989); and also appointed two staff members, Monsignor Jean-Francois Arrighi and Father Thomas Stransky CSP. The office opened in October 1960.

The SPCU began official contacts with leaders in the Anglican, Orthodox and Protestant Churches. It evaluated their suggestions for the Council themes and, if need be, used these for its own draft work or passed them on to other Preparatory Commissions. The SPCU negotiated with the world confessional bodies for the participation of their delegated observers in the Council: 169 persons, including substitutes, during the four sessions.

From 1960 to 1962, the SPCU prepared five drafts: *On Ecumenism, On Religious Freedom, On the Necessity of Praying for Unity, On the Word of God and its Function in the Church* and *On the Jews*.

As the Council convened (11 October 1962), the SPCU was the only Preparatory Commission that had not been dissolved. Although it had prepared five drafts, it was not empowered to submit them directly to the Council floor. On 19 October, John XXIII raised the SPCU status to that of a Conciliar Commission with the same corresponding rights and obligations.

By the Council's end, the SPCU had been responsible for the promulgated documents: on Ecumenism (*Unitatis Redintegratio*); on Religious Freedom (*Dignitatis Humanae*); on the Relation of the Church to the Non-Christian Religions (*Nostra Aetate*); and on Divine Revelation (*Dei Verbum*), co-drafted with the Theological Commission.

After the Council, Paul VI confirmed the SPCU as a permanent office of the Holy See (3 January 1966). Later, he specified its structure and competence in the reorganization of the Roman curia (15 August 1967).

The SPCU's contacts with other Christian communions had initiated the personal and organizational relations which in the post-conciliar period, led to the active presence of SPCU-delegated observers at confessional and inter-confessional gatherings, and to a variegated series of international and national bilateral dialogues. The SPCU has been co-sponsoring the international theological dialogues with the Lutheran World Federation (1965), the Anglican Communion (1966), the World Methodist Council (1966), the Old Catholic Churches of the Union of Utrecht (1966), the World Alliance of Reformed Churches (1968), the Pentecostals (1972), the Disciples of Christ (1977), the Evangelicals (1977), the Orthodox Church (1979), and the Baptist World Alliance (1984).

In 1966 was held the first annual meeting of the joint working group between the Holy See and the World Council of Churches. This group recommends to the parent bodies both the agenda and the means of collaboration in studies and action.

The SPCU broke through old walls of distance and suspicion by arranging visits of Christian leaders to the pope. The first such meeting in the Vatican was between John XXIII and the Archbishop of Canterbury, Geoffrey Fisher (December 1960). Many in the Vatican tried to downplay this visit, but not so that of Archbishop Michael Ramsey to Pope Paul VI in 1966. Again, the initial SPCU relations with the Orthodox led to the embrace of Paul VI and Ecumenical Patriarch Athenagoras in Jerusalem (January 1964), to the lifting of the anathemas between the Sees of Rome and of Constantinople at the Council's end (7 December 1965), and to later frequent contact, especially through delegations, to and from the Greek Orthodox and other Eastern Orthodox local churches. What were at first historic breakthroughs have now become normal Christian courtesies.

Since the Council the SPCU has been issuing norms and guidelines on specific topics: of major import was the *Directory, Part One* (1967) on diocesan and national ecumenical commissions, on mutual recognitions of baptisms, and on sharing 'spiritual activities', including liturgical worship; *Part Two* (1969) was on ecumenical principles and practices at the university and seminary levels. As part of the detailed implementation of the 1983 *Code of Canon Law*, Rome promulgated an extensive updated ecumenical *Directory* in 1990.

In bearing the Holy See's competence for Jewish religious concerns, the SPCU formed, with the International Jewish Committee for Interreligious Consultations, the Catholic/Jewish International Liaison Committee. Since 1970 the group has met annually. In 1974 Paul VI set up the Commission for Religious Relations with the Jews; its president is *ex officio* the SPCU president. In 1975 the Commission issued *Guidelines and Suggestions* for implementing Vatican II's statement on the Jews (*Nostra Aetate* 4); and in 1985, notes on the Catholic presentation of *Jews and Judaism in Preaching and Catechesis*.

In John Paul II's restructuring of the Roman curia, the SPCU became one of twelve Pontifical Councils. The new Council (PCCU) retains all the SPCU's original post-conciliar mandates; among them, 'to interpret correctly ecumenical principles' and 'to apply with opportune initiatives and activities the ecumenical duty to restore unity among Christians'. All curial offices are juridically equal among themselves, but they must submit documents which 'touch on doctrines as to faith and morals' to the Congregation for the Doctrine of the Faith for its judgement prior to publication. One understandably questions, in the post-Willebrands era, how the two bodies will resolve differences on the content, for example, of multilateral and bilateral dialogues in which the PCCU is a partner through its designated members, including its staff.

9B The Secretariat for Promoting Christian Unity: Bibliography

Stransky, T. F. (1982) 'An Historical Sketch of the SPCU', in Stransky, T. F., and Sheerin, J., eds, *Doing the Truth in Charity* (Holy See ecumenical documents, 1964–80). New York, Paulist Press, pp. 1–15.

Stransky, T. F. (1986) 'The Foundations of the SPCU', in Stacpoole, pp. 62–87.

The three to four times a year SPCU (now PCCU) *Information Service*, 00120 Vatican City, Europe.

9C The Secretariat for Non-Christians

AYLWARD SHORTER

The Secretariat for Non-Christians, now known as the Council for Inter-Religious Dialogue, was founded by Pope Paul VI in May 1964. It was clearly a fruit of the Second Vatican Council. Already, in his opening address to the Council's second session in 1963, Paul VI had announced his intention to create the Secretariat. Its *raison d'être* was to be a sign of the Church's concern for the spiritual needs of all humanity and a means of dialogue with other believers in God, as well as with all people of good will. As such, it reflected several of the Council's major themes, particularly its positive appraisal of non-Christian religions and its emphasis on dialogue instead of on apologetics or polemics. The pope's encyclical letter, *Ecclesiam Suam*, of the same year spelt out the terms of this dialogue and became, in many ways, the charter of the new Secretariat.

The new Secretariat received more from the Council than it was able to give. It was not in any way an organ of the Council, and was not entitled to submit drafts to it. This was pointed out when it was suggested that the statement on the Jews, which had become open to misinterpretation in the Middle East, might be handed over to the Secretariat for redrafting. However, the Secretariat profited from the presence of the Council fathers and *periti* in Rome to set up its own structures and choose its first consultors. Meetings began in 1964 and 1965, at which time the statement on the Jews was being incorporated into a wider document on non-Christian religions. This Declaration (*Nostra Aetate*) was issued by the Council in October 1965, and became at once a major guiding document for the Secretariat.

During the first nine years of its existence, Cardinal Paul Marella, the first president, and Pierre Humbertclaude, the first secretary, laid the foundations of the Secretariat. Paul VI's decree *Regimini Ecclesiae Universae* determined its shape. In addition to its officials, members and consultors, there was to be a special section on Islam. This office began the custom, continued ever since, of issuing a message to Muslims each year at the beginning of Ramadan. Five years later two further sections were created for traditional religions and Asian religions. Much of the Secretariat's time was devoted in the first years to publications. Its *Bulletin*, and its other publications, were designed to inform, analyse and document the problems of dialogue with non-Christians.

This activity was termed *prédialogue*, and its aim was to promote mutual understanding between people of different faiths and to acquire an objective knowledge of their varied spiritualities. The attempt was also made to stimulate local episcopal conferences along the same lines. They were to set up their own commissions for non-Christians, or at least charge an expert with the duty of dialogue.

In 1973 Cardinal Sergio Pignedoli and Monsignor Pietro Rossano succeeded as President and Secretary respectively. The new President had been Secretary of the Propaganda Fide Congregation and possessed a wide range of contacts in the world. He was also a man of considerable personal warmth and accessibility. His presidency, which was cut short by his sudden death in 1980, was characterized by an energy and outreach which brought the Secretariat into contact with many religious traditions in every continent. The Secretariat hosted the visits of numerous religious leaders to Rome, but, more importantly, conducted its own visits and encounters in other countries. Within the space of four years, the Secretariat had held fifteen meetings in different countries, most of them organized by local consultors.

These encounters were not without risk. One of them, the encounter with Muslims at Tripoli in February 1976, led to a celebrated gaffe, when an Arabic text containing anti-Zionist propositions was read and approved, though not signed, by the Vatican representatives (see *The Tablet*, 1976, p. 170).

From 1980 to 1984, Archbishop Jean Jadot acted as Pro-President of the Secretariat. This appointment saw the abandonment of overseas meetings sponsored by the Secretariat. Instead, the aim was to visit the local episcopal conferences and to co-ordinate their own encounters with non-Christians. There was also a new policy for the Secretariat to take part in congresses and encounters sponsored by other bodies. Along these lines the most important development has been the collaboration with the Secretariat's counterpart in the World Council of Churches, the Working Unit for People of Living Faiths and Ideologies.

The first plenary assembly of the Secretariat had been held in 1979, and had asked the Secretariat to prepare a document to clarify the relationship between dialogue and mission. This document was finalized at a second plenary assembly in 1984. Shortly afterwards, Archbishop Jadot retired as Pro-President. Monsignor Rossano had left the Secretariat the year before on being named an auxiliary bishop of Rome and Rector of the Lateran University.

The new President was Cardinal Francis Arinze of Nigeria, and Marcello Zago OMI held the post of Secretary for four years, being followed in 1987 by Michael Fitzgerald of the Missionaries of Africa (White Fathers). The advent of an African President has naturally led to a new emphasis on traditional religion, and an enquiry on the subject is currently in progress among the episcopal conferences of Africa. The meeting of religious leaders to pray with the pope for peace at Assisi in October 1986 was another important landmark for the Secretariat. In July 1988, as a result of a simplification of curial structures, the Secretariat for non-Christians was renamed the Council for Inter-religious Dialogue. The new name better expresses the positive approach and purpose of the Secretariat.

9C The Secretariat for Non-Christians: Bibliography

Arinze, F. A. (1985) 'Prospects of Evangelization with Reference to the Areas of the Non-Christian Religions', (3. History of the Secretariat for Non-Christians), in *Secretariatus pro Non-Christianis: Bulletin*. Rome, vol. 20/2, no. 59, pp. 111–40.

Rossano, P. (1979) 'The Secretariat for Non-Christians from the beginnings to the present day: history, ideas, problems', in *Secretariatus pro Non-Christianis: Bulletin*, Rome, vol. 14/2–3, no. 41–2, pp. 88–109.

The Tablet (1976) 'An Unfortunate Mistake', 14 February.

9D Justice and Peace

JOSEPH GREMILLION

The Pontifical Council (formerly Commission) Justice and Peace is the ecclesial initiative and structure authorized by Vatican II to promote and co-ordinate Catholic social ministry adapted to the modern world, along lines set forth by *Gaudium et Spes*. This sort of pastoral concern had been launched within the Church by the 1891 encyclical of Pope Leo XIII, *Rerum Novarum*, 'On the Condition of Labour', and it gathered momentum under the stimulus of the two world wars and ensuing economic and political crises of global dimensions.

Recognizing these signs of the times, Pope John XXIII convoked Vatican II to respond to them by updating the Church. He opened the Council's vision of the world and pointed the way with his opportune encyclicals *Mater et Magistra*, 'Christianity and Social Progress' (1961), and *Pacem in Terris*, 'Peace on Earth' (1963). Stimulated by these papal pointers and their own pastoral motives, Council members formed three volunteer groups to promote within Vatican II their special concerns for the poor, for peace, and for world justice and development.

Prominent among these lobbies were Bishops Helder Camara of Brazil, Angelo Fernandes of India and Edward Swanstrom of the United States, together with Gerald Mahon, at that time Superior General of the Mill Hill Fathers, and Cardinals Suenens of Belgium and Raul Silva of Chile. With over a hundred informal collaborators, these three groups planned and promoted their interrelated causes in drafting committees and open discussion of the Council, as well as behind the scenes. Besides updating social doctrine, their practical aim was to institutionalize follow-up after Vatican II through a social ministry office within the Roman curia and a co-operating network among Church bodies planet-wide. On its final voting day, 7 December 1965, the Council approved its 'Pastoral Constitution of the Church in the Modern World', *Gaudium et Spes*, which states:

> Taking into account the immensity of the hardships which still afflict a large section of humanity, and with a view to fostering everywhere the justice and love of Christ for the poor, the Council suggests that it would be most opportune to create some organization of the universal Church whose task it would be to arouse the Catholic community to promote the progress of areas which are in want and foster social justice among nations (*GS* 90).

In January 1967 Paul VI established the Pontifical Commission Justice and Peace as an official body of the Vatican curia for arousing the whole Church to its mission of promoting social justice and development, peace and human rights. The pope himself compared the Commission to a cock on the Church's steeple for awakening both world and Church. With a staff that grew by 1970 to a dozen professionals, and with the help of lay members of international stature such as Barbara Ward, Vittorino Veronese, James Norris, Marga Klompe, August Vanistandael, Kinhide Mushakoji and Candido Mendes, the

188

Commission conceived and fostered a global Catholic movement with seven main goals and features:

1 Creation of centres, channels and programmes for Justice and Peace promotion, ministry and communication within all principal structures of the Church: among Vatican offices and nunciatures, Bishops' Conferences, dioceses and parishes; generalates of religious, their provincialates, local houses and institutions; organizations of faithful and their specialized movements; retreat houses, spiritual centres.

2 Fostering and deepening theologies of the 'Church in the World', and their spread through faculties and seminaries; insertion of social teaching into liturgy, preaching, pastoral ministry and education networks.

3 Conception and preparation of Justice and Peace literature, books and articles, through research centres, editors and publishers; by encyclicals, papal addresses, bishops' pastorals and regional documents such as those of Medellín; and their circulation through the above networks and via news media.

4 Promotion of social ministry as a vocation, and of social science studies and leader training, to provide lay and clergy personnel for the Justice and Peace movement and structures at all levels.

5 Sponsorship and encouragement of conferences and media events *ad hoc*, and of Justice and Peace themes within ecclesial sessions – such as Medellín and Puebla Assemblies, 1968 and 1979; Synods on Justice, 1971, and Evangelization of Culture, 1974; Annual World Day of Peace on January First; Assisi Interreligious Peace Assembly of 1986; also comparable activities at national and local levels.

6 Ecumenical and interreligious co-operation, especially with World Council of Churches and national affiliates.

7 Consultation and co-ordination with governmental bodies at all levels, including United Nations and European Community; also with universities, foundations and professional associations.

In the twenty-five years since the Council, most of these far-ranging and even rather presumptuous programmes have advanced to a notable degree. Justice and Peace has indeed become a 'constitutive dimension' of Christian teaching and ecclesial consciousness, of pastoral ministry and canonical structure within the Catholic Church.

Only six years after the Council, 'Justice in the World' had become so prominent in the Catholic agenda that the 1971 Synod of Bishops was devoted to that subject, strongly reinforcing Vatican II's this-world thrust among the Church's many concurrent concerns. Pope Paul had himself urged this incarnational direction through his encyclical on 'The Development of Peoples', *Populorum Progressio*, in 1967.

During the Medellín Assembly of Latin American Bishops a year later, work groups were formed on Justice and on Peace, in which Gustavo Gutierrez was very active. The reports of Medellín brought to English readers early inklings of 'The theology of liberation' then being born, to be fully revealed by the Gutierrez book of that title published in 1973. In view of his inspirational role

189

at Medellín, Gutierrez was invited to a colloquium entitled 'Toward a Theology of Development', sponsored in 1969 at Geneva by SODEPAX, the Committee on Society, Development and Peace formed by the World Council of Churches and the Pontifical Commission Justice and Peace. Gutierrez presented there a 100-page paper on liberation theology which became, by his own admission, the prototype for his famous book. The 1960s had been declared 'decade of development'. It was at this point that the rather patronizing word 'development' as expressive of the true way to respond to the world's needs gave way theologically to the far more radical model of 'liberation'. By this date and into the early 1970s, Justice and Peace leaders began to deduce that their apostolate must include the encouragement for and articulation of *ecclesiologies* adequate to the new potential of 'Church in the World' opened by Vatican II. In May 1971 Paul VI confirmed this orientation with the social theology of his 'Call to Action' message, *Octogesima Adveniens*. Six months later the Synod statement 'Justice in the World' deepened these theological vistas and widened their pastoral scope. Among proximate drafters of that noted document were Bishops Ramon Torrella and Helder Camara, with Fathers Philip Land and Vincent Cosmao. One oft-quoted sentence of the Synod statement sums up the Church's *social aggiornamento* as conceived and promoted post-Vatican II:

> Action on behalf of justice and participation in the transformation of the world fully appear to us as a constitutive dimension of the preaching of the Gospel, or, in other words, of the Church's mission for the redemption of the human race and its liberation from every oppressive situation (*Justice in the World*, Flannery 2, p. 90).

These new Justice and Peace guidelines – Pope Paul's encyclical on development, the Medellín Assembly, *Octogesima Adveniens* and the synod on justice – had by 1971 enunciated a pattern for the Church's social mission well beyond what one finds in the Council itself. They inspired and guided the wider take-off of the social mission and its understanding in the years since, during which much more has appeared: several additional Roman documents, scores of national pastorals, hundreds of books.

Seventy-five conferences of bishops have created and staffed national offices, as have 500 dioceses. Latin America held its second great conference, at Puebla in 1979, and other regions have done the same in Africa and Asia. Religious orders have provided hundreds of trained specialists to staff newly formed social centres of provinces and dioceses, and train thousands of others annually to work in this field in scores of institutes and universities. Justice and Peace ministry has become a favoured vocation among laity as well as religious. About 4,000 of the 19,500 parishes of the United States now offer social-ministry programmes, as compared with a hundred at most before Vatican II.

The selection of Cardinal Karol Wojtyla as pope in 1978 has proven propitious for a continued Justice and Peace momentum. Although still in its teens, the movement had become under Paul VI so widespread and structured that even a revisionist successor could hardly have destroyed it; however, John Paul II has brought ever greater stature and scope to its work. Besides his social encyclicals *Laborem Exercens*, 'On Human Work', and *Sollicitudo Rei*

Socialis, 'The Social Concerns of the Church', plus a constant stream of addresses on related subjects, especially during his forty international visits to all continents, the Polish pope has elevated the role of Justice and Peace within the Roman curia and throughout the Church. Besides raising its canonical status to that of a full-fledged Council of the Vatican, John Paul has named top-ranking prelates as full-time executives of the office.

Cardinal Bernardin Gantin served as president until his transfer to be prefect of the Congregation of Bishops, and was succeeded at Justice and Peace by Cardinal Roger Etchegaray, for many years director of the *Mission de France* and head of the European Conference of Bishops, then archbishop of Marseilles. The current secretary general of the Synod, Archbishop Jan Schotte, served for a decade as secretary and vice-president of Justice and Peace, a post now filled by Bishop Jorge Mejia, formerly editor of *Criterio*, the distinguished Argentine review, who was also very active at Medellín and Puebla, and more recently in charge of Jewish relations world-wide in the Vatican's ecumenical secretariat.

Relations between Justice and Peace leadership at Vatican and at national levels have become more significant and at times more tense as the Roman Catholic body attained greater stature while local churches exercised increasing ecclesial self-confidence in line with the spirit of collegiality. Two cases in the 1980s, concerning Latin America's theology of liberation and the 'encyclical-like' pastorals of the United States bishops on peace and the economy, illustrate these new dynamics of tension and complementarity between the papacy and local churches.

Brazil became the focus of contention over liberation theology when Cardinal Joseph Ratzinger, head of the Congregation for the Doctrine of the Faith, issued in 1984 a formal Instruction severely criticizing this ecclesiology which had begun animating much of the regional church of Latin America since its 1968 Medellín Assembly. A few months after Ratzinger's critique, he summoned to Rome Brazil's best-known liberation theologian, Leonardo Boff, to be examined and placed under a formal ban of silence on theological subjects.

After ten months of weighty exchanges, public and private, Pope John Paul held a summit session in March 1986 to settle the issue, with leading Brazilian bishops, Ratzinger and other Vatican cardinals. Within a few days the ban of silence against Boff was lifted, and the pope sent Cardinal Gantin, Vatican prefect over bishops world-wide and former president of Justice and Peace, to deliver in person a very cordial letter to the annual meeting of the Brazilian bishops. In it John Paul praised the theological renewal begun under their auspices as 'a chance to renovate all Catholic theology'.

Simultaneously, Ratzinger issued a second document, 'Instruction on Christian Freedom and Liberation' (*Libertatis Conscientia*, 5 April 1986), over 12,000 words in length. Viewed as a Magna Carta for liberation theology, this document shows Vatican approval for many fresh ecclesial approaches of the Latin American Church since Medellín and Puebla, including:

> The special *option for the poor*, [which] manifests the universality of the church's being and mission . . . . The *new basic communities* [which] are a great hope for the church. If they really live in unity with the local church and the universal church, they will be a

191

real expression of communion . . . . Similarly, a *theological reflection* developed from a *particular experience* can constitute a very positive contribution (68–70, emphasis added).

These and other themes of Ratzinger's instruction – on use of violence in promoting social reform, the relation between work for the Kingdom of God and work for justice in this world, and the experience of oppression as a beginning point for theology – offer hope that the creative potential of ecclesial awareness within the plural cultures of today's changing world will be more appreciated by the Apostolic See, alongside our classical heritage of Europe and the West. These cultural sub-strata for Church-in-the-world theologies will take on great significance as the several ecclesial regions mature in Africa and Asia, as well as in the Americas.

The transnational scope of world peace and economic justice of the two pastorals from the United States Bishops' Conference in the 1980s involved perforce transnational participation for their preparation, at new levels of authority and collegiality. In 1983 a first-of-its-kind session was held in the Vatican on the peace pastoral draft, involving Cardinal Joseph Bernardin and his staff from the United States conference, with representatives of seven European conferences: those of Germany, England, Scotland, France, Italy, Netherlands and Belgium, among whom were three cardinals. Cardinal Casaroli and Archbishop Silvestrini represented the Holy See's foreign affairs office, with Ratzinger presiding and Archbishop Schotte, then head of Justice and Peace, as presenter and rapporteur.

While the issues of pacifism, just-war theory and disarmament were prominent, this historic first in collegial praxis raised the ecclesiological question of American pastorals of 'encyclical-like' scope extending beyond national borders, into the global sphere reserved till now to the papacy. The American bishops explained that as pastors and national leaders within a superpower, they must address moral judgements about global use of their country's economic, political and military might.

The Holy See has now accepted these complementary roles of consultation with Church leaders of those areas and peoples affected, and the second great American pastoral, on economic justice in 1986, became another occasion for such complementary action, including representatives of the Latin American Episcopal Conference, CELAM, at the Vatican's request. The consultation took place in Miami, where the Holy See was represented by Bishop Mejia, the Argentinian vice-president of Justice and Peace. United States policy in Central America and the mounting burden of international debt on third world peoples were the top subjects of this inter-American ecclesial consultation, under Vatican oversight.

These two cases merely signal future complications and promise as Justice and Peace matures and spreads around the globe. This updated social apostolate launched by Vatican II has already engendered new degrees of consciousness and engagement both for Church and for world at complementary levels, with long-range ecclesial consequences of some depth yet to unfold. Justice and Peace is thus adding a fresh and fruitful 'constitutive dimension' to the Church in the modern world for today and towards tomorrow.

9D Justice and Peace: Bibliography

Benestad, B., and Butler, F. (1981) *Quest for Justice: Statements of U.S. Catholic Bishops on the Political and Social Order*, 1966–80. Washington, US Catholic Conference.

Cox, H. (1988) *The Silencing of Leonardo Boff: The Vatican and the Future of World Christianity*. Oak Park, Ill., Meyer-Stone Books; London, Collins.

Dorr, D. (1983) *Option for the Poor: A Hundred Years of Vatican Social Teaching*. Dublin, Gill & Macmillan; Maryknoll, New York, Orbis Books.

Eagleson, J., and Scharper, P., eds (1979) *Puebla and Beyond: Documentation and Commentary*. Maryknoll, New York, Orbis Books.

Gremillion, J., ed. (1976) *The Gospel of Peace and Justice: Catholic Social Teaching Since Pope John*. Maryknoll, New York, Orbis Books.

Gutierrez, G. (1973) *A Theology of Liberation*. Maryknoll, New York, Orbis Books.

Henriot, P., *et al.* (1988) *Catholic Social Teaching* (outlines of eighteen documents, from *Rerum Novarum* 1891 to US Pastoral on the Economy 1986). Maryknoll, New York, Orbis Books; Melbourne, Australia, Collins Dove.

Hug, J., ed. (1983) *Tracing the Spirit: Communities, Social Action and Theological Reflection*. New York, Paulist Press.

9E The International Theological Commission

WALTER H. PRINCIPE csb

On 28 October 1967 the doctrinal commission of the First Synod of Bishops responded to wishes of many of its members by proposing a commission

> composed of theologians of diverse schools, to be appointed for a definite term, all men of intellectual ability, recognised as scholars, who reside in various parts of both the Western and the Eastern Church, whose duty it will be, acting with all lawful academic freedom, to assist the Holy See, and especially the Sacred Congregation for the Doctrine of the Faith principally in connection with questions of greater importance.

It was suggested that the pope should select members from those nominated by the Episcopal Conferences (Flannery 2, p. 670); these were to consult Catholic universities and faculties of theology in their region (see Delhaye, 1985, p. 303).

Although this proposal reflected the bishops' immediate concerns about opinions considered dangerous, it also arose from their experience of working together with theologians from many nations at the Council: this collaboration had led the conciliar fathers to challenge and modify the limited theological vision of the Roman curial participants. Wishing to maintain a more universal, richly diverse theological outlook at the service of the pastorate, they strongly approved the proposal by a vote of 124 to 14, with 2 abstentions and 39 approvals *iuxta modum*.

A whole year was to pass before the pope's decision to form the Commission was announced to episcopal conferences (see Flannery 2, p. 671; cf. *AAS*, vol. 61, 1969, pp. 431–2); only on 11 and 24 April 1969 did Paul VI establish the International Theological Commission within the Congregation for the Doctrine of the Faith, approve its statutes 'experimentally', and have them published (*AAS*, vol. 61, 1969, pp. 540–1; English in *Herder Correspondence*, 6, 1969, pp. 214–15). The names of the thirty members were then announced (see *OR*, 1 May 1969), and finally, two years after the bishops' original vote, the first meeting was held, in October 1969. This 'astonishing delay' was the result of various tensions and of opposition against non-Roman theologians coming from the 'consultors' working within the Congregation for the Doctrine of the Faith (thus Delhaye, 1985, pp. 303–4). After a trial period, John Paul II, on 6 August 1982, promulgated the Theological Commission's definitive statutes (*AAS*, vol. 74, 1982, pp. 1201–5), which were influenced in part by those of the Pontifical Biblical Commission. The president of the Commission is the cardinal prefect of the Congregation for the Doctrine of the Faith, who consults episcopal conferences and then proposes for papal nomination thirty members 'from diverse schools and nations, eminent for their science and fidelity to the Magisterium of the Church' (*Annuario Pontificio*, 1988, pp. 1577–8; it lists members annually; see ibid., p. 1138, for the members named in 1986).

Although the Commission is not part of the Congregation for the Doctrine of the Faith and has its own norms, the cardinal prefect of the Congregation none the less wears two hats because he presides over the annual full meeting; he also appoints the general secretary, who is very influential in organizing activities of the Commission. The individual themes of meetings have often been determined by the pope working with the cardinal prefect of the Congregation for the Doctrine of the Faith, the Secretary of State, and the presidents of bishops' synods, sometimes in response to requests from other pontifical commissions; at other times, discussion among members of the Commission has led to the choice of a theme. Sub-commissions, whose chair and members are appointed by the president from among those on the Commission, select the authors and scope of papers. They revise drafts of documents in response to discussions at plenary meetings or to members' written suggestions, and, sometimes after a special meeting, submit the final draft for vote by mail or at the next year's meeting. When the Commission approves a document by a vote 'in specific form', it takes responsibility for the entire text; approval 'in generic form' implies that the Commission accepts responsibility for only the main ideas of the text. Approved documents are offered to the pope after examination by the Secretariat of State for possible political implications (this was a concern, for example, in the document on human rights); they are also given to the Congregation for the Doctrine of the Faith for its use (see *Annuario Pontificio*, 1988, p. 1578, and Delhaye, 1985, p. 311). The individual documents are regularly published in various journals, and collections of the documents have recently appeared (*Commission Théologique Internationale: Textes et Documents 1969–1985*).[1]

Many well-known and influential theologians have been appointed, for example, B. Ahern, J. Alfaro, C. Arévalo, H. Urs von Balthasar, W. Burghardt, Y. Congar, Ph. Delhaye, W. Kasper, K. Lehmann, M.-J. Le Guillou, B. Lonergan, H. de Lubac, O. Semmelroth, C. Peter, G. Philips, K. Rahner, J. Ratzinger, R. Schnackenburg, H. Schürmann, B. Sesboüé, J.-M. Tillard, C. Vagaggini, J. Walgrave. However, the omission of prominent authors less favoured by the Vatican curia has been noticed (see 'The Thirty Theologians', 1969, pp. 210–11).

The Commission concentrates on one topic each year. These have been the Catholic priesthood (1970), unity of faith and theological pluralism (1972), the apostolicity of the Church and apostolic succession (1973), Christian moral doctrine and its norms (1974), the magisterium and theology (1975), human development and Christian salvation (1976), the sacrament of matrimony (1977), selected questions on Christology (1979), theology, Christology, and anthropology (1981), reconciliation and penance (1982), the dignity and rights of the human person (1983), selected questions of ecclesiology (1984), Christ's consciousness of himself and his mission (1985), faith and inculturation (1987), Mary (1987), interpretation of dogmas (1988), and themes related to the nature of the moral law (1989). The documents of 1973 and 1974 were approved 'in generic form'; all others have been approved 'in specific form'.

The presentation of documents has varied. Earlier documents were often in the form of 'theses', which were sometimes published together with commentaries written by individual members. Such commentaries helped to flesh out the skeletal theses, but did not engage the Commission. From 1976 to 1988

195

more developed essay-type 'conclusions' have been produced; these make better reading. A useful procedure has been publication not only of the conclusions, but also of the essays written by the members to help prepare the annual meeting. This was done for the documents of 1970, 1974, 1976, 1977 and 1983 (references in Delhaye, 1985, pp. 24, 86, 154, 216, and 296 respectively).

On the whole, the Commission has functioned neither as an autonomous teaching body nor, as was hoped by some curialists, as a group useful only for consultation and documentation. It has addressed some important issues, although often in a restricted Western European Catholic context. It has provided thoughtful texts that may serve to guide pastors and teachers concerned to present an approved if cautious theology. Its publications, however, have failed to capture the attention of most theologians or of many pastors and teachers. This inattention has produced a certain malaise among some Commission members, especially after their diligent efforts to produce the documents. The response made by the president and the general secretary to this malaise has been that the documents have at least been valuable for the Roman congregations and for some of the bishops' synods, even if they have had small influence outside the Vatican.

Although such an influence on the Roman congregations and bishops' synods was indeed one of the original aims of the bishops in establishing the Commission, it is questionable whether this aim has been realized. For example, many decisions and documents on important matters are regularly issued by the pope or the Vatican curia with little or no consultation of the Commission – which meets only once a year on a specific topic. Again, subtle controls limit the ability of the Commission to address questions with complete freedom.[2] For one thing, the pope and the curia strongly influence the choice of members of the Commission. Moreover, although free, lively discussion takes place at the meetings and through the internal communications of the Commission, within its working some of the influential members (including, it has been averred, a circle of the *Communio* journal group) see to it that the conclusions of the discussions remain in line with particular opinions of the pope, or with previous official pronouncements. Hence the Commission often seems to be more the mouthpiece of prevailing Vatican official opinions than an expression of the diverse theological views quite consistent with Catholic faith.

For example, the conclusions about penance and reconciliation (1982) ignored the pastoral possibilities shown from history, and also reflected John Paul II's opposition to general absolution; earlier statements of the Holy Office or of Pius XII hovered over the Commission's discussions of Christ's human knowledge and self-consciousness (1981, 1985); rights of Christians within the Church could be stated but, as in the new *Code of Canon Law*, silence was to be maintained about the corresponding duties of those holding authority in the Church (1983); the insights of scriptural scholarship, often challenging to received official positions, fail to have much impact on the views of the Commission; little interest or sympathy has been shown to women's (and so to some men's) issues; ecumenical matters and the conclusions of bilateral

196

dialogues have only remote impact;[3] diverse Eastern or third-world theologies have been passed over or, in cases like liberation theology, been viewed with suspicion.

The limited interest of the documents is partially owing to their being consensus statements. To achieve such a consensus, the theses or conclusions issuing from the discussions have had to be so modified, and legitimately different theological views so watered down, that the texts lack vitality and fail to stimulate. Since in this process the number of votes remains secret, an impression of unanimity is fostered. To overcome these weaknesses, some members have suggested that on any topic a consensus statement be replaced with a survey of different theological positions compatible with Catholic faith, somewhat in the form of a 'disputed question'. So far this constructive suggestion has been rejected. In fact, Cardinal Ratzinger now holds that 'within [the Commission] the opinions of thirty theologians must be reduced to a common denominator', that the Commission's 'specific nature is its capacity to disengage a common theological fund from multiple viewpoints', and that 'within a legitimate theological pluralism theology remains one and theologians must be able to speak with the same voice on a determinate subject' (*Commission Théologique*, 1988, Préface, p. 8).[4]

The cardinal's statement is inconsistent with his own earlier theses approved by the Commission in 1972 (ibid., pp. 51–2); it stands in opposition to Vatican II's statements about Eastern Churches recognizing the value of 'legitimate variety' as applied to 'differences in theological expressions of doctrine', and asserting that their 'various theological formulations are often to be considered complementary rather than conflicting' (*Unitatis Redintegratio* 17). It forgets that Paul VI in his inaugural address to the Commission said: 'We willingly allow for the progress and variety of the theological sciences, that is, for the "pluralism" which seems to characterize modern culture today', and that he assured the members of his intention 'to respect the freedom of expression rightfully belonging to theological science, and the need for research inherent to its progress' (Pope Paul VI, 1969, pp. 715–16). It also ignores the frequent calls by popes and bishops' synods for inculturation of the gospel, which must include inculturation of the faith in diverse but not contradictory theologies. This need for theological pluralism had already been indicated by the statutes of the Commission calling for appointment of theologians from 'different theological schools and nations'. As a result of the search for an overriding consensus and of other procedures within the Commission, there were several resignations (including this author's after the 1980–5 term), while some among those who vigorously sought different outlooks were not reappointed.

It is unclear to what extent the Episcopal Conferences have a voice in proposing members; even when they are consulted, the final choice remains with the cardinal prefect of the Congregation for the Doctrine of the Faith and the pope. This procedure has meant that the Commission is largely representative of European theology and its outlook; theologians from European countries have regularly numbered about two-thirds of the membership, and even those appointed from outside Europe often reflect European theology in method and interests (the South American members' opposition to liberation theology is a case in point). Most theologians on the Commission have been professors in Catholic institutions where interaction with other religious or humanistic traditions is often minimal. The present Commission is the first to have native Asiatics and laymen, or more than one African theologian. Despite the original synodal proposal, Eastern Catholics have had little representation or voice. No women theologians have been appointed.

The choice of membership, the control of themes for discussion, and the restrictive procedures are some of the reasons why the Commission has, in large part, addressed inner-Church questions. Insufficient attention has been paid to many contributions or challenges of contemporary thought, to the meeting of Christianity with other living faiths and religions, to the methods and outlook of African, Asian, North and South American theologians, to ecumenical questions, or to women's studies or issues about women's role in the Church.

From all this it is evident that if the International Theological Commission is truly to represent the legitimate variety of creative, culturally adapted Catholic theologies and thereby fulfil the original intentions of the bishops' synod, considerable changes will be required.

Notes

1 Paris, Cerf, 1987. A collection of the documents in English is being prepared. See also *Comisión Teológica Internacional: Documentos 1970–1979*. Madrid, CETE, 1983; single documents were published for succeeding years.

2 For an example of a less than subtle control, see the account in W. Principe, 'The History of Theology: Fortress or Launching Pad?', in *The Sources of Theology*, Current Issues in Theology, vol. 3, ed. J.P. Boule and G. Kilcourse. Louisville, Ky., Bellarmine College, 1988, pp. 334–5. Also available in *CTSA Proceedings*, vol. 43, 1988, pp. 34–5.

3 Yet Paul VI stated that the work of the Commission had as one 'important' goal that of 'finding in the firmness of our faith the mysterious secret of a persuasive language for ecumenical dialogue – a dialogue designed to reestablish . . . perfect and happy communion with our brothers who are still separated from us' (Pope Paul VI, 1969, p. 716). Another goal set by the pope can hardly be said to have been attained, that is, the goal that 'concerns our art of teaching, which is termed kerygmatic, and our ability to proclaim the message of Divine Revelation and human salvation' (ibid.).

4 '. . . au sein de [la Commission] les opinions de trente théologiens doivent être ramenées à un dénominateur commun. Sa spécificité réside dans sa capacité à dégager de la multiplicité des points de vue un fonds théologiquement commun; au sein d'un pluralisme théologique légitime, la théologie reste une et les théologiens doivent être capables de parler d'une même voix sur un sujet déterminé.'

9E The International Theological Commission: Bibliography

Commission Théologique Internationale, Textes et Documents (1969–1985) (1988) Préface du Cardinal Ratzinger. Paris, Cerf.

Delhaye, Ph. (1985) 'L'après Vatican II et la constitution de la Commission Théologique Internationale: Contribution à l'histoire post-conciliaire', *Revue théologique de Louvain*, vol. 16, pp. 288–315.

Pope Paul VI (1969) 'Membris Commissionis Theologicae Internationalis, primum plenarium Coetum habentibus', *AAS*, vol. 61, pp. 713–16.

Rahner, K. (1969) 'Defending the Faith, Modern Style', *The Tablet*, 25 October, pp. 1057–8 (Résumé of speech to the first meeting of the International Theological Commission, Monday, 6 October 1969).

'Statuta "ad experimentum" Commissionis Theologicae' (1969) *AAS*, vol. 61, pp. 540–1.

'Statuta Commissionis Theologicae Internationalis forma stabili definitaque approbantur' (1982) *AAS*, vol. 74, pp. 1202–5.

'The Thirty Theologians' (1969) *Herder Correspondence*, vol. 6, pp. 210–15.

9F The Synod of Bishops

PETER HEBBLETHWAITE

Syn-od (from the Greek *sunodos*, common way) is a term used from antiquity for meetings of bishops. After the Council of Trent it came to be restricted to assemblies on the level of the diocese, largely controlled from above and with no serious discussion. Pope John held a diocesan synod in Rome in 1960. It endorsed 755 wide-ranging articles which, among other things, placed the opera and race tracks out of bounds for clerics, and warned against faith healers and psychiatrists.

The 'Synod' with which this chapter will deal is a modern development. In a speech at Nijmegen in 1961, the year before the Second Vatican Council met, Cardinal Bernard Alfrink, archbishop of Utrecht, called for some way of associating the world's bishops with the central government of the Church. In his *vota* for Vatican II (not revealed until much later) he recommended a 'legislative council' to help the pope on the model of the permanent synods of the Eastern Churches (Grootaers, 1984, pp. 803–4).

It is not surprising, therefore, that Maximos IV Saigh, Melchite patriarch of Antioch, should have become the chief advocate of the Synod at the Council. Speaking in French, as was his custom, Maximos said on 6 November 1963:

> A small group of bishops, representing the whole college, would have the task of helping the Pope in the general government of the whole Church. This group could form the real 'sacred college' of the universal Church. It could include the principal bishops of the Church.

He went on to enumerate them, beginning with Patriarchs. In Maximos's mind, some members of the Synod would have to be permanently in Rome, in order to act as 'the supreme, executive and decision-making council of the Church'. 'All the Roman Congregations,' he added, 'should be subordinate to it' (Laurentin, 1964, p. 118).

Maximos's 'model' of the Synod, prompted by Oriental experience, represented the most radical proposal for the new body. It trapped Paul VI in a dilemma. On the one hand, he realized the political difficulty of subordinating the Roman Congregations to the Synod. Yet on the other, he wanted somehow to involve the world's bishops in the government of the Church. As he admitted in his address to the opening of the second session in 1963:

> For us personally your discussion [on episcopacy] will provide the doctrinal and practical standards by which our apostolic office, endowed though it is with the fulness and sufficiency of power, may receive more help and support, in ways to be determined (*modi et rationes*), from a more effective and responsible collaboration with our beloved and venerable brothers in the episcopate (XR 2, p. 355).

In November 1963, over 500 bishops presented a memorandum to the pope urging him to flesh out this proposal, but there was hardly any conciliar debate about the shape of this future body, and Paul VI kept the *modi et rationes* very close to his chest.

So it was something of a surprise when, at the start of the fourth and final session of the Council on 14 September 1965, Paul VI announced the setting up, in accordance with the wishes of the Council, of an episcopal synod of bishops to be chosen for the greater part by the episcopal conferences and approved by us, which will be convened, according to the needs of the Church, by the Roman pontiff, for consultation and collaboration when for the general good of the Church this will seem most opportune to us. We consider it superfluous to add that this collaboration of the episcopate is meant to be of the greatest help to the Holy See and to the whole Church. And in a special way it can be of use in the day-to-day work of the Roman Curia to which we owe so much gratitude for its effective help. Just as the bishops in their dioceses, so we too always need a Curia for carrying out our apostolic responsibilities. Further details will be brought to the notice of this assembly as soon as possible (XR 4 1965, pp. 276–7).

In fact, the *motu proprio*, *Apostolica Sollicitudo*, setting up the Synod was already drafted: it was read out to the Council the very next day in the pope's presence.

Apostolica Sollicitudo (Abbott, pp. 720–4) was received with applause, and thus fulfilled Paul VI's immediate aim of starting the final session with a concession (as he saw it) to the progressive majority, crestfallen by the 'black week' at the end of the previous session. The Synod was established on a permanent basis ('by its nature perpetual'): so it would be difficult to suppress it altogether. The vast majority of its members – all but 15 per cent – were to be elected by episcopal conferences. They were: patriarchs and major archbishops of Oriental Churches (thus covering the Ukrainian Catholic Church, which does not have a patriarch); bishops elected 'for their theoretical and especially their practical knowledge of the matters to be discussed', one for conferences under twenty-five, two for those under fifty, three for those under one hundred, and four for the rest; ten religious superiors; the cardinals in charge of Roman dicasteries.[1] That came to a total of some 210 to 230 for an 'ordinary' Synod.

In addition, an 'Extraordinary' Synod was provided for in which *presidents* of episcopal conferences replace the elected members. There have been two Extraordinary Synods, in 1969 to consider the aftermath of *Humanae Vitae*, and in 1985 to celebrate twenty years after Vatican II. Paul VI briefly toyed with the idea that an Extraordinary Synod should elect his successor; a conclave constituted along these lines would be more truly representative of the Church than the college of cardinals (even though many cardinals would have been there as presidents of their conferences). This idea was abandoned, but the pale ghost of it remained in the decision to exclude cardinals over eighty years old from the conclave: so membership of the college of cardinals did not confer the *right* to elect the bishop of Rome. Though it came to nothing, this illustrates the Synod's unrealized potential.

A third type of synod, called 'Special', was envisaged for a region or country. Paul VI never made use of this opportunity. John Paul II called a special synod, in 1980, to consider 'the pastoral work of the Church in the Netherlands in the present situation, so that the Church will reveal itself more as a communion'. Though it conformed to the letter of the *motu proprio*, some theologians said that the Dutch synod violated the spirit of the law which stresses the *regional* character of such meetings: a Belgian archbishop was co-president and the presence of prefects of curial congregations meant that the Dutch bishops were outnumbered, thus demonstrating, said Giuseppe Alberigo, 'the sovereign will of the Pope in dealing with a collegial organ' (quoted in Granfield, 1987, p. 89). Later, special synods were called for Africa and for Europe.

But whichever type of synod is envisaged, the 'sovereign will of the Pope' appears in the founding document with the utmost clarity. The pope calls the Synod when and as he chooses, confirms its membership, determines its agenda, appoints its president and secretary, decides how its results are to be communicated, settles where it will be held, and presides over it (through a delegate). It is, moreover, said to be 'immediately subject to the Roman pontiff' (3).

Nevertheless, the Synod as envisaged by *Apostolica Sollicitudo* was not a completely toothless and spineless creation. Though not a decision-making body, there was the hope that it might become one some day: 'By its very nature the task of the Synod is to inform and give advice. It may also have deliberative power, when such power is conferred upon it by the Sovereign Pontiff.' Yet its elective system guaranteed a relative autonomy, and its purpose could not be ensured without some freedom of speech. Three aims were stated:

1 To encourage close and valued assistance between the sovereign pontiff and the bishops of the entire world.
2 To ensure that direct and real information is provided on questions and situations touching upon the internal action of the Church and its necessary activity in the world of today.
3 To facilitate agreement on essential points of doctrine and on methods of procedure in the life of the Church.

But the 'assistance' hoped for in (1) and the 'agreement' aspired to in (3) would only be of use if there were the genuine exchange of information about the life of the Church envisaged in (2). So come what may, the Synod had an essential function in the life of the post-conciliar Church: to continue the collaborative experience of the Council and keep the local churches in touch with each other and the bishop of Rome.

There was much theological debate in the post-conciliar period about whether the acts of a synod should be considered *collegial* acts. Edward Schillebeeckx and Angel Antón contended that Bishops attended the Synod as 'representatives of the entire Catholic episcopacy' (*'partes agens totius catholici episcopatus'*, *Lumen Gentium* 22) rather than as delegates of the pope. Therefore, the Synod meets the requirements of a strictly collegial act so long as the pope accepts its advice or ratifies its decisions – should it be allowed to make any (see the discussion in Granfield, 1987, pp. 90–2).

The counter-argument, however, was that only the entire episcopal body, the whole *corpus episcoporum*, can perform strictly collegial acts. This is the position followed in the *Code of Canon Law* and in the 1985 Synod of Bishops, which declared in effect that only an ecumenical Council could express 'effective' collegiality. However, the Synod could still embody 'affective' collegiality, that spirit of co-operation which is 'the sign and instrument of the collegial spirit'.

This debate still goes on. However arid and fruitless it may seem, it concerns the very nature of the post-conciliar Church. Is it to be a monarchical Church in continuity with Vatican I, or a collegial Church in continuity with Vatican II? The reason the debate will go on is that Paul VI in *Apostolica Sollicitudo* produced a diplomatic compromise solution designed to satisfy the bishops at the Council without offending the Roman curia. He also remarked that the Synod, 'like all human institutions, can be still more perfected with the passage of time'. The truth of that may be seen in the simple fact that there has not been a Synod since 1967 that did not reflect critically on its own methods and procedures.

Rather than attempt to write the history of the seven Ordinary and two Extraordinary Synods, it will be more useful to consider them as part of the experience of collegiality in the Church.

The Synod of 1967 was important, mainly because it was the first (see Hebblethwaite, 1968). It attempted to do too much in too short a time. Its five topics came from a variety of disparate sources. They were (1) principles for the revision of the *Code of Canon Law*; (2) a document from Cardinal Alfredo Ottaviani 'On Dangerous Modern Opinions and also Atheism'; (3) a report on seminaries; (4) mixed marriages; and (5) liturgy.

The most practically important of these themes was the last: for the liturgical reform mandated by the Council, by now under way, was contested at every step by an impenitent right-wing in which Archbishop Marcel Lefebvre was already active. Paul VI could use the Synod to enlist the continued support of the bishops for this vast project and ensure its 'reception' throughout the whole Church.

The debate 'On Dangerous Modern Opinions' was like a throwback to the Council. The negative and alarmist tone of the curially prepared document was criticized on all sides. Cardinal Suenens rode again. Even Cardinal Heenan praised the work of theologians and said we could do without 'another Syllabus of Errors'. 'A poor text gives the Fathers of the Synod a chance to be prophetic,' remarked a Frenchman.

The debate was important for two reasons. The prepared draft had clearly to be thrown out, and a doctrinal commission was hastily elected to produce an alternative. The election aroused great excitement: it meant that the Synod was taking charge of its own texts, acting in a more responsible manner. It was no curial rubber-stamp.

But there was another very practical consequence. The Holy Office, though theoretically 'reformed', could no longer be allowed to define the theological agenda. There was a more and more insistent (and therefore co-ordinated) demand for the setting up of a permanent International Theological Commission. The proposal, accepted by a considerable majority, was implemented on 11 April 1969 (see Chapter 9E). This was the first instance of a synodal recommendation taking effect.

However, this major achievement came too late to affect a series of measures which seemed to suggest that collegiality was in abeyance. The encyclicals *Sacerdotalis Caelibatus* (1967) and *Humanae Vitae* (1968) had been prepared without collegial consultation. The question was not whether Paul VI *could* issue such documents, but whether he *should*. The mildest thing Suenens could find to say about them was that they would have carried more weight and had more credibility if they had been preceded by widespread consultation. Third-world bishops objected to not being consulted about another document, *Sollicitudo Omnium Ecclesiarum* (26 June 1969), which, while purportedly 'reforming' the papal diplomatic service, left episcopal conferences largely subordinate to the Vatican representative.

But there can be no doubt that the furore created around *Humanae Vitae* was the principal motive for the decision to make the 1969 Synod an Extraordinary Synod and assign collegiality as its theme (see Grootaers, 1981, pp. 25–9). The announcement was made in December 1968, just six months after *Humanae Vitae*. Three questions were on the agenda:

1 A doctrinal approach to collegial unity and ecclesial hierarchy.
2 Improvement of the relationship between episcopal conferences and the Holy See.
3 Improvement of the relations between episcopal conferences.

The central question was how the relationship between what was then called the 'centre' and the 'periphery' should be understood, so that greater autonomy for episcopal conferences could be achieved without infringing upon the pope's freedom of action. Cardinal Edouardo Pironio from Argentina provided the theological key to the problem:

> The community of the bishops with the Pope should not be understood as though the Pope was the only centre of unity, while bishops represented merely diversity. The college of bishops, united with the Pope, is itself a principle of unity. The bishop represents the particular church in which the universal Church dwells. The Roman Pontiff is the defender of legitimate diversity to the extent that he favours the cultural diversity of the Churches and prevents the absorption of particular Churches.

Pironio was secretary general of CELAM. Paul VI had been to Medellín the previous year to open their historic conference.

For the first time the Synod broke up into nine language-based discussion groups (*circuli minores*). This meant less emphasis on the big speech in the Aula (sometimes addressed to the gallery), and improved the level of communication. There was surprising unanimity. Differences between 'progressives' and 'conservatives' seemed less relevant. The 1969 Synod made it clear that the bishops *wanted* to collaborate with the pope in all matters of importance (above all in the preparation of pontifical documents and decrees), in order to strengthen the Church's unity and discipline. It was a tacit, if unemphatic, restatement of the point made by Suenens. One cannot prove cause and effect, but it is a fact that Paul VI issued no more encyclicals in the remaining nine years of his pontificate.

The other main achievement of the Extraordinary Synod of 1969 concerned the Synod itelf as institution. The bishops wanted a more effective secretariat, controlled by a body representing the episcopal conferences, with power to choose the topic for the Synod. There was a more radical version of this proposal, known as the 'Poma-plan' (after Cardinal Antonio Poma, President of the Italian Episcopal Conference, a man known to be close to Paul VI). This would have made the Synod secretariat a body truly representative of the episcopal conferences. it would consist of twenty elected members and be permanently responsible for the liaison between the pope and the episcopal conferences. It would meet several times a year, and be responsible for planning the next Synod.

Paul VI met this suggestion half way. On 23 March 1970, the Synod Council was set up, consisting of fifteen members, twelve elected by the Synod (three per continent) and three named by the pope. It would meet twice a year, usually in spring and autumn, and have the task of preparing the next Synod.[2] It never had the broader function envisaged by Poma, which was closer to the original idea of Alfrink and Maximos.

The 1971 Synod had two themes, priestly ministry and justice in the world. It was the first Synod to take place in the custom-built auditorium above Pier Luigi Nervi's new audience hall. It was the first Synod to involve lay experts like Barbara Ward, and to consult lay people in advance through the national Justice and Peace Commissions. This showed how a synod could healthily 'conscientize' the whole Church.

The distinctive voice of Latin America made itself felt in *Justice in the World*, the Synod's final document, notably in its insistence that 'action on behalf of justice and participation in the tranformation of the world fully appear to us as a *constitutive* dimension of the preaching of the Gospel' (Flannery 2, p. 696).[3] It was not, therefore, an optional extra. Liberation theology could take off from there. Crucially important also was the following principle: 'While the Church is bound to give witness to justice, she recognizes that anyone who ventures to speak about justice must first be just in their eyes' (Flannery 2, p. 703). This was then applied to the Church's own lifestyle (the Church should not be 'an island of wealth in an ocean of poverty') – and judicial procedures (the accused 'had the right to know their accusers and also the right to a proper defence').

Though banal enough in secular terms, such statements were novel from this source. They influenced many religious orders in the next decade. But they posed a problem for Paul VI. Such documents were clearly addressed to the whole Church, if not the whole world. But was it the business of the Synod to be writing documents at all? It did not fulfil its function 'to inform and give advice' to the pope by making such pronouncements. On the last day, Synod president Cardinal Léon-Etienne Duval warned that 'the Synod of Bishops cannot and ought not to be thought of as a mini-council (*veluti parvum concilium*)', and he recommended for next time a 'simplified procedure' and concentration on a more manageable topic.[4] This was seen as a rebuke.

Thus paradoxically the Synod that had produced the best document so far ended in unhappiness. This mood was compounded by the feeling that the Synod's views on the ordination of married men had been misrepresented. In the debate on priestly ministry there had been urgent pleas, especially but not exclusively from the younger churches, that they be allowed to ordain suitable married men where otherwise the Eucharist, to which all the baptized had a right, could not be assured. To resolve this question the Synod was invited to consider two propositions:

> *Formula A*: Excepting always the right of the Supreme Pontiff, the priestly ordination of married men is not permitted, even in particular cases.
>
> *Formula B*: It belongs solely to the Supreme Pontiff, in particular cases, by reason of the needs and the good of the universal Church, to allow the priestly ordination of married men who are of mature age and proven life (Flannery 2, p. 689–90).[5]

The Synod was asked to vote for one or other of these propositions. Formula A got 107 votes, Formula B got 87. Those who voted for the ordination of married men admitted defeat, but pointed out that it was not by the two-thirds majority required by a Council (not that they were a Council). They could also claim that they had a majority of *elected* members. What was galling was that their honestly given advice was swept aside as though it had never existed. In his closing speech Paul VI said:

> From your discussions it emerges that the bishops of the entire Catholic world want to keep integrally this absolute gift by which the priest consecrates himself to God; a not negligable part of this gift – in the Latin Church – is consecrated celibacy (Paul VI, 1971, p. 873).

There was not a word about the ordination of married men. This raised the question: if the Synod of Bishops cannot put a question on the Church's agenda, who can?

The preparations for the 1974 Synod were for the first time entrusted to the new Synod Council elected in 1971. As late as October 1973 it looked as though its theme would be Christian marriage, but it was pointed out that this would involve a reopening of the *Humanae Vitae* wounds. Though 'Evangelization' may have seemed a less controversial topic, in fact it addressed very directly the question of liberation theology (and therefore the Synod of 1971), as can be seen in the following passage from its position-paper:

> There are those who describe evangelization as though it were something only on the spiritual and religious level, meant only to free men from the bonds of sin. Others, however, describe Christ as the new Moses and consider the Gospel is ordered only towards human development, at least in the present moment of human history.

It is easy to say that this was a 'false dichotomy', but false or not it dogged the whole proceedings, and meant that for the first time the Synod was not only unable to produce a document of its own, but was unable to 'conclude' at all. So it simply dumped a series of confused propositions in the papal lap and invited the pope to sort them out.

This he did magnificently in *Evangelii Nuntiandi*, published on 8 December 1975 (Flannery 2, pp. 711–61). It can be considered the high point in the history of the Synod so far. For here was a text that was at once synodal and papal, and therefore deeply collegial. The Synod provided the raw experience and many of the insights, while Paul VI articulated them using his 'charism of discernment'. It makes important new statements about, for example, liberation theology (*Evangelii Nuntiandi* 38–9), basic communities, but, above all, on

> the close links between evangelization and human advancement, that is development and liberation. There is a link in the anthropological order because the person to be evangelized is not an abstract being but someone subject to social and economic factors. There is also a connection in the theological sphere because the plan of creation cannot be isolated from the plan of redemption. There is, finally, a connection in the evangelical order, that is the order of charity; for how can the new law be proclaimed unless it promotes a true practical advancement of man in a spirit of justice and peace.

That is very different in tone and content from *Ecclesiam Suam* (1964), Paul's first encyclical. If he went on learning throughout his pontificate, this was largely because of the Synod.

By the time of the 1977 Synod on Catechesis, however, Paul VI was tiring. His eightieth birthday was celebrated, slightly belatedly, during the Synod. He was unable to respond to the mass of material presented to him. This was now deemed to include the various interventions, reports from the discussion groups, the 'message' to the world, and the final list of conclusions summarized in thirty-four 'propositions' – in short, practically everything said at the Synod.

John Paul II, present at the 1977 Synod and elected pope on 16 October 1978, completed the unfinished task by an apostolic exhortation, *Catechesi Tradendae*, published on the first anniversary of his election. It was obviously not easy to make the transition from participant to president, and John Paul II's reading of the Synod, though not unfaithful, nevertheless reflected his own concerns as much as those of the majority of the Synod members.

Thus John Paul revived the notion of 'Catholic social doctrine' (abandoned by Paul VI) and claimed it went back to the patristic era (*Catechesi Tradendae* 29). The document is full of warnings about the extremely limited nature of 'ecumenical catechesis' (33) and the danger of theologians troubling the minds of young people with 'outlandish theories, useless questions, and unproductive discussions' (61). The tone was different – almost a revival of Ottaviani's 'On Dangerous Modern Opinions' of 1967. But more fundamentally, *Catechesi Tradendae* set the pattern for future Synods.

Thanks to Paul VI's compromises, the Synod had always been somewhat ambivalent: was it the organ of the bishops or of the pope? Of course, a dialectic was involved which we have seen at work in the Synods of Paul VI, and the institution could be said to have grown towards maturity in his pontificate. But in the pontificate of John Paul II, one-half of the dialectic seems to have been suppressed, and the Synod became simply the organ of the pope.

This can be seen in the choice of topics, each of which reflected a major personal worry of John Paul II, often dating back to the 1970s. Thus Christian Marriage (1980) provided an opportunity to restate the validity of *Humanae Vitae* against all attempts to find 'pastoral' solutions, or learn from the fact that a large number of Catholics did not accept the encyclical. Reconciliation (1983) provided a chance to stress the merits of individual confession over 'general absolution', which many bishops found pastorally useful. The Role of the Laity in the Church and the World (1987) revealed suspicion of 'lay ministries', a desire to distinguish sharply between priestly ministry (in the Church) and lay apostolate (in the world), and a resolve to bolster 'new movements', like Comunione e Liberazione and Opus Dei, that the pope believed expressed the 'charismatic nature' of the Church as it moved towards the end of the twentieth century.

Habits die hard, and many bishops continued to act as though the Synod still had its traditional function of 'informing and advising' the pope. The forms remained. Never was there so much 'consultation' of the faithful than before the 1987 Synod, which concerned them. Many home truths were spoken, many hopes expressed. But the home truths were ignored, and the hopes dashed.

Jan Grootaers and Joseph Selling wrote a book called *The 1980 Synod of Bishops 'On the Role of the Family'* (Louvain University Press, 1983). They summarize the process by which the Synod is turned into a rally round the papal throne. Though speaking of 1980, what they say applies to all the Synods of the pontificate. In the first stage (a week to ten days) there is always great optimism as reports are given in the name of episcopal conferences. There are sometimes memorable speeches, a great sense of freedom, and always a rich sense of the diversity of Catholicism. But the *relatio* (or position-paper) which makes the link between the debates in the Synod hall and the discussion groups is usually found inadequate to convey the richness of the debate. Still cheerfulness continues as the work of replying to the questions posed by the *relator* goes on. Language and the accident of the alphabet determine who goes where. The third stage involves drafting a series of 'propositions' which represent the conclusions of the Synod. These are voted upon, reworked and gradually steered in the direction of insignificance. The last phases happen in impenetrable secrecy, so that all a bishop can say, when asked at the airport on his return home what the Synod did, is: 'You will have to wait for the document of the Holy Father.'

Though the forty-five concluding propositions of the 1987 Synod on the Laity were never officially published, the secrecy did not prove impenetrable, and the post-synodal exhortation, *Christifideles Laici*, published in April 1989, was reasonably faithful to them. There were two disappointments, however. The reconsideration of the 1972 document *Ministeria Quaedam* on lay minis- teries was entrusted to a special, anonymous commission with no clear indication about whether its brief was to extend lay ministries (including those of women) or cut them down. The Synod's recommendation that 'new movements' (such as Communion and Liberation) should be in the first place under the local bishop or episcopal conference was simply ignored. But in other respects, *Christifideles Laici* was a much richer document than the Synod propositions. Its key-word was *participation*. It urged the participation of women and men in all consultative bodies from parish councils to diocesan Councils, and in the preparation of documents. But since there is no machinery for implementation, it may all prove to be so much hot air.

This feeling is getting through to the bishops themselves. In October 1988 the Synod Council considered a proposal to increase the interval between Synods from three to five years. *The Tablet* reported: 'Bishops are understood to want more time to prepare for a meeting of the Synod and to apply its conclusions afterwards, and are reluctant to spend a month away from their dioceses for what may turn out to be rather intangible results' (5 November 1988, p. 1287). That verdict sounds rather like an epitaph. But the Synod, as founded by Paul VI, is a *permanent* body, and when some pope wants to try the adventure of collegiality, he will have recourse to it with gratitude.

Notes

1 There was some ambiguity about the curial cardinals. They were not included among the 'members' of the Synod, but were merely said to be present (*intersunt*), which suggested a role of 'observers'. But the ambiguity was soon resolved: they were members. See R. Laurentin, *L'Enjeu du Synode, Suite du Concile*. Paris, Seuil, 1967, pp. 98–9.

2 This is enshrined in the *Code of Canon Law*, canon 348.

3 In *The Christian Faith in the Doctrinal Documents of the Church*, ed. J. Neuner and J. Dupuis, London, Collins, 1983, no. 2159, the word 'transmission' replaces 'transformation' in this text, thus making nonsense of it.

4 P. Hebblethwaite, 'The Future of the Synod' *The Month*, January 1972, p. 4. Note also in the same issue John Harriott's 'The Difficulty of Justice', which lists ten reasons why the final Synod document was an advance on *Gaudium et Spes*, *Populorum Progressio*, and *Octogesima Adveniens*.

5 Flannery gives the whole document called 'The Ministerial Priesthood' (pp. 672–94) but curiously attributes it here and in the index to 30 November 1967. 'Priestly Ministry' became the pleonastic 'Ministerial Priesthood' at the request of Cardinal Karol Wojtyla, anxious to preserve the 'essential distinction' between the ordained priesthood and other forms of ministry.

9F The Synod of Bishops: Bibliography

Granfield, P. (1987) *The Limits of the Papacy*. London, Darton, Longman and Todd.

Grootaers, J. (1981), *De Vatican II à Jean Paul II, Le Grand Tournant de l'Eglise Catholique*. Paris, le Centurion.

Grootaers, J. (1984) *'Une restauration de la théologie de l'épiscopat: contribution du Cardinal Alfrink à la préparation de Vatican II'*, in *Glaube im Prozess*. Für Karl Rahner, Herder.

Grootaers, J., and Selling, J. (1983) *The 1980 Synod on the Family*. Louvain University Press.

Hebblethwaite, P. (1968) *Inside the Synod*. Dublin, Gill & Macmillan.

Hebblethwaite, P. (1985) *Synod Extraordinary*. London, Darton, Longman and Todd.

Laurentin, R. (1964) *Bilan de la Deuxième Session*. Paris, Seuil.

Paolo VI (1971) *Insegnamenti*, vol. IX. Vatican Polyglot Press.

9G The Revision of Canon Law

LADISLAS ÖRSY sj

On the Feast of the Conversion of Paul, 25 January 1959, when Pope John XXIII announced his intention to call a diocesan synod for Rome and an Ecumenical Council for the Universal Church, he added that 'they will lead happily to the much desired and much attended revision of the *Code of Canon Law*, which should accompany and crown these two events with practical applications'. The pope clearly had an integrated project in his mind: first, the insights and proclamations of the two assemblies, then the provisions of the laws. As it happened, the Roman synod shrunk into insignificance, but the Council's significance rose beyond all expectations. What happened to the third project, the renewal of canon law?

The process of the revision of canon law began right after the first session of the Council: a steady stream of legislative enactments touching on various aspects of ecclesiastical life was produced by the Holy See and has continued ever since. Moreover, shortly before he died in 1963, Pope John appointed a commission to revise the *Code* which has been in effect since 1917. The work of this group was brought to completion on 25 January 1983, when John Paul II promulgated the new *Code*, only the second such collection in the history of the Church.

The *Code*, in spite of its title, is more than a book of legal rights and duties. Some of its canons are statements of belief, pure and simple. Some others repeat long-held theological opinions, some reflect tenets inherited from scholastic philosophy, a few of them are spiritual exhortations. To interpret any given rule in such a multi-layered document requires a sophisticated approach; an unwary reader may easily attach a sanction to an exhortation or miss the seriousness of a legal obligation.

The contents of the *Code* are grouped into seven books: 1. *General Norms*, including rules for the interpretation of the laws and a great deal on ecclesiastical offices; 2. *The People of God*, on the rights and duties of the faithful, also on the primacy, episcopacy and consecrated life; 3. *The Teaching Office of the Church*, especially in reference to all kinds of educational institutions; 4. *The Sanctifying Office of the Church*, containing the norms for the administration of the sacraments, for other forms of worship and for sacred times and places; 5. *The Temporal Goods of the Church*, regulating the acquisition and administration of property; 6. *Sanctions*, giving the definitions of public offences and of the corresponding penalties; 7. *Processes*, defining the structures and competencies of the courts and determining the patterns of judicial and administrative procedures.

More importantly and transcending the above divisions, the canons are grouped somewhat loosely around three major themes reflecting the threefold task of the Church: governing, teaching and sanctifying. This division is modelled on the three aspects of the mission of Christ: he came as King, Prophet and Priest. This gives a religious framework to the *Code* and distinguishes it from secular books of law.

Now the question: has the *Code* really 'crowned' the work of the Council?

Certainly not in the sense that the *Code* would have concluded the process started by the Council. Vatican II was not a passing event which could be closed with an appropriate set of laws. It was the beginning of a movement *in the Spirit*, which continues and will do so for a long time to come. The bishops went home, but before they did so, they rekindled in the Church an attitude of mind which is marked by a spirit of enquiry into the mysteries of salvation. St Anselm of Canterbury once described this search as faith seeking understanding. The human spirit, however, cannot rest with understanding alone; faith seeks also action. Thus, new norms for action in the form of laws, customs and usages had to follow. Yet neither the *Code* nor any other law could conclude the process started by the Council; they were and remain part of a larger movement.

Yet this is not a full answer. The question still remains, how far has the new *Code* succeeded in translating the insights of the Council into practical norms?

A fair overall judgement may well be that, through the instrumentality of the *Code* and the legislation preceding and following it, the Church has done a great deal to adjust its institutions, structures and discipline to the vision of the Council, but as yet it has not completed the task. Much done, but much remains to be done. This complex situation is the result of several factors.

One is that the Council often had a rich insight into a point of doctrine, but without fully explaining it; however, it is difficult to enact a practical norm for the application of an insight that has not been well defined.

Another is that the *Code* was prepared during the time when the Church was absorbing the teaching of the Council and there were dissensions among the faithful; in such a climate, a good policy for the legislator is to seek reasonable compromises.

Finally, to bring concrete changes into the external world, as laws are meant to do, is always a slow and painful process; it is rarely wise to do it all at once. There is a paradox in all this: we have a *Code* that does not go the whole way in applying Vatican II, but it faithfully reflects the state of the Church as it was in the years after Vatican II.

Some major themes taken from both the Council and the *Code* will illustrate well the progress made and the task still to be achieved.

THE CHURCH AS COMMUNION

The Council saw the Church as the one people of God, the hierarchy being in the service of the whole body (*Lumen Gentium* chs 2 & 3). The *Code* reflects the understanding of the Church as the *communio* of the faithful where all have the same Spirit: it states clearly the equal dignity of all, the fundamental rights and duties of the faithful; for the first time in the history of the Church, a genuine bill of rights has been promulgated. The *Code* puts much emphasis, however, on the 'power to govern', *potestas regiminis*, which must be reserved for those who received orders; lay persons, men or women, can only co-operate with it but not share in it. History tells a different story: non-ordained persons did occasionally exercise 'jurisdiction' and did participate in important decision-making processes, including synods and Councils.

ECUMENISM

The Council saw in the Roman communion a fullness not to be found elsewhere, but perceived also that the Church of Christ embraced other churches and ecclesial communities (see *Lumen Gentium* 8; *Unitatis Redintegratio* repeatedly); it spoke often of our 'separated brethren' with whom we are united, and from whom we are divided. The drafters of the *Code* faced a formidable task: it is near impossible to handle a seemingly contradictory situation (one and divided at the same time) by precise legislation; add to this the variety of relationships with so many communities. None the less, the *Code* displays an openness not seen before in canon law.

All are bound to work for the unity of the Christian churches. In mixed marriages the conscience of the non-Catholic ought to be respected. There are some basic rules for the sharing of the sacraments, but obviously that matter is not concluded. Dialogues between the Roman Church and other communities are going on.

EPISCOPAL COLLEGIALITY

The Council stated that the episcopal college has full and supreme power in the universal Church, no less than the pope (*Lumen Gentium* 22). Now, if the pope wants to exercise his power, he has institutional structures built up over many centuries at his disposal; no such structures, however, exist for the college, except for an ecumenical Council – a rare event in the life of the Church. Yet, if the Spirit assists the college no less than the pope, ways and means should be found to let the college use its power for the benefit of the Church. This can be a project for the future; the *Code* has hardly made the first steps towards it.

PARTICULAR CHURCHES

The Council saw in particular churches a source of enrichment for the universal Church (*Lumen Gentium* 13), but this can happen only if they have enough freedom to develop in their own way, as did the early Christian communities in various cultures, such as Syrian, Greek, Roman, and others. This freedom is especially important at this turning point of history when young churches full of energy are gaining strength in Africa, Asia and other continents. The present canon law offers little or no help for such evolution, and we all are the poorer for it.

CONSECRATED LIFE

The emphasis that the Council put on the charismatic nature of the life of religious orders and congregations (see *Perfectae Caritatis*) is fairly reflected in the *Code*. Questions are, however, raised as to whether the *Code*'s well-defined categories (religious institutes, secular institutes, institutes of apostolic life) correspond to the variety of charisms that the Spirit may in fact distribute.

TEACHING OFFICE

Vatican II, no less than Vatican I, stated clearly that the subject of infallibility applies to the whole Church, although an ecumenical Council or a pope can define in the name of the Church the content of our faith (see in particular *Lumen Gentium* 12 and 22). The *Code* focuses almost exclusively on the teaching office of the episcopate; it gives little consideration or scope to the 'supernatural appreciation of the faith (*sensus fidei*) of the whole people . . . aroused and sustained by the Spirit of truth'.

MARRIAGE

The Council stressed the religious dimensions of Christian marriage, and praised the mutual love that must sustain it (*Gaudium et Spes* 47–52). The *Code* made a significant effort to revise the body of relevant laws which developed over a millennium, but kept a good deal of it as well. The result is that new ideas about personal commitment and relationship coexist uneasily with some old legal categories and medieval psychological theories. The ensuing tensions are often resolved by judicial interpretations; thus the law keeps evolving.

OFFENCES AND PENALTIES

The spirit of the Council undoubtedly had its effect on the law of offences and penalties, which was for a long time the most archaic and complicated part of the Church's legal system. The norms of the *Code* are far less detailed and far more humane. Automatic penalties have been retained for a few major crimes only (they could have been omitted totally without any loss to justice); in most cases, broad discretion is left to the judgement of the courts or of the competent superiors.

COURTS AND PROCEDURES

Following again the spirit of the Council, the *Code* provides a somewhat simpler and more efficient judicial system than the one that existed before. In theory, the system is open to all issues of justice; in practice, our courts have

213

become marriage tribunals. The need for competent courts to resolve, fairly and speedily, all kinds of conflicts is pressing.

These are outstanding examples of how the insights of the Council have been translated into canonical norms. If the translation does not appear perfect, let us recall that while God reveals the truth, human persons make the laws.

The movement that the Council has started or rekindled is still gaining momentum: as the Christian community progresses in vision, it must progress also in legislation. A never-ending task – ultimately sustained by the Spirit.

9G The Revision of Canon Law: Bibliography

'Canon Law' in *Encyclopaedia Britannica*, forthcoming edition.
The Code of Canon Law in English Translation (1983). London, Collins.
Coriden, J. A., *et al*, (1985) *The Code of Canon Law: A Text and Commentary*. New York, Paulist Press.
Index to the Code of Canon Law in English Translation (1984). London, Collins.
Örsy, L. (1985) *From Vision to Legislation: From the Council to a Code of Laws*. Milwaukee, WI, Marquette University Press.
Örsy, L. (1988) *Marriage in Canon Law: Texts and Comments, Reflections and Questions*. Wilmington, DE, Michael Glazier.
Richstatter, T. (1977) *Liturgical Law Today: New Style, New Spirit*. Chicago, Franciscan Herald Press.
Robinson, G. (1984) *Marriage, Divorce and Nullity: A Guide to the Annulment Process in the Catholic Church*. Melbourne, Dove Communications.

10

UNFINISHED BUSINESS

10A General Overview

F. J. LAISHLEY

> At the outset of every piece of art there is a will to break a part of time out of the unmerciful flow of life and make it available to others (Joseph Conrad).

The title of this chapter should not surprise, for in reality the business of a Council is never finished. It is the purpose of this chapter to elucidate and illustrate this theme in regard to Vatican II. To achieve this, there is required more than a chronicle of events and views since the Council. Even if this account were presented in terms of the development and (sometimes) the resolution of controversies arising out of the unresolved tensions in the Council debates themselves, only a part of the task would be accomplished. What is more fundamentally required is, in the first place, at least a brief account of a basic hermeneutics or interpretation theory that can aid the understanding of the necessarily unfinished nature of conciliar, and of all theological, business, and then the working out of this in the themes examined in this chapter. Three aspects of this task seem immediately relevant:

1 To reflect on *the historical nature* of understanding, which in the case of the Council means highlighting its epoch-making character as a watershed between an ahistorical and an historical method in doing theology. This will underline the necessarily provisional character of thinking and decision-making, and help to explain subsequent conflicts in these terms.

2 To sketch *the interpretative nature* of all conceptualized experience which can assist understanding of the necessarily pluralist character of theological practice and theory, and hence the still unfinished debates between different perspectives.

3 To indicate the *continuously expanding* (or contracting) *horizons* of the theologies expressed in the Council documents as they are received in the world-wide communities of the Roman Catholic Church, arising from continuous change in perspective and response to changing needs.

HISTORICAL METHOD

What was at stake in Vatican II was nothing less than the long overdue coming to terms on the part of the Roman Catholic Church with the modern world: that is to say, the social, political and intellectual movements predominantly occurring in Europe since the late eighteenth century (see Gilkey, 1975, ch. 1). This reorientation could not be achieved in the four years of the Council, and much of the unfinished business we are concerned with can be seen as response to modernity. A great deal has been written about the social and structural immobilism of the pre-conciliar Church (Alberigo and Jossua, p. 12) and of its corresponding essentialist theology. This does not need repetition. What do bear a brief examination, however, are the underlying categories of thought for the interpretation of this phenomenon and of the counter-flow of modernity in the existentialist ideas which had been gathering momentum for decades, largely outside official circles, and which were to break through in the views of many leading speakers at the Council.

At this hermeneutical level it seems legitimate to speak of contrasting basic structural tendencies in thinking, whereas at the level of particular themes and discussions (the level of contents), the reality is more diverse. During the Council itself, Monsignor Philips of Louvain had identified these tendencies, which still exist, as follows:

> [The first] moves easily in the world of abstract and changeless ideas, but risks being locked into that world and mistaking concepts for the mystery that transcends them . . . . The second type [of theologian] . . . is convinced that his vision of the truth is not identifiable in all its forms with the truth itself . . . . He has a keener sense of history (in Alberigo and Jossua, p. 218).

In what follows, more attention is given to the conceptuality of modernity, since this is of more recent development.

The basic issue here in the use of these labels lies below the particular merits of competing theologies; it lies in the diverse ways of giving an account of the *enduring consistencies* (or universal elements, as traditionally named) in human experience. For herein lies the coherence of one's world-view. In an essentialist mode one is speaking of a framework which abstracts from the diverse complexities of things as they exist and concentrate on what is, in fact, an absolute, timeless conceptualization of these enduring elements. This account rests on the further assumption of the mind's capacity to rise above the changing conditions of existence and view all from a godlike perspective. Theological theories, of revelation for example, are then easily elaborated in terms of a participation in the timeless truth of God which is equally easily conceived of (because abstract) in propositional terms. The strength lies in evident continuity and certainty; the weakness stems from the immobility which, in the end, generates unreality. That is to say, the whole construct is ahistorical.

Existentialist thought, on the other hand, was but the latest of the modern ways to attempt to give a proper place to historical consciousness. The accent was on the uniqueness, the irreducibility, of personal experience, but this necessarily involved the time-conditioned processes of personal and social history. The *enduring consistencies* could then be thought of in terms of analogies of experience from within experience. Likeness was the paradigm, not identity or sameness. For theology, therefore, speaking about God increasingly renounced descriptive language and tendencies to univocity, and increasingly also the language of participation, and rooted its reference to God in the conditions of possibility of human finite existence. The 'Word of God' could then be seen, not as external to humanity, but as words of men which could challenge human beings to face the unconditioned ground of their being. The whole perspective is situated within history, and the theological task becomes akin to that of art as portrayed by Conrad: it is not to break out of the flow of time into another world, but to break a part of time out of the flow of time, or to break through the crust of the superficial to disclose the hidden human and divine depths of experience (see Ruggieri, in Alberigo and Jossua, pp. 91ff.); and in so doing, to create effective symbols of that depth. 'Christianity is the common life of human beings in a transfigured form' (ibid., p. 103).

INTERPRETATION

Interpretation theory of an essentialist type tends to bypass the subjective aspects of our mental activity with a non-critical realist stance. But the tide of modern theory since Kant has forced theology to come to terms with those subjective aspects of knowing, of understanding and of all human activity (Jeanrond, 1988, pp. 175ff.). The mind operates within a framework of space and time and its own organizing categories, and we each have our own perspective on the events to which we have access in partial and incomplete, even if overlapping, ways. This realization raises in a new way questions of objectivity and truth. It is important to see that truth questions cannot be resolved simply by correspondence theories, whereby truth is defined as conformity of the mind and reality; for the mind is an aspect of reality, operating from within a total reality. But it is equally important to realize that, in acknowledging the rightful place of subjective considerations, objectivity is not lost in a mere coherence of, or self-consistent pattern of, ideas without any extra-conceptual reference. Ultimately, in an historical framework, the resolution of such questions lies in the realization that thinking and understanding are 'transparent moments' within the totality of lived reality.

Several things follow that are relevant to theology. Firstly, intellectual method does not begin with the idea, with theory, and then apply it to situations. Still less is all reduced to the idea. But experience in all its pluriformity precedes theory, which is, in turn, a particular organizational tool for the interpretation of life from within. Secondly, conceptual frameworks do not mirror 'what is the case' in a one-to-one relationship; concepts, and all communications (images, gestures, etc.), are symbolic mediations, partial and incomplete expressions, of the richness of life. As such they may generically be

217

called 'models of interpretation', and we all communicate through differently conceived models. Aspects of this approach have been developed by Avery Dulles in his own way in *Models of the Church* and *Models of Revelation*. Thirdly, we have the possibility of a renewed approach to mystery, not as a 'truth above reason yet revealed', but as the richness of the experience of life and, at depth, of God which escapes adequate statement. Thus the more modest claim is made for theological languages: they are particular interpretative frameworks for that which, in its fullness, escapes them. And a critical function is restored to theology, as to all reflection, in that the presuppositions and standpoints of any utterance can and should be examined constantly. Finally, no single theological system can be created: synthesis is not the aim, but the careful mapping of theologies as analogical expressions of experience. In a word, pluralism is a permanent feature of all theology.

EXPANDING HORIZONS

As one might guess from the above, one of the critical hermeneutical tensions in the modern world has been that between the perceiving subject and its object – whether text or event, whether present or past; in a phrase, between subjectivity and objectivity. In this tension is found the 'ugly trench' between the necessary truths of reason and the contingent events of human history; also, the breach between science and religion. Essentialist tendencies bypass the tension in claiming plain objectivity for religious and theological truth. But it is only in recognizing that the standpoint of the subject enters into the definition of 'the real', that the real is relational and that neither pure subjectivity nor pure objectivity is given, that a fuller approach can be evolved. As regards theology in this connection, the historical critical method vindicated to a large extent the objective search for the literal sense of Scripture. But it has been left to hermeneutics to integrate that approach within the ever expanding horizons of historically evolving reception on the part of ever-new communities. The 'literal sense' is itself situated within its own historical and cultural horizon, not as a nugget of meaning which is locked in the treasure chest of the Bible. Meaning is always meaning *for* a recipient and so necessarily relational. Reception therefore of the word – scriptural and theological – is seen to be an ongoing process of reflection in ever changing contexts (see Schneiders, 1978).

Of these contemporary contexts, perhaps the most important theologically is the shift from an existentialist framework (in the 1960s), historical but individualist and geared to understanding the world, to a political one (in the 1970s), historical but social and prepared to use political and conflictual models for interpreting the Christian meaning of events and geared to changing the oppressive conditions of the lives of the masses. The 1980s have seen a further shift, not complete nor unopposed by the earlier movements, to a new conservatism and, typically, a neo-Augustinian pessimism about the world (Alberigo and Jossua, p. 254). These contexts affect the interpretation of the Council and will enter into later discussions.

DIVERGENCE IN INTERPRETATION

It has been the argument of this chapter so far that the business of a Council remains always unfinished, and the basic tension within our post-conciliar period does not lie between two sides taken on this or that reform (a feature which on its own is inevitable and healthy), but at a deeper level between those who accept historicity and pluralism fully and those who still basically think that the 'business' should end and a permanent, normative, stability return. At this stage it is useful to illustrate this from main themes of the Council in their subsequent history.

That we are not dealing with clear-cut 'battle lines' can be seen from the fact that it was John XXIII himself who, having introduced the idea of a certain historicity of understanding, none the less spoke of it in terms of a distinction between the truths of faith and the way in which they are enunciated (*EV*, *Documenti*, p. 45). This distinction was taken up in 1973 in *Mysterium Ecclesiae* (Flannery 2, p. 433), suggesting a changeless kernel and changeable expressions. But it is this very concept of a kernel that is at issue. Is theology dealing with a recognizably universal element that can be applied diversely (a deductive approach), or with analogues of concrete experience which plot a more or less coherent trajectory (an inductive approach)?

The method in the Council itself shifted towards an inductive one in *Gaudium et Spes*, but the tension continued. As recently as *Sollicitudo Rei Socialis* (1987), we find the method of expository vision and application employed. The result is a flawed universalism which speaks in generalities of an inspirational nature, but lacks concrete policy. On the other hand, efforts by local hierarchies to develop effective teaching based on wide consultation in an inductive method (as by the United States bishops in their recent pastoral *Economic Justice for All*) have met with unease at the centre, and suspicion that the local hierarchy was endangering its teaching role.

The immobilism of the pre-Vatican II institution was challenged on (almost) every side, along with the monolithic theocratic claim to absolute certainty and unchallengeable divine authority within the field of faith and morals, which has not infrequently been referred to as 'creeping infallibilism'. But the tensions have not gone away. There is a whole spectrum of positions between the monolithic and the pluralist on matters such as the relation of the local churches to the centre, the relation of other Churches to the Roman Catholic Church, and of the latter to other religions. It is important to map out carefully the actual positions in dispute, but also, as here, to point up the ahistorical and historical tendencies at work.

In further matters of Christian social relationships, in ethics, the ahistorical/ deductive and the historical/inductive polarization is particularly acute. On the one hand, the view in possession leans towards an absolute, normative, ontological concept of human nature as a basis for moral deduction on matters such as birth control, to be discussed below. On the other, there lies an existential view of human beings as historically and culturally conditioned but analogous in their humanness.

219

In liturgy, the use of Latin had given the Mass of Pius V a presumption of timelessness and had reinforced clerical exclusivity. The introduction of the vernacular was a first recognition of changing cultural factors, and a first step in the restoration of the liturgy as a symbolic expression for and of the whole people. Vernacular texts were first seen as translations of relatively timeless normative Latin texts, but advances into linguistic pluralism were fortunately made, even though the tradition of the normative text dies hard.

A deeper problem is seen in the theology of mission and the growth of Christianity in a plurality of cultures. From 'indigenization' in the 1960s to 'inculturation' in the 1970s, onward to 'contextualization' and the constructing of local theologies in the 1980s, milestones mark a slow progress away from the concept of a changeless gospel being translated into different cultures and towards a dialogue of analogous forms. 'Inculturation does not move from a world of essences to history, but from history to history, from Jerusalem to the ends of the earth' (Richard, 1987, p. 109).

These polarities flow from the diverse concepts of revelation already referred to. In counterpoint to this, the concept of tradition contains a similar ambiguity. Is tradition a series of fixed points enshrining doctrine (e.g. 'transubstantiation') and practice (e.g. the threefold structure of orders as we have it today), or are the *enduring consistencies* of tradition historically conditioned and particular symbols which activate understanding and encounter with the inexpressible faithfulness of God for their age, and as such are expressible as further analogous symbols hitherto undreamed of?

It will be the task of subsequent sections to review in some detail some of the main issues touched on here. Those selected are not chosen at random, but as *foci* of whole areas of theology of an ever-widening relevance: from ecclesiology in its internal, Roman Catholic relations (10B) to ecclesiology in relation to other churches (10C); from anthropology and the concept of human nature (10D), to the strictly theological issues relating to the kind of God Christians worship (10E).

10A General Overview: Bibliography

Gilkey, L. (1975) *Catholicism Confronts Modernity* (A Protestant View). New York, Seabury.

Jeanrond, W. G. (1988) 'Hermeneutics and Christian Praxis', *Journal of Literature and Theology*, vol. 2, no. 2 September, pp. 174–88.

Palmer, R. E. (1969) *Hermeneutics*. Evanston, North West University Press.

Richard, L., ed. (1987) *Vatican II, the Unfinished Agenda*. New York, Paulist Press.

Schneiders, S. M. (1978) 'Faith, Hermeneutics, and the Literal Sense of Scripture', *Theological Studies*, vol. 39, pp. 719–36.

Schneiders, S. M. (1982) 'The Paschal Imagination: Objectivity and Subjectivity in New Testament Interpretation', *Theological Studies*, vol. 43, pp. 52–68.

10B Ecclesial and Theological Pluralism

The theme of this chapter has been that the business of a Council always remains unfinished because of the historicity, the pluralist nature, and the changing context of human experience. The underlying polarization, therefore, in Vatican II and since has to be understood in terms not primarily of this or that divergence of views, but of the tension between the historical cast of mind and one that sees the mind as having possession of timeless truths, as being guided by definitive statements in a permanent and stable conceptual structure.

In this section the aim is to examine the way this tension is enshrined in (broadly) political matters, that is to say, in the structures of power in the Catholic Church. Here then we are to see the tension in ideas transposed into terms of power. On the one hand are those who see their Church as a body of persons fundamentally equal in status, as a segment of the Body of Christ, whose (certainly necessary) structures are formed from within the Body and exist solely in function of that Body and at its service. It is a model of universal access. On the other, there are those who see their Church as essentially composed of those who possess authority and the power to exercise it, and the rest who do not, even though they make one Body. The authority is conveyed directly, in some sense from above, from God, in a way therefore immune to change except for externals. It is a model of limited access. Here we look at developments only in some of the most important areas for internal Roman Catholic relations: the local church and the universal Church; collegiality and the appointment of bishops; and authority to teach.

LOCAL CHURCH AND UNIVERSAL CHURCH

Lumen Gentium 23 encapsulates the tension, and will be the starting point: '(The individual bishops are the visible source and foundation of unity in their own) particular churches, which are constituted after the model of the universal church: it is in these and formed out of them that the one and unique Catholic Church exists' (my brackets, Flannery 1, p. 376). The first clause after the bracketed clause suggests an existent, ideal, universal Church model for the construction of local churches: the second, a diverse historical growth of local churches into a complex unity based on intrinsic analogies between them. In the first case, history is abandoned for a Platonizing analysis of the present situation; in the second, the recognition is expressed that only concrete particular churches exist with their developing relations. Both views recognize that a cohesive body needs a principle and a structure of unity, but the first hypostatizes the principle and creates a structure elevated above the whole, while the second sees the principle to lie dynamically within the diverse communities which give birth to structures that foster their unity and that have as their *raison d'être* responsive service.

In spite of this radical ambiguity, the post-conciliar period saw a great development in participating structures in local churches from Holland to

Brazil, which expressed their geographical and cultural uniqueness and diversity. Much good has been done. But only up to a point. And that point is reached when the Roman authorities, working on a fundamentally idealist model of a centralizing type, perceive a threat to the hierarchic, dualist, structure as they understand it. The Dutch were the first (1968) to hold a National Pastoral Council (for a brief but good account of which, see Hebblethwaite, 1975, ch. 3). Its collapse came when its activity in the direction of local autonomy and decision-making from below was perceived as a threat by Rome. Yet the question is not one of the need for focuses of unity, local and universal (this is accepted), but of the form and extent of authority and power exercised. And this no Council has defined (see Vorgrimler 1, pp. 218–19).

The main developments in local identity, however, were taking place further away in poor countries. A milestone for all later developments was passed in the Latin American Bishops' Conference at Medellín (1968). Here we have a focus for an enormous growth in practice and theory which exemplifies in the main an historical perspective, the root of later conflict with Rome.

The starting point here is the unique local social experience (in this case of suffocating political oppression): not for these people an abstract conceptual system which is applied to events. This oppressive experience is seen as demeaning human beings and therefore challenges Christian engagement to change things. The perspective here is one that recognizes human life itself as a theological *locus*, because the goal of Christian transformation is to become fully human, since God became human in Christ.

The goal is not an other-worldly one directed to individual and inner salvation of souls. Social and political analysis becomes a theological tool and the aims pursued are, in the first instance, social betterment rather than individual conversion, since social sin and institutionalized violence are seen as the primary target. But it is the community structures from the grass roots of experience that concern us most here. They are Basic Christian Communities, from within which this historical, interpretative and contextualized theology is done. For here in all its diversity is a movement among local churches in consonance with an historical consciousness, churches of the people, churches of the poor. And though it was the social theology that met much criticism from Rome, it was above all the threat of the emergence of a 'people's Church' which motivated Cardinal Ratzinger's *Instruction* of liberation theology (see Segundo, 1985, ch. 4), and was an element in the imposition of a year's silence on Leonardo Boff.

COLLEGIALITY

If we now look at the leadership structures within the local–universal Church relations we find the same tensions transposed. One of the problems for the conciliar period was that reforming theological voices did not speak in complete harmony. Attacking immobilism had been a joint aim, but there the unanimity ended. Yves Congar, who had done so much to restore an historical perspective to theology and who had identified the hypostatization of power and its historical roots in *Power and Poverty in the Church*, himself allowed a dualism to remain in his ecclesiology. Anxious to support the ultimate primacy of the Church as a communion of persons constructed under God by the creative co-operation of all its members (*L'Eglise à faire*), he yet allowed, in *Lay People in the Church*, a second unintegrated strand of apostolic and sacramental authority deriving directly from Christ (*L'Eglise donnée*), thus giving support to the continuing clericalization of the Church's leadership.

In contrast, Hans Küng in *The Church* adopted a thoroughgoing theology of the primary role of the people of God as a community endowed with diverse charisms of the Spirit, among which the charisms of leadership, at each level, had a significant place, but in service to the whole and responsible to the whole.

It is the theology articulated by Congar, almost in spite of himself, which none the less expresses the theory of a uniquely privileged access to hierarchic power in the Roman Catholic Church, and which predominates in official circles today. It is the theology of Küng that represents a revival of the conciliar tradition in the Catholic Church, not in the earlier sense of the superiority of Council over pope, but in terms of a collegiality at every level in which a pope can exercise his special role only within the context of the leaders of the other local churches (*'primus inter pares'*). The extent to which this historical and pluralist model has been able to make an impact on the former one – with its roots in Vatican I – has been limited, and raises the question of the extent to which the implications of an historical consciousness were assimilated even by its protagonists at Vatican II. This in turn points to the subtle shades of opinion within 'majority' and 'minority' views, and underlines the unfinished nature of theological business. Let us look at one case.

The final version of *Lumen Gentium* 22, on the relation of pope and bishops, had included the crucial word 'also' (*quoque*), added to the penultimate version: ' . . . the episcopal order is (also) the subject of supreme and full power over the universal Church' (Abbott, p. 43 does not include here the 'also', though he does do so in the translation of the *nota praevia* (Abbott, p. 100); Flannery has it in neither place). But if 'also', who *else*? The pope alone. And the real advances in the self-consciousness of local churches spoken of above has to be offset by the growing immediacy of the papal role, augmented by modern means of travel and communication, coupled with the fact that all the collegial structures emerging from Vatican II are consultative, not legislative. Hence the decline in the impact of the episcopal synods.

> Many theologians believed that in the process of reception the new – that is, the concept of the *collegium* – would play an explosive role. . . . The normative element (they hoped) would prove to be not the compromise finally written into the document but that which was new in comparison with the existing tradition. . . . This view was not accurate (Vischer, in Alberigo and Jossua, pp. 241–2).

The appointment of bishops provides an illustrative case. Increasing centralization over 150 years (designed to keep the Roman Catholic Church free from state interference) means that today all bishops are, formally speaking, appointed by the pope, although, generally speaking, local rights of election by cathedral chapters have been incorporated into the process. But increasingly the concept of the local bishop as the symbol embodying the unity of the local church in collegial unity with other churches, including the Roman Church, is being overriden in favour of a concept of the bishop as the local representative of the pope.

The role of papal nuncios has been of more importance here than collegial considerations. The well-publicized views of Cardinal Ratzinger on the lack of a theological rationale for Bishops' Conferences further undermines concepts of collegiality and the recent papal interventions in the appointments at Cologne (*The Tablet*, 24/31 December 1988) and at Salzburg (*The Tablet*, 14 January 1989), overriding capitular rights in the election, not to mention the earlier intervention to limit the episcopal rights of Archbishop Raymond Hunthausen, all point in the direction of a growing devaluation of the local church in the interests of further building up the Roman curial structures as the administrative organ of a 'concrete universal' Church.

But the movement for the historicity of consciousness has one more card to play. The features of the modern world that have promoted an expansion of the papal role rather than its diminishment, are also the features that are forcing Christians of different traditions closer together. As the claims of unity are forcing attention back into history, synodical history can claim to have a future because it has had a past longer than the jurisdictional immediacy of the present papal role (Tillard, 1983, *passim*). And it is only through coming to terms with history that the errors of history – our Christian divisions – can be overcome, since it is increasingly apparent that it is only through the implementation of synodical or conciliar models that the unity of Christians could be achieved.

THEOLOGICAL PLURALISM

In the context of this chapter, the role of theology can be said to be that of maintaining historical, pluralist and contextual understanding of Christian faith. But as reflection on lived experience from within that experience, theology is at the service of the community as a whole and of those entrusted with decision-making (itself always provisional) as to how best human and Christian life is to be carried on in the light of that reflection. The balance between these two functions is a delicate one.

The tensions created in the Council between the legitimate claims of theological thought and those of executive (hierarchic) power have given rise to much unfinished business. On the one hand, there are the conciliar expressions of rights of conscience and religious liberty, (not to mention the United Nations Charter of Human Rights on freedom of speech), and on the other, there is a backlog of institutional theory stemming from the early nineteenth century (Congar, 1976, pp. 94ff.) which radically subordinates critical reflection to its own executive power claiming to be *the* magisterium, the sole source of authentic teaching and rule.

Küng's *Infallible?* (1970) reasserted, in adversarial style, the claims of the

224

theological expert over against official claims to infallibility on an absolute model. Work by Congar, Avery Dulles, Mary Daly and others (gathered in *Concilium*, no. 148) on the plurality of teaching roles in the community sought to restate the vital dialectic. Dulles wrote in terms of three *charismata*, the apostolic, the prophetic, and the theological ministries (elsewhere he wrote of 'two *magisteria*'); Congar, and Boff after him, criticized the compartmentalized division between 'teaching' and 'taught' Church, affirming that both labels mark roles that belong to all in the Church at different times.

Daly, now admittedly a 'post-Catholic', prefers the theologian to renounce any 'magisterium', and speaks instead of a socratic role. Increasingly this critical function, including the right to dissent, is under threat in the present, as recently in the cases of Schillebeeckx, Boff, and Charles Curran. The *Cologne Declaration* of 27 January 1989, signed by 163 theologians from Germany, Austria, Switzerland and the Netherlands (text in *The Tablet*, 4 February 1989), argues forcibly against the neglect of the rights of local churches in the appointment of bishops, the refusal of official permission to teach to critical voices, and the attempt to establish the pope's doctrinal competence in an inadmissible way. Vatican II's project of coming to grips with modernity favours at a hermeneutic level the theologians' concerns. The Council was a plunge into the waters of pluralism or it was nothing.

10B Ecclesial and Theological Pluralism: Bibliography

Congar, Y. (1976), 'Histoire du mot "Magistère"', and 'Bref historique des formes du "Magistère" et de ses relations avec les docteurs", *Revue des Sciences Philosophiques et Theologiques*, vol. 60, pp. 85–98 and 99–112.

Dulles, A. (1982) *A Church to Believe in*. New York, Crossroad.

Hebblethwaite, P. (1975) *The Runaway Church*. London, Collins. Revised Edition (Fount Paper).

Küng, H., and Moltmann, J., eds (1981) *Who Has the Say in the Church?*, *Concilium*, no. 148, August.

Segundo, J. (1985) *Theology and the Church*. London, Geoffrey Chapman.

Sweeney, G. (1977), ch. 9 (On the appointment of bishops) in Hastings, A., ed. *Bishops and Writers*. Wheathampstead, Anthony Clarke.

Tillard, J. (1983) *The Bishop of Rome*. London, SPCK.

10C Intercommunion

That Vatican II was most fundamentally a struggle to come to terms with the historicity of human consciousness has been the main argument of, and has provided the main criterion for, this chapter's interpretation of what occurred in the Council, and of what has happened since 1965. It has favoured historicity and its implications against various ahistorical forms, as providing a more adequate way of interpreting human religious experience and Christian social practice. Intercommunion, the symbolic focus of ecumenism, provides another illustration of the tension between these two forms of understanding. For to make claims for historicity is to make claims for pluralism in forms of life and of thought, and this, in ecclesiological terms, has meant claiming a priority for concrete local churches. Extended one stage further, this implies a methodology for inter-church dialogue which begins from the existing churches as analogues of Christian community life, and sees their diverse histories as trajectories more or less coherent in pattern with their origins and therefore with each other, and more or less imperfect in their struggle to overcome all manner of division – a factor pointed out by Congar as long ago as 1937 in his historic work *Chrétiens Désunis*.

This interpretation rejects that other approach which posits a 'concrete universal' – one actual true Church – to which all others must conform, an approach that existed in the Roman Catholic Church prior to Vatican II, but which is hardly sustainable as a serious interpretation of the documentary evidence of the Council with its recognition of other *churches* (*Unitatis Redintegratio*, 3, etc.), not to mention the door left ajar to pluralism in the famous 'subsists in' clause (*Lumen Gentium* 8). More serious, however, has been another ambiguity. On the one hand, there are views that see not the present reality this time, but the future goal of ecumenism as a 'concrete universal', as one structurally united Church sharing the idealist aim of one faith expressible as such in precise form. Over against these are views that see full unity as an eschatological goal which cannot be instantiated as such either in form or formula, and which, therefore, appeals to a 'conciliar fellowship where mutual recognition of ministry and sacraments would exist within a framework of separately governed churches' (Derr, 1983, p. 6). Intercommunion, the sharing in the Eucharistic table and all that that symbolizes, makes sense on this view in the context of an eschatological dynamism.

DEVELOPMENTS SINCE 1965

1 Where *Lumen Gentium* fractionally opened an ecclesiological door, the decree on ecumenism left a symbolic, sacramental door ajar. In speaking in general terms of worship in common (*communicatio in sacris*) but not directly envisaging the Eucharist, it says: 'The expression of unity very generally forbids common worship. Grace to be obtained sometimes commends it' (*Unitatis Redintegratio* 8).

2 A genuine tide of urgency for unity, however diversely understood,

226

followed in the wake of the Council, especially among many of the Churches' leaders who had been participants or first-hand observers at the Council and among the theologically aware. This existed alongside a great deal of inertia and incomprehension. Encouraging *rapprochements* were made between the East and Rome and between Canterbury and Rome. In this context, a degree of openness in regard to intercommunion was expressed in *Ad Totam Ecclesiam* (the Directory concerning Ecumenical Matters: Part One) of 14 May 1967 (Flannery 1, pp. 483ff.). Since the Orthodox Churches are seen as having valid sacraments, especially orders, there is considerable openness: 'This offers ecclesiological and sacramental grounds for allowing and even encouraging some sharing in liturgical worship – even Eucharistic – with these Churches "given suitable circumstances and the approval of church authorities" (*UR* 15)' (Flannery 1, p. 496). This is also understood of Catholics receiving in Orthodox churches. 'Spiritual need' is included as a reason in favour. With regard to the Churches of the Reformation, the first statement is always that intercommunion is forbidden, primarily due to deficiency in orders. 'Nevertheless, since the sacraments are both signs of unity and sources of grace (see *UR* 8) the Church can for adequate reasons allow access to those sacraments to a separated brother' (Flannery 1, p. 499). The criteria are danger of death or urgent need (if there is not access to one's own minister), if the request is spontaneously made and a faith in the sacrament in harmony with that of the Catholic Church is expressed. Catholics may never communicate at non-Roman Catholic Eucharists.

3 In 1970 a firmer line was taken officially in the Unity Secretariat's *Dans ces derniers temps* of 7 January (Flannery 1, pp. 502ff.). The earlier phrase referring to lack of access to a minister of another communion becomes a firm condition (para.7), to all intents and purposes ruling out intercommunion in normal circumstances.

4 Then in 1972, when the inter-Church *Groupe des Dombes* (McAdoo, 1973, pp. 51ff.) was arriving at a shared expression of Eucharistic faith which enabled them to conclude with the recommendation that 'access to communion should not be refused for reasons of eucharistic faith to Christians of another denomination whose own faith is that professed above' (p. 64), a further Roman document of the Unity Secretariat, *In Quibus rerum Circumstantiis* of 1 June 1972 (Flannery 1, pp. 554ff.), reinforced the official line with a deeper theological rationale based on 'the strict relationship between the mystery of the Church and the mystery of the Eucharist [which] can never be altered' (p. 557). Agreed statements on the theology of the Eucharist were not to affect practical discipline.

5 World-wide practice has not, however, been so clear-cut or so uniform, but considerable effort has been expended (witness the many documents) to sustain the official practice. One example of a directive that mitigated the 'lack of access' condition was that of the bishop of Superior, Wisconsin, who none the less carefully defined cases for Eucharistic hospitality mostly restricted to family occasions (*Ecumenical Trends* 7).

6 This family setting has raised the question of intercommunion in an acute form throughout the post-conciliar years. Inter-Church families (where both

wife and husband are committed to their own, different, traditions) often feel acute spiritual need of sharing across the divides in sacramental Communion and their experience, movingly documented for England in *Sharing Communion*, is hard to gainsay.

7 Meanwhile other influences have turned attention away from intercommunion as a symbol of post-conciliar tension: the serious impatience of younger people (often highly articulate); the diminished interest in sacramental issues and the growth in outward-looking social involvement (see Girault, in Alberigo and Jossua, ch. 8), even while the official policy remains as firm as ever in the pontificate of John Paul II. Such factors and the issues associated with celibacy (10E) have jointly produced influences diminishing Eucharistic concern, while it also seems true that sharing Communion within the denominations has in actual fact increased.

COMMENT

The fundamental tension can be expressed in the question: Is sharing the Eucharist to be seen solely as the seal on unity achieved, or should it be seen as also a means to create unity? In the official 'seal' argument there is an internal tension which should first be pointed out: on the one hand, there is a partial recognition of other Churches and their sacramental structure. Insistence on the 'lack of access' argument as a basic condition for admission of non-Roman Catholics to Catholic Communion suggests that such access, where possible, does integrate the person in their own Church's sacramental structure with its own degree of validity as means of grace. On the other hand, the insistence on the invalidity of orders in the other Churches of the West tends to a position that the sacramental forms of other Churches is 'completely null and utterly void'.

But if there is a tension in a minor key within the official stand, the major tension lies between the official position and those who argue for much greater flexibility. These include those who would support an 'open table' (as almost universally nowadays in the Churches of the Reformation), but also those who would see the question of participation in the Eucharist as best decided by ability to express a faith-filled desire for the Eucharist as a sacramental symbol of the presence of the living Lord, living and active in the community whose hospitality one shares, but not requiring formulaic precision.

The two tendencies we have traced throughout this chapter show themselves again here. Without saying that all who pursue greater historicity of consciousness favour *de facto* an 'open table' approach, this position expresses most clearly an acceptance of the historical diversity and pluralism of actual church communities as they struggle towards a greater 'conciliar fellowship'.

No community is perfect, and no community's Eucharist is a perfect symbol, but all embody analogously Christian presence in the world. Here it is all a matter of degree. But the official Roman Catholic position enunciates in terms of sacramental discipline an absolute, ahistorical, idea of unity present in the Roman Catholic Church (and if the validity/invalidity argument is pursued, it is difficult to see how even partial embodiment is possible elsewhere). In other words, the official position appears to express obliquely the 'one, true Church' claims of pre-Vatican II Catholicism, and with them the former 'one, true Eucharist' claims.

The way forward suggested by a historical hermeneutics is to recognize the vital distinction between concrete, incomplete, realities (however complex and widely interwoven their interrelationships in time and space) – in our case, Christian Churches – and reflectively acquired and abstract universals. The 'universality' of an inductive ecclesiology lies not in absolutizing any particular form or formula (symbol), but in the lived openness of its continuing process of enquiry, its method, its pursuit of truth as an heuristic 'wherever it may lead' (a truly eschatological pursuit); while accepting particular, revisable structures and expressions as helpful milestones on the way. Symbolically or sacramentally expressed, this would suggest a theology of Eucharist which favours, rather than opposes, intercommunion as an important means to promote unity to an ever-greater degree, when it is celebrated as the historical memorial of the Lord Jesus from whom all communities derive their source and present life, awaiting meanwhile his final coming, the eschaton we cannot conceive of.

10C Intercommunion: Bibliography

Derr, T. S. (1983) *Barriers to Ecumenism*. New York, Orbis Books.
Duquoc, C. (1986) *Provisional Churches*. London, SCM.
Ecumenical Trends (1973) vol. 11, no. 2, May.
McAdoo, H. ed. (1973) *Modern Eucharistic Agreement*. London, SPCK.
Reardon, R., and Finch, M., eds (1983) *Sharing Communion*. An appeal to the Churches by Inter-Church Families. London, Collins.

10D Birth Control

The publication of *Humanae Vitae* in July 1968 provided a vivid focus for the tensions of the immediate post-conciliar period, and created, for vast numbers of ordinary people, shock waves whose reverberations will echo for many years to come. Underlying the particular issues of moral practice and theory, of institutional authority and world population, lay the deeper issue of attitudes to the way human nature itself was interpreted. Is there a constitutive core of humanness? Is it permanent? Can it be known? These questions bring us back to the fundamental theme of this chapter: the tension between an ahistorical and an historical interpretation of human reality. For at the heart of the pain and conflict created has been the clash between two broad conceptualizations of natural law. On the one hand stands the claim to an absolute, god-given and changeless law of human nature which could be known by natural reason and be reinforced by revelation. On the other is the recognition that such an ahistorical absolute is not given in consciousness from whatever source. What does exist are culturally and historically conditioned analogues of human experience.

DEVELOPMENT SINCE 1965

The events of the conciliar period set the scene. In 1963 John XXIII had established an international commission whose terms of reference expanded as did its membership. Under Paul VI its brief was to consider the Church's position on marital sexuality. Meanwhile, the discussions leading to *Gaudium et Spes* and its teaching on marriage (*GS* 47–52) expressed the familiar tensions we have examined in other spheres. Concern for an holistic, personal, doctrine of marriage which took account of historical perspectives predominated, but those who supported an absolute, supra-historical interpretation of human nature, and consequently of the nature of the marriage act, made a strong showing. 'This turning away from a narrow analysis of the marriage act to a view of the married vocation as a whole is momentous' (Vorgrimler 5, p. 239). But incumbent on both schools of thought was the necessity of finding more adequate ways of expressing the *enduring consistencies* of human experience (see 10A), loosely referred to as 'human nature', since none of the participants wished to support a pure situationism. However, opportunity was not given in the Council. The matter was referred by Paul VI to the Commission.

The Commission's report was leaked to the press in April 1967 (see *The Tablet*, 1967, p. 451ff. and 510ff.). This took up the historical, holistic and personalist categories adumbrated in *Gaudium et Spes* and worked them through. The sense of history enabled the majority who signed the report to envisage a development and change in the traditional doctrine, which was seen as designed to protect the enduring values of sex, marriage and procreation which the Commission also wished to preserve, but as formulated in a too limited and severely inadequate way. The holistic and personal outlook enabled the signatories to affirm that 'the morality of sexual acts between

230

married people takes its meaning first of all and specifically from the ordering of their actions in a fruitful married life. . . . It does not then depend upon the direct fecundity of each and every particular act' (ibid. p. 451). The objective criteria are 'the various values and needs duly and harmoniously evaluated' (ibid., p. 452), concerned, that is, with total human meaning (ibid., p. 512).

By contrast, the conservative case, presented in a position paper signed by a minority on the Commission of four named theologians (*The Tablet*, 1967, pp. 478ff.) argued against any change in the official teaching, resting its case on the 'principle' of a *specific ordering* of each free, generative action to procreation in the strict sense' (ibid., p. 484) and maintaining consequently that any contraception is morally evil. This principle, in turn, rests on twin pillars: on a theory of moral absolutes (that certain classes of moral act are intrinsically evil and absolutely forbidden, for example, 'homicide' (ibid., p. 478); and on the constant claim of the leadership of the Roman Catholic Church to make universally binding prohibitions of such acts (ibid., pp. 480–1). What is defined as intrinsically evil is said to be evil by reason of 'natural law' (ibid., p. 478), not in the sense that the precept is directly 'read off' human biology, as it were, but because such law asserts that human life itself (and all that concerns its origin and ending, therefore) 'is not under man's dominion' (ibid., p. 480).

Paul VI reserved the pain of decision to himself. In July 1968 *Humanae Vitae* was published and, in spite of deeply felt passages expressing pastoral understanding, the encyclical decided in favour of the line of argument of the minority and against change. It was not that Paul VI ignored personal values; the question is whether he succeeded in integrating the different dimensions or levels of human being – biological, psychological, personal – into a unity. The biological, it would seem, remains determinative.

There are considerable obscurities in all the opposing arguments. Only a brief comment is possible. The core of the argument appears to be focused (unwillingly in the case of the majority on the Commission) on bodily, that is, sexual, functioning. It is then a question of *how far* this functioning ('nature'), as being the embodiment of human personal meanings, can be and is altered by these meanings. For Paul VI it would appear, the body and its functioning, in carrying personal meanings, can be co-ordinated with, but cannot be radically altered by, overall meanings. It is still necessary to 'obey' the nature of each sexual act. There is a 'two-tier', dualistic, approach here that favours the changelessness of the naturally 'given'. On the other hand, the (majority) report is saying that personal values control the whole reality of all human levels of being. Biology is not ignored, but it does not exist except as integrated in the human totality. So it is not individual sexual acts but the overall health, dignity and responsible parenthood of the couple that counts. There is here only one story, one history.

The lack of consultation in the production of the encyclical, as well as the content, led to a crisis in its reception; a crisis that in turn led both to anguished confusion and to the maturing of many individual consciences. Conferences of bishops did not take public issue with the teaching, but many so wrestled with the problems created for ordinary people that the result could rarely be seen as simply an endorsement of the document. But the official teaching and the reactions to it, whether of assent or dissent, have remained very much as they were in the immediate aftermath. The 'essential' and 'existential' tendencies were followed through. Officially, the Declaration of the Congregation for the Doctrine of the Faith on Certain Problems of Sexual Ethics, *Personae Humanae*, in December 1975 (Flannery 2, pp. 486–99) reiterated that 'man's true dignity cannot be achieved unless the essential order of his nature be observed' (Flannery 2, p. 487). While historical changes occur, the unchangeable principles 'transcend historical circumstances' (ibid.). Theologically, the literature *pro* and *con* multiplied (see contrasting papers in *Theological Studies*, vol. 39, 1978). The synod of the family in 1980 was the occasion for John Paul II to issue his subsequent letter *Familiaris Consortio* (Flannery 2, pp. 815–98), in which valuable insights into personal values are accompanied by a strong reiteration of the position of *Humanae Vitae* (29 and 32). Other restatements have followed.

The teaching of *Humanae Vitae* was not infallible (Lambruschini, in Mahoney, 1987, p. 271), but assent was due to it as an authentic (meaning authoritative) pronouncement of the magisterium. The whole issue of authority and dissent has lain behind the moral questions (see 10B). Most recently, events have taken a most disturbing turn. John Paul II has declared that to dispute the teaching of the encyclical was '"the equivalent of refusing to God himself the obedience of our intelligence", and could threaten the very cornerstones of Christian doctrine' (*The Tablet*, 1988, p. 1378). The authoritarian effects of an absolutist moral and intellectual framework could not be more clearly illustrated.

COMMENT

The depth of the conflicts aroused is to be explained by the radically opposed conceptual frameworks which clash at this focal point. The first affirms that a kernel of permanent created reality exists, embodied in a particular way in the physical constitution of the human being. Furthermore, it is possible to enunciate this essence in permanently valid precepts of natural law, or, more modestly, it is possible to reach this kernel by making allowances in some way for the new recognized cultural conditioning that accidentally affects the changeless nature (see Flannery 2, p. 487). The result is a deductive ethic which does not admit even that it is offering one interpretational framework among a number. Ranged against this is an array of positions which concur in the assertion that no such univocal kernel exists, still less is it possible to enunciate it. What exists are historically conditioned forms of human life. Inductive methods provide generalized guidelines for particular cultures.

But where this range of views differs internally is over the *extent* to which general statements can be made about human beings, and hence over the criteria used.

1 A not surprisingly sweeping reaction to deductive ethics with its authoritarian character has led many to opt for a situationist ethic which may be rather generally described as placing the norm, the criterion for moral action, solely

in the individual person's situation as perceived by them in their freedom. There is no law of nature. Variations of this extreme individualist reaction have been tried without much success in moral theology, and we will not be pursuing them here.

In the present-day context, to accuse a person of adopting situation ethics is usually a form of abuse and a poor substitute for argument. But it cannot be denied that a great deal of confused thinking verging on a situationist position arose, all with the best of motives, where the unique situation of persons, especially of married couples in their loving relationship, was at issue. The consciousness of a unique personal element in the relationship obscured, perhaps, the possibility of further, more generalized, norms.

2 Other still relative but more general ethical norms have been formulated by many ethicians both in society at large and within religious bodies over a much longer time span than that since 1965. Here the only generalizations possible would be within the limits of a particular culture or era. Vigorous arguments can be formulated for this range of positions, but they would take us too far afield. For these views there is not, at any rate, anything constitutive of our humanity.

3 More typical for our purposes has been the elaboration of an existentialist ethic (see Rahner, 1963) which both acknowledges the unique element of experience in the existence of persons in relationship, and also recognizes that this is a modification of a more general human situation. What *exists*, for Rahner and others, are human beings in analogous (i.e. inextricably like and unlike) relationships. Moral absolutes as previously conceived do not provide an adequate analysis of moral states of affairs, which are always particular and have to be assessed in their concrete circumstances. (For a good account, see Mahoney, 1987, pp. 311ff.)

For people and actions conceived thus, moral precepts, whether in ethics or in moral theology, provide guidelines for responsible particular decisions, not absolute commands. But it remains true, in this perspective, that the physical and socio-psychological make-up of human beings (always in the concrete) does provide some of the agenda for decision, though not the decisions themselves. One strength of an existentialist-type ethical theory is that it bids fair to reintegrate the subjective and objective elements in morality. There is no further question of 'objectively wrong' but 'subjectively right' (excusable?), since only concrete human acts of persons occur and they are then more or less adequate responses to concrete situations which comprise a complex web of social and psychological conditions and of a degree of personal, graced, freedom. Such theories also take the historical seriously, in eschewing an ahistorical concept of an absolute natural and moral law: as such, they have provided much of the alternative framework to that of *Humanae Vitae*.

Where the earlier existentialist ethic has proved uncertain, however, is in its way of handling the *enduring consistencies*, the analogies, of experience, which the model of natural law is itself an attempt to cope with. There is more than a hint of an enduring essence which exists in diverse ways (the familiar 'kernel'). What seems to be required here is further reflection on the nature of moral norms, conceived not on the model of law at all, but as heuristic principles

('principles for finding one's way'), on the lines of 'love in all that you do'. These are paradoxically empty of content (at least at first), but yet indicate directions in which to look for analogies of behaviours. Expressing a method rather than a content, they teach us how to proceed, not what to do. *This* has to be arrived at inductively. What human beings share is, then, not a constitution but a dynamism, a 'radar beam' searching for the good, a historical process – not absolute rules.

All this makes wide discussion and therefore the legitimacy of dissent a constitutive part of the process of finding the concrete norms for the here and now.

What has become apparent is that once again, in the discussions of the papal commission and in the subsequent reactions to *Humanae Vitae*, we find hermeneutical attitudes to the historicity of consciousness underlying the vast complexity of the particular issues.

10D Birth Control: Bibliography

Mahoney, J. (1987) *The Making of Moral Theology: A Study of the Roman Catholic Tradition*. Oxford, Clarendon Press.

Rahner, K. (1963) 'On the Question of a Formal Existential Ethics' in *Theological Investigations*, vol. 2. London, Darton, Longman and Todd, pp. 217–34.

Theological Studies, (1978) vol. 39, especially the articles by Komonchak, J. A., '*Humanae Vitae* and its reception: Ecclesiological Reflections' (pp. 221–57), and by Ford, J. C. and Grisez, G. 'Contraception: the Infallibility of the Ordinary Magisterium' (pp. 258–312).

10E Celibacy

The issue of celibacy serves as a focus in the Roman Catholic Church for a whole range of issues concerned with priestly ministry, and all circle around the central question of mediation between God and human beings. We have already seen the dualism, albeit mitigated, implied in a Congar-type theology of office in the Church, which in consequence offers a degree of support to the still-active traces of a sacral, mediatorial view of priestly ministry. Celibacy as a cultic symbol of 'the man set apart' for the service of the divine fits well into this pattern. Over against this stands the more fully human-centred ecclesiology of those like Küng and Schillebeeckx, whose theology of office focuses on the charism of leadership from within the community which is itself the Spirit-animated Body of Christ.

In this paradigm the symbolic value of celibacy for the ministry becomes much more problematic in the face of the pressing pastoral needs of people deprived of the Eucharist. Celibate ministry may well be seen in this perspective as one symbolic form, freely chosen, of commitment to a demanding service of others, much as a nurse or a teacher might remain single without any comparison being possible with those, equally committed, who marry; it may also be seen as a symbol of commitment to what the *world* really is, a finite reality grounded in the transcendent God, as in the case of a monk. But it cannot be seen as an ahistorical, cultic symbol of service given to an other-worldly God, a God apart.

It is important to note that the dualist position is not seen any more, even by its protagonists, as *determinative* for ministry: none argue that there is a necessary theological connection between priestly ministry and celibacy. But the cultic symbol is still powerfully *operative*: it provides an ideological rationale for what is acknowledged to be a juridical linkage. The final comment of this chapter will argue that this providing of a theological rationale for a juridical obligation obscures some very important theological concerns and leaves the status of the prescription unclear.

DEVELOPMENTS SINCE 1965

1 Vatican II left many unresolved problems in regard to the ministerial priesthood (see Duquoc, in Alberigo and Jossua, ch. 14). Radical questioning of the traditional model of sacral priesthood, defined in terms of sacred power to consecrate and absolve, was initiated, but no fully worked-out alternative was proposed. Debate on celibacy was precluded by Paul VI, and so *Presbyterorum Ordinis*, while reaffirming the discipline of celibacy for the ordained in the Latin Church, made only a general statement that 'there are many ways in which celibacy is in harmony with the priesthood' (*PO* 16).

Paul had, however, invited written comments, and Maximos IV Sayegh wrote pithily: 'In case of necessity the priesthood must not be sacrificed to celibacy but celibacy to the priesthood' (Hickey, 1986, p. 56). Thus a three-way tension was created: the traditional discipline was reaffirmed without discussion; pressure to mitigate the discipline for pastoral reasons lay barely hidden below the surface; and the underlying theological accounts were in disarray.

2 The reaffirmation of the discipline of celibacy for the ordained, a formal requirement at least since the Second Lateran Council of 1139, has been a constant feature of the last twenty-five years. Paul VI issued his encyclical *Sacerdotalis Caelibatus* in 1967 (Flannery 2, pp. 285–317); the Synod of 1971 also endorsed the position (Flannery 2, p. 689), as did the *Letter to Priests* of John Paul II in 1979 (Flannery 2, p. 354). The sustaining arguments have widened to include the human considerations (which are also theological) mentioned in the introductory remarks to this section, but the anomaly remains: it is impossible satisfactorily to give universal juridical expression to what is essentially a charism.

3 The pressure therefore to modify the traditional stance has been widespread. The right of all priests to marry has been vigorously espoused, for example in the Netherlands, but the main pressure has been in favour of the ordination of married men to alleviate the dearth of priests, especially in poorer countries. This was the burden of Maximos IV's letter and particular needs were expressed in Africa (see Hastings, 1967) and in Indonesia (see Hickey, 1986, pp. 64–9). The Synod of 1971 did debate celibacy in its discussion of priestly ministry in general. A large number of bishops spoke in favour of ordaining married men, but the majority vote in the event went against, recognizing, however, the right of the pope to act. The one area where this action has been taken has been in regard to the ordination of married convert clergy in Germany, in Australia, in the United States, a possibility already envisaged by Paul VI in *Sacerdotalis Caelibatus* 42. A particularly significant body of opinion, principally among clergy in the support of ordination for married men, has been formed in Britain. The Movement for the Ordination of Married Men (MOMM) produces a regular Bulletin of documentation covering relevant matters world-wide; it has the tacit approval of the bishops.

4 Meanwhile, the fluid state of the theology of the subject has taken its toll. The increased emphasis on human values and the rejection of the sacral model with its authority structures led significant numbers of priests to leave the active ministry. A darker side of these twenty-five years has been the official treatment of many of those who have left. Initially more tolerant (see the 1971 Synod, Flannery 2, p. 689), this treatment has grown more harsh as the present policy sought to stem the exodus by demeaning questionnaires and by protracted delays, amounting sometimes to refusal. Little sign is given that the institutional Church has failed many of its priests. The emphasis is all the other way. But national organizations of those who have left the active ministry, like the Advent Group in Britain and Corpus in the United States, are working to secure that the lessons of their personal experience and theological reflection are not lost to the churches at large. These movements have so flourished that international conferences are now held.

5 Finally, the contrasting theologies of ministry have developed over the years. The traditional sacral model lost many of its features, especially in the personalist theology of John Paul II, who puts great emphasis on celibacy as a

236

gift of availability for service of people (Flannery 2, p. 355). But the general theology of ministry remains in a Congar-type dualistic mould: its *essential* difference (Flannery 2, p. 351, quoting *Lumen Gentium* 10) as a participation in the priesthood of Christ, from the participatory priesthood of the laity, means a gift given directly from Christ who is conceived of as distinct from his people. And the prohibition, often repeated by John Paul II (but not to be found in the Synod of 1971) (Flannery 2, p. 685), of involvement by priests in political activity, is symptomatic of a concept of a modified sacrality, a holy precinct of activity which sets the priest apart.

An alternative theology emphasizes charism. It sees official ministry as a charism of leadership, of service, among all the charisms with which the baptized are endowed. All are gifts of the Spirit, not 'transferable' (and so unique to the person, 'essentially' different from those of others!). But all emerge from within the Body of Christ: there is no need to foster a dualistic interpretation of ordained ministry. Then, too, leadership is not predefined abstractly in its structures. It will contribute to building up a community in whatever manner serves the goals of the community. This will usually be through the symbolic means of word and sacrament, but social involvement is often likely to be appropriate. Life does not have compartments, and the sacraments comment on and illuminate life. Many movements developed in the 1960s and 1970s to give concrete expression to these insights, for example, Priests for the Third World in Argentina, L'Assemblée des Prêtres Solidaires in France, and other groupings also. The tension adumbrated in the Council remains.

COMMENT

The main argument of this chapter could not be more clearly illustrated than by an intervention at the 1971 Synod, by Bishop Santos Ascarza of Chile, on two contrasting methodologies:

> The first starts from scripture and the priesthood of Christ in order to determine the purpose, scope and meaning of the priestly ministry once and for all, and then proceeds to draw appropriate conclusions for our time. It is clear but abstract. The other method starts from the signs of the times, the crisis in the priesthood and the conditions in which the apostolate is developing, and then discerns what Christ is asking of us today.

This is not a purely theoretical matter. In the context of comment on the phenomenon of celibate clergy pronouncing authoritatively on the sexual lives of the married, Peter McCaffrey says:

> The obligation (of celibacy) serves as a symbol for a certain type of thinking about the nature of revealed truth and its implications . . ., namely, that by comparison with any inductively achieved insight into the conditions of moral choice, the Roman Catholic priesthood has something better to offer, since its members are able to draw uniquely valid deductions as to the details of people's religious and interpersonal obligations. Priests are able to do this because they work from the only correctly conceptualised account of the overall purpose of human existence (MOMM, *Bulletin*, 5, p. 23).

237

It is this position and its modifications that has been under critical examination throughout this chapter. It is the concern of this final comment to indicate that from what has been called a historically conscious perspective, celibacy might very well be chosen freely for particular, contingent and humanly intelligible reasons, but that the reasoning which accepts that celibacy has no logically necessary link with priestly ministry, yet still defends the universal linkage by various theoretical arguments, rests in fact on a suspect ahistorical hermeneutics which has been radically challenged by the very event of Vatican II. Four theoretical arguments will be considered, all of which disclose in different ways doubtful *theological* views, that is, views of the God we worship.

1 The 'ritual purity' argument has in the past demanded abstention from sexual relations as a condition for celebrating the Eucharist the next day (see Lawrence, 1979, p. 572). This Manichaean, Platonizing argument has been explicitly rejected by contemporary documents (e.g. by John Paul II; Flannery 2, p. 254). None the less, suspicion of the body and of sexual expression riddles Christian minds, and still operates in an unreflective way, buttressing the evaluation of celibacy as an 'other-wordly' value and a rejection of this world. The difficulty for the Judaeo-Christian tradition is that one of its pillars is the rejection of 'nature religion', that is, the divinizing of world, of nature, and so of sexuality. This rejection explains the polemic of the first chapters of Genesis. But too great a swing towards an other-worldly God in fact denies the created goodness of the world and distorts the image of God.

2 But the relation of God to nature has further pitfalls in store. Between confusion of God with nature and separation of God entirely from nature is yet a third unsatisfactory path which bedevils the theology of celibacy. This path accepts the goodness of creation, but sees in human creation an overly close relation (not identification) with God. It presents nature, especially human nature, as an *icon* of God and often means by this that there are certain necessary and informative symbols that reveal God in human nature.

Here lies the rationale behind the argument for the maleness of the priest, and the celibacy of the clergy likewise, 'in the image of Christ'. This seems to be the logic behind the argumentation of the present pope and can be found in the theological synthesis of H.U. von Balthasar. But while the world is an icon or sacrament of God, especially in Christ, the relation between God and world is not in any way logically necessary but contingent. There are no deductions to be drawn of a descriptive nature. Christ's humanness (and his maleness and his celibacy) tell us something about the *fact* of the goodness of God, of God's commitment to humanity. They tell us nothing about the description of God for God has no description.

How God stands to the world is a matter of transcendental reference, of love and truth which are heuristic notions, not content-ful descriptions. And as a result, celibacy must remain as a possible witness to commitment to other human beings or to the sheer reality of God as transcendent horizon of our lives (and therefore to the relativity of life). But there is no necessary connection between celibacy and particular forms of ecclesial service.

3 The argument that celibacy enabled a person to serve God with 'undivided

heart' is seen in many of the documents (e.g. Flannery 2, p. 292 (Paul VI), p. 688 (1971 Synod)). Its implications are dualist and Platonizing, confusing the unqualified (transcendental) commitment to God which is the vocation of all human beings (the 'universal call to holiness' of *Lumen Gentium* ch. 5) with particular styles of commitment to human beings. The implicit thrust is to compartmentalize the divine and the human and to put the 'priest' in a precinct apart from the ordinary concerns of life, devaluing the latter and canonizing the former as a symbol of the eternal. But the married are equally called to holiness and the celibate gives *divided* attention to this or that human being or group. Commitment to Christ, the sacrament of God, is not in competition with commitment to a wife or husband; but to live certain styles of commitment to other people may be incompatible with marriage. What must not happen is to set God in opposition to God's creation, to humanly good concerns.

4 The theoretical arguments for celibacy appeared flawed. Above all, the understanding of God is put at risk. Is there a less than theological rationale underlying an invariant link between celibacy and priestly ministry? Duquoc identifies such a rationale in the defence of the ministerial priesthood as a clerical *state of life*:

> The only plausible hypothesis seems to me, therefore, to be the following: the by now centuries-old practice of the Church, having once responded to real interests, has been theorised into a quasi-dogmatic system, which, by canonising that practice, makes it impossible to perceive the new needs of the community. In other words, an ecclesial practice, one of the concerns of which was the vitality of the communities, having been formalised into an essential structure of the Church, perpetuates itself independently of the network of relationships of which it originally formed a part (Duquoc 24 March, 1979, p. 309).

This dissociative structure he calls Platonizing in inspiration and we are brought full circle in our concern to differentiate between an abstract, ahistorical tendency and a fully historical consciousness. The tension underlying the unfinished business of Vatican II is to be found here and the struggle to take history fully seriously will persist. Two dimensions of this struggle have been evident throughout: to explore the implications of historicity is one; to combat resistance to accepting historical consciousness is the other.

10E Celibacy: Bibliography

Duquoc, C. (1979) 'Concepts of Ministry 1 and 2', two articles in *The Tablet*, 10 and 24 March, pp. 231–2 and pp. 309–11.

Hastings, A. (1967) *Church and Mission in Modern Africa*. London, Burns & Oates.

Hickey, R. (1986) *A Married Priesthood in the Catholic Church*. Darlington, Liverpool Institute of Socio-Religious studies (LISS), Occasional Papers 2.

Lawrence, C. H. (1979) 'Clerical Celibacy', *The Tablet*, 16 June, pp. 572–3.

Movement for the Ordination of Married Men (MOMM). *Information Bulletins* nos. 1–9, September 1982–October 1988. Liverpool, LISS.

11

ASPECTS OF CHURCH LIFE SINCE THE COUNCIL

11A Devotion

MARGARET HEBBLETHWAITE

Before Vatican II, the devotional practices of Catholics were easier to pin down than they became after the Council. There was a recognizable culture expressed in prayers specific to Catholics and in many devotions performed in Church. Examples of these would be the lighting of candles before statues of the saints, the stations of the cross, visits to the Blessed Sacrament, the rosary recited in common and the first Friday of the month devotion of confession and Communion. Benediction was a regular – often weekly – devotion of great popular appeal: reverence and love were fostered in a rite that enriched the senses of smell – with clouds of incense; of hearing – with sweet singing; and of sight – with the awe-inspiring presence of a consecrated host, exposed in a golden, spiky monstrance. In addition to Mass on Sundays and holidays of obligation, the good Catholic would go to confession monthly and abstain from meat on Fridays.

In terms of purely private devotion, prayers were taught by rote. The devout Catholic would have a short formula for morning prayer (usually the morning offering), for grace before and after meals, for night prayer (commending the soul into the arms of God in case one died in the night), and maybe even the Angelus at midday. The Salve Regina, the Memorare, the De Profundis and the rosary (with the names of all fifteen mysteries) were prayers that every good Catholic would know.

The revolution of thought resulting from the Council hit all these traditional practices hard. Some customs persisted for a while with older Catholics, but were not passed on to the next generation, though there has been a little restoration of the older styles of spirituality in certain circles during the 1980s. The Madonna of Medjugorje (see 11H), for example, is said to urge the saying of the rosary, fasting and frequent confession. John Paul II has encouraged the recovery of practices like Friday abstinence along with Marian devotion. But it is too early to know whether such restoration will be permanent, and the general thrust of post-Conciliar spirituality has been characterized by a widespread collapse of the older devotional system.

Better education, a search for meaning and relevance, and a new confidence in the Catholic Church's ability to change and grow under the guidance of the Holy Spirit, have all led to a critical reappraisal of many customary practices.

Questions crept in as to whether the Lord had rather instituted the Eucharist for us to share in a common meal, than for us to kneel down and worship and then replace in the tabernacle: numbers dropped at benediction, until the rite became almost extinct. Devotion at Mass changed from gazing with love in silence on one's knees – maybe even telling the rosary while the mysterious rites proceeded in barely audible foreign words – to more standing, singing, participating and responding.

In the same mood of urged participation, weekly communicating has become the almost universal norm, bringing to completion a trend towards frequent Communion that had been growing since the late nineteenth century. Mortal sin came to be seen as an exceptional state of affairs that you could not fall into very easily, so that even while the frequency of Communion was increasing, the frequency of confession was declining sharply. Today it is probably only a minority of Catholics who receive the sacrament of penance on any regular basis, even before Easter, unless as part of a communal liturgy of reconciliation. Many came to feel that their sinfulness could no longer be summed up in the neat lists of offences they used to confess, that the dark atmosphere of the confessional box fostered a morbid sense of guilt, and that the priest was no longer the person they would look to in matters of moral guidance.

Friday abstinence was abolished as an obligatory practice, though the idea of a Friday penance was to be continued, with people choosing their own one rather than having a standard practice imposed for all (and one that for many had lost any religious meaning other than marking out Catholics as different). In practice, however, the idea of mortification became almost completely lost: penance was thought to smack of gloom, but the new mood was the celebration of freedom.

Post-Conciliar Catholics no longer wanted to say set prayers learnt word for word, but to find spontaneous words from the heart. They were not prepared to structure their day around fixed prayer markers, but rather preferred to pray when and how the Spirit led them. External frameworks gave way to an increased sense of individual responsibility for the shaping of one's spiritual life.

The decline of specifically Catholic devotions was accompanied by a growth of an ecumenically shared spirituality. Popular religious art and holy pictures went through a transformation. Images became less identifiably Catholic: sacred hearts and crowned virgins were on the decrease; golden sunsets, billowing waves, snow-clad mountain peaks and leafy glades took their place, usually with a short text in the corner and often in the form of a poster to stick on the wall rather than a card to slip in a missal.

Spiritual reading boomed, no longer in the short didactic style of the pious leaflet, but in books for the more mature reader, including the spiritual classics as well as a wealth of new writings. The Bible was read and studied by many ordinary Catholics for the first time. Courses of spirituality abounded. The retreat movement flourished, but its style had changed. There was less silence and more group dynamics; less preaching and more sharing. Silence did, however, continue in Ignatian retreats, which blossomed now in most areas of the world as a practice for laity as much as for clergy and religious; but even the Ignatian exercises went through a radical transformation as the preached retreat was almost entirely replaced by the personally directed retreat.

There was, then, a great ecumenical convergence, as the old devotions peculiar to Catholics were replaced by practices shared by Christians of many denominations. They read the same books, they bought the same pictures, sometimes they even went to the same pilgrimage places (like the ecumenical, monastic community of Taizé in France, to which tens of thousands of young people flock every year).

Along with the openness to other Christian denominations went an openness to other faiths and diverse cultures. Eastern traditions of meditation began to exert a more widespread influence, and Anthony De Mello's book, *Sadhana*, which included some Hindu and Buddhist exercises, became a world best-seller. 'Inculturation' has also led to liturgical experiment with, for example, the Indian practice of *arati* (waving a tray of flowers with a lamp as a sign of respect), or with the use of drum and dance in African liturgy. It has led to iconographical experiment with black Christs and even female Christs, and to linguistic experiment with the spread of inclusive (that is, non-sexist) language, both for the believer and also sometimes for God, in public and in private devotion. This development still causes much disturbance between those who find such language culturally appropriate and those who do not.

There has been a sensitivity to spiritual values coming from sources that need not be specifically religious. For example, as the green movement gains ground, there is increasing reverence for creation and a growing sense of human stewardship of the world. Creation-centred spirituality is a term that began to gain prominence in the later 1980s, associated especially with the Californian Dominican, Matthew Fox, whose name became more widely known after he was asked to observe a period of silence by the Vatican.

Community is one of the strongest of the new values, and this has been felt at all possible levels of devotional life. Even the habit of sharing coffee after the parish Mass has reflected this change from private to communal spirituality. Sacramental preparation for first Communion changed from a me-and-Jesus emphasis to an expression of communal sharing: the Brusselmans programme, one of the most popular first-Communion courses in Western Europe and North America, uses celebration as the key to Eucharistic understanding, and involves parents, catechists and the whole parish community in the sacramental preparation.

Residential communities of laity started in a few places (some relationship could be claimed with the secular commune movement of the 1960s). Some religious orders, including the Benedictines, fostered the growth of lay communities in loose association with them, or of laity living in the religious community without vows on a temporary basis. Usually these were no longer based on 'third order' principles (that is, a version of the religious life adapted for laity in 'the world', still very dependent on male, first-order leadership – second orders were of nuns): rather they were experiments in new forms of Christian lifestyle.

Many of the traditional lay movements and associations declined in numbers (such as the Legion of Mary, the St Vincent de Paul Society, the Union of Catholic Mothers and the Catholic Women's League). New movements grew that fostered group sharing and community building (such as the Christian Life Communities, Marriage Encounter, charismatic prayer groups and the neo-conservative Comunione e Liberazione (see 11I).

Some movements that were already looking to the future have made the transition successfully from pre-Conciliar foundation to a thriving presence in the post-Conciliar Church. The Focolare movement, founded by Chiara Lubich during the Second World War, is an example of this. Each *focolare* or 'hearth' is the place where a spiritual family meets and lives: the members of a *focolare* – all women or all men – are usually drawn from different denominations and different countries, but they find a common spirituality in their fellowship and in reflecting on the same New Testament passage circulated by Chiara Lubich each month with her comments. The strong community base, together with the ecumenical composition, has enabled this movement to do well in the new mood after the Council.

The charismatic renewal expresses community experience of a different kind. The renewal is a world-wide, ecumenical movement which, since the early 1960s, has brought Pentecostal experiences and practices out of the confines of the specifically Pentecostal churches and into all the mainline Christian denominations. Catholics have been involved since 1967, beginning with some American Catholics at Duquesne University, and spreading through the United States and Canada, and then throughout the world. At Pentecost 1975, when there was an International Congress of the Renewal in Rome, 10,000 participants from over sixty countries gathered.

Charismatics pray aloud (often in tongues), raise their hands aloft to heaven, sing stirring folk hymns with an emphasis on praise, give public testimony to God's grace in their lives, give cries of 'alleluia' and 'praise the Lord' in spontaneous response, 'prophesy' in words of consolation or exhortation, and lay hands on each other to pray for healing (often with dramatic success). Most groups run an initiating course called 'Life in the Spirit seminars'. At one of the later seminars the members are 'baptized in the Holy Spirit': hands are laid on them, and often there are emotional responses such as tears, falling down on the ground, and so on. The aim is to recover the Spirit-filled experiences of the Church as recorded in the Acts of the Apostles, where speaking in tongues, prophesying and healing were clear marks of the Christian communities.

When Catholics speak of the baptism in the Spirit they do not devalue the gift of the Spirit in the sacrament of baptism: rather they see this new outpouring as the breaking forth into conscious experience of the Spirit who has already been given. They associate the charismatic renewal with Pope John's call at the Council for the Spirit to come on the Church as a 'new Pentecost'. The most famous Catholic adherent of the charismatic renewal has been Cardinal Suenens of Belgium, who, with his speeches at Vatican II, was one of the first to bring the Pauline idea of 'charisms' back into the vocabulary of the contemporary Church.

Another new form of community development is the proliferation of base communities (also known as Basic Ecclesial Communities, or Basic Christian

Communities (see 12I). These are found chiefly in Latin America and in the Philippines, where their growth is integrally connected with liberation theology. Base communities are the ecclesial context in which liberation theology can occur, and they make a point of so uniting faith with life that religious devotion cannot be compartmentalized nor become a private affair.

Base communities are neighbourhood-based but not residential; they are smaller than the parish, more participatory in liturgy, and more outgoing in social commitment. In this 'new way of being Church', old devotions are supplanted by a communal spirituality giving high priority to Scripture reading and discussion. Rather than being totally dependent on the leadership of a priest, the poor, the illiterate and the oppressed gain the confidence to interpret the Scriptures in the light of the reality of their lives. If there is a priest, the community will gather for the Eucharist, but if none is available there will be celebrations of the liturgy of the word, or Communion services using preconsecrated hosts and led by lay leaders and catechists (known in some places as 'delegates of the word').

A base community meeting would typically include the discussion of local problems, the reading of a passage of Scripture, and a group reflection on how the biblical message could be put into practice in the concrete situation confronting the community. Particular projects of social or political commitment are undertaken by members of the community in mutual solidarity, while prayer and singing express the struggle to bring the Kingdom of God into this world. This strongly incarnational flavour is captured, for example, in the famous opening words of the Nicaraguan *Misa Campesina*: 'You are the God of the poor, The human, simple God, The God who sweats in the street, The God with a sunburnt face.'

Base communities see themselves as founded solidly on Vatican II, particularly on the incarnational insights of *Gaudium et Spes* and the promotion of the laity in *Apostolicam Actuositatem*; and they see the ideas of the Council as being importantly carried forward by the Latin American bishops' meetings at Medellín and Puebla, which specifically encouraged the formation of base communities. At the same time, they believe they are recovering a sense of what it meant in the first century to be an evangelizing community of Christians, before the edifice of the institution obscured the freshness of the gospel appeal.

It is still too early to assess how devotional practice will settle down after the Council in the long run. There are some signs, for example in the large numbers of pilgrims flocking to Medjugorje, that many people feel lost without a strong support system with an immediate appeal and clear external markers. But at the same time the move towards individual discernment by the mature, responsible adult is a process that is difficult to reverse; and the discovery of the strength of the small, supportive community is a value that, once found, will be hard to lose again.

11A Devotion: Bibliography

Brusselmans, C., and Haggerty, B. A. (1984) *We Celebrate the Eucharist.* New York, Silver Burdett Company.

De Mello, A. (1978) *Sadhana: A Way to God.* India, Gujarat Sahitya Prakash.

Fox, M. (1983) *Original Blessing: A Primer in Creation Spirituality.* New Mexico, Bear & Co.

Gonzalez Balado, J. L. (1980) *The Story of Taizé.* Oxford, Mowbray (first published in Spanish 1976).

Hughes, G. W. (1985) *God of Surprises.* London, Darton, Longman and Todd.

Marins, J., Trevisan, T. M., and Chanona, C. (1989) *The Church from the Roots: Basic Ecclesial Communities.* London, CAFOD.

Morley, J., and Ward, H., eds (1986) *Celebrating Women.* London, Movement for the Ordination of Women and Women in Theology.

Sobrino, J. (1988) *The Spirituality of Liberation: Toward Political Holiness.* New York, Orbis Books (first published in Spanish 1985).

Suenens, L. J. (1975) *A New Pentecost.* London, Darton, Longman and Todd (first published in French 1974).

The Life in the Spirit Seminars Team Manual: Catholic edition, developed by the Word of God, Michigan, Ann Arbor. Ann Arbor, Michigan, Servant Books, 1971, Catholic edition 1979.

The Way, periodical of contemporary Christian spirituality, Heythrop College, London.

Wakefield, G. S. (1983) *A Dictionary of Christian Spirituality.* London, SCM.

11B The State of the Priesthood

MICHAEL GAINE

The most striking thing about the priesthood in the twenty-five years since Vatican II is the unprecedentedly large number of those leaving it, and the way that the official Church has reacted to this situation. On the basis of figures published by the Secretariat of State in the *Statistical Yearbook of the Church*,

Table 1 Absolute numbers of priests leaving the active ministry between 1964 and 1986 (abstracted from the *Statistical Yearbook of the Church* for those years.)

Year	Diocesan priests	Religious priests	Joint total
1964	371	269	640
1965	579	549	1,128
1966	730	688	1,418
1967	771	988	1,759
1968	1,059	1,237	2,296
1969	1,780	1,259	3,039
1970	1,848	1,530	3,378
1971	1,894	1,834	3,728
1972	1,964	1,635	3,599
1973	1,868	1,822	3,690
1974	1,778	1,686	3,464
1975	1,560	1,441	3,001
1976	1,329	1,350	2,679
1977	1,429	1,077	2,506
1978	1,253	784	2,037
1979	1,056	520	1,576
1980	901	660	1,561
1981	800	460	1,260
1982	685	541	1,226
1983	603	655	1,258
1984	601	448	1,049
1985	546	456	1,002
1986	633	424	1,057
Total	26,038	22,313	48,351

annually since 1971, it appears that some 50,000 priests left the active ministry, with or without a dispensation, between 1964 and 1986 (see Table 1). CORPUS (Corps of Reserve Priests United for Service), an American mutual-support group of married priests and their spouses which claims 3,500 married

246

Table 2 Absolute number of secular priests by continent for the year 1985, also expressed in each category as a percentage of those incardinated at the beginning of 1985

A Summary

Continent	Numbers on 1 January	Ordinations Nos.	%	Deaths Nos.	%	Departures Nos.	%	Transfers Nos.	Balance Nos.	%	Numbers on 31 Dec
Africa	7,715	492	6.38	81	1.05	23	0.30	51	439	5.03	8,154
The Americas	64,845	1,523	2.35	1,090	1.68	239	0.37	78	272	0.30	65,117
(North America)	(41,666)	(612)	(1.47)	(752)	(1.80)	(167)	(0.40)	(49)	(−258)	(−0.73)	(41,408)
Asia	15,702	645	4.11	171	1.09	48	0.31	−34	392	2.71	16,094
Europe	162,927	2,097	1.29	3,400	2.09	219	0.13	−336	−1,858	−0.93	161,069
Oceania	2,900	65	2.24	37	1.28	17	0.59	−26	−15	0.37	2,885
World total	254,089	4,822	1.90	4,779	1.88	546	0.21	−267	−770	−0.19	253,319

Notes 1 These figures have been abstracted and collated from pp. 137 and 146 of the 1987 edition of the *Statistical Yearbook of the Church*

2 The statistics are further complicated by the considerable number of priests who transfer from one diocese to another, or from the secular priesthood to the religious life, or vice versa

3 Both in terms of absolute numbers or percentages, the changes in any one year may appear miniscule. Nevertheless, the cumulative effect of a constant small trend over a number of years can become catastrophic for the viability of a particular 'population'.

priests on its mailing list, reckons that a truer estimate of departures world-wide for this period would be 100,000. Either of these figures needs to be considered against the fact that there was an estimated total of 425,000 priests, secular and regular, throughout the world in 1969. Just over two-thirds of those whose age was known were under 55 at that time.

All the indications are that the priests who left were young or middle-aged. Although the number of ordinations has dropped, it has always been much greater than the number of those who leave. None the less, over that period the number of deaths combined with departures has always been greater than the number of ordinations. As a result, the total number of priests has dropped from the 425,000 of 1969 to an estimated 399,400 in 1985, a decrease of nearly 26,000 over a twenty-six-year period, during which time world population has been increasing rapidly. In addition, in many countries the clergy are an ageing group and this will contribute to a continuing decline in numbers.

These trends are not spread consistently around the globe. Thus, North America, Europe, and Oceania have suffered a persistent decline in the number of their priests, while many countries in Africa and Asia have experienced an increase, and their seminary population also has increased rapidly since the beginning of the decade. Although this is encouraging news, the increase in the number of their priests has not kept pace with the size and growth of their Catholic populations. As a result, many Catholic communities are left without the Eucharist for months on end. When a priest does visit them, he is a stranger – rather than the leader of that community presiding at its Eucharistic celebration. At other times, a catechist will lead a Scripture service, or a Eucharistic minister may distribute hosts that have been consecrated previously, sometimes in another place. A different but related trend may be observed in Europe and the United States, where there is a growing number of priestless parishes. Table 2 gives a snapshot of the situation on different continents in 1985 as regards secular priests. The figures speak for themselves, but it is worth pointing out that well over half the secular priests in the world still work in Europe, although far fewer than half of the world's Catholics live there.

Again, there are wide variations between countries within this European total. Thus, at the beginning of 1985 there were some 22,400 priests in Poland, and one-third of all newly ordained priests in Europe was Polish. Unlike most other first world countries, Poland has experienced a steady increase in the number of vocations to the priesthood. It is interesting to speculate on the extent to which this is the result of the fact that the present pope is himself a Pole, and also that the Church has been seen as a powerful symbol of resistance against communist domination.

WHY HAVE SO MANY LEFT THE PRIESTHOOD?

As most of those who leave active priesthood have subsequently married, it is tempting to suggest that this was the motive for their departure. It may well have been so for many, but many other reasons are operative as well. Thus, a large study carried out by the National Opinion Research Centre of Chicago in the early 1970s for the United States Catholic Conference found that the major reason for priests leaving the active priesthood was loneliness, rather than simply the desire to get married. This was closely followed by dissatisfaction over the lack of communication and co-operation by their ecclesiastical superiors. Particularly in the Western world, where psychoanalytic concepts have become part of everyday thinking, the idea has become widespread that priests, along with other members of the caring professions, can suffer from a complex psychological syndrome known as 'burn out', caused by excessive and conflicting demands without any adequate support system. Other reasons have been, for instance, where a priest has felt morally compelled to become politically active over an ethical issue such as nuclear disarmament or the redistribution of land, and his bishop has forbidden this. Or again, a priest may 'withdraw his labour' as a protest against the failure of his bishops to implement the changes of Vatican II. Sometimes bishops and provincials give priests a long leave of absence from pastoral and liturgical duties while they 'reflect on their vocation'. For many, this is a transitional phase before they leave the active priesthood, but they do not feature in local or global statistics of departure.

Many of these priests who seek a dispensation from celibacy do not wish to leave the active priesthood. It is Church regulations that force them to abandon that commitment to the service of the people of God if they are to be excused from the commitment to celibacy. It is interesting to observe how many laicized priests seek secular employment in the caring professions.

Even when priests do not leave the active priesthood in order to get married, it is understandable that they would marry once the main motive for their celibacy, that is, to become a priest, had ceased. Many of the older generation of priests were brought up to regard celibacy as a condition of their priesthood rather than as a separate charism.

A second report, commissioned by the American bishops, was completed in spring 1988, but was not published by their Committee on Priestly Life and Ministry until January 1989. It seems that celibacy has become an even more salient motive for departure over the twenty years since the previous report. It paints a sad picture, saying that many United States priests feel trapped, overworked, frustrated, and that their morale is low. The report continues, 'Generally every study or commentary done on the priesthood and shortage of vocations mentions sexuality – and specifically mandatory celibacy – as a major reason a) for leaving the priesthood, b) for shortage of vocations, and c) for the loneliness and unhappiness of those who stay'. It says that sexual tensions involve not only questions of 'personal and inter-personal levels of sexuality' for individual priests, but also what might be called the 'politics of sexuality', which includes 'the issues surrounding feminism, married clergy, optional celibacy, and the role of homosexuals in the ministry, to name but a few'.

Another source of frustration for priests, the report says, is that 'some solutions to the clergy shortage are precluded from discussion and that not all pastoral solutions and options can be explored'. Those most commonly referred to are the ordination of married men, effective use of laicized priests, and expanded roles for women in the ministry.

249

A survey of United States Bishops by Father Terrance Sweeney in 1986 was based on 145 replies from the nation's 312 Catholic bishops. It found that nearly one-quarter of those who replied would allow Catholic priests to marry; 20 per cent would approve of asking married and resigned priests to return to active ministry; and 30 per cent would approve of ordaining women as deacons (but less than 8 per cent as priests). There was pressure from the Vatican for these results to be suppressed, but Sweeney resigned from the priesthood rather than destroy his research findings. There is evidence from many countries in Europe and North America that an increasing number of bishops, priests, and lay people believe that celibacy should be optional for priests, but this is rarely voiced in public for fear of Vatican disapproval. Indeed, the Bishops' Conference of Zambia was forbidden to discuss the issue of priestly celibacy in 1969 when the Congregation for the Propagation of the Faith discovered that they had been discussing the possibility of ordaining mature married men to the priesthood.

It can be argued that a genuine *sensus fidelium* cannot be based on ignorance. It will only emerge when there is free, informed discussion amongst the faithful.

THE CHURCH'S RESPONSE

In the latter half of the eighteenth century there had been a vigorous debate in European Catholic circles over the issue of compulsory priestly celibacy. When the 'reformers' of the French Revolution insisted on clerical marriage, this idea became tainted with the violence and anti-clericalism of the Revolution. For nearly 200 years the debate remained unacceptable in Catholic circles. Compulsory celibacy became regarded as a matter almost of doctrine rather than merely of Church discipline. This remained true even though we had the example of the Eastern Catholic Churches (e.g. of the Ukrainian rite) who are in full communion with Rome but who retain the older tradition of a married priesthood (although there are a few maverick historians who seek to argue that compulsory celibacy is of apostolic origin).

When the first wave of priests sought laicization in the late 1960s for the reasons explained above, dispensations were granted fairly readily. However, the whole business was shrouded in secrecy. It was a common condition for the granting of a dispensation that the individual had to promise not to live or work within a 50-mile radius of any parish in which he had worked. The aim of this rule was so that the 'simple faithful would not be scandalized' by realizing that a priest might wish to leave the active priesthood.

Another element in the Church's response has been to deal in a punitive manner with those who leave the active priesthood. The canonical procedures involved were demeaning for the individual and his prospective partner. They looked for signs of mental instability, or a history of sexual misconduct as a reason for granting a dispensation. By this device the growing number of departures could be interpreted as an accumulation of personal failures rather than as an institutional crisis arising partly from an inadequate official theology of vocation and ministry. Both pope and bishops have frequently used the terms 'defection' and 'Judas' for those who leave the active priesthood, so as to reinforce the sense of commitment among those who remain.

Those who were granted dispensations were effectively reduced to the status of second-class Catholics. They were forbidden to act as Eucharistic ministers, or as reader at Mass; forbidden to conduct retreats or to teach theology in Catholic institutions of higher education.

Those who left the active priesthood and attempted a civil marriage without a dispensation before October 1983 automatically incurred excommunication, specially reserved to the Holy See under the 1917 *Code of Canon Law*. Under the new (1983) *Code*, such a person is automatically suspended *a divinis*, with the threat of further penalties. There were literally thousands of excommunicated priests in our midst because of this harsh legislation. Does the Catholic Church have to have scapegoats in order to preserve its cherished values, or should these values commend themselves to the people of God in their own right?

When Pope John Paul II came to the papal throne in October 1978, he virtually halted the granting of dispensations, and this is reflected in the lower figures for departures in the years that followed. This new policy was formulated in 1980 in new procedural norms for laicization which were sent *sub secreto* to all local ordinaries and heads of religious congregations. They were soon 'leaked' in various journals. Basically, they stated that a dispensation would be granted only to older priests who had left the active ministry for a number of years.

The pastoral objective of these norms was to discourage priests from thinking of laicization as a possibility in the short term, and to give those who had left the active ministry time to reflect and change their minds before their change of status was juridically confirmed. In practice, however, the change has had many harmful effects. We do not know how many applications have been delayed in the pipe-line, nor how many priests whose applications have been refused have remained reluctantly in the priesthood. (However, in 1986 it was rumoured in Vatican circles that 5,800 applications were still awaiting dispensations since 1978.) The Belgian group, Hors-les-Murs, in a recent issue of their *Bulletin*, published a series of case studies of Belgian priests living in concubinage in a variety of different circumstances accepted by fellow priests in a team ministry, or a wider community. There is more scattered, anecdotal evidence to suggest that this has become more widespread in recent years. Sadly, it is always the women involved who are psychologically and socially (and often also economically) the losers in such situations.

Apart from attempting to stem the flow of priests from the active ministry by such means, the Church has also sought to supplement the declining number and proportion of priests by formally encouraging other ministries. Thus there have emerged lay readers at Mass (who may not read the Gospel); Eucharistic ministers who may conduct Eucharistic services using hosts previously consecrated by a priest; and religious sisters and brothers who conduct retreats and prayer meetings, or who act as chaplains to prisons, educational institutions, or priestless parishes.

There have been two other major attempts to supplement the declining ratio of priests to lay people in most parts of the world. The first was the deliberate reintroduction and fostering of the permanent diaconate. This was introduced as a panic measure, without thinking clearly through its theological implications. In addition, against all Western tradition and practice for a thousand years, it was decided that *married* men could be ordained to the permanent diaconate. However, the canonical rules regarding the diaconate present a Catch 22 situation. Many committed men enter the diaconate as a substitute for the priesthood, which they cannot enter because they are married (a hurtful situation which defines a wife as an obex to priestly ordination). If their wife dies they cannot proceed to the priesthood without dispensation because their diaconate is *permanent*, nor can they remarry.

A question mark hangs over the diaconate. When it was first introduced in 1968, many saw the deacon's role as being the leaven in the mass, penetrating the world of work after the fashion of the priest workers in France. Others saw it in very clerical terms. Some bishops faced with the lack of clear objectives for the diaconate have declared a moratorium and have ceased to ordain permanent deacons.

Since 1968, over 12,000 permanent deacons have been ordained (67 per cent in North America, and 20 per cent in Europe, but only 10 per cent in South America). Some 94 per cent of these deacons have other occupations; 90 per cent of them are married. It is striking that in the third world, where the absolute shortage of priests remains greatest, least use has been made of this intended, but essentially inadequate, substitute.

The second attempt to improve the declining priest/people ratio has been the recent increase in the number of convert married clergymen being ordained into the Roman Catholic priesthood. This phenomenon is discussed later.

The world-wide Catholic population rose from 784 million in 1969 to 866.7 million in 1985. By 1985, 3,180 of the Church's parishes and quasi-parishes were without priests. Lay people were in charge of 872 parishes (40 per cent of which were in France). Women religious administered 783 (with 53 per cent of them in Latin America). Permanent deacons were in charge of 212 (mainly in North and South America); religious brothers accounted for 77; and about 1,236 pastoral centres had no one in charge. At the beginning of 1989, the archbishop of Detroit announced that 31 out of the 212 parishes in Detroit were to be closed, and a further 25 were to be given until the end of the year to prove their viability.

In the face of such a drastic decline in the priest/people ratio in so many countries, the Vatican has produced a document on the 'formation' of priests in preparation for the 1990 synod on that topic. The document acknowledges that humanity is going through a cultural and spiritual crisis and that 'absolute norms and reference to the past as the source of wisdom have been rejected'. However, it makes no mention of sensitive subjects such as married priests, or the ordination of married men. A paragraph on celibacy makes it clear that the Secretariat still does not envisage debate on these topics at the synod. This is a sad denial of any real collegiality and, objectively, a straight refusal to acknowledge the existence of the most basic theological and pastoral issues. While that refusal continues, any reforms can be no more than cosmetic.

ARE THERE SIGNS OF HOPE FOR THE LAST DECADE OF THE
CENTURY?

Yes! There are, but too few as yet to suggest any real will for the implementation of change. They include:

1 Doing the right thing for the wrong reason: because of the shortage of
priests, the Church is slowly accepting a diversification of ministries, different
from but not subordinate to the ordained priesthood. However, a damaging
form of clericalism still remains entrenched in titles (e.g. Your Eminence,
Monsignor, or Canon), dress, etc. Again, where they do exist, married deacons
are often in danger of succumbing to clericalization.

2 The increasing number of convert married clergymen who are being
ordained to the priesthood. This practice began fifty years ago when Pope Pius
XII gave permission for the ordination of convert Lutheran clergymen in
Germany. Archbishop Goody in Australia in 1969, and more recently the
Bishops' Conferences of the United States and England, sought the same
permission, and by 1990 some 70 convert married episcopalian clergy had been
ordained or were in preparation for ordination in the USA, and three had been
ordained in England. Unfortunately, in most cases they are being assigned to
non-parochial duties (sometimes so that they can earn a salary with which to
support their families, but more often so that they will have a low profile). If
and when such cases become more common, it will highlight the anomaly
whereby a committed married lay Catholic who feels a sense of vocation to the
priesthood cannot be ordained, while a convert married clergyman may be.

The fact that obligatory priestly celibacy is a matter not of doctrine but of
ecclesiastical regulation is further underlined by the fact that on 31 March
1989, the granting of dispensations from celibacy was transferred from the
Congregation for the Doctrine of the Faith to the Congregation for the
Sacraments.

If we demonstrate our desire for unity with the other Christian Churches by
acceptance of diversity in non-essentials, we must surely prepare ourselves to
acccept their tradition of a married clergy into our midst, and then the
anomolies will be even further highlighted.

3 It is to be hoped that the synod of 1990 will discuss openly and seriously
the need for totally new styles of priesthood, which might include a married
priesthood, a non-stipendiary priesthood where priests would support themselves (and their families) by working in secular employment, women priests,
and maybe even priests who would commit themselves for only a limited
number of years to be engaged in active pastoral and sacramental work. It is
such an openness of choice, rather than punitive legislation, which could
increase the number of priests to serve the growing Catholic population.

These are not wild and maverick suggestions. Thus Cardinal Hume,
delivering a paper on his vision of the local church at a seminar for European
bishops held at Bruges in June 1985, said:

> Now I, for one, value very much the tradition of celibacy in the Latin church and would very much wish to see it preserved. I do, however, foresee the ordaining to the priesthood of married men in certain parts of the world as the only way to bring the sacraments of Eucharist and Reconciliation to the people.

He was further reported as saying, 'I would say that there is a shortage [of priests] in every country and culture.' Similar beliefs have been expressed by many individual bishops and by some conferences of bishops.

While such ideas were unthinkable they could not be spoken; once spoken, they have become more widely accepted and their implementation now seems inevitable (although it is unlikely that they would be permitted in the lifetime of the present pope with his very traditional Polish background).

11B The State of the Priesthood: Bibliography

The best available source of statistics of the priesthood of the Roman Catholic Church is the *Statistical Yearbook of the Church*, which has been published each year since 1971 by the Vatican Secretariat of State. Each volume contains extensive data on every aspect of Church life for the calendar year two years previous to the date of publication (so that in 1988 we have figures from 1967 to 1986). It was originally published in Italian, but now all the text is given in Latin, English and French in each volume.

Unfortunately, because of the variations in the definition and compilation procedures, these figures can only be taken as broad generalizations about Church life and membership. Because definitions and presentation have varied considerably over twenty years, some comparisons become impossible, and one can make only informed guesses about the biases involved in others. (This is a comment not about the compilers, but about the necessarily flawed nature of this material.)

One interesting example is with regard to religious priests who left the active ministry (with or without dispensation). This information was not given for several years, while it was given for secular priests from the beginning. When it was given for religious priests it was labelled 'departures', while for secular priests it was given under the obnoxious heading of 'defections'. It included only those who left congregations of pontifical rite.

Three useful periodical sources are:

1 A series of files on Church and ministries which contained abstracts of books and articles on theology, sociology, history and ecumenism in this area. They were produced between 1970 and 1972 by Prospective (a Belgian organization now defunct).

2 A quarterly bulletin entitled *Ministries and Communities* (since 1975) (Louvain, *Pro Mundi Vita*).

3 MOMM (Movement for the Ordination of Married Men) *Information Bulletin* issued periodically: editor M. Gaine, St Mary's, Highfield Street, Liverpool L3 6AA.

Other analytic studies include:
Bessiere, G., *et al.* (1985) *Les volets du presbytere sont ouverts 2000 pretres racontent*. Paris, Desclee de Brouwer.
Fichter, J. H. (1968) *America's Forgotten Priests – What They Are Saying*. New York, Harper & Row.

Greeley, A. M. (1972) *Priests in the United States: Reflections on a Survey*. New York, Doubleday.

Grollenberg, L. *et al.* (1980) *Minister? Pastor? Prophet? Grass-roots leadership in the churches*. London, SCM.

Hickey, R. (1986) *A Married Priesthood in the Catholic Church*. Liverpool, LISS.

Hoge, D. R. *et al.* (1984) *Research on Men's Vocations to the Priesthood and the Religious Life*, with commentaries by Joseph Komonchak, Richard P. McBrien and Philip J. Murinon. Washington, DC, US Catholic Conference.

Kennedy, E., and Hechler, V. J. (1971) *The Catholic Priest in the United States: Psychological Investigations*. Washington, DC, US Catholic Conference.

Rice, D. (1990) *Shattered Vows: Exodus from the Priesthood*. London, Michael Joseph.

Sanford, J. (1982) *Ministry Burnout*. New Jersey, Paulist Press.

Schillebeeckx, E. (1981) *Ministry: a Case for Change*. London, SCM.

Schillebeeckx, E. (1985) *The Church with a Human Face: a New and Expanded Theology of Ministry*. New York, Crossroad.

Secretariat for 1990 Synod (1989) 'The Formation of Priests in the Circumstances of the Present Day', *Briefing*, vol. 19, no. 13, 23 June.

Thurian, M. (1983) *Priesthood and Ministry*. London, Mowbray.

Vera, H. (1982) *The Professionalization and Professionalism of Catholic Priests*. Gainesville, Florida, University Press.

11C The Society of Jesus

PETER HEBBLETHWAITE

The 27th General of the Jesuits ('General' is not a military term, but an adjective, *praepositus generalis*), the Belgian John Baptist Janssens, died on 5 October 1964, as the fraught third session of the Council was getting under way. The general congregation to elect his successor could not be held until after the Council session, if only because there were so many Jesuits busy as Council *periti*, including those like Henri de Lubac, Jean Daniélou and Karl Rahner, whom Janssens had been forced to ban and silence in the 1950s.

So when the 31st general congregation assembled on 7 May 1965, its most important task was to elect a General who would bid farewell to the pontificate of Pius XII and bring the Society of Jesus into the world of Vatican II. The representatives of the world's 35,000 Jesuits chose 58-year-old Pedro Arrupe, born in Bilbao, Spain.

The first Basque to be elected General since St Ignatius, the founder, Arrupe (invariably known as Don Pedro) brought to the office considerable international experience. A medical student before he joined the Jesuits in 1927, he studied in Belgium, Holland and the United States before setting off for Japan in 1939. When the A-bomb fell he was novice-master in Hiroshima, and turned the house into a hospital. Later he became Provincial of the Japanese international province made up of volunteers.

In addition to this international experience, Arrupe had an undoubted charism which enabled him to rethink the Jesuit vocation in the post-Vatican II world. He was able to profit from the work on Jesuit origins and spirituality that had been going on, especially since the Second World War.

In Rome, the *Monumenta Historica Societatis Jesu* made better known figures like Jerome Nadal, first Secretary of the Society, who toured Europe spreading the principle of *in actione contemplativus* (contemplative in action) that was to be the hallmark of Jesuit spirituality. In *Manresa* the Spanish Jesuits filled out the historical record, restored the text of Ignatius's *Autobiography* and produced critical editions of *The Spiritual Exercises*. With *Christus*, founded by Maurice Giuliani in 1953, the French Jesuits turned these ideas into a form accessible to religious women and lay people, and a decade later the British Jesuits did the same for the English-speaking world with *The Way*.

So Arrupe did not have to start from scratch in his redefinition of Jesuit identity. From Nadal, Arrupe learned that Ignatius possessed a *gratia capitalis*, a founder's grace, the essence of which was that it was *communicable*. Where was it to be found? Not in the *Constitutions* but in *The Spiritual Exercises*. The *Exercises* provide the key to the *Constitutions*. Ignatius said that 'the internal guidance of the Holy Spirit' ought to be sufficient without written texts, but that experience suggested a few rules should be laid down to spell out that internal guidance. Yet the internal guidance remained prior, and the activity of 'discernment of spirits', that is, the path towards 'finding God in all things and all things in God' (in Ignatius's phrase), is what defines Jesuit spirituality. Jesuits are not defined by a particular work: *a priori* they are neither monks nor schoolmasters nor theologians; they may turn out to be clowns, script-writers, philosophers, gurus, literary critics, newspaper editors, peaceniks (Dan Berrigan), revolutionaries (Fernando Cardenal).

All these possibilities – and many more – came to pass under Pedro Arrupe's stewardship. Unlike his stay-at-home predecessors, he travelled the whole world proclaiming the Jesuit *charisma*, but still more importantly he seemed to embody it. Paul VI appeared delighted. Before Arrupe's election, he had invited the Jesuits to consider atheism as their speciality: 'It is the special task of the Society of Jesus to defend religion and Holy Church in the most tragic times. We entrust to it the charge of opposing atheism' (*ut atheismo obsistant*) (Hebblethwaite, 1967, p. 44). This was obviously not an invitation to start a crusade, for only a month before Paul VI had set up the Secretariat for Non-Believers intended to 'study atheism'. What did that mean? *Usus docebit*, Paul VI told its first President, Cardinal König: 'You will find out by experience' (Hebblethwaite, 1967, p. 41).

But Arrupe already gave some hints about how he intended to 'obstruct atheism'. 'The battle against atheism,' he said, 'is an aspect of the battle against poverty which was one cause of the mass exodus of the working classes from the Church.' He made disturbing remarks: 'The voice of young Jesuits is the voice of the modern world within the order.' He talked about 'the superior-in-the-community' rather than 'the superior-over-the-community'. Such ideas also had great success among the religious women who shared Jesuit spirituality.

By the 1970s a reaction began to set in. Bishops used their visits to Rome, now much more frequent, to bombard Arrupe with complaints about 'laxity'. In France, Jesuits were alleged to have said Mass in boiler-suits, in California a theory of the 'third way' (a special relationship with a woman that was intimate but chaste) led to predictable shipwrecks, while in Latin America the complaint was more likely to be that a Jesuit had joined the guerrillas. Arrupe picked his way through the slanders and said: 'My first instinct is always to defend what you do, but please make it easier for me to defend you.'

A fifth column of right-wing Jesuits added to the alarm of the Vatican. By 1974 numbers had dwindled to 29,436 and there were only half the numbers of scholastics. Arrupe met this situation by summoning a general congregation, the 32nd. It was unprecedented, for the sole function of previous congregations had been to elect a new General. The carefully prepared 32nd was invited to renew – or withdraw – Arrupe's mandate.

In the event, his policies were massively endorsed by the 32nd general congregation, though not without warnings about storm clouds from Paul VI. There seems to have been a genuine misunderstanding about the abolition of 'grades' – the distinction between 'professed fathers' and 'spiritual coadjutors' – which, claimed the papal advisers, would undermine the essence of the Society.

Arrupe was able to go ahead with a renewed mandate and a fresh team. In particular, the 32nd congregation stressed that the work of justice was not an optional extra in the preaching of the gospel, but rather a constitutive dimension of it. 'If we obey this decree,' Arrupe predicted with complete accuracy, 'we will have martyrs.' To Roman ears, Arrupe sounded more and more 'extreme'. For example, he thought that 'for hundreds of millions of Catholics the real crisis of faith comes not from "materialism" or "unrestrained theological discussion", but from the brutal poverty of their existence.'

Bold in the later years of Paul VI, such language seemed positively reckless in the pontificate of John Paul II. Arrupe quite simply had a different analysis of the Church's problems. He had written weighty letters on 'Priest Workers' and 'Marxist Analysis', which had wide influence partly because of the silence of the official magisterium on such issues. Arrupe was privately accused of 'setting up a parallel magisterium'. But before any steps could be taken against him, he suffered a stroke on 7 August 1981, which left him paralysed down one side and unable to speak. He was on his way back from inspecting the Jesuit Refugee Service in Thailand.

With Arrupe incapacitated, the normal procedure would have been for a Vicar-General to be appointed to set about preparing the 33rd general congregation to elect his successor. But this juridical process was interrupted. The Vicar-General Arrupe named, Fr Vincent O'Keefe, was set aside, and an 80-year-old, almost blind, Jesuit, Fr Paolo Dezza, was named 'personal delegate of the Supreme Pontiff to the Society of Jesus', a hitherto unheard-of post. The 33rd general congregation was indefinitely postponed. Some compared it to a 'second suppression' of the Jesuits. It was not that, but it was clearly designed to 'restore order'.

By 27 February 1982, Pope John Paul came close to admitting he had made a mistake. He told a meeting of Jesuit superiors that they had 'passed the test [*la prova*]' with flying colours. They had neither risen in revolt nor waxed indignant. They kept a dignified silence. It must also be said that Fr Dezza, former confessor of Pius XII, played a brilliant tactical game, keeping Arrupe's curial team intact, and playing for time. The anomalous situation could not be allowed to continue indefinitely, so normal service was resumed in September–October 1983 when the 33rd general congregation elected on the first ballot a Dutchman, Fr Peter-Hans Kolvenbach.

Kolvenbach's international experience came from being provincial in the Lebanon and rector of the Oriental Institute in Rome. He is the first General to come from an Eastern rite – the Armenian Church – and the first to be elected while his predecessor was still alive. The first thing he did on being elected was to embrace Arrupe and thank him for his exemplary obedience. There was not a dry eye in the Jesuit curia. His style has been more low-key and laconic than Arrupe's, but the documents of the 33rd general congregation and Kolvenbach's subsequent letters prove that the Jesuits have not repudiated Arrupe or the policies he inspired. They have, on the contrary, continued to see him as a symbol of the spiritual renewal the Council called for.

11C The Society of Jesus: Bibliography

Arrupe, P. (1975) *A Planet to Heal*, introduction by J. Harriott. Rome, Ignatian Center of Spirituality.

Arrupe, P. (1980) *Justice with Faith Today*. St Louis, USA, Institute of Jesuit Sources.

Hebblethwaite (1967) *The Council Fathers and Atheism*. New York, Paulist Press.

Lamet, P. M. (1989) *Arrupe: una Explosión en la Iglesia*. Madrid, Temas de Huy.

Woodrow, A. (1984) *Les Jésuites, Histoire des Pouvoirs*. Paris, Clattès.

11D The Place of Women in the Church

ROSEMARY RADFORD RUETHER

An essay on the teachings of Vatican II on women would be brief enough. Women are seldom discussed in the documents as a social group with particular problems and concerns. They are mentioned in only a few sentences in the decree on the Apostolate of the Laity and the Pastoral Constitution on the Church in the Modern World. Nevertheless, the new openness of the Catholic Church to the changes created in modern Western societies by liberal, democratic principles, including changes in women's status and roles, was an important turning point. The Second Vatican Council created an atmosphere where a discussion among Catholics of women's rights in society and in the Church seemed possible.

In the previous century feminist liberal reformers had received only negative responses from the Catholic Church. In the 1920s the Vatican and various national episcopacies expressed themselves in opposition to women's suffrage. In the United States, the American Catholic bishops supported the National Association opposed to Women's Suffrage. In a speech to this organization by James Cardinal Gibbons of Baltimore on 7 December 1916, the cardinal declared that suffrage was incompatible with women's role as mother and wife:

> When a woman enters the political arena she goes outside the sphere for which she was intended. She gains nothing by that journey. On the other hand, she loses that exclusiveness, respect and dignity to which she is entitled in her home (Gibbons, 1916).

This hostility to women's rights prompted a group of British Catholic women to form the Catholic Women's Suffrage Society (later called the St Joan's Alliance) in 1910 to educate each other and the Church on the compatibility of Catholicism and feminist reforms. The St Joan's Alliance became an international organization in the 1920s and continued to work on women's concerns throughout the world in the following decades.

In 1959, with the announcement of the coming Ecumenical Council, the Alliance began to work on a series of requests for greater participation of women in the life of the Council and the Church. In 1961 it forwarded a request to the Vatican that women be included in the diaconate. In 1963 it responded to the statement in the papal encyclical *Pacem in Terris* (41) that declared that the right to follow a vocation to the priesthood was a basic human right, by requesting that the Vatican consider the possibility of the ordination of women to the priesthood.[1]

These interventions, however, received little response. When the delegates to the Council assembled in Rome in October 1962, women were conspicuously absent. The clerical male culture of woman-shunning was shockingly demonstrated early in the Council when a woman news reporter was denied Communion. The uproar over this incident brought some soul searching. On 4 December 1962, Cardinal Leon-Joseph Suenens made a famous intervention in which he called for an additional document that would consider the role of the Church in the modern world. During this intervention he noted the absence of women by declaring that 'half of the Church' was excluded from the conciliar deliberations.[2]

By the beginning of the second session of the Council some women *auditrices* were appointed, and, by the end of the Council, their numbers had grown to twelve lay women and ten women religious. Prominent among them was Sister Luke Tobin SL, Superior of the Sisters of Loreto in the United States and then head of the Leadership Conference of Women Religious. Sister Luke Tobin was and continues to be a major supporter of Catholic feminism. Three of the women's auditors, including Luke Tobin, were appointed to commissions which drafted the final Council documents. The major commissions to which they were appointed were the Church in the Modern World and the Apostolate on the Laity.

The women auditors were granted voice but not vote in these commissions. Their presence played a major role in the inclusion of some mention of women's rights in these two documents. In a recent interview, Luke Tobin recalled a meeting of the commission on the Church in the Modern World in which the French theologian Yves Congar made a long and flowery speech on women's virtues. He then looked at one of the women auditors, Australian Rosemary Goldie, head of the Vatican Commission on the Laity, and asked her opinion of his words. She replied that he could dispense with the flowery rhetoric; what concerned women was that they be treated as the fully human persons that they are.

This forthright approach is echoed in the three statements concerning women in the final document of the commission on the Church in the Modern World, *Gaudium et Spes*. In the introduction it is said that 'where they have not won it, women claim for themselves an equity with men before the law and in fact' (*Gaudium et Spes* 9). In the section on the family, although the importance of the mother's role in child-raising was duly noted, it was also said that this role of woman as mother should not be used to underrate 'the legitimate social progress of women' (*GS* 52). Finally, in the section on the right of every person to culture, it is said that 'women are now employed in almost every area of life. It is appropriate that they should be able to assume their full proper role in accordance with their own nature. Everyone should acknowledge and favour the proper and necessary participation of women in cultural life' (*GS* 60). Perhaps the most important statement of *Gaudium et Spes* for women is the inclusion of sex discrimination among the unjust prejudices that must be 'overcome and eradicated as contrary to God's intent', along with discriminations based on race, colour, social condition, language and religion (*GS* 29).

These endorsements of women's rights echo the most comprehensive papal declaration of support for the principles of democratic liberties, Pope John XXIII's *Pacem in Terris*, issued in April 1963. The encyclical endorses the liberal tenet that all human beings have essentially the same human nature and, from this nature, derive the same basic human rights. Women are included in this egalitarian doctrine of human nature with the ringing statement that, 'Since women are becoming ever more conscious of their human dignity, they will not tolerate being treated as mere material instruments, but demand rights befitting a human person in both domestic and in public life' (41).

This endorsement of liberal, democratic principles, however, did not extend to the life of the Church. The Second Vatican Council effected a reconciliation of Catholicism with liberalism for secular society, but exempted the Church from these same principles of human rights. Thus it is not surprising that much less is said about women's role in the ministry of the Church than was said in endorsement of women's civil rights.

One brief statement in the Decree on the Apostolate of the Laity (*Apostolicam Actuositatem*), which was inserted only in the final drafting of the document, notices women as members of the laity: 'Since in our times women have an ever more active share in the whole life of society, it is very important that they participate more widely also in the various fields of the Church's apostolate' (*AA* 9). It is significant that this call for an expanded role of women in the ministry of the laity is derived from women's expanded roles in civil society, rather than from the nature of the Christian community itself.

The controversial issue of artificial contraception, which began to surface during the sessions of the Council, was put on the shelf by Pope Paul VI. He decided that a reconsideration of this question should be made the work of a specially appointed papal commission. This commission was to be made up of a wide range of experts, not only moral theologians, but also sociologists, physicians and married couples. The pope was concerned to receive input from the practical sciences and also from those with personal experience of the problems of conjugal love and parenting. Three married couples, from the United States, from French Canada and from France respectively, were members of the Pontifical Commission on Population, Family and Birth. There was also one woman sociologist from the Philippines. This was one of the first times that women were full members of a papal commission.[3]

The Commission met from 1964 to 1966. During its sessions, the personal testimony of married couples made a strong impression on the clerical moralists, who were used to thinking about sexuality and reproduction in scholastic categories. As a result, a significantly changed understanding of the relation of sexuality and family planning began to emerge in the discussions. This was reflected in the final report of the Commission, which recommended the acceptance of artificial contraception as morally legitimate within the context of committed, child-raising marriages.[4]

However, Pope Paul VI was unable to accept this conclusion of his Commission. In 1968 he reaffirmed the traditional ban on artificial birth control in his encyclical *Humanae Vitae*. This encyclical evoked a storm of protest from lay people, as well as from some priests and moral theologians. Most lay Catholics have chosen simply to ignore the Church's teachings on birth control, and to practise contraception. For most Catholics, this refusal to comply with Church teaching on this subject is no longer done in bad conscience. Rather it is assumed, especially by the educated lay person, that a new moral consensus has been developed, and it is the Vatican that is out of step with the consensus of the Church.

The conflict over contraception is of particular importance for Catholic women. Without reliable contraception it is scarcely possible for married women to combine family life with significant contributions to society. The Catholic Church's hesitancy to endorse women's social development outside the family reflects a desire to confine and define women by their reproductive role. The hierarchy has assumed that, for a woman, a decision to do something else other than mothering is a decision for celibacy.

Catholicism traditionally split women into two categories, celibate women under vows and married women, with the former seen as the superior vocation to the latter. One of the important developments in the post-Vatican II period has been an increasing rejection by both nuns and lay women of this hierarchical division among women. Already in the Council the lay and religious women auditors realized that they had far more in common as women than what divided them by states of life.

The birth-control issue has proven in post-conciliar Catholicism to be a conflict that refuses to go away. For Catholic women, the decision to form an independent conscience on birth control transformed them from passive victims of 'nature' into moral agents. In so doing, women were declaring that they were moral persons in their own right, who can and must be the primary decision-makers about the effects of sexuality on their bodies and their lives. The continued struggle between the Catholic hierarchy and Catholic women over reproductive rights reflects, perhaps more than anything else, a patriarchal clericalism that is unable to accept women's autonomous personhood.

The Second Vatican Council precipitated a host of expectations of renewal which its hierarchical leadership has been unwilling or unable to fulfil. Perhaps potentially the most explosive of these conflicts is between the male hierarchy and Catholic women. There are three major areas where this conflict has erupted. First, there is the area of reproductive rights. Secondly, there is the relation between nuns and the hierarchy, and, finally, there is the question of women's ordination. Surrounding all these questions is a pervasive conflict between two different models of ecclesiology, the traditional Roman concept of the Church as a hierarchical clerical corporation, and the populist view, that took its charter from the Vatican II Constitution on the Church, of the Church as 'the people of God'.

The call in the Decree on the Renewal of Religious Life (*Perfectae Caritatis*) for 'a continuous return to the sources of all Christian life and to the original inspiration behind a given community and an adjustment of the community to the changed conditions of the times' (*PC 2*) was taken by Catholic nuns, especially in North America, as a charter for a comprehensive democratization of the polity of their communities and a diversification of their ministries. Believing that the religious habit was an anachronism, reflecting earlier styles of female dress and an impediment to their work today, most orders greatly modified or abandoned such dress, thus bringing them closer to lay women.

Many women religious came to believe that their ministry must involve systematic change for social justice, not just charity work. Religious women became the forefront of ministries to the poor in urban areas and in the third world. In the 1970s, American nuns, under the Leadership Conference of

Religious Women, consciously adopted the goals of the feminist movement and declared themselves in solidarity with it.[5]

This autonomy, democratization and social involvement has sparked increasing conflict between Catholic nuns and the Vatican, particularly in the pontificate of John Paul II. Several nuns have been forced to choose between giving up their political involvements and leaving their orders (see Kolbenschlag, 1986, on the conflict between the Vatican and the Sisters of Mercy of the Union). The Vatican has ordered religious communities to submit their revised constitutions to Rome for approval, and has refused to accept many of the changes. This has created an increasing feeling of antagonism between religious women and Rome.

A third major area of conflict between Catholic women and the hierarchy lies in expanded roles of women in ministry, ultimately leading to the ordination of women to the priesthood. This subject, barely discussed at Vatican II, was out in the open by the early 1970s. Protestant churches had begun to ordain women in the nineteenth century, but only in the 1960s did the number of Protestant women ministers begin to increase significantly. With this development came a rapid increase of women in seminaries, including Catholic seminaries. A feminist critique of sexist anthropology, theology and exegesis began to be written, with Catholic feminist theologians often at the forefront of this debate.[6]

In 1975, United States Catholic women organized the first Women's Ordination Conference in Detroit. Planned for 600, the conference was swamped by applicants and finally closed its registration with 1,200. The conference resulted in the formation of a national organization, the Women's Ordination Conference, dedicated both to the promotion of women's ordination and also the renewal of priestly ministry. Catholic women declared that they were not just interested in being admitted to a clerical club, but wanted the priestly ministry significantly transformed to express a participatory understanding of the Church as a ministering community (see Gardiner, 1976).

The following year the Vatican responded to these developments, particularly to the decision of the American Episcopal Church to ordain women to the priesthood, by issuing a decree that reaffirmed the exclusion of women from ordained ministry on the grounds that women were incapable of 'imaging Christ'. The argument of the declaration responded to recent changes in the status of women in secular society by claiming that the Church has 'always' supported women's equality in society. The exclusion from ministry was removed to a separate plane related to sacramental symbolism, but no longer based on the traditional Catholic argument of women's natural inferiority.[7]

This argument, far from ending the discussion, crystallized the opposition of Catholic feminists to what they saw as a sinfully sexist theological anthropology. By the early 1980s the sense of a crisis between the hierarchy and Catholic women had grown so acute that the American Catholic bishops sponsored an official dialogue between the Catholic Bishops' Committee on Women and the Women's Ordination Conference.

One result of this dialogue was the decision of the American Catholic bishops to write a pastoral on women. This pastoral, issued in draft form in

April 1988 (second draft, April 1990), has been widely criticized by Catholic feminists. It is seen as still highly clerical and paternalistic, offering only an expanded role in lay ministry, but continuing to accept the view that women are incapable of being ordained to the priesthood (see the US National Conference of Catholic Bishops, 1988; and Ruether, 1988, pp. 175–6).

The conflict between the hierarchy and the growing consciousness of Catholic women is by no means limited to North America. Feminist theological networks have developed in Western Europe in the 1980s. Through the Ecumenical Association of Third World Theologians, Catholic and Protestant women from Asia, Africa and Latin America met in national, regional and then global meetings to discuss the feminist contextualization of liberation theology (see Fabella and Oduyoye, 1988). With the increasing crisis of the celibate male priesthood, more and more of the ministry in Catholic parishes is being done by theologically trained lay women. Such women in pastoral ministry are practical exemplars of an alternative, more inclusive model of ministry.

Thus the conflict between Catholic women and the hierarchy, in part released by the Vatican Council, shows no signs of lessening in the decades to come. The underlying issue is not simply the token inclusion of a few women in the hierarchy, but rather a more comprehensive questioning of this hierarchical pattern of Church government, seen as derived far more from feudalism and absolute monarchy than from the gospel.

Two different visions of the Church collide in this conflict; the vision of the Church as monarchy, ordered monolithically from above, and the vision of the Church as a community of people at the base, jointly participating in theological reflection and practical decisions and committed to helping shape a just society.[8] Since many of the populists refuse to leave the Catholic Church, and the hierarchalists are becoming ever more entrenched and aggressive, these groups are likely both to continue to coexist within the Catholic Church and to become more polarized in the future.

Notes

1 This information is derived from pamphlets of the American branch of the St Joan's International Alliance and from a 1978 personal letter from its long-time American leader, Frances McGillicuddy. The text of the petition to the Vatican is cited in the preface by Arlene and Leonard Swidler to Ida Raming's *The Exclusion of Women from the Priesthood: Divine Law or Sex Discrimination*, trans Norman Adams, Metuchen, New Jersey, Scarecrow Press, 1976, p. xvii.

2 This and subsequent information on the women auditors at Vatican II comes from an interview with Sister Luke Tobin, 27 December 1988.

3 The three married women were Mrs Patrick Crowley from Chicago, Illinois, Mrs Laurent Potvin, Ottawa, Ontario, and Mrs Henri Rendu from Paris, France. Dr Mercedes Concepcion, professor of demography from the University of the Philippines in Manila, was the other female member of the Commission.

4 This information on the papal birth-control commission is derived from a 1986 interview with Mrs Patty Crowley, who, together with her husband, Pat Crowley, headed the American Christian Family Movement and were appointed as members of the birth control commission. For the history of the commission, see also

R.B. Kaiser, *The Politics of Sex and Religion*. Kansas City, Mo, Leaven Press, 1986.

5 A number of pamphlets and study packets were written by the LCWR between 1972–6 to bring American Catholic nuns into solidarity with feminist principles and goals. See, for example, *The Status and Role of Women in the Church*, LCWR pamphlet, 1976.

6 Among the leading United States Catholic feminist theologians are Elizabeth S. Fiorenza, Rosemary Radford Ruether, Ann Carr and Mary Hunt. Mary Daly, the leading post-Christian feminist, also comes from a Catholic background. See Mary Jo Weaver, *New Catholic Women: A Contemporary Challenge to Traditional Religious Authority*. San Francisco, Harper & Row, 1985; also *The Inside Stories: Thirteen Valient Women Challenge the Church*, ed. A. Milhaven. Mystic, Conn., Twenty-third Publications, 1987.

7 'Declaration on the Question of the Admission of Women to the Ministerial Priesthood', Congregation for the Doctrine of the Faith, The Vatican, 15 October 1976. For critical commentary on this document, see *Women Priests: A Catholic Commentary on the Vatican Declaration*, ed. L. and A. Swidler. New York, Paulist Press, 1977.

8 For a dicussion of the base community model of the Church, from the perspective of liberation theology, see L. Boff, *Ecclesiogenesis: The Base Community Reinvents the Church*. Maryknoll, New York, Orbis Books, 1986. For a feminist version of the base community ecclesiology, see R. Ruether, *Woman-church: Theology and Practice of Feminist Liturgical Communities*. San Francisco, Harper & Row, 1985.

11D The Place of Women in the Church: Bibliography

Fabella, V. and Oduyoye, eds (1988) *With Passion and Compassion: Third World Women Doing Theology*. Maryknoll, New York, Orbis Books.

Gardiner, A.M., ed. (1976) *Women and the Catholic Priesthood: An Expanded Vision: Proceedings of the Detroit Ordination Conference*. New York, Paulist Press.

Gibbons, J. (1916). 'Cardinal Gibbons says women should keep from the polls', extract from a message from His Eminence, James Cardinal Gibbons to the National Association Opposed to Women's Suffrage, Washington, DC, 7 December. Massachusetts, Sophia Smith Collection, Smith College.

Kolbenschlag, M., ed. (1986) *Authority and Community in Conflict*. Kansas City, Mo, Sheed & Ward.

Ruether, R. (1988) 'Catholic Bishops and Women's Concerns', *Christianity and Crisis*, 16 May, pp. 175–6.

The US National Conference of Catholic Bishops (1988) 'Partners in the Mystery of Redemption: A Pastoral Response to Women's Concerns for Church and Society', Washington, DC, April.

11E Marriage and Sexuality

THEODORE DAVEY cp

The preparatory document on marriage and sexuality produced by the Theological Commission in 1962 for the Council was designed to emphasize the changeless nature of the Church's teaching. In fact, it merely served to close a chapter over 1,000 years long, in which marriage was seen to contain within itself its own objective ends or purposes established by God and independent of human experience. The teaching was clear: the one and only purpose of marriage was the procreation and rearing of children; subordinate to this was the mutual help and physical love husband and wife would share.

When eventually the Council came to consider marriage in *Gaudium et Spes*, under the general title of 'Some more urgent problems', the bishops forcefully expressed the inadequacy of the traditional view. They quite simply refused to see marriage in terms of a legal contract within which human love was institutionally irrelevant, and instead spoke of it as being an 'intimate partnership of life and love', and 'the mutual giving of two persons (*GS* 48). In spite of many requests to use the familiar word 'contract' in describing marriage, the bishops refused (Vorgrimler 5, p. 232). This was not simply playing with words, but was a response to a crucial question that had been posed with increasing concern since the 1930s, and would be much discussed in the years following the Council: has human love a central place in marriage, or is procreation its justifying and overriding value?

Attempts were made in the years immediately following the Council to say that *Gaudium et Spes* was merely a 'pastoral' document, that is, that it had not substantially altered our view of what marriage is, theologically or canonically. But this proved increasingly difficult to sustain as reflection on the conciliar texts and on human experience itself intensified, leading to the publication of the revised *Code of Canon Law* in 1983. In this new *Code* an attempt was made to translate the theological insights of Vatican II into practical norms, and Pope John Paul II in his letter of promulgation made this quite clear when he wrote:

> If, however, it is impossible to translate perfectly into canonical language the conciliar image of the Church, nevertheless the *Code* must always be referred to this image as the primary pattern whose outline the *Code* ought to express in so far as it can by its very nature.

The following description of marriage is to be found there: man and woman by an irrevocable covenant mutually give and accept one another to establish a marriage (canon 1057/2).

I would like to concentrate on two main areas of development: (1) covenant and nullity; (2) divorce, remarriage and the Eucharist.

COVENANT AND NULLITY

The move from a contract about an exchange of physical sexual rights, to marriage seen as a covenant relationship embracing the whole of life, of which

267

the procreative is an important part, but still only a part, is the single most important development since the Council. When marriage is seen as self-gift, then love becomes the central value, to which all others are subordinated – for what is married love but the lifelong gift of oneself? It has been pointed out that the marital covenant engages the whole of the spouses' lives, while contract is concerned with more limited services and for a determined period of time. Furthermore, contracts, made between persons about things, can be terminated by mutual agreement (the rationale behind much divorce legislation in the Western world). But in the Christian view, covenants are witnessed by God, who guarantees them. Significantly, too, marriage covenants can only be made by people who are emotionally and spiritually mature. This puts greater demands on intended spouses, and has led to a considerable emphasis on marriage preparation in the Church.

This covenantal aspect of marriage corresponds to what Christians are experiencing today, when they say that the primary task of marriage is not procreation but growth in love. Through their experience of each other, they experience the divine. The bishops of England and Wales underline this when they say:

> An enriched theology of marriage will have to take into account the growth of human relationships, the need for true communication within marriage, and the understanding of sexual intercourse both as a life-giving act and as a communication of love and self to one's partner (1980, p. 36).

It is sometimes objected that post-conciliar reflection has undervalued fruitfulness as one of the chief elements in the marriage relationship. However, one might equally argue that it has been set within a broader context, where the entire relationship is seen as life-giving. Pastorally this is also a most valuable insight for those couples whose marriage is childless, or who marry in later life.

This personalist view of marriage was developed in the encyclical *Humanae Vitae*, where Pope Paul VI enumerates the characteristics of human marital love, stressing that it is a very special kind of personal friendship, where man and woman are equal companions. However, by moving away from a view of marriage seen essentially as a contract about an exchange of physical sexual rights, one is compelled again to consider the persons involved in the 'covenant'.

The pessimism of Augustine about sexual expression in marriage has been repudiated by the Council and the post-conciliar Church. However, it has to be admitted that little was said in Council about human sexuality, and various authors have pointed out that in the intervening years the need to understand sexuality within a theological framework has not been achieved. A study commissioned by the Catholic Theological Society of America, *Human Sexuality: New Directions in American Catholic Thought* (1977), was an attempt, but was received with considerable criticism. A more recent essay by Theodore Mackin, 'How to Understand the Sacrament of Marriage' (Roberts, 1987, pp. 47–56), goes some way to remedying this lack. He makes the point that, for priest theologians at least, we have a problem of theological method here, in that understanding the place of sexuality in the sacrament depends on information that can only be supplied by Christian spouses who have a grasp of sacramental theology, and can, at the same time, reflect intelligently on their own experience.

By the 1970s it was seen that the redefining of marriage begun at the Council was having an effect on pastoral practice. Most people could marry under the contractual view, but the covenantal understanding was a different matter. As a result, the new *Code of Canon Law* introduced two factors to emphasize the change: firstly, soundness of judgement with regard to understanding the obligations to be assumed on marriage was stressed as vitally important, so much so that without this 'discretion' marriage becomes impossible. Secondly, people intending to marry must have the psychological ability to accept and cope with such lifelong obligations (canon 1095). As we have seen, of the obligations to be assumed on marriage, the central one is the right to a community of life and love. Just what such a community consists in is presently being explored by the Church's nullity tribunals.

These tribunals have had a new lease of life in the post-conciliar period. They received their present form some 240 years ago under Pope Benedict XIV, and remain substantially the same today. Based on the assumption that every request for nullity is 'controversial', they are called upon to adjudicate in circumstances in reality very different from those envisaged by Benedict. The reality today is that people in increasing numbers divorce and remarry, and then ask the Church to make a decision on the status of their first marriage; the object being a return to the sacramental life of the community. Their operation remains uneven, so that accusations of 'geographical injustice' are frequently made. The classic dilemma then occurs, of either providing a well-trained and well-staffed tribunal working for the care of the divorced, at considerable expense, or having an inadequate tribunal where delays are a matter of course, and individuals feel alienated at a time when they expect help and compassion. The present canonical system is far beyond the resources of many local churches outside the West.

Influential voices suggest that the present tribunal system should be transformed into an instrument of pastoral care, with healing as the objective, rather than the Church seeming to be preoccupied with the administration of the law. One of the tasks of a marriage tribunal is to help people form their consciences. That an alternative system of fulfilling this duty can be found, remains one of the objectives of pastoral theology (Örsy, 1988, p. 283).

DIVORCE, REMARRIAGE AND THE EUCHARIST

The Council said little about divorce; the agenda of pressing problems was large, and this particular pastoral issue gave no indication then of the way it would become the most urgent problem of social pathology in the 1970s and 1980s. However, with the changes of legislation in even so-called Catholic countries over the last twenty years, questions of divorce and remarriage have forced themselves on to the pastoral agenda, and show no signs of disappearing.

The central theological question here is: how can the Church preserve its teaching on the permanence of marriage, seen as central to the gospel, and yet at the same time act as an agent of reconciliation and healing to those men and women, who, in the words of Pope Paul VI: 'through inadequate preparation, human weakness or the harmful pressures of a permissive society, have experienced the breakdown of a love which they certainly wanted to be more permanent'. The question remains unresolved to the present day, but has become more acute as the result of another development initiated by the Council, namely, the centrality of the Eucharist in Christian living. In a Church that was required to enforce the legislation of the Fourth Council of the Lateran on annual reception of the Eucharist, and without divorce as a factor, there was no dilemma.

The traditional response has been that when divorce occurs in a consummated marriage between two baptized persons, and one or other of whom remarries, then the right to the Eucharist has been forfeited. The only way it can be recovered is by returning to the first spouse. If this cannot be done because of compelling obligations arising from the second union, then those involved must live as though they were not married; this is the 'solution' referred to as the 'brother and sister' marriage.

This theological stance is based on the notion that Christians in such a second union are living in a permanent state of sin; they are also imperfect symbols of what the marriages of Christians should signify. But most serious of all, they are objects of scandal to the community and to the world at large. This is seen as 'theological' scandal, since if remarriage after divorce is not a sin, what is it? And if it is not sinful to remarry (while one's first partner is still alive), what is wrong with it? And if there is nothing wrong with it, what has become of indissolubility?

For the last fifteen years or so, moral theologians have made an exhaustive analysis and critique of these arguments, so much so, that the 'state of sin' argument very rapidly vanished. The chief reason was based on the realization that judgement of human virtue and sinfulness is God's prerogative – human judgement in such matters being totally fallible. But the two other bases for refusing to separate the Eucharist from remarriage remain. The 1980 Synod of Bishops on marriage and family life debated this issue, but was unable to reach any pastoral conclusions. And when Pope John Paul II issued his exhortation on marriage and the family in 1981, *Familiaris Consortio* (Flannery 2, pp. 815–98), he too felt unable to change the traditional stance, saying:

> Their state [the divorced and remarried] and condition of life are objectively opposed to that union of love between Christ and the Church that is signified by the Eucharist . . . and the faithful would be misled and confused about the doctrine of indissolubility (84).

A careful reading of *Familiaris Consortio*, however, gives one reason to conclude that the pope is not closing the pastoral debate, but is stating that up to the present these two theological arguments have not been sufficiently clarified, 'we are in the midst of a development that has not reached its final goal yet' (Örsy, 1988, p. 290). Thus, for example, if a community did not conclude that the Church was changing its doctrine on the indissolubility of marriage, then clearly the 'scandal' argument would no longer hold. It can be asserted too, that the scandal the community is receiving at present is caused by the exclusion of people from the Eucharist, and not by their reception.

The argument that the divorced and remarried are imperfect symbols is disquieting, if for no other reason than because in a Church all of whose members are sinners, it must lead to a further question: 'Who then can be admitted to the Eucharist?' (For a wide ranging discussion of this whole question, see Kelly, 1982, pp. 64–105.)

11E Marriage and Sexuality: Bibliography

Bishops' Conference of England and Wales (1980), *The Easter People*. Slough, St Paul Publications.

Kelly, K. (1982) *Divorce and Second Marriage*. London, Collins.

Mackin, T. (1982) *What Is Marriage?* New York, Paulist Press.

Örsy, L. (1988) *Marriage in Canon Law: Texts and Comments, Reflections and Questions*. Wilmington, DE, Michael Glazier.

Roberts, W. P., ed. (1987) *Commitment to Partnership*. New York, Paulist Press.

Saxton, S., ed. (1984) *The Changing Family: Reflections on Familiaris Consortio*.

11F Abortion

JAMES TUNSTEAD BURTCHAELL CSC

The documents of Vatican II embody no concern that abortion was taken to be an urgent issue in the middle of the 1960s. It is given brief mention in *Gaudium et Spes*, the Council's most comprehensive statement on the moral issues of the day: 'From the moment of its conception life must be guarded with the greatest care, while abortion and infanticide are unspeakable crimes' (*GS* 51). Abortion had been dealt with rarely in the abundant literature of encyclicals and discourses of Pius XII. John XXIII did not include it in his agenda of social concerns in *Mater et Magistra* (except obliquely, 194) or *Pacem in Terris*, nor is there any mention of it in Paul VI's great moral statement, *Populorum Progressio*.

Reliable statistics on abortion were just emerging at that time, but the world was already well on its way to its present traffic in abortions, which are estimated at about 40,000,000 annually.

At the time of the Council, abortion had already been firmly established as a prime element of the population control programmes within the communist bloc. When the birth rate was to be augmented, abortion was severely punished, but when the state wished to curb population it was permitted, encouraged, or even required. In Europe and North America, the 1960s saw the organization of articulate and aggressive movements to repeal traditional criminal laws that forbade abortion – movements that succeeded in making abortion-on-demand legal by 1967 in Great Britain and 1973 in the United States. Advocacy of abortion to control population growth was effectively urged upon the economically developing countries of the third world by affluent governments and philanthropic foundations as a condition of continued subsidy. Within a short span of time, a practice that had been furtive, criminal and 'unspeakable' was transformed into one of the most aggressively advocated measures of social engineering in the world.

Abortion had, of course, been rigorously forbidden in Catholic teaching. Catholics were either slow or loath to notice that the incidence of abortion was especially high in certain countries where Catholics predominated, for example, Hungary, Argentina, Poland, Austria. In Latin America it had long been a principal method of birth control. In pluralistic populations within North America and Western Europe, surveys would soon indicate that Catholic women resorted to abortion about as frequently as did mothers of other religious allegiance. Even more suggestive was evidence from opinion polls that Catholic respondents displayed a range of opinion on the morality of abortion that varied by only a few percentage points from the judgements of their fellow citizens. Here was a foundational tenet of the Church's moral teaching on personal and social justice that apparently found no significant echo in either the convictions or the practice of many Catholic people.

One sees here striking evidence that the faith and its moral sequelae may have very little grip on national populations where a traditional Catholicism has decayed into a nominal – perhaps no more than tribal – identity. There has been a wistful assumption that large segments of the Catholic community whose membership has degenerated from active commitment to passive tradition might still be tethered to the faith by sentiment, if not by conviction. But evidence referring to abortion would suggest that these Catholics are less than marginal in their allegiance. Although they are likely to be identified as Catholics by social scientists, and are themselves more likely than lapsed members from other religious groups to continue identifying themselves as Catholics, they have in many respects – perhaps in most – ceased to be interactive parties to the community of belief.

One very instinctive finding has been that polar attitudes towards abortion (that it is reprehensible, or allowable, in virtually all cases) correspond not to one's specific religious affiliation, but to whether or not one is religiously active. In a word, Catholics in general do not tend to embody the official teaching of their Church on abortion, except to the extent that they are vitally involved in the interactive life of their faith community.

Yet even practising Catholics had been little exposed to strenuous exhortation on this subject. Abortion had scarcely been mentioned in the scholarship of moral theology or in parochial preaching. When it began to be promoted actively in the 1960s, there was for a long while only a feeble response in the Church. Three reasons may explain this moral lethargy or confusion.

The abortion movement has been largely sponsored as a function of concern about over-population, and Paul VI's encyclical *Humanae Vitae* (1968) long inhibited public participation by Catholics in the population debate. Rather than interpreting the birth-control issue in the context of a contemporary resentment towards childbearing, Pope Paul had rested his entire argument upon a distinction between 'natural' and 'artificial' methods of having sex without reproduction. So long as Catholics were prevented from openly challenging that argument, the Church appeared, at best, to be indifferent to the issue of over-population and, at worst, to be provoking unwanted pregnancies and the ensuing abortions. Though Pope John Paul II has been forthright in the defence of the unborn, his equally vigorous rejection of contraception has in some ways put these two exhortations at apparent odds with each other.

Abortion has also been a prominent agenda item of the contemporary feminist movement. In their early, aggressive campaign to gain parity for women, feminist spokeswomen have wished to emancipate women from the inexorable obligations of the marital and maternal bond, and thus downgraded home-making and motherhood. Catholic resistance was inevitable to a movement that portrayed the needs of women as opposed to, rather than allied with, the advantage of men and children. Unfortunately, this resistance has been more conservative and nay-saying than inspired. Rather than entering the controversy as a partisan for women on terms that derived from Christian wisdom, the Church appeared to be hostile to the legitimate and timely appeal of women for fair treatment. This discredit was not alleviated by the Church's readiness to recruit women for virtually every ministry in the Church, but to refuse them access to ordained office.

A third disability in the Catholic moral treatment of abortion derives from the contemporary disarray of moral theology. Ethics as studied by Catholics had long been an adjunct of the Church's penitential ministry, and therefore under close surveillance. The long Vatican habit of treating moral theology more as a matter of discipline than as one of enquiry, had a stunting effect. Ironically, it was the freedom of expression sponsored by Vatican II that made many Catholic moralists embarrassed by the recent lack of scholarly rigour in their field. For some of them, the most attractive academic alternative has been an ethic descended from Enlightenment liberalism, with its intense priority upon the liberty of the individual. In the atmosphere of an abruptly emancipated discourse within the Church, not a few moralists found this doctrine of moral autonomy attractive, and found that on these terms they could find no very persuasive argument to inhibit the choice of any mother to eliminate a child unwanted and unborn (the more recent extension of abortion advocacy to infanticide for handicapped newborns has extended the issue). Thus there are many ostensibly Catholic theologians whose recent embrace of individualism as a theological starting point has muted their voice on behalf of the unborn.

With the rise of public controversy, Catholics eventually appeared as prominent and forceful opponents of abortion. This has led to a curious internal division among social activists, however. The movement of social awareness and active advocacy for the disadvantaged, which found new momentum in Vatican II, has taken special interest in certain causes. Warfare, especially involving the threat of nuclear arms; destitution and chronic poverty; civil rights for ethnic minorities; totalitarian rule; alcohol and drug abuse; capital punishment; the physically and mentally handicapped; shelter for refugees: all these are causes to which Catholics have rallied in a prophetic way. There has been an awkward distance, thus far, between some of these movements for social justice and succour and the movement to protect the unborn and newborn.

More is at stake than the old ideological divide between 'liberal' and 'conservative' causes. The estrangement may be due partly to the readiness of one group to interpret the aborting mother only as a victim, and the propensity of the other group to target her only as a destroyer. Also, the pro-life advocates, for some of whom this has been the first social justice cause to provoke their consciences to public witness, are often newcomers to social activism, whereas the other causes have veteran supporters. Those veterans respond with annoyance to the alleged concentration of pro-life advocates upon a single issue, whereas the latter distrust the commitments of those who treat an atrocity with an annual death toll equal to that of all of the Second World War as coequal with other misfortunes. A lively debate has arisen regarding the proper target issues of an authentically consistent ethic supportive of human life.

The evidence suggests that abortion has been one of these issues towards which Vatican II did not turn its gaze, but one that calls for a better integrated and prophetic wisdom about the advocacy of the most helpless.

11F Abortion: Bibliography

Bernardin, J. (1988) *Consistent Ethic of Life*. Kansas City, Sheed & Ward.

Burtchaell, J. T. (1982) *Rachel Weeping, and Other Essays on Abortion*. Kansas City, Andrews and McMeel.

Burtchaell, J. T. (1989) *The Giving and Taking of Life*. Notre Dame, University of Notre Dame Press.

Callahan, D. (1970) *Abortion: Law, Choice and Morality*. New York, Macmillan.

Connery, J. (1977) *Abortion: The Development of the Roman Catholic Perspective*. Chicago, Loyola University Press.

Glendon, M. A. (1987) *Abortion and Divorce in Western Law: American Failures, European Challenges*. Cambridge, MA, Harvard University Press.

Noonan, J. T., Jr, ed. (1970) *The Morality of Abortion: Legal and Historical Perspectives*. Cambridge, MA, Harvard University Press.

Noonan, J. T., Jr (1979) *A Private Choice: Abortion in America in the Seventies*. New York, Free Press.

Stevas, N. St John- (1963) *The Right to Life*. London, Hodder & Stoughton.

11G Homosexuality

TIMOTHY C. POTTS

The Second Vatican Council said nothing about homosexuality – not surprisingly, perhaps, considering that very little was being said about it anywhere else in the mid-1960s. The Stonewall riot in New York, when homosexual men resisted police harassment publicly for the first time, did not occur until 1969, while sexual acts between consenting males in private were only decriminalized in England and Wales two years earlier. The trigger to open discussion of the matter among Catholics was *Humanae Vitae* (1968), which, by confounding widespread expectations regarding teaching on birth control, led to general questioning of the sexual ethic developed in the Church since the early Middle Ages and still prevalent, just at a time when sexual orientation began to be talked about more widely in society as a whole.

One of the earliest statements on homosexuality came from the United States Bishops' Conference in 1973, in the form of *Principles to Guide Confessors in Questions of Homosexuality*. This recognized that people do not choose their sexual orientation and that psychiatric techniques to change it are often inappropriate. Homosexual people are to be encouraged to form stable friendships, even with other homosexuals. But 'homosexual acts are a grave transgression of the goals of human sexuality and of human personality' and, although responsibility may be mitigated in some cases, homosexual people are in general responsible for their actions. So confessors should help them to work out an ascetical plan of life with a view to controlling their inclinations.

The first explicit pronouncement from the Vatican on the topic came in a Declaration on Certain Questions concerning Sexual Ethics (*Personae Humanae*) from the Congregation for the Doctrine of the Faith issued on 29 December 1975 (Flannery 2, pp. 486–99). The central theme of the declaration is that any sexual behaviour that does not have reproduction as its goal is, objectively, seriously wrong; moreover, that this includes premarital heterosexual activity, homosexual activity and masturbation. Regarding homosexual people, the declaration endorses a distinction between those whose orientation is either innate or an incurable pathological constitution, and others, in whom it is transitory or at least curable. But, even for the former, 'homosexual relations within a sincere communion of life and love' are inadmissible, for 'in sacred Scripture they are condemned as a serious depravity and even presented as the sad consequence of rejecting God' (8). Yet homosexual people are to be 'treated with understanding and sustained in the hope of overcoming their personal difficulties and their inability to fit into society. Their culpability will be judged with prudence.' (10).

Meanwhile, gay Catholic organizations were springing up, especially in the English-speaking world. In the United States, Dignity was founded in 1969 to offer pastoral care and campaign for change in official attitudes, including among its aims 'to work for the development of the Church's sexual theology and for the acceptance of gays as full and equal members of the one Christ'. In Britain, a Catholic gay group founded in London in 1973 led, early in 1976, to

276

the formation of Quest, a title chosen to express that its members 'are seeking ways of reconciling the full practice of their Catholic faith with the full expression of their homosexual natures in loving Christian relationships'. In the same year, J.J. McNeill's *The Church and the Homosexual* appeared, after a two-year delay during which the Vatican brought pressure to bear upon the Jesuit General to prevent its publication. This was not the first work on the topic by a priest; Marc Oraison (1975) had already argued for change but, writing in French, commanded a much smaller audience. McNeill, a moral theologian, first reviewed scriptural texts commonly cited in condemnation of homosexuality, then tradition, concluding that neither shows that a homo-sexual orientation is contrary to the will of God. He went on to argue for the possibility of morally good homosexual relationships, given certain conditions such as mutuality, fidelity, unselfishness, etc.

In 1977, an influential report, *Human Sexuality*, commissioned by the Catholic Theological Society of America, appeared. This contained a section on homosexuality, beginning with a Scripture survey that owed much to McNeill. The report then described four current approaches to the morality of homosexuality and concluded with some pastoral reflections, among which was:

> Christian homosexuals have the same needs and rights to the Sacraments as heterosexuals. In determining whether or not to administer absolution or give Holy Communion to a homosexual, a pastor can be guided by the general principle of fundamental moral theology that only a certain moral obligation may be imposed. *Ubi dubium, ibi libertas*. An invincible doubt, whether of law or of fact, permits one to follow a true and solidly probable opinion in favour of liberty.

Moreover, in view of all the material on homosexuality canvassed in the report, 'solidly probable opinion can be invoked in favour of permitting a homosexual freedom of conscience and free access to the sacraments . . . a homosexual engaging in homosexual acts in good conscience has the same rights of conscience and the same rights to the sacraments as a married couple practising birth control in good conscience' (p. 216).

Urged by Quest, in 1977 the National Conference of Priests asked the Bishops' Conference of England and Wales to set up a working party to look at the Church's pastoral approach to homosexuality. The result was *An Introduction to the Pastoral Care of Homosexual People*, issued by the Social Welfare Commission of the Bishops' Conference in 1979 – a year in which the Church of England and the Methodists also produced reports on homosexuality. The authors of this document drew a sharp distinction between homosexuality as a state or condition, which, they considered 'as such is neither morally good nor bad. . . . It is morally neutral', and homosexual acts, of which 'scripture and the ongoing tradition of Christianity make quite clear . . . are immoral'. But they followed the lead of *Human Sexuality* on pastoral practice and social questions, declaring that 'The Church has a serious responsibility to work towards the elimination of any injustices perpetrated on homosexuals by society' (13).

Support for gay rights was further emphasized by the Council for Church and Society of the Dutch Bishops' Conference in *Homosexual People in Society* (also 1979). The types of discrimination to which homosexual people are liable were spelled out in detail, with the conclusion that 'any appeal to the Scriptures in order to condemn a homosexual orientation and to transfer that condemnation into social discrimination must be rejected as an abuse of Scripture'. The document explicitly avoids moral judgement about homosexual activity, but points to the dangers both of confusing orientation with behaviour and of trying to separate them too rigidly.

In October 1979, Pope John Paul II visited the United States and, in addressing its bishops, commended them for their pastoral letter of 1976, *To Live in Christ Jesus*, and for saying *inter alia*, 'Homosexual activity . . . as distinguished from homosexual orientation, is morally wrong'. For the next six years, little was heard from the Vatican or bishops, and the period was characterized more by scholarly studies, of which one of the most important was by the heterosexual Protestant biblical scholar Scroggs (1983), arguing that the New Testament texts did not have homosexuality in its modern sense or manifestations in mind at all, but were aimed at male prostitution in the ancient world. While adopting no position himself on the morality of homosexual acts, Scroggs concludes that the New Testament texts commonly cited in condemnation of it are, in fact, irrelevant, and that we must look more widely to the Bible for general principles that bear on the matter.

Disturbed by increasing challenges to the traditional Christian view of homosexuality, the Congregation for the Doctrine of the Faith issued a letter to the bishops in October 1986 on *The Pastoral Care of Homosexual Persons*. It begins by recalling the distinction between the homosexual condition and individual homosexual actions but, instead of saying that the former is morally neutral, says that it is an 'objective disorder' because, though not a sin, it is a tendency towards evil. This introduces an ambiguity, which persists throughout the letter, between a moral and a medical model of homosexuality (see Moore, 1989). There follows a review of biblical texts relating to homosexual acts, which is essentially fundamentalist in its method and shows no acquaintance with any of the scriptural work noted above.

Going on to practical matters, the letter turns its back on any duty to oppose injustice to homosexuals, instructing the bishops to oppose, instead, gay rights legislation, as, indeed, some have consistently done (e.g. Cardinal O'Connor in New York). The letter deplores 'violent malice in speech or action' against lesbians and gays, but the force of this is much reduced by an immediately preceding accusation that they are careless of the lives of other people, and a subsequent remark that no one should be surprised by violent reactions to gay-rights campaigns. Finally, the letter turns to what is supposed to be its main topic, asking bishops to develop forms of gay ministry and commending priests who engage in it. Conditions, however, are attached: it must be clearly stated that homosexual activity is immoral, priests engaging in gay ministry must agree with the letter, and gay organizations that oppose, are ambiguous about or even merely neglect the Congregation's view must not be allowed to meet on Church property.

In terms of its effects, this document is best described as a dead letter.

Dignity responded in 1987 'that gay and lesbian people can express their sexuality physically in an unitive manner that is loving, life giving and life affirming', adding that 'it emphatically disagrees with and calls for a re-examination of the magisterial teachings on "homosexual activity"', referring to the 1986 Pastoral and the Vatican letter. In consequence, it has been denied the use of Church premises for its meetings. Difficulties have also been put in the way of priests engaged in gay ministry. Quest was more cautious, emphasizing its pastoral role and disclaiming any view, as an organization, on the morality of homosexuality – perhaps rather disingenuously, in view of its original aims. Nevertheless, the strategy has paid off, to the extent that it enjoys increasing support among the bishops of England and Wales, where there is a tacit agreement to say nothing about the Vatican letter and carry on as before.

It seems evident that moral questions concerning homosexuality cannot be resolved in isolation. The Vatican's objection to homosexual activity is, basically, the same as its objection to contraception: that neither are even potentially reproductive. The central issue is whether every kind of sexual activity that is not potentially reproductive is wrong, either on philosophical or on theological grounds. Vatican II, by dropping previous insistence on reproduction as the *primary* end of sexual intercourse (*Gaudium et Spes* 48–50), seemed to open the way to justification of certain non-reproductive uses of sexuality, but so far it has been left to individual theologians to explore this avenue.

11G Homosexuality: Bibliography

Boswell, J. (1980) *Christianity, Social Tolerance, and Homosexuality.* Chicago and London, University of Chicago Press.

Coleman, P. (1980) *Christian Attitudes to Homosexuality.* London, SPCK.

Kosnik, A., *et al.*, eds (1977) *Human Sexuality: New Directions in Catholic Thought.* London, Search Press.

McNeill, J.J. (1977) *The Church and the Homosexual.* London, Darton, Longman and Todd.

Moore, G. (1989) 'Are Homosexuals Sick?', *New Blackfriars*, vol. 70, pp. 15–19.

Nugent, R., ed. (1983) *A Challenge to Love: Gay and Lesbian Catholics in the Church.* New York, Crossroad.

Oraison, M. (1975 ET 1977) *The Homosexual Question.* London, Search Press.

Scroggs, R. (1983) *The New Testament and Homosexuality.* Philadelphia, Fortress Press.

11H Marian Apparitions

C. J. MAUNDER

A BRIEF OVERVIEW OF APPARITION CULTS SINCE 1960

Over a period almost concurrent with the Second Vatican Council (1961–5), four girls in a Spanish mountain village, San Sebastian de Garabandal, claimed to have seen the Virgin Mary on many occasions. Their visions were attended by an abundance of spectacular phenomena, including the appearance of a supernatural host; the message they passed on was focused on a perceived decline in reverence for the Eucharist, and included these memorable words: 'Many cardinals, bishops, and priests are on the road to perdition, and are taking many souls with them'.

The Garabandal movement was and is not opposed to the Council *per se*. Its members (many from the United States) anticipated a spread of communism and a decline in traditional Catholic piety, yet they did not lose confidence in the papacy or in the possibility of ultimate favour from the Church, although the local bishops suppressed the movement for many years. Two cases of apparitions are, however, noted for their schismatic tendency: Palmar de Troya (near Seville, 1968–), where one of the visionaries proclaimed himself pope in 1976, and Bayside (New York, 1975–), where it was claimed that a communist double of Paul VI had usurped his place in the Vatican. Under-standably, these paranoid and elitist movements have been condemned by the hierarchy.

Notable Marian visions and miracles outside Europe have not, on the whole, aroused controversy: those at Akita (Japan, 1973–81), Betania (Venezuela, 1976–84), Cuapa (Nicaragua, 1980), and Kibeho (Rwanda, 1985–) gained some degree of approval from the local bishop. The visions of light at Zeitoun (Cairo, 1968–71), seen by many Christians and Muslims, were recognized as genuine Marian phenomena by the Coptic patriarch. Other recent cases have been recorded in Mexico, Syria, Argentina, South Korea, Egypt and else-where.

Europe has not been without its own recent reports of apparitions: in particular, Ireland and Italy. The notable cases in Ireland are Melleray (1985, where the message included a warning for the Church and comfort for Ireland), Inchigeela (1985–), and Bessbrook (1987–); in Italy, San Damiano (1961–70, a case that became controversial), Schio, and Oliveto Citra (both 1985–). Many modern apparition cults include long and intricate messages more reminiscent of revelations to nuns over the centuries than of the famous public apparitions. This is the result of the better-educated and mature status of many visionaries (e.g. the women seers of San Lorenzo del Escorial, Spain, 1980–, and Surbiton, England, 1983–; the latter publicizes devotion to the 'Divine Innocence' – special devotions are often the subject of Marian visions).

Apparitions during the latter part of the post-conciliar period have not displayed the anxious opposition to change that marked earlier cases. Never-theless, they have continued the twin theme of old: (1) the need to re-establish the basics of Catholic piety (in particular, confession, penance and the Eucharist), and (2) the possibility of disaster in an unbelieving world. These considerations have constituted the major part of the message resulting from daily apparitions at Medjugorje, Yugoslavia (1981–). In addition, Medjugorje has emphasized some central conciliar themes – ecumenism, parish renewal, the importance of Scripture, Christocentricity – in such a way as to attract the condemnation of the extreme conservative French group, the 'Contre-Réforme Catholique'; there is also a continuation of the Fatima tradition of concern for world peace, with the onus for this placed on individual and group spirituality.

Medjugorje's well-known controversy has arisen from ecclesiastical tension between the local Franciscans and the bishop of Mostar. On the other hand, the Croat nationalism feared by the communist authorities has not material-ized, and they now encourage the foreign pilgrims who bring currency into an economy in crisis. However, the link between separatist nationalism and Catholic piety is a delicate issue in Eastern Europe generally; the apparitions at Hrushiw (Ukraine, 1987–) are cast in a nationalist mould.

PAPAL TEACHING ON THE MARIAN APPARITION SHRINES

The Council demanded that, 'the cult, especially the liturgical cult, of the Blessed Virgin, be generously fostered', and sought a middle way between the divergent tendencies of indifference and exaggeration (*Lumen Gentium* 67). Paul VI did not regard Fatima as an example of the 'vain credulity' rejected by the Council, and visited the shrine on the fiftieth anniversary of the apparitions (1967). John Paul II was willing to follow his predecessors in consecrating the world to the Immaculate Heart (1982 and 1984) according to the wishes of the Fatima visionary, Sister Lucia.

Paul VI felt the need to clarify and expand the brief conciliar treatment of the Marian cult, and published the apostolic exhortation *Marialis Cultus* in 1974. Here he outlined the way in which the Marian movement might conform to a distinctly post-conciliar spirituality. The careful exposition of devotion using the rosary (42ff.) is especially relevant to the Marian shrines, where this prayer has been a central feature, since Lourdes (1858) in particular. The use of the rosary before and after, but not during, Mass at Medjugorje is reported to be the instruction of the Virgin, but also echoes *Marialis Cultus* 48.

John Paul II has been prominent in his own distinctively Polish devotion to Our Lady, often expressed in pilgrimage to Jasna Gora. He has made a point of visiting Marian apparition shrines when on tour (e.g. Lourdes, Knock, Fatima, Beauraing, Banneux). The encyclical announcing the Marian year of 1987–8, *Redemptoris Mater* (1987), speaks at length of the Church following Mary in her own earthly pilgrimage to the cross. Like Paul VI, John Paul II is concerned to confirm and expand the conciliar treatment of Mary; his new and original emphasis is on the 'presence of Mary' (28), and implicit in his references to shrines is the fact that the apparitions are a special sign of her

281

presence. In addition, *Redemptoris Mater* alludes to a central concern at both Garabandal and Medjugorje in linking the Eucharist with devotion to Mary as a fact evident in the 'pastoral practice of the Marian shrines' (44).

THE WAY FORWARD

The concerned and often controversial debate over the Marian apparitions and shrines suggests the need for clarification in three major areas, so as to keep the Marian cult in line with the renewal dynamic of Vatican II (a task made easier by the fact that apparition phenomena exhibit quite spontaneously the developments and moods of the contemporary Church):

1 the links between conciliar and papal teaching on social and religious commitment on the one hand, and the Marian cult on the other, so as to elucidate and develop the call to commitment passed on by many visionaries.

2 Catholic teaching on visionary prophecy, so as to show how the worlds of apocalyptic and everyday faith may be held in a healthy balance.

3 The official position on episcopal responsibility for apparition cults, giving clear indications as to the circumstances in which this is likely to be overriden by the national or international hierarchy.

11H Marian Apparitions: Bibliography

Craig, M. (1988) *Spark from Heaven: Mystery of the Madonna of Medjugorje*, London, Hodder & Stoughton.
Doyle, D. N. (1985) 'Marian Apparitions', *One in Christ*, no. 1, pp. 78–83.
Laurentin, R. (1990) *The Apparitions of the Blessed Virgin Mary Today*. Dublin, Veritas.
O'Carroll, M. (1986) *Medjugorje: Facts, Documents, Theology*. Dublin, Veritas.
Pelletier, J. A. (1971) *Our Lady comes to Garabandal*.
Rahner, K. (1963) *Visions and Prophecies*. Questiones Disputatae. London, Search Press.

11I The Conservative Reaction

MICHAEL J. WALSH

The dedication of part 2 of Michael Davies's three-volume study, *Liturgical Revolution*, reads: 'With respect and gratitude to Archbishop Marcel Lefebvre and all the members of the International Group of Fathers (*Coetus Internationalis Patrum*) who strove to uphold the traditional Catholic Faith throughout The Second Vatican Council'. The text on the inside of the front cover accuses the London-based Catholic Truth Society of publishing 'a misleading and factually inaccurate pamphlet intended to discredit Archbishop Lefebvre in the eyes of British Catholics'. The three volumes chronicle what is, in Davies's eyes, an attempt to 'Protestantize' the Roman liturgy. He was himself a convert, and he believed he found in *Pope Paul's New Mass* (the title of volume 3) an approximation to *Cranmer's Godly Order* (the title of volume 1).

In the United Kingdom, Davies's attack has been one of the more sustained ones upon the changes consequent upon Vatican II. But although his comments are wide-ranging, in practice his chief antagonism is reserved for matters liturgical: another of his publications is entitled *Communion in the Hand and Similar Frauds*. Such concentration upon the ritual aspects of the Church's life is a common feature of conservative movements. Few perhaps go as far as Davies in their rejection of the changes in the liturgy, but alarm at 'innovations' such as the reception of Communion while standing rather than kneeling, as Communion in the hand, at the use of lay people to distribute the sacred species, are common features.

Opposition to the new liturgy may be found among groups in opposition to the Council, but is not coterminous with them even though some of the Council's more radical supporters present it as such. Yet if the liturgy will not provide an adequate touchstone by which to gauge conservative reaction to Vatican II, it is difficult to find one single criterion. The Abbé George de Nantes dates his disillusionment with the Council to John XXIII's opening speech on 11 October 1962 (up to that point, he claims, he had 'joyously welcomed' Vatican II). His conviction that the pope had fallen into heresy, however, he attributes to the *Ordo Missae* promulgated on 3 April 1969, and more particularly to a conversation he had three months later with a Dominican, Guèrard de Lauriers, who, he reported, 'told me that Paul VI was no longer pope. Convicted of heresy by article 7 [of the new *Ordo*, defining the Mass], his fall from the papacy was immediate, obvious and formal'. For a time, de Nantes was a leading proponent of those who believe that, with the pope having fallen into schism, there is now no pontiff – the 'Sede vacante' theory. He later came to repudiate a strict interpretation of this theory as impracticable, and concocted his own version, according to which Paul VI, as a man, had erred, but must now submit himself to the judgement of Paul VI as pope – an appeal to the pope against the pope.

De Nantes's opposition to the Council occasioned his suspension from all priestly activities in December 1965. He was condemned by the Congregation for the Doctrine of the Faith in August 1969, and among the charges laid

283

against him was that of appealing to the Roman clergy to proceed to a canonical deposition of Paul VI. 'I reject the new religion, I refuse *aggiornamento* as an inspiration of the devil, and I nevertheless remain a full member and son of the Church. The tyranny of the Reformers has met a setback', he wrote in his monthly newsletter *La Contre Reforme Catholique* for July 1970. In recent years his writing has become increasingly apocalyptic and has taken on a strongly anti-Semitic tone. But his precise complaints about the post-conciliar Church, apart from the new *Ordo*, are difficult to pin down. One Council document continues to crop up in his newsletter, that on religious liberty (*Dignitatis Humanae*): 'freedom of conscience and of religion is an error', he wrote shortly before the Declaration was approved, 'insulting to God and pernicious for all human society'.

It is a view he shares with Archbishop Marcel Lefebvre. For both of them, the Council reversed a century and a half of opposition to the French Revolution by endorsing *liberté* (= declaration on religious freedom), *egalité* (= the doctrine of collegiality enshrined in *Lumen Gentium*) and *fraternité* (= ecumenism). Though there is little sympathy between Lefebvre's Society of St Pius X and de Nantes's League of the Counter-Reformation, their objections to the post-Vatican II Church are very similar. For both, the rejection of the new Mass is central. Thus *Catholic: The Voice of Catholic Orthodoxy*, a Lefebvrist monthly published in Australia, listed as 26th among the 'Sixty-Two Reasons why, in conscience, we cannot attend the New Mass': 'Because the New Mass was made in accordance with the Protestant definition of the Mass'. The document then goes on to cite the same paragraph 7 of the new *Ordo* quoted by Guèrard de Lauriers.

Lefebvre's conviction that the Church has sided with the principles of 1789 is quite explicit: 'The Council consummated marriage with the Revolution', he said at Lille in August 1976:

> but what the Revolution brought about is nothing besides what the Council has done . . . . From this adulterous union between the Church and the Revolution can come only bastards. This union shows itself by the dialogue, on equal terms, between truth and falsity. It is not possible to dialogue with Protestants: we love them, and that is why we want to convert them. It is not possible to dialogue with free-masons or Communists for one cannot dialogue with the devil!

Equally explicit seems Rome's conviction that, at the heart of the problem with Lefebvre's Society of St Pius X, founded in Switzerland in 1970 with a seminary opened shortly afterwards at Ecône, there is the new liturgy and no more. Hence the Congregation for Divine Worship in 1984 made it easier for the Tridentine Rite to be celebrated. Those who have left the Society of St Pius X since its formal break with Rome after the episcopal consecrations by Lefebvre in June 1988, have also been permitted to continue using the old form of the Mass. Lefebvre, on the other hand, has made it clear that, though the form of the *missa normativa* may be abhorrent to him, it is only one aspect of the Church's deviation from the truth, 'I do not reject everything about the Council', he has written, 'but I still think it is the greatest disaster not only of this century but of any century since the foundation of the Church.'

Why it should have been such a disaster was explained to a reporter of *L'actualité religieuse* by two Lefebvrist seminarians. 'The Church has a divine Constitution', they said, 'it cannot be changed. Man needs order, was made for order. If the Catholic Church brings its structures tumbling down, then there is order no longer, and one looks for something else' (15 April 1988, p. 9). From that perspective, it does not matter what the changes were that the Council brought about: that it made any changes at all was sufficient to condemn it. The case of the liturgy (the most dramatic changes in which, of course, happened long after the Council) was only the most obvious.

The seminarians' concern for order is as much a political statement as it is a theological one. Both de Nantes and Lefebvre have displayed strongly conservative political tendencies. The Abbé de Nantes was born in Toulon in 1924 to parents who were royalist members of the Action Française, and he was himself as a teenager associated with the Vichy State of Marshal Pétain. For his right-wing sympathies he was banished from the diocese of Paris, into which he had been ordained in 1948, and then worked for publications associated with Action Française for three years. In 1958 he became a member of the diocese of Troyes, and founded a community of missionaries, but his opposition to the French withdrawal from Algeria led to his imprisonment, and to his removal from his parish. Lefebvre, twenty years older than de Nantes, had closer personal experience of the Action Française, and was a student at the French College in Rome at a time when the College was strongly influenced by the *integriste* movement of Maurras. Though as a missionary bishop in Africa he was active in promoting black priests to the episcopate, eventually himself resigning his see of Dakar in 1962 to make way for an African, he was also prominent in the promotion of French culture in the areas for which he held responsibility. Since then he has been a strong supporter of military regimes in Latin America, and has appeared in the company of far-right politicians both in France and in Spain.

The same conservative trends in both politics and theology are to be found in a whole string of movements within the contemporary Church, of which organizations such as Comunione e Liberazione and Opus Dei are only the best known examples. There are many others such as Fiducia, Sodalitium Vitae, Tradition, Family and Property. Some of these, especially the last, are actively political. Others, the Focolarini (at least in Latin America where it has aroused considerable suspicion), the Neo-Catechumenate, the Priests' Marian Movement, preach a conservative, interiorized, piety which evades the commitment to social activism to be found in conciliar documents, particularly *Gaudium et Spes*, and later papal encyclicals. A number of congregations have emerged which represent this trend within religious life. When Ramon Tejero was ordained priest into one such group, the Servants of the Poor in the Third World, in January 1989, the occasion was marked in Madrid by a demonstration by fascist sympathizers – the new priest's father, then a colonel in the Guardia Civil, had led an abortive coup against the Spanish government in 1981.

The most powerful of these religious orders and institutes is undoubtedly Opus Dei. Founded in Madrid by Josémaría Escrivá de Balaguer in 1928,

Opus did not assume a recognizable structure until the years immediately following the Spanish Civil War. Its spirituality and its spiritual vocabulary owe much to the period of Franco's *cruzada* and the 'National Catholicism' of Spain of the 1940s and early 1950s. Opus members remained closely allied to the Franco government, even when the Church in Spain withdrew its support, and more recently prominent Opus members have been associated with right-wing regimes in various countries of Latin America.

In 1945 Escrivá moved to Rome, and members of his institute began to play an active part in the various congregations. Two years later Opus became the first 'secular institute' – a solution to the problem of its juridical status which, though at first being welcomed, was later quietly dropped. Opus became the first, and so far only, 'personal prelature' in 1982 with Alvaro del Portillo, one of the founder's earliest associates (Escrivá himself died in 1975), as its first head.

Opus Dei's traditionalism can be seen in its retention of a Latin liturgy and in a variety of practices of piety and mortification which have died out elsewhere in the Church. But its hostility to Vatican II goes deeper. Escrivá spent the last years of his life in visits to his followers in various parts of the world, warning them against a liberal interpretation of the Council. They have been identified in Peru, for example, as leading opponents of liberation theology.

It is instructive to compare the secretive Opus Dei with the very much more outgoing Comunione e Liberazione founded in 1954 as Gioventu Studentesca (it took its present name in 1970). Its founder, Luigi Giussani, now a monsignor but in 1954 a layman lecturing in theology in Milan, was dissatisfied with the youth wing of the Italian Catholic Action and began his own organization as an actively anti-communist movement. It is much larger than Opus, claiming 70,000 members in Italy alone (Opus claims approximately that number world-wide), but has a similar structure in that it is basically lay, with a small proportion of members making a full-time commitment to it. Unlike Opus, however, it is openly active in the political sphere as a right-wing pressure group.

The theological stance of CL, as it is known, is more difficult to quantify. Some commentators put it among charismatic movements, and its followers tend to share with charismatics an unquestioning certitude about their faith and its primary importance in daily life. There is a degree of triumphalism about their Catholicism that is out of keeping with the Council, and they have allied themselves closely with conservative bishops in Latin America, particularly with Cardinal Lopez Trujillo of Medellín, Colombia. In 1981 it launched a magazine entitled *Incontri* to support Lopez Trujillo's campaign against liberation theology. This magazine was not a success, and was revamped as the much more popular *30 Giorni*, now available (with a Jesuit editor) in an English-language edition published in San Francisco.

While it is obviously true that conservative reaction to the Council is not synonymous with opposition to liberation theology, in Latin America (the home of half the world's Catholics) there is a clear link. Liberation theology is an articulation of the principles enunciated in the 1968 gathering at Medellín,

Colombia, called by the Conference of Bishops of Latin America (CELAM) to give practical application in that continent to the documents of the Council. The Medellín principles have never formally been repudiated: they were indeed endorsed, somewhat hesitantly, by a further CELAM conference at Puebla, Mexico, in 1979.

But the bishops of Latin America have not been left free to decide for themselves the interpretation of the Council within their own jurisdiction. From as early as 1971 Roman appointments to bishoprics in Latin America, as they became vacant, have reflected a choice of clergy who can be identified as being in the conservative tradition. The complexion of Bishops' Conferences is changing across the continent – quite swiftly in countries such as Peru, for example, with a relatively small number of bishops; more slowly, but inexorably, in the much more radical Brazil, which has the world's largest conference of bishops.

Because so much of the Council was of necessity a compromise between radically different tendencies, it is of course possible to draw fairly conservative conclusions from its documents. Moreover, there was undoubtedly a development in the thinking of the Council fathers as the sessions went by, and the more conservative interpretations are to be found if one concentrates on the earlier documents to the relative exclusion of the insights of the later ones. Or again one can argue, as did Dietrich von Hildebrand in *Trojan Horse in the City of God*, that interpreters have misunderstood the true thrust of the Council: 'It would be difficult to conceive a greater contrast than that existing between the official documents of Vatican II and the superficial, insipid pronouncements of various theologians and laymen that have been breaking out everywhere like some infectious disease', he wrote (Hildebrand, 1967, p. 3).

Many of the movements mentioned above endorse such a judgement. Few if any of these and similar institutions would admit to hostility towards Vatican II. One of them, perhaps the most prestigious, claims indeed to have pre-empted the Council: Opus Dei had made as its own the teaching of Vatican II on the laity long before the 1960s, thanks to the particular charism of its founder. But, while it is of course true that Opus had campaigned for the formal approval of 'secular institutes', it has remained a solidly clerical organization, in which the laity who are full members are subjected to a quasi-monastic spirituality. But whether Opus's traditionalism in liturgical practice, in its devotions, and in its theology is appropriately described as a conservative reaction to Vatican II depends upon how Vatican II is to be understood.

One thing is clear. The understanding of Vatican II, and of the Church's tradition in general, among members of Opus and other conservative movements, is now closely aligned with that of Rome, and has been so at least throughout the pontificate of John Paul II. An increasing number of bishops have been chosen from among Opus clergy, and of clergy sympathetic to Opus, for sees in Latin America and elsewhere.

Although it is the conservative/traditionalist movements in the Church that have attracted most attention during the past few years, their importance in the total picture of the Church remains small compared to that of episcopal conferences, and the impact of the movements may finally depend upon the extent to which they come to dominate even the hierarchy.

11I The Conservative Reaction: Bibliography

Buckley, J. C. (1988) 'The Neo Catechumenate', *Priest and People*, vol. 2, no. 5, June, pp. 175ff.

Buckley, J. C. (1989) 'The Church within a Church', *The Tablet*, vol. 243, no. 7752, 11 February, pp. 149ff. On the neo-catechumenate.

Congar, Y. (1977) *Challenge to the Church: The Case of Archbishop Lefebvre*. London, Collins.

Gennarini, G. (1988) 'The Neo Catechumenate', *The Tablet*, vol. 242, no. 7705, 17 March, pp. 328ff.

Hebblethwaite, P. (1975) *The Runaway Church*. London, Collins.

Hildebrand, D. von (1967) *Trojan Horse in the City of God*. Chicago, Franciscan Herald Press.

Lernoux, P. (1989) *People of God: The Struggle for World Catholicism*. New York, Viking.

Manigne, J. P. *et al.* (1988) 'L'Affaire Lefebvre', *L'Actualité Religieuse*, no. 55, April, pp. 6–31.

Menozzi, D. (1987) 'Opposition to the Council', in Alberigo and Jossua, pp. 325–48.

Moynihan, R. (1988) 'Valiant for God', *The Tablet*, vol. 242, no. 7701, 20 February, pp. 194f.

Robertson, E. (1988) 'Holy Families', *The Tablet*, vol. 242, no. 7703, 5 March, pp. 266f.

Shaw, R. (1988) 'Judged by Opus Dei', *The Tablet*, vol. 242, no. 7702, 27 February, pp. 234ff.

Walsh, M. (1989) *The Secret World of Opus Dei*. London, Grafton.

11J Church and State

DERMOT KEOGH

The pontificates of John XXIII and Paul VI were characterized by a spirit of ecclesiastical self-confidence and Christian optimism. Encyclicals such as *Mater et Magistra* (15 May 1961) and *Pacem in Terris* (11 April 1963) by the former, and *Populorum Progressio* (26 March 1967) by the latter, reflected a confident engagement with the secular world free from the dualism of earlier teaching. The Second Vatican Council, the work of both popes, produced two documents in particular which formed the basis for new thinking on the relationship between Church and state; the Pastoral Constitution on the Church in the Modern World (*Gaudium et Spes*) and the Declaration on Religious Freedom (*Dignitatis Humanae*) were a reflection of that spirit of hope.

They were not, however, milestones in human history. The Catholic Church was still catching up with the twentieth century. However, in the words of John Courtney Murray, the Declaration on Religious Freedom in conjunction with the Constitution on the Church in the Modern World 'had opened the way towards a new confidence in ecumenical relations and a new straightforwardness in relationships between the Church and the world' – and a 'new era in the relations between the People of God and the People Temporal' (Abbott, p. 673). This new approach to Church and state, shorthand for the above, had cleared up the 'long-standing ambiguity' that Courtney Murray went on to describe as follows: 'The Church does not deal with secular order in terms of a double standard – freedom for the Church when Catholics are a minority, privilege for the Church and intolerance for others when Catholics are a majority.' Cautious, and perhaps even disappointed at the wording of the final documents, he predicted none the less that 'the ripples will run far'. That is certainly accurate if one examines the way in which some sections of the hierarchies of the third world, in particular, have taken the teaching of Vatican II in this area, as was the case with meetings of the Latin American Episcopal Conference (CELAM). Other episcopal conferences in Africa and Asia also proved to be both innovative and radical (for instance, of recent years, South Africa).

Under the leadership of Pope Paul VI, policies influenced by the spirit of *aggiornamento* encouraged the local churches to make pastoral decisions that had a relevance to domestic needs. Giovanni Battista Montini had spent most of his adult life in the Secretariat of State. While he never lost touch with the cut and thrust of secular Italian politics, he was also very much aware of the richness in diversity of the Catholic Church. In his letter *Octogesima Adveniens* to the president of the Council of the Laity and of the Pontifical Commission Justice and Peace, Cardinal Maurice Roy published on the eightieth anniversary of *Rerum Novarum*, 14 May 1971, Paul VI recognized the diversity of the historical and political situations in which the Church found itself throughout the world – Western democracy, military dictatorships, bureaucratic–authoritarian régimes, totalitarian régimes and revolutionary single-party states – and resisted the temptation to propound a single centrist solution:

In the face of such widely varying situations it is difficult for us to utter a unified message and to put forward a solution which has universal validity. Such is not our ambition, nor is it our mission. It is up to the Christian communities to analyse with objectivity the situation which is proper to their own country.

Vatican II had dealt a severe blow to ultramontanism on the one hand and to the ahistorical approach to Church–state relations on the other. Theocracy, confessionalism and Erastianism or Caesaropapism were not considered either appropriate or acceptable models to employ in the latter part of the twentieth century. Separation of Church and state, somewhat on the North American model, was the option that had most appeal; but whatever model was finally pursued, it had to fulfil two criteria:

Whether the arrangement respects human rights, particularly the right to religious liberty, and whether it respects the internal liberty of the Church, which needs freedom to choose its own officials, to set its internal policies and laws, to engage in missionary and evangelizing activity, to cooperate across national boundaries, to minister to oppressed or dissident groups, and to proclaim its moral and social teaching (Langan, 1987, pp. 206–9).

Events in Western Europe in the late 1960s and early 1970s provide a good example of Vatican decentralism (an oxymoron some might say) in action. The Catholic Church in Spain, which once enjoyed the 'privileges' of being an established Church under the watchful eye of General Franco, played an important role in the country's transition to democracy. By the time of the death of the dictator in 1975, the Church in Spain was ceasing to resemble the model of Catholicism which had brought 'altar' and 'throne' together during the Civil War *cruzada* in the 1930s. Franco had given the traditionalist bishops exactly what churchmen of the nineteenth century had sought – state-guaranteed orthodoxy within a political system of very limited diversity which outlawed liberalism, democracy, communism and socialism. Franco's Spain was as close to the nineteenth-century ideal of 'thesis' as made no difference: civil society recognized only the rights of the Catholic Church.

However, in the Secretariat of State, Montini witnessed the inequalities and the inadequacies of such a system where, under the concordat of 27 August 1953, Franco enjoyed right of presentation. The Catholic Church was recognized as *the* Church of Spain. There were many other concessions granted: tax concessions on Church property, the clergy received pay from the state, Church marriage was binding in civil law, and there was recognition of the jurisdiction of religious courts. The establishment of the Catholic Church as a state religion by Franco was certainly in violation of the principles of the Vatican II Declaration on Religious Freedom (see Lannon, 1987). It was a status much more befitting the thinking of the nineteenth century, and Giovanni Montini must have seen its dangers.

This anomalous position of 'privilege' was inherited by Cardinal Archbishop Enrique y Tarancón when he took over the archdiocese of Madrid and the presidency of the Spanish Episcopal Conference in 1971 in a period of transition. The disestablishment of the Catholic Church was a necessary corollary of the return to democracy. In classical nineteenth-century terminology, 'thesis' was no longer defensible in justice. It was time for 'hypothesis', where the Church had come to accept the divisions in society and sought only the right to preach freely, to educate, and to own property. During his ten-year tenure, Tarancón helped implement the teaching of Vatican II and, in so doing, infuriated the Spanish right to the point where posters carried in demonstrations in the early 1970s read: *Tarancón al paredón* (Tarancón to the firing squad).

Tarancón survived to see Spain become a democracy again, and with a socialist government. Article 16 (section 3) of the new constitution of 1978 states that 'there shall be no State religion'. Some recognition is given to the role of the Catholic Church in the same section, but it is not very emphatic: 'The public authorities shall take the religious beliefs of Spanish society into account and shall in consequence maintain appropriate co-operation with the Catholic Church and the other confessions.' There is, therefore, a clear separation of Church and state in the constitution where, at the same time, 'freedom of ideology, religion and worship of individuals and communities is guaranteed, with no other restriction of their expression as may be necessary to maintain public order as protected by law' (article 16, section 1). Spain is no longer a confessional state. A series of bilateral agreements with the Vatican has modified the 1953 concordat which, even in the time of Franco, was a source of conflict between Rome and Franco. The state payment of clergy is being phased out. A divorce law was introduced in 1980, which was a source of contention between Church and state. The transition to democracy in Spain has, despite obvious areas of dispute between Church and state, not seen the emergence of a confessional political party. That was discouraged by Tarancón and the wisdom of that decision is self-evident. Spain is a very important example of how it was possible for the Catholic Church to help in the transition to democracy. Tarancón's willingness to help actively in the dismantling of the confessional state has shown him to have been one of the shrewdest episcopal interpreters of the teaching of Vatican II in Western Europe. The Catholic Church has learned to play with confidence its role in a democracy where a socialism of a sort has been the dominant political influence of the 1980s. Here is a new Church–state 'hypothesis' with relevance for the latter part of the twentieth century.

The transition from authoritarianism to democracy made the Church in both Spain and Portugal work out a new *modus vivendi* with the leaders of the respective representative leaders in Madrid and Lisbon. Italy, however, had made an earlier return to democracy after the fall of Mussolini. Postwar republican Italy afforded special protection for the Catholic Church under the new constitution. Article 7 stated that 'the State and the Catholic Church are, each in its own sphere, independent and sovereign, their relations are regulated by the Lateran Agreements. Such amendments to these Agreements as are accepted by both parties do not require any procedure of constitutional revision' (Wiskemann, 1971). The passage of that article had provoked a great debate about the role of the Church in Italian society. The distinguished professor of law at the University of Florence, Piero Calamandrai, opposed the idea of incorporating the Lateran Pacts into the constitution, as he found it impossible to reconcile religious freedom and freedom of conscience with the confessional state of which the 1929 agreements with Benito Mussolini were the symbol (see Jemelo, 1960, p. 293; for one of the best recent studies on this topic, see Pollard, 1985). This echoed the moderate criticisms of the relations between the Catholic Church and the state in the fascist period.

Daniel Binchy, in his classic study *Church and State in Fascist Italy*, quotes an experienced British observer of the Roman scene who defined the settlement of 1929 as 'a deal in futures' (Binchy, 1941, p. 734). In reality, it was a pact that brought short-term gains, a financial settlement, recognition of the sovereignty of the Vatican, and guaranteed rights and privileges under a concordat. That there was conflict between Church and fascism throughout the 1930s does not negate the fact that there was a politics of accommodation in the 1920s with Mussolini's regime, partially as a means of securing the agreements of 1929. But the approach of Pius XI, in his final years a fierce anti-fascist, revealed certain inadequacies in the pope's strategy of dealing with a dictatorship which had infringed the civil and human rights of so many Italians. Vatican hostility to Don Luigi Sturzo's aconfessional *Partito Popolare Italiano* certainly shortened the life of that organization and led to the exiling of its leader. The preference for a hierarchically controlled Catholic Action, rather than an independent (if Catholic-inspired) political party, weakened the independent action of the one organization left in the country that could have stood up to the dictator. This revealed, on the part of the Vatican and the Italian bishops, a hierarchy of preference for the protection of the Church's institutional needs rather than human rights. Writing in exile in 1939, Sturzo stated prophetically:

> What form the hierarchy of Church and State will assume tomorrow cannot be foreseen today, but we may venture to affirm that it will be in the ethical–social sphere . . . The arrogant concept of a state above everything, the centre of complete unification, the fount of ethics, the expression of the common will, mystical aspiration of the unity of a people, has resulted in the totalitarian monster, Communist, Nazi, Fascist, which today holds Europe in a triple stranglehold. A new breath of mystical spirituality and of pacifying reorganisation must come (and cannot fail to come) from Christianity, in its character as a personal religion, universal and autonomous, profoundly felt and vigorously actuated by the faithful who are partakers in the mystical body of Christ, then Church and State will find again their rhythm of social duality and spiritual unification (Sturzo, 1939, pp. 562–3).

However, it took the Vatican and the Catholic Church in Italy quite some time to acquire the 'rhythm' of social duality and spiritual unification that Sturzo had written about. The continued presence of the Christian Democratic Party, in government from 1948 until the 1990s, together with article 7 of the constitution, gave the Catholic Church a comfortable confessionalism with little incentive to want to change. However, the gradual secularization of Italian society brought Church and state into conflict over a series of predictable issues. In 1970 Italy's first divorce law was passed. The same year the law banning the use of contraception and the dissemination of information on birth control was removed. A referendum to repeal the divorce law – pushed by the Catholic Church and the Christian Democrats – was defeated decisively in 1974. (Some 19 million voted to retain divorce [59.1 per cent] with 13 million against.) The same fate befell the attempt to repeal the abortion law of 1978. When the referendum was held in May 1981, only 30 per cent voted for repeal. With fewer vocations to the priesthood and the religious life, declining Mass attendance and a severe drop-off in the numbers attending confession, the Italian Church had finally to conclude a new *modus vivendi* with the state. Thus, in 1984, a new treaty ended sixteen years of highly stylized diplomacy between the Cardinal Secretary of State, Agostino Casaroli, and an Italian government led by the socialist Prime Minister, Bettino Craxi. Leaving in place two of the original Lateran accords, the revised concordat, or treaty, radically revised the relationship between Church and state. It was a document of fourteen articles and an additional protocol – only sixteen pages in length.

Vatican II is mentioned twice in the preamble of the new agreement with reference to the changes promoted by the Church, and its statements on religious liberty and the relationship between Church and state. But there is no mention of Catholicism being the state religion of Italy. The first article affirms the independence and sovereignty of both Church and state. State recognition of the Catholic Church's liberty to pursue her pastoral mission of evangelization and sanctification is stated, while the Church is also guaranteed the freedom to organize, to hold public worship, etc. The Italian government also recognized the particular significance of Rome for Catholics. Other articles go into detail on ecclesiastical organization and the position of the clergy. However, the Church made substantial concessions on marriage law and religious instruction. Religious instruction in state schools became optional. (It had previously been the 'foundation and crowning of public education'.) This was among the most contentious issues. However, the agreement did give full freedom to Catholic schools. In the area of Church annulments, the Vatican agreed that this was to be subject to a decision by civil courts if one of the parties requested it. The clergy were exempted from military service. On the question of the payment of clergy and religious, there was an agreement to phase the system out by 1990.

It would be incorrect to perceive this agreement simply as the result of negotiating weakness on the part of the Church. The document can be presented as a piece of Vatican realpolitik. Alternatively, it can be presented as the result of the application of Vatican II principles governing questions of religious freedom and Church and state. Both elements are certainly present. Overall, the agreement showed the realism of Cardinal Casaroli at a time when the temporal power of the papacy had become something of an embarrassment with the collapse of the Banco Ambrosiano. The very signing of the agreement with the government of Giovanni Spadolini had to be postponed at least on one occasion in 1982 when the scandal developed. On 25 May 1984, the Vatican Bank (Institute for Religious Works, IOR) agreed to pay up to 250 million dollars 'in recognition of moral involvement', but 'on the basis of non-culpability' to 109 creditor banks. The IOR had been involved in complicated share deals with the ill-fated Banco Ambrosiano. This was a definite case of an institution with a spiritual mission 'trading in futures'.

Reviewing the experience in Western Europe over the past fifty years, a

293

large question mark must be placed over the morality and the prudence of regulating Church–state relations by concordat. The Italian accord of 1929, the German concordat of 1933, the Portuguese concordat of 1940 and the Spanish concordat of 1953 all highlight the difficulties of trying to deal in a quasi-definitive way with states controlled by dictators. Perhaps it is best left to the local church to make judgements in accordance with particular pastoral needs. In that way, there is less danger of the international and political 'interests' of the Church being given precedence over more 'narrow' local pastoral interests. Moreover, such agreements with the Vatican can be utilized for propaganda purposes by dictatorial regimes to attempt to win international credibility. In these circumstances, it is often virtually impossible to sustain a distinction between *regime* and *state*. Pius XII and Paul VI were very much aware of the deficiencies of the system. Having to negotiate from a weak position is an argument against the continued practice of this system. But there is a more solid theological argument available based on the teaching of Vatican II interpreted in the following way:

> To some it may appear that the Church would do well and in the end be better off to eschew all such pacts with civil societies, that its spiritual nature and mission would stand out more clearly if it remained aloof from pacts and treaties, which belong to the 'political' order and are often accompanied by the manoeuvering and sharp practice of human diplomacy .... (Donlon, pp. 119–20).

Ireland is a traditionally Catholic country which has sedulously avoided the signing of a concordat. Both Church and state have fought shy of allowing the Vatican to play too familiar a role in local ecclesiastical affairs. Both Church and state have enjoyed a certain intimacy in relations. But that has stopped short of establishing a confessional state as, indeed, some of the hierarchy tried to do in the 1930s. A number of prominent clergymen wished to follow the 'thesis' model where, as the president of the day, Eamon de Valera favoured the 'hypothesis' model. This tension resulted in a very intense exchange of views in the lead up to the promulgation of the 1937 constitution. The drafting process moved from 'a one, true church' formula to a set of words which deeply upset a number of leading clergymen. In the end, de Valera devised the following formula:

> I. 1 The State acknowledges that the homage of public worship is due to Almighty God. It shall hold His Name in reverence, and shall respect and honour religion.
>
> 2 The State recognises the special position of the Catholic Apostolic and Roman Church as the guardian of the Faith professed by the great majority of the citizens.
>
> 3 The State recognises the Church of Ireland, the Presbyterian Church in Ireland, the Methodist Church in Ireland, the Religious Society of Friends in Ireland, as well as the Jewish Congregations and the other religious denominations existing in Ireland at the date of the coming into operation of this Constitution.

Although article 44 was considered at the time to have been a personal triumph for de Valera and a victory over the ultramontane element in the Irish hierarchy, it was to come under severe criticism by the 1960s. An All-Party committee of Dáil Eireann stated the following:

these provisions give offence to non-Catholics and are also a useful weapon in the hands of those who are anxious to emphasise the differences between North and South. They are also defective in that they make no provision for religious denominations which did not exist in Ireland at the time the Constitution came into operation, in contrast to later provisions of the Article which apply universally to all denominations.

The last sentence was a reference to the remaining provisions of article 44 which guaranteed certain rights and freedom from discrimination. (That section of the article on religion followed very closely the wording of the corresponding article in the 1922 constitution.) The report went on to state, quoting Vatican II, that the Catholic Church 'does not seek any special recognition or privilege as compared with other religions.' The deletion of the 'offending' sections of article 44 was recommended. Two years later, in 1967, Cardinal William Conway of Armagh stated that he would not personally 'shed a tear if the relevant sub-sections of Article 44 were to disappear' (Whyte, 1980, pp. 349–50). In 1972, the article was accordingly amended by referendum.

Twelve years later, a delegation of the Irish hierarchy addressed the New Ireland Forum, which had been set up by Dr Garret FitzGerald to discuss the country's future. Consistent with the line adopted by Cardinal Conway, Bishop Cahal Daly, stated the following:

> The Catholic Church in Ireland totally rejects the concept of a confessional state. We have not sought and we do not seek a Catholic State for a Catholic people. We believe that the alliance of Church and State is harmful for the Church and harmful for the State. We rejoiced when that ambiguous formula regarding the special position of the Catholic Church was struck out of the Constitution by the electorate of the Republic. The Catholic Church in Ireland has no power and seeks no power except the power of the gospel it preaches and the consciences and convictions of those who freely accept that teaching .... So far as the Catholic Church and questions of public morality are concerned, the position of the Church over recent decades has been clear and consistent. We have repeatedly declared that we in no way seek to have the moral teaching of the Catholic Church become the criterion of constitutional change or to have the principles of Catholic faith enshrined in civil law.

That was a clear repudiation of the 'thesis' model of Church–state relations, and the then Minister for Foreign Affairs, Mr Peter Barry, applauded this approach on 16 September 1985 in the presence of a number of leading members of the hierarchy and the Cardinal Secretary of State, Agostino Casaroli, at a luncheon in Iveagh House, Dublin. He stated two basic principles upon which relations between Church and state should operate: (1) Every church and religious denomination had, subject to the provisions of the Constitution, the right to speak out on any issue they wish. (2) The members of the Oireachtas had the right to legislate in accordance with their conscience in what they considered to be the best interest of the Irish people. That may mean, he added, not following the advice of one, or even any, of the churches.

The 1970s and 1980s, in particular, had witnessed a number of bruising exchanges between churchmen and successive governments over, for example, the introduction of legislation to permit the sale of contraceptives. In 1983 there was a referendum to amend the constitution to prevent, as one side saw it, the possibility of abortion being brought into the country through the courts. In 1985, the government failed to win a referendum to remove the constitutional ban on divorce. In all these exchanges, it was not always clear whether sections of the hierarchy and militant elements of the laity, in particular, properly appreciated the principles governing Church–state relations as outlined by Cahal Daly or Peter Barry. There remained in the 1980s in Ireland a strong suspicion about the state, which had been so much a feature of the hierarchy's Church–state thinking from the 1930s to the 1950s.

Residual feelings of anti-statism were reinforced by the reaction to the papal visit to Ireland in autumn 1979, which brought to the fore a level of orthodox lay militancy antagonized by the 'moral drift' of the 1960s and 1970s. This took place at a time when the pontificate of John Paul II had moved very far away from the 'hands off' policies of Pope Paul VI ('In the face of such widely varying situations it is difficult for us to utter a unified message and to put forward a solution which has universal validity'). In Ireland of the 1980s, Vatican centralism became much more obtrusive in two ways: the papal nuncio, Gaetano Alibrandi, became more assertive in domestic Church–state affairs, and Vatican influence was spread indirectly by the appointment of a number of bishops who were selected for their conservatism and for their likely ability to act independently of the national conference of bishops – an institution that has come under criticism from the cardinal prefect of the Sacred Congregation for the Doctrine of the Faith, Joseph Ratzinger. The pressure to move away from the search for local solutions can only be partially successful, but it can be extremely disruptive of Church–state relations as individual bishops and organized lay groups 'take on' the state in a confrontational manner. That danger will only be partially avoided in Ireland. In Latin America, the consequences can be far more serious.

The undemocratic centralism of the pontificate of Pope John Paul II has, of course, had its impact on Ireland. But in the third world, and Latin America in particular, the effect has been far greater. The positive impact of his many visits to Latin America, where his message has been far from monochrome social conservatism, has been vitiated by the underlying Vatican support for the appointment of conservative bishops throughout the continent. This process has been referred to as the 'new restoration' by the Belgian sociologist, Francois Houtart (Houtart, 1989). It has created major tensions within CELAM and almost provoked the secession of the Brazilian bishops from that body. Paradoxically, while this trend towards episcopal conservatism may well damage the Church, it may also lead to greater harmony between Church and state in many Latin American countries where the regimes much prefer to see less emphasis on the social teaching of the gospel. A few examples to demonstrate that point will suffice. The hierarchy in Argentina enjoyed a good relationship with the military dictatorship between 1976 and 1983 and found it far less congenial to work with the democracy of President Raul Alfonsin. In Central America, many members of the hierarchy have continued to maintain close relations with the military, notwithstanding their terrible human-rights record. El Salvador is a case in point. In Nicaragua, the hierarchy failed to establish a working relationship with the revolutionary Sandinista government, despite the fact that there were priests in the cabinet. Let us take the case of Argentina first.

There is at least one outstanding example in Latin America of the Church–state integralism advocated in prewar days by the French atheist, Charles Maurras. Argentina between 1976 and 1983 provides the most tragic examples of a 'royalist' Church–state relationship where the hierarchy failed completely as a body to adapt to the teachings of Vatican II. This has been vividly demonstrated in the writings of Emilio F. Mignone, a Catholic human-rights worker, who lost his daughter in the 'dirty war' which began with the military coup of 1976. She was among the 'disappeared'. He estimates that about 30,000 died in the clandestine repression, while a further 10,000 were held without due process and thousands more were forced into exile. His daughter's crime was to have given Christian witness in a slum on the outskirts of Buenos Aires working with the poor. As a Christian, she opposed the military takeover. She favoured a Church divested of state privileges and dependent solely upon the power of the poor. But that was not how the overwhelming majority of Argentinian bishops perceived their historical role. With very few exceptions they supported the coup. Dr Mignone has argued that the executive commission of the bishops' conference met with General Jorge Rafael Videla and Admiral Emilio E. Massera – two of the main conspirators who were jailed following the return to constitutional government in 1983 – the evening before the coup. The meeting, which took place at the headquarters of the episcopal conference, was to inform the bishops of the plans of the armed forces to take over the government. A further meeting took place on the day of the *coup d'état* between the three members of the military junta and the archbishop of Paraná, Adolfo Servando Tortolo, who was then president of the episcopal conference of Argentina.

Mignone argues that the armed forces placed great importance on the support of the episcopacy to give legitimacy to the coup. The bishops, in consequence, were the only body in the country with sufficient influence to oppose meaningfully the policy of 'disappearances'. As a group they refused to do so. Their neo-Constantinian view of the role of the Church was hardly in accord with the teaching of Vatican II: 'She [the Church] has the right to pass moral judgments, even on matters touching the political order, whenever basic personal rights or the salvation of souls make such judgments necessary' (*Gaudium et Spes* 76). There was a clear case for such a public testimony, but it was at no time in evidence. The hierarchy appeared satisfied with general statements of principle which remained unapplied in any pastoral context.

The elaboration of the teaching of Vatican II, as expressed in the documents of the CELAM Conference at Puebla (1978) and Medellín (1968), was not in evidence in the official statements of the Argentinian hierarchy during this period. In very few other countries in Latin America were the contradictions between a post-Vatican II model of the Church and a royalist 'state Church' so much in evidence as here, where bishops accepted pensions from a dictatorship responsible for the deaths of thousands of people.

The personal and ideological closeness between most Argentinian bishops and the armed forces had deep historical roots. The local hierarchy had done little to respond to the teaching of Vatican II and CELAM. In the repression that followed, sixteen priests were among the detained 'disappeared'. Two French missionary nuns, Alice Domon and Leonie Duquet, were killed in December 1977 by the military. Together with thousands of other Christians, these victims had operated on an understanding of the gospel imperative to challenge and change unjust social structures. Paul VI said in 1967:

> We want to be clearly understood: the present situation must be faced with courage and the injustice linked with it must be fought against and overcome. Development demands bold transformations, innovations that go deep. Urgent reforms should be undertaken without delay. It is for each one to take a share in them with generosity, particularly those whose education, position and opportunities afford them wide scope for action (*Populorum Progressio* 32).

Responding to that call, some members of the Argentinian Church in the period of the 'dirty war' did not choose to live a silent lie. Many who had rejected a royalist concept of Church paid for their witness with their lives. The lesson of allowing close relations to develop between bishops and military has not been learned fully yet in Argentina. The creation of the military diocese, a ruling from the Vatican that came into effect on 21 July 1986, provides for the spiritual care of members of the armed forces under their own military bishop distinct from the ordinary diocese. The failure to integrate the armed forces into the ordinary parish structures – and the provision of specially trained chaplains – is something that has great dangers for Argentina and for Latin America as a whole.

Vatican II appeared to have passed the majority of Argentinian bishops by. Some would have found it difficult to deal even with Leo XIII's *Rerum Novarum*. Paul VI's *Populorum Progressio* and the earlier teaching of Vatican II on religious freedom appear only to have had a negative impact. They sought the security of the *patronato*, even if it was administered by a military dictatorship. In contrast, the very opposite occurred in one of the smallest countries in Latin America, El Salvador, where the charismatic archbishop of San Salvador, Oscar Arnulfo Romero – earlier himself a conservative – sought to implement the teaching of Vatican II, Medellín and Puebla, even if that meant confrontation with the military who did not differ very much in mentality from their Argentinian counterparts. In opting for the poor, Romero placed himself in conflict with the wealthy and the powerful. His concept of Church led him to seek no privileges or concessions from the state – just the respect of the government for the rights of the peasants and urban poor. Operating from a position of powerlessness, Romero finally constituted such a threat to the state that he was murdered in 1980 by members of the armed forces. He gained little support in his lifetime as archbishop from the majority of his fellow bishops or from the papal nuncio. This was an example of what has happened so many times in Latin America when conservative bishops feel emboldened with the support of a nuncio (and, it is felt by extension, the Vatican) to oppose the witness of a man such as Romero.

The Catholic Church in Nicaragua, not unlike the Church in Cuba after the revolution there in 1959, partially lost an important historical opportunity to play a leading role in rebuilding that society in the post-Somoza era. in the weeks following the overthrow of the dictator, there was episcopal uncertainty about the nature of the new political configuration. Although it was a revolution made substantially by Christians, the Nicaraguan hierarchy produced a pastoral letter expressing fears about the march of political events. However, only four months later, on 17 November 1979, all seven Nicaraguan bishops signed a joint pastoral on 'Christian Commitment'.

It is interesting to chronicle what had occurred in the meantime to bring about the change of episcopal policy. There was overwhelming popular Christian support for the revolution, demonstrated by the presence of priests in four key ministries. And the religious also gave strong support to the government, through the Confederation of Religious (CONFER). In the general atmosphere of euphoria and international approval of the revolution, all the Christian groups felt the need for some pastoral orientation from the hierarchy which would provide a blueprint for a positive Catholic contribution to the 'process'. So Archbishop Obando y Bravo asked some local Jesuits and one of Latin America's best-known and respected liberation theologians to draft a paper which was to form the basis of the November pastoral. This document was the subject of a week of intense and sometimes heated discussion among members of the hierarchy. Monsignor Pietro Sambi, the Vatican's chargé d'affaires in Managua, provided liaison between the various groups throughout all the negotiations. Two of the pastoral's most solid supporters were Bishop Ruben Lopez Ardon of Estelí and Bishop Julian Barni of Matagalpa. Its main critic was Bishop Pablo A. Vega of Juigalpa, who ensured that it was never read in his diocese.

At this point, Archbishop Obando y Bravo played a constructive and decisive role. He had a reputation as a man of courage because of his outspoken opposition to the Somoza regime in the 1970s. He had played the role of intermediary on two occasions when Sandinistas had taken hostages and were demanding the freeing of political prisoners and transport out of the country. He was closely identified with the martyred editor of La Prensa, Pedro Joaquín Chamorro Cardenal. During the final offensive that toppled Somoza, he issued a pastoral along with the other bishops which legitimized the insurrection. That document placed the lives of each of the signatories in danger.

But while the hierarchy recognized the right of the people to rise up against a tyrant, they were not prepared for what was to happen after Somoza's downfall. The hierarchy had supported the insurrection, but what would their attitude be to the revolution?

The Sandinistas won the various power struggles that followed the 1979 victory – and the broadly based anti-Somoza coalition of 1979 fragmented afterwards. As the Sandinistas gained the upper hand, Obando y Bravo's opposition to the government seemed to increase. After the revolution, the government nominated a team of three to conduct permanent, structured dialogue with the hierarchy. Unhappily that initiative was never put into practice, and the deteriorating relations between the archdiocese of Managua and the government were certainly exacerbated by the lack of dialogue.

Suspicion and misunderstanding were allowed to grow on both sides and, in a small country like Nicaragua, the dispute became highly personalized at times.

The lack of dialogue did not, however, mean a breakdown in relations between Church and state. Catholic groups of many sorts helped keep open the avenues of communication.

Despite Vatican sanction, four priests served in senior positions in the Sandinista government defeated in the general election in March 1990. All had to suspend their priestly functions, and one had to leave his religious order in order to carry on his 'political' role. Miguel D'Escoto, a Maryknoll Father, was Minister for Foreign Affairs. Ernesto Cardenal, a diocesan priest, was Minister for Culture. He is also a well-known poet. His brother, Fernando Cardenal, is a Jesuit (now outside the order) who was Minister for Education; previous to that he held various positions within government. Edgar Parrales is a diocesan priest, and was Nicaraguan ambassador to the Organization of American States. All four were ordered by the Vatican to quit their posts. All four refused. This was perceived as acting in defiance of Vatican policy and Pope John Paul II publicly reprimanded Ernesto Cardenal on the airport tarmac when he arrived in Managua on 4 March 1983.

While it is generally accepted that priests should not occupy government positions in the latter part of the twentieth century, a case can be made for an exception to that general rule in a third world country where there may not be a plentiful supply of administrative expertise. Of course, there have been plenty of precedents in the earlier part of the twentieth century – Ignaz Seipel, chancellor of Austria five times from 1922–4 and 1926–9, being one of the most important. Ill health forced him to retire but even then he became foreign minister for a short time in 1930. The Cardinal Secretary of State, Eugenio Pacelli, told the Irish envoy to the Vatican in the early 1930s that Seipel's role was justified on the principle that anti-Church forces would gain in strength if he was not there. If that was so in Austria at that period, then it was certainly possible to make the same argument for the maintenance of priests in the Sandinista government – indeed, especially if one accepts Cardinal Obando y Bravo's negative judgement of the Sandinistas. The divided church in Nicaragua is a tragedy for Catholicism in Latin America. It was all the more tragic because it was so unnecessary.

This chapter has examined briefly the contribution of Vatican II to Catholic thinking on Church–state relations and the application of those ideas to a range of contrasting situations. This was far from being a Copernican revolution. But it was of profound importance, particularly as many of the ideas were actively allowed to be applied in different countries by Popes John XXIII and Paul VI. Had he lived, Pope John Paul I would probably also have been in that same tradition. It was a church that had regained its self-confidence in the world. The traditional defensiveness associated with Catholicism appeared to have been replaced by the assertiveness of a Church that no longer felt threatened by 'the world'. That had radical implications for a Church that had been close to the 'temporal powers' in many countries of the world, enjoying the benefits of an alliance between 'throne and altar'. The revolution in Portugal in 1974 swept away the privileges that the Catholic Church had enjoyed under Salazar and his successor. In Spain, the Catholic church played an important role in the peaceful transition to democracy and voluntarily gave up its position as the 'established' Church. In Italy, Cardinal Casaroli loosened the ties between Church and state. But there was still a desire to find a legal basis for that new relationship, as there was also in Spain. Ireland too, despite its really more intensely Catholic character in modern times than either Spain or Italy, is moving very slowly away from a situation where sectional religious concepts are reflected in legislation. This has, however, been complicated by the recent shift in emphasis of Vatican thinking on Church and state.

In Latin America, Church–state relations continued to exist in certain countries as if Vatican II had never taken place. Argentina was the case chosen for discussion here. There the majority of the hierarchy felt much more comfortable with a repressive military regime than with the democracy that replaced it in 1983. In Central America, El Salvador and Nicaragua proved two contrasting studies. In the case of the former, Archbishop Oscar Romero had a profound influence as he sought to implement the teaching of Vatican II as interpreted by Medellín and other meetings of CELAM. His implementation of the concept that the Church should stand with the poor cost him his life in a country where the ruling elites would have much preferred to deal with a Church seeking the patronage and protection of the state. Nicaragua is an example of the dynamics of Church–state relations in a third world country which has overthrown a dictatorial dynasty. The resulting twists and turns have helped reveal the shift in policy from Paul VI to John Paul II. The 'new restoration' has the most profound implications for the future of Catholicism. The emergence of a populist papacy has supplanted diplomacy with direct contact in individual countries, and in some a nuncio has further played the role of surrogate pope. In general, the pattern of Church–state relations is moving away from Pope Paul's admission that he had neither the ambition nor the mission to put forward a single solution of universal validity. With more consistently conservative episcopal appointments, the Church in parts of Latin America at least might even appear to be moving back towards an alliance of Church and state and away from the ideal of Cahal Daly rooted in the vision of Vatican II, that the Church seeks 'only the freedom to proclaim the gospel'.

11J Church and State: Bibliography

Binchy, D. (1941) *Church and State in Fascist Italy*. Oxford University Press.
Donlon, S. E. ( ) 'Concordats – Theological Questions'. *New Catholic Encyclopedia*, vol. 1, pp. 119–20.
Houtart, F. (1989) 'CELAM: The Forgetting of Origins' in Keogh, D., ed. *The Church and Politics in Latin America*. London, Macmillan.
Jemelo, A. (1960) *Church and State in Italy, 1850–1950*. Oxford University Press.
Keogh, D. (1986) *The Vatican, the Bishops and Irish Politics 1919–1939*. Cambridge University Press.

Modern Catholicism

Langan, J. (1987) 'Church and State' in Lane, D., Collins, M., and Komonchak, J. A., eds *Dictionary of Theology*. Dublin, Gill & Macmillan.

Lannon, F. (1987) *Privilege, Persecution and Prophecy: The Catholic Church in Spain 1875–1975*. Oxford, Clarendon Press.

Mignone, E. (1988) *Witness to the Truth: The Complicity of Church and Dictatorship in Argentina*. New York, Orbis Books.

Pollard, J. (1985) *The Vatican and Italian Fascism 1929–1932: A Study in Conflict*. Cambridge University Press.

Sturzo, L. (1939) *Church and State*. London, Geoffrey Bles.

Whyte, J. (1980) *Church and State in Modern Ireland 1923–1979*. Dublin, Gill & Macmillan.

Wiskemann, E. (1971) *Italy since 1945*. London, Macmillan.

11K War and the Nuclear Dilemma

BRIAN WICKER

INTRODUCTION

The moral dilemma of nuclear deterrence lies in the belief that you have to threaten nuclear war in order to prevent it. This threat inevitably includes the intentional killing of innocent human beings. According to clear Catholic teaching, it is illegitimate to carry out any such threat, or even to intend to carry it out, on however small a scale. Yet this threat has certainly helped to keep a peace of sorts, by inducing caution on the part of the superpowers, and inhibiting any temptation to go to war. Here then lies a seemingly insoluble moral crux. For this is quite certain, and constantly reiterated by all Catholic teaching in modern times: that there is an overwhelming imperative *both* to abjure war *and* to abjure any intentional killing of the innocent.

PACEM IN TERRIS AND GAUDIUM ET SPES

Pope John XXIII's dying testament to the world, *Pacem in Terris*, published in 1963, set the agenda for the Second Vatican Council's debates on the nuclear dilemma. In it the pope said that justice, humanity and right reason all condemned the arms race, and required the banning of nuclear weapons. He denied the suggestion, widely accepted at the time, that a balance of armaments was necessary to the maintenance of peace, suggesting on the contrary that it simply fuelled the arms race. (A point reiterated by Pope Paul VI later, in his message to the first United Nations Special Session on Disarmament in 1978.) Pope John went further, and even asserted that 'it is no longer rational to believe that war can still be an apt means of vindicating violated rights'. Nevertheless, he recognized the deterrent effect of the possession of nuclear weapons, and for this reason did not go so far as to condemn their possession as such.

The Council's own treatment of these questions was, in one particular, more specific than that of the encyclical, but in another was less so. In its concern to justify the right of a nation to defend itself, by a discriminate and proportionate use of force as a last resort when all other means have failed, the Council decided in the end not to adopt Pope John's declaration as to the irrationality of any form of war in the nuclear age. On the other hand, it did settle once and for all the question of indiscriminate attacks on centres of civilian population. 'Any act of war aimed indiscriminately at the destruction of entire cities or extensive areas along with their population is a crime against God and man himself. It merits unequivocal and unhesitating condemnation.'

This statement (the one absolute anathema uttered by the whole Council) must be read as a judgement not only on the area bombing of cities in the

Second World War, but also on the envisaged destruction of cities and civilian centres under the various nuclear strategies that had been adopted by the nuclear powers. During the debates leading up to the ratification of the final text of *Gaudium et Spes* in the third and fourth sessions, in 1964 and 1965, some speakers argued that there were still some military installations remote enough from civilian centres, to be legitimate targets of nuclear attack. They thought this fact could justify the possession of nuclear weapons for a credible deterrent, since the threat could, in some extreme circumstances, be carried out while avoiding any intentional killing of innocent non-combatants. But a majority found this argument unrealistic. Furthermore, fears were widely expressed that any such endorsement of nuclear deterrence would be liable to lead the Church into complacency and moral confusion, or mislead people into imagining that peace could be built on fear rather than on mutual trust and genuine disarmament.

In the end, then, chapter 5 of *Gaudium et Spes* left open a loophole through which the emerging nuclear strategies of the 1960s, 1970s and 1980s would eventually be driven, without any clear condemnation from the Church. True, the inevitable arms race that followed was consistently condemned for its robbing the poor of their basic needs. But the central moral crux of nuclear deterrence was evaded. The Council nevertheless did succeed in sowing an abiding and profound distrust, in the minds of all its participants, of any purely technical solution to the essentially moral, political and spiritual problem of preserving peace in the nuclear age. Following Pope John XXIII, it insisted that mutual trust and effective disarmament were necessary for true peace to be established, because the arms race was 'an utterly treacherous trap for humanity . . . which ensnares the poor to an intolerable degree'. Yet the deeper problem, of how to reconcile the right of self-defence for nations with the essentially uncontrollable and indiscriminate nature of modern war, was left unresolved.

COLD WAR AND THE ARMS RACE, 1965–82

Because the most difficult but most crucial moral dilemmas were left unresolved by the Council, it was difficult for the Church to do much more, during the period of arms-racing and cold war that followed, than to plead and cajole. During the race towards nuclear parity between the superpowers which led up to the SALT I agreement, popes and bishops found little new to say. True, some positive steps were taken: such as the establishment of pontifical and national commissions for justice and peace, and of an annual world day of peace: and, against the background of nuclear competition and stalled negotiations for force reductions in Europe, Paul VI and John Paul II continued to plead for international trust, support for international organizations, the priority of the needs of the world's poor. They continued to denounce the wickedness of the arms trade and the fragility of nuclear deterrence as a means of keeping the peace.

THE POPE AND THE BISHOPS, 1982–83

It was the introduction of new intermediate-range nuclear forces into Europe (SS20s, Pershing IIs and Ground-launched Cruise Missiles), and the chorus of disapproval that followed, that led to the next significant development of Catholic thought about the nuclear dilemma. In 1979 Cardinal Krol of the United States, speaking for the United States bishops in support of ratification of the SALT I Treaty, had made some very significant points which eventually led the whole conference of American Bishops in 1980 to devote a pastoral letter to the question of peace in the nuclear age. They set about this in a novel manner, modelling themselves partly on the American tradition of public hearings as used by the Congress. They invited many experts, from very many persuasions and positions, to address them or give evidence, before a drafting committee produced an initial text for circulation and comment.

The initial text adopted as its own several of the points first made by Cardinal Krol. For example, it described nuclear deterrence as 'objectively sinful' and as tolerable at all only on very narrow grounds. These involved the frank admission that Catholic moral requirements were at odds with some important elements of the American government's own policy. The text condemned all 'first use' of nuclear weapons; any second use aimed at military targets that were close enough to civilian centres of population to make non-combatant casualties on a large scale inevitable; and any threats of such use. 'Not only the use, but also the declared intent to use them involved in our deterrent policy is wrong', it said, quoting Krol. The case for tolerating nuclear deterrence at all was solely as the lesser of two evils: that is, its too rapid abandonment might lead to even greater harm. But this toleration was legitimate only as long as there were real hopes for success in negotiations leading to the reduction and eventual complete phasing-out of nuclear weapons.

An immense amount of comment on the first draft was received, from many quarters. This led perhaps inevitably to its modification in the final version of the pastoral letter, and many of Cardinal Krol's points were seriously weakened. In the end, deterrence was not labelled as a 'sinful situation' as such, nor did the bishops quite commit themselves to being at odds with their government's declaratory policy on the targeting of innocent civilians, despite deep scepticism about the claims of government that it was not aiming at 'populations as such'.

Although the clear condemnation of any first use of nuclear weapons remained, much of the discussion now centred on the risks of escalation and the application of the criterion of proportionality – inherently a much more hazardous criterion to apply than that of avoiding the intentional killing of the innocent. All in all, the final text's toleration of nuclear deterrence, while strictly qualified, did not seem so crisply confined in narrow limits, by unambiguous moral criteria, as in the first draft. As the question of risks loomed larger in the text, the more critical moral problem of intentions seemed to have been diminished. Furthermore, the attempt to forbid first use (thus

305

challenging a fundamental tenet of NATO policy) and the profound scepticism about any use whatsoever, which the final text embodied, while still tolerating deterrence itself, seemed to many critics inconsistent or even incoherent.

The changes in the texts of the American bishops' pastoral letter have to be understood in the light of Pope John Paul II's intervention at the United Nations in 1982. At the second Special Session on Disarmament, the pope took the opportunity to issue his own statement. One short paragraph has become a *locus classicus* for all subsequent discussion:

> In current conditions, 'deterrence' based on balance, certainly not as an end in itself but as a stage on the way toward a progressive disarmament, may still be judged morally acceptable. Nonetheless, in order to ensure peace, it is indispensable not to be satisfied with this minimum, which is always susceptible to the real danger of explosion.

Now, it is possible to interpret this position as confirming Cardinal Krol's views, and those of the American bishops' first draft. But more permissive interpretations were clearly also possible, and these allowed a wide variety of opinions to be expressed in the spate of statements issued by various national episcopal conferences in the following year.

The French bishops produced the most audacious defence of nuclear deterrence, even though in doing so they had to admit that the policy that they appeared to be justifying was clearly in conflict with the absolute anathema uttered by the Council on the targeting of cities. Nuclear deterrence was certainly an 'occasion of sin', but it was a 'necessary' one. It was the lesser of two evils, and anyhow 'the threat is not the use'. In saying this, the French bishops resorted to the notion of what they called 'the logic of distress', meaning that nuclear deterrence could not be fitted into the ethical norms governing less agonizing situations. In similar vein, the German bishops wrote in their letter of a need for an 'emergency ethics' to cope with the nuclear dilemma.

The appeal to an 'emergency ethics', or an 'ethic of distress' cut no ice with some of the other Bishops' Conferences. The Scots roundly said that if it was wrong to use the weapons, then it was wrong to threaten to do so. The Irish reminded their readers of Pius XII's injunction, that it is sometimes better to suffer an injustice than to inflict it. The Dutch insisted that nuclear deterrence must not be used for any purpose beyond the deterrence of war itself, that is, it must not become an instrument of political pressure. The East Germans flatly denied that there could be any justified use of nuclear weapons under any circumstances. The English hedged their bets. In an article in *The Times*, Cardinal Hume admitted that 'to condemn all use and yet to accept deterrence places us in a seemingly contradictory position' – a statement with which all clear-headed analysts would agree. Yet the cardinal went on to claim, rightly, that 'the acceptance of deterrence on strict conditions and as a temporary expedient leading to progressive disarmament is emerging as the most widely accepted view of the Roman Catholic Church.' Unfortunately, the obvious questions that this position immediately raises have not yet been tackled: how temporary is temporary? How concrete and clear must the hopes of disarmament be? What kinds of disarmament, and how much of it, would be needed to satisfy the criterion?

It is difficult to avoid the conclusion that during the period from 1979 to 1983, what once appeared to be a strong presumption against tolerating any form of nuclear deterrence has turned into a resigned readiness to go along with it, for as long as the most influential politicians and strategists say is necessary.

SDI AND MR GORBACHEV

In 1983 the American bishops committed themselves to continuing their study of the nuclear dilemma. In 1988 they produced their first 'update'. In this they tried to apply their previous arguments to the new strategic situation produced by the SDI project and by the rise to power of a reforming USSR government. However, little that is really new emerges from their analysis. On SDI they express support for a fairly familiar list of objectives: deep cuts in strategic systems, conventional arms control, a ban on chemical weapons and on nuclear weapon testing, non-proliferation, and strict adherence to the narrow interpretation of the ABM Treaty. They are very sceptical about the morality and feasibility of SDI, and reject the MX missile as destabilizing, but are less certain about the Trident submarine missile programme.

This document is one of the most considered discussions by a senior Catholic source since Mr Gorbachev came on the world scene. It is therefore disappointing that it does not directly address some of the most important recent arguments made on both sides of the deterrence debate. The bishops say they are not convinced by the arguments of writers such as Finnis, Grisez and Boyle, who claim that there can be no effective nuclear deterrence without the intention to attack cities directly, or even to indulge in the virtual annihilation of the enemy society. On the other hand, neither are they persuaded of the possibility of 'discriminate deterrence' as advocated by the prestigious American Commission on Integrated Long-Term Strategy.

Perhaps they have been influenced by suggestions that it might be possible to mount a 'counterforce' deterrent that did not involve any conditional intention to attack the innocent. Whatever the explanation, the recent arguments on each side are so crucial to the nuclear dilemma that it is a pity that the American bishops did not feel able to go into them thoroughly, as they did in their original letter.

At the time of writing,the most recent papal statement has come from Pope John Paul II in his 1988 address to the Diplomatic Corps. He reiterates the main themes that are common to all Catholic authorities in the nuclear-deterrence field. 'Mutual assured destruction' cannot be a reliable basis for long-term peace. Nuclear deterrence is tolerable at all only on the condition 'of remaining fundamentally transitional and oriented towards the search for another type of international relationship'. It must lead 'to a progressive search for a new balance at the lowest possible level of weapons so as to arrive eventually at the elimination of the atomic weapon itself'.

More recently, following a speech by the papal Secretary of State, Cardinal

Casaroli, to a UN gathering in 1986 which pointedly raised the question of the morality of deterrence *threats* as such, Archbishop Sodano, Secretary of the Church's Council for Public Affairs, said to a Paris Chemical Weapons conference in January 1989 that 'the threat of recourse to chemical weapons capable of indiscriminately destroying so many human lives . . . cannot be justified on any ethical grounds'. If, as the archbishop went on to imply, this condemnation of the very threat of mass destruction applies equally to nuclear weapons, the consequences for the Church's stand against nuclear deterrence seem to be far-reaching.

CONCLUSION

Despite the inconclusiveness of Catholic teaching on the nuclear dilemma, a few guidelines seem clear. It is unanimously agreed that no strategy that harbours an intention to attack cities or extensive areas along with their population is morally tolerable. This means that any strategy that includes such attacks, even in retaliation as a last resort, is excluded. Whether the *threat* to make such attacks is itself excluded, in the absence of any real intention to carry it out, is another matter: but a strategy based on bluff of this kind is anyhow not likely to deter for long. Secondly, nuclear deterrence can be no more than a temporary expedient. The goal of completely phasing-out nuclear weapons (a de-nuclearized world) is part and parcel of Catholic thought on the issue: there can be no question of nuclear deterrence remaining a permanent part of any legitimate policy. Thirdly, any strategy that is adopted must facilitate actual disarmament: arms control, though very important, by itself is not enough.

Whether it is possible to design a nuclear deterrence policy that fully respects these criteria is far from clear. The attempt has not seriously been made. While it remains true that the central moral crux of nuclear deterrence has not been adequately faced by the Church, the radicalness of the criteria that are already agreed must not be underestimated. It would certainly be very difficult, and probably impossible, to maintain nuclear deterrence in anything like its present form if they were fully taken into account.

11K War and the Nuclear Dilemma: Bibliography

The literature on the nuclear dilemma is already vast. The following very brief list includes only those works that have been referred to above, or that are of particular value or relevance to the Catholic debate.

Conference of the Bishops of England and Wales (1984) Pastoral Letter, 29 January.

Dutch Conference of Bishops (1983) *Peace and Justice*.

East German Conference of Bishops (1983) *Pastoral Letter of the GDR Catholic Bishops on Peace*.

Finnis, J., Boyle, J. M., and Grisez, G. (1987) *Nuclear Deterrence, Morality and Realism*. Oxford University Press.

French Conference of Bishops (1983) *Gagner La Paiz* (Winning the Peace).

Hume, B. (1983) 'Towards a Nuclear Morality', *The Times*, 17 November.

Ikle, F., and Wohlstetter, A. (1988) *Discriminate Deterrence*. Washington.

Irish Conference of Bishops (1983) *The Storm That Threatens*. Dublin.

Murnion, P. (1983) *Catholics and Nuclear War*. London, Geoffrey Chapman.

O'Brien, W. V., and Langan, J. (1986) *The Nuclear Dilemma and the Just War Tradition*. Lexington, MA.

Pope John Paul II (1982) *Message to the Second Special Session of the UN on Disarmament*.

Ruston, R. (1989) *A Say in the End of the World*. Oxford.

Scottish Conference of Bishops (1982) *Statement*, 16 March.

Stein, W. (1961) *Nuclear Weapons and Christian Conscience*. London, Merlin Press.

United States Catholic Conference (1983) *The Challenge of Peace: God's Promise and Our Response*. London, Catholic Truth Society.

US Bishops ad hoc Committee for the Moral Evaluation of Deterrence (1988) 'A Report on the Challenge of Peace and Policy Developments 1983–88', *Origins*, vol. 18, no. 9, 21 July.

Walzer, M. (1977) *Just and Unjust Wars*. London, Penguin.

West German Conference of Bishops (1983) *Justice Creates Peace*.

Wicker, B. (1985) *Nuclear Deterrence: What Does the Church Teach?* London, Catholic Truth Society.

12

THE EFFECT OF THE COUNCIL ON WORLD CATHOLICISM

12A Africa

PATRICK A. KALILOMBE M AFR

In the quarter century following the closing of the Council, the Church in Africa nearly doubled its size (see Table 1).

Table 1

	Mid-1970	*Mid-1985*
All Christians	142,962,732	236,278,850
Roman Catholics	52,813,760	89,722,420
Muslims	141,884,235	215,816,700
Tribal religions	64,266,229	63,880,140

Source: Barrett, 1982, p. 782.

This tremendous growth is consonant with trends since the beginning of this century, but to what extent and in what ways is it related to Vatican II? Statistics alone cannot give an answer; other indications need to be taken into account.

AFRICA'S PRESENCE AT THE SECOND VATICAN COUNCIL

The presence of Africa at Vatican II was marginal and by proxy. Just 311 (8 per cent) of the 2,625 Council fathers represented Africa and, of these, only 60 were Africans, the others being expatriates or missionaries (Hastings, 1979, p. 173). Although technically and juridically the Church was no longer 'missionary', it is hardly possible to imagine that the African Church counted very much as an influence on the Council. Apart from regular interventions from the principal spokesman, Cardinal L. Rugambwa, only sporadic voices were heard from Africa.

It is obvious from an examination of the sixteen documents that the Council was largely a forum for the concerns of the Churches of Europe and America in the 1960s. These were especially in the area of patristics, liturgical, biblical and ecumenical studies, and in catechetics, issues that had been under consideration at least since the modernist crisis in the first decade of the twentieth

310

century (see Thils *et al.* 1973). In many ways, this was indeed a courageous, if belated, response to the agenda of the Reformation, an attempt to come to terms with a modern, industrialized Western world.

Africa's problems and preoccupations, therefore, came only indirectly: they did not determine the central perspective from which the Council's deliberations were moving. Africa's questions were not those of a long-established Church, but of a newborn community trying to find its place in a fast-moving continent. It can therefore be said that, while Africa has had to look back on the Council to seek guidance over the past twenty-five years, Africa had little effect on Vatican II itself. Moreover, real acquaintance with the documents must not be exaggerated, even though efforts were made to publish them and diffuse their message widely in the African continent (see Hastings, 1968). After all, Africa is largely a non-literate continent.

However, one result of the Council was that Africa's prelates learned to feel that they belonged together, and should work in collaboration. Foundations were laid here for AMECEA (Association of Member Episcopal Conferences in Eastern Africa) which was followed by the formation of similar organizations across the continent. In 1969 these regional conferences were to form the Symposium of Episcopal Conferences of Africa and Madagascar (SECAM).

AFRICA'S CONCERNS DURING AND AFTER VATICAN II

In the 1950s and 1960s most countries of Africa were struggling for their independence from colonial powers. Ghana's independence in 1957 set the pace, followed by 'winds of change' in British, French and Belgian colonies. The decolonization of the former Portuguese territories in 1975 signalled a second, less conclusive phase of the independence struggle: the special case of Southern Africa. Although Zimbabwe became free in 1980, the struggle still continues in neighbouring Namibia and South Africa. The question of freedom and independence is, therefore, still on Africa's agenda.

Political independence, however, was only the starting point for more perplexing problems: how do you forge real national unity out of diverse tribes, ethnic groups and regional interests? There are numerous examples of tribal and sectional struggles, resulting in insecurity and violence, displacement of persons and loss of life, which are strangely typical of post-independent Africa (Mazrui and Tidy, 1984).

There has been a tendency towards despotic governments, civil or military, and a disregard of human rights by privileged, powerful minorities (see Okullu, 1974; and Ela, 1980). Poverty and powerlessness of the masses, over against absurd enrichment of the few, are becoming the mark of the African continent. It is important, however, to understand this discouraging development against the global structure of world economic and socio-political dynamics. At the root of the failure of decades of development plans, the breakdown of national economies and the accumulation of debts, is the dependent nature of third world economies and politics (Strahm, 1978; or Gheddo, 1973).

311

Inevitably, the Church in Africa has been part and parcel of this experience. Its self-image, its priorities and the way it has attempted to move forward have been determined by the need to respond to this situation. At the same time, the twenty-five years after Vatican II have also been dominated by the issues of transition from a dependent, missionary-guided Church to a self-determining local Church. There seem to be two main directions in which Africa's Catholic Church is moving.

One is the tendency to cling to the past and its assurance of security: an emphasis on the universality of the Church, and 'fidelity' to Rome as the guarantee of orthodoxy and clear identity. The other is for more 'localization' of the African Church, made possible by a greater decentralization and a more enterprising inculturation. This does not propose the weakening of Church unity, but rather a unity through pluriformity. These two directions coexist in a basically healthy dialectic, even if they express themselves in the rather ominous form of tension between a hierarchically oriented group (which is by no means primarily composed of bishops) and an academically oriented group of theologians, intellectuals and some reforming pastoral workers (see *Pro Mundi Vita*, 1985, 1986, 1987).

THE ROLE OF SECAM AND THE QUESTION OF THE 'AFRICAN COUNCIL'

The marginal presence of Africa at Vatican II is in marked contrast with the active participation in the later Roman synods. It is through SECAM that the consciousness of the African Catholic Church has been taking shape, and thanks to SECAM that it could be effective and influential at the 1974 Synod on Evangelization in the Modern World, and at subsequent assemblies (see SECAM, 1984; SECAM, 1987; and SECAM, 1988). The areas of concern arise directly from the African situation: theological and biblical stimulation, inculturation, Small Christian Communities, ecumenism (Islam and traditional religions), justice and peace (refugees, relations with national governments, apartheid in Southern Africa), and social communications.

In the various assemblies of SECAM the call for an African Council has been repeated time and again, and on 6 January 1989, thirty years after the suggestion was first made by the pioneering authors of *Des prêtres noirs s'intérrogent*, Pope John Paul II announced that a special assembly for Africa in the form of a Special Synod was going to take place. The proposal has been to do for Africa what CELAM's Second General Assembly at Medellín in 1968 did for Latin America: provide a comprehensive examination of the Church in the present-day transformation of Africa in the light of Vatican II. Whatever such a Synod turns out to be, in the highly Roman-Controlled shape now envisaged, it should in principle be Africa's golden opportunity to come to terms with those orientations of Vatican II that are of special relevance to the continent's present struggles.

THE VATICAN II DOCUMENTS AND AFRICA'S PRESENT AND FUTURE

Which documents of Vatican II have proved to be of special significance for the African Catholic Church, and in what way will they guide its search for a hopeful future? Discussions, especially within SECAM, indicate four areas of concern for the Church, and one can assume that documents relating to these priorities will be the most significant. The four are: (1) ecclesiology; (2) inculturation; (3) ecumenism; (4) the Church in modern Africa.

1 Ecclesiology

The central theme is the Church itself: What is it? What is it for? How should it exist and function? In the conciliar document *Ad Gentes*, these questions are addressed, although in such a way that Africa is seen not in its own light, but as the universal Church's field for expansion. The crucial text is in n.6: 'The special end of missionary activity is the evangelization and the implantation of the Church among peoples or groups in which it has not yet taken root.' The notion of 'implantation' suggests that something transplanted in new soil is expected to grow into a similar shape and to function in the same way as the original prototype, in this case, the Western Catholic Church. *Christus Dominus* (Pastoral Office of Bishops), *Presbyterorum Ordinis* (Ministry and Life of Priests), *Optatam Totius* (Training of Priests) and even *Perfectae Caritatis* (Renewal of Religious Life) deal with questions that arise primarily from Western Catholicism, tacitly assuming that their solution is applicable to Africa, with a few minor adjustments. The same is true of *Apostolicam Actuositatem* (Apostolate of Lay People) and *Orientalium Ecclesiarum* (Catholic Eastern Churches), although Coptic and Ethiopian Church traditions have been present in Africa for centuries. *Lumen Gentium*, the basic document on the Church, offers very useful guidance when studied with the assumption of implantation in mind.

And yet for Africa, the starting point has to be the fact that the Church was introduced there under the shadow of Vatican I. Africans have always, therefore, had to face two major tasks: to assimilate and find meaningful identity within this highly hierarchical and centralized religious organization, and to find in this religion from abroad the satisfaction of those basic values that traditional culture and religion used to cater for. The hierarchical authority and world-wide communal belonging were very attractive to African neophytes, but these same values could also be in conflict with the traditional localized community participation and the effect of African culture's world-view on everyday life.

In the Protestant tradition this has led to the rise of African independent churches, one of the most impressive expressions of African initiatives in religion (see Barrett, 1968 and 1971; and Sundkler, 1961). Among Catholics this has not happened with the same frequency, but the need for the Church to

313

take the shape of traditional religious expressions is no less great. Some ecclesiological principles of Vatican II have given rise to the vision of Small Christian Communities, which are seen increasingly as the most appropriate shape of the Church in Africa. They attempt to meet the requirements of communion with the world-wide universal Church while at the same time responding to the imperatives of inculturation. That they are an initiative from the hierarchy, rather than from the grassroots as in Latin America, demonstrates the additional problem of developing effective authority and power structures for the young African churches (Healey, 1986).

2 Inculturation

This is firstly a theological question: how divine revelation and God's salvific project for humanity is related to the various cultures and their histories. The implantation model of Christianity's coming to Africa makes the question eminently relevant: should the Church take root in Africa by espousing ready-made foreign cultural forms?

Movements to reclaim African history and to repair its fractured culture were at work even before the Council proclaimed the need for 'Africanizing' Christianity, but for a long time these were largely restricted to intellectual circles, or were pre-empted by politicians. Ordinary people, including a wide section of Westernized Africans, have not been taken up by campaigns for African Authenticity, adaptation, indigenization, or simply Africanization. One reason for this may be that 'inculturation' seems to imply a return to an outmoded and irrelevant past, when people would rather move forward towards modernity. Moreover, in the context of apartheid South Africa, reclaiming African traditional values carried with it the danger of playing into the hands of racist-motivated segregation policies. This underlines the need for determining precisely the nature and aims of inculturation. It is not an idle wish to create an amusing folklore, but a need to carry forward fundamental values from traditional culture, so that present and future generations can build a meaningful way of life on a valid African foundation (see Waliggo et al. 1986; and Shorter, 1988).

Sacrosanctum Concilium, the document on the sacred liturgy, was especially significant for the inculturation process. As the independent churches had shown initiatives in inculturation, so this document opened the door for Catholics. With the use of local languages in the liturgy, other possible areas of inculturation developed almost as a matter of course: local tunes, art and symbolism. It is significant that this project of inculturation is being implemented by African theologians and biblicists. This should ensure that the flourishing growth of local productions is not merely superficial adaptation, but addresses the real theological questions of the situation.

The Ecumenical Association of Third World Theologians (EATWOT), founded in 1976, and the Ecumenical Association of African Theologians (EAAT), started the following year, have been significant in promoting and co-ordinating contextual theological exploration among both Catholics and

314

Protestants. Parallel to this is the Congress of African Biblical Exegetes, started in 1978. Catholics in these movements have been finding inspiration and guidance in the Vatican II documents, and following the recommendations of *Dei Verbum*, Scriptures are being made increasingly available in the vernacular. SECAM's biblical centre for Africa and Madagascar (BICAM) has undertaken to promote the knowledge and use of the Bible, especially at the grassroots level. More than anything else, it is this contact with the Word of God in local languages that promises to stimulate inculturation within the African Catholic Church, as it has done with the independence movement in the Protestant tradition.

3 Ecumenism

The Vatican II documents that are of interest to Africa on the issue of ecumenism are: *Unitatis Redintegratio*, centred on relations between the Roman Catholic Church and other Christian bodies; *Nostra Aetate*, a tantalizingly short declaration of principles of relations with non-Christian religions; and *Dignitatis Humanae*, which grapples with fundamental attitudes of ecumenism. Here, as in other documents, the commanding viewpoint is the Western Catholic Church, and the churches in Africa are simply subsumed under it, with few allusions to questions from other perspectives. The principles that guide the discussion appear quite revolutionary in comparison with the assumptions of only a few decades earlier. It is clear that we have here a radical change from a 'Christendom' mentality to a realistic appraisal of religious pluralism.

The problem for the Catholic Church in Africa has always been that of uncritically espousing the Western standpoint, in this case without making allowance for the influence of the Christendom mentality in attitudes to other religions in the faith it received from the West. Between 1976 and 1981 the All Africa Conference of Churches conducted a joint research project with AMECEA to assess ecumenical initiatives in Eastern Africa (see Mugambi, Mutiso-Mbinda and Vollbrecht, 1982). Although the conclusions were basically encouraging, there was evidence of widespread uncertainty and confusion, which seem to stem, in the last analysis, from the fact that Africans do not yet feel assured in taking seriously the implications of their different context and history.

The Roman Catholic Church in Africa has to deal with three religious challenges. It has to find a way of relating to other Christian churches, not least the growing number of independent churches, without feeling committed unquestioningly to the ideas and practices of the Western Church. Next is the question of relating to Muslims, whose numbers in Africa are almost as great as Christians, and whose relations with African peoples and cultures are different from those in Europe and America. SECAM is beginning to work out new approaches to the challenge of Christian–Muslim relationships in the African context. Thirdly, there is an equal need to revise the Church's relationship with Africa's own traditional religions. Again, the principles found in the

315

Vatican II documents will guide the Church as it probes deeper into God's gracious and salvific dealings with all peoples, and moves forward into creative ecumenical ventures, seeking to overcome past negative attitudes.

4 The Church in modern Africa

Vatican II's *aggiornamento* is singularly represented in *Gaudium et Spes* (The Church in the Modern World). Twenty-five years later, this document appears over-optimistic, but nevertheless, it managed to identify the main issues in the present-day world and attempted to relate them to the presence and mission of the Church. Questions about justice and peace, development, human rights and dignity were on Africa's agenda long before the Council, and have become even more pressing in the post-conciliar years.

Africa has paid special attention to later pronouncements which took up for further application principles found in the conciliar documents. The 1971 Roman synod on issues of justice, peace and development was particularly relevant, and in its wake, diocesan and regional offices on these questions have sprung up all over the continent, and their activities found an effective forum for co-ordination in the Pan African Seminar of Lesotho (1988).

Concern about justice and peace, and indeed the whole complex of questions about the Church's role in modern Africa, falls into two areas: the newly independent states north of the Limpopo, and the region of southern Africa. In the newly independent states, the question is how to make real for everyone the freedom gained at independence. Towards this end, the Church is searching for ways of standing on the side of the struggling masses, and becoming the prophetic voice of the marginalized and the oppressed (see *Pro Mundi Vita*, 1974). In southern Africa the task is to oppose more explicitly the system of apartheid and its destructive effects. This area includes neighbouring states whose fragile independence is constantly threatened by South Africa, and the front-line states who are a special target for South Africa's destabilizing manoeuvres because they are bridgeheads for black resistance and struggle. In this situation, the Catholic Church is working with other Churches and democratic agencies to put an end to apartheid, and to create the vision of a harmonious and equitable post-apatheid South Africa.

Church leadership is central in these efforts to spell out the Church's prophetic role. The churches are among the very few areas where an independent, credible reserve of people's autonomy and power can be found, for the sad predicament of most African states is the absence of democracy and participation. Citizens find themselves deprived of any real voice, and so Church leaders become potential mouthpieces. They can speak without fear or favour, because the source of their authority is outside the pale of the power-holders. Episcopal conferences, often speaking through charismatic figures like Cardinal E. Nsubuga in Uganda, Archbishop Zubeir Wako in Sudan, or Archbishop Hurley in South Africa, have often become the voice of courage and hope. IMBISA in South Africa is a forum through which the Catholic Church's contribution to the future of that country is channelled.

This demands from the Church leadership a spirituality of independence from co-option by local powers, and of courage and integrity. It asks them, too,to become ambassadors of their people to the outside. Since the oppressive and exploitative agents in African countries draw their strength from alliances with overseas powers, the forces of freedom and justice also need to seek support from international allies. The advantage of the Catholic Church lies in its capacity to mobilize a world-wide conscience and to link local struggles with wider organizations. And that is why such a continental body as SECAM is a great sign of hope. In the principles of Vatican II it finds a source of tremendous support in time and space.

CONCLUSION

Over the twenty-five years beginning with the closing of the Second Vatican Council in 1965 and reaching into the 1990s, a trajectory can be discerned in the way the church in Africa has been relating to the issues dealt with at the Council. During the Council itself, and for some years following it, the Council's agenda was only partially and indirectly related to the preoccupations of Africa: decolonization and national independence, development, the search for a localized Church, and the teething problems of newly independent states. Structures for expressing and mobilizing a continent-wide ecclesial consciousness were still tentative. The African Church seemed simply to follow the Western responses to the conciliar programme. Only later, especially beginning with the mid-1970s, and thanks to the growing influence of SECAM, has there begun to emerge a specifically African response to Vatican II. It is to be hoped that the proposed African Council will help the continent to sharpen this response and make it effective.

12A Africa: Bibliography

Barrett, D. B. (1968) *Schism and Renewal in Africa*. Nairobi/Addis Ababa/Lusaka, Oxford University Press.

Barrett, D. B., ed. (1971) *African Initiatives in Religion*. Nairobi, East African Publishing House.

Barrett, D. B., ed. (1982) *World Christian Encyclopedia*. Nairobi/Oxford/New York, Oxford University Press.

Buhlmann, W. (1977) *The Coming of the Third Church*. Maryknoll, New York, Orbis Books.

Des pretres noirs s'interrogent (1957) Coll. Paris, Les Editions du Cerf.

Ela, J.-M. (1980) *African Cry*. Maryknoll, New York, Orbis Books.

Gheddo, P. (1973) *Why is the Third World Poor?* Maryknoll, New York, Orbis Books.

Hastings, A. (1968) *A Concise Guide to the Documents of the Second Vatican Council*, 2 vols. London, Darton, Longman and Todd.

Hastings, A. (1979) *A History of African Christianity 1950–1975*. Cambridge/London/New York/Melbourne, Cambridge University Press.

Hastings, A. (1989) *African Catholicism*. London, SCM,

Healey, J. G. (1986) 'Basic Christian Communities: Church-Centred or World-Centred?' (*Missionalia*, vol. 14, no. 1, April, pp. 14–32).

Mazrui, A. A., and Tidy, M. (1984) *Nationalism and New States in Africa*. Nairobi/Ibadan/London/Portsmouth, NH.

Mugambi, J., Mutiso-Mbinda, J., and Vollbrecht, J. (1982) *Ecumenical Initiatives in Eastern Africa*. Nairobi, AACC/AMECEA.

Okullu, H. (1974) *Church and Politics in East Africa*. Nairobi, Uzima Press.

Personnalite africaine et catholicisme (1963) Coll. Paris, Presence Africaine.

Pro Mundi Vita (1974) Special Note n. 34, 'The Church in the African States'.

Pro Mundi Vita (1985) Bulletin 102, 3, 'Vatican II: Twenty Years on'.

Pro Mundi Vita (1986) Bulletin 107, 4, 'The Laity and the Extraordinary Synod 1985'.

Pro Mundi Vita (1987) Bulletin 110, 3, 'The Laity in the Field'.

Pro Mundi Vita (1988) Studies, 2, 'The Church in the World: Panorama 1987'.

SECAM (1984) Acts of the 7th Assembly (Kinshasa).

SECAM (1987) Newsletter, n.5 (December).

SECAM (1988) Pan African Seminar on Justice and Peace (Roma, Lesotho).

Shorter, A. (1988) *Toward a Theology of Inculturation*. London, Geoffrey Chapman.

Strahm, R. H. (1978) *Pourquoi sont-ils si pauvres?* Neuchatel, A la Baconniere.

Sundkler, B. (1961) *Bantu Prophets in South Africa*, 2nd edn. London, Oxford University Press.

Thils, G., *et al*. (1973) *L'Ecclesiologia dal Vaticano I al Vaticano II*. Brescia, Editrice La Scuola.

Ukpong, J. (1988) 'Theological Literature from Africa', *Concilium*, no. 199, pp.67–75.

Vandrisse, J. (1989) 'Luce Verde per il Sinodo Nero', *30 Giorni*, February, pp.70–2.

Waliggo, J. M., *et al*. (1986) *Inculturation: Its Meaning and Urgency*. Kampala/Nairobi, St Paul Publications.

12B Latin America

ENRIQUE DUSSEL

The Latin American Church has been so profoundly influenced by the Second Vatican Council – from the time it was summoned in 1959, throughout its sessions and even more since 1965 – that everything which has taken place in the Church since bears some relation to it. It is, perhaps the continent where the Council has made the most profound and far-reaching impact. Moreover, those indications of an anti-conciliar 'restoration' which can be seen in Latin America since 1972, and more pronouncedly since 1979, also testify to the importance of the Council for the present day in so far as they are attempts to erase the renewal prophetically called for by Vatican II.

THE INFLUENCE OF THE COUNCIL DURING ITS DELIBERATIONS, 1962–5

John XXIII immediately won the hearts of the Latin American people when he officially announced the summoning of the Council on 25 January 1959 at St Paul's-without-the-walls. Latin America was already in a state of excitement, as this was the second major event of that year: at the beginning of January Fidel Castro had freed Cuba from the Batista dictatorship and inaugurated the first socialist government of the continent. *Mater et Magistra*, the social encyclical of 1961, would later receive an equally positive welcome in Latin America from among groups of militant Christians.

Although not yet reformed, the Church in Latin America was sufficiently organized as to be able to cope with the renewal process that was now approaching. The founding of the Latin American episcopal conference CELAM in 1955 and the strong, forward-looking personality of Monsignor Manuel Larrain, bishop of Talca (Chile) and later president of CELAM, had put at the disposal of the bishops – here as in no other continent – a structure of co-ordination and execution that would function harmoniously and effectively within the Council and in the whole of the Latin American continent. The 620 Latin American bishops who participated in the Council (including the Caribbean, they made up 22 per cent of the total) convened in Rome in the years 1962–5 the VII, VIII and IX assemblies of CELAM, in addition to numerous other national and regional reunions. Leading bishops like Monsignor Larrain intervened verbally in the debates: Sergio Mendez Arceo (Mexico) on the relation of church and state, on the Virgin Mary and on liturgy; Kremerer (Argentina) on the diaconate; Henriquez (Venezuela) on the laity; Devoto (Argentina) on ecclesiology. In the majority of cases the Council opened up the minds of the bishops from a provincial regionalism to a universal outlook and to the responsibility of collegiality.

This spirit remains to the present day. However, very little if anything referring directly to Latin America found its way into the final documents of the Council. We can recall, for example:

319

Nations on the road to progress, like those recently made independent, desire to participate in the goods of modern civilisation, not only in the political field but also economically, and to play their part freely on the world scene. Still they continually fall behind while very often their dependence on wealthier nations deepens more rapidly, even in the economic sphere. People hounded by hunger call upon those better off (*Gaudium et Spes* 9).

No important Latin American theologian's voice was heard in the Council. The future liberation theologians were still students or only young priests and activists, not really aware of being at all different from the rest.

TRANSFORMATION OF THE CHURCH IN THE LIGHT OF THE COUNCIL, 1965–72

From the first summoning of the Council there was developing a new tradition that would eventually be formulated as 'The Church of the Poor'. (John XXIII was the first to use the phrase, and it is confirmed by John Paul II in his social encyclical, *Laborem Exercens*.) The repercussion of the Council was enormous and immediate throughout the whole continent. If collegiality can be said to have been its most important institutional achievement, then the Latin American Church entered into a new period under the leadership of the bishops collegially united in CELAM. The prophetic spirit came initially mainly from above, from bishops, priests and religious, and then it gradually began to emerge from below. As Monsignor Larrain expressed it:'CELAM is the first case in the whole of church history where the concept of episcopal collegiality has been realised' (*Criterio*, 13.5.1965). In the same way, a little afterwards in a preparatory document for the Roman synod of 1967, the Latin American bishops said:'We have rediscovered ecclesial communion which at the apostolic level is called collegiality'.

While all this was going on, Camilo Torres Restrepo, a priest turned revolutionary, died on15 February 1966, showing a new link between faith and politics. The reconciliation between the Church and the world, which in Europe took the form of a dialogue with the modern world, was found inLatin America in the discovery of the *compromiso* or commitment to the poor, who made up the great majority of humankind. *Pacem in Terris* (1963) and especially *Populorum Progressio* (1967) were received with great joy. In the same way, the Declaration of the Bishops of the Third World of 31 July 1966 created an awareness of the Church's social responsibility. The Latin American bishops met to discuss education, the secular apostolate and joint pastoral activity (Baños, June 1966); the role of the Church in the development and integration of Latin America (Mar del Plata, 1966); Pastoral care (the University, Buga, 1967), which launched a student movement throughout the continent and which was to coincide with the events of 1968 in Europe and the US; vocations (Lima 1967), where seminaries and the theological education of future priests were reformed; an indigenous pastoral and missionary programme (Melgar, April 1968), where the question of indigenization penetrated the ecclesial consciousness; and social pastoral strategy (Itapoan, 1968), where they studied how to put into practice a social doctrine for the continent. All these meetings reformed the structures of the Church in the spirit of the Second Vatican Council, and prepared the way for the Second General Conference of the Latin American episcopate at Medellín, Colombia, in 1968, which might be called the Latin American Council of the twentieth century. Its theme was 'The presence of the Church in the present day transformation of Latin America'. Medellín was the mature fruit of Vatican II. It was not a mere application nor an adaptation; it was the genuine expression of the Latin American Church. It was the realization of a council in the third world, much more important than the first Latin American continental council of 1899.

> The Latin American Church centered its attention on man [note: not on the Church], man of this continent who is living a decisive moment of his historic process .... This indicates that we are on the threshold of a new historic epoch of our continent, full of longing for a total emancipation, for liberation from all servitude, a time of personal maturation and collective integration. In this painful period of gestation we can see the signs of a future new civilisation. (*Medellín*, pp. 43–6)

The Latin American Church, even more than the universal Church, has been transformed under the inspiration of the renewal of Vatican II. It has modified its national and Latin American structures, the 'spirit' of its institutions. It has taken on a new face towards the poor of the continent. It has come to play a significant part in the life of Latin America. It is no longer a distant, clerical body, churchy, exclusively inward-looking. It has gone into the streets and has won a place in Latin American civilization as perhaps never before, and this has been not 'from above' but 'from below'. Liberation theology is the considered result of this profound renewal. It is its theoretical and reflective expression.

The Latin American Pastoral Institute (IPLA) (in Quito since 1967), the Liturgical Institute (Medellín), Catechetics (Manizales), Youth (Bogotà) and others form the new prophetic generation of the Church. Meetings of episcopal renewal have brought about a profound change in the collegial body. The religious orders and congregations have brought about a radical reform in their lifestyle, their chapters and their rules. The Latin American Confederation of Religious (CLAR) originated in Lima in 1964 and became the greatest realization of the spirit of the Second Vatican Council, since it preserved a healthy independence from the Roman curia. When the latter tried to restore central control, CLAR allowed the orders a salutary, prophetic liberty, in keeping with their charism. The commitment to the poor was to be a light to guide the orders to a return to the fulfilment of their rules. It would reinterpret from the vantage point of the poor motives that inspired their founders. These reforms were to be a major pivot for the preservation of the renewal of the Church begun by the Council. On an historic occasion, from 25 January to 2 March 1972, the provincial superiors of the continent met at Medellín for a course of study and decision-making. In their political involvement the laity passed from expressing themselves in terms of Christian democracy to a more revolutionary standpoint, and for this young Christians from all the activist movements of Latin America met together. The political left was evangelized from within.

321

THE CHURCH OF THE POOR AND THE ANTI-CONCILIAR MOVEMENT, 1972–9

The post-conciliar renewal in Latin America was so profound and rapid that the conservative groups were left disconcerted, without an organization, or possibility of reply. Nevertheless, some of the more conservative members of the Roman curia, although swept aside, had never accepted defeat. Relying on groups opposed to the Council and to the 1968 Assembly of Medellín – for instance CEDIAL, an institute founded by Roger Vekemans, – they now began to bring about changes in the organizations most active in reforming the Church. In Rome itself the Secretariat of Justice and Peace was dismantled. And in a move clearly orchestrated from the nunciatures – and in particular from La Paz, Bolivia – CELAM totally changed its orientation at the XIV Ordinary Assemby at Sucre, Bolivia. In 1972, Alfonso Lopez Trujillo was chosen as secretary general. This date coincided with a sharp swing to the right in Latin America, and a general repression under military dictatorship in almost all the countries of the continent: Brazil 1964, Bolivia 1971, Uruguay and Chile 1973, Peru 1975, Argentina 1976. This produced a new situation contrary to the spirit of the Council.

Those elements in the Church that had been inspired by the Council identified even more clearly with the oppressed, and the Church of the Poor emerged as a clear point of reference for them. We see this in the bishops of the north-east of Brazil who issued the pastoral letter 'I have heard the Cry of My People':

> Only they, the people of the fields and the cities, united in work, in faith and in hope, can be this Church of Christ which invites, this Church which works for liberation. And it is only in the measure in which we enter into the waters of the Gospel that we become Church, Church-People, People of God.

The Council had defined the Church as the People of God. The experience of poverty, repression and martyrdom of the Latin American Church developed this concept with more precision and pertinence for the third world. The Church, the People of God, was the People of the Poor. The Church of the Poor aligned itself with the social mass of the oppressed and exploited; they took part in its life, and soon the poor themselves made the Church. Basic ecclesial communities arose. The Church is now a Church from out of the poor. This is the history of its people, this is its self-awareness, this is its struggle. There has been a change from a commitment to the poor, to being, as a Church, the people of the poor. This was the most profound fruit of the Council, the most authentic reformation, a return to its origins in the first three centuries. It too became a Church of martyrs, from the priest, Antonio Pereira Neto, in Brazil 1969, to Enrique Angelelli, bishop of La Rioja, in Argentina 1976, and Oscar Romero in El Salvador 1980: three bishops, amongst dozens of priests and religious, and thousands of laity, leaders of communities, catechists and so on, who died for their faith.

After the Council and as part of a renewal in liturgy and spirituality, there was at first an attempt to purge the temple of images, symbols and remains of a pre-Christian culture, which were dismissed as folklore, superstition and fetishism. But soon the importance of popular culture and of ancestral religion was realized. The historical awareness of what it meant to be Latin American brought a re-evaluation of the religiosity of the people and the creation of a popular pastoral care that provided great scope for a prophetic renewal. In this way, the Church came into contact with a people that had had to invent a popular religion in the face of an institutional Church that had been enthusiastic 'romanizers' since the second half of the nineteenth century. This has been a major factor in the life of the Church since the Council, and a development of it, in as much as it shows the importance of the discovery of the value of indigenous cultures.

From 1972 to 1979, the Church, faithful to the spirit of the Council continued its prophetic and missionary work. The secretary general of the Communist Party of Chile, Luis Corvalán, wrote:

> In these conditions religion loses its character of opium of the people and, on the contrary, in the measure in which the church sides with man, one can say that instead of alienating, it is an inspirational factor in the fight for peace, liberty and justice (*Excelsior*, Mexico, 2.6.1977).

As in the previous period, it is not possible to give a comprehensive account of all that the Council inspired in Latin America. Its spirit is found in numerous places. But there is a whole sector of the Church, associated with the now changed CELAM, which had by 1979 gained complete institutional control, and is dismantling bit by bit the reforms that were effected in the light of the Council. The structures that were the motive force of the renewal are being dissolved. They have been centralized and transferred to Medellín, and all the former officials and professors excluded. Liberation theologians are being systematically persecuted, and not one of them assisted at the 1979 conference at Puebla. Everything is being centralized in Rome, in the Council for Latin America (CAL). The hard-won autonomy of CELAM has been lost and its power of decision taken away. Above all, the Congregation of Bishops in Rome, and its prefect, Monsignor Sebastiano Baggio, see to it that bishops of a conservative frame of mind are appointed in Latin America, ones who are opposed to the directives of the 1968 Medellín Assembly and the Second Vatican Council. The conference of Puebla was called to give a new direction to the pastoral activity of the Church. This was only successful in part because of the presence of many bishops who had lived through the experience of ecclesial reform during the years 1962–8. Franz Hengsbach, bishop of Essen, a sympathizer of Opus Dei and a chaplain to the German Army, was nominated president of Adveniat, which aimed to divert economic relief to those works that lay within the new spirit. They excluded those projects that were associated with the Church of the Poor, the theology of liberation or the formation of leaders who had clear political objectives. José Comblin wrote that support for the Council and the liberation 'was condemned as being suspect of subversion'.

THE 'RESTORATION' AND A DEEPER GROWTH IN THE SPIRIT OF THE COUNCIL, 1979–89

The influence of the Council has continued on its way in the last ten years and has perhaps become more radical. The opposition to the spirit of the Council, to collegiality and to the Church as the People of God is now better organized and has gained control of CELAM. But the option for the People of God and People of the Poor has also grown and deepened; it has been tested by persecution and martyrdom, and at the same time has gained hope from victories which, although limited, have clearly shown its potential.

Since the Third General Conference of the Bishops at Puebla in 1979 there has been an organized opposition to those who continue in the spirit of Medellín. No bishop has been nominated anywhere in the continent who has shown himself to be a prophet in defence of the poor. The necessary condition is obedience to Rome. The reality is that one is coming to see the bishop as a Roman delegate to the local community, and not a pastor to the community. Against the whole history of the Church, the nuncios are the only people consulted in the choice of bishops. Collegiality has been replaced by the autonomous individuality of each bishop who is directly related to Rome. The spirit of a national and continental episcopate has been lost and there is special persecution of the Episcopal Conference of Brazil. There is a parallel Church to the People of God as the Church of the Poor. The same goes for the Basic Communities. There is a methodical dismantling of the Latin American post-conciliar reforms. The bishops of the Council and of Medellín are being systematically replaced. Either they have to resign because of age, or death takes them in the midst of their labours. Leonidas Proano died in the odour of sanctity in 1988, he was 'the bishop of the indians' in Ecuador, and is the latest example. The exclusion of liberation theologians, the reform of the seminaries in a pre-conciliar way, the prohibition of a true solidarity with the poor in social action and enterprise, the weakness of the defence of human rights (under the pretext of not entering into politics), the solidarity with those in power and the ruling classes: all this illustrates a restoration that is contrary to the spirit of the Second Vatican Council.

Nevertheless, there are many hopeful signs of the presence and permanence of the Council in Latin America. The prophetic spirit has grown since the Sandinista Revolution in Nicaragua in 1979 – the first revolution where Christians formed a full and integral part – the movements of liberation in Central America, the enormous expansion of the Basic Communities. There are more than 100,000 in Brazil and very many in Mexico, Central America, Colombia, Peru, etc. These must be considered for their qualitative rather than quantitative importance. There is the first systematization of liberation theology in the collection of fifty volumes of the 'Theology and Liberation' series of books. There is the authority that belongs to the Church of the martyrs which has been tested for its faith in the commitment to the oppressed in all countries of Latin America. There is the renewing action of the religious who in the majority belong to the tradition that was initiated in the 1960s.

There is the Christian commitment of the laity in the process of the democratization of Latin American society after the military dictatorships of right-wing Catholic inspiration. There is the richness of a spirituality that imbibes the experience of a popular religiosity with its age-old wisdom and long suffering. All these are signs of today's presence of the Second Vatican Council in Latin America.

Before such a profound reform as that realized by the Council in the Latin American Church, it would seem normal that we should take a few steps back. The question that poses itself today is whether it will return to the position it held before the Council began. The composition of both CELAM in Latin America and the Consistory in Rome give cause for anxiety. But the Holy Spirit breathes where and when he will and the oppressed long for their liberation and in their suffering have great hope in his 'Church of the Poor'.

12B Latin America: Bibliography

Dussel, E. (1979) *De Medellin a Puebla: una decada de sangre y esperanza (1968–1979)*. Mexico City, CEE-Edicol.

Dussel, E. (1983) *Historia de la Iglesia en América Latina: Coloniaje y Liberación (1492–1983)*. Madrid, Esquila Missional.

Dussel, E. (1986) *Los Ultimos 50 Años (1930–1985) en la História de la Iglesia en América Latina*. Bogota, Indo American Press.

Dussel, E. (1985) *Hipótesis para una Historia de la Teologia en America Latina*. Bogota, Indo American Press.

Lernoux, P. (1980) *Cry of the People*. New York, Doubleday.

Prien, H. J. (1985) *La História del Cristianismo en America Latina*. Salamanca, Sigueme.

12C North America

GERALD P. FOGARTY sj

From the retrospect of twenty-five years, Vatican II represented a watershed in the Catholic Church in North America, not only because of the changes the Council introduced, but also because of the altered status Catholics had in American society. While the focus of this section will be the United States, many of the events had their parallel in Canada as well. In the 1950s, the American Church was not prepared for a Council. Immediately after the Second World War, there had been a new outbreak of anti-Catholicism, led by Paul Blanshard and the organization called Protestants and Other Americans United for the Separation of Church and State. They argued for the incompatibility of Catholicism and American democracy. When Senator John F. Kennedy declared his candidacy for the presidency in 1958, they demanded that he address himself to two issues: aid to parochial schools and establishing diplomatic relations with the Vatican. In a speech before the Houston (Texas) Ministerial Association, Kennedy stated emphatically that if there were ever a conflict between his conscience (not the Church) and his office, he would resign. Kennedy's answer assuaged some of his critics, and his election as the first Catholic president of the United States seemed to symbolize that Catholics were now truly Americans. Yet his election failed to address the relationship between Catholicism, or religion in general, and American public policy. This would become a neuralgic question for Catholics in the post-conciliar age.

Catholics were still a people set apart. The Latin liturgy made them different from the Protestant majority. While it seemed to express the timelessness of the Church, its uniformity had also helped unify the diverse ethnic and language groups that made up the American Catholic Church. As a group, American Catholics were still working class in origin and conscious of their ethnic roots. They were loyal to their Church that, from the beginning of immigration in the early nineteenth century, had provided not only a place of worship, but also identity and protection in a sometimes hostile environment. 'National' parishes, each with their own parochial schools, reinforced ethnic identity that in turn shored up religious identity. Only after the Second World War did Catholics begin to go to colleges and universities in numbers comparable to their Protestant counterparts. With education came upward mobility to the middle class, and outward mobility from the urban centres with their ethnic neighbourhoods and parishes to the suburbs with their homogeneous populations. Yet, even for these newly educated and affluent Catholics, there was little awareness that change was in the offing. Parochial schools rose alongside the large new churches surrounded by parking lots. Imperceptibly at first, the Church was coming to play a different role in the laity's life – no longer was it the protector against a hostile society; no longer did it reinforce ethnic identity; no longer was the priest one of the best-educated men in the community and therefore a natural leader. These Catholics were now assimilated and educated, but were theologically unprepared for the changes that would sweep the Church with Vatican II.

The bishops, too, expected little change in the Church. But here there was a paradox. In the nineteenth century, the bishops of the United States had had a strong tradition of collegiality. Not only did they hold Councils on a regular basis, but they consciously expressed their conviction that it was the college of bishops under the presidency of the bishop of Rome that was infallible. The twentieth-century American bishops, however, had little awareness of collegiality. They had, it is true, an episcopal conference, the National Catholic Welfare Conference, but this had been merely tolerated by the Vatican in 1922, and the bishops did not think of it in terms of collegial activity – it was merely consultative and its standing departments existed only to co-ordinate Catholic efforts on a national level.

The bishops' ignorance of their own history reflected a woeful lack of scholarly life. American Catholic intellectual life, only in its infancy in the late nineteenth century, virtually ceased after the condemnation of Americanism (1899) and of modernism (1907). In its place was an almost slavish adherence to Roman manuals of theology and obedience to the letter of the law.

There were, however, some exceptions to this intellectual slumber. In 1937, biblical scholars of the United States and Canada formed the Catholic Biblical Association of America, which, by the 1950s, had become a scholarly organization, seeking to implement and express the new biblical orientation mandated by Pius XII in 1943. By the late 1950s, American biblical scholars fell under attack as the American Church reflected the assaults being made on the Pontifical Biblical Institute in Rome. Meanwhile, in the 1940s, the Jesuit theologian John Courtney Murray had again broached the subject of the compatibility of American religious liberty with Catholic teaching – the issue underlying Americanism in the 1890s – but he came under fire and ceased writing in 1955 (Pelotte, 1976). The same year, Monsignor John Tracy Ellis, professor of Church history at the Catholic University of America, published an important essay lamenting the lack of American Catholic intellectual life (Ellis, 1955).

Weak though it was in scholarly activity, the American Church had achieved success in other areas. Beginning in 1887, its bishops had defended the rights of the labouring class which, unlike that in Europe, remained the faithful backbone of the Church. The American Church, furthermore, had a long experience of religious pluralism and of co-operation and association with non-Catholics – an issue the Council would address under the more formal title of ecumenism.

During the Council, the issues that most drew American attention were religious liberty and ecumenism. In 1963 Cardinal Francis Spellman of New York was instrumental in having Murray named a *peritus* at the Council and went on to promote the Council's declaration on religious liberty. The American bishops, with a few notable exceptions, played less of a role in shaping such key documents as the dogmatic constitutions on the Church and Revelation (Fogarty, 1982, pp. 390–400; Fogarty, 1989, pp. 322–44). But the conciliar teaching that most immediately affected American Catholics was the constitution on liturgical renewal in 1964 and the subsequent use of vernacular languages. What had seemed so absolute and unchangeable, so timeless and

327

ahistorical, what had previously set Catholics apart from other Americans and yet united them among themselves, now became the symbol of a Church immersed in human history and change. In the archdiocese of Baltimore, Fr Gomar de Pauw anticipated Archbishop Marcel Lefebvre's tradionalist movement in 1965 and was disciplined by Cardinal Lawrence Shehan of Baltimore (Hennesey, 1981, p. 315).

Ecumenism, too, was a novelty after the Council. The bishops established formal 'dialogue' committees with Protestants, Jews, and the Orthodox. Ecumenical prayer services became commonplace. As such gatherings ceased to make the news, they symbolized the end of an era of hostility.

Dramatic though the liturgical renewal and ecumenical movement were for American Catholics, there were other changes that became increasingly evident. The end of the Council coincided with the end of an era in American Catholicism. Catholics in the United States had long sought to show they were truly American by patriotic service in the nation's wars. No sooner had the Council ended, however, than American Catholics found their nation involved in an unpopular war in Vietnam. For the first time in history, Catholics in large numbers challenged their nation's policy. Some priests, notably the Berrigan brothers, the Josephite Philip and the Jesuit Daniel, even went to jail for their anti-war activities (Hennesey, 1981) pp. 318–21). Other priests turned to political life to oppose the war and influence American society. In 1970 Robert F. Drinan SJ, professor of law at Boston College, won election to the House of Representatives. In 1972, Robert J. Cornell, O. Praem., of Wisconsin won the first of two terms in Congress. In 1980, however, as Drinan was preparing to run for a sixth term, Pope John Paul II, through the Jesuit General, Pedro Arrupe, commanded him to withdraw from the race. A few days later, Cornell, who was again running, was also ordered to withdraw. The papal prohibition on holding elective and certain appointed offices was subsequently extended to religious women. Priests and nuns could well criticize their government, but they were to restrict their activities to the more traditionally religious sphere.

In the meantime, however, the bishops had gradually joined the criticism of the Vietnam war. In 1968, they issued a pastoral letter espousing selective conscientious objection to a particular war (Nolan, 1983, vol. 3 p. 193). By 1971, they passed a resolution that stated: 'whatever good we hope to achieve through continued involvement in this war is now outweighed by the destruction of human life and of moral values which it inflicts' (ibid., pp. 289–91). By 1980, they had begun to challenge American foreign policy in Central America. American Catholic leaders no longer identified patriotism with military service. American Catholics also began taking positions in other controversial areas of American life. Long used to obeying the law, priests, sisters and lay people joined in the civil-rights demonstrations in favour of racial desegregation (Hennesey, 1981, p. 315).

On a more institutional level, the United States bishops, in accordance with the Council, abolished the old Welfare Conference and formed two new organizations, the National Conference of Catholic Bishops (NCCB) and the United States Catholic Conference (USCC), a standing secretariat in Washington DC that co-ordinates Catholic efforts on the national level in such areas as education, legal matters, social concerns, and justice and peace. As it had done on civil rights and the Vietnam war, the Bishops' Conference became more critical of American policy. Like the people they led, the bishops of the 1980s were products of different experiences. Two-thirds of them had been appointed since the Council. On the one hand, they did not have to shepherd their flocks through the anti-Catholicism of the late 1950s. On the other, while they had not participated in the Council, they had been nurtured by the Council's teaching, especially the Pastoral Constitution on the Church in the Modern World. In 1983, they issued a controversial pastoral letter, 'The Challenge of Peace', in which they asserted that a policy of nuclear deterrence was morally tolerable only as long as it led to negotiations for bilateral nuclear disarmament (Nolan, 1983, vol. 4, pp. 493–581). The pastoral was the result of widespread consultation, public hearings, and critical reactions to preliminary drafts. Though the process had been previously used, the topic of nuclear war drew public attention and opposition from some Catholics. The bishops now regarded their obligations as pastors and duties as citizens to mean that they might have to criticize government policy. Three years later, they issued another controversial pastoral, 'Economic Justice for All' (NCCB, 1986). Following the same process of publishing drafts and consulting experts in economics as well as theology, they criticized the nation's domestic and foreign economic policy. This pastoral letter provoked a 'lay pastoral', rebuking the bishops for intruding into a non-religious realm.

The laity's public disagreement with the bishops was a relatively new phenomenon in American Catholicism. 'Dissent' had entered Catholic vocabulary in response to Paul VI's 1968 encyclical *Humanae Vitae*, reiterating the Church's prohibition of artificial contraception. Priests, religious and lay people protested against the pope's teaching. For the first time, there was widespread public dissent from papal teaching among American Catholics. In their pastoral letter for 1968, 'Human Life in Our Day', the bishops acknowledged that there could be 'theological dissent from the magisterium . . . only if the reasons are serious and well-founded, if the manner of the dissent does not question or impugn the teaching authority of the Church and is such as not to give scandal' (Nolan, 1983, vol. 3, p. 174). Washington was a particular focus of attention. Cardinal Patrick O'Boyle, the archbishop, immediately disciplined several of his priests.

But Washington was also the focus of attention because it was the site of the Catholic University of America. As early as 1967, Fr Charles Curran had drawn attention when several bishops on the board of trustees refused to renew his contract because of his teaching that the prohibition of artificial contraception was not binding in conscience. After a faculty and student boycott of classes closed down the university, the trustees reserved their decision and granted him tenure. In 1986, however, Curran's case came up again when the Congregation for the Doctrine of the Faith demanded that he retract certain of his writings. When Curran refused, Cardinal James Hickey, the archbishop of Washington and chancellor of the university, removed his canonical mission to teach as a Catholic theologian. Refusing a post in another school of the university that did not come under a pontifical charter, Curran sued the

329

university in a civil court for violating its contractual relations with him, but in 1989 the court upheld the university.

The Curran case was symptomatic of greater tensions in the American Church. By the 1970s, the laity was divided as it never had been before. On the far right were those who wanted to return the Church to the state they imagined had existed before. These adopted an ecclesiology that essentially made bishops delegates of the pope. In the words of Cardinal Joseph Bernardin, archbishop of Chicago, in 1984:

> Many Catholics see bishops as mere branch managers with the significant authority and leadership in Rome. That is why some bypass the local bishop or even the episcopal conference in sending letters to the Pro-Nuncio or directly to the Holy See. While they surely have the right to do this, this practice often belies a faulty ecclesiology. Whereas the lines of authority are clear and each bishop is directly subject to the Holy Father, the danger remains that this mentality can reduce both the efficiency and the legitimate authority of the local bishop (Bernardin, 1985, p. 322).

A letter-writing campaign to Rome had already contributed to an apostolic visitation of Archbishop Raymond Hunthausen of Seattle and, late in 1985, to the appointment of Donald Wuerl as auxiliary bishop with special faculties over certain aspects of the administration of the archdiocese. By the summer of 1986, the situation became so untenable that Hunthausen announced his inability to administer his diocese under such restrictions. While the bishops at their annual meeting in November expressed their sympathy for Hunthausen, they refrained from any direct criticism of the Vatican's action (*Origins*, 1986, pp. 361, 363–4; 400–5). The Holy See, nevertheless, appointed a new committee to investigate the situation. Consisting of Cardinal Bernardin, Cardinal John J. O'Connor of New York, and Archbishop John R. Quinn of San Francisco, the committee was instrumental in working out a compromise, according to which Wuerl was assigned as auxiliary bishop of Pittsburgh and Hunthausen accepted a coadjutor (*Origins*, 1987, pp. 37, 39–41). Early in 1988, Wuerl was named bishop of Pittsburgh with the transfer of Bishop Anthony J. Bevilacqua from that see to the archdiocese of Philadelphia.

On the liberal side, the issues of concern to the laity varied from the meaning of participation in the Church to the ordination of women. Some interpreted the biblical notion of the 'People of God', used by Vatican II, to mean the American political concept, 'We the People', with the result that they sought to make the Church more democratic in structure. The role of women in the Church took on greater significance as an ecclesial reflection of the movement for women's liberation, particularly in the United States. In November 1976, the 'Call to Action', the first national assembly of the clergy and laity in the United States since 1893, recommended a fuller participation of women in the Church. The same year, however, the Congregation for the Doctrine of the Faith issued a declaration that priestly ordination was to be restricted to men. The Congregation's argument – that as Christ was a male, the person who offered sacrifice in his place should also be male – may have been a signal to the Orthodox Churches that the Catholic Church would not change its practice while in dialogue. But in the United States, the Women's Ordination

Conference (WOC) had already been founded. It held three national meetings in Detroit in 1975, in Baltimore in 1978, and in St Louis in 1985 (Rader, 1988, p. 189). In 1979 the Catholic Biblical Association of America published a report that Scripture in itself did not preclude the ordination of women (*Origins*, 1982, pp. 1, 3–9). Continuing dialogue with various women's organizations, the NCCB issued a draft pastoral on women for reaction in 1988. Each diocese in the country held hearings on the draft which is currently undergoing further revision.

While some feminists, such as Elisabeth Schüssler-Fiorenza, are deeply critical of the male-dominated Church (Rader, 1988, pp. 190–1 and 194–5), the women's movement is also a sign of increased lay activity in the American Church. This new activity is partly a result of the dramatic decline in religious and priestly vocations in the years following the Council and of the departures from the active ministry and religious life. In 1965 there were 58,632 priests, 179,954 religious women, and 12,271 religious brothers; by 1988 these numbers had declined respectively to 53,522, 106,912 and 7,069. The number of seminarians decreased from almost 49,000 to less than 11,000. An estimated 10,000 priests left the active ministry between 1966 and 1978 (Dolan, 1985, pp. 436–7), and this exodus was not limited to priests. In the fall of 1969, Bishop James Shannon, auxiliary bishop of Minneapolis-St Paul resigned from the priesthood; he was followed two years later by Bishop Bernard J. Kelly, auxiliary of Providence. Lay men and especially lay women took on increasing roles not only as lectors, but also as extraordinary ministers of the Eucharist.

The decline in clerical and religious personnel also affected Catholic education on every level. In 1965 the number of Catholic colleges and universities climaxed at 309; in 1986 there were 243. Much of this decline was the result of the closing of small, financially unstable institutions, but much of it also reflected a Catholic population who chose publicly supported institutions or prestigious private institutions for the higher education of its children. Despite the relatively large number of Catholic institutions that remain, few are truly distinguished as major research centres (Dolan, 1985, p. 443). On the primary and secondary level, the story is much the same. In 1965 there were 10,879 elementary schools, a number that dropped to 7,865 in 1986. High schools declined in numbers from 2,413 in 1965 to 1,418 in 1986, (Hennesey, 1981, p. 323; *The Official Catholic Directory Anno Domini 1965*, 1986, 'General Summary').

Mass attendance declined from 71 per cent in 1964 to roughly 53 per cent in 1985 (Gallup and Castelli, 1987, pp. 194–5). American Catholics are still a church-going population. They gave Pope John Paul II an enthusiastic welcome in his two pastoral visits to the United States, the first in the fall of 1979 and the second in the fall of 1987. Yet, while they applauded his condemnation of the arms race and materialism at the United Nations in 1979, many rejected his denunciation of birth control, abortion, homosexuality, and the ordination of women (Dolan, 1985, pp. 453–4). American Catholic values had begun to mirror American society at large, and this meant privatizing religion.

One clue to the general shift in Catholic attitudes is abortion as a personal and political issue. In 1960 Kennedy had to answer questions about diplomatic relations with the Vatican and government aid to parochial schools. In 1984 Geraldine Ferraro, a Catholic and Democratic candidate for vice president, was asked where she stood on abortion. She replied that she was personally opposed to it, but would not impose her views on others. She initially appealed to Kennedy's position, which had gone unchallenged at the time, because the questions were ones on which Catholics could legitimately disagree. But abortion was a pressing moral question. Ferraro met public rebuke from Archbishop O'Connor of New York and Archbishop Bernard Law of Boston. Catholic politicians publicly disagreed. Governor Mario Cuomo of New York argued that the Catholic-elected official was sworn to uphold the law. Representative Henry Hyde of Illinois spoke in favour of legislation either prohibiting or restricting abortion. Some Catholics, including several religious women, signed a statement in the *New York Times* arguing that abortion was a private decision. Two of the nuns refused to retract their statement and were subsequently dismissed from their order.

Public dissent from Catholic teaching was something new in the American Church, and caused Vatican concern about American Catholic loyalty to the magisterium. This shaped the context of a special meeting of the American archbishops with Vatican officials in March 1989. The American bishops had originally requested a meeting with the pope and his advisers in relation to the Hunthausen case and other matters, but they dropped their request after the papal visit of 1987. The pope, however, asked all the metropolitans to meet with him and the curia for a week in Rome. Openly exchanging views, the Americans described the pluralistic culture within which they evangelized, defended American procedures in areas such as granting marriage annulments, and explained the American women's movement. In some ways, the Roman meeting was reminiscent of perennial areas of misunderstanding between the Vatican and the American hierarchy, such as the freedom Americans cherish. In the past, the American style of episcopal leadership gave rise to tension with the Vatican, the resolution of which evidenced the vitality of the American Church (see Fogarty, 1988, pp. 3–9). At the same time that the Holy See's relations with the American hierarchy are occasionally strained, it has drawn closer to the United States government. In 1984, with little opposition, President Ronald Reagan initiated diplomatic relations with the Holy See, a controversial issue in 1960.

The American Church currently numbers over 52 million, or roughly 22 per cent of the population. In 1990 it is considerably different from what it had been in 1965; yet some characteristics of the past remain. It educated its earlier, largely European, immigrants into the middle class. Yet it still remains a Church of immigrants, now largely Hispanic. It continues to minister to the residents of the nation's inner cities, now largely black. It is still practical, rather than intellectual. It has had its own unique struggle in implementing Vatican II. Its bishops still voice their concern for the poor and working class, but they have expanded their pastoral horizons to criticize the nation's domestic and foreign policies.

12C North America: Bibliography

Bernardin, J. (1985) 'Changing Styles of Episcopal Leadership,' *US Catholic Historian*, vol. 4, p. 322.

Dolan, J. P. (1985) *the American Catholic Experience: A History from Colonial Times to the Present*. Garden City, New York, Doubleday.

Ellis, J. T. (1955) 'American Catholics and the Intellectual Life' *Thought*, vol. 30, pp. 351–88.

Fogarty, G. P. (1982) *The Vatican and the American Hierarchy from 1870 to 1965*. Stuttgart, Anton Hiersemann Verlag.

Fogarty, G. P. (1988) 'Rome and the U.S. Bishops, Contending Ecclesiologies: A Historical Perspective' *Church*, vol. 4, Fall, pp. 3–9.

Fogarty, G. P. (1989) *American Catholic Biblical Scholarship: A History from the Early Republic to Vatican II*. San Francisco, Harper & Row.

Gallup, G. and Castelli, J. (1987) *The American Catholic People; Their Beliefs, Practices, and Values*. Garden City, New York, Doubleday.

Hennesey, J. (1981) *American Catholics: A History of the Roman Catholic Community in the United States*. New York, Oxford University Press.

NCCB (National Conference of Catholic Bishops) (1986) *Economic Justice for All: Pastoral Letter on Catholic Social Teaching and the U.S. Economy*. Washington DC, National Conference of Catholic Bishops.

Nolan, H.J., ed. (1983) *Pastoral Letters of the United States Catholic Bishops*. 4 vols. Washington DC, National Conference of Catholic Bishops.

The Official Catholic Directory Anno Domini 1965 (1965) Willmette, Ill., P. J. Kenedy & Sons, 'General Summary'.

The Official Catholic Directory Anno Domini 1986 (1986) Willmette, Ill., P. J. Kenedy & Sons, 'General Summary'.

The Official Catholic Directory Anno Domini 1988 (1988) Willmette, Ill., P. J. Kenedy & Sons, 'General Summary'.

Origins (1982) vol. 12, 20 May, pp. 1, 3–9.

Origins (1986) vol. 16, 6 November, pp. 361, 363–4; 20 November, pp. 400–5.

Origins (1987) vol. 17, 4 June, pp. 37, 39–41.

Pelotte, D. E. (1976) *John Courtney Murray, S.J.: Theologian in Conflict*. New York, Paulist Press.

Rader, R. (1988) 'Catholicism Feminism: Its Impact on United States Catholic Women', in Kennelly, K., ed., *American Catholic Women: A Historical Exploration*. New York, Macmillan, pp. 182–98.

12D Australia and New Zealand

ELIZABETH ISICHEI

A study of Catholicism in New Zealand and Australia since Vatican II begins with it a problem of perspective. Should one focus on local manifestations of world-wide changes (such as a decline in recruitment to the priesthood and religious orders), or on those issues perceived as most central by these local churches (such as Catholic schools)? What is the basis of comparison? If one see Catholic mass attendance figures, for instance, in terms of the past, they show a decline – from about 50 per cent to about 25 per cent of those who call themselves Catholic in census returns. But no Church has a higher attendance ratio, and a 1989 study in Auckland, New Zealand, showed that only 12.5 per cent of the general population attend church at all.

Australian and New Zealand society is generally accepted as profoundly secularized (though some Australian studies have questioned this). In the words of a young Dominican, '85 per cent of New Zealanders aren't interested in formal religion and wouldn't be caught dead near a church ....It seems to me we're now catering for the fringe – about 15 per cent at most' (Parker, 1989, pp. 56 and 64). Secularization has deeply affected the attitudes and lifestyles of those who are still practising Catholics. But in some ways this secularization is more apparent than real. Many are alienated from the churches, but engaged in various forms of inward quest that may lead them, for instance, to Eastern-style meditation or Gestalt-psychology workshops. This has influenced Catholicism in two ways – some are alienated from it, and others pursue a more individualistic spirituality within it.

There are many similarities between Australian and New Zealand society, and the position of Catholicism within them. Nevertheless, perhaps the differences are more instructive than the similarities. Australian Catholicism is much larger. People who call themselves Catholic in Australian census returns outnumber the entire population of New Zealand. In 1981 a quarter of all Australians (3,786,505 out of 14,576,330) called themselves Catholic; in New Zealand in the same year, it was 14.4 per cent of a population of 3,175,737 – 456,858. In both countries the Catholic population was originally mainly Irish and working class. In the years after the Second World War, this was modified by a gradual process of embourgeoisement and, in Australia, by extensive immigration. Australian Catholicism impinges much more on public life. It has had a major corporate impact – seen most spectacularly in the splitting of the Labour Party in the 1950s, which excluded it from Federal office until 1972. Partly because of its sheer size, it has produced much more writing of various kinds, including vigorous weeklies and periodicals (New Zealand in 1990 has one monthly and one, struggling, conservative weekly). Australia has greater financial resources, and its buildings make a major contribution to urban landscapes.

It is an apparent paradox in Australasian Catholic life that Vatican II was initially received with euphoria, and yet was followed by what seemed to be catastrophic decline – church attendances shrank, as did the proportion of

Catholic children attending church schools; fewer were recruited to the priesthood and religious life; and existing members left to an unprecedented degree. There was little doubt about the initial euphoria. In the words of an Australian priest:

> The Vatican II years were a springtime in Catholicism. To many it seemed that the church was at last shaking off outmoded accretions from the past, and that it was becoming more relevant to contemporary men and women, and hence more Christian (Campion, 1982, p. 172).

People were alienated to both the left and the right in the years that followed. Some radicals left the Church – or retreated into apathy – because the Church did not change fast enough. Others were perplexed and alienated by the speed of change, especially in the liturgy – as Latin gave way to English, Benediction disappeared, and the churches were largely stripped of their statuary. Religious, perhaps, felt the crisis most, for they had made the greatest personal investment in their religion. As their members grew fewer and older (the average age of Australian nuns is 58), the very continuation of their orders sometimes seemed in doubt. A member of a community who are all in their late seventies told me that they had been through a process of grieving, as if for death.

A New Zealand Marist, who is also a Cambridge-trained anthropologist, has analysed the period of malaise and angst that followed the initial euphoria. 'Disorientation gives way to feelings of chaos, malaise, anger, fear of the future, even despair' (Arbuckle, 1987, pp. 25–7). People emerged from this in various ways. 'Some are escapist, e.g. forms of fundamentalism or reverse naturism' – such as the tiny Lefebvrist movement. Some emerge with a new sense of religious and cultural identity – which must not be allowed to fossilize into immutable custom, lest a new period of chaos and malaise develop. In the account that follows, we shall analyse a few key areas of encounter and growth – justice issues, especially in the area of cultural encounter; the identity crisis of priests and religious; the changing role of the laity, especially women; and the changing function and content of Catholic education.

JUSTICE ISSUES

Michael King, one of many New Zealand Catholic intellectuals who drifted away from the Church in the 1960s and 1970s, described in his autobiography the happy certainties of a day that was irrevocably lost:

> We saw no gap between rich and poor . . . no broken homes, no alcoholics, no homosexuals, no psychiatric cases, no Maori experiencing discrimination, no people under stress. We saw only people like ourselves: Catholic, middle-class, largely Irish in origin, all comfortably provided for. We presumed we were a microcosm of New Zealand and of the world as it ought to be. And if the world was not like that, it was largely the world's fault (King, 1985, p. 61).

For both Australians and New Zealanders, justice issues had two dimensions – local and international. In New Zealand, at the heart of all justice issues lay the relationship between the indigenous people, the Maori (about 12 per cent of the population), and the white settler ('pakeha') majority. Until about 1970, the unquestioned policy was assimilationist. It was believed that Maori and pakeha should be treated in the same way and would, and should, become one people.

It was not realized that this in fact meant the assimilation of Maori to the dominant settler culture, and that, although equal under the law, they were in fact impoverished and marginalized in their own land. In every index of well-being, from life expectancy to home ownership, Maori people, and especially women, are disadvantaged. As so often in the world, change came not from a change in white sensibilities, but through Maori action. By the mid-1980s biculturalism had become an official government policy, a policy rooted in the 1840 Treaty of Waitangi.

The Catholic Church, like other denominations, did not pioneer this policy, but supported it strongly. Despite official support, attitudes among Catholics generally mirrored divisions in society as a whole. Some became strongly committed to biculturalism. For some, indeed, it became the major commitment of their lives. Others opposed it – an opposition rooted essentially in the natural insecurities of a settler population. But it was also pointed out that biculturalism tended to make other minorities – including immigrant Polynesians – invisible.

The denominational loyalties of Maori Catholics had been forged in rural areas, where mass attendance was part of community life. 'Maori Missions' under Mill Hill Fathers, often of foreign extraction, saw mission as gift rather than encounter. From the 1950s on, as Maori people became increasingly urbanized, they became profoundly alienated from a Church that seemed to have little to offer them. The Dominican Michael Shirres stated that only 2–3 per cent of Maori Catholics still practised their faith. Many aspired to a Maori Church, under a Maori bishop. Bishop Max Takuira Mariu, appointed in 1988, is, in fact, this, though not in name (his title is that of auxiliary bishop of Waikato diocese).

White attitudes to traditional Maori religion ranged from those of Shirres – who stated that Maori divinities were created spirits under God, like angels – to those of the correspondent in the conservative *Tablet*, who believed 'Maori culture is totally permeated by witchcraft, by the satanic supernatural' (*The Tablet*, 6 July 1974, p. 10).

It is clear that Maori Catholic theology will be done by Maori and not by pakeha, however well intentioned, and will be done by the traditional Maori method of discussion and consensus (as soon as Mariu was appointed he began to hold meetings, *hui*, the length and breadth of New Zealand).

A striking innovation in New Zealand in the late 1980s was the increasing tendency of the Church to pronounce on political issues. A Labour government came to power and was re-elected in 1987. In an attempt to solve New Zealand's economic problems, it followed policies that dramatically increased unemployment. Cardinal Thomas Williams publicly attacked these policies, briefly adding the word Cardinalnomics to New Zealand's political jargon – 'a callously cold-blooded programme of despoiling lower-income earners and bloating those on high incomes' (Totara Point sermon, 28 February 1988, typescript).

The Australian Church was also challenged by the position of indigenous people. The Aborigines form a much smaller proportion of the population than the Maori; their poverty and marginalization are much greater. Some live in urban ghettos, many in remote rural areas in the north. There has been only one Aborigine priest – Patrick Dodson. Ordained in 1975, he left the priesthood six years later. The Church has expressed increasing concern for racial justice. When Australians celebrated their bicentenary with much pomp and circumstance in 1988, a pastoral letter from the bishops pointed out that it marked the last day when the Aborigines totally possessed their land. The autobiography of that truly prophetic Australian Catholic, Shirley Smith ('MumShirl') mirrors the transition from welfare to justice among Aborigines themselves. Significantly, she is a sickness beneficiary and illiterate – her story was ghost-written.

But it was the encounter with Catholic immigrants that impinged on parish life much more. 'Post war migrants and their children have added over one million affiliates to the Australian Catholic church' (Lewins, 1983, p. 74). The official – and Church – policy of assimilation to the Anglo majority left many migrants alienated or marginalized. One Italian called Australian Catholicism 'soup without salt' (Campion, 1988, p. 181). Gradually, Anglo-Australians became aware of the poverty and unhappiness many migrants endured (in one five-year period a quarter returned to Europe), and became more responsive to their needs.

Australia's Catholic Commission for Justice and Peace was established in 1972. Its New Zealand Counterpart, the Commission for Evangelization, Justice and Peace, began in the following year. Significantly, it was renamed the Commission for Justice, Peace and Development in 1988. These bodies were intended to speak with a prophetic voice on local and international issues, and to generate resources for aid. New Zealand's JPD, under the leadership of a Maori layman, Manuka Henare, has been especially identified with biculturalism. Many Catholics were unable to identify with the radical witness of these organizations, and both became a focus of dispute and controversy. In 1988 the Australian body was replaced by a new one, dominated by bishops.

Catholics were divided similarly by international issues. The memoirs of a New Zealand Mercy sister show how the war in Vietnam caused an unprecedented polarization in her convent. 'Many of us were strongly opposed to New Zealand's involvement in Vietnam. It was bewildering to many nuns ....Might not the communists overrun New Zealand if they were not stopped in Vietnam?' (O'Regan, 1986, pp. 98–9). The same polarization occurred on a larger and more public stage in Australia. Cardinal Gilroy believed that the Vietnam war was part of a communist expansion that threatened Australia. Catholics for Peace (founded in 1967) thought otherwise. Springbok tours were to be equally divisive.

337

PRIESTS AND RELIGIOUS

Priests and religious in the pre-Vatican II Church were of great symbolic importance, and the leadership of priests was unquestioned. A decline in recruitment, and especially departures from the priesthood and religious life, spread ripples far beyond those immediately involved. There were 14,622 women religious in Australia in 1966 and 10,575 in 1985 – an absolute decline of 28 per cent made still more significant by an expanding population.

Women religious responded with especial earnestness to the call to rethink the original charism of their orders. Perhaps their relative marginalization and powerlessness in the Church made it easier for them to do so. Often, they discovered that their founder's original call to work among the poor had gradually mutated into the running of schools for middle-class pupils and the running of hospitals for middle-class patients. They dismantled the many artificialities of their lives – the serge habit, the detailed regulations. But instead of a new springtime in religious life, what followed often looked more like collapse. Once decline set in, it was difficult to reverse. It is not easy for a young woman to join an ageing community; she will experience isolation, and be cast in the role of caregiver. Some prospective entrants have been warned that in their *own* old age, care may well be lacking.

An age of major corporate undertakings in religious life gave way to one of individual initiative. Some have found this empowering and liberating – like the 80-year-old Sacré Coeur nun in Wellington, who works with apparently unlimited energy among the old. Some of those who left had long been unhappy; as with priests, it was now possible to leave without becoming a social outcast.

The decline in religious and priestly vocations is, of course, world-wide. Is it a consequence of increasing secularization, or of a new understanding of the priesthood of all believers, consequent on Vatican II? Is it a temporary setback, like the crisis in religious orders during and after the French Revolution, or does it herald a lasting change of direction in the spiritual life?

The same problems – lack of new recruits and an exodus of some existing members – affected the priesthood. Many left to marry: the Australian priest, Michael Parer, describes in his strikingly frank autobiography a life in which celibacy had become a torment. After 1981 laicization and release from the vow of celibacy became more difficult to obtain:

> . . .six years ago John resigned from the priesthood and applied for a dispensation from the vow of celibacy. He hasn't heard a word since. After waiting three years he married Jane . . . how can I be reconciled with the church when it won't be reconciled with me? (*Zealandia*, 1 May 1988, p. 10.)

It became ever more widely accepted that celibacy was not a necessary dimension of priesthood. Some priests – like some distinguished lay people – left because they had given up the faith. 'I found the church to be no longer a helpful or credible framework in which to live my life' (Parer and Petersen, 1971, p. 16). The protagonist in Thomas Keneally's Australian novel *Three*

Cheers for the Paraclete, Father James Maitland, is oppressed for his theology, although Maitland writes under a pseudonym. An Australian convert poet wrote these words for an ex-priest:

> . . . your stand a cry
> from this southern Church of Silence where to speak
> what's in the heart is some dishonour . . .
> >   Days
> reel us in . . .
> Snap-frozen in some seminary,
> the Word, secured against the ubiquitous shock
> of honest air or breath, rots as it thaws (Bruce Dawe, 'At Mass').

In 1988 there were no first-year seminarians from either of New Zealand's two largest dioceses, or in its largest religious order of priests. There were in 1989 forty-one seminarians in New Zealand's national seminary in Mosgiel; there are 120 in Fiji, at the seminary for the island, Pacific. This has led to suggestions that 'they hopefully in the near future, will be able to help us in a reversed mission' (Denis Browne, Bishop of Auckland, in Parker, 1989, p. 69).

Opus Dei was introduced to Australia in 1963, and to New Zealand in 1989. A recent book by an Australian priest echoes criticisms that have often been made elsewhere – right-wing political involvement, elitism, discrimination against women, and theological conservatism (Collins, 1986, pp. 103–10). Similar points were made in an anonymous article in the New Zealand periodical *Accent*. Such allegations are strengthened by Opus Dei's secrecy. But they were not sustained at an enquiry at the University of New South Wales in 1974.

THE LAITY

Humanae Vitae impinged more profoundly on the life of the average lay person than all the deliberations of Vatican II. Some priests and lay people opposed it publicly. The Australian bishops at first took a strongly ultramontane line; six years later they issued a declaration of such masterly ambiguity that both sides cited it in their favour.

Some couples practised contraception and obeyed the Church in all else. Some could not live in apparent disobedience to the magisterium and left. Some lacked the robustness of conscience to take a decision and live by it, agonizing over the issue for years and going from confessor to confessor. Those who obeyed *Humanae Vitae*, often at the cost of much suffering, bitterly resented those who did not. But the general pattern was clear – it has been estimated that 85 per cent of Australian Catholics under 45 now use contraceptives.

Many who first discovered liberty of conscience in relation to *Humanae Vitae* went on to apply it to many other areas of life, including compulsory Sunday Mass. Auricular confession declined – a world-wide phenomenon that is not yet fully understood, but can perhaps be most plausibly explained in terms of this new robustness of conscience. Partly as a concomitant of theological pluralism, the fear of hell, which had coerced so much Catholic piety, declined. In May 1988 the Sydney *Bulletin* ran a cover story on the decline of hell. It included the results of a survey which showed that only 54.7 per cent of Australian Catholics believed in it.

Several categories of people are chronically marginalized in Catholicism – the divorced and remarried and those living in gay relationships. Some have sufficient inner confidence to continue to frequent the sacraments; many leave the Church altogether. The Auckland priest, Felix Donnelly, attacked the Church's blanket condemnation of homosexuality and was silenced.

In March 1985 a bill was introduced to decriminalize homosexuality in New Zealand. After a bitter public controversy, it was passed. Catholics were found in both camps; Cardinal Thomas Williams was among the opponents.

Both divorced and gay Catholics find that the inflexibilities of Church theory are tempered in pastoral practice. The Beginning Experience is an important New Zealand support group for the divorced and others newly alone. 'Acceptance' in Australia and 'Ascent' in New Zealand cater for gay Catholics. They have their own chaplains and hold retreats, special Masses and social functions. Many believe that the Church's blanket condemnation of gay love leads to promiscuity, and that it would be better to encourage fidelity and stable relationships. It is also profoundly threatening to gay people's self-esteem. When AIDS and 'safe sex' became an issue, the bishops adhered to the official line – that the young should avoid AIDS by adhering to traditional Catholic sexual morality. Some religious found a new meaning for their lives in work for AIDS victims. Cynics compared this with repainting the ambulance at the bottom of the cliff . . .

Paradoxically, while Vatican II affirmed lay spirituality, many lay organizations – including all sodalities – ceased to exist, among them, the Holy Name Society, and the Children of Mary. Others became pale shadows of their former selves, such as the Legion of Mary. The St Vincent de Paul Society survived, and the Catholic Women's League flourished, becoming New Zealand's strongest lay Catholic movement, although its members are mainly older women. Movements strongly geared to a specifically lay apostolate – Young Catholic Workers and the Christian Family Movement – crumbled away. Liturgical changes created openings for lay Readers, Extraordinary Ministers of the Eucharist and so on; these roles were subordinate to the priestly, and in a sense fostered traditional attitudes and relationships.

Changes in the liturgy and the reorganizing of church interiors, consequent on these, led to much agonized protest. This was partly the result of the lack of a sense of history, and the belief that the state of affairs in 1960 had always pertained in the universal Church. But it was not sheer mindless conservatism. To many Catholics, the unchanging Latin of the Mass was a symbol of an eternally unchanging God. Many lay people had developed what was essentially a practice of contemplative prayer against the background of the traditional Mass's silences, and found enforced participation disagreeable. Folk hymns and upbeat services with guitars were intended to attract the young, but many of the young stayed away and the elderly who remained were disaffected. A New Zealand priest compared the new services with Terylene copes – artificial, but not gripping. One remembers the words of Kierkegaard that the churches have reversed Christ's miracle, and turned wine into water.

In general, Catholic churches became more like their Protestant counterparts, with services in the vernacular, and the disappearance or decline of many of the things that had pained Protestant susceptibilities – indulgences, medals, statues, auricular confession. Rapprochement between Catholics and Protestants became easier. In 1988 the Catholic Church joined the National Council of Churches to form the Conference of Churches in Aotearoa-New Zealand. (The Orthodox Churches joined this, but not the Baptist Union.)

While some priests, religious and lay people drifted into discouragement and indifference, others found new directions for their lives. Some found it in the charismatic movement – perhaps the most genuinely ecumenical section of the Church. This has its critics, not least for its tendency to theological and social conservatism. But its lively services and warm fellowship have enriched many lives.

Some charismatics have formed convenant communities, though these have tended to lack staying power. Some Catholics, especially the young, have joined Pentecostal/fundamentalist churches, which offer the certainties and the strong social cohesion once provided by Catholicism. Not all communities are charismatic, of course. Some seek to develop an alternative lifestyle, and relate to the poor and marginalized. 'Hesed' in Melbourne, a community working among street people which has lasted for sixteen years, is a striking example. Religious took the lead in pioneering various forms of self-exploration, which have now become familiar in Catholic retreat houses – the Myers-Briggs personality indicator, Enneagrams and so on. Marriage Encounter courses have become popular, though their cost makes them inaccessible to many.

O'Farrell in his magisterial study of Australian Catholicism believes that a tendency of the 1970s was

> to diminish substantially and dampen Catholic intellectual life . . . the causes of this were numerous. The extreme radicalism of some intellectuals discredited intellectual activity generally in the eyes of the traditionalists. Theorists became disillusioned and discouraged when confronted by opposition or resistant practicalities (O'Farrell, 1985, p. 423).

One index of this was the decline or extinction of a number of Catholic periodicals. He also describes the redirection of Catholic intellectual energies into detailed historical studies or novels, poetry and drama.

The post-Vatican II years were particularly difficult for women, who sought to reconcile their Catholic inheritance with insights absorbed from the growing feminist movement. Some concluded that the Church was irremediably sexist and left. Among those who stayed there were many divisions and much ambiguity. Vatican II had little to offer feminists. In the insightful words of a theologian from Sri Lanka:

> It had no real sense of the struggles of the poor, the working class, of women, of oppressed racial groups. It did not deal seriously with racism and white supremacy, with sexism and male dominance, with classism and capitalist exploitation (Balasuriya Tissa, *Planetary Theology*, quoted in L. Richard, D. Harrington and J.W. O'Malley, eds, *Vatican II, the Unfinished Agenda*, New Jersey, 1988, p. 193).

341

Some Catholic women, and many evangelicals, were opposed to feminism, feeling their identity and self-esteem as wives and homemakers imperilled. When a 30,000 dollar survey into sexism in New Zealand Catholicism was commissioned, women took a leading role in organizing an unsuccessful petition against it. When a regular columnist in *The Tablet* (a priest who wrote under a pseudonym) was asked about the ordination of women, he replied that they were as incapable of it as an animal is of baptism.

Catholic women experienced some difficulty in working with other feminists, especially since more liberal abortion laws were a standard part of the feminist agenda. Many strongly supported the ordination of women, though probably few outside the ranks of religious had any desire to be ordained. What they wanted was a radical rethinking of hierarchical and clerical structures.

SCHOOLS

Until some point in the 1960s, the necessity of Catholic schools was one of the major premises of Australasian Catholicism. Parents who did not send their children to an accessible Catholic school were excommunicated. The occasional critics who pointed out that they were not necessarily the best preparation for life in a pluralist society, and that there was no Catholic version of standard school subjects such as chemistry, were unwelcome; when Fr Patrick Crudden suggested in 1980 that the future of Australian education lay with state schools, he was dismissed from his post as director of Catholic education in Melbourne archdiocese. Catholic schools absorbed a disproportionate amount of Church resources; the solution seemed to most Catholics to lie in state subsidies. It was experienced as a burning injustice that Catholics supported both the state schools (by their taxes) and their own schools. This discontent was expressed dramatically in Australia in the Goulburn 'strike' of 1962 when Catholic schools were closed for a week, and the children sought admission to state schools. An increasing school population – the result of the postwar baby boom, and the declining number of religious teaching in schools – created a situation of intolerable pressure, as the religious were replaced by lay teachers on standard salaries. The obligation to send children to Catholic schools was quietly abandoned. State aid became a reality in both Australia and New Zealand in the 1970s, but in both countries half the Catholic children attend state schools. The future and functions of Catholic schools continue to be a matter of debate. So does the content of their religious curricula.

ASSESSMENT

Many have undoubtedly experienced the changes of the last thirty years as 'chaos'. Some have left the Church entirely, including some of the brightest and best. Some have drifted into secularized apathy. When Pope John Paul II visited New Zealand in 1986, attendances were unexpectedly low and many memorabilia remained unsold. Did this reflect apathy or a rejection of a conservative pope? Possibly both.

The local Catholic press tends to be gloomy. This gloom is probably ill-founded. We have come to take many of the gains of the last thirty years for granted – such as the fact that Catholics now read and study the Bible. But I interviewed Catholics in their late fifties who remember 'Knox and Cox' (Knox's Bible, Cox's commentary) as a high point in their spiritual journey. No one would wish to return to the denominational hostilities of the past, when children from Catholic and state schools regularly fought and insulted each other. The piety of the past was partly coerced by fear: the hell-fire sermons that are still so vividly remembered. Morris West's novel about the Christian Brothers in Australia (published in 1946 – significantly, under a pseudonym) shows the unhappiness that often existed within religious orders, as does much other literature. There can be no doubt that many who left had long been unhappy, and that many others have now moved closer to the charism of their founders. It has even been suggested that some are being 'founded' for the first time. A religious priest in his thirties told me, 'I would think I'm in the midst of chaos . . . . I'm not especially worried about that. I think it's more important that I really address where religious life is at the moment, so that it can re-vision and revitalize . . .' Many Catholics – priests, religious and lay – have moved through years of rapid change without an identity crisis of any kind, lighting candles that illumined many lives. Gerard Crotty was a Marist brother who died of cancer at the age of 30 in 1988. He was an outstandingly gifted composer. Near death, he said: 'Sometimes I have the feeling that I've already made the move into heaven . . .'

POSTLUDE

Partly as a result of Vatican II, there is a much deeper appreciation of the lay calling. Many idealists now find their vocation in lay work in the third world, or in youth movements such as Antioch. New Zealanders regard two twentieth-century figures as prophetic – the artist Colin McCahon, and the poet James K. Baxter. A Jesuit told me that they were major influences in his vocation. McCahon belonged to no church, but his paintings made extensive use of Catholic symbols, such as the Stations of the Cross, the Sacred Heart and the rosary.

New Zealand's greatest poet, James K. Baxter, died in 1972. A recovered alcoholic, and a convert to Catholicism, his piety was of the most traditional kind, and he loved scapulars, statues, medals and rosaries. He identified profoundly with Maori culture, and the social critique in his poems was the more powerful because of his own radicalized lifestyle. He broke away from bourgeois comfort, founding a short-lived commune on the Wanganui river. He did not claim to be a plaster saint, but the love of his fellow men, which burns through his poems, speaks to us still.

Prophetic utterance is only one division of Catholic life. Most Catholics live, as it were, with a perpetual squint, endeavouring to focus at the same time on

343

the world that is too much with us, late and soon, and on the bright light of eternity. This kind of double vision is not particularly satisfactory, and rather uncomfortable. A case study of a Catholic village on a little island off the shores of Papua New Guinea uses words that are equally applicable to the urban parishes of Australia and New Zealand: 'There is no need to assume that anyone completely escapes the discomfort of confusion and dissidence.'

12D Australia and New Zealand: Bibliography

The abundant literature on Australian Catholicism since Vatican II contrasts sharply with the dearth on New Zealand. The focus on New Zealand in this chapter is intended to redress a little of this imbalance, and also reflects the natural bias of a New Zealander!

New Zealand
Arbuckle, G. (1987) *Strategies for Growth in Religious Life*. New South Wales (This is an important book by a New Zealand Marist).
Arbuckle, G. (1988) *Out of Chaos, Refounding Religious Congregations*. New York (see comment for above reference).
Donnelly, F. (1982) *One Priest's Life* Auckland. An autobiography.
Isichei, E. (199) *A History of New Zealand Catholicism since 1960*. (This is a study in preparation, based largely on interviews.)
King, M. (1985) *Being Pakeha*. Auckland. An autobiography.
O'Regan P. (1986) *A Changing Order*. Wellington. A Mercy Sister's life an autobiography.
Parker, A. (1989) 'Faith, Hope and Charity: Catholics in Crisis', *Metro*, July.
Simmons, E.R. (1978) *A Brief History of the Catholic Church in New Zealand*. Auckland, 'The Post-War Years', pp. 105–17.
Simmons, E.R. (1982) *In Cruce Salus, A History of the Diocese of Auckland 1848–1980*. Auckland, chs 24 and 25, pp. 257–74.

Australia
Campion, E. (1982) *Rockchoppers, Growing up Catholic in Australia*. Ringwood, Victoria.
Campion, E. (1988) *Australian Catholics*. Harmondsworth, Penguin.
Collins, P. (1986) *Mixed Blessings, John Paul II and the Church of the Eighties*. Ringwood, Victoria.
Keneally, T. (1968) *Three Cheers for the Paraclete*. Sydney.
Lewins, F. W. (1983) 'Wholes and Parts: Some Aspects of the Relationship between the Australian Church and Martyrs', in A. W. Black and P. E. Glasner, *Practice and Belief: Studies in the Sociology of Australian Religion*. Sydney.
O'Farrell, P. (1985) *The Catholic Church and Community, An Australian History*, revised edn. Kensington, New South Wales, chs 7 and 8, pp. 406–48.
Parer, M., and Peterson, T. (1971) *Prophets and Losses in the Priesthood*. Sydney. Covers New Zealand as well.

12E Eastern Europe

GRAZYNA SIKORSKA

THE POSTWAR YEARS

At the end of the Second World War large areas of Eastern Europe fell under Soviet political control and together with the USSR formed the 'Eastern bloc'. In accordance with Soviet policy, atheism became part of the official state ideology in every one of these communist countries. Yet although the ultimate objective everywhere was the eradication of religion, the priority given to achieving this and the practical policies adopted by communist governments differed considerably, both from country to country and over the years. Official attitudes depended on a variety of considerations: the different denominations involved and their own tradition of relations with the state, as well as foreign policy, internal politics, economic conditions within the country, ideological preoccupations and nationalist pressure. The same variable factors applied within the Soviet Union itself. For example, local conditions led the Soviet Communist Party to ban the Eastern Rite Catholic Church in Ukraine and aggressively persecute the Roman Catholic Church in Belorussia, while allowing greater freedom for Lithuanian Catholics. Outside the Soviet-dominated Eastern bloc, the communist states Yugoslavia and Albania had their own distinctive policies towards religion. In Yugoslavia, religious practice has been tolerated within rather widely defined limits, while Albania is the only state in the world where religion is illegal, and all public expression of faith severely punished. In the other seven countries of the region – the Soviet Union, Poland, East Germany, Czechoslovakia, Bulgaria, Romania and Hungary – the struggle against religion gradually became less violent over the decades and a *modus vivendi* was reached in most countries. Nevertheless, the state offices for Church affairs – established after the war in all Eastern European countries – subjected the activities of the churches to open state control. Articles of the Criminal Code were used (to varying degrees in the various countries) to prosecute those who did not comply with its directives on religious practice.

When the Second Vatican Council was being held in Rome, the Roman Catholic Church in the entire Eastern bloc was still suffering the aftermath of the mass arrests and imprisonment of the early 1950s. Indeed, in Hungary priests were being arrested and bishops disciplined at the time of the Council, and in the Soviet Union the savage campaign against religion launched by Khrushchev in 1959 was well under way. In Belorussia, where not a single new priest had been allowed since the end of the war, in Bulgaria, where about seventy priests were trying to extend their pastoral care over 70,000 believers, or in Czechoslovakia, where the Party had allowed a maximum of three ordinations every year since 1960, the Second Vatican Council was no doubt of little more than academic interest to local Catholic communities whose very survival still seemed threatened. Believers in Eastern Europe – in so far as they were aware at all of the Council's existence and activity – realized that implementation of the Council's decisions would depend more on the communist parties than the Roman Catholic Church itself. That this was indeed so was demonstrated in Czechoslovakia during the Prague Spring of 1968, with its brief lifting of Party control. In the space of a few months several initiatives involving the laity were launched. A Catholic journal, *Via*, came into being to provide a platform for theological debate. In July 1968 representatives from all over Czechoslovakia, including fourteen bishops, met to draw up a charter for religious freedom. During that meeting an Association for Conciliar Renewal was born. Set up in the spirit of the Second Vatican Council, the movement's objectives were the spiritual renewal of the Church and service to society. The Warsaw Pact invasion of August 1968 and the subsequent loss of the Church's new-found freedom sealed the fate of both *Via* and the Association. Equally short-lived was a pastoral Council of priests and lay Catholics set up in 1968 in the archdiocese of Prague by Bishop Tomasek. No official pastoral Council was allowed by the communist authorities after that, though in some places unofficial Councils did exist and – in some places at least – work successfully.

Communism and Catholicism were from the outset viewed as ideologically irreconcilable by both the communists and the Vatican. Pope Pius XII spoke out publicly against communism. On 1 July 1949 the Holy Office issued a decree which threatened to excommunicate Catholics who belonged to or supported a communist party or propagated communist ideas. For their part, communist governments sought to obstruct contacts between local churches and Rome, and put pressure on priests to join social organizations which would explicitly support government policies. In some countries attempts were even made to set up national Catholic Churches, independent of the Vatican. However, in Eastern Europe the government did not achieve substantial success, or match the achievement of the Chinese authorities with the Catholic Patriotic Association.

John XXIII's encyclical *Pacem in Terris* inaugurated a new phase. Ideological irreconcilability was no longer seen as ruling out practical coexistence. The encyclical advocated qualified co-operation with communists and was greeted with interest by the Eastern European communist governments. It was undoubtedly John XXIII's new approach to communism that enabled every Eastern European Roman Catholic Church (apart from that in Albania) to have an official delegation participating in some sessions of the Council. However, only Yugoslavia's bishops could travel to Rome freely. As far as the other countries were concerned, the presence of individual bishops or other representatives depended solely on the whim of the Party. For example, eight Czechoslovak bishops were not allowed to go to Rome, while Cardinal Beran, who was present at the final session, was not allowed to go back to Czechoslovakia afterwards and remained in Rome until his death. In Poland, the Party used the occasion to try to split the hierarchy by refusing passports to some bishops while giving passports to their respective auxiliary bishops.

A NEW APPROACH TO MARXISM

All communist governments noted that the Council did not condemn communism. In Hungary, the Council's attitude to communism was welcomed by the state authorities and a Church hierarchy still demoralized by the repression of the 1950s. The Council's decisions gave leeway to Hungarian bishops to co-operate with Marxists, mainly in the sphere of politics. It became easier for the bishops to justify enforcing the clause in the Church–state agreement, signed in 1950, requiring them to 'initiate proceedings against those churchmen who opposed the legally based order of the Hungarian People's Republic'. Priests judged guilty were transferred or even dismissed by the bishops. Later, Cardinal Lekai was to formulate his 'small steps' policy: in return for support given by the Church to the Communist Party's political programme, the Church would receive small concessions.

In 1964 an agreement was signed between Hungary and the Vatican which recognized the state's right to give prior approval for the appointment of bishops and stipulated that Church leaders must swear to uphold the laws of the Hungarian People's Republic. Five new bishops were appointed. This very limited agreement did not, however, spare the Church continuing persecution by the state. Throughout the 1960s arrests and trials continued of priests accused of illegal religious activity – such as instructing the young outside the limited facilities provided at parish level; priests' licences were still withdrawn from time to time.

In 1966 the Vatican and Yugoslavia signed a protocol. The Yugoslav bishops were not present during the formal negotiations at which the text was agreed, and indeed one of the clauses of the protocol – a reference to possible 'terrorist' activities by priests – caused them offence. In the protocol, the state recognized the Vatican's jurisdiction over spiritual and ecclesiastical matters within the Roman Catholic Church, and in return the Vatican agreed that the clergy would steer clear of direct political involvement. This ensured, for instance, that bishops could be appointed freely and keep up open contact with Rome. By 1970, full diplomatic relations had been restored between the Vatican and Yugoslavia.

Outside Yugoslavia and Hungary formal agreements between communist states and the Vatican did not materialize. The Soviet, Czechoslovak, Bulgarian and Romanian Parties continued to regard the Catholic Church as one of the obstacles on the way to building a new socialist society, and remained confident that their policies would eventually remove it. The Catholic Church in East Germany, with its 'fortress mentality' as well as 'minority complex', did everything possible to avoid contact with the state. The East German hierarchy consciously and resolutely avoided public utterances on political, social or economic subjects, except when it considered that state policies ran directly counter to Christian principles. Subjects on which it did speak out included abortion, universal Marxist education, the state-sponsored Youth Dedication ceremonies (the *Jugendweihe*) and the lack of provision for conscientious objectors.

Before 1968 Marxist–Christian dialogue was fashionable in some Polish intellectual circles but, to the mass of believers as well as to the hierarchy, co-operation with the communist authorities remained merely a sad if necessary consequence of Poland's geopolitical position in Europe. The Roman Catholic Church in Poland kept its co-operation to a minimum. It helped the Communist Party retain political power at times of national crisis, but did so only for the sake of national survival. At the same time the Church used all means at its disposal to promote Catholic teachings on social and ethical questions, regardless of what the official communist ideology might say.

AVAILABILITY OF COUNCIL DOCUMENTS

One of the immediate effects of the Second Vatican Council in Yugoslavia was the birth of a bulletin *Glas Koncila*, which published news of the Council. The bulletin supported the proposed changes in the liturgy and published the liturgical texts which were widely distributed. Its circulation soared, and in 1970 reached around 180,000, higher than any other weekly in Yugoslavia. Although the original intention had been to cease publishing it at the end of the Council, it was so successful that it was allowed to continue. There was no pre-publication censorship and only three issues were banned after publication. It was largely due to the influence of *Glas Koncila* that the changes (especially the liturgical changes) proposed by the Council were introduced more quickly in Yugoslavia than in any other Eastern European Country.

Conciliar documents, as well as details of every session, were also relatively well known in Poland. The Polish hiearchy, led by Cardinal Wyszynski, showed a unique inventiveness in involving Polish Catholics in the Council. Throughout every conciliar session, night vigils were held at the Marian shrine of Jasna Gora, and Catholics were encouraged to make 'conciliar vows', which were noted down in a special book and presented to the pope. A number of pastoral letters about the Council's work and its decisions were read out in all churches, and 'conciliar' sermons were preached. The state prevented large-scale publishing of books of conciliar documents and evaluations of them, but various academic works on the Council were produced. As early as 1966, the Council's documents, with theological, historical and pastoral commentaries, were published. Translations of Western theologians appeared in religious periodicals. The Polish Church itself contributed to an academic discussion on the meaning of the Council. In 1972 the Polish Theological Society in Krakow published a book, *U Podstaw Odnowy* (the Basis of Renewal), by the then Cardinal Wojtyla. In 1967 an auxiliary bishop of Lodz, Bogdan Bejze, began publishing a series of books, 'W Nurcie Zagadnien Posoborowych' (The Main Issues of the Council). Some 3,000 theses connected with the Council were produced at the Catholic University of Lublin (KUL) between 1980 and 1982 alone. The majority remained in manuscript form because of the state's strict control on religious publishing.

In other Eastern European countries the conciliar documents were much less readily available. In Hungary the last of them were not published before the mid-1970s. Conciliar documents were translated into Czech and Slovak and published in a limited edition of the Czechoslovak Catholic periodical *Duchovni Pastyr* (Spiritual Pastor), soon after the Council ended. A complete set of documents was published in Slovak by Academia Christiana in Rome, in 1968–70, and in Czech (also in Rome) in 1983. Several thousand copies were printed, but it was impossible to send them openly to Czechoslovakia. The documents of the Council were not published in the Soviet Union. Thus they remained unavailable to priests and lay people in Lithuania, Latvia, Belorussia and other Catholic areas.

IMPLEMENTATION OF THE COUNCIL'S REFORMS

Religious education was perhaps one of the most difficult problems confronting the churches in the Soviet Union and Eastern Europe. Poland was in a unique position. The Catholic University of Lublin thrived, together with the Theological Academy in Warsaw and several other theological institutes. However, even in Poland, religious instruction was barred from schools in 1959. It was not until 1980 that the state officially renounced its right to supervise catechetical instruction in churches and dictate what could and could not be taught. However, a new subject – 'religious studies' – was then introduced in secondary schools as a counterbalance, propagating Marxism as the only acceptable scientific world outlook. In Czechoslovakia, Hungary and East Germany, religious instruction was allowed but a number of administrative measures discouraged children from taking part. After 1976 Hungarian Catholic parishes were allowed to organize restricted religious instruction for children on church premises. In the Soviet Union, Bulgaria and Romania, religious instruction remained forbidden by law.

Other measures used by the communist authorities to make it difficult for the Church to preach the gospel included limiting the Church's access to the state-controlled mass media, or denying access altogether, and severe restrictions on the number of Bibles available in the country. Only in Hungary and Yugoslavia were there enough Bibles available to meet the basic needs of believers. In the German Democratic Republic fair numbers were available, but not enough to meet requirements. In Poland, despite relatively high production, supply did not altogether meet demand. As in many Eastern-bloc countries, believers were prepared to pay more than the official selling price to obtain a copy. In Czechoslovakia severe restrictions were imposed by the authorities on the number of Bibles which could be printed or imported. Only in 1988 did Cardinal Tomasek secure permission to import 100,000 copies of the Bible and 10,000 copies of the Breviary – the first to appear in Czech since the Second Vatican Council. In Romania, there were no new prayer books or catechisms until 1976, and it was only in 1980 that 10,000 copies of the New Testament in Romanian were allowed into the country. The high price of the Bible acted as a disincentive, and the priest – the only person who could distribute the Bible legally – had to inform his superiors of the identity of every

349

individual purchasing one. In Bulgaria, the first Bible to be published since the Second World War did not appear until 1983, in a print-run of 28,000 copies. There is no Belorussian Bible. In Lithuania, the Old Testament was almost unavailable even to the clergy.

The liturgical reforms of the Second Vatican Council – including the use of the vernacular and the new liturgy of the word – provided excellent opportunities for teaching the faith. Christian instruction could now be carried out legally during preparation for the sacraments in the context of the Mass.

In Romania, the state authorities tried to use liturgical reform to undermine the unity of the country's Catholic Church. The authorities fomented disunity among three major national groups of Catholics – Romanians, Hungarians and Germans – by favouring first one group and then the other.

Although the authorities did not make it so, the use of the vernacular for Mass proved to be a controversial issue in the Soviet Union, especially outside the Baltic Republics. Many mixed Catholic communities, consisting of various nationalities, feared that reform would mean the inevitable use of the Russian language, and in consequence would be an unexpected bonus for the Soviet authorities in their campaign of Russification among national minorities.

In Poland, liturgical reform was introduced – under Cardinal Wyszynski's deliberate guidance – only in slow stages. The new conciliar Polish missal was not finally introduced in churches until 1987.

Another factor in the slow introduction of the new post-conciliar liturgy in the various countries of Eastern Europe was the lack of new liturgical books. In Lithuania, only five volumes of new texts were published. None were published elsewhere in the Soviet Union. Not surprisingly, in some churches, part of the Mass is still said in Latin, and there are many churches in the USSR where the priest does not face the people during the Mass.

In Bulgaria, it took Bishop Simeon Kokov ten years to translate ten volumes of liturgical books. However, the Bulgarian state authorities refused the Church permission to publish the new liturgical texts and they circulated in cyclostyled form. In 1988 the Church was finally allowed to bring into the country copies of liturgical texts published in Bulgarian in Rome, and to import 200 Eastern-rite liturgical books.

In Czechoslovakia, from 1965 provisional translations were used, then in 1969 the final texts of parts of the Mass were published. Between 1970 and 1973 the remaining liturgical texts appeared in duplicated form. The whole missal in Czech was not printed until 1985, and even then in Rome.

In Hungary, the vernacular was gradually and without controversy introduced into the liturgy. The Hungarian missal was published in 1965, and from the following year Mass was celebrated in the vernacular. The Eucharistic prayer in Hungarian was introduced in 1968.

THE LAITY AND ECUMENISM

Deep historical divisions have worked against interdenominational relations in all Eastern European countries. The existing divisions were merely sharpened where the secular authorities actively pursued policies of setting one denomination against another while officially promoting ecumenism through state-sponsored Church leaders. The authorities' policies inspired fears that ecumenism was no more than a government ploy to encourage the Church to neglect local concerns in favour of prestigious international contacts.

Nevertheless, in all Eastern European countries ecumenism has made some progress. In Poland, 'Christian Unity Weeks' have been organized annually, an ecumenical institute has been established at the Catholic University of Lublin, and ecumenism was introduced as a separate degree course at the Catholic Theological Academy in Warsaw.

In some places the existence of a perceived 'common adversary' seems to have brought believers of different denominations together. In Lithuania, the Catholic Committee for the Defence of Believers' Rights spoke on a number of occasions on behalf of non-Catholic Christian victims of persecution, while Russian Orthodox dissidents have assisted Catholic activists in meeting the Western press. There are many accounts of truly ecumenical personal relationships between East European Church leaders, parish priests and ministers. In Hungary, it is within the basis community movement that the spirit of ecumenism has been strongest. In the GDR, Protestants and Catholics often acquire land jointly in new housing areas, many joint non-sacramental services are performed, and isolated Catholic people in villages are sometimes given pastoral care by the local Protestant pastor.

In Poland, the German Democratic Republic and Yugoslavia, entrance to seminary remained outside the control of the state. In other Eastern European countries the number and selection of students was state controlled. In Bulgaria, there is still no seminary at all, though since 1988 the authorities have sanctioned the ordination of three priests annually. In Czechoslovakia, lecturers at the two Roman Catholic seminaries permitted by the communist authorities were selected by the state from members of *Pacem in Terris,* an association of clergy close to the regime and proscribed by the Vatican. Moreover, in all Eastern European countries outside Poland, the GDR and Yugoslavia, all priests needed a state 'licence' to perform their pastoral duties, and in most Eastern European countries there were restrictions on a priest performing any religious function outside his prescribed parish, including saying Mass or hearing confession.

Considering the severe shortage of priests (apart from in Poland and the GDR) and the fact that monastic orders had been dissolved in many Eastern European countries, the Decreee on the Apostolate of the Laity was particularly relevant to Eastern Europe. In Hungary, a programme for licensed lay men to perform pastoral services was approved by the Church and the state. It has not been a great success, a result largely of opposition from the ranks of the older clergy. There were in fact substantial reasons why the decree was greeted with caution by some Eastern European bishops and clergy. According to Soviet legislation on religion, 'parish councils' were made responsible for the activities of 'religious associations' at the local level. In the 1960s, their role became even more prominent while the priest was reduced to the status of an employee of the parish. These 'parish councils', often

351

infiltrated by local Party activists, became over the years a very useful tool which the state could use to put pressure on the Church.

There were other factors that slowed down the active involvement of the laity in Church life. Until the late 1980s, no Catholic lay associations could exist officially in Eastern Europe. Only in Poland did the authorities sanction the existence of five Intellectuals' Clubs formed in 1956. Moreover, in some countries, for example the Soviet Union and Bulgaria, the decree on the missionary activity of the Church came into direct conflict with legislation that permits anti-religious propaganda, but prohibits the canvassing of any belief that conflicts with the state's official Marxist–Leninist ideology.

In the GDR, with Vatican approval, the authorities did allow married men to hold services in isolated places. These services consisted of the Liturgy of the Word and the distribution of Communion. Permission for this was first given in 1965. By 1979 there were about 500 of these lay assistants. Thus a lay ministry sprung up with special responsibility for the pastoral care of the old and chronically sick, as well as for residents of new housing estates. It was also thanks to the massive involvement of the laity that an impressive programme of Christian education, commended by the Vatican, has been developed in the GDR in the last twenty years. 'Religious Children's Weeks' are organized regularly for schoolchildren, as are 'Happy Hours given to the Lord' for the pre-school age group.

The 1970s saw mounting frustration within the Churches of Eastern Europe about the many restrictions imposed by the authorities. Believers began to act on the belief that they should organize their religious life without asking or informing the authorities. Conciliar renewal movements have taken root in a number of Eastern European countries. It is in Poland that such movements have been most widespread, the most important being the 'Light-Life' renewal movement. 'Light-Life', which Pope John Paul II described as 'the ecclesiology of the Second Vatican Council translated into action', has been undoubtedly one of the most dynamic and complex renewal movements to appear in the universal Church. Such movements in Poland have attracted an increasing number of people, especially the young, disillusioned with the state ideology and searching for alternative sources of meaning in life. Some 500,000 young Poles have received Christian instruction within the Light-Life movement alone, and have been affected by its brand of 'Polish Theology of Liberation in the Spirit', formulated by the movement's leader, Fr Franciszek Blachnicki. By the end of the 1970s in Poland, 'illegal' churches were being constructed without the state's permission, 'Believers' Self-Defence Committees' were being set up, unofficial religious literature (*samizdat*) was being produced, and informal discussion groups, as well as Weeks of Christian Culture and academic courses, were being organized with the full backing of the clergy and Polish bishops.

In Lithuania too, an increasingly active laity felt itself obliged to defend the Church, at considerable personal sacrifice, against moral and physical attacks by the authorities. Both the Committee for the Defence of Believers' Rights and the *Chronicle of the Lithuanian Catholic Church*, published in *samizdat* since 1972, were the result of close co-operation between clergy and laity.

The religious *samizdat* which sprang up in Czechoslovakia in the mid-1970s – often produced by lay-people – was of a quantity and quality unequalled in Eastern Europe. Between 1977 and 1981 alone, 700 titles were published. The works of writers and theologians banned by the state have been printed as well as translations of foreign literature. The circulation of the monthly *Informace o Cirkvi* (Information about the Church) with a counterpart published independently in Slovakia, and of *Teologicke Texty* (Theological Texts) – an invaluable quarterly for the clergy and educated laity – is larger than that of all secular *samizdat* in Czechoslavakia put together.

In Hungary, given new impetus by the Council's decisions, the dynamic 'small group' movement has experienced considerable development, spreading the conciliar vision of the Church. There are between 4,000 and 6,000 'basis groups' in Hungary, mainly in urban areas, involving some 100 priests and 60,000 to 100,000 lay people. None of them were systematically encouraged by the hierarchy until the 1980s. One basis group, 'the Bush' led by the charismatic Fr Gyorgy Bulanyi, with 2,000 members and over 100 groups, has been rejected outright by the Hungarian bishops because of his advocacy of pacifism, his vision of a new Church order, his emphasis on individual conscience, and his definition of the priesthood. In the early 1980s several priests belonging to the movement were suspended or banished to remote parishes by the hierarchy. Seminarians were refused ordination unless they left the movement, and in 1982 Fr Bulanyi himself was placed under a *suspensio a divinis*. The Vatican did not come down unequivocally on either side until 1987 when it condemned some of Bulanyi's views.

On 16 October 1978, Cardinal Wojtyla of Krakow was elected pope, taking the name of John Paul II. The impact of his election on Eastern Europe cannot be overestimated. It was seen by Catholic Poles as God's reward to the Polish nation for its faithfulness to Christ and his Church. The election of a pope from Poland gave an enormous morale boost to the Catholics in all Eastern European countries and increased their self-confidence. It also gave fresh hope to a region which, until then, had often felt misunderstood and even forsaken by the Vatican.

In June 1979, John Paul II made his first pilgrimage to his native country. The pope's speeches to his countrymen stressed human dignity derived from man's unique relationship with God – a direct challenge to Marxism. He left Poles with a clear message: 'the future of Poland depends on how many people are mature enough to be non-conformists'. Ten months after his visit the 'Solidarity' movement was born. Solidarity was not simply a free trade union with over 10 million members. A central part of its message was a return to Christian values.

THE RETREAT OF COMMUNISM

With Solidarity, the Roman Catholic Church in Poland entered a golden age. Religious expression, which had largely been suppressed for so many years, bubbled up in joyful and spontaneous ways. The imposition of martial law on 13 December 1981 halted the process of democratization of the system.

Solidarity went temporarily underground. Nevertheless, the ideals lived on. Outside Poland they were defended and propagated world-wide by John Paul II. In Poland, a new theology of inner freedom was taking root, especially after its best-known exponent and propagator, Fr Jerzy Popieluszko, was murdered by members of the Security Forces in October 1984. Fr Popieluszko was quickly adopted by Poles as a martyr for the truth and as an example to follow. Fr Popieluszko's teaching and example gained the papal seal of approval in 1987 when, during his third visit to Poland, John Paul II made a special pilgrimage to the grave of the murdered priest. The failure of the government's 'ideological verification' campaign of 1985 was symptomatic of the collapse of the political system which led to the fall of the communist government in 1989.

In May 1989 – shortly before the departure from office of the communist government – the Polish Parliament ratified three decrees regulating relations between Church and state. For the first time, the communist state granted the Church legal status. In practice, this meant that the Church no longer required permission for new buildings, and that it could set up its own enterprises, hospitals, schools, publishing houses, TV and radio networks and other institutions. The second decree guaranteed the equality of all citizens regardless of their beliefs, thus ending discrimination against Catholics in public life. The third decree included all clergy in the national system of social benefits. In August 1989, a non-communist and devout Catholic, Tadeusz Mazowiecki, became the first non-communist prime minister of Poland since the communist takeover. For the first time since the 1940s, a government in Eastern Europe ceased to be a monopoly of atheists.

In other parts of Eastern Europe hardline communism was losing its grip. The loosening of ideological control from Moscow affected every country. Gorbachev's example of *glasnost* combined with his avowed policy of non-interference in the internal affairs of the Soviet Union's East European allies were major contributing factors in the rapid collapse of the totalitarian system. The process of *perestroika* begun by President Gorbachev in the USSR aroused new hope among religious believers throughout Eastern Europe.

In the USSR the Catholic Church benefited in various ways from *glasnost* and *perestroika*. Catholic prisoners of conscience, mainly from Lithuania and Ukraine, were all released after 1987. The two exiled Lithuanian bishops were allowed to return to their dioceses. A number of well-known church buildings, confiscated by the state in past years, were returned to Lithuanian Catholics. The most famous of these was Vilnius Cathedral, formerly used as a storehouse and art gallery. It was returned to religious use at a service attended by at least 10,000 Catholics. The Soviet authorities allowed publication to begin of two official Catholic journals – *Kataliku Pasaulis* (Catholic World) in Lithuania, and *Katolu Dzeive* (Catholic Life) in Latvia. The new social and political movements that developed in Latvia and Lithuania after 1986 established links with the Churches – in Lithuania with the Catholic Church in particular – and supported the calls of religious leaders for changes in the Soviet law to legalize religious instruction for children and charitable activity by the churches. An amendment to the Lithuanian constitution, adopted in 1989, granted legal status to the Church for the first time under Soviet rule.

Under *glasnost* members of the banned Ukrainian Catholic Church began a public campaign for legalization, and bishops and priests openly declared their allegiance to the Church. A breakthrough was achieved in December 1989 when the government's Council for Religious Affairs in Kiev declared that their formerly clandestine parishes could register with the authorities and function openly. Registration by hundreds of such parishes was accompanied by the reoccupation of church buildings, which since 1946 had either been in the hands of the Russian Orthodox Church or were closed down.

In February 1989 in Prague Cathedral, Cardinal Tomasek celebrated a Mass in which the superiors of six monastic orders participated. Monks, who were wearing their habits for the first time since 1950, turned to the cardinal, requesting him to press the authorities to recognize the existence of monastic orders in Czechoslovakia. Only one year before, Cardinal Tomasek had endorsed a 31-point petition for greater religious freedom drawn up by lay Catholics and signed by 600,000 people. A few months later he reiterated in a pastoral letter his belief in the importance of the laity. 'For years little has been said of the responsibility of the laity for the Church. I was called a general without troops. It is important that you [believers] do speak out.' He also urged: 'Do not be afraid to live a religious life in the spirit of the Second Vatican Council both inside and outside the Church.' The new government with a non-communist majority, which came to power in December 1989, abandoned Marxism–Leninism. It moved fast to loosen the tight restrictions on religious activity. Agreement was soon reached with the Vatican on filling vacant dioceses, permission was granted for three new seminaries, and religious instruction could again take place on church premises. New laws on the churches – which would end the requirement for clergy to hold a state licence – began the drafting stage. The priests' movement *Pacem in Terris*, closely linked to the old regime, announced its dissolution in December 1989.

In Hungary, the State Office for Church Affairs, which had been the Communist Party's main instrument for controlling religious life since the Stalinist era, was dissolved on 1 July 1989. The abolition of the Office symbolized the government's declared aim of abandoning the struggle against religion and interference in the internal affairs of the churches. Within the Communist Party – later renamed the Socialist Party – atheism was no longer a prerequisite for membership.

The GDR, Bulgaria and Romania all experienced popular unrest in 1989, which led to the fall of hardline communist regimes. In the GDR and Bulgaria, new governments promised free elections and moved to lift political restrictions. In Romania, the Ceausescu regime was overthrown and a new National Salvation Front of ex-communists and non-communists took power.

The GDR Catholic Church had already become more outspoken on political topics before the fall of the old regime, following the government's moves against a Protestant group in a Berlin church in November 1987 and the rise of social unrest. The readiness to speak out was intensified after the transfer of Cardinal Meisner from Berlin and his replacement with Georg Sterzinsky. A last-ditch communist attempt to reassert atheism, through a 'League of Freethinkers', fizzled out.

The new governments of Bulgaria and Romania immediately promised religious freedom, together with social and political reform. In Bulgaria new laws were proposed. In Romania the government revoked the 1948 decree banning the Eastern-rite Catholic Church.

The year 1989 proved a turning point in relations between Eastern European governments and the Catholic Church. New governments not controlled by communists ended the forty-year-old domination of the Church imposed by their communist predecessors. In the Soviet Union, new legislation, long delayed, was intended to govern future Church–state relations, including some degree of government control. Other governments abandoned their policy of interference and confined themselves to a purely administrative monitoring of Church affairs within another ministry, such as culture or education. Only Albania remained committed to atheism.

12E Eastern Europe: Bibliography

Alexander, S. (1979) *Church and State in Yugoslavia since 1945*. Cambridge University Press.

Andras, E. and Movel, J. (1983) *Church in Transition: Hungary's Catholic Church from 1945 to 1962*. Vienna, The Hungarian Institute for the Sociology of Religion.

Beeson, T. (1982) *Discretion and Valour*, 2nd ed. London, Collins.

Bourdeaux, M. (1979) *Land of Crosses*. Chulmleigh, Devon, Augustine Publishing Co.

Brown, J. (1988) *Conscience and Captivity: Religion in Eastern Europe*. Washington, DC, Ethics and Public Policy Center.

Dunn, D. (1979) *Detente and Papal-Communist Relations 1962–1978*. Boulder, CO, Westview Press.

Eibner, J. (1989) 'A New Deal in Hungary', *The Tablet*, 11 March, pp. 272–3.

Knauft, W. (1980) *Katholische Kirche in der DDR (Gemeinden in der Bewahrung 1945–80)*. Mainz, Grunewald.

Krzeminski, I. (1986) 'Solidarity – the meaning of the experience. A sociological survey', *Religion in Communist Lands*, vol. 14, no. 1, pp. 4–16.

Krzeminski, I. (1985), 'Czechoslovakia: The Church at the Crossroads', *Religion in Communist Lands*, vol. 13, no. 3, pp. 250–60.

Luxmoore, J. (1987) 'The Polish Church under Martial Law', *Religion in Communist Lands*, vol. 15, no. 2, pp. 124–66.

Polgar, S. (1964) 'A Summary of the Situation of the Hungarian Catholic Church', *Religion in Communist Lands*, vol. 12, no. 1, pp. 11–41.

Walters, P. (1988) *World Christianity: Eastern Europe*. Eastbourne, MARC.

Wildmann, J. (1986) 'Hungary: from the Ruling Church to the Church of the People', *Religion in Communist Lands*. vol. 14, no. 2, pp. 160–79.

12F Western Europe

JAN KERKHOFS sj

European society has changed greatly since 1965: automation, new systems of communication, popular tourism, the socialization of education and culture. Many people are experiencing the effects of a dual economy, of unemployment, of pollution, drugs, terrorism and AIDS. The general trend towards urbanization continues, and the number of farmers has shrunk even further. Twelve states are preparing for economic integration in 1992. Meanwhile, a mutation has taken place in family life. *Humanae Vitae* (1968) notwithstanding, even in 'Catholic' countries (with the exception of Ireland) the birth rate, in general, remains below replacement level. Divorce is on the increase, while many people do not even marry at all – though the family still scores very high in the opinion polls.

According to the survey carried out by the European Value Systems Study Group (EVSSG) in 1981–2, 54 per cent of Western Europeans claim to be Roman Catholic, 31 per cent belong to the Protestant or Free Churches, 2 per cent say they are members of other religions, while 12 per cent claim to have no religion. Only 5 per cent say that they are convinced atheists. In Europe as a whole, Sunday church-going has decreased – often drastically. People's relationship to the Church has weakened, and this has been true to a greater extent among women than among men, although the latter tends to be less 'religious' in any case.

Table 1 People with 'No-religion' according to country (*percentage*)

(FR=France; NL=Netherlands; B=Belgium; SP=Spain; UK=United Kingdom; FRG=Federal Republic of Germany; IT=Italy; DK=Denmark; IR=Ireland)

	FR	NL	B	SP	UK	FRG	IT	DK	IR
Age group									
18–24	38	47	24	15	14	9	9	6	2
25–34	45	45	16	19	10	15	12	9	2
55–64	16	26	13	5	4	8	4	4	1

The 'New Age' is spreading among the urban population who are searching for new forms of religiosity, and the influence of sects reaches even into the countryside. Whereas Marxism is on the decline, Muslims have never been so numerous. Public opinion is characterized by pluralism of ideologies and of lifestyles, and tolerance of widely divergent moral attitudes (with regard to abortion, euthanasia, homosexuality, etc.).

Between 1965 and 1990, there were many changes in the *Zeitgeist*, changes that were not foreseen, or that had been underestimated by the fathers of the Council. Whereas *Gaudium et Spes* hinted optimistically at a reading of the 'signs of the times', this reading has become increasingly complex. Science is looked at more critically (by ecologists, for example). Neo-liberalism and the all-pervading power of economics contrast with new forms of poverty. Meanwhile, thousands of small groups and some influential new movements (e.g. Amnesty International) or *movimenti* (such as Comunione e Liberazione) have built up national and international networks. The concern for peace and human rights has become part of public opinion as never before.

In this context of the new tensions between individualism and solidarity, the local churches are trying to put into practice the spirit of the Council. Probably the most striking feature of this short, post-conciliar period is the role of the laity in shaping the Church-to-be. Never since the late Middle Ages have these churches been expressing their synodal nature so strongly.

THE SYNODAL MOVEMENT

The deep need to apply the orientations of the Council at the local level was felt immediately after Vatican II. Often this feeling was nation-wide, especially in the northern, more Germanic parts of Europe. The first main impetus came from the Netherlands, where for the first time since the Reformation Catholics became aware of their position as a majority. Already during the last session of the Council, the Dutch bishops had sent a letter to their flock in which they announced a 'provincial council', which they later, in 1966, baptized a 'Pastoral Council of the Dutch Ecclesiastical Province'. Cardinal Alfrink provided the general orientation: 'We are a Church on the move, and in that movement we desire to follow the Lord.' In his opening address (January 1968), he stressed the need for participation. 'We envisage that from these common exchanges will result the governing style which the Church requires today.' The episcopate was clearly championing a model of authority centred on the concept of collegiality, involving priests and laity. Typically, the final documents concentrate on: authority; mission and development work; ethics, family and youth; the practice of the faith in a secularized world; religious life and ministry; evangelization; ecumenism; Jewish–Christian relationships; and peace. Celibacy was one of the burning issues. At the end of the Pastoral Council (1970), it was decided to set up a permanent National Pastoral Council. This proposal, however, was rejected by the Vatican Congregation for the Clergy in 1972. The bishops had to give in and opted for the formula of a loose 'National Pastoral Consultation' which did not even meet once a year. In the meantime, Rome managed to split the once homogeneous episcopal conference by appointing conservative bishops. After the special Dutch Synod in Rome (1980), which dealt mainly with the distinction between priests and the lay ministry, the faithful became increasingly polarized, with a small group looking for strong leadership, while the majority wished for real participation.

While the Dutch held their conciliar meetings, the Danes had already held their own 'Diocesan Synod' (1969) covering the whole country. At this Synod, too, the laity were in the majority, and here, also, community life and co-responsibility were stressed, as well as a serious commitment to ecumenism. The creation of personal parishes, in addition to territorial ones, was accepted in principle. A more open approach to issues such as optional celibacy, mixed marriages, allowing remarried divorcees to receive the sacraments in certain cases, and, shortly after *Humanae Vitae*, family planning, received strong majority support. For many years, the Holy See failed to react officially to the synodal requests of this small Nordic Church.

Meanwhile, in the Federal Republic of Germany, a vast operational machine was preparing the most important national synod in Europe. Thanks largely to the impetus of the German Catholic youth organizations, and stimulated by the Dutch initiative and the diocesan Synod of Hildesheim (1968), the Bishops' Conference decided, in 1969, to hold a national synod which would follow the canonical rules (*inter alia*, involving a majority of clergy – 164 – in comparison with 153 laity). The Bishops' Conference of the German Democratic Republic, in turn, decided to hold its synod at the same time. In preparation for the synod in the Federal Republic, several public opinion polls were held, and these revealed, primarily, the need for a deepening and up-dating of the faith. The synod therefore intended to 'apply, in Germany, the decisions of Vatican II' (Cardinal Döpfner). Ten commissions prepared working documents on: faith; liturgy; Christian diaconia; marriage and the family; social action; pastoral structure; ministries and charisms; forms of co-responsibility; education; and ecumenical and international collaboration. Between 1971 and 1975 eight sessions were held in the cathedral of Würzburg. The climate was one of high optimism (particularly with regard to ecumenism), but there was also deep disappointment (regarding *Humanae Vitae*, the problem of remarried divorcees, and the bishops' refusal to discuss the ordination of married men). This vast amount of work resulted in an impressive volume entitled *Gemeinsame Synode der Bistümer in der Bundesrepublik Deutschland, Beschlüsse der Vollversammlung*, 1976, considered by many as an improvement on a number of the Vatican II texts.

In 1975, too, the synod of Dresden (German Democratic Republic) came to an end. In the particular context of persecution, the discussions focused on deepening the experience of the faith in the scattered communities of a Church in diaspora, and its strengthening by catechetics within the family.

In the same period (1972–5), Austria and Switzerland held their synods, but using a different method, and with much greater success in the latter country. The main work was done at the diocesan level. In Austria, no real national synod took place; indeed, in two dioceses (Eisenstadt and Feldkirch) it was impossible to organize even diocesan synods. Unlike Germany, no efforts were made to mobilize the media. Nevertheless, in Austria, largely thanks to the dynamism of the archdiocese of Vienna, an overall synodal process took care of the much-needed cross-fertilization between the dioceses. The cautious attitude of the bishops met with widespread apathy among the faithful. When the delegates finally did agree upon a series of proposals, the bishops refused to endorse anything which, in their opinion, deviated too much from tradition.

The synod in Switzerland, on the contrary, was firmly rooted in the Swiss context of democracy and regionalism. The debates were preceded by broad consultation and the media were actively involved. Meetings were held on the diocesan level (on seven occasions), at the level of the linguistic communities, and at the national level. The final session was celebrated on the same day, 30 November 1975, in the cathedrals of the seven dioceses. Thus the Swiss achieved unity in diversity. In a very balanced way all the matters mentioned in respect of the Dutch, Danish and German synods were debated openly. Courageous final votes were taken. Here Vatican II was really in dialogue with the local culture. As in Holland, the bishops tried to ensure follow-up by creating a permanent 'Interdiocesan Pastoral Forum' – but this too was rejected by the Vatican. The bishops had to make do with occasional consultations. These were held in 1978, 1981 and 1983, and dealt mainly with the problems of ecclesial communities and ministries. Once again, Rome's fear of a revival of nationalism and autonomy discouraged post-conciliar enthusiasm.

Like Denmark, Luxemburg is also covered by one single diocese. In 1971, a diocesan synod, preceded by a wide public opinion poll, resulted in the setting up of a permanent Diocesan Pastoral Council. The need for socio-political commitment among the faithful was particularly stressed.

In two other countries nationwide 'pastoral consultations' were held, but they differed both in method and in impact. In 1977, the National Conference of Priests in England and Wales proposed that a national pastoral meeting be held in Liverpool in 1980, and this idea was accepted by the bishops. The preparatory documents were discussed widely, and over 100,000 people sent replies. Cardinal Hume, who gave the whole enterprise his full backing, wrote:

> For the first time the whole Church – bishops, priests, religious and lay people – has been asked to take stock of its life and work, to deepen and renew its prayer and spirituality, and then to suggest a way forward for the future. Nothing like this has ever been attempted before in England and Wales.

More than 2,000 delegates gathered at the National Pastoral Congress. They had prepared recommendations for pastoral options and strategies, while the bishops promised to take them seriously. The central idea was the Church as people of God, with a focus on co-responsibility, parishes as a communion of communities, liturgical renewal and – in certain cases – Eucharistic hospitality, ecumenism, and regular in-service training of priests. There was more positive teaching on sexuality, and a re-examination of the Church's teaching on contraception and the remarriage of those who were divorced; the diaconate for women; and serious consideration of the ordination of married men. A renewal of methods of evangelization and a greater commitment on behalf of Justice and Peace were also recommended. Some two months later, most, though not all, of the recommendations were accepted by the bishops in their message, *The Easter People*.

Finally, in Belgium, the five Flemish dioceses have had a permanent 'Interdiocesan Pastoral Consultation' since 1970. It is a body that is unique in Europe, with about 125 elected members, and meets three times a year in the presence of the bishops. The statements and the recommendations of this Consultation have covered all the issues dealt with in the aforementioned synods. Before each Roman Synod of Bishops, this 'Consultation' prepares its own list of recommendations for the Belgian bishop-delegate.

In most of these countries, in the mid-1980s, meetings of former members of synods, consultations, as well as publications made evaluations of the huge investment involved. With few exceptions, the general tone was one of disappointment, mainly with regard to the attitude of the Holy See, which had dismissed most of the recommendations addressed to Rome. In a climate often described as one of 'restoration', the previous commitment often turned into a feeling of resignation, while many people have come to expect more from engagement in small communities or from initiatives within their own dioceses than from structural change. Moreover, many newly appointed bishops are facing, or are causing, polarization, while the number of priests is rapidly shrinking.

While Northern Europe was involved to a greater extent in national synods than the Latin countries, a number of diocesan synods (e.g. Rome, 1988) or sometimes regional ones, as for example in several parts of Spain, tried to bring the spirit of Vatican II nearer home. In France, in particular, these new models of participation had, at first, to cope with the tension between the working class and those of more middle-class backgrounds, with the latter claiming that they were underrepresented. Since 1985, however, the number of synods has increased rapidly (in 1988, more than twenty dioceses were holding or preparing to hold a synod). The polarization between those who are traditional and those who are more progressive has, on occasion, had a restraining influence, as has the spectre of Archbishop Lefebvre and his followers.

In Spain, too, several diocesan or regional synods were organized, without, however, influencing the situation at the national level to any great extent. In Italy, some dioceses organized diocesan synods (e.g. Bolzano, Ivrea, etc.), but the real revelations of participation in the Church in Italy were the two national *convegni*, one on 'Evangelization and Human Promotion' (Rome, 1976) and the other – with 2,000 participants, including Pope John Paul II – on 'Christian Reconciliation and the Human Community' (Loretto, 1985). Though both meetings gave only general guidelines, they revealed a serious polarization in the Italian Church, mainly with regard to models for Christian involvement in politics (cf. the older Catholic Action movements which stressed dialogue in a pluralistic society versus the new *movimenti* with their Church-centredness).

In all these synods, as in the dynamic synod of the diocese of Rottenburg (1987), delegates were conscious of the growing minority status of Christian believers in Western society, and of the dramatic consequences of the shortage of priests and religious. They acknowledged the need for warmer and more lively communities, for more open relations between clergy and laity, for new forms of lay ministries and ordained ministry, and for a more creative approach to the evangelization of the modern world. The dialectic between the longing for more democratic procedures (with the acceptance of a great variety of charisms and models of organization) and the need for coherence of the 'little flock' around the bishop were accepted as a challenge and a cross. But the willingness to participate was overwhelming. In the French diocese of Le Mans, for example, 650 teams prepared the synod of 1988 over a period of two years, which enabled Bishop Gilson to declare: 'Since the Council we have continued to repeat that the Church is a people. Through uninterrupted sowing, we finally reap the harvest.' Out of 200,000 baptized Catholics, 25,000 participated in the election of 350 members of the synod. The laity were in the majority, and the ninety priests were chosen by their peers. There were equal numbers of men and women delegates, and fifty delegates had to come from the 16–25 age group. Here, as in many other places, the particular Church is becoming a reality. At the same time, at the grassroot level the previous model of the monarchical parish priest is disappearing.

LAY INVOLVEMENT AT PARISH LEVEL

Although the growing number of unchurched people has reduced many parish communities to small groups (in most countries Sunday church-going has decreased by 50 per cent or more since 1965), and though the number of young people who have received no religious instruction at all is appalling, probably never before have so many of the faithful been involved in catechetics, liturgy, parish councils, pastoral teams, prayer and Bible groups, pressure groups for peace and justice, etc. After Vatican II, something happened at the ground level in the Church. According to all the public opinion polls, a vast majority of practising Catholics fully endorse this evolution, as do most of the priests. Moreover, often inspired by Latin America, in Western Europe too, and in urban areas in particular, thousands of base communities are bringing the gospel nearer to daily life.

Table 2

Year	Diocesan priests	Women religious	Lay brothers	Deacons
1970	185,026	561,389	39,474	166
1986	159,682*	483,563	30,929	2,923

*Of this number, about 28,000 belong to Eastern European countries.

At the same time, however, and again at the ground level, a minority is looking back with nostalgia to the days when they could expect to receive clear guidelines 'from above'; they wish to relegate the clergy to a sacred 'separate' category; they are afraid of the political consequences of linking faith and justice, and they stress the need to return to the 'traditional' Catholic identity, with its order, its uniformity and its immutability. For many such Catholics, the pope and Our Lady are more central in their 'hierarchy of truths' than the God of Jesus Christ and the Holy Spirit. One often has the impression that these faithful, often well-organized and financially powerful though small in number, refuse the practical 'reception' of the Council with the as-yet unfinished agenda of the *aggiornamento* for which the majority is looking. In the meantime, many pastors are torn between yesterday and tomorrow, as they try to take into account the fears of the noisy minority and the desire for prophetic leadership expressed in Councils, synods, youth movements and Catholic women's organizations.

Nevertheless, parish communities are increasingly becoming aware that they have reached a point of no return. The reality of priestless parishes and ageing priests is forcing them to deepen the theology of the People of God, and to make the laity co-responsible even in the area of ministry. Though Europe still has some 50 per cent of traditional Church personnel, the decrease in the numbers of women religious and lay brothers was dramatic even before Vatican II, while after the Council, except in a few areas such as Poland, the number of priests has continued to diminish. Table 2, although it conceals the reversed pyramid of age, reveals the trend in Europe (East and West). As a consequence of this trend, many thousands of parishes in Europe have no resident priest. This is the case in France, Germany, Austria, and Switzerland in particular, and is rapidly becoming true of Belgium, the Netherlands and Great Britain also. Meanwhile, hundreds of thousands of lay people, mainly women, are involved in catechetics, assistance to the sick and the dying, and the organization of liturgical celebrations. In many theological faculties, lay students outnumber seminarians, and the percentage of women is steadily growing. These shifts are among the most significant that have taken place since the Council, and will have a major influence on the future.

In the meantime, in many countries where Catholics and Protestants coexist, ecumenism at grassroot level has changed the previous picture of more strictly separated Churches. Mixed marriages are on the increase everywhere, and often represent 30–50 per cent of marriages. In England and Wales, some 30 per cent of Catholics who married during the 1950s entered into a mixed marriage; in contrast, in the 1970s the figure was 67 per cent. In 1985, one-third of all marriages celebrated in a Catholic church in the Federal Republic of Germany involved a non-Catholic partner; in the German Democratic Republic it was over 50 per cent. This is also the case in twelve of the twenty-six cantons of Switzerland, and in most Dutch dioceses. Everywhere the need for Eucharistic hospitality is felt, and too often the children of these mixed marriages fall into a religious 'no-man's land'. Increasingly, ministers of different Churches are looking for new forms of co-operation.

In many parishes, the Pastoral Constitution *Gaudium et Spes* and often, too, a modified form of liberation theology, opened eyes to the need for a new relationship between Church and world, one that would be less self-defensive than in the previous Church–state love–hate relations. National and local Justice and Peace Commissions, or similar committees, began not only to interpret the Church's social doctrine, but also to make their own reading of the 'signs of the times' in their own particular context. Thanks to these 'conscientizers', many Catholics, for the first time in European history, became aware that they were called to defend the human rights of Christians and non-Christians in Europe, abroad, and even within the Church itself. Thus Justice and Faith became closely linked. In most countries, national episcopal agencies for overseas development aid were set up, inspired by the example of Misereor and Adveniat in Germany. Their influence in parishes and schools is immense. Not only have they channelled billions of dollars to the poorer regions of the world, they have also helped Europeans to become less self-centred in their attitude towards the Southern hemisphere. Likewise,

Pax Christi became the most influential peace movement in Europe, and indeed for many years was the only bridge between the Roman Catholic and the Russian Orthodox Churches. Chiefly due to its network, many Catholic movements have recently responded positively to the call for an ecumenical 'Conciliar Process for Justice, Peace and the Integrity of Creation'.

As a conclusion, we could agree with what the Flemish 'Christians for Europe' Foundation suggested in the hall of the European Parliament in Brussels, in the presence of the chairpersons of the Commission of Episcopal Conferences of the European Community, the European Laity Forum, and the European Conferences of Priests and Religious Superiors: 'We urgently need a Council of the Catholic Church in Europe to promote the inculturation of the Gospel in today's Europe.' Thus, twenty-five years after Vatican II, European Catholics are facing many new challenges – challenges that were not even mentioned at that Council. If politicians and economists meet together to prepare a new Europe, why should Christians not do so too?

12F Western Europe: Bibliography

Calvaruso, C., and Abbruzzese, S. (1985) *Indagine sui valori in Italia, Dai post-materialismi alla ricerca di senso*. Torino, Sei.

Coleman, J. A. (1978) *The Evolution of Dutch Catholicism 1958–1974*. Berkeley, University of California.

de França, L. (1981) *Comportamento religioso da populaçao Portuguesa*. Lisboa, Moraes ed.

Harding, S., Phillips, D., and Fogarty, M. (1986) *Contrasting Values in Western Europe, Unity, Diversity and Change*. London, Macmillan.

Hervieu-Léger, D. (1986) *Vers un nouveau christianisme?* Paris, Cerf.

Noelle-Neumann, E., and Köcher, R. (1987) *Die verletzte Nation*. Stuttgart, DVA.

König, F. and Rahner, K. eds (1983) *Europa, Horizonte der Hoffnung*. Graz, Styria.

Orizo, F. O. (1983) *España entre la apatia y el cambio social*. Madrid, Mapfre.

Pro Mundi Vita (Brussels-Louvain): Christian Country Profiles from 1962 to 1989.

Synode (1976) (Gemeinsame) der Bistümer in der Bundesrepublik Deutschland, Offizielle Gesamtausgabe, Freiburg i.Br., Herder.

Valadier, P. (1987) *L'Eglise en procès, catholicisme et société moderne*. Paris, Calmann-Lévy.

Voyé, L., Dobbelaere, K. eds (1985) *La Belgique et ses dieux*. Louvain, Cabay-Recherches sociologiques.

12G Great Britain and Ireland

V. ALAN McCLELLAND

Reflecting in 1967 upon the Second Vatican Council, Canon Bernard Pawley, the first representative of the archbishops of Canterbury and York in Rome, pointed out the remarkable difference in the commitment to Catholicism of the Latin countries on the one hand, where 'the Church is either languishing in a state of neglect or facing the active hostility of people who have forsaken it' and, on the other hand, the much stronger condition of the Church in those countries such as England and the United States, 'where the immense thrust of Irish vitality has given it a vigour which is the envy of all its neighbours' (Pawley. 1967, p. 23). Perhaps the intensity of that 'Irish vitality' goes far in explaining why the Irish experience of Vatican II has held fewer traumas and given rise to less apparent internal divisiveness than has been the case in the more varied, cosmopolitan and racially mixed minority Catholicism of some 4 million adherents in England and Wales. The homogeneity of the Catholic population in Ireland – and to a less marked degree also in Scotland – helped to smooth the path of ecclesiastical reform and adaptation, invigorated by an episcopate already closely knit together by ties of social origin and education. It is an interesting fact that of the 189 members of the Irish episcopacy functioning between 1870 and 1987, no fewer that 140 had been students at St Patrick's College, Maynooth, and that 67 per cent of the bishops had occupied academic posts there or elsewhere before their elevation. If we remind ourselves, too, that in the mid-1960s over 72 per cent of the students entering Maynooth came from centres of population of less than 1,000 inhabitants and that the majority of students in the college were sons of farmers, shopkeepers or tradesmen (a fact that exactly replicates the position appertaining in the first quarter of the nineteenth century), it becomes understandable why an unusual degree of co-operation in social and liturgical matters has been evident in the leadership of the Irish Church. This demography contrasts, for instance, with the situation in Scotland where, since 1900, the substantial majority of theological students has come from mainly urban industrial locations and from working-class families. Again, while the Church in England and Wales is often regarded as being mainly Irish in its social composition, Robert Nowell has argued convincingly that 'for the most part (its members) have become so thoroughly assimilated as to retain little positive sense of Irish identification' (Cumming and Burns, 1980, p. 24). The basic social grounding of the contemporary Irish Church is, then, decisively different from that of England, Scotland or Wales as they have developed.

In the introductory paragraphs to *Sacrosanctum Concilium* (4 December 1963), the centrality of liturgical change in the reforms engendered by the Council is emphasized. The liturgy, it was stated, 'daily builds up those who are in the Church, making of them a holy temple of the Lord, a dwelling-place for God in the spirit, to the mature measure of the fullness of Christ' (*SC* 2). In first place of attention was the liturgy of the Mass and the need to give greater

365

emphasis within it to the proclamation of the word – with all that implied in terms of vernacular usage and didactory explication. Writing in 1985, Sean MacReamoinn saw this liturgical renewal as the main success story of Vatican II in Ireland: 'The new norms have been generally well implemented and accepted,' he wrote. 'The Vernacular is taken for granted, both in Irish and English, there is little nostalgia for the "old ways", and no Latin Mass Society.' Furthermore, he declared, 'Mass attendance figures are still over-all very high and, while the quality of participation varies widely, at its weakest it compares more than favourably with pre-council days: at its best it is very impressive indeed' (Falconer, McDonagh and MacReamoinn, 1985, p. 5).

Indeed, the Irish bishops, under the dynamic leadership of the new primate, William Conway, moved swiftly in response to *Sacrosanctum Concilium*. In the same month of its promulgation, the Irish Episcopal Commission for Liturgy was appointed, assisted by five advisory committees for music, sacred art and architecture, pastoral liturgy, catechetics and translations. This was followed a year later by the establishment of the Irish Commission for Liturgy, which was to achieve much dynamism under the leadership of Joseph Cunnane, future Archbishop of Tuam. Several journals embraced the cause, not least *The Furrow, Doctrine and Life*, and *New Liturgy*. The vernacular was introduced smoothly and gradually, beginning on the first Sunday of Lent in 1965 and leading to full use of the Roman canon and new Eucharistic prayers in the vernacular on 1 December 1968. Both Irish and English versions were confirmed by Rome in the following year. In 1972, a Liturgy Centre was established in Carlow College as a diocesan enterprise. After a short spell located at Portarlington, it returned to Carlow in 1978 and became the Irish Institute for Pastoral Liturgy under the directorship of Fr Sean Swayne. The influence of this institution in conducting courses and disseminating literature was to have an enormous impact upon Irish post-conciliar life. The Irish Commission for Liturgy, also established in 1987, undertook to produce a number of specific liturgical reforms, notably in regard to the Exposition and Benediction of the Blessed Sacrament and other congregational devotions. In spite of linguistic infelicities perpetrated by the International Committee on English in the Liturgy (ICEL), under the chairmanship from 1965 to 1971 of Cardinal Gordon Gray of St Andrews and Edinburgh, in spite of the loss of rubrical control which led here and there to unauthorized liturgical experimentation, and in spite of interference with old-established forms of ritual and symbol, the changes initiated by Vatican II in Church worship were accepted in Ireland without widespread protest or complaint. The situation in England and Wales was more complex.

In a joint report in October 1984 on liturgical renewal in the British Isles (including Ireland), delivered at a meeting of national presidents and secretaries in charge of renewal at an international gathering in Rome, differences in national response were recorded. The Irish people, it was declared, had reacted 'with enthusiasm' to liturgical renewal, whereas

in England and Wales and Scotland the response was at times rather more cautious and this caution was reinforced by a somewhat legalistic application of liturgical norms. This difference is still to be seen today in that while there exist one or two minority groups in England, Wales and Scotland opposed to liturgical change, such groups are almost unknown in Ireland.

Opposition in England and Wales tended to emerge from clearly defined groups of converts, 'old Catholic families' and sections of the intelligentsia, some of whom were opposed to the loss of Latin, and others to all forms of rubrical change, or new presentations. Not all bishops, however, were as sensitive to their difficulties as Bishop Thomas Holland, the recently appointed Bishop of Salford, who pointed out in 1965 that he retained a certain sympathy for those wishing to have the option of the traditional language of liturgical celebration, and forecast that the nucleus of Latin-lovers he had encountered could well provide a strong point of resistance to the total loss of Latin in the liturgy. His plea for episcopal tolerance, indeed, might have fallen on more favourable ears if Archbishop Francis Grimshaw of Birmingham had not had to lay down the chairmanship of the Liturgy Commission of the English-speaking countries shortly before his death in 1965. His successor all too often saw virtue in uniformity, and was constitutionally disinclined to compromise on liturgical matters. The year in which George Patrick Dwyer became Archbishop of Birmingham saw the formation of the Latin Mass Society.

In the first batch of information sent to enquirers about the Society, in response to an advertisement in *The Guardian*, Hugh Byrne, one of the chief inspirers of the movement, indicated that a love of the Latin language was not to be the only reason why opposition to liturgical change was necessary. 'What is so remarkable,' he demanded, 'about the 1960s that for the first time in history the Church seems to be in the grip of an almost neurotic mania of "moving with the times" when the very reason of her being – witness the Gospels and the Imitation of Christ – is *to stand fast on fundamentals in a changing world?*' Byrne added, 'many of our clergy are hiding their timidity beneath a veneer of loyalty'. In adopting the new liturgical norms, the hierarchy was accused of acting 'unwisely and impetuously'; the Latin Mass Society was to be the focal point of loyal dissent.

Painfully sensitive to the accusation that liturgical reform was being thrust upon the Church without adequate consultation with the laity, Archbishop Heenan, shortly before his elevation to the cardinalate, prescribed that during the month of January 1965 meetings were to be held in all parishes of the Westminster diocese to enable people to give their views on changes in the liturgy. Other bishops began to follow this example. The initiative was, however, too tardy. Heenan established a diocesan liturgical commission in London in March 1965, initially composed of four diocesan clergy, four religious and four laity. He at first tried to defuse the quarrel with traditionalists by prescribing that on Sundays in churches where more than two Masses were to be offered, one had to be in Latin. He informed his clergy: 'It is our duty to follow faithfully the new instructions while treating our people with consideration.' He urged them to 'explain gently what is happening in the Church and refrain from decrying the traditional ways our people have been brought up to revere and love.'

The English and Welsh bishops, along with their Scottish and Irish counterparts, generally supported the idea of having common liturgical texts for the English-speaking countries, but Heenan informed Archbishop Dwyer (who was a vice-chairman of ICEL) that he did not believe it to be important to have the same pattern of language in England, Australia and the United States. If Heenan's view had prevailed, some of the opposition to the clinical translations over the next twenty years would have been obviated. The constant complaints by a number of bishops in both England and Scotland, as well as by members of the Latin Mass Society, was that decisions were being taken by ICEL and its officials without adequate consultation with the local churches. Heenan, indeed, was out of sympathy with the ICEL translations and what he considered to be the 'American-style' adopted. It left him with a vague impression of 'a child's reading book', to some extent because of the virtual abandonment of relative clauses in the texts. Indeed, among a number of the English bishops there was a feeling of frustration, typified by Heenan's comment in April 1969 that 'individual bishops and even the national conference of bishops have very little to do with the liturgical changes'. The experts decided, and 'we are told to implement the instructions in our own way'. Later in the same year he was able to add: 'If it depended only on Catholics in the British Isles there would be very few liturgical changes.'

The strength of minority lay reaction to liturgical change in England and Wales, a combination of dissatisfaction with the ICEL translations and a longing for the old-established form of celebration of Mass, led the Latin Mass Society in 1971 to seek the restoration of what it began to call 'the Tridentine Mass', that uniform rubric celebration laid down 'in perpetuity' by Pius V. In October of 1971, Heenan was received by Paul VI and sought a limited use of the old rite, to go some way to meeting this demand. He followed up his verbal request by a formal statement emphasizing

> the wish of many zealous Catholics – among whom are many converts – to be allowed on special occasions to use the old rite of Holy Mass. It is very difficult for them to give up the Latin Mass which they have learned to love in the old rite. Most Catholics are quite happy with the new rite but some of the older people (like some of the older priests) would be grateful if they could occasionally have the so-called Tridentine Mass after it is officially withdrawn at the end of this year.

The request was granted. The application for the concession, however, had been made without formal consultation with Heenan's episcopal confrères, and was not greeted with much enthusiasm by a number of them. Heenan's was a typically English gesture of compromise, nevertheless, and it helped to contain what could have developed into a nasty and difficult case of open defiance. Heenan himself had voted *non placet* to the Missa Normativa but, as he told a correspondent in 1970, 'I am an old-fashioned Catholic and the word of the Vicar of Christ is enough for me . . .' In that year, the Latin Mass Society formally changed its constitution to concentrate efforts upon securing the preservation of the Tridentine rite, but perhaps it is not too fanciful to see in Heenan's concession a grain of hope for the traditionalists, which ensured subsequently that few of them would flock to the standard of Archbishop Marcel Lefebvre.

In 1988, Pope John Paul II in *Ecclesia Dei* permitted the more frequent celebration of the Tridentine rite subject to the approval of local ordinaries. The bishops have been slow to respond to the papal initiative, but Cardinal Basil Hume in February 1989 permitted three weekly Sunday Masses to be offered in designated churches of his diocese, for an experimental period of six months, thus giving a lead in the implementation of *Ecclesia Dei*. At the time of writing, attendance has not indicated any great need for an increase in the number of such masses in London. The poor response made to the concessions offered by *Ecclesia Dei*, however, indicate the true level of acceptance of *Sacrosanctum Concilium* twenty-five years on. Such acceptance was emphasized in a public way by the National Pastoral Congress held in Liverpool in 1980, which called for even greater liturgical change and more uniformity in the pace of such change between dioceses, in addition to seeking a re-examination of *Humanae Vitae* and requesting a better deal for divorced Catholics.

As in Ireland, liturgical changes did not lead to organized opposition on a large scale in Scotland, a particularly remarkable fact in view of the absence of liturgical experimentation there before the Council. In 1980, as a result of a Gallup Poll commissioned by the Archbishop of Glasgow and the Bishop of Motherwell, it appeared that only some 15 per cent of the population was still yearning for the Tridentine Latin Mass, although a considerably higher proportion (56 per cent) registered disquiet at the disappearance or reduction of other traditional Catholic devotions. Weekly Mass attendance was still high at 54 per cent. The Scottish hierarchy, a more cohesive force than that of England and Wales, approached liturgical change in a gradual and, hence, more uniform way.

Maura Hyland, a teacher and catechist, writing recently on her perception of the Catholic Church in Ireland some twenty years after Vatican II, accounted for the apparent success of some of the changes induced by the Council in that country to 'rampant clericalism'. She explained

> Two factors seem to be involved. Firstly, we have a laity who for years had been trained to do as they were told, without expecting to be consulted, and without any sense of responsibilty for the decisions that were taken by others. They are, only slowly, being re-educated to take ownership of the Church, to recognise their potential, and to be aware of their duty to make their voice heard. Secondly, we have a clergy who are trained to see themselves as authority figures, running one-man shows, and are slow to face the risk of dialogue, of showing responsibility, or even of taking seriously the voice and experience of the laity. In this situation, many lay people react with anger and frustration, and many of the clergy by becoming even more authoritarian and withdrawn (Falconer, McDonagh and MacReamoinn, 1985, pp. 95–6).

This rationalization does less than justice to the efforts of the Irish hierarchy in implementing the determination arising from its Mulrany meeting in 1974 that 'the main thrust of the Irish Church over the next five years should be implementation of the principle of the involvement of the laity in the spiritual mission of the Church'. A series of perceptive articles appeared in *The Furrow* between 1978 and 1983 that indicated the nature and the enormity of the task the bishops had set for themselves. In the first of these (October 1978), the

Jesuit Michael Gallagher considered the immediate danger to the task of such renewal to be not one of unbelief, but of shallow belief affected by 'the sheer materialism' of the Irish environment, and opening up a context 'not openly at war with Christianity but in fact hostile to the survival of real faith'. The full Church on Sunday, indeed, 'could blind one not only to the growing absenteeism but to the hidden spiritual malnutrition of those present'. New support activities involving the fullest lay participation would be needed to counter these tendencies, aggravated by a growing young population and a rapid process of urbanization. In short, to Gallagher, Irish Catholics in the 1980s seemed to be 'over-sacramentalized and under-evangelized', the problem being that 'sacramental attendance is experienced by many as a matter of obedience or duty rather than as a spiritual nourishment, a meeting with the Lord'.

The seriousness of the problems associated in Ireland with rapid urbanization becomes manifest when we reflect that only some 15 per cent of Irish people are now engaged in agriculture as a full-time occupation. This indicates a potential contraction of the Church's main area of support, and will bring in its wake serious repercussions for ecclesiastical management and vocations.

The diminution of vocations to the priesthood, manifest in all countries of Western Europe since the Council, has not affected Ireland with the same intensity. This is illustrated by the fact that today there is one priest to 647 Catholics in Ireland, while the corresponding figure for Europe as a whole is one to 1,200. Decline in vocations cannot be ascribed simply to rapid industrial development and materialism; it also owes something to the ecclesiology of Vatican II which gave rise to confusion concerning the roles of priests and religious. In Ireland, the problem was least serious in the diocesan priesthood where the number of priests in 1988 was only 3 per cent fewer than in 1970, although it is apparent that the educational level of many aspirants steadily deteriorated over that period of time. At Maynooth today, only about 10 per cent of the clerical students meet the standard appropriate for degree work compared with what was a norm for acceptance a decade ago. Nevertheless, more students were accepted for Irish dioceses in 1987, for instance, than in any of the years from 1970 to 1975. If the secular priesthood in Ireland has not experienced the traumatic losses of personnel common elsewhere in Western Europe, the religious congregations have suffered more greatly. There has been a 31 per cent decline since 1970 in priests who are members of such bodies, a 44 per cent decline in brothers and 25 per cent decline in sisters. This erosion has led to a serious withdrawal from missionary endeavour abroad, and to a more gradual withdrawal from work at home in schools and colleges. One consequence of this change has been an increased participation of the laity in hitherto exclusive ecclesiastical concerns. The pattern is repeated in England and Wales where, for instance, in the decade 1977 to 1989 there was a more than 50 per cent decline in the number of women religious engaged in teaching in Catholic secondary schools, and where, since 1960, independent Catholic schools have been reduced by over a third. The Council, too, forced many orders and congregations to reconsider employing large numbers of their subjects in teaching the children of wealthy and privileged parents.

If the liturgical revival in Ireland, engendered by Vatican II, has been a success, Fr Peter Connolly has considered the sectarian conflict, which erupted in Northern Ireland five years after the Council, to have brought 'shame, discredit and scandal to the more sensitive and concerned Christian' (*The Furrow*, December 1979, p. 756). The conflict provided 'an occasion of deep soul-searching in the face of a moral dilemma of the most extreme and radical kind'. The continuing spiral of violence in Northern Ireland – and the problems that spiral has posed for episcopal leadership in the Church – has cast a deep shadow over the capacity of the Irish Church in its internal struggle for pastoral renewal. The heart of the Irish spiritual problem was analysed in the four-volume *Survey of Religious Practice, Attitudes and Beliefs* published in Dublin in 1973–4. Undertaken for the Catholic bishops of the Republic, the survey reported that

> Irish religious practice is sustained to an inadmissible extent by rule and law, social custom and a sense of duty, a framework of authority and sanction rather than by a personal commitment of mind and heart, so that such belief or faith is extremely vulnerable in a rapidly changing society.

This lack of interiorization of religious faith has persisted, while the clergy have diverted attention from it by propogating new responsibilities in social welfare schemes and third world relief. The Northern problem, however, is not one of unmitigated gloom. The scale of the social unrest has led to a number of remarkable ventures in the ecumenical field which have attempted to bridge the sectarian divide, not all of them, of course, inspired by the institutional Church *per se*: the Corrymeela Community, Protestant and Catholic Encounter, People Together, the Glencree Reconciliation Centre, the Irish School of Ecumenics in Dublin. Professor Liam Ryan has encapsulated this religious and moral dichotomy in his statement that 'the essence of religious belief in Ireland today is that conflicting values and beliefs are held by the same person. The struggle of faith goes on within people and not only between them. And as people's values and beliefs are conflicting, actual behaviour often becomes a moral compromise' (*The Furrow*, January 1983, p. 5). Perhaps the lesson to be learned from all this is that 'growth' rather than 'formation' is the necessary strategic catalyst in Ireland, a process relying less upon formal teaching agencies and more upon social interaction that turns Christian life into personal encounter.

In Scotland and in England and Wales the great emphasis placed upon the necessity of denominational schools to copper-fasten the teachings and approaches of the Council distinguishes those countries from the perceived needs of the more religiously homogeneous Catholic Ireland. The Council had re-emphasized the importance of conscience in the living of the Christian life, and had presented the tenet that the teaching programme of the Church was not simply a matter for the pope and the bishops to present the laity with a vision of the straight and narrow path that leads to salvation. But, in reality, when personal initiatives were embodied in institutional form, tensions sometimes developed. The chequered history of Corpus Christi College in London is a useful example.

The impetus for the foundation of a national catechetical centre along the lines of *Lumen Vitae* presented itself in England at the beginning of 1965, when the Provincial of the Sion Nuns approached the then Archbishop Heenan with a view to using their surplus school property in Bayswater to train qualified Catholic school teachers to assume headships of departments of religious education in Catholic secondary schools. The archbishop was enthusiastic, acted rapidly, and sought the support of his episcopal confrères. By March he had announced the establishment of a catechetical college for 120 students which would train Catholic teachers to deliver the message of Vatican II to the schools. As principal, he named Fr Hubert Richards who, along with his friends Fr Charles Davis and Fr Peter de Rosa, were at the centre of some disquiet in the diocesan seminary where Richards was teaching Scripture. An opportunity came for Davis to join the staff of the Jesuit Seminary at Heythrop, while Richards petitioned for his colleague, de Rosa, to be appointed vice-principal at Corpus Christi. Neither had school-teaching experience in a state school. The initial syllabus of studies, indeed, with its large slabs of theology and anthropology, gave early and ample evidence that the new college was not going to confine its activities to catechetical formation. Soon, indeed, it seemed to be taking on an aura of an institute of speculative theology. The college opened with only a dozen lay people, but with two dozen priests and nearly fifty nuns as students.

By April 1966, Cardinal Heenan was in receipt of a large number of complaints about the teaching at the college, and he had begun to show unease about the type of applicants being admitted, about the nature of the speculative theology being offered, and in regard to the adequacy of certain pedagogical approaches. Twelve months later, complaints were arriving at Archbishop's House and the Apostolic Delegation from bishops, priests and lay people in various parts of the country, some undoubtedly ill-founded and based upon hearsay, but others seemed to be of substance. The Apostolic Delegation asked Heenan to provide 'accurate and exhaustive information' of the position in order that a report could be sent to the Holy See. Part of the college's undoing related to a series of popular lectures given to over a thousand people in the evenings by way of an 'extra mural' programme, concerning which the Catholic Education Council had articulated anxiety. Richards argued that some people would be upset by *any* attempt at theological renewal, but by 1968, the bishops were so alarmed at the volume of complaints, that Heenan asked the Council of Major Religious Superiors to ensure that only mature priests, brothers and nuns were sent to the college. Episcopal confidence was further shaken on 2 August 1968 with the publication of a letter in *The Times* inspired from the college by the vice-principal and containing fifty-five signatures, attacking the papal encyclical *Humanae Vitae*. From that date, bishops were reluctant to send priests to study at Corpus Christi. By the autumn of 1970, in fact, not a single diocese in England, Wales or Scotland, except Westminster, had a priest there. If the college was to survive it would have to return to its original function, a matter made more urgent by the resignation and subsequent abandoning of the priesthood in 1971 of the vice-principal and another member of staff. In the summer of that year, the cardinal refused to sanction a list of visiting lecturers the principal was proposing to invite, although, as Heenan put it, 'with another type of audience these men might be admirable'. As a consequence of this act, the remaining college staff resigned, declaring to the cardinal, 'there is between us such a divergence of understanding on the nature of religious education that it would be inappropriate for us to remain as a staff in charge of your college'. The institution limped on under new management for a while before it closed in 1975. The Corpus Christi affair did more that anything else to ensure that the English penchant for caution prevailed.

The crisis of authority that arose with the publication of *Humanae Vitae* in August 1968 was not simply one arising from disappointment of raised expectations of change in the Church's teaching on contraception. It provided the key to open a Pandora's box of contextual theological issues: the understanding of natural law; the primacy of conscience; the interconnection between law and love; the nature of infallibility; the duty of obedience to the magisterium. To the signatories of the *Times* letter, the primacy of conscience was paramount and *Humanae Vitae* seemed to them to be lacking in compassion and in understanding of the modern world; it seemed out of kilter with the main thrust of the Council and an obstacle to ecumenical dialogue. On the other hand, Maurice Reidy (*The Furrow*, October 1978, p. 629) has regarded the strength of the encyclical as resting in its insistence 'on the presence of a personal and procreative dimension in what is undoubtedly a personal and procreative faculty'. In the encyclical the pope sought especially from priests 'the sincere obedience, inward as well as outward, which is due to the magisterium of the church' arising from 'the special light of the Holy Spirit' enjoyed by the pastors of the church 'in teaching the truth'. Heenan was faced with a difficult task. Although he had been pro-prefect of the final commission that had reported to the pope, he had not received advanced warning of the encyclical. He told the apostolic delegate: 'As it is we are left to repair the damage!' By September 1968, twelve priests had been censured by their bishops and more were soon to follow, opposition to *Humanae Vitae* being most vocal among those working in the provinces of Westminster and Southwark. Guidelines were drawn up by the episcopal conference to deal with priests opposing the teaching. Large-scale reprisals were likely to do harm but, on the other hand, inaction by the bishops could destroy the magisterium. Individual bishops were to interview priests who had publicly opposed the encyclical and had not withdrawn their opposition. The priests involved were to be required not to preach or teach against *Humanae Vitae*, and to declare faithfully its objective teaching in the confessional. Dissidents who persisted were to be maintained by the diocese until they found other employment. Most bishops adhered to the general norms which had been laid down, although attitudes and approaches differed in practice from place to place.

The ability of Catholic theologians to relate to non-Catholics working in the same field had been one of the arguments used by Hubert Richards at Corpus Christi College in favour of the principal's freedom of action in the devising of courses and the appointing of staff. It was the same argument that inspired the seminaries in England to build close relationships with neighbouring universities. At the height of the *Humanae Vitae* furore, Ushaw was engaged in doing so with Durham University, and Heythrop College was negotiating to become a school of London University, which it did in 1969.

In April 1965, the Jesuits had entered into a convention with the English and Welsh hierarchy to convert their main house of studies, Heythrop College, which was then situated at Chipping Norton in Oxfordshire, into an Athenaeum empowered by the Roman Congregation of Seminaries and Universities to grant Roman degrees to all qualified candidates. It was planned to establish halls of residence on a site adjacent to the college for various religious congregations and for the diocesan clergy. The expense of developing the site, however, and the dearth of vocations to the priesthood, led Cardinal Heenan and the Jesuit superiors to consider relocating the Athenaeum near to an English university with a view to securing degrees in theology from that source. Oxford, Bristol, Nottingham, Manchester and London were all considered in turn. By July 1969 the Senate of London University had agreed to admit the college (to be established in London in the former Cavendish Square College of Education) to membership, as a School in the Faculty of Theology. This was seen as a first step to full collegiate status. The development was envisaged as a major thrust forward in the education of the laity in theology and, it was thought, would make good, too, some of the deficiencies of Corpus Christi College. The move would help the cause of ecumenism if association and co-operation between theologians of different religious denominations could be facilitated. It provided a stimulus in the long term for the relocation of the Westminster diocesan seminary in London, and thus opened up a new educational dimension in priestly formation.

Perhaps the foundation of Heythrop, in the long term, has done more for the cause of ecumenism in England than some of the more overtly formal initiatives. The Augustinian Gabriel Daly and the Presbyterian Alan Falconer, in an interesting article in *Freedom to Hope?*, have wondered whether the work of ARCIC (the Anglican/Roman Catholic International Commission) has been entirely beneficial. 'The production of agreed statements,' they write, 'is indeed a necessary procedure in promoting Christian unity, but is no substitute for active dialogue at all levels in the Church.' The framers of such statements 'are a tiny minority totally dependent for the success of their labours upon the enthusiasm and industry of others in disseminating their documents. David Lapsley has called them a manifestation of "the elite discussing the exotic"' (pp. 30–1). In this statement the authors have highlighted the strengths and weaknesses of ecumenical dialogue in Ireland and Great Britain since the Council. The Agreed Statements with the Church of England have been spectacular achievements of ecumenical dialogue, as, in its way, has been the social and working relationship of Archbishop Worlock of Liverpool with his Anglican counterpart, Bishop David Sheppard. Inter-Church dialogue at grassroots level, however, has been patchy and spasmodic despite the good work of several diocesan commissions on ecumenism. Of more direct impact than the somewhat rarified work of ARCIC, has been the mutual recognition since 1967 of the rite of Christian baptism and the subsequent modification of the Catholic Church's attitude to mixed marriages, with written promises no longer being demanded of the non-Catholic partner in relation to the upbringing of children of the marriage. Anglicans have seen *Humanae Vitae* as a hindrance to unity, undoubtedly, but English Catholics have been equally concerned about the unpredictability of synodical decisions in the Church of England, and by ongoing debates on the rights of homosexual clergy, remarriage in church of divorced persons, and the ordination of women priests and bishops.

In spite of these difficulties, it is with Cardinal Hume and Archbishop Worlock, who both succeeded to their metropolitan sees in 1976, that ecumenism in England and Wales began to assume the importance envisioned by the Council. Cardinal Heenan and his fellow bishops had coped with the difficult tasks of breaking down barriers, of softening ancient prejudices, of removing misunderstandings and misgivings. The major task of those years had been with what Hume has described as 'organizational ecumenism' within a context of what Michael Jackson has called 'ecclesial parallelism'. That in itself, however, was a necessary foundation upon which to build.

The Hume years have been characterized by three seminal developments. The first, to which we have already alluded, was the National Pastoral Congress in Liverpool in 1980. In some ways, the openness and frank speaking of the delegates, their commitment to ecumenical advance and their enthusiasm for possible Roman Catholic membership of the British Council of Churches took the episcopate by surprise. The Congress was the inspiration of Archbishop Worlock, who was already giving a firm lead in ecumenical relationships by his close association with the Anglican bishop of Liverpool. That story has been told with sincerity and commitment in their joint publication: *Better Together: Christian Partnership in a Hurt City* (1988).

The second event arose directly from the invitation to Pope John Paul II, following the National Pastoral Congress, to visit England, Wales and Scotland in 1982, some three years after his journey to Ireland. The spirit of euphoria that had revitalized the Irish Church as a consequence of the pope's visit there gave an earnest of what the 1982 event might engender. When the pope came, the symbolic journey to Canterbury Cathedral, the meeting with various Church leaders that ensued, and the invitation to them to embark on further talks in Rome, established ecumenical activity upon a path from which there could be no retreat. In the common declaration that Pope John Paul II signed with Dr Runcie was the statement: 'Our aim is not limited to the union of our two Communions alone, to the exclusion of other Christians, but rather extends to the fulfilment of God's will for the visible unity of all His people.'

In the following year, the English and Welsh bishops designated ecclesiology as the focus of future ecumenical discussions, and in 1984 resolved to collaborate with the British Council of Churches in a major conference in 1987 on the nature of the Church. From this beginning, the Inter-Church Process developed, which ultimately led to the agreement at Swanwick in the autumn of 1987. Thirty-three Churches were represented, and there were participants from Scotland and Ireland. New ecumenical 'instruments' emerged, one for each of England, Wales and Scotland, and an international one for Great Britain and Ireland. The new 'instruments' would enable the development of relationships between the Churches without prejudice to the normal authority structures and decision-making processes of each participant body.

Cardinal Hume in his recent book, *Towards a Civilisation of Love*, has declared that he believes the Swanwick conference (at which he had recommended Roman Catholics to move from a situation of co-operation to one of commitment) to be 'one of those rare occasions when the Council Decree on Ecumenism took flesh and was seen to be alive and full of hope and promise'. He added: 'As Roman Catholics we cannot undertake initiatives or take decisions except in complete harmony with Peter and the Universal Church.' There could be no way forward 'in doctrinal fudge and compromise'. We hope, he wrote, 'to bring to the dialogue and the work for unity all that we are and all the richness of our intentions'. That message and model presents the ecumenical blueprint for the 1990s.

12G Great Britain and Ireland: Bibliography

(1973) *The Church 2,000: An Interim Report of the Joint Working Party set up to discuss the Preparation of a National Pastoral Strategy for England and Wales*. London, Catholic Information Services.

Cumming, J., and Burns, F., eds (1980) *The Church Now: An Inquiry into the Present State of the Catholic Church in Britain and Ireland*. London, Burns & Oates.

Daly, C. (1978) *Violence in Ireland and Christian Conscience*. Dublin, Veritas.

Falconer, A., McDonagh, E., MacReamoinn, S., eds (1985) *Freedom to Hope? The Catholic Church in Ireland Twenty Years After Vatican II*. Dublin, The Columba Press.

Hastings, A. ed. (1977) *Bishops and Writers: Aspects of the Evolution of Modern English Catholicism*. Wheathampstead, Anthony Clarke Books.

Hastings, A. (1986) *A History of English Christianity 1920–1985*. London, Collins.

Holland, T. (1989) *For Better For Worse*. Salford Diocesan Catholic Childrens' Rescue Society.

Hornsby-Smith, M., and Lee, R. (1979) *Roman Catholic Opinion: A Study of Catholics in England and Wales*. Guildford, University of Surrey.

Hornsby-Smith, M. (1987) *Roman Catholics in England: Studies in Social Structure since the Second World War*. Cambridge University Press.

Hume, B. (1988) *Towards a Civilisation of Love: Being Church in Today's World*. London, Hodder & Stoughton.

McClelland, V. A., ed. (1988) *Christian Education in a Pluralist Society*. London, Routledge.

McRoberts, D., ed. (1979) *Modern Scots Catholicism 1879–1978*. Glasgow, John S. Burns.

Pawley, B. C., ed. (1967) *The Second Vatican Council: Studies by Eight Anglican Observers*. Oxford University Press.

Worlock, D., and Sheppard, D. (1988) *Better Together: Christian Partnership in a Hurt City*. London, Penguin.

12H India and Sri Lanka

BENNY M. AGUIAR

The Second Vatican Council came to the countries of the Indian subcontinent in the first flush of their independence. Long before Europe had emerged from the Dark Ages these countries had been the home of ancient civilizations and great religions. Christianity had come to these parts early in its first millennium, but it was only after the fifteenth century that it spread beyond Kerala to other parts of India and to Sri Lanka. Unfortunately, along with the gospel message there came the veneer of a culture that tore the new converts from their roots, giving them new names, new habits and customs, even new languages. Their liturgy was the Latin liturgy, their churches were built in pseudo-Gothic or Baroque styles, their religious art, paintings and music were cheap importations from the West.

Perhaps it was the Constitution of the Church in the Modern World to which the South Asian bishops made their greatest contribution. One of the most striking speeches was made by Archbishop Angelo Fernandes of Delhi:

> While speaking of the world of our time, let us not deceive ourselves. The majority of human beings belong to the so called third world, a world composed of people undergoing profound changes, but who for the most part are weighed down by wretched poverty. In fact, many of them live in conditions unworthy of human beings, conditions which on no account should be tolerated by the human race.

One Council father after another had taken up this appeal, and it was out of this that the Commission for Justice and Peace emerged.

Apart from the chronic state of underdevelopment, after the Council ended the monsoons failed for two successive years and the rice fields lay barren and dry. So great was the drought that tribal people in the interior were living off roots and the leaves of trees. The immediate need was to feed the hungry, but if India was to avoid famine her agriculture had to be modernized.

Hearkening to the Council's call, missionaries took up pick-axe and shovel to work in the fields. Besides distributing foodstuffs, they embarked on projects for digging wells, laying roads, loaning tractors for ploughing and harvesting, providing fertilizers and pesticides, constructing godowns for storage of grain, organizing co-operatives, and making surveys for long-term projects. Aid poured in from voluntary organizations like Caritas, Catholic Relief Services, Misereor, Secours Catholique, Oxfam and Cafod.

The critical food situation gave a fillip to another of the Council's themes – ecumenism. The division among Christians had long been a scandal to non-Christians in mission countries. So when the Council gave the go-ahead, Catholics joined with Protestants in common prayers, exchanging pulpits, and singing Christmas carols on the beaches. But it was on the food front that Christians gave their best witness. Responding to the call of India's health minister, Mr Asoka Mehta, several church-related and other voluntary agencies banded together to form one service agency. AFPRO (Action for Food Production) was thus born, bringing together CRS, Caritas, Corags, The Indian Social Institute and the Council of Churches (Protestant) in India.

Closely connected with development was the problem of population. With 2 per cent of the world's land, India had 14 per cent of its population. The growth rate was 3.5 per cent; because while the death rate had slowed down, the birth rate had not diminished. Every year 11 million, or the equivalent of the population of Australia, was being added to India's population, which, by the year 2000, was feared would reach 1,000 million. All efforts to increase food supply were simply cancelled out by the growth in numbers. We have to keep running only to stand still, Mrs Gandhi declared. The only solution, as an International Conference on Population organized by the Jesuit Indian Social Institute and attended by delegates from Afghanistan, Bangladesh, India and Sri Lanka, concluded, was an integrated plan of socio-economic development that would include family planning as one of its important elements. India's government went ahead with the most drastic plans to reduce population growth by every possible means.

The Indian bishops as a whole did not share this preoccupation. When India's minister of health and family planning, Dr Sushila Nayar, asked for the 'support of religious leaders, teachers and others' to accelerate the pace of the birth-control campaign, Archbishop R. Arulappa called on Indian Catholics to organize themselves against the movement. In Kerala, Bishop Jerome Fernandes of Quilon clashed with the government adviser, Mr N.E.S. Raghavachari, saying the methods employed by the government were wicked. India's difficulties were due not to over-population, but to the government's errors in handling economic problems. Shortly before *Humanae Vitae*, India's minister for health, Mr S. Chandrashekar, went to the Vatican to meet Pope Paul VI. After the audience, the Indian embassy issued a press release that claimed the pope said he was 'examining the whole problem of population and the need for birth control'.

Monsignor Fausto Vallainc, the Holy See's press officer, quickly issued a correction. 'The Holy Father,' he said, spoke not of birth control but 'family planning in accordance with the law of God . . . . He expressed the view that the people of India constitute her true riches and that the country with careful utilization of the resources could feed a population of a thousand million.' Mr Chandrashekar's visit to the Vatican raised a furore in the Indian Parliament. When *Humanae Vitae* came out, Cardinal Gracias hailed it as 'an authentic pronouncement of the magisterium'. Catholics, he said, may not agree with the contraceptive and sterilization policies of the government. The standing committee of the Bishops' Conference directed priests, religious and laity to spread the text of the encyclical, and speak without ambiguity.

If economic development and population control constituted one side of the early post-conciliar agenda, forms of worship and the correct approach to Hindu religion and Indian culture formed the other. The first fruits of the Council were reforms in the liturgy. Vernacular replaced Latin, and the altar was brought forward to look more like a table. But the norms of adapting the liturgy to the particular genius and culture of the people have still to be applied. The Council had set the churches in Asia on the path of inculturation and dialogue, but it would quickly prove hardly less contentious an issue than that of population control.

Some progress had already been made in the field of religious art. Christian themes were being depicted in the manner of Moghul and ancient Indian paintings. In the realm of Indian dance, music and drama, Fr George Proksch SVD had achieved remarkable success. As regards philosophy and theology, there had been attempts to show Christ could be reached through a study of the Vedas and Upanishads, and philosophers like Shankaracharya and Ramanuja. As for dialogue, the Abbé Monchanin had started a contemplative monastic ashram on the banks of the Cauvery near Trichinopoly. Here he met Hindu sadhus and holy men and mingled with the common people to learn how on the mystical plane Christian beliefs like the Holy Trinity were foreshadowed in the Hindu insight of Sat-Chit-Ananda or Being, Knowledge and Bliss. He was joined later by Swami Abhishiktananda (Dom Le Saux) and Bede Griffiths.

For the mass of Catholics in India, however, Hinduism was a religion steeped in mythology, superstition and error. Any idea that non-Christian religions could possibly be ways of salvation, and that they often reflect rays of that truth that enlightens all men, was alien to their minds. If God could have spoken through non-Christian scriptures, if the relationship between Hindus and Christians was to be marked by dialogue rather than conversion, if the aim of Christian educational institutions was to make Hindus better Hindus or Muslims better Muslims, then what was the point of the vast missionary endeavour of the Church down the ages? In other words, could mission and dialogue be compatible?

Three years after the Council, a survey showed that it had made no real impact in India. Its documents were little read, and still less put into practice. The hierarchy and clergy still thought in pre-conciliar terms, and the laity sheepishly followed them. Diocesan and parish councils were rare. Where they existed, it was for matters like fund-raising, and not pastoral administration. Catholics in India, concluded the survey, had for too long lived in a ghetto to be aware of the changing reality around them.

ALL-INDIA SEMINAR

The great breakthrough seemed to come with the Church in India Seminar in Bangalore in 1969. Its purpose was to define the Church's mission in the light of the Council documents, to establish priorities for action, and get every Catholic involved in Church renewal. Preparatory seminars were held all over the country. Some 9,000 copies of a questionnaire were circulated, and background and orientation papers drawn up on the basis of the replies received. 'The thoroughgoing response and the thoroughgoing preparations,' said Raimundo Pannikar, 'allow us to hope that this time something more than an empty gesture or a cry without echo or a rhetorical attitude is going to take place.'

In his message to the seminar, Pope Paul VI had called it 'a great moment in the history of your country', and an opportunity 'to trace out the path of a great renewal of the Church in India.' When on Pentecost Sunday, 25 May

1969, the seminar ended, the 500 or so delegates broke out into thunderous applause as Cardinal Gracias hailed it as a second spring and new Pentecost.

The high point of the seminar was the resolution on rites. Ever since the synod of Diamper in the sixteenth century, when Rome attempted to bring the ancient Syrian churches in India into line with its own theology and practices, there had been mistrust and rivalry between Latins and Orientals. Churches, hospitals and colleges were built sometimes in the same street, vying with each other in splendour. Intermarriages were rare. At the preparatory seminar in Kerala, there had been a move for a merger of the three rites, the Syro-Malabar, the Syro-Malankara and the Latin, but a powerful section opposed it on the grounds that the decree on oriental churches forbade any change in their structures. The Bangalore seminar resolution did not call for an outright merger, but only for a study by a special committee of the areas where there was more than one jurisdiction to bring about a working arrangement. The hope was that as the three rites gradually Indianized, they would converge into a common Indian rite. The resolution was fiercely contested, but was passed amid great applause and acclamation, when Syro-Malankara Archbishop Mar Gregorios announced he had persuaded members of his community to accept it. 'We have awakened from a long slumber of two thousand years,' he said. 'We have to go forward hand in hand. I offer my wholehearted co-operation for the good of the Church in India.'

Another great moment was the passing of the resolution on responsible parenthood. Excitement reached fever pitch when the president of the assembly for the day, Mr George Verghese Kananthanam KSG gave up the chair to demand that the entire resolution be withdrawn. The safest guide to conscience, he said, was the Holy Father. Difficultes in following the encyclical *Humanae Vitae* could be considerably reduced by resort to the sacraments. The way to heaven was narrow, and not as wide as the resolution made it out to be. His challenge was taken up by Mr S. Santiago of the Indian Social Institute, Delhi. Natural law was not the monopoly of a single religion, he said. The views of the World Council of Churches and of international organizations should be taken into account. As heated arguments moved back and forth, Cardinal Gracias called for calm and a quiet discussion. The resolution was finally passed omitting the world 'unreliable' before 'rhythm method'. The seminar, the resolution said, appreciated the values of marriage brought out by the encyclical, but wanted to place before the Holy Father and the Synod of Bishops the many pastoral problems that had arisen in its wake: and appealed for more effective guidance to 'enable the Church to fulfil better its salvific mission'.

A novel feature of the seminar was the Indian Rite Mass. A hundred priests walked barefoot to the altar, the chief celebrant vested in a saffron shawl wrapped round his shoulders. Nuns and lay people squatted on the floor. As the priests came in, they made an 'aṅjali hasta' (a profound bow with hands joined) to the crucifix. Instead of kissing the altar, they touched it with their fingers which they then brought to their foreheads. Then followed the lighting of the seven wicks of a tall, slender brass lamp, which signified Christ the light of the world. At the offertory there was the 'aarti', the waving around of a thali or brass platter filled with fruits, a broken coconut, some joss sticks and the bread and wine. At the elevation, the celebrants prostrated themselves full length on the floor in a gesture called the 'panchanga pranama'. The sign of peace was given by placing the hands of the giver between the hands of the recipient. All these gestures were part of a package of twelve points which were approved by Rome for use as and when the episcopal conference or the local bishops thought fit. But while there was unanimous approval to adapt the liturgy to India's cultural and religious heritage, there was considerable objection to the clause 'integrating authentic forms of Indian worship'; 168 voted for and 134 against, while nearly 200 abstained.

Thus, though technically the twelve points were approved, there was considerable hesitation in accepting what seemed to many a gradual conversion of the liturgy into a poor imitation of Hindu temple worship. The decree on the missions, *Ad Gentes*, envisaged 'a more thorough adaptation' to the culture and spiritual tradition of the people covering the whole extent of life. But why, the opponents objected, should this adaptation be confined only to Hindu worship. Indian culture was a composite of many strands. Why not incorporate Muslim forms of worship as well? Moreover, could these gestures and symbols be extricated from the myths, superstitions and errors in which they were embedded? The 'aarti' was not really an offertory, but a rite for driving out evil spirits. The 'anjali hasta' or profound bow with hands joined was a salutation to human beings and lesser gods and could not replace genuflection. The mystic syllable 'OM', which was used instead of 'Amen', was Shiva's cry of joy after relations with his wife.

Controversy round the twelve points raged for many years, and took a serious turn when the All India Laity Congress, a traditionalist organization, launched a diatribe against what it called the Hinduization of the liturgy, and took Father Amalorpavadas, director of the National Biblical, Catechetical and Liturgical Centre, to court for having built a chapel with grill windows depicting the Hindu Trimurti and the Dancing Shiva. Only a few of the twelve points have been accepted in most dioceses.

Still worse was the fate of the Indian anaphora or Eucharistic prayer, which Rome at first welcomed. Composed by students and professors of the Jesuit theological faculty in Kurseong, the text used phrases and expressions resonant of the Vedas and Hindu scriptures. At a meeting of the Indian Bishops' Conference, Cardinal Parecattil endorsed it, but since the total vote fell short by one of the required two-thirds majority the proposal was lost. Rome insisted that on such an important matter, a two-thirds majority was essential. In 1975 Cardinal Knox issued an instruction forbidding the use of the Indian anaphora, the reading of non-Christian scriptures in the liturgy of the word, and unauthorized experimentation in the rites of the Mass.

A resolution of the seminar that fared slightly better was the one that encouraged the setting up of contemplative monastic ashrams. An ashram is a place of intense and sustained spiritual quest, centred round a person of deep spiritual experience, the guru. The food is vegetarian and the lifestyle simple, it is open to all who seek peace and enlightenment through yoga and meditation. Christian ashrams already existed in Shantivanam near

Trichinopoly where Bede Griffiths continued the attempts to make Monchanin's dream come true, after Abhishiktananda left for Uttarkashi in the Himalayas to live with Hindu sanyasis. At Kurisumula in the high ranges of Kerala, Francis Acharya directed an ashram combining the Cistercian pattern of life and the Antiochene Rule of the Syro-Malankara rite. As a result of the resolution, other Christian ashrams sprang up in Poona, Madras, Varanasi and elsewhere.

These ashrams became centres of an ongoing dialogue with non-Christians, especially Hindus. In Aikiya Alayam in Madras, Father Ignatius Hirudayam held monthly meetings devoted to prayer, meditation, inter-faith research and dialogue. In the live-ins at Shantivanam, participants shared their reflections on the Gospels and the Bhagavad-Gita. 'We must be humble, shedding all superiority complex in our approach to other religions . . . . In God's providence every religion has a part to play in leading men to their destiny,' said Cardinal Parecattil at the World Conference of Religions held in Cochin in November 1981. The conference was a kind of summit meeting of all the dialogue groups that had sprung up in various parts of the country on the initiative of the Dialogue Commission of the Indian Bishops' Conference. A similar experience was repeated most recently in October 1988 in Bombay, when nearly 200 Hindus, Muslims, Christians, Buddhists, Sikhs, Parsis and Jains, including a few delegates from Sri Lanka, 'lived together', and found that when confronted with each other's beliefs and spiritual practices, the normal result was most often a deepening and enrichment of one's own faith.

Another seminar that had great influence on Church renewal was the Asian Seminar on Religion and Development held in Bangalore in July–August 1973. It drew participants from several countries in Asia, including Ceylon and Bangladesh. It was conducted by Father Francois Houtart of Louvain, who had done sociological surveys of Ceylon and Kerala. Until then, development had been seen mainly as increased agricultural production through self-help projects. This seminar gave a radically new twist. Emergency relief and even long-term self-help projects now came to be regarded as a band-aid that only served to maintain the status quo. A deeper analysis of problems called for a radical transformation of the economic and political power structures.

In Ceylon and Kerala, Father Houtart had found a striking similarity with Latin America: a dualistic type of society, a minority group monopolizing power, culture and economic consumption. A social analysis of the Indian situation revealed that the top 10 per cent spent 30 per cent of the country's income, while the bottom 10 per cent spent only 2 per cent. The rich were getting richer and the poor poorer. Caste differences reinforced class discrimination. Religion in the past had often played the role of 'legitimizer' of the power structure. The task of the Church now was to disengage from the feudal ruling groups, the capitalist forces and structures, and identify herself with the struggle of the oppressed.

Reactions to this new approach were predictable. One bishop denounced it as simplistic, materialistic and Marxist. Another wondered why suddenly now there was talk of oppressors and oppressed. But the leaven began to spread. Jesuits in Bihar and Maharashtra were shocked at the physical and mental serfdom of the tribals and the low castes among whom they worked and took up the struggle against bonded labour. They broke the hold of money-lenders who had cheated the tribals of their land and of the fruits of their labour. In Bombay, the Jesuits carried out an evaluation of their institutions, found they were catering to the elite or the middle classes, and decided it was time to go out to the slums and the villages.

In Goa, Redemptorist priests spearheaded the struggle of the small fishermen against those who used trawlers and purse seine nets that swept away fish roe during the spawning season. In Kerala, a similar agitation became front-page news when priests and nuns who were leading it by remote control jumped into the fray, courted arrest and went on a hunger strike in front of government offices. Asked why she did not work for the sick and the needy like Mother Teresa instead of engaging in this kind of agitation, Sister Alice, a medical mission sister who had gone on an indefinite fast, said her charism was different.

The theology of liberation had thus come with a bang to the Indian scene. This was largely the result of some individual theologians, but also of the Indian Theological Association and the Ecumenical Association of Third World Theologians (EATWOT). Theology, they said, arises from a genuine encounter with God in the actual situation of human suffering. Traditional theology was too closely linked with Western culture, capitalism, colonialism and male domination; too heavily dependent on Greek philosophy.

In Sri Lanka, Bishop Leo Nanayakkara and Fr Tissa Balasuriya founded a new seminary on two main ideas: Asia is a continent of poverty and a continent of religions and cultures. These two ideas became also the basis of Fr Alois Pieris's theology. 'Theology in Asia,' he said, 'is the Christian apocalypse of the non-Christian experience of liberation.'

Nothing illustrates better the shattering of the hopes for conciliar renewal than the fate of the proposal for a National Pastoral Council. Voted on by a large majority at the Bangalore seminar and accepted by the Bishops' Conference, it was meant to be an expression of the collegiality of clergy, laity and hierarchy, and to draw its strength from diocesan pastoral councils and parish councils. But just when it was about to be set up, the Vatican issued a directive that pastoral councils could only be associated with the local or universal Church, and must not be held at a national level. The Follow Up Committee of the seminar urged the bishops to dialogue with Rome, but Rome was adamant. The proposal was dropped and a National Advisory Council (NAC) was set up instead.

The NAC fared little better. The themes it discussed were indeed important – Self-reliance, response to urgent needs, development and liberation – but the members were all nominated, the level of discussion not always consistent, and the NAC never really knew how much of its advice was taken by the bishops. It was, moreover, kept in the dark about some very crucial issues including finance. The result was complete stagnation in almost every avenue of Church renewal. An attempt was made in 1983 to revive the NAC, and even to get a clearance for the National Pastoral Council from Rome, but failed. Since then, the NAC has been almost defunct, as even the Bishops' Conference became bogged down in the internecine rivalry between the Latin and the Syro-Malabar and Syro-Malankara rites.

True the resolution on rites had been the high point of the 1969 Church in India Seminar. But as efforts towards greater inculturation proved increasingly fruitless, the prospect of the emergence of a common Indian rite receded from view. At the same time, as a result of the Council documents, especially *Orientalium Ecclesiarum* the Syro-Malabar and Syro-Malankara churches acquired a growing consciousness of their rights and equality with the Latin Church. They too were of apostolic origin, with their own liturgy, devotions, spirituality, theology and ecclesiastical administration, and they resented the fact that as a result of Portuguese domination, they had been prevented from undertaking missionary work outside Kerala. Some 70 per cent of the missionary personnel in the country, they said, belonged to the Syro-Malabar Church, but had to change their rite to evangelize. Some 24 per cent of the total Catholic population were members of the Syro-Malabar Church, but thousands had been lost when they migrated to the major and small cities of the north. A countrywide report by the apostolic visitor, Mar Anthony Padiyara, painted a distressing picture of their spiritual condition. With no other choice but to follow an alien liturgy, tradition and practice, they felt themselves to be second-class citizens.

The Indian Bishops' Conference thus became the battleground for the conflicting claims of Latins and Orientals, with the latter claiming jurisdiction for their bishops over their faithful who had settled in Latin dioceses, and the former clinging to the principle of 'one territory one jurisdiction' and pointing to the perils and confusion of 'double jurisdiction'. The battle was taken to the Extraordinary Synod of Bishops in Rome in 1985, where the Oriental bishops claimed that the stand of the Latin bishops was clearly contradictory of the Vatican Council decree on Oriental Churches, and the Latin bishops insisted that in a missionary country like India there could be place only for one common Indian Church. Most of the priests and faithful of the Eastern rites who had settled outside Kerala would not like to return to their original Church, they added. The matter was submitted to a high-ranking pontifical commission of cardinals and bishops, and on 28 May 1987 Pope John Paul II announced his decision that each of the three Churches had the right to form their own episcopal conference, though the national body could continue to look after common concerns; that all three had the right and obligation to evangelize; and that the pastoral care of Eastern-rite faithful settled in Latin dioceses should be entrusted to their own priests and, where circumstances warrant (as in the Bombay–Poona region), to their own bishops: a major victory for Orientals over Latins, whose consequences it will take time to identify.

As for the diocesan pastoral councils and the parish councils, a survey conducted in 1987 showed that most dioceses in India still do not have them. Those that exist hardly function. Their members are handpicked and have no real say, except for fund raising and other unimportant matters. Since by definition they are consultative, they have a built-in futility. They are not accepted as ordinary elements in diocesan or parish administration.

The changes brought about by the Vatican Council in south-west Asia may well be described as cosmetic. Not even 50 per cent of the liturgical reform envisioned by the Council has been put into effect. Only two or three of the twelve points of inculturation have been introduced. Catholics, including priests and nuns, involved in the struggle for social justice and liberation, have been marginalized as trouble-makers and Marxists who disturb the simple faith of people. Some 75 per cent of the Indian laity have never heard of the Council.

Some of the blame for this stagnation must be laid at the door of the Council documents themselves, which are often vague and ambivalent. Then there has been the over-cautious and even obstructive attitude of the Vatican that has blocked proposals like the National Pastoral Council. Nor has the attitude of the Church leadership been very encouraging. Frequent exhortations to 'hasten slowly', and warnings that though 'change is necessary, continuity is essential', have often led to one step forward and one step backward. The laity too have mostly been sheepish, looking to the clergy and hierarchy for initiative or guidance, just as the bishops in their turn have been constantly looking over their shoulders to Rome – which has given eager hearing to the traditionalists.

Yet the labours of so many in so many directions over the last twenty-five years cannot have been in vain. A ferment has been created by the numerous seminars, consultations and conferences that cannot but bear fruit in due time. Basic Christian Communities, charismatic and other post-conciliar movements, as well as the centres for dialogue and social justice, are keeping the flame of the Council alive. There remains hope for the future that the doors of post-conciliar renewal have not been closed.

12H India and Sri Lanka: Bibliography

Abhishiktananda, S. (1969) *Hindu–Christian Meeting Point*. Bombay, Institute of Indian Culture.

Amolorpavadas, D. S. (1981) *The Indian Church in the Struggle for a New Society*. Bangalore, NBCLC.

Griffiths, B. (1982) *The Marriage of East and West*. London, Collins.

Griffiths, B. (1986) *Essays Towards a Hindu-Christian Dialogue*. Bangalore, Asian Trading Corporation.

Houtart, F. (1968) *The Eleventh Hour*. London, Burns & Oates.

Kappen, S. (1977) *Jesus and Freedom*, New York, Orbis Books.

Mundadan, A. M., ed. (1988) *Cardinal Parecattil: The Man, His Vision and His Contribution*. Alwaye, Star Publications.

Pannikar, R. (1981) *The Unknown Christ of Hinduism*. London, Darton, Longman and Todd.

Perumalil, H. C., and Hambye, E. R., eds (1972) *Christianity in India – History in Ecumenical Perspective*. Alleppey, Prakasam Publications.

Pieris, A. (1988) *An Asian Theology of Liberation*. New York, Orbis Books.
Vandana, A. (1978) *Gurus, Ashrams and Christians*. London, Darton, Longman and Todd.
Weber, J. G. (1977) *In Quest of the Absolute: The Life and Work of Jules Monchanin*. London, Mowbray.

12I The Philippines

MARY JOHN MANANZAN osb

INTRODUCTION

The close of the Second Vatican Council coincided with the 400th anniversary of the Catholic Church in the Philippines, by far the most considerable Catholic community in east Asia. The Church had just assessed its four centuries of history and was ready to make a new beginning. Vatican II provided an added impulse to this openness to renewal. Its impact on the life of the Church was caused not so much, or not only, by its decrees, but by what we may call a 'paradigm shift'. It did away with the wall of orthodoxy that kept the Church insulated from the developments of the world. And this opening created tremendous possibilities and opportunities of development in all directions.

The first imperative of the Church was reformulation of its new self-understanding and of re-directing its mission. Taking 'participation' as keyword for a summary of Vatican II, Bishop Francisco Claver outlines the main changes that came about:

> There is a shift of focus from hierarchical leadership to lay fellowship, from the institution to its membership, from canonical concerns to the life problems of the people. It is not that hierarchy, institution and ecclesiastical law are no longer of consequence. They still are, but like the Sabbath they are put in the perspective they are meant to be in: at the service of people . . . not the other way around (Claver, 1985, p. 318).

How this 'paradigm shift' affected the Philippine Church will be discussed in relation to: (1) pastoral ministry and Basic Christian Communities (BCC); (2) missionary reorientation; (3) liturgical and spiritual renewal; (4) *aggiornamento* in the religious life; (5) participation of the laity; (6) efforts at ecumenism; (7) theological redirection.

PASTORAL MINISTRY AND BASIC CHRISTIAN COMMUNITIES (BCC)

Three major documents, *Lumen Gentium*, *Ad Gentes*, and *Gaudium et Spes*, ushered in a deep and thorough going self-reflection in the Church which had a lasting consequence on pastoral ministry. The Church saw itself as the people of God, requiring the co-responsibility and participation of the laity. It stressed the importance of the local church and of gathering a worshipping community. It facilitated collegiality among the bishops and subsidiarity within the structures of the Church.

In the Philippines where there was and is an acute shortage of priests, especially in rural areas, these principles were concretized in the establishment

387

of Basic Christian Communities. Karl Gaspar and Bert Cacayan have described the beginnings of this new endeavour:

> In the local church of the Philippines, it was the Mindanao-Sulu church with its Pastoral Conferences (MSPC) that provided the lead in officially endorsing BCC, when in 1971 it had a conference that took as its theme – 'Building Basic Christian Communities'. Other dioceses followed suit, and before long the Catholic Bishops' Conference of the Philippines (CBCP) also gave its official sanction. From then on it spread like wildfire through most of the dioceses in the Philippines (Gaspar and Cacayan, 1981, p. 64).

Inspired by the Communidad Ecclesia de Base of Latin America and taking them as models, the Maryknoll Fathers adopted the BCC in the Prelature of Tagum in Davao del Norte, Davao Oriental, setting up grassroots structures called *Gagmay'ng Kristohanong Katilingban*. The initial efforts were centred in bringing the people together to celebrate meaningful liturgies. Remote *barrios* were visited, and community seminars were held to discuss the new theological and pastoral development ushered in by Vatican II. The training of lay leaders became a main concern and main project. Volunteer catechists and youth leaders were organized. Meaningful preparation for the reception of the sacraments was given.

In the 1970s, the Church's concern for total human development widened the scope of the BCC. Social-action centres were set up which provided not only social services and income-generating activities, but also engaged in organizing the farmers, labourers and the youth. However, their priority was in the area of co-operatives, credit unions, consumers' co-ops and such like.

The BCCs began to get interested in similar projects and initiated self-help projects and community-education programmes.

With the declaration of martial law in 1972, the situation in the Philippines became critical. Economic conditions worsened, militarization escalated, prices rose and violation of human rights intensified. It was during this early period of martial law, when the secular groups had to go underground, that the Church people were radicalized because they were the ones left above ground to continue the legal struggle against the Marcos dictatorship. Church people began to link themselves with the basic masses in struggling for their human rights. Nuns and priests in rallies and mass demonstrations became a common sight. Many religious left institutional education to work and struggle directly among and with the poor. Some even began to live in the slum areas with the urban poor. The Rural and Urban Missionaries were formed, which were intercongregational and who opted to be with the masses. However, it has to be said that while rank-and-file religious were becoming more and more involved with the fate of the masses, the Church hierarchy opted for a 'critical collaboration' with the Marcos regime, which was more collaboration than critical.

The progressive elements in the Church saw the need for educating the people to justice. The introduction of social analysis in 1975 and Alinsky's principles of organizing in 1976 influenced the direction of the BCC and the social-action apostolate. These were included in the conscientization programmes of lay leaders and catechists. These resulted in the politicization of the people. In some places, the pastoral programmes became BCC-CO (Basic Christian Communities with Community Organization).

In 1977 the National Secretariat for Social Action (NASSA) identified as its thrust the organization of peasants; farmers were given seminars and were organized.

The increasing concern of the BCC in pursuing human rights of the poor, the deprived and oppressed, met with harassment and repression from the military government. In a military report, the armed forces claimed that 'the Basic Christian Communities have become the most potent political force of the Church in the Philippines today' (Gaspar and Cacayan, 1981, p. 63). As time went on, it was not only the military who were suspicious; conservative bishops and priests who felt the BCC should concentrate only on spiritual matters became alarmed. In some dioceses there were accusations of left-wing infiltration of the BCC, and the instrumentalization of Church structures. Assessing the potentials and limitations of the BCC, Gaspar and Cacayan conclude:

> In the context of Philippine realities today, the BCC can play a significant role in the struggle for liberation. However, it is not within its means to resolve the basic contradictions now intensifying in the Philippine society. It cannot be the leading force. But it can serve as the venue for reflection, where the people inspired by the Gospel discern their task in bringing about God's kingdom of justice and freedom (Gaspar and Cacayan, 1981, p. 70).

This involvement of Church people in the struggle of the masses hastened the downfall of the Marcos regime, especially when the Church hierarchy began to question its moral authority after the assassination of Ninoy Aquino. This event awakened the middle class, including the hierarchy, which began to write pastoral letters against the regime, the strongest of which was the pastoral letter on the electoral fraud of the snap elections in 1986. This, together with the defection of the national defence secretary, Juan Ponce Enrile, and the chief of the armed forces, Fidel Ramos, led to the famous EDSA event of February 1986, which was characterized by the active participation of Church people on the invitation of Cardinal Sin using traditional folk religiosity to stop the tanks. This event marked the end of the Marcos regime, and the inauguration of the Aquino administration.

Although there was a change in the leadership, there has actually been no change in the structure of society, in the economic development model of the country, in the relationship of classes. In other words, there occurred no social revolution. This has made the Church people who had been in solidarity with the masses continue to struggle for justice, while the Church hierarchy basically supports the Aquino administration. Since there has been an intensification of the 'red scare', the Basic Christian Communities, which have become suspects because of their political involvement, are gradually being transformed into 'basic ecclesial communities', which have a more inner-church focus than the former BCC-CO. This has lessened their social impact.

MISSIONARY REORIENTATION

When *Ad Gentes* categorically stated that the 'pilgrim church is missionary by her very nature' (*AG* 1,2), the Church in the Philippines was jolted out of its missionary dormancy into a realization of its significant role as the only Christian country in Asia. First of all, there was a realization that it is humankind itself that is the Kingdom of God, and not only the Church. The Church is the 'privileged instrument' instituted, raised up by Christ to work within the world, to work within history to help prepare humankind to become the Kingdom of God.

The Church has awakened to the fact that even in the Philippines there are those 'who do not yet believe in Christ', and that the Church's task is not mainly to convert them, to promote their total human liberation. For this purpose, the Episcopal Commission for Tribal Filipinos was established.

The realization that in the new age of mission there no longer is a one-way movement from metropolitan churches of the old world to younger churches of the colonies, but that every local church must be a sending church, has emboldened the Philippine Church to establish the Philippine Missionary Society. In a report on the International Mission Conference held in December 1979, during which seventy Filipino missionaries received their Mission Cross, Bishop Rosales wrote:

> We have been a receiving church for more than four hundred years now. Perhaps that time is in large measure over, that more and more time for sending is upon us . . . . It is surely a source of joy that more than five hundred of our Filipino Catholics have answered that call, and given the yes of their best years and efforts. And we can be confident, I believe that this missionary generosity will not die down but will grow in coming years (Rosales, 1981, p. 14).

It is also significant that in that International Mission Conference that the Philippines hosted, the pervasive influence of the orientation of Vatican II was evident already in delineating the focus of mission in Asia today. We read:

> The starting point of Mission Theology in the Asian context is the present day situation of the realities of Asia. This situation, read in the light of the Gospel and with the faith that the Holy Spirit is present and active in world history, had led discerning Asians to point out the following as the tasks of mission in Asia today. The focus of evangelization is the local church which, in order to be fully built up, must engage:
> a) in a dialogue with the local churches
> b) in life dialogue and solidarity with the masses of the poor and oppressed in the region
> c) in dialogue with the religious traditions of our Asian neighbours (International Mission Conference, 1981, p. 5).

LITURGICAL AND SPIRITUAL RENEWAL

In fact, the liturgical and biblical renewal antedate the Vatican Council. In a way, spade work had been done for the two documents *Dei Verbum* (on Divine

Revelation) and the *Sacrosanctum Concilium* (on the Sacred Liturgy), but these documents brought the initial efforts of renewal to full blossoming. There was a time when the Catholic Church 'kept the Bible from the people'. In the Philippines, to be reading the Bible before Vatican II was a sign of being a Protestant! From being 'forbidden', the reading of the Bible was not only encouraged, but almost commanded. Its centrality in the liturgy was pre-scribed. Bible-study groups sprouted all over the Philippines. Prayer groups started with the reading of Scriptures. The study of Scriptures was re-emphasized in religious formation houses. The Basic Christian Communities discovered the empowering effect of the Bible on the people who began to read it in the context of their lives.

The Philippine Church has a history of identification with the Spanish colonization of the country. Having no major non-Christian religions to dialogue with besides Islam in the south, inculturation in the Philippines means contributing to the discovery of the Filipinos' identity as a people, investigating why there is a syncretic reception of the message of Christianity, delving into the value systems of the people, the world vision of the pre-Spanish Filipino, and of present cultural minorities in the hope of truly assimilating Christianity and putting an end to what Fr Bulatao calls 'split level Christianity'. Recently there has been a growing interest in understanding the dynamics of folk religiosity in the hope of harnessing its liberative potentiality.

Having understood evangelization as integral, total, historical and social, involving the whole person (not only the soul) in the context of a social milieu and including liberation from concrete evils and working out of concrete blessings inculturation must include the dimension of contextualization. Not only is the history and culture of the people considered, but likewise the people's present economic, political, and cultural situation of oppression, and how the Church can truly incarnate herself in their midst and together with them struggle for a more just and more humane society.

One of the earliest biblical theologians to discover this was Fr Carlos Abesamis, who spent more than twenty years developing the biblical basis for a contextualized theology in the Philippines. He and other progressive biblical theologians have given seminar-workshops and published manuals used by Basic Christian Communities all over the country.

Parallel to and even pre-dating biblical renewal, is the liturgical renewal. It is in the liturgy that the attempts of inculturation are most manifest. After Vatican II the churches lost no time in adopting indigenous languages in the celebration of the liturgy. Hymnbooks in the national language were published, liturgical seminar workshops, consultations and congresses were held.

According to a report by Bishop Dosado, a major approved adaptation had been in the marriage rite, where the Ritus Toletanus (marriage rite originating in Toledo, Spain, using arrhae, veils and cord adapted in the Philippines) was merged with the new Roman Ordo Matrimonii and Ordo Missae. Then the renewal of marriage was added, a rite of revalidation and presidential prayers in Filipino adapted to the cultural pattern of the Filipino. However he adds:

> Our most ambitious project has been the Misa ng Bayan (People's Mass) in Tagalog and English, made in 1975–1976. In it we proposed a revision of the Order of Mass, including two Eucharistic Prayers on the basis of our literary, social and other cultural forms and customs. The project was unanimously endorsed by our Archbishops' Conference and accepted and approved, but then it has remained unconfirmed by the Apostolic See up to the present (Dosado, 1985, p. 55).

He also thinks that the Roman rite is so alien to the mentality of the Filipino people that there is a need 'to express what is alive in them'. He sees the need of loosening the tight rule of experimentation in this regard.

A development that some consider as going beyond the intentions of the Council, but that is considered by those who do it as liturgy according to its essence as 'public service', is the incorporation of people's concerns, economic–political–social, in the liturgical celebration – making use of testimonies of different sectors, of victims of injustice, of the poor, usually accompanied by dance, progressive songs or mimes. In the years of martial law there were street stations of the cross, people's Masses, para-liturgical services during rallies, pickets, vigils and funerals of salvaged victims, and prayer services for specific issues.

In the more personal aspect of the spiritual renewal, the most immediate change was the reaction to the institutional, legalistic aspects of the Church and an emphasis on the personal and interpersonal. This saw the growth of charismatic movements, the *cursillos*, the introduction of the Focolare Movement, and the beginning of the Christian Family Movement. It is a pity, however, that some of these movements that started with the best intentions have become fundamentalistic in their attitude, and have served as escapes from the social issues that confront society. There are also movements like Opus Dei, which appear to seek to return to pre-Vatican II days.

In more progressive circles there are those whose involvement in the struggle of the masses has developed into a socially oriented spirituality, which they call 'integral spirituality'; this seeks to develop a holistic dynamism between one's social commitment and one's life of prayer.

Finally, the effect of inculturation and dialogue with other religions has aroused an interest in the Oriental forms of spirituality, and the thirteen-year-old Zen Center of the Philippines (founded in 1976) has today a flourishing membership among Catholics.

AGGIORNAMENTO IN THE RELIGIOUS LIFE

The consequences of Vatican II have been more dramatic on religious women than on religious men in the Philippines, maybe because the former have suffered more limitations throughout the ages. One of the weaknesses of the Council was its failure to address the issue of women, even if Pope John XXIII already mentioned as one of the signs of the times the concern over this in his encyclical *Pacem in Terris*. However, even if the Council failed to address the issue of women, the spirit of openness and renewal has greatly affected the lives of religious women since.

The document *Perfectae Caritatis* urged religious congregations to go back to their original charisma. This impelled their members to go back to their sources and redefine their identity, and had far-reaching consequences on religious women in the Philippines. Some congregations reoriented their apostolates, gave up their educational institutions to recapture their primary commitment to the poor. Outstanding examples are the ICM Sisters, who gave up their highly prestigious St Theresa's College, and the Maryknoll Sisters, who gave over Maryknoll College to lay ownership and administration. Other congregations such as the Benedictine Sisters, Franciscan Sisters, and the Good Shepherd Sisters reoriented their institutions in response to the 'signs of the times', which called for a new social orientation and commitment to justice. Many sisters gave up work with institutions to give direct service to the poor, particularly the urban and rural poor, the workers, the slum dwellers. Both rural and urban missionaries initiated an inter-congregational apostolate, which put an end to the individualistic and even competitive attitudes of pre-Vatican II days.

In 1982 the National Organization of Women Religious of the Philippines was founded, based on a conviction that the religious should be in solidarity with the poor, deprived and oppressed in their efforts to build a more just society.

Religious women have since then been in the forefront of the 'progressive Church', leading cause-oriented organizations like the Task Force Detainees, the Women's National Federation, GABRIELA, the AMRSP Justice and Peace Commission, the Citizen's Alliance for Consumer Protection. A sister was appointed a member of the Presidential Commission on Human Rights, and another sister was appointed a member of the Constitutional Convention that drafted the 1987 Philippine Constitution.

In other words, the state of economic and political crisis in the Philippines enabled Filipino religious women to transcend personalistic preoccupations and move through the door opened by Vatican II and the changes it encouraged in the structures and lifestyle of convent life into the wider concerns of society. As one writer puts it:

> They have broken out of their mouldy medieval world, shaken off the dust of centuries and gone past those ivy-colored walls that once set them so apart and made them so strangely different . . . . Many sisters have come a long way, a very long hard way. But they're more fully WOMAN. They are beginning to immerse themselves in a world they once 'fled because it is evil', and many are blazing new trails off to outdo even their saintly Mother Foundress (Doyo, 1983, p. 1).

PARTICIPATION OF THE LAITY

In the Philippines efforts to implement the decree on the Apostolate of the Laity have been very evident in the formation of Basic Christian Communities, where lay readers are given more responsibility (especially in regions where there are no priests) in para-liturgical celebrations, distribution of the Holy Eucharist, funeral services and pre-marriage counselling.

Modern Catholicism

Lay people have been encouraged to be active in the promotion of social justice, and to have an influential role in policy-making bodies in society. The Bishop's-Businessmen's Conference was founded to keep this social orientation in the Church alive through fora, symposia, and seminars on current economic, political and social issues. Lay religious associations, prayer groups and Bible study groups have sprouted all over the country. And these lay groups are co-ordinated by the Council of the Laity of the Philippines.

In spite of these efforts, however, there is a glaring failure in the continuing discrimination and subordination of women in the Church. In spite of the fact that women continue to be the ones most active in the Church, they are still relegated to minor roles in the liturgy and are still barred from the decision-making bodies within the Church. In fact, the laity in general have not yet been given leadership, even in Church organizations.

The conclusion of the FABC's first Bishops' Institute for Lay Apostolate in Taiwan in 1984 applies to the lay people in the Philippines. In its final statement, we read:

> Despite some inspiring examples of lay involvement in the Church in East Asia, we have come to the clear realization that there is a big gap between the vision of the Church as the people of God, promulgated by Vatican II almost 20 years ago, and the actual situation existing in our Church today. Dialogue, sharing, co-responsibility are words that we use regularly, but now we clearly see that the vast majority of our laity do not share in dialogue with their clergy, nor do they share the responsibility for the works of the Church with their clergy in a partnership of brotherhood.
>
> In some situations this gap between the vision of Vatican II and the reality as we live it may be due to passivity of the laity who tend to leave the 'leading to the clergy'. In other situations it may be due to an unwillingness on the part of the clergy to share responsibility ('Bishops' Institute for Lay Apostolate', 1985, pp. 4–5),

EFFORTS AT ECUMENISM

In the Philippines, the only significant non-Christian religion is Islam, which is professed by 5 per cent of the Filipinos, mostly in the south. Some efforts have been made to create a dialogue with Muslims, and a Muslim Christian Secretariat has been established in Sulu. Some priests, sisters and lay people have studied Islam to facilitate this work, the Muslim–Christian dialogues have been held on a national level. Complicating the matter, however, is the continuing war between the Christian government and the Moro National Liberation Front, which has economic rather than religious roots.

In relation to the Protestant Church, ecumenism has come a long way from the time when it was considered a mortal sin for a Catholic to enter a Protestant church or to take part in its services. However, apart from the attitude of cordiality, the hierarchical Church has not in reality budged from its position that unity will come about only when the 'separated brethren' have come back to the fold. Being the majority Church (85 per cent of Filipinos are Catholics) has not made it easy for the Catholic Church to develop an attitude that is not more or less oppressive towards minority churches.

However, there has been a qualitative leap in ecumenism, not in official quarters but among the rank and file Christians. This is not so much the result of the initiative of Church authorities, but because of the situation of crisis that brought people of different creeds together. I wrote the following in 1979:

> Church people, confronted by worsening conditions of society, were diverted from their differences in doctrine and religious practices and they focused their attention on a common crisis. Especially immediately following the declaration of Martial Law in 1972 when all militant opposition groups had to lie low, church people found themselves in the forefront faced with the unique opportunity of fulfilling their prophetic role. As such they were forced to do serious study of the situation. Some even arrived at common political options that further eliminated religious obstacles to ecumenical cooperation. It became quite common to meet each other in the same exposure areas, to be in the same panel at some symposium, to link arm in arm at some demonstration or picket, to be co-facilitators in conscientization seminars, to be co-workers at community organizing projects . . . . Even such a sensitive area as worship became a practical meeting point, because for some time it was only in common worship that people could give expression to their grievances (Mananzan, 1979, pp. 32–3).

THEOLOGICAL REDIRECTION

Theology is reflection on the practice of faith. With the changes that have come about in the practice of Christian life, it is inevitable that they would be reflected in theological discussions.

Vatican II's insistence on the reading of the signs of the times brought about the contextualization of theology. It is precisely this factor that made the Latin American bishops not quite satisfied with the decrees of Vatican II, because they were still too European and did not quite answer the needs of their people. Medellín was the attempt at contextualization that gave birth to liberation theology.

Inspired by this theology, Filipino theologians involved in the struggle against the dictatorship of martial law days began to reflect on the situation of poverty, injustice and oppression that confronted them. Equipped with tools of social analysis, they sought to understand together with economists and sociologists the causes of the people's problem. Emboldened by their discernment in the Gospels of Christ's preferential option for the poor, they immersed themselves among the struggling people and together with them read, and reflected on, the Bible, drawing from it the inspiration and strength to 'announce the good news' and to 'denounce the bad news'. The change of the locus of theologizing provided them with a new perspective – that of the struggling poor and oppressed. They understood that theologizing could not primarily be an academic exercise, but must be geared to transforming action. This ecumenical and interdisciplinary group who wanted to focus on context and process describe their efforts as steps towards a 'theology of struggle'.

There remains of course a mainstream theology that keeps well within the parameter of Vatican II, and would consider the theology just described as going beyond the bounds of the Council. Another recent development in

Philippine theology that would likewise be judged by mainstream theology as going beyond the Council, are the initial attempts at theologizing from the perspective of Filipino women. An association of theologically trained women who are affiliated with the Ecumenical Association of Third World Theologians have met on a national level, continental level and intercontinental level with women from Asia, Africa and Latin America to discuss theology from the perspective of third-world women. In their own milieu they have set for themselves the following goals in the Church with regard to women:

> The agenda of renewal must include all aspects of Theology from the reinterpretation of scriptures, to historical-critical reflection of church doctrine from the women's point of view, to rediscovery of the great women of church history, to the fundamental questioning of the church's hierarchical structure, its constricting prescriptions, its discriminatory practice and the sexist language of its liturgy (Mananzan, 1988, p. 119).

APPRAISAL AND CONCLUSION

It seems evident that the Second Vatican Council has indeed ushered in a new era in the Church, though in east Asia generally, outside the Philippines, the impact may not be as dramatic – because of the minority position of the Church, and the lack of successful inculturation up to this day in spite of efforts in this regard. But in the Philippines the life of the Church has been profoundly changed. This, however, is not only the result of direct prescriptions of the Council, but because the openness it has generated has made Church people react with greater creativity, innovativeness, and even daring in the face of the situation of crisis that they found themselves in from the 1970s up to the present. Some observers may judge it as going beyond the Council. But perhaps the success of a Council is not so much in the implementation of its decrees as in the vitality and dynamism that it generated, which by their very nature must go beyond it.

12I The Philippines: Bibliography

'Bishops' Institute for Lay Apostolate' (1985) *East Asian Pastoral Review*, vol. XXII, no. 1.

Claver, F. (1985) *The Church in Asia Twenty Years After Vatican II*.

Dosado, J. (1985) 'Twenty Years of liturgical Renewal, An Asian View', *Philippine Studies*, vol. 20.

Doyo, C. (1983) 'The Sisters Have Come a Long Way' *Panorama* – Sunday Supplement of *Bulletin Today*, 29 May.

Gaspar, C., and Cacayan, A. (1981) 'BCC in a Rural Setting', *Witness*, vol. I, no. 4.

Gomez-Berlana, F. (1980) 'The International Missions Congress and Evangelization in Asia Today', *Boletin Ecclesiastico de Filipinas*, vol. LIV, September–October.

Mananzan, M. J. (1979) 'A Practice of Ecumenism Among Church Women', *Tugon*, vol. I, no. 1.

Mananzan, M. J. (1988) 'Women and Religion', *Woman and Religion*, Women's Studies Series no. 2.

Rosales, G. (1981) *Towards a New Age of Mission*. Manila, Manila Theological Conference Office.

13

ECUMENICAL RELATIONS

GEORGE H. TAVARD

Since Vatican II, the relationships of the Catholic Church to other Christian Churches and various ecumenical agencies have developed to a remarkable extent. This development is evidently related to the reception of the decree *Unitatis Redintegratio* in the thought and practice of the Catholic Church. This itself has been fostered by the activity of the Secretariat for Christian Unity; this was created by John XXIII, and entrusted by Paul VI with the responsibility of leadership in implementing the conciliar decree at the universal level. It has also depended on the actions of the ecumenical offices and commissions that have been established by episcopal conferences throughout the world. Yet by their very nature, such relations are not unilateral. They are possible only where the desire of Catholics for better ecumenical relations is met by an interest, among other Christians, in having positive relations to the Catholic Church and its members.

Since Vatican II, ecumenism in the Catholic Church has therefore had two fundamental dimensions; these may be suggested by two questions. First, how did the Catholic Church enter the modern ecumenical movement, which had already been active for over fifty years by 1962–5? Second, how has the ecumenical opening of Vatican II affected, and possibly transformed, the ecumenical movement? The first question evokes principally the opening of relations with the World Council of Churches. The second relates chiefly to the initiation and growth of bilateral dialogues with Orthodox, Anglican and Protestant Churches. Before this, however, one should enquire on what principles the Church could thus open itself to the search for Christian unity.

13A The Principles of an Ecumenical Opening

When it became a permanent office of the Roman curia, the Secretariat for Christian Unity was assigned the task of helping the clergy and faithful to overcome the retrenchment mentality of the Counter Reformation. This mentality had marked the encyclicals *Satis Cognitum* of Leo XIII (1896), *Mortalium Animos* of Pius XI (1928), *Mystici Corporis* of Pius XII (1943), and several documents of the Holy Office concerning participation in ecumenical activities, notably the *monitum* of 5 June 1948 and the rather more positive instruction of 20 December 1949, *Ecclesia Catholica*. It was at that time assumed, without deep investigation, that the ecumenical movement is, theologically, Protestant. Correlatively, it was held that Catholics have no need to search for Christian unity, this unity being simply given to those who are in union with the chair of Peter in Rome. This union is effective in the Roman Catholic Church, which Pius XII therefore identified with the Mystical Body of Christ. It was generally feared that the involvement of Catholics in ecumenical matters, beyond the unionism that works and prays for conversion, could easily lead to indifferentism (the assumption that all forms of Christianity are equal: this was the danger to which Pius XI drew attention in *Mortalium Animos*) or to a false irenicism (as denounced by Pius XII in *Humani Generis*: the ecumenical approach might threaten fidelity to the true doctrine of the nature and identity of the Church). It was often feared that friendly dealings with Protestants might encourage on their part a proselytism that would attempt to convert Catholics to lesser forms of Christianity, especially in countries – as was the case in Latin America, and as it has become increasingly so in Western Europe – where there are many baptized and nominal Catholics, where actual church attendance is scarce, and where there are few vocations to the priesthood.

Even before the Council, however, several lines of thought had begun to soften the harsh lines of the papal stance. First, there was the continuing interest shown by a number of Latin theologians and bishops in the Oriental rites and their theology, and, by a natural consequence, in the life and thought of the Orthodox Church. From 1907 to 1936 the Congresses of Velehrad, in Czechoslovakia, had been the main theological expression of this interest, which was still, however, marked by unionism. Secondly, there was the Week of Prayer for Christian Unity (18–25 January), the origin of which goes back to the Italian priest Vincent Pallotti (1795–1850). By the time of Vatican II, it had undergone transformations in regard to the time (first, after the Epiphany, then before Pentecost, finally in January between the feasts of the conversion of St Paul and of the chair of Peter) and purpose.

It had started with Fr Paul Watson of Graymoor (1863–1940), himself a convert from Anglicanism, as an 'octave of prayer' for the conversion of non-Catholic Christians. Then, with Abbé Paul Couturier (1881–1953), the tireless inspirer of 'spiritual emulation' among Christians of all denominations, it became a 'week of universal prayer for Christian unity' when and as Christ wills it. Thirdly, there was the Una Sancta movement in Germany, which was focused on prayer and dialogue; its founder, Max Josef Metzger (1887–1944), was executed after the attempt on Hitler's life. Fourthly, a Catholic theology of ecumenism had been initiated in France, notably by Yves Congar; the solidity of it had been tested, since 1937, in the unofficial ecumenical dialogue of the 'Groupe des Dombes', itself inspired by Couturier.

Most of these trends converged in a 'Catholic Conference for Ecumenical Questions', created in the Netherlands by a professor of theology, Jan Willebrands, in 1948. As all this shows, the problem was not to create a Catholic ecumenism. It was to co-ordinate the existing forms of Catholic involvement in the ecumenical movement, and to channel this co-ordination into official policy. But on what principles should this be done? 'Catholic principles of ecumenism' were clearly stated in the conciliar decree, but how they could be applied remained to be seen. They had to be made concrete and practical. This was the purpose of the *Directory* for Ecumenism, published in 1967 (part I) and 1970 (part II).

The *Directory for the Application of the Decisions of the Second Ecumenical Council of the Vatican concerning Ecumenical Matters* was planned in the Secretariat for Unity before and during Vatican II. The first part examines four sets of problems: (1) the organization of ecumenical work at diocesan and regional levels; (2) the recognition of baptism given in other Churches; (3) prayer for unity; (4) the question of *communicatio in sacris* (participating in common worship). A brief summary of these four sections will be given here.

1 Dioceses and Conferences of Bishops should create an ecumenical commission for their territory. The task of these commissions will be to promote ecumenical activities, to provide guidance for clergy and laity, to appoint experts who will engage in ecumenical dialogues, to organize consultations among Catholics and with other Christians, to co-ordinate information and to learn from one another.

2 The purpose of this section is to put an end to the widespread abuse that consists in baptizing conditionally those who have been baptized in other Churches, when they wish to enter the Catholic Church.

3 This part tries to urge and facilitate the promotion of 'spiritual ecumenism', along the lines of Couturier. It points to times that are especially appropriate for prayer for Christian unity.

4 This section examines several aspects of the problem of sharing prayer with other Christians. It distinguishes between 'sharing spiritual resources', including prayer, and 'sharing liturgical worship'. The first is generally encouraged. The second is seen to need careful regulation, in keeping with the decree *Unitatis Redintegratio* (8). The problem here was to overcome a narrow interpretation of canon 1258 in the *Code* of 1917 that generally prevailed, especially in Anglo-Saxon countries. The text makes a distinction between the Orthodox Church and the Churches of the West. The principle of 'reciprocity' ought to be 'given the greatest possible attention': the sharing of worship should not be one-sided. The principle of mutual agreement complements

this: there should be no participation in the sacraments given in the Orthodox Church without the agreement of the authorities of this Church.

In regard to the Western, chiefly Protestant, Churches, however, the principle of reciprocity cannot apply to the same degree, since the Catholic Church does not recognize the validity of their orders (with the exception of the Old Catholics). It follows that in cases of 'urgent need', Catholics may give the sacraments to members of other Churches, but may not ask for sacraments that the Catholic Church does not consider valid. Yet they may generally share in the prayers and chants of Communion services. The text, however, maintains that the reader of Scripture and the homilist ought to belong to the same Church as the one who presides, on account of the close ties that should exist between the word and the sacrament.

Over the years, however, this last regulation has been widely ignored. Furthermore, unauthorized intercommunion, sometimes justified as a prophetic gesture, has become widespread among Catholic laity and even clergy. The concern about validity has found little echo outside canonical and theological circles. For this reason, the Secretariat, in 1972, issued a new 'Instruction concerning cases when other Christians may be admitted to eucharistic communion in the Catholic Church'. This text reaffirmed the principle that there is an 'essential relation between eucharistic communion and ecclesial communion'. It confirmed that the bishop has 'fairly wide discretionary power' in this area, but it maintained that an invitation to receive the Catholic Eucharist is not proper when other Christians can easily receive Communion in their own communities.

The second part of the *Directory* deals with 'Ecumenism in higher education'. The purpose of this text was to promote the education of Catholics, laity and clergy, in ecumenical matters. The text is in four parts: I: General Principles; II: Ecumenism in Religious Education; III: Guidelines for Ecumenical Education; IV: Institutional and Personal Co-operation between Catholics and other Christians. It recommends special courses, and the insertion of an ecumenical concern in all courses of religion and theology; the adaptation of ecumenical education to the capacity and culture of different audiences; the opening of centres of formation and information; the careful choice and supervision of textbooks for religious education.

The general welcome given by Catholics to *Unitatis Redintegratio* and the careful indications of the *Directory* were largely responsible for the specific way in which the Catholic Church entered the ecumenical movement after Vatican II. A preference for bilateral dialogues with other Churches, in which doctrine and theology are discussed, is undeniable. Pope Paul VI himself, in his first encyclical, *Ecclesiam Suam* (1964), described the structure and life of the Church as being radically dialogical. Even the approach to the World Council of Churches, which went much further than could have been expected in the light of the pre-conciliar restrictions, was itself conceived on the mode of dialogue.

At the time of writing, a revised and updated version of the *Directory* for ecumenism is being prepared by the Council (until recently Secretariat) for Christian Unity. The *New Directory* (like the change of name from Secretariat

401

to Council) may come to signify a shift of emphasis in Roman ecumenical attitudes which have, from the 1960s to the late 1980s, been remarkably consistent under the immediate control, for more than twenty years, of Cardinal Willebrands.

13A The Principles of an Ecumenical Opening: Bibliography

Dulles, A. (1974) *Church Membership as a Catholic and Ecumenical Problem*. Milwaukee, Marquette University.

Ehrenström, N., and Gassmann, H. (1975) *Confessions in Dialogue, A Survey of Bilateral Conversations among World Confessional Families, 1959–1974*, 3rd edn, (Faith and Order Papers, no. 74). Geneva, World Council of Churches.

Fries, H. and Rahner, K. (1983) *Unity of the Churches. An Actual Possibility*. New York, Paulist Press.

Goodall, N. (1972) *Ecumenical Progress: A Decade of Change in the Ecumenical Movement, 1961–1971*. London, Oxford University Press.

Puglisi, J. F. and Voicu, S. J. (1984) *A Bibliography of Interchurch and Interconfessional Dialogues*. Rome, Centro pro Unione.

Sheard, R. B. (1987) *Interreligious Dialogue in the Catholic Church since Vatican II: An Historical and Theological Study*, Toronto Studies in Theology, no. 31. Lewiston, New York, E. Mullen.

Stransky, T. and Hotchkin, J., eds (1981) *John Paul II: Addresses and Homilies on Ecumenism, 1978–1980*. Washington, USCC Publications.

Stransky, T. and Sheerin, J. eds (1982) *Doing the Truth in Charity: Statements of Popes Paul VI, John Paul I, John Paul II, and the Secretariat for Promoting Christian Unity, 1964–1980*. New York, Paulist Press.

13B The World Council of Churches (WCC)

On the basis of *Unitatis Redintegratio* and the *Directory*, the Church approached the WCC. This was the first obvious partner for an ecumenical dialogue. The WCC had come into existence in Amsterdam in 1948, and had established its headquarters in Geneva. Conceived as an association of Churches that confess Jesus Christ as Lord and Saviour, the WCC embodied a type of ecumenism in which both Protestant and Orthodox could take part. The Catholic Church was not a member. In 1969, Paul VI declared the question of membership 'not yet mature enough for a positive decision'. But multi-level relationships have grown between the two institutions. A 'Joint Working Group' was created early in 1965, after the third session of the Council. Informal soundings and meetings in view of such an organ had in fact begun before Vatican II, in 1960. The mission of the Joint Working Group is 'to work out the principles which should be observed in further collaboration and the methods which should be used'. It has become the central instrument of communication and collaboration between the Catholic Church and the WCC.

The Joint Working Group has worked through subcommissions in charge of specific questions (on Catholicity and apostolicity, mixed marriages, prayer for unity, and proselytism). Already by 1967, at the time of the second report of the Joint Working Group, these questions had multiplied. In addition to the previous topics, the Group intended to study the following. Under the theme of Faith and Worship: the Week of Prayer for Christian Unity, the date of Easter, and the authority of the Bible; under that of Unity and Mission: the common witness of the Churches, and non-Christian religions; under that of Laity and Unity: the role of the laity, the co-operation of men and women, education; under that of Service to Humanity: peace and justice, service activities, international affairs. The question of co-operation in the translation of the Bible was also brought to the fore. Contacts with the United Bible Societies had begun as early as 1963. They developed into a systematic collaboration, with the joint publication of *Guiding Principles for Interconfessional Collaboration in Translating the Bible* (1968). In 1967, the Joint Working Group issued a 'Working Paper' in ecumenical dialogue. The Secretariat for Unity drew on this paper in its later 'working instrument', entitled 'Reflections and Suggestions concerning Ecumenical Dialogue' (1970). Since these beginnings, the Joint Working Group has continued, at the rate of one meeting a year, to assist and report on the relationships between the two bodies. In February 1975, the Secretariat for Christian Unity published a paper on 'Ecumenical Collaboration at the Regional, National, and Local Levels', which was the result of co-operation with representatives of Diocesan Ecumenical Commissions (meeting in Rome in November 1972) and with the WCC Secretariat for Relations with Christian Councils.

Given the welcome extended to WCC observers at Vatican II, the presence of Catholic observers at meetings of the WCC was desirable. The question had been discussed before the Council. In 1952, the Catholic bishop of Sweden had sent observers to the Faith and Order Conference in Lund. In 1954, however, Cardinal Stritch vetoed the presence of Catholic observers at the Evanston

Assembly. The few Catholic theologians who attended were present as journalists. In 1961, the Holy See took a broader view and sent five observers to the New Delhi assembly of the WCC. This practice has continued at the WCC plenary meetings of Upsala, 1968, Nairobi, 1975, and Vancouver, 1983, at the meetings of the WCC's Central Committee, at those of the World Conference on Faith and Order, Montreal, 1963, and at numerous other gatherings. In 1969 the Faith and Order Commission, made up of individuals in good standing in their Churches, but not of official representatives, began to co-opt a few Catholic theologians. These (ten, later increased to twelve) have taken part in its work, notably in the long preparation of the Lima document on *Baptism, Eucharist, and Ministry* (1983). Likewise, there has been active Catholic participation, through a number of consultants, in the Commission on World Mission and Evangelism.

The Church's relations with the WCC have in turn inspired some regional and local units (Conferences of Bishops, dioceses) to increase their own relations with the ecumenical agencies of their area. By 1971, the Catholic Church had full membership in eleven national Councils of Churches. In the United States, many dioceses are full members of the Council of Churches of their state. The relationships of the Catholic Church with the WCC have also grown through personal relations established between their leaders. This began with a brief visit of Paul VI to the headquarters of the WCC in Geneva, on 10 June 1969. In response to a formal welcome from the general secretary that remained on the cool side, the pope spoke very warmly, though he did cause some surprise with his self-identification as Peter: 'Our name is Peter.' Yet as general secretary Carson Blake noted in his subsequent report to the Central Committee of the WCC (August 1969), it is a basic principle of ecumenical co-operation that each side always remains free to formulate its faith in its integrity. Fifteen years later (12 June 1984), the welcome extended to John Paul II was much warmer. It began with common prayer, and there was, after the formal speeches, an informal exchange of questions and answers. In turn, the general secretaries of the WCC have had occasion to visit the Secretariat for Christian Unity and to be received by the pope at the Vatican (e.g. Philip Potter, November 1971; Emilio Castro, April 1986). Philip Potter even gave a major address on 'evangelization' at the Synod of Bishops of 1974.

It is difficult to draw a unified conclusion from this overview of developing collaboration between the Catholic Church and the WCC. Activities are many-faceted, the levels of interaction diverse. Mutual trust is growing, yet not without occasional misunderstandings. Given the inner diversity of the WCC, the deepest input towards an ecumenical consensus in doctrine and theology cannot emerge along the Rome–Geneva axis (with the partial exception, to which we will return, of the BEM). We should now turn to the bilateral dialogues between Churches. These are the most original contribution of Vatican II and the Secretariat for Unity to the Ecumenical Movement.

13C   The Orthodox Church

The ties between the Orthodox (Eastern) Church and the Catholic (Western) Church are clear from history. In spite of the schism of 1054, there have always been close relationships between the two sides in certain regions. The Catholic Church, however, claims that it is not only Western and Latin, since a number of Churches following the Eastern rites are in communion with the bishop of Rome rather than with the patriarch of Constantinople. Vatican II itself adopted a decree on the Eastern Churches in communion with Rome (*Orientalium Ecclesiarum*). It is largely because of the existence of these Churches that the Vatican and the Catholic Church have commonly treated relations with Oriental Christians as a global problem: unity is to be effected between Churches, by way of relations from Church to Church, rather than between isolated believers, through individual instruction and conversion. The proper model for such inter-church relations is that of two Churches talking together. This is the basic reason for the deep involvement of the Catholic Church since Vatican II in bilateral dialogues. Yet the ecumenical rapprochement with the Orthodox Church did not start in the form of a dialogue. It was initiated by Paul VI through a number of prophetic gestures.

DURING VATICAN II

These prophetic gestures began before the end of Vatican II. They started as soon as Paul VI was elected bishop of Rome: all the Oriental patriarchs were officially informed of the election by a letter from Cardinal Bea. Moreover, Paul VI wrote personally to ecumenical Patriarch Athenagoras on 20 September 1963, the first such communication since 1054. There followed, on 5 and 6 January 1964, the momentous meeting of Paul VI and Athenagoras during their pilgrimages to Jerusalem. And since the Orthodox Church is made of autocephalous Churches, Paul VI also approached some of the other patriarchs. He thus addressed a telegram of congratulations to Patriarch Alexis of Moscow for the feast of Easter. He decided to return to Greece the relic of St Andrew (the patron saint of Constantinople) that had been entrusted to Pope Pius II for safekeeping in 1462. A Roman delegation took it back to Patras in September 1964, during the third session of the Council. In November 1964, at the Third Pan-Orthodox Conference of Rhodes, the Orthodox Churches discussed their relations with Rome. On 15 February 1965, two envoys of Patriarch Athenagoras I visited Paul VI to acquaint him with the desires expressed at Rhodes: there should be on both sides a general, spiritual, preparation for dialogue, and a theological dialogue should be initiated later. In return, Cardinal Bea travelled to Istanbul in early April on an official visit. Two delegates of the secretariat (Willebrands and Duprey) visited Patriarch Alexis in May and June of the same year, and the Catholicos of Georgia. Not forgetting the Ancient Oriental Churches (of so-called Monophysite origin), they also visited the Supreme Catholicos of All the Armenians in Erevan.

Toward the end of the fourth session of the Council, Paul VI and

Athenagoras reached the proper conclusion: the mutual excommunications pronounced in Constantinople in 1054 between the papal legate, Humbert de Moyenmoutier, and Patriarch Michael Cerularios had become obsolete. In November 1965 a special commission of the two Churches agreed on a joint declaration that the excommunications were to be 'removed from the memory and the midst of the Church . . ., and committed to oblivion'. On 7 December this declaration was solemnly proclaimed at the Council in Rome and at the Orthodox liturgy at the patriarchal residence of the Phanar in Istanbul.

AFTER VATICAN II

With regard to the Orthodox Church, *Unitatis Redintegratio* had seen the ecumenical problem as one of restoring the communion that had existed in the past. Pending theological and doctrinal questions, however important in themselves, were deemed to be secondary. This understanding of the matter was clearly shared by Pope Paul VI and by Patriarch Athenagoras. The policy of ecumenical gestures, in view of an eventual restoration of communion, was therefore pursued on both sides. On 25–26 July 1967 Paul VI paid a visit to the ecumenical patriarch in Istanbul, and made a pilgrimage to Ephesus. In return, Athenagoras I visited Rome in the following October (26–28).

Meanwhile, similar gestures of progressive reconciliation brought the Ancient Oriental Churches and the Catholic Church closer together. On 8–12 May 1968, the Supreme Catholicos of All the Armenians, Vasken I, along with two other patriarchs and many bishops of his Church, paid an official visit to Pope Paul VI. In November 1971, Cardinal Willebrands attended the enthronement of the new Coptic patriarch in Cairo.

It soon became clear, however, that gestures of friendship and mutual esteem were not enough. Letters between bishops were exchanged, especially for the great feasts of the liturgical calendar. Mutual visits of delegates continued on a regular basis. On 8 February 1971, in a letter to the ecumenical patriarch, Paul VI stated that the communion of the two Churches was 'already almost full', and expressed his desire for an eventual concelebration. On 21 March, Athenagoras responded that if the two Churches 'are separated for causes known to the Lord, they are not divided in the substance of communion in the mystery of Jesus, God made man, and of his divine-human Church'. On 24 January 1972, a delegation from the patriarchate presented Paul VI with a copy of the *Tomos Agapis*, a volume containing documents on Vatican–Phanar relations from 1958 to 1970. But the list of possible symbolic gestures is soon exhausted. In fact, the only remarkable gesture that was made after 1969 was that of Paul VI in 1975, when, on the tenth anniversary of the lifting of the anathemas, he received an Orthodox delegation that was headed by Bishop Meliton, a member of the Holy Synod of Constantinople. To the surprise of everyone present, Paul VI knelt before him and kissed the feet of Bishop Meliton!

The policy of gestures ought to be supported by attempts to reach a theological agreement on the questions that have traditionally been debated between Eastern and Western Christians. Orthodox and Catholic prelates and theologians meet more and more frequently, notably in the context of WCC activities and discussions. But this is not sufficient to overcome distrust and disagreement between the two ancient traditions. These derive ultimately from the differing orientations of the Greek and the Latin fathers. They were exacerbated in the past by political circumstances. They bear on such matters as the uncanonical insertion of *Filioque* in the Latin creed, the corresponding doctrine of the *Filioque*, the nature of the primacy of the bishop of Rome as the first patriarch and the successor of Peter, the Western doctrine of papal infallibility, the imagery and understanding of purgatory, the doctrine and dogmatization of Mary's Immaculate Conception, and the dogmatization of Mary's Assumption.

Discussion of these questions by theologians of the two Churches has always been delicate. In fact, the first theological conversations, that took place under Paul VI, preferred to deal with matters arising from the problems and divisions of the modern world. A Russian Orthodox delegation headed by the metropolitan of Leningrad, Nikodim, met with a Catholic delegation in Leningrad (1967), Bari (1970) and Zagorsk (1973), to discuss 'the role of the Christian in the developing society'. This continued at Trent (1975) on the topic, 'the Christian proclamation of salvation in a changing world'. Such meetings are made difficult by what Cardinal Willebrands, at the plenary meeting of the Secretariat in February 1984, called 'the negative effects of extra-ecclesial tensions'. Yet there have been times when relations between Rome and Moscow have been especially close. In December 1969 the Russian Orthodox Church decided to admit Catholics to Holy Communion when the latter find themselves without the services of a Catholic priest (as would be the case in most cities of the Soviet Union). On 30 May 1971, Cardinal Willebrands addressed a local Council of the Russian Orthodox Church at Zagorsk. Later meetings of a joint delegation examined the notion of catholicity (Odessa, March 1980) and 'The Diaconal Function of the Church, especially in the service of peace' (Venice, October 1987). In 1988 a delegation representing the Catholic Church was invited to take part in the celebrations of the conversion of Prince Vladimir of Kiev (988), the event that introduced Christianity into Russia. It was headed by Cardinal Casaroli. On occasion, Roman delegations have also visited all the other patriarchates of the Orthodox Church, the ancient ones (Antioch (Beyrouth), Alexandria, Jerusalem) as well as the new ones (in Romania and Bulgaria), and the patriarchates and catholicates of the Ancient Oriental Churches.

The theological aspects and causes of Eastern–Western dissensions were indeed studied in local theological dialogues, some of which were anterior to Vatican Council II. But relations with the Orthodox Church should go beyond the level of practical co-operation, mutual esteem and friendship, and this requires that the theological problems be cleared at the level of the universal Church. After the schism of 1054 this was attempted at the second Council of Lyons (1274) and the Council of Florence (1439). In both cases the solutions arrived at proved untenable. But would the Churches be less bold and enterprising today than they were in the Middle Ages and at the Renaissance?

Patriarch Athenagoras died (January 1973) too soon to take this new step. He was succeeded by Dimitrios I.

One condition for a renewal of dialogue at the highest level was imperative. Since the Orthodox Church, which accepts the decisions of Ecumenical Councils, rejects the findings of the two synods of Lyons and Florence, these assemblies should not be considered ecumenical in the context of Orthodox–Catholic relations. Paul VI boldly opened the way in 1974. Sending Cardinal Willebrands to Lyons for the anniversary of the Council, he did not call it ecumenical, in spite of all the catholic textbooks to the contrary. Instead, he identified it as the 'Second General Council of Lyons', the 'sixth of the General Synods held in the Western world'. It was Paul VI's conviction, already expressed to Patriarch Athenagoras in 1967, that the political causes of dissent had now been removed by history: the way should soon be ready for taking a new look together at the theological problems. The first step was taken in 1975: on the anniversary of the lifting of the anathemas, Patriarch Dimitrios I announced that the Orthodox Churches together had decided to create an 'Inter-Orthodox Theological Commission for the Preparation by the Orthodox Church of the Theological Dialogue with the Catholic Church'. In response, Paul VI immediately named a 'Catholic Preparatory Commission for Theological Dialogue with the Orthodox Churches'. A 'Joint Coordinating Group' was established between them. It met in March–April 1978 and agreed on a proposal for an effective dialogue.

The major contribution of John Paul II to Orthodox–Catholic relations has been his co-operation with Patriarch Dimitrios I. The pope went to Istanbul to visit the patriarch in November 1979; and the patriarch returned the visit and was received at the Vatican in December 1987. Between these two meetings they decided to implement the theological dialogue foreseen by their predecessors. A 'Catholic–Orthodox Joint Commission for Ecumenical Dialogue' was established in 1980. It held its first meeting in May–June of that year (Patmos and Rhodes). Three sub-commissions were created, to study the 'mystery of the Church and the Eucharist in the light of the mystery of the Holy Trinity'. A synthesis of the result was drafted by a Co-ordinating Committee (Venice, May 1981). The meetings of the full Joint Commission are carefully prepared by this Co-ordinating Committee. They have been held in July 1982 (Munich, where a topic was chosen: 'Faith, Sacraments, and the Unity of the Church'), June 1984 (Crete), June 1986 (Bari), June 1987 (Bari, where a statement on the topic was adopted), June 1988 (New Valamo, Finland, where discussion began on another topic: 'The sacrament of Orders, Apostolic Succession, and the sanctification and unity of the people of God').

On numerous occasions John Paul II has expressed his great hopes that the dialogue with Orthodoxy will lead to a restoration of communion that will effectively heal the schism of 1054. In his encyclicals (especially *Redemptor Hominis* (1979), n. 1, *Dominum et Vivificantem* (1986), n. 2, n. 49, and *Redemptoris Mater* (1987), n. 52), he has taken the year 2000, the symbolic end of the second millennium after the birth of Christ, as a symbol of redemption and renovation. Can the rapprochement between Catholics and Orthodox have matured enough by that time to make a renewal of full communion possible?

This, it would seem, is the hope of the present pope. It is certainly to be prayed and worked for. Neither good will nor serious thought are lacking. Mutual visits and correspondence continue to promote friendship between Rome and all the Orthodox Churches. The Ancient Oriental Churches, though themselves out of communion with Constantinople, are involved in this vast undertaking.

Yet other forces may be at work that may make the expected outcome of reunion more Utopian than realistic. There are such forces in the progressive retrenchment of the Catholic magisterium on a strict, if not regressive, interpretation of Vatican II; in the official encouragement of an exuberant Marian piety focused on the dogma of the Immaculate Conception, not accepted in the Oriental tradition; and in the echoes that the spectacular activities and proclamations of excommunciated Archbishop Lefebvre undoubtedly evoke among some of the faithful.

13C The Orthodox Church: Bibliography

Stormon, E. J., ed. (1987) *Towards the Healing of Schism: The Sees of Rome and Constantinople. Public Statements and Correspondence between the Holy See and the Ecumenical Patriarchate, 1958–1984.* New York, Paulist Press.

13D The Anglican Communion

Unitatis Redintegratio referred to the Anglican communion as having a 'special place' among the Churches issued from the Reformation, in that 'Catholic traditions and structures partially subsist' in it (*UR* 13). But it had not drawn any consequences from this as to the ecclesial status of the *Ecclesia Anglicana*. This was to be the task of bilateral dialogues between the Churches. A national dialogue between Anglicanism and Roman Catholicism started in the United States in 1965 towards the end of the Council. It was soon followed by an international dialogue involving the entirety of the Anglican communion. In March 1966 the archbishop of Canterbury, Michael Ramsey, paid an official visit to Pope Paul VI, at the end of which they stated their intent 'to inaugurate . . . a serious dialogue which, founded on the gospels and on the ancient common traditions, may lead to that unity in truth for which Christ prayed'. The Joint Preparatory Commission that was then created met three times between January 1967 and January 1968. Its findings and recommendations are contained in the 'Malta Report' (2 January 1968). Among other points, this report affirmed two fundamental principles. First, the dialogue between the two communions must be forward-looking: 'We cannot resolve our differences by mere reconsideration of, and judgment upon, the past. We must press on in confident faith that new light will be given us to lead us to our goal' (n. 18). Second, since there exists 'a particular difficulty in regard to Anglican Orders' in the light of their condemnation as 'null' by Pope Leo XIII (in *Apostolicae Curae*, 1896), a context must be established for reconsideration of this problem: such a context can be no other than 'the theology of the Church'. Thus, for the start, ecclesiology emerged as the general concern of the coming dialogue. The Malta Report also recommended the formation of a more permanent forum for an international dialogue: the Anglican–Roman Catholic International Conversations (ARCIC). As this first commission of ARCIC was succeeded in 1983 by a second, one should distinguish between ARCIC-I, inspired by Paul VI, and ARCIC-II, created by John Paul II.

THE WORK OF ARCIC-I

ARCIC-I functioned from 1970 to 1981. It held thirteen plenary meetings. It published four Agreed Statements (*Eucharistic Doctrine*, Windsor 1971; *Ministry and Ordination*, Canterbury 1973; *Authority in the Church I*, Venice 1976; *Authority in the Church II*, Windsor 1981), and three sets of 'Elucidations' that were destined to answer questions and face objections regarding the published statements (on *Eucharistic Doctrine*, Salisbury 1979; on *Ministry and Ordination*, Salisbury 1979; on *Authority in the Church I*, Windsor, 1981). Finally, all its Agreed Statements and Elucidations were bound together under the title *The Final Report* (1981), and ARCIC-I prefaced the publication with some reflections on the ecclesiology that was instrumental in its work. The highlights of these documents will be indicated.

ARCIC-I set an example of ecumenical methodology when it decided

410

systematically to avoid theological terms to which past controversies have given polemical connotations. It worked on the basis, implicit in the first Agreed Statement, explicit in the later ones and the introduction, of an ecclesiology of *koinonia* (communion). The point of departure being the Eucharist, the Church is seen as 'expressed and proclaimed' in the Eucharist, that is, as the community that is 'centred in, and partaking of [Christ's] body and blood' (*Eucharistic Doctrine* n. 3). The Eucharist is itself perceived as 'mystery', a complex sacramental event in which Christ, 'crucified and risen', is present in the Holy Spirit 'through bread and wine'. Past polemics about sacrifices are overcome in the biblical notion of *anamnesis* or 'memorial', in which 'the totality of God's action' in Christ (n. 5) is offered to the community of believers. The medieval term, 'transubstantiation', that evokes philosophical categories that are largely foreign to the modern mind, is avoided. Yet faith affirms that the action of God brings about the 'real presence' of Christ through 'the prayer of thanksgiving, a word of faith addressed to the Father . . . so that in communion we eat the flesh of Christ and drink his blood' (n. 10).

In the Catholic tradition that is recognized by the two Churches, the Eucharist is tied to ministry, orders and ordination. The ordained ministry should be seen on the backdrop of the ministry of the whole Church and its members, 'whose purpose is always to build up the community (*koinonia*)' (*Ministry and Ordination*, n. 3). Originating in the sending of the Son by the Father, it was given its paradigm in the mission of the apostles. It was differentiated in the early times of the Church between *episcopoi* (bishops) and *presbyteroi* (priests), to whom deacons were associated. This ministry has a historical genesis and development. Its task is the 'oversight' of the community in the work of reconciliation. Like the 'priesthood of the people of God' that is conveyed in baptism, it is theologically dependent on the High Priesthood of Christ; yet it is 'not an extension of the common Christian priesthood but belongs to another realm of the gifts of the Spirit' (n. 13). Ordination by laying on of hands is the act through which ministers are chosen, empowered and sent. In these two statements, ARCIC-I lays claim to having reached 'substantial agreement' on the doctrine of the Eucharist (*Eucharistic Doctrine*, n. 12), 'a consensus . . . on essential matters' regarding the ministry (*Ministry and Ordination*, n. 17).

The treatment of authority in the Church was in two stages, because an area emerged in which no such consensus could yet be obtained. In the first stage the principles regarding Christian authority and its diversification in several types of lay, episcopal, conciliar and primatial authority within the *koinonia* were the object of a consensus which could imply, it was suggested, 'a unity at the level of faith which not only justifies but requires action to bring about closer sharing between our two communions in life, worship, and mission' (*Authority I*, n. 26). In the second stage, controversial questions were faced regarding the place of Peter in the New Testament, the language of *jus divinum* ('divine right') as it is used in relation to authority in the Church, the 'jurisdiction' that is attributed to the bishop of Rome in Roman Catholic theology and canon law, the 'infallibility' that is ascribed to him by Vatican Councils I and II. ARCIC-I agreed on 'the need of a universal primacy in a

411

united Church' (n. 31). But it could not, at this point of the dialogue, determine how the traditional Anglican form of authority could be safeguarded under the universal primacy of the bishop of Rome. The undeniable convergence on the matter of authority that is formulated, along with its substantial agreement on the doctrine of Eucharist, ministry and ordination, should serve, as the Commission stated several times, to help solve lingering problems and narrow or even eliminate remaining differences. As is stated in the conclusion of *The Final Report*, the dialogue should lead 'not merely to the achievement of doctrinal agreement, which is central to our reconciliation, but to the far greater goal of organic unity'.

THE RECEPTION OF *THE FINAL REPORT*

The first three reports had been published one by one, with the explicit authorization of Pope Paul VI and of the archbishop of Canterbury. Their reception in the theological circles of both Churches had been good, although some expressed reservation. The questions and objections that were answered in the *Elucidations* of 1979 and 1981 did not touch the substance of the agreed statements. They pointed to historical controversies; or to doctrinal questions of the past that have lost some of their importance; or to remaining points of secondary moment; or to the decision of Leo XIII regarding Anglican orders; or they questioned the extent of the consensus reached (agreement in theology or agreement in faith?); or they wondered about the exact meaning of 'substantial agreement' in the mind of the Commission. ARCIC-I certainly intended to formulate an agreement in faith. It called it substantial because the agreement related to the heart of the Christian faith on the three topics that were examined ('essential matters where it considers that doctrine admits no divergence', (*Ministry and Ordination*, n. 17), and because the commission esteemed that whatever questions or problems still remained could be 'resolved on the principles here established' (*Eucharistic Doctrine*, n. 12). The last agreed statement and the *Final Report* in its entirety could not be 'elucidated', as ARCIC-I went out of existence with their adoption.

As ARCIC-I ended its work, the Church was faced with a question about which there had hitherto been little reflection: what is the normal process of reception for a document that has been endorsed by an official theological commission of two Churches? The authorization given by Paul VI and Archbishop Ramsey to publish ARCIC's doctrinal statements before their acceptance or approval by the Churches' authorities was itself a new type of action, without antecedent or parallel in the practice of the Roman curia. Since the Counter Reformation, the Roman curia in general had dealt with doctrinal questions by way of disciplinary decisions and magisterial pronouncements that left no room for debate.

Paul VI, however, had tentatively opened a gate to an exercise of persuasive authority that was much closer to the normal functioning of Anglicanism than to customary Roman Catholic practice. In line with this, the reception of the agreed statements should have been given the time needed for free theological discussion in as many centres as possible, so that the competent authorities in the two Churches could eventually arrive at a considered judgement in the light of these reactions and evaluations, and then be able to take whatever practical steps forward may then be advisable.

OTHER LEVELS OF DIALOGUE

While ARCIC-I was working, a special International Commission on 'The Theology of Marriage and Mixed Marriages' studied the vexed question of mixed marriages. Its conclusions came out in June 1975 in the form of a Joint Report. Meanwhile, a number of ecumenical dialogues have brought together Anglicans and Roman Catholics at a national or regional level, notably in the British Isles, the United States, Canada, Australia, and South Africa. One cannot review all their findings here. Yet several documents should be mentioned. The agreed statement of 1975 on 'The Purpose of the Church' by the American dialogue (often called ARC-USA), brought further light to the theme of the Church *koinonia*. 'The Twelve Year Report' (December 1977) of the same national dialogue summed up and evaluated the first twelve years of its work (it started in 1965 before the end of Vatican II). On 22 December 1983 it proposed some pointers for the construction of a modern Christian anthropology: *Images of God: Reflections on Christian Anthropology*.

The urgency of this topic arose from the question of the ordination of women, raised unexpectedly on 29 July 1974. Since 1970, women could be ordained to the diaconate in the Episcopal Church. In 1974, several bishops, acting outside the canons of this Church, ordained several women to the priesthood. In fact, this had already been done in the diocese of Hong Kong in 1944, 1971 and 1973. But it was the American action that raised the question for the Anglican Communion as a whole, and thereby for the entire Catholic tradition as it faces the emancipation of women in modern society. In June 1975, ARC-USA organized a special consultation on the ordination of women. In October of the same year it issued a statement on ⁺he matter. Meanwhile, the General Convention of the Episcopal Church in 1976 proceeded to validate the illegal act of 1974, and henceforth to authorize the ordination of women. Other provinces of the Anglican communion followed on the same line, approving the legitimacy of the ordination of women, even in areas where such ordinations were considered premature or socially unsuitable.

In spite of the repeated assurance of Anglican bishops, duly acknowledged in the context of the bilateral dialogues, that these ordinations were not intended to alter the traditional nature of the Catholic priesthood, the emerging Anglican position threw cold water on the warm relations with Roman Catholics that were in the making. In an exchange of letters initiated by Donald Coggan, archbishop of Canterbury, Pope Paul VI declared with deep sadness that the ordination of women in the Anglican Communion was placing 'a grave and new obstacle and threat' on the path to unity (10 February 1976). In March 1978, a special Joint Consultation was held in Versailles (France) between the Secretariat for Christian Unity and the Anglican Consultative

413

Council. ARC-USA has discussed the question several times. All these meetings, however, can do little more than recognize the deadlock. Yet they suggest, as was perceived by ARC-USA, that it is urgent to work jointly on a Christian anthropology for the modern context of life. In the meantime, however, the election of women as bishops in the Anglican Communion must make the issue even more serious for ecumenical relations. The Lambeth Conference of 1988 has approved such a step by an overwhelming majority, and the first woman bishop was elected in Massachusetts later the same year.

FURTHER STEPS IN THE RECEPTION OF THE *FINAL REPORT*

The process of reception was vitiated from the start, when the Congregation for the Doctrine of the Faith intervened along the lines ordinarily followed by its predecessor, the Holy office. The *Final Report* was released to the public at a press conference in London, on 29 March 1982. Two days before, on 27 March, the 'Observations' of the Congregation had already been addressed to the two chairmen of ARCIC-I by the prefect of the Congregation. On 2 April, five days after the release of the *Final Report*, these 'Observations on the Final Report of ARCIC' were sent to the national conferences of bishops, most of which, for obvious reasons, had not yet seen the *Final Report*. The 'Observations' were a hasty composition, and not of a very high calibre. They betrayed a degree of ignorance concerning the Anglican Communion and its history that could easily have been avoided by more consultation. Others pointed to a number of pending questions, most of them secondary, that had been listed by ARCIC itself. Still others were theological points tied to the language of the Counter Reformation, that ARCIC had systematically shunned out of ecumenical sensitivity. Above all, the 'Observations' declared: 'It is not yet possible to say that a truly "substantial" agreement has been reached on the totality of the questions studied by the Commission.' Here, the Congregation employed the word 'substantial' in a more scholastic sense than that of ARCIC, where the term was simply used as it is current in plain English. The ensuing denial of the position of ARCIC-I was self-evidently off the point. Yet this became responsible for the hesitancy of most conferences of bishops to speak in a more positive way of the work of ARCIC-I, for disappointment on the part of those who deemed the work of ARCIC-I worthy of more serious theological treatment, and for widespread confusion in the people of God. It indirectly pointed to the difficulty of a normal process of reception in the present organization of the Catholic Church, as it showed up a built-in weakness of the Roman curia, which had not yet incorporated ecumenical requirements into its mode of functioning. In spite of this, however, most conferences of bishops have addressed their own remarks on the *Final Report* to the Secretariat for Christian Unity. Their collation into one document is not finished at the time of writing.

Meanwhile, the process of reception of the *Final Report* in the churches of the Anglican Communion reached a major stage at the 12th Lambeth Conference (Summer 1988). The statements on Eucharist and on Ministry, with their Elucidations, were recognized as 'consonant in substance with the faith of Anglicans', and 'a sufficient basis for taking the next step forward' towards reconciliation. This next step, however, was not identified. The statements on Authority, I and II, with the Elucidations of I, were 'welcome as a firm basis for the direction and agenda of the continuing dialogue'. In other words, further work needs to be done, on the basis proposed by ARCIC-I, relating to 'the concept of a universal primacy in conjunction with collegiality as an instrument of unity [and on] the character of such a primacy in practice'. This further work is the task of ARCIC-II.

THE WORK OF ARCIC-II

ARCIC-II was created on 10 November 1982. It was assigned three general tasks: 'to examine . . . the outstanding differences', especially the doctrine of justification by faith and questions of morality; 'to study all that hinders the mutual recognition of the ministries of our Communions', especially *Apostolicae Curae* and the question of the ordination of women; and 'to recommend practical steps' with a view to 'full communion'.

ARCIC-I therefore started with the doctrine of justification, which it examined as an aspect of the theology of salvation, in the context of an ecclesiology of *koinonia*. Its first agreed statement, *Salvation and the Church*, was released on 22 January 1987. It has since turned its attention to problems relating to orders and ordination. Among these problems is the continuing practice of the Roman Catholic magisterium to abide by the decision of Pope Leo XIII against the validity of Anglican orders (*Apostolicae Curae*, 1896). ARCIC-I alluded to this when it argued that its agreed statements were 'setting a new context' for the solution of the question of ordination. The perspective of ARCIC-II in this area was clarified by Cardinal Willebrands in a letter of 13 July 1987 to the co-chairmen of ARCIC-II. The president of the Secretariat for Christian Unity endorsed the notion that a new context is in the making. He noted that the question of the validity of Anglican orders has taken new aspects since the decision of Leo XIII. The liturgical renewal of the two Communions, the dialogue of the last twenty years, and the 'profound study' of the work of ARCIC-I that is taking place, may lead to a reassessment of what Leo XIII called the *nativa indoles*, the 'innate character', of the Anglican ordinal.

SOME ECUMENICAL GESTURES

As in their relations with the Orthodox Church, both Paul VI and John Paul II have realized that gestures of good will and ecumenical commitment are at least as important as the steps that are being taken to arrive at a doctrinal consensus among Western Christians. While important in their consequences, the gestures have been less spectacular than those of Paul VI toward Orthodoxy. The creation of an 'Anglican Centre' in Rome in October 1966 was encouraged by Paul VI. This was more than symbolic, as this centre and its library are helping Catholic scholars to study the history and theology of Anglicanism. In October 1966 the anniversary of the Malines Conversations, celebrated in Belgium, was graced by a telegram from Paul VI. On certain occasions, Paul VI invited visiting Anglican bishops to bless the people with him.

The ecumenical gestures of John Paul II have been made chiefly in the context of his 'pastoral journeys' to various countries, when he willingly meets with pastors and theologians of diverse Churches. This began with the papal visits to Ireland and to the United States in September–October 1979. Prayers in common are organized. In Informal meetings, the pope listens to the views of Protestant Christians and speaks with them. In May 1982 the papal visit to England was the occasion for a common declaration in Canterbury Cathedral. This has served as the charter for ARCIC-II. In it, Pope John Paul II and Archbishop Runcie announced the formation of the new commission, formulated its goals, invited the members of their two Churches to 'collaboration and prayer', and hailed the efforts towards the reunion of all Christians as a 'renewed challenge to abandon ourselves completely to the truth of the Gospel'.

13D The Anglican Communion: Bibliography

Bired, D. J. (1987) '"The Anglican Communion Occupies a Special Place." An Examination of the Background, Development and Reception in the Roman Catholic Church of the Text on the Special Place of the Anglican Communion in *Unitatis Redintegratio*', PhD thesis, Pittsburgh, Dusquesne University.

Clarke. A., and Davey, C., eds. (1974) *Anglican–Roman Catholic Dialogue: The Work of the Preparatory Commission*. London, Oxford University Press.

Mairiri Nididde, J. C. (1987) 'Primacy in the Communion of Churches: A Study in Anglican–Catholic Dialogue'. PhD thesis, Rome, Urbaniana University.

Mikulanis, D. L. (1986) 'Authority in the Church from the Perspective of Recent Anglican–Roman Catholic Dialogues', Rome, PhD thesis. Thomas Aquinas University.

Not Strangers but Pilgrims: Churches Together in Pilgrimage. (1989) London, British Council of Churches/CTS.

Ryan H., and Wright, J. R., eds (1972) *Episcopalians and Roman Catholics: Can They Ever Get Together?* Denville, Dimension Books.

Tavard, G. H. (1990) *A Review of Anglican Orders. The Problem – and the Solution*. Collegeville, MN, Liturgical Press.

Witmer, J., and Wright, J. R. (1986) *Called to Full Unity: Documents on Anglican–Roman Catholic Relations, 1966–1983*. Washington, USCC Publications.

Wright, J. R., ed. (1979) *A Communion of Communions: One Eucharistic Fellowship*. New York, Seabury Press.

13E The Protestant Churches

Ecumenical dialogues opened, after Vatican Council II, with almost all the Protestant Churches directly issued from the Reformation and with some of the more recent Churches and ecclesial communities. International dialogues take place between the Catholic Church and the following agencies:

1 the Lutheran World Federation, since 1965;

2 the World Methodist Council since 1967;

3 the World Alliance of Reformed Churches, since 1970;

4 the Disciples (Christian Church), since 1967;

5 representatives of classical Pentecostal Churches, since 1972 (with a 'Final Report' in 1982);

6 representatives of several evangelical and missionary associations, for a dialogue on mission (in 1977, 1982 and 1984);

7 a group of Baptist scholars and religious leaders (annual meetings since 1984);

8 the United Bible Societies, for the purpose of collaboration in translating the Bible into the many languages of the world (since 1967, with 'Guidelines' for joint translations published in 1968 and 1987).

In addition, a tripartite dialogue on 'the theology of marriage and the problem of mixed marriages' has been held between Reformed, Lutherans and Catholics. It began in November 1971, issued its report in 1976, and met again in 1980 to evaluate the reactions to its report. There are also national and regional dialogues in many parts of the world. Special comments will be made on the international dialogues with Lutherans and with Methodists, and, on account of their intrinsic importance, on the unofficial dialogue of the 'Groupe des Dombes' and on the reports of 'Lutherans and Catholics in Dialogue in the USA'.

THE LUTHERAN/ROMAN CATHOLIC JOINT COMMISSION

This international dialogue started in 1965. It has produced three major documents and several shorter statements. *The Gospel and the Church* (often called 'The Malta Report'), 1972, is an overview of traditional pending questions, with an indication of the evolution of the topic since the Reformation. *The Eucharist*, 1981, is in part a 'joint witness' to the traditional Eucharistic doctrine, with a description of 'common tasks' that still need to be done in regard to the Eucharistic presence, the notion of sacrifice, the practice of Communion, and the liturgy itself. The Commission has also issued reports on the Confession of Augsburg: *All under One Christ* (1980). In 1981 it published *The Ministry in the Church*. On the occasion of the 500th anniversary of Luther's birth, it composed *Martin Luther – Witness to Jesus Christ* (6 May 1983). For its next major topic the Commission entered new ground, ground that no other dialogue had yet approached. Picking up a concern it had touched upon in *Ways to Community*, 1980, it wrote *Facing Unity*, 1985. This attempts to foresee and outline the possible ways in which the official reconciliation of Lutherans and Catholics can take place. After surveying several modes of reunion that have been tried or suggested through the ecumenical movement, the Commission proposes a way that will lead the two traditions to a community of faith, hence to a community in sacraments, and finally to a community of service (service being identified here as the service of pastoral leadership in the Christian community).

Encouragement was given to the growing fellowship of Lutherans and Catholics when Pope John Paul II visited the Lutheran *Christuskirche* in Rome, and preached from its pulpit during a celebration of the word (11 December 1983).

THE JOINT COMMISSION WITH THE WORLD METHODIST COUNCIL

This dialogue has opted for another style, one that gives as much weight to experience as to doctrine. It has not reached the theological level of the dialogue with Lutheranism, yet its contribution to the growth of ecumenical understanding is impressive. It functions on a quinquennial basis, renewing its membership and changing its topic every five years on the occasion of the plenary meetings of the World Methodist Council. Since its beginning in 1967 it has thus produced four reports. These tend to be general surveys dealing with a variety of topics. Yet they are unified by a central concern: practical Christian spirituality (received at the WMC meeting in Denver, 1971), salvation and the Christian life (Dublin, 1976), the Holy Spirit and Christian experience (Honolulu, 1981), and the nature of the Church (Nairobi, 1986).

THE 'GROUPE DES DOMBES'

Named after the Trappist monastery where it has met since 1968, this is the oldest continuing ecumenical dialogue. It was started in 1937 under the impulse of Abbé Couturier. It includes Lutherans (Evangelical) and Reformed (Calvinists) from France and Switzerland, and occasionally from Belgium. It did not publish its findings until 1963, when it decided to release the 'theses' that it had arrived at in 1956 ('Original Sin'), 1957 ('The Mediation of Christ'), 1958 ('The Church as Body of Christ'), 1959 ('Pastoral Activity in the Church'), 1960 ('Apostolicity of the Church'), 1961 ('Priesthood and Ministry of the Church'), and 1962 ('The Priestly action of Christ in the Church's Priestly Activity'). Later theses were published in 1967 ('Intercommunion'), 1968 ('Apostolic Succession'), 1969 ('The Holy Spirit'), 1970 ('The Communion of Saints'). From 1971 on, the group has followed the example of the official dialogues and composed full-size statements: on *Eucharistic Faith* (1971), *The Reconciliation of Ministries* (1972), *The Episcopal Ministry* (1976), *The Holy Spirit, the Church and the Sacraments* (1979), *The Ministry of*

Communion in the Church Universal (1985). Although they remain unofficial, these conversations are promising, as, aided by the cultural unity of the group, they reflect the Calvinist tradition at a level of theological depth that the more international official dialogue with the Alliance of Reformed Churches has not been able to reach.

'LUTHERANS AND ROMAN CATHOLICS IN DIALOGUE' IN THE UNITED STATES

Of the innumerable national dialogues between Protestants and Catholics, this has been the most important because of the pioneering scope of its reports. It has published increasingly lengthy common statements on 'The Nicene Creed as Dogma of the Church' (1965), 'One Baptism for the Remission of Sins' (1966), 'The Eucharist as Sacrifice' (1967), 'Eucharist and Ministry' (1970), 'Papal Primacy and the Universal Church' (1974), 'Teaching Authority and Infallibility in the Church' (1980), and 'Justification by Faith' (1985). It has also sponsored studies by a group of scholars from several Churches, whose findings were published as *Peter in the New Testament* (1973) and *Mary in the New Testament* (1978). The document of 1970 made a bold suggestion for the eventual recognition of Lutheran ordinations. That of 1985 formulated a consensus on justification by faith that goes a long way towards overcoming the principal problem of the Reformation. At the present time, this dialogue is studying 'Mary and the Saints'.

BAPTISM, EUCHARIST, AND MINISTRY AND ITS RECEPTION

One should at this point return to the Faith and Order Commission of the WCC. In 1982 this Commission published an agreement entitled, *Baptism, Eucharist, and Ministry*, often called 'the Lima Report', from the city where it was released. This statement encapsulates the furthest advance towards Catholicity that can be made for the moment by the generality of the Protestant Churches. It takes the form of a consensus, with indication of lingering problems, and agreements to disagree where this is appropriate. It relates to Catholic–Protestant relations in two ways. First, a number of Catholic theologians, members of Faith and Order, took part in the long discussions that prepared it, and in the final redaction. Second, the official Catholic response to the BEM was released by the Secretariat for Unity in August 1987. Both the method and the quality of this response show that some ecumenical progress has been made in the working of the Roman curia since 1982, when the Congregation for the Doctrine of the Faith gave its premature response to ARCIC's *Final Report*.

The process was co-ordinated by the Secretariat for Christian Unity. It started in 1982 with a consultation of the national conferences of bishops, of Catholic universities, and of some other competent organizations. The answers were then received, analysed, and sorted out by a team of consultants, who then drafted a general Catholic response. Lastly, this draft was given its final form in collaboration between the Secretariat and the Congregation for the Doctrine of the Faith. This question of method and process is important for all Catholic–Protestant relations. Ever since the Reformation, problems of content and teaching have always been compounded by problems of style and approach. Protestants have been repelled by the magisterial mode of authority in the Catholic Church no less than by the objective content of its teaching and discipline. Much of the effort for better relations in view of an eventual organic unity should therefore bear on style and method.

As to its content, the official Catholic response to *Baptism, Eucharist and Ministry* praises the openness and honesty of the report, its appreciation of Catholic positions, the weight it gives to tradition as the proper locus for interpreting Scripture, the theological depth at which most questions are treated. It agrees with the 'holistic approach' to Christian unity that is apparent in the report, and with the urgency of keeping the goal of organic unity in mind through all ecumenical activities. At the same time, it indicates several areas that stand in need of further clarification (as on infant baptism), where an agreement to disagree is not satisfactory (as on whether ordination is a sacrament), where there is insufficient consideration of some theological or doctrinal point (as on ordination of women). In particular, it regrets that the study of ministry paid no attention to the traditional ministry of the bishop of Rome at the service of the Universal Church.

CONCLUSION

The Catholic response to *Baptism, Eucharist and Ministry* may serve as a marker in the ecumenical relations of the Catholic Church. The quality of these relations rests for a large part on the extensive network of meetings and consultations that have been established between the Catholic Church at its many levels, and the corresponding levels of the Orthodox, Anglican and Protestant Churches. It evidently also depends on a multitude of non-theological factors, and especially on the extra-ecclesial conditions of the world, with its divisions, at one level, between flourishing and impoverished countries, at another between rival political systems and conflicting ideologies. But a relatively short period of trial and error on the part of the Roman magisterium leads to the conclusion that the quality of ecumenical relations depends to a large extent on intra-ecclesial conditions, and specifically on harmony and understanding within the Roman curia, between Rome and the national episcopal conferences, and between the agencies and people at work at the diocesan and local levels.

Much progress has undoubtedly been made since Vatican II. The principles and recommendations of *Unitatis Redintegratio* have been generally proven correct by experience. Yet much more needs to be done. The results of the dialogues between scholars are still largely unknown to the laity and clergy who make up the people of God. The process of ecumenical education at the ground level has hardly begun. Conflicts between diverse tendencies in public opinion within the Church (that are often labelled, for lack of better terms, traditionalist and conservative, or progressive and liberal) commonly thrive on differing appreciations of ecumenical activities. Faced with the threat of internal dissent, the Catholic magisterium tends to fall back on reticent attitudes. Thus there is ground to think that the interpretation, by episcopal authority, of the careful conciliar formula on *communicatio in sacris* has been excessively restrictive. Yet this may still belong to the hesitancies of the beginnings.

13E The Protestant Churches: Bibliography

Lutheran:

Burgess, J. and Tavard, G. (1980) *Studies for Lutheran–Catholic Dialogue*. Minneapolis, Augsburg.

Lutherans and Catholics in Dialogue, vol. III. Washington, USCC Publications; 1967; vol. IV, Washington, USCC Publications, 1970; vol. V, Minneapolis, Augsburg, 1974; vol. VI, Minneapolis, Augsburg, 1980; vol. VII, Minneapolis, Augsburg, 1985.

Presbyterian:

Pour la Communion des Eglises: L'Apport du Groupe des Dombes, 1937–1987 (1988) Paris, Le Centurion.

Reconsiderations: Roman Catholic–Presbyterian and Reformed Theological Conversations. (1967) New York, World Horizons.

Vischer L., and Karrer, A. (1988) *Reformed and Roman Catholics in Dialogue. A Survey of the Dialogues at National Levels.* Geneva, World Alliance of Reformed Churches.

Pentecostal:

Sandidge, J. L. (1987) *Roman Catholic/Pentecostal Dialogue, 1977–1982. A Study in Developing Ecumenism*, 2 vols. Frankfurt-am-Main, Verlag Peter Lang.

14

CATHOLIC THEOLOGY IN THE POST-CONCILIAR PERIOD

JOHN McDADE sj

> Tired of the old descriptions of the world,
> The latest freed man rose at six and sat
> On the edge of his bed. He said,
>   I suppose there is
> A doctrine to this landscape . . . (Wallace Stevens, 'The Latest Freed Man')

The quest for a doctrine appropriate to the landscape may be taken as an image of the development of Catholic theology since Vatican II: it symbolizes the way in which Catholic theology in the post-conciliar period is dependent upon the Council's readjustment of the landscape of contemporary Catholic identity. In addition, it presents a theme that will become central to post-conciliar theology: the priority of the 'landscape' of lived experience in the articulation of theological 'doctrine'. As the features of Catholic faith-experience were altered by the Council, the consequent theological reflection followed contours different from those that preceded it.

The Council correctly did not regard theology as the primary agent of reformation and change within the Church. Neither was the Council directly responsible for a renewal of Catholic theology: this had been underway, chiefly in France and Germany, since the 1930s. Although the lines of theological continuity between pre- and post-conciliar theology – expressed in the foundational work of Rahner, Congar, Daniélou, de Lubac, von Balthasar, and Chenu – continue to shape the reception of the Council they inspired, they no longer supply the central perspective of post-conciliar theology. Vatican II's contribution to theology is not primarily in its formal acceptance of a particular approach, for example, to ecclesiology or to revelation; although its documents on these matters are immensely significant, the Council's importance for theology lies rather in the new location it proposed for theological reflection.

This most ecclesial of Councils proposed, in *Gaudium et Spes*, that the Church ought to be characterized by a profound engagement with the reality of the world's experience: no longer a Church set apart from the world within an institutional Christendom, but a Church that enters into profound solidarity with the experiences of human society, and takes humanity seriously in the unfolding of its history. This new location of the Church's identity prescribes a new location for theology, and a revaluation of what is to count as properly theological activity. If human history becomes an indispensable *locus revelationis* for the Church – and I take this to be the principal theological orientation of the Council, and the central *intuition maîtresse* of post-conciliar theology – then human history becomes the *locus theologicus* for the post-conciliar theologian. The implications of this new location for Catholic theology can be illuminated, again with the help of a quotation from Wallace Stevens; writing about the need to construct a modern poetic language, he describes its contemporary task:

> . . . It has not always had
> To find: the scene was set; it repeated what
> Was in the script.
>   Then the theatre was changed
> To something else. Its past was a souvenir.
> It has to be living, to learn the speech of the place.
> It has to face the men of the time and to meet
> The women of the time. It has to think about war
> And it has to find what will suffice. It has
> To construct a new stage. ('Of Modern Poetry')

The new stage on which post-conciliar theology is to speak is set unambiguously in the middle of human history and experience. (This also has the effect of revivifying biblical and historical theology – the study of the 'script' of inherited tradition – because the relationship of the various texts to their contexts illuminates the character of theology as something 'enacted' in varying cultural milieux.) As with 'modern poetry', so with theology: the audience must be offered utterances – 'wholly/Containing the mind, below which it cannot descend/Beyond which it has no will to rise' – in which a contemporary audience can recognize the truth of its experience.

It is no accident that Rahner's transcendental theology, which sees itself as the articulation of unthematized human experience, becomes such an important influence on post-conciliar theology: its background lay in the epistemology of Maréchal, the French Jesuit. The point of Rahner's use of it is to disclose the ultimately 'mystical' character of all human subjectivity as an 'immediate, preconceptual experience of God' (Imhof and Biallowons, 1986, p. 182). *Homo est capax Mysterii*: human beings, in their very constitution, are oriented towards the self-communication of God; by establishing the transcendental character of human subjectivity as a constitutive moment of revelation, Rahner provides post-conciliar theology with its most ambitious image of the co-naturality of the Creator and the creature, dynamically oriented towards one another. His statement, 'man as subject is the event of God's absolute self-communication', is the basis of a fundamental theology with considerable implications for how the themes of grace, Christology and revelation are related (Rahner, 1978, p. 119).

Christian theology of every age must address the question of how Jesus is significant for the nature of reality: the foundational post-biblical response is given by the apologists in their development of a '*Logos* Theology', and Rahner's theological anthropology stands in this tradition of attempting to provide an ontologico-metaphysical account of the correlation of the mystery of the triune God and the mystery of humanity, in the light of which a Christology can move from its metaphorical roots towards an ontology.

For Rahner, human beings are not only capable of God's self-communication, but *because* they exist at all, that self-communication is what constitutes them as creatures. Rahner presents God's revelation in Jesus as the 'grammar' that brings to articulate expression the mystery of the God–world relationship, and by considering Christology and salvation within the context of the God–world relationship, he enables post-conciliar theology to develop a new 'paradigm' for itself in which the concerns of anthropology and history become central. In an interview in 1974, he raises the question of what is 'the fundamental and basic conception' within Christian theology: his answer is neither incarnation nor soteriology, but 'the divinization of the world through the Spirit of God' (Imhof and Biallowons, 1986, p. 126). Hence, history and society cannot be left out of the task of 'speaking about God', because they are the very context in which the 'divinization' of the world occurs. Theology, then, must address the dynamic of the Spirit's action in that world. This reply, which takes the doctrine of creation as the over-arching conceptual framework of theology, and which moves behind the inherited doctrines in order to reveal their significance within the metaphysics of the God–world relationship, summarizes perfectly the concern of post-conciliar theologians to take the world seriously in its reality and development. It is an answer that exemplifies the post-conciliar concern to explore alternative ways in which the classic doctrinal truths can be shown to have an anthropological and metaphysical significance, and Rahner's contribution to this field is immense.

Acerbi is correct in identifying anthropology as the 'conceptual medium' through which post-conciliar theology, principally under the influence of Rahner, constructs a new model of the relationship between the Church and the world:

> To establish at their centre the 'mystery' of man, created and redeemed, is to proclaim that at the heart of human history is the 'mystery of Christ', in which man and his activity find their meaning and their fulfilment (Acerbi, 1981, pp. 81–2).

That the mystery of Christ is to be found within the *humanum*, within the complex of human experience and history, directs theologians to issues concerning the *context* within which theology is constructed. The agenda of theology then necessarily involves questions about its engagement with the world in its development, its orientation within particular social situations, and fundamental questions about its methodology and hermeneutics. And it is through the introduction of this horizon within the sphere of proper 'speech about God' that theology is most deeply affected in the post-Vatican II period.

A condition for this enterprise – labelled by Gordon Kaufmann as 'Catholicism confronts Modernity' – is that the Church enter into solidarity with the experiences of contemporary society, in order to make the world's experience *its* experience. This insight implies that the post-Vatican II Church demands a different theological agenda in which anthropology, history and the impact of social relations on theology become central concerns for a Church that begins to consider itself as the articulate heart of the world's implicit experience of God and the Kingdom. Post-Vatican II theology does not register significant developments in doctrine, but it attempts to answer the essentially pastoral question, 'What is the appropriate theology for this world, and for a Church committed to the good of this world?' New human and social matrices, which focus on the historicity and contextuality of *all* theological understanding, become constitutive of valid theological reflection if the theologian's primary concern becomes the character of the world's development into God's kingdom.

A simple illustration will make the point: the *Dictionnaire de Théologie Catholique*, published between 1903 and 1950, has either no article, or an insufficient treatment, of human and social themes that later became central to post-Vatican II theology: *Work*: nothing; *Family*: nothing; *Woman*: nothing; *Economy*: nothing; *Politics*: nothing; *History*: nothing; *World*: nothing; *Life*: an article of eternal life; *Laity*: nothing apart from an article on laicism (a heresy); *Technology*: nothing; *Sex*: nothing; *Power*: 103 columns on 'the power of the pope in the temporal order'. After the Council, these anthropological and social themes assumed a central, constitutive role in theological reflection (Congar, 1986, p. 144).

In the years immediately following Vatican II, because of the need to disseminate and clarify the work of the Council, theology is directly and consciously tied to the Council in an interpretative and expository way. To judge by *Concilium*, this lasts until 1973; after this point, it is significant that Vatican II ceases to be the primary point of reference for theology, which then concerns itself more with the trajectory which it regards as continuous with the 'mind' of the Council.

> From 1974 onwards, then, the dogmatic issues became much more closely related to man's problems 'in the world'. The point of reference was no longer the Second Vatican Council . . . but the situation in the world and the Church since the Council (Schillebeeckx, 1983, p. 16).

The immediate theological exposition of the conciliar decrees soon gives way to a critical engagement with the realities of the world and its history, and to an exploration of the implications of this development for theological understanding. It is this area that deserves to be characterized as the 'theological reception' of the Council, and it is significant that theologians do not see their task as tied to the categories of the Council.

The creative focus of post-conciliar theology is found in the orientation offered in *Gaudium et Spes*. Rahner argues that this pastoral constitution prescribes for theology the acquisition of 'a kind of knowledge essential to her activity, which, however, does not spring from divine revelation but from human experience' (Rahner, 1972, p. 7). The kind of knowledge that the Church requires for its theology

> is won from a secular experience, scientifically and systematically gained through modern history, sociology, scientific psychology and futurology . . . a totally new kind of profane experience, previously non-existent, and loaded with all the dangerous, dubious and provisional qualities which are associated with strange, scientific, 'empirical' manipulation (Rahner, 1972, p.7).

The Church is no longer merely involved with the world that God created, but also with that world that 'man is building as *his* work, as an embodiment of *his* decisions, dreams, utopias and of his scientific reflection'. Rahner seems to me to be advocating the expansion of the second option offered by Jean Calvin at the beginning of his *Institutes of Christian Religion*:

> Our wisdom in so far as it ought to be deemed true and solid wisdom, consists almost entirely of two parts: the knowledge of God and of ourselves. But as these are connected together by many ties, it is not easy to determine which of the two precedes and gives birth to the other.

Post-conciliar theology, for the most part, follows this second option, and directs its attention towards what Rahner calls 'the world of an immense future in process of being planned' (Rahner, 1972, p. 6). Hence the perspectives that it employs will necessarily include those offered by critical secular disciplines. This, of course, adds to the inherent difficulty of all theologizing: 1989 was neither a better nor a worse year in which to theologize than 1289, but it could be argued that the context of a pluralistic modernity poses considerably more painful challenges to 'speech about God' than did the Middle Ages.

David Tracy's remark that 'the problem of the contemporary systematic theologian . . . is actually *to do* systematic theology' is prompted by the complexity of intellectual horizons within which theology tries to find its voice. (Tracy, 1975, p. 238). But this is not a difficulty for those who begin, in Barthian fashion, with Calvin's first option, starting from the controlling features of God's revelation. Eloquent and confident reaffirmation of the historical fc ms of Christian belief mark this theological tradition. Within post-conciliar Catholic theology, this approach is given magisterial expression in the writings of von Balthasar. His stature as a major theologian within the great tradition must, however, contrast with his relative isolation within the dominant trajectory of post-conciliar theology which chooses Calvin's second option – the *lectio difficilior*, in my opinion – of beginning with the complexity of 'our knowledge of ourselves'. Von Balthasar's detachment from the 'anthropological turn' that characterizes Catholic theology in this period, is given dramatic expression in his bitter attack on Rahner in his book *Cordula oder der Ernstfall* in 1966. At issue for Balthasar is Rahner's linear convergence of the dynamism of the human spirit and the corresponding shape of God's revelation, and his consequent treatment of Jesus as the undialectical fulfilment of human potentialities: according to von Balthasar, this negates the necessity of a *theologia crucis* as a central feature in Christian theology, and evacuates Christianity of its scandalous character. Only faithful witness to the point of martyrdom testifies to the irruption of revelation within the world; anything less than this, such as an attempt to transpose the dynamism of selfhood into a constitutive feature of revelation, is a betrayal (Williams, 1986).

Rather than probe further into this particular debate, however, it seems better to highlight the differences between von Balthasar and Schillebeeckx – partly because they exemplify divergent tendencies within the Catholic Church; partly because it focuses the question of the 'theological reception' of the Council; and partly because Schillebeeckx is, in many ways, the representative post-Vatican II theologian whose development offers a microcosm of the theological initiatives prompted by the Council. Von Balthasar, on the other hand, offers a theological exposition in a different key: a patristic eloquence in which there is a felicitous interpenetration of classical Christian themes and cultural breadth. Where Schillebeeckx seems to be attempting to 'rebuild' theology from foundations in contemporary experience and praxis, von Balthasar offers a comprehensive theological system to the post-conciliar Church in which doxology, not praxis, is the keynote, and in which the full sweep of the Church's thinking takes priority over the particular development. Although these two individuals are cited, I take them to represent divergent tendencies in the wake of the Council: Schillebeeckx, devoted to fostering a critically involved Catholicism of local churches, and directing the Church's attention towards the possibility of a 'political love and holiness' in the contemporary world (Schillebeeckx, 1986, p. 272); von Balthasar, composing 'a meditative act of homage to the Lord of the Church . . . an act of adoration before Christ in the name of the Bride-Church' (von Balthasar, 1982, pp. 555–6). For von Balthasar, 'only the saint who does what he thinks and intuits is a Christian theologian in the full sense of the word' (p. 556).

Von Balthasar follows Anselm and Barth in holding that theology has its own starting point, method and articulation, which derive from our taking seriously 'the *auctoritas Dei revelantis* in all its indissoluble concrete reality' (von Balthasar, 1982, p. 154). Where the dominant theological 'consensus' is in danger of suggesting that its autonomy has been 'hijacked' by the methods and disciplines it employs, von Balthasar strictly monitors the influence of cognate disciplines: God's revelation in Jesus has an incomparable radiance which is not to be dissolved by the criteria of secular disciplines, nor by an over-enthusiastic handling of critical exegesis. (He has read the Barth–Harnack correspondence carefully.) In his hands, theology has the character of an obediential *nachdenken*, an obediential 'thinking after', in which the Christian mind and heart shapes its understanding in conformity with the given pattern of God's revelation; and this von Balthasar expounds with copious reference to the high culture of European humanism. He described his work as fostering, as a presupposition to *aggiornamento*, 'a reflection on the specifically Christian element itself, a purification, a deepening, a centring of its idea, which alone renders us capable of representing it, radiating it, translating it believably in the world' (Riches, 1986, p. 196).

Earlier we used the image of 'location' to characterize the character of post-Vatican II theology: von Balthasar writes his theology at the centre of the contemplative Church's experience. It is only if theology is grounded in an experiential sense of God's engagement with us, and only if it is an expressive articulation of the depth of Christian experience, that it can claim its character as 'a meditative act of homage to the Lord of the Church' (von Balthasar, 1982, p. 555). His major works, *Herrlichkeit, Theodramatik, Theologik*, are shaped by the need to find categories in which the 'knowledge appropriate to faith' may be given adequate and appropriate expression without distortion. So, for example, he writes a theological aesthetics, in which the perception of aesthetic truth is analogically related to the perception of divine truth in revelation: thus the aesthetic analogy of 'form' and 'radiance' can be developed in a Trinitarian theology in which the incarnation of the Son is the assumption of a 'created

427

form' – the humanity of Jesus – in which radiates the depth of divine love and glory, the fullness of God's self-revelation. In his Son, God honours his creatures by 'becoming world' (von Balthasar, 1982, p. 302), and Jesus stands as the archetypal expression both of the nature of divine love and of valid creaturely existence.

This Johannine and 'epiphanic' Christology – an ancient Christological style, of which von Balthasar is almost the sole contemporary exponent – is developed in the direction of a 'theological dramatics', in which the contemplation of the 'form' of Jesus' life requires elucidation as the focus of the 'drama' of the self-emptying love of God for the sinful creation. Von Balthasar presents the crucifixion as God's engagement with the creation whose freedom opposes divine love. In his death, Jesus 'recapitulates' the disobedient creation, and integrates in his obedient love humanity's imperfect and partial forms of love. The Son in his death enters into solidarity with not only the frailty of the sinner, but also those who, in the exercise of their relative freedom, have 'damned themselves'. This theme is the heart of von Balthasar's profound consideration of the Trinity as a mystery of self-emptying love, in which the dying Son gives to his love for the Father 'the character of obedience to such a degree that in it he experiences the complete godlessness of lost man' (von Balthasar, 1975, p. 51). This 'theology of Holy Saturday' is a masterly reworking of the ancient theme of the descent of the dead Son to Sheol, and it is a remarkable treatment, perhaps unique in contemporary theology, which revives the power of figurative and mythical categories within theological discourse.

The central features of his Christology shape von Balthasar's conservatively symbolic ecclesiology: the 'form' of the Church's identity must be an ever-greater approximation to the 'form' of the Son. Von Balthasar discusses the character of the Church with reference to the 'constellation' of figures who surround Jesus and the emergence of the infant Church of the resurrection: Mary (pre-eminently), Peter, John, James the brother of the Lord, Paul, and the collegial Twelve. He treats them as archetypes of 'privileged participation in Christ's all-sustaining experience of God' (von Balthasar, 1982, p. 350) and as irreducible dimensions of the invariant structure of the Church's identity.

Where most other post-conciliar writers on ecclesiology focus on the status of the local church within the Catholic communion, von Balthasar's reading of Lumen Gentium is deliberately meditative, symbolic and all-inclusive. He writes a typological ecclesiology in which the Marian dimension is central: Mary is the prototype of the Church's responsive faithfulness, the 'body-image' of ecclesial life, and the responsive centre from which ecclesial faith in Christ flows. The Marian dimension is like a 'protective mantle' which encompasses the Petrine and hierarchical functions within the Church. Mary is the real type and abiding centre of the Church, the one whose lay holiness underlies the communio which is to be realized through the Petrine and collegial ministry of the apostles. He pursues Mary's position as 'type' of the Church in a way that relativizes hierarchy: the deepest dimension of the Church's identity is lay, faithful and feminine. Hence his insistence that the ordination of women to priesthood and episcopacy would damage 'the precedence of the feminine aspect of the Church over the masculine' (von Balthasar, 1986, p. 194). From a very different perspective, he is in partial agreement with the feminist critique of the androcentric character of the Church, and argues that a Church that has lost its female/contemplative/Marian centre is unbearably masculine and distorted.

Peter, and therefore the papacy, exercises his ministry within the ambit of Marian fidelity; he is *simul justus et peccator*, since he is the most publicly acknowledged example of inadequate discipleship, rivalling only Judas in his failure of faith – hence the continuing 'scandal' of the Petrine office and the inevitability of a continuing anti-Roman feeling within the Church. The Petrine ministry must be exercised with reference to the collegiality of the Twelve, to the principle of 'abiding love' that John represents, to inherited 'tradition and law', represented by James the brother of the Lord, and to 'charismatic ministry and adaptation', symbolized by Paul. Thus the Church is structurally complex, composed of distinct, interrelated principles, from which can come either destructive tension, as in the Reformation, or an integration in a continuing process of 'individuation' as the principles interact with one another.

In his writings, symbols are allowed to function 'heuristically' as part of the disclosure of theological truth, and as central to theology's grasp of the divine mystery. In von Balthasar's hands, Catholic theology feels again the power of symbol, metaphor and dramatic categories within a theology caught in the tension between what *can* be said and what *must* be brought to expression. His is perhaps the last great theological synthesis in which there is the full flowering of European Christian humanism. More than any other contemporary theologian, he is able to restore to theology an eloquence in which biblical, cultural and philosophical dimensions find their place within the context of a richly symbolic theology.

With Schillebeeckx, we enter a quite different theological world from that occupied by von Balthasar, whose work does not require the stimulus of a particular social context: it seems to float, angel-like, above the particularity of human history, touching earth only to ascend again for further improvements to the theological edifice. Schillebeeckx, on the other hand, writes a theology that is multi-disciplinary, secularly involved, and committed to fostering the prophetic character of local 'critical' communities, both in relationship to the universal Church and to the society in which they live. Schillebeeckx's work is characterized by the introduction of an innovative repertoire of approaches and methods within the theological agenda: historical–critical exegesis of Scripture; a phenomenology of the relationship of experience and faith; literary–critical and other hermeneutical approaches; linguistic philosophy and Marxist critical theory; the approach of the Frankfurt School to ideology and critical negativity – all these find their place within Schillebeeckx's theological method.

The centripetal intensity of von Balthasar's work remains detached from the proposal of Küng and Schillebeeckx that there is a post-Vatican II theological consensus wherein the contemporary task is to formulate 'a theology of Christian origins and centre enunciated within the horizon of the contemporary world'. Küng and Schillebeeckx envisage an elliptical movement between the 'two poles' of theology: 'God's revelational address in the history of Israel and the history of Jesus', and 'our own human world of experience' (Küng, 1980, p. 3). Like all generalizations, its validity stands in tension with its programmatic character, which still leaves many of the central questions unexamined: for example, what is the correlation between the historical–critical exegesis of Scripture, post-biblical doctrinal traditions and contemporary ecclesial experience? Can the post-biblical doctrinal tradition be said to exercise a 'normative' role within this scheme?

The reorientation given to Schillebeeckx's work from 1965 onwards is instructive: the explicitly Thomist framework is set aside and his subsequent writings no longer depend upon a single metaphysical framework. Epistemology, the phenomenology of experience and theology's character as a 'communicative praxis', which is always in danger of exhibiting ideological bias, become more significant concerns. A developing emphasis on 'experience' as the central point of entry into the *interpretandum* of theology enables him to establish mutually critical correlations between the expression given within New Testament contexts to the early Christian experience, and the structurally analogous, but conceptually different, experience of contemporary Christianity. Compare, for example, the Christology of his 1958 work, *Christ the Sacrament*, with his 1974 *Jesus: An Experiment in Christology*, and *Christ: The Christian Experience in the Modern World*: in the pre-conciliar work, the hypostatic union is the point of departure. In the later works, there is the concern to establish contacts between exegesis and Christology, and to trace the developing trajectories of Christological interpretations, not solely in order to reconstruct them, but in order that the analogous complex of interpretation and experience in twentieth-century Christianity might be stimulated. He interprets the New Testament writings in order to arrive

at an exact understanding of the way in which these Christians gave new expression to the traditional message of the gospel or apostolic faith on the basis of new experiences and demands with which they themselves were in critical solidarity.

That then raises the question for us, what are the historical circumstances in which we, in the year 1980, must pick up the threads of apostolic belief? Where must our Christian *critical solidarity* find its focal point today, taking into account present-day experiences and demands? (Schillebeeckx, 1980, p. 653.)

The task of theology, then, is not to update a previously constituted body of truth – interpretative hermeneutics is insufficient – but to articulate present experiences so that they stand in a creative and critical relationship to the tradition. 'The practice of the community is the sphere in which theology is born' (Schillebeeckx, 1985, p. 12). For Schillebeeckx, contemporary experience and understanding carry a claim to authority because they come from the continuing practice of discipleship, and contribute the perspective through which the preceding tradition is appropriated. The theological task is the formulation of a theological understanding ('theory') that interacts with the expression of Christian life in the contemporary context ('praxis'); and so he describes theology as 'the self-consciousness of Christian praxis' whose 'point of departure is the contemporary praxis of the church' (Schillebeeckx, 1986,

p. 118). Thereby a structural analogy is created between the theory and praxis of the *past* and the theory and praxis of the *present*. For Schillebeeckx, the crucial relationship is not between the formulations of the past and present, but between the 'praxis' that gave rise to the 'theory' of the past and the corresponding elements in the present situation. He shifts the focus of theology from past experience theoretically considered, and hermeneutically related to the present situation, to present ecclesial experience or 'praxis', which is both the object of the theologian's reflection and the perspective in which the past is retrieved.

This reformulation of the nature of theology's task arises from Schillebeeckx's appropriation of the 'neo-Marxist' analysis of the relationship between theory and praxis, applied to the character of 'authentic' theology: the qualification is important, because Schillebeeckx's reading of critical theory convinced him that all human communication in history, even the proclamation and interpretation of the gospel, can be distorted in the interest of maintaining unjust social structures within both society and the Church. Hence the need for theology to include, as part of its internal self-correction, a sensitivity to the 'ideology critique' of the Frankfurt School. As a corrective mechanism, an essential component of 'authentic' theology will be its commitment to 'liberative and emancipatory praxis': he argues that in contemporary society, it is impossible to believe in a Christianity that is not at one with the movement to emancipate mankind. The effect of this is that Catholic theology is made to recognize that the anthropological and social co-ordinates within which it is constructed form part of its criteria of authenticity.

Although we have examined this point only in the writings of Schillebeeckx, it is the unifying feature within a broad range of particular theological developments. If I stress the quality of particularity, it is because it is impossible to present the theology of the post-Vatican II Church as though it were a unitary and coherent development: the revision of tradition undertaken by the Council, and the variety of perspectives that it introduced into the life of the Church, preclude the emergence of a theological coherence such as was found, in a neo-scholastic form, prior to the Council.

For example, it is noticeable that the vitality of French theology *before* the Council contrasts with its relative poverty since then. In an open letter to Congar in 1970, Küng wrote: 'Between the Second World War and Vatican II, it was French theology above all which called for a renewal of the Church and of theology. Why is French theology so silent since the Council?' Claude Geffré finds an answer in the contrast between the intra-ecclesial character of pre-conciliar French theology, which 'took shape through contact with the sources of Tradition, developed at the heart of faith and at the service of the institution of the Church', and the difficulties experienced by contemporary French theologians in trying to engage with contemporary French intellectual life. The earlier theology met the expectations of a Church that felt the need to reform itself from within the dynamism of its forgotten traditions: Geffré identifies three features of postwar French theology: a return to biblical and patristic sources, an intense interest in ecclesiological research and a pastoral and ecumenical orientation (Geffré, 1982).

431

By contrast, post-conciliar French theology has a different set of questions, which centre on the confrontation of faith with a modernity in which theology feels the bracing effect of the radical criticism of religious language emerging from philosophical movements, such as structuralism and linguistics, and the critical human sciences such as sociology and psychology. French post-conciliar theology is characterized by this dialogue with the human sciences: and while this does not enable theological production on the same level as before the Council, that engagement is a sign of the hard task that faces theology in dialogue with post-Christian European atheism. May 1968 was the watershed when the model of the 'old masters' was abandoned by younger theologians to be replaced by that of structuralism.

Rahner's judgement that Vatican II signals the emergence of a 'world Church' from an initially Judaeo-Christian, and subsequently European, cultural matrix, indicates that the Council marks the end of a Church and a theology dominated by European norms. If the Council bestowed on the Church the obligation to foster an appreciation of the particularity of the social and ecclesial contexts in which communities lived, it comes as no surprise that theology since the Council should be marked by particularity. The renewal of theology and its accompanying 'practice' in the life of the Church will therefore be variegated, localized and inevitably uneven: the determining characteristic that shapes the degree of growth seems to be the urgency with which the concerns of a particular context can be positively aligned both with a living community of faith and with generative elements in the tradition. It is also notable that theology conducted in third-world contexts is better able to foster theological initiatives than its European and North American counterpart.

So, for example, European political theology – in Catholic theology, closely identified with the writings of Johann Baptist Metz – has had little impact on the life of Christian Europe, compared with what has been achieved by Latin American liberation theology in its context, and the potential influence of Asian theologies in dialogue with the soteriological and cultural traditions of Hinduism and Buddhism.

Like liberation theologies, political theology is concerned with mediating the Christian faith in ways that can transform the social and political world. In particular, Metz pays attention to the alienation produced by contemporary forms of individualism: Christianity, in its 'privatized' and 'bourgeois' forms, has been distorted by the modernity it claimed to be confronting since the Enlightenment. The result has been that the Church has been unable to exercise its socially critical functions in Western societies, having been adapted and domesticated by liberal capitalism. Political theology aims at restoring a dialectical approach which, on the one hand, 'retrieves' genuine values from the Christian tradition that have been ignored in the West's appropriation of Christianity, and, on the other hand, 'unmasks' the alienating distortions in forms of Christianity in which the gospel has lost the capacity to be prophetic.

Political theology tries to identify the context in which European theology *should* be done: if one were to identify key features of contemporary European experience, the horrors of two world wars centred on Europe, and its current position between two competing empires, would be high on the list. It is not unreasonable to expect that European theologians would take these events as central to their agenda, but do they? Matthew Lamb comments:

> Faced with two world wars, massive militarism, increasing poverty in the midst of incredible affluence, modern theologians tended either to treat all these issues as moral problems calling for greater individual efforts, or to see them as requiring a total re-formation of creedal symbols and theological concepts. As ecclesial institutions are rent with the controversies spawned by conservative reactions and liberal assimilation, the concrete possibilities for the churches to exercise socially critical functions are diminished. The church does not change the modern world, rather modernity fashions the church into its own image (Lamb, 1987, p. 777).

This is a sharp rebuke to European theology. But at the moment, it seems fair to say that political theology has done no more than begin to address the question of an appropriate agenda for itself. The European movement still has the character of a university-based project, lacking real contact with a faith-community actively searching for a theological understanding of its social experience. It is overwhelmingly 'critical' in character, but it has been able to do little more than fulminate against the 'privatized' and 'bourgeois' character of contemporary Europe; this judgement is more a comment on the complexity of constructing a 'contextual' theology in capitalist Europe than on the inadequacies of its political theologians.

But if Western theology has had difficulty in coping with the social complexity of the developed world, it has begun to feel the effect of significant questions about the status and role of women, both in the Church and in the wider society: it is a focus of social, economic and anthropological concerns which has given an impetus to theological reflection principally in the areas of ecclesiology and theological anthropology. It arises precisely out of an awareness that the anthropological and social co-ordinates of theology cannot be ignored if theology is to be rooted in human reality. From the recognition that the primary interpretative 'pole' of Christian theology has been predominantly masculine, and frequently misogynist, feminist theology forms a critical response to a pervasive bias both in the tradition and in the contemporary Church. It is potentially one of the important *particular* developments within Catholic theology since the Council; it seems to me to be an indispensable attempt to create for theology a perspective on the nature of our humanity which, for complex socio-psychological reasons, it has failed to articulate in its earlier traditions. It illustrates the way in which theology is led to reflect critically on the poles of tradition and contemporary experience. Rosemary Radford Ruether comments that 'since women lack major bodies of tradition which spring from their own experience and point of view, they are in effect probing the primary basis of theology in direct religious experience as a major foundation for new theological symbol-making' (Ruether, 1987, pp. 394–5). She also remarks that 'whether feminist theology will remain primarily as a reform and renewal movement within existing historical religions, such as Christianity, or whether it may give rise to a significant new movement of religious expression is unclear' (p. 396).

This judgement raises the question of the relationship of such particular theological developments to the broader community of the Church. The diversity of social and cultural contexts within which theology is conducted issues in patterns of theological reflection that will not be co-extensive with one another. Although the Catholic Church has come to terms with diachronic pluralism in theology – the 'development of doctrine' across the centuries – in the post-Vatican II period it has prescribed for itself the experience of synchronic pluralism – a range of co-ordinating formulations of Catholic faith-experience. We have still to face the implications of this development for a Church whose traditional values are order and consistency. It is significant that a theologian such as Schillebeeckx, and the broader movement of Latin American liberation theology, have deliberately 'targeted' their theology towards the needs of particular communities of faith. Around the time that Schillebeeckx began to integrate critical theology within the practice of theology – 1968–73 – he made a conscious decision to identify himself with the critical communities in Dutch Catholicism: Schillebeeckx's writings are directed towards fostering communities of politically committed Christians whose 'critical remembering' of Jesus is a prophetic and critical force in history, both with regard to the Church's fidelity to the gospel and the primacy of the local community within the Church's structure, and with regard to society's treatment of the poor within its economic systems.

The most significant 'particular' development within Catholicism is, of course, the emergence of liberation theology in Latin America. In many ways, it stands as the most dramatic expression of the 'paradigm shift' brought about in post-conciliar Catholic theology. It offers a way of doing theology that originates, develops and culminates in response to the destructive experiences that characterize the lives of the majority of human beings: oppression, injustice, hunger and persecution – life-threatening factors that are the result of social structures – become central concerns in the articulation of Christian responsibility in the modern world. And it is essentially a contextual theology, in which the attempt to formulate a 'universal' theology valid for the whole Church – the European 'temptation' – is abandoned in favour of developing a theological understanding through contact with the demands of particular social and historical situations.

The 1968 meeting of the Latin American bishops at Medellín focused attention on the massive poverty of the continent, and on the social and political factors responsible for the oppression of the poor. Following *Gaudium et Spes*'s recognition of a 'new humanism' in which human beings were defined primarily by their joint responsibility for history, the bishops denounced what they saw as the 'institutionalized violence' of Latin American society, and demanded 'urgent and profoundly renovating transformations' in the social structures of their countries. Each episcopal conference was called upon to present 'the Church as a catalyst in the temporal realm in an authentic attitude of service', and to encourage the efforts of the people to create and develop their own grassroots organizations for the 'redress and consolidation of their rights and the search for justice'. It is important to underline the official episcopal approval for the developments that subsequently took place: the developed form of liberation theology emerges directly in response to the Latin American bishops' interpretation of the Council, and of *Gaudium et Spes* in particular.

434

Liberation theology presents an understanding of Christian truth from the determinative experience of most human beings today: the experience of poverty and injustice. From this point of view, it presents the most sustained attempt by post-conciliar Catholicism to interpret Christian truth in solidarity with the 'wretched of the earth' – the weak and the hungry, the 'non-persons' within social structures that exclude them and keep them in a powerless position. It is the most dramatic attempt by Catholic theology to locate the mystery of Christ within the *humanum*, within the complex of human experience and history: it affirms that only solidarity with the experience of humanity in experiencing and countering injustice and poverty provides the *locus theologicus* required by the character of the gospel. When confronted with the extent and depth of structural injustice in the world, Christian theology has the right to speak only if it is conducted in solidarity with those who are suffering, and is directed towards their liberation from oppression. According to this approach, theology will be directed towards grasping the relevance of themes that will entail structural changes in socio-historical contexts marked by domination and oppression. Hence Juan Luis Segundo's insistence that liberation theology also marks 'the liberation of theology' from falsifying versions of itself which ignore the demands of the context in which it is conducted. Boff offers the following picture of the theologian and his/her task:

> Theologians do not live in the clouds. They are social actors with a particular place in society. They produce knowledge, data and meanings by using instruments that the situation offers them and permits them to utilize. Their findings are also addressed to a particular audience. Thus theologians are framed within the overall social context. The themes and emphases of a given Christology flow from what seems relevant to the theologian on the basis of his or her social standpoint. In that sense we must maintain that no Christology is or can be neutral. Every Christology is partisan and committed. Willingly or unwillingly christological discourse is voiced in a given social setting with all the conflicting interests that pervade it. That holds true as well for theological discourse that claims to be 'purely' theological, historical, traditional, ecclesial, and apolitical. Normally such discourse adopts the position of those who hold power in the existing system. If a different kind of Christology with its own commitments appears on the scene and confronts the older 'apolitical' Christology, the latter will soon discover its social locale, forget its 'apolitical' nature, and reveal itself as a religious reinforcement of the existing status quo (Boff, 1980, pp. 265–6).

The conflictual character of the modern world, acknowledged in *Gaudium et Spes*, becomes part of theology's evaluation of itself, and part of the internal critique it requires if it is to respond to the Church's re-evaluation of its identity in the modern world. Earlier we quoted Hans Urs von Balthasar's view that what the Church needs is 'a reflection on the specifically Christian element itself, a purification, a deepening, a centring of its idea, which alone renders us capable of representing it, radiating it, translating it believably in the world': liberation theologians see their theological method as precisely such a reflection which restores to theology its evangelical and prophetic character. What von Balthasar achieves by spiralling inwards towards the Church's contemplative experience as the proper source of theology, liberationists achieve by proposing a purification of the relationship of theology to its context.

435

Liberation theology presents answers to questions which, because they are simple, are always the most difficult and the most instructive to face: What is theology? Why do it? Where is it done? Who does it? To the first three questions, liberation theology answers that theology is a 'critical reflection on historical praxis, undertaken on behalf of the poor in situations of oppression and injustice'. But, according to Gutierrez, the final question, 'Who does theology?', should be answered by 'the poor themselves'. He speaks of the 'irruption of the poor' within the historical process of Latin America, within the Church, and within theological reflection (Gutierrez, 1981).

Leonardo Boff argues that liberation theology has contributed several insights to theology in general: it has set the poor at the forefront of the theological agenda; it has recaptured the Christian vision of transforming the world; it has empowered the poor by making them, not the objects, but the responsible subjects of the task of theology; it has identified the proper 'location' of theology not in the university or institute of learning, but in the Christian community in its experience of identifying with the cause of the poor; its evangelical practice in situations of oppression is a partial realization of the total liberation to which Christ bears witness; it has, for the first time in Church history, expressed the experience of the oppressed as a central datum of theological reflection (Boff, 1988).

Because this theology is a reflection on a commitment to the cause of the poor, it cannot remain content with simply offering a new theoretical interpretation of Christian belief: the question 'What is to be done?' becomes central to theology, which is no longer exclusively the *intellectus fidei*, but an understanding based on the form that Christian love should take in a specific situation. Hence the importance of a commitment to action with, and on behalf of, the poor, since that option is both the beginning and the end of the interpretative circle of theological praxis. As Gutierrez puts it:

> The theology of liberation seeks to understand faith from within this historical praxis . . . this is the fundamental hermeneutical circle: from humanity to God and from God to humanity, from history to faith and from faith to history, from the love of one's brothers and sisters to the love of the Father and from the love of the Father to love of one's brothers and sisters, from human justice to God's holiness and from God's holiness to human justice. . . . theology in Latin America is an understanding of the faith from an option and a commitment. It will be an understanding of the faith from a point of departure in real, effective solidarity with the exploited classes, oppressed ethnic groups, and despised cultures of Latin America. It will be a reflection that starts out from a commitment to create a just society (Gutierrez, 1983, pp. 60ff.).

Boff identifies features of liberation theology's approach to Christology that are general enough to be applicable to the tenor of the whole movement: the *anthropological* element takes priority over the *ecclesiastical*: the focus is not the Church, but 'the human person that it should help, raise up and humanize'. An over-ecclesial approach impedes attempts to 'create a new incarnation of the church outside of the inherited traditional framework of a Greco-Roman understanding of the world'. The *social* perspective takes priority over the *personal*: concentration should be on the social context rather than on individual conversion. The *utopian* element – openness to the future and its transformation – takes priority over the *factual*, the existing state of affairs. The *critical* takes priority over the *dogmatic*: the possibilities inherent in the concrete situation for developing a new self-understanding take priority over inherited versions of Christian experience. The practice of discipleship (*orthopraxis*) is the basis of a correct understanding of faith (*orthodoxy*) (Boff, 1980, p. 44). This entire scheme is a project for a new human person, a new future, a new self-understanding, new social structures, and, to some extent, a new 'aspect' of revelation disclosed through contemporary discipleship.

This movement has presented theology with an alternative and challenging re-evaluation of its identity: rather than consider it as a 'new' theology, it seems more accurate to describe it as a prophetic renewal and re-centring of theological reflection. Several liberation theologians have drawn a distinction between what they see as the 'academic' theology of Europe and their own 'liberating' vision of the character of theology: European theology being more concerned with hermeneutical shifts in understanding, and Latin American theology being more concerned with changing the conditions of social life. Yet it seems more accurate to regard the distinction between these two theological models as different approaches to the fundamental question of *atheism*. Western theology's dialogue with philosophical and critical disciplines is prompted by a desire to develop an understanding of Christianity within a culture that no longer feels the need for, or recognizes the possibility of, religious truth; equally, the trajectory taken by liberation theology attacks a virulent form of atheism that perpetuates social structures which deform the image of God in human beings.

Liberation theology claims, it seems to me, to be the 'correct' way of doing theology; this should not be understood as a claim that what is achieved in Latin America can be exported elsewhere. Its exponents insist that other social contexts require theologies that are appropriate to different exigencies. But there comes the suggestion that the 'method' it employs has a universal validity. Liberation theologians have attacked Western 'academic' theology for seeking to adjust the Christian belief-system while being naïvely and culpably optimistic about the possibility of making 'neutral' theological statements unrelated to the processes of history. Theology must take different forms, according to its starting point, approach, conceptual structures and cultural context.

Avery Dulles points out that history offers many examples of 'contextual' theology, such as the homiletic theology of the Church fathers, the contemplative theology of the monastic tradition, and the scholastic theologies of the medieval universities: against the attempt to reduce the diversity of approaches required, he judges that 'in our own day the various demands of widely differing audiences would seem to call for a corresponding variety of theologies. The kerygmatic, patristic, and transcendental currents, as well as political and liberation theology . . . have seemed to answer to real needs' (Dulles, 1980, p. 48) His appeal for a recognition of pluralism in theological approaches includes also theological reflection in an *ecumenical* context, without appeal to the doctrinal standards of a particular Church, and in an *interfaith* context, without expressed faith in Christ or the Church.

437

But what happens to Catholic theology when it is conducted in an interfaith context? The Council moved the Church away from a dismissal of the other religions – 'error has no rights' – towards a positive recognition of their place within the universal availability of God's grace. Post-conciliar theology has begun to exhibit the enrichment that can occur when genuine dialogue with other religious traditions is allowed to present a different perspective on theological reflection. But rather than consider how Western Catholic theologians have dealt theoretically with the status of other religions – Rahner's proposal of 'anonymous Christians' is the most celebrated model – I want to draw attention to the writings of Aloysius Pieris, a Sri Lankan Jesuit, who is one of the finest theologians to emerge in the third world since the Council. I regard him as important because he exemplifies the expansion and renewal of Catholic theology in contextual dialogue with non-Christian cultural and religious traditions. In addition, he shows the impact of liberation theology outside the Latin American context, and it is the particular conjunction of these two elements that makes his writings such a challenge to the Catholic Church *in* Asia to become a fully inculturated Church *of* Asia, and no longer the outpost of a European colonial mission.

The double focus of his work, *An Asian Theology of Liberation*, is the conjunction of two realities, the poverty and the religiousness of Asia. He argues that Christian theology will not address the poverty of Asia unless it does so within a context of dialogue with Asian religious interpretations of poverty, and that it will not carry out authentic inter-faith dialogue unless that dialogue is based on a concern for the poor. 'Liberation' and 'inculturation' are for him two names for the same process in the Asian context. Like the Latin American theologians, he argues that the validity of a theology lies in its origin, development and culmination in the praxis/process of liberation, through which the Church's identity is established:

> The same praxis of liberation that makes a theology valid also creates the indigenous identity of the local church that overlaps with that theology. The genesis of a liberation theology overlaps with the genesis of an authentically local church. That is to say, a liberation theology begins to be formulated only when a given Christian community begins to be drawn into a local people's struggle for *full humanity* and through that struggle begins to sink its roots into the life and culture of these people, most of whom are non-Christians (Pieris, 1988, p. 111).

Christianity failed to make an impression in Asia because of its association with the mammon of commercial and colonial exploitation, and because it failed to enter into the monastic spirit of non-Christian soteriologies such as Buddhism. Pieris comments on the fact that the Asian Church at the moment has no theology of its own, yet the cultures that host it teem with theology! He is also sharply critical of what he sees as Christian 'theological vandalism': the various attempts to detach Oriental techniques of prayer from the soteriological ethos of Eastern religions in order to serve Christian spirituality, without respect for the integrity of these faiths. Pieris judges that Christian theology in Asia is 'the occult language of its colonial founders to be understood only by the initiated': it must now be given time 'to step into the baptismal waters of Asian religion and to pass through passion and death on the cross of Asian poverty' (Pieris,

1988, p. 63). He sees this developing – significantly on the fringes of the institutional Church – in *theological communities* composed of Christians and non-Christians who form basic human communes with the poor, sharing the common patrimony of a *religiousness* that their (voluntary or enforced) *poverty* generates' (p.125).

Like Gutierrez, he speaks of the 'irruption' of the poor within theology, but his concern is that the vast majority of the poor express their ultimate concern and symbolize their struggle for liberation in the idiom of non-Christian religions and cultures. 'Therefore a theology that does not speak to or speak through this non-Christian peoplehood is an esoteric luxury of a Christian minority' (p. 87). The Asian theological dilemma is that 'the theologians are not (yet) poor, and the poor are not (yet) theologians'; it can be resolved only where theologians and the poor become mutually reconciled 'through a process of mutual evangelization' in which 'theologians are awakened into the liberative dimension of poverty and the poor are conscientized into the liberative potentialities of their religiousness' (p. 41). For Pieris, this process is integral to the establishment of local churches in Asia. Like the liberationists in Latin America, he sees 'theological communities of the poor' as creative *loci* for theology; but unlike Catholic Latin America, the initiatives in Asia will come rather from non-Christian sages who, in poverty, interpret Jesus:

> My surmise is that a meaningful discourse on the 'Son of God' will come about in Asian cultures mainly through an in-depth dialogue between *those* peripheral Christian communities and *these* non-Christian disciples of Christ trying to retell the story of Jesus to one another in terms of the one, absolute, triune mystery of salvation (Pieris, 1988, p. 65).

This is a vision of a Catholic Asian theology in which a significant role is given to *non-Christians* in their shared experience of poverty and in their encounter with Jesus within their own soteriological perspectives: non-Christian thought could then become a source of Asian Catholic theology. The growth of basic communities formed according to this model would coincide with a re-evangelization of the Church as a whole, a revision of its ministries, and 'the reawakening of the poor themselves to their irreplacable role in the liberative revolution that Jesus referred to as the kingdom' (p. 40).

It is an example of the post-conciliar insight into the priority of the 'landscape' of lived experience in the articulation of theological 'doctrine', adapted in a way that gives a central role to Asian poverty and religiousness. It is also an instance of post-conciliar Catholicism's insight that the mystery of Christ is to be found within the *humanum*, within the complex of human experience and culture, and that the *humanum* – in this case, the religiousness of the non-Christian Asian poor – could be a new source of revelation for the Asian Church. Pieris's approach raises again the question of the *sources* of Catholic theology. Both he and the liberation theologians insist on the centrality of the poor in the Church's articulation of its faith: it is they who should be taken as proper subjects of theologizing. Pieris's proposal that non-Christian reflection on Jesus should be given a special status in Asian theology is perhaps the most radical instance of the 'de-centring' of Catholic theology since the Council.

In this respect, Pieris is typical of the movement of theology since the Council, as exemplified in the approach of liberation theologians and Schillebeeckx: if the reception of Vatican II is characterized by a relocation of the Church's identity within the reality of the world's history and experience, then theology will be relocated in a similar fashion. The centre of theology can no longer be the Church's experience of its inner holiness: this is the weakness of von Balthasar's approach. His is a magnificent theological achievement based on a view of theology as a quintessentially intra-ecclesial activity that parallels contemplation. But, it seems to me, the Council required of theology something different, something that the liberationists have glimpsed, interpreted and offered to the rest of the Church: that theology should have the character of a shared hope between the world's experience and a Church that has begun to share the complexity of that experience. It also required theology to attend to the universal availability of God's grace within the development of the world's history. The centre of the theology, then, is not the Church, but the world's history as it is constructed by human beings, and through which the mystery of grace is brought to fulfilment. The theological lines of development since the Council exhibit a diversity and vitality that comes from rediscovering that theology is something to be 'done' in a way that affects the present conditions of humanity. In this respect, the sensitivity shown by theologians to the anthropological and social co-ordinates of theology – an almost universal characteristic of contemporary Catholic practice – is a necessary aspect of post-conciliar awareness. Equally, the close association between human movements of liberation and Christian theology – one of the most notable and controversial features of contemporary Catholic theology – seems to me to be an almost inevitable development of the Council's promptings to the Church, and an authentic development of the 'practice' of theology.

In this inevitably selective presentation of Catholic theology since the Council, I have tried to indicate some of the paths that theologians have taken in response to the Council, or, perhaps more accurately, to indicate the ways in which theologians have tried to accompany the Church in the paths of development it prescribed for itself in the early 1960s. I have approached the development of post-conciliar theology in so far as it bears upon the relationship of the Church to the world, since that is, in my opinion, the central focus of the Church's reassessment of its identity undertaken at the Council. Clearly, important areas have not been addressed in this chapter: moral theology, sacramental theology, fundamental theology, ecumenical theology and, perhaps most regrettably, the impact of biblical study on the different dimensions of theological reflection.

Most (inevitably European) Catholic theology since Trent has been dominated by a concern to define Catholic positions in relation to Protestantism; Vatican II basically moved beyond this posture to focus attention on those whose human experience does not issue in any Christian formulations. Although there must be *direct* ecumenical dialogue with Christians of other Churches, the 'conversation partners' to whom post-conciliar theology is directed are non-believers. Rahner judges that 'Christian theology for today's heathen is also the best ecumenical theology':

All churches and Christian communions will only find the same language and a common confession of faith, not in the first place by discussing present doctrinal differences as they have emerged from the past, but by all taking pains to learn the new language of the future which is to serve to proclaim the Gospel of Christ . . . . We do not have the 1,000 volumes on 'atheism' which would be needed if we were to justify the innumerable books on Mariology which we do have (Rahner, 1972, p. 23).

While the period is not marked by doctrinal development in any major area, this is not to suggest that there is doctrinal lassitude, but rather that the centre of interest is in establishing local theologies appropriate to the lived experience of the community. The difficulties inherent in this 'localizing' approach will, one suspects, be more and more evident in the future as these developments prompt the Church to address the question of synchronic pluralism in theological statements; although formulations may be within the ambit of acceptably orthodox opinions, it is likely that controversy about the direction of the developments will be exacerbated as Rome endeavours to 'rein in' the rebellious horses.

In the last decade, the Vatican Congregation for the Faith has taken action against several theologians: requiring clarification on disputed points (Schillebeeckx), silencing a theologian for a period, and prohibiting publication or teaching (Boff and Pohier), declaring that a theologian is not suitable to teach Catholic theology (Curran), or withdrawing the right to be called a Catholic theologian (Küng). The Congregation's actions have not been precipitate – twelve years in the case of Küng and seven years in the case of Curran – but it signals a determination, on the part of Roman authorities, to constrain theological development within narrower limits than were generally envisaged in the more sanguine atmosphere of the 1960s. (It is significant that in the debates following the publication of *Humanae Vitae* in 1968, the Vatican itself issued no censures or excommunications.)

The exact form the theological development has taken could not, of course, have been predicted by the Council fathers; but nor should these developments be set in opposition to the 'mind' of the Council fathers, as though theologians have 'gone beyond' what the Council intended. After thirty years, a marriage relationship is a more complex experience than a young couple envisage on their wedding night; similarly, the cultural optimism of the early 1960s, in which the Council was set, and the centralized Eurocentrism of the Church on the eve of the Council, offer limited vantage points from which to assess the Church's experience of the last thirty years. One has to stress 'experience', because theology since the Council has been rooted in the Church's experience of asking difficult questions about what it means to be the Church of Christ in the contemporary world; it has had to find ways of understanding itself as a living, varied, changing community whose identity is established, not prior to, but as a function of, its relationship to the world in which God's Kingdom grows. This has led to a preference, on the part of theology, for inductive approaches, in which the context in which theology is conducted becomes a constitutive feature of theological reflection.

In particular, Catholic theology shows a widespread sensitivity to the need for partiality in social matters: within a short space of time, liberation theology has had a profound effect on world-wide Catholic theology. Its influence is felt throughout the Church, and it could be argued that it has already replaced transcendental neo-Thomism as the most pervasive theological approach in the life of the contemporary Church. If at the heart of human history is the 'mystery of Christ', and if at the heart of contemporary history is poverty and oppression on a massive scale, then theology is led to see the contemporary form of its task as a reversal of the maxim *ubi ecclesia, ibi Christus* ('Where the Church is, there is Christ'). It becomes, instead, *ubi Christus, ibi ecclesia* ('Where Christ is, there is the Church'), and is expanded to mean, 'Where the poor are suffering, there must the Church (and its theology) be'. The development of this evangelical insight into the quasi-sacramental character of the poor has prompted Catholic theology to develop new approaches to hermeneutics and methodology, in which a central role is given to the exigencies of the world's experience in becoming God's Kingdom. Since the Council, theology has acquired a compelling sense of its place in this development.

Rahner's judgement is that Vatican II marks a change in the Church's identity in the direction of being a 'world Church', comparable only to the reorientation at the beginning of its history when it moved outwards from its Jewish matrix towards being a (European) Church of the Gentiles. In the thirty years since the Council, we see the beginnings of this process – inevitably *only* the beginnings – but the signs of theological vigour required for the genesis of the 'world Church' are unmistakable.

14 Catholic Theology in the Post – conciliar Period: Bibliography

Acerbi, A. (1981) 'Receiving Vatican II in a Changed Historical Context; *Concilium*, no. 146, pp. 77–84.

Balthasar, H.U. von (1968) *Man in History: A Theological Study*. London, Sheed & Ward.

Balthasar, H.U. von (1975) *Elucidations*. London, SPCK.

Balthasar, H.U. von (1982) *The Glory of the Lord: A Theological Aesthetics, I: Seeing the Form*. Edinburgh, T. & T. Clark.

Balthasar, H.U. von (1986) *New Elucidations*. San Francisco, Ignatius Press.

Boff, L. (1980) *Jesus Christ Liberator*. London, SPCK. pp. 265–6.

Boff, L. (1986) *Ecclesiogenesis: The Base Communities Reinvent the Church*. London, Collins.

Boff, L. (1988) 'What are Third World Theologies?', *Concilium*, no. 199, pp. 3–13.

Congar, Y. (1986) 'Moving Towards a Pilgrim Church', in Stacpoole, pp. 129–52.

Dulles, A. (1974) *Models of the Church*. New York, Doubleday.

Dulles, A. (1980) 'Ecumenism and Theological Method', *Journal of Ecumenical Studies*, vol. 17, pp. 40–8.

Dulles, A. (1987) *The Catholicity of the Church*. Oxford, Clarendon Press.

Geffré, C. (1982) 'Silence et promesses de la theologie, catholique française', *Revue de Théologie et de Philosophie*, vol. 114, pp. 227–45.

Gutierrez, G. (1981) 'The Irruption of the Poor in Latin America and the Christian Communities of the Common People', in S. Torres and J. Eagleton, eds, *The Challenge of Basic Christian Communities*. New York, Orbis Books, pp. 107–23.

Guttierrez, G. (1983) *The Power of the Poor in History*. London, SCM.

Imhof, P., and Biallowons, H., eds (1986) *Karl Rahner in Dialogue: Conversations and Interviews 1965–1982*. New York, Crossroad.

Küng, H. (1965) *Structures of the Church*. London, Burns & Oates.

Küng, H. (1967) *The Church*. London, Burns & Oates.

Küng, H. (1971) *Infallible: An Enquiry*. London, Collins.

Küng, H. (1977) *On Being A Christian*. London, Collins.

Küng, H. (1980a) *Does God Exist? An Answer for Today*. London, Collins.

Küng, H. (1980b) 'Toward a New Consensus in Catholic (and Ecumenical) Theology', *Journal of Ecumenical Studies*, vol. 17, pp. 1–17.

Lamb, M. (1987) 'Political Theology', in J.A. Komonchak, M. Collins, and D. Lane, eds, *The New Dictionary of Theology*. Dublin, Gill & Macmillan, pp. 772–977.

Lash, N. (1988) *Easter in Ordinary*. London, SCM.

Lonergan, B., (1972) *Method in Theology*. London, Darton, Longman and Todd.

Metz, J. B. (1969) *Theology of the World*. London, Burns & Oates.

Metz, J. B. (1980) *Faith in History and Society*. London, Burns & Oates.

Mussner, F. (1984) *Tractate on the Jews: the Significance of Judaism for Christian Faith*. London, SPCK.

Pieris, A. (1988) *An Asian Theology of Liberation*. Edinburgh, T. & T. Clark.

Rahner, K. (1961–89) *Theological Investigations, vols. 1–22*. London, Darton, Longman and Todd.

Rahner, K. (1972) 'The Second Vatican Council's Challenge to Theology' in *Theological Investigations IX*. London, Darton, Longman and Todd.

Rahner, K. (1975) *The Trinity*. London, Burns & Oates.

Rahner, K. (1978) *Foundations of Christian Faith*. London, Darton, Longman and Todd.

Riches, J. (1986) *The Analogy of Beauty*. Edinburgh, T. & T. Clark.

Schillebeeckx, E. (1979), *Jesus: An Experiment in Christology*. London, Collins.

Schillebeeckx, E. (1980) *Christ: The Christian Experience in the Modern World*. London, SCM.

Schillebeeckx, E. (1983) 'You Cannot Arbitrarily Make Something of the Gospel!' *Concilium*, no. 170, pp. 15–19.

Schillebeeckx, E. (1985) *The Church with a Human Face*. London, SCM.

Schillebeeckx, E. (1986) *The Schillebeeckx Reader*, ed. R. J. Schreiter. Edinburgh, T. & T. Clark.

Segundo, J. L. (1973–4) *A Theology for Artisans of a New Humanity*. 5 vols. New York, Orbis Books.

Segundo, J. L. (1977) *The Liberation of Theology*. Dublin, Gill & Macmillan.

Sobrino, J. (1978) *Christology at the Crossroads*. London, SCM.

Tracy, D. (1975) *Blessed Rage for Order*. New York, Seabury Press, p. 238.

Williams, R. (1986) 'Balthasar and Rahner', in J. Riches, ed., *The Analogy of Beauty: The Theology of Hans Urs von Balthasar*. Edinburgh, T. & T. Clark, pp. 11–34.

15

JOHN PAUL I

PETER HEBBLETHWAITE

Albino Luciani, who briefly reigned as John Paul I in 1978, was the first pope born in the twentieth century and the first to have working-class parents. He was elected because the August conclave of 1978 was looking for a non-curial Italian with pastoral experience. Despite the brevity of his pontificate – a mere thirty-three days – he left his mark on the papal institution in two chief ways.

The first was by his unprecedented choice of a double-barrelled name. He explained why in his first address to the Roman crowd on Sunday, 27 August. He was fulfilling a debt of gratitude. Pope John had made him a bishop in 1958; Pope Paul appointed him patriarch of Venice, Pope John's old see, and made him a cardinal in 1973. He modestly said that he did not have the 'wisdom of heart' of Pope John nor the 'preparation and culture' of Pope Paul. His motto (borrowed from St Charles Borromeo) was *Humilitas*. And he meant it.

But the double-barrelled John Paul had a deeper significance. Luciani knew that Popes John and Paul were popularly contrasted, with John symbolizing openness to 'all men of good will', while Paul was perceived as a hesitant worrier. By calling himself John Paul, Luciani was refusing to separate them. To have called himself John XXIV or Paul VII would have been divisive. By appealing to the heritage of both and dying early, he almost imposed this 'name of promise' on his successor.

The second achievement of his brief reign was to simplify the papal style. Hitherto, popes had been crowned with the tiara – the triple crown of Asiatic origin – which symbolized power, including the now vanished temporal power. Paul VI had been thus crowned, though he stopped wearing the tiara. But if the start of the papal ministry was not marked by a coronation ceremony, how should it be marked? 'Enthronement' was briefly toyed with, but Pope John Paul wanted to relegate the *sedia gestatoria* (portable throne) along with the ostrich feathers to the Vatican lumber room. In the end he simply 'inaugurated his pastoral ministry as supreme pastor' on Sunday, 3 September 1978, anniversary of the outbreak of war in 1939 and feast of St Gregory the Great. John Paul was good at devising such symbols.

But he was not just displaying 'humility'. He was making a point about the petrine office. All the papal titles that theologians had proscribed as unscriptural or even pagan – Vicar of Christ, Supreme Pontiff, Head of the Church – were abandoned in favour of the Bishop of Rome. Instead of the tiara he received the pallium, presented to archbishops 'from the tomb of St Peter' since the fourth century. It is placed on the shoulders, and resembles a yoke; made of lamb's wool, it evokes the pastoral nature of all offices in the Church.

Gregory the Great, he said at the Angelus that same day, had been the patron of his seminary at Belluno in the province of Venice. He recalled Gregory's love of the poor, reluctance to become pope, and his memorable remark that 'the emperor wants a monkey to be a lion'. Gregory also defined the bishop of Rome as 'the servant of the servants of God'.

Obviously, the rhetoric of service can be used to mask the ideology of power; but John Paul I did not give the impression that he was playing that game. His pontificate has the pathos of any life cut short. But there was enough evidence from his past to suggest that, had it been longer, the authoritarian streak might have come to the fore, and the famous smile might have turned into a grimace.

Though present at all four sessions of the Council as bishop of Vittorio Veneto, he never spoke in the Aula. He seems to have regarded this period as a time for study and reading. He stayed out of intrigues. He had the greatest difficulty with the decree on religious freedom, *Dignitatis Humanae*. Cardinal Alfredo Ottaviani had taught him in his Belluno Seminary that 'error has no rights'. Luciani admitted: 'I studied the question in depth and reached the conclusion that we had been wholly wrong.' Better bluntness than following the crowd.

A somewhat idealistic picture was painted subsequently of Luciani as the very model of a post-conciliar bishop, inspired by Antonio Rosmini's prophetic *The Five Wounds of the Church*. True, Luciani had written a thesis on Rosmini, but on his conception of the soul. Yet his pastoral priorities came from Rosmini: liturgical reform, education of the clergy, the need for poverty in the Church. He was at least prepared to entertain the question of electing bishops – while concluding that it would be too divisive.

He carried over all these attitudes to the much more sophisticated diocese of Venice in 1970. He was also vice president of the Italian episcopal conference in 1972–5. He extended his range of contacts by hosting two meetings of ARCIC, and four encounters with Orthodox Christians. He notoriously quarrelled with Archbishop Paul Marcinkus, president of the Vatican Bank, and declared that 'the poor are the true treasure of the Church'. He kept up with his reading and welcomed into the world Louise Brown, the first 'test-tube baby', just before Paul VI's death.

But on the other hand, he thundered against 'false pluralism' in the run-up to the divorce referendum of 1974, denouncing 'self-appointed theologians'. He castigated these jumped-up disturbers of the peace at the 1974 synod on evangelization. This marked his first appearance on the international Catholic scene. He did not sound like a closet liberal.

'He that heareth you, heareth me,' he explained to the Eucharistic Congress at Pescara in 1977, is specifically addressed to bishops. 'Authority,' he declared, 'exists for the service of the faithful, entirely and solely for their good, so that they are more younger brothers of the pastors than subjects, responsible crewmen aboard the barque of the Church rather than mere passengers.' In all of this, one has to allow for the Italian context in which to admit that the laity are 'responsible crewmen' is progress.

The brief pontificate did not provide enough evidence to say how he would have developed. The Russian Orthodox Metropolitan Nikodim died in his arms on 5 September. On 21 September he addressed a group of United States bishops on one of his favourite themes, the family as the domestic Church with the parents as 'the first and best catechists'. He was himself a skilled catechist with a talent for communication (witness his book of letters to famous people, *Illustrissimi*). But on his first and last sortie from the Vatican on 23 September, he revived the *sedia gestatoria* (in response to popular demand, it was alleged) and denounced in St John Lateran, his cathedral, false notions of 'creativity' that had led to 'liturgical excesses'. Though no doubt true, it hardly seemed the most urgent message from the new bishop of Rome to his diocese. The people from the shanty-towns who had been bussed in to see the 'workers' pope' were puzzled.

The death of John Paul, probably late on the night of 28 September 1978, was made needlessly mysterious by the disinformation put out by the Vatican Press Office. Unable to admit that the body had been discovered by Sister Vincenza, who brought him a cup of chocolate every morning at 5.30, the Press Office said he was found by his Irish priest-secretary, John Magee. His last reading was said to have been *The Imitation of Christ*, which, though not true, was a reasonable guess. The Vatican, in other words, sanitized the story, thus giving rise to 'no smoke without fire' theories about the 'real' cause of death.

David Yallop's book, *In God's Name*, has been a bestseller. Where facts run out, he liberally invents (claiming, for example, to have had an interview with Sr Vincenza at a time when, in fact, she was dead). He also has too many suspects, and totally fails to explain how the conspirators, reacting hostilely to six new nominations, could put their murder plot into action so swiftly on the night of 27 September 1978.

John Cornwell's *A Thief in the Night* shows a much better grasp of the characters and the issues involved. He agrees that John Paul I was 'murdered' in the sense that his grave medical problems were cavalierly ignored by his entourage. He needed treatment and did not get it. This was more incompetence than ill-will, part of the 'tough-it-out' approach to illness often found among religious people. But it was culpable. The final lesson of John Paul I is that future *papabili* should submit to a proper medical examination.

15 John Paul I: Bibliography

Cornwell, J. (1989) *A Thief in the Night*. London, Viking Penguin.

Hebblethwaite P. (1978) *The Year of Three Popes*. London, Collins.

Luciani, A. (1978) *Illustrissimi*. London, Collins (letters to famous people of the past).

Willi, V. J. (1987) *'Im Namen des Teufels?'* Steim-am-Rhein, Switzerland, Christiana (conceived as an answer to David Yallop's bestseller, *In God's Name*, London, Cape, 1984).

16

JOHN PAUL II

PETER HEBBLETHWAITE

To try to assess an incomplete pontificate is a daunting task, all the more when one does not know how much longer it will last. Karol Wojtyla was born at Wadowice, a market town not far from Kraków in southern Poland, on 18 May 1920. Thus if he lives on he will be 75 (the usual retirement age for bishops) in 1995, and 80 (the imposed retirement age for cardinals) in the year 2000. Both Pope John and Pope Paul were over 80 when they died.

Having declared 1990–2000 the decade of evangelization, he would be hardly likely to want to resign before seeing it through and preserving the Church from the anxieties that beset the end of any millennium. He sees his mission as that of bringing 'the joy of faith to a troubled world' (to use one of the headings of *Redemptor Hominis,* his first encyclical).

The second difficulty in speaking of a living pope lies in the nature of his office and the hopes it arouses or disappoints. A pope has the right to expect loyalty, respectful attention to his words, and if one were forced to the conclusion that the Holy Spirit had abandoned the pope altogether, then one would in practice have despaired of the Catholic Church. But these qualifications do not mean that one should not be free to speak frankly.

The best approach to this problem was well put by Melchior Cano, the great Dominican theologian, at the Council of Trent: 'Peter has no need of our lies or flattery. Those who blindly and indiscriminately defend every decision of the Supreme Pontiff are the very people who do most to undermine the authority of the Holy See – they destroy instead of strengthening its foundations.'

The emphasis here will fall upon the relationship between the pope and Vatican II. What does he really think about Vatican II? In his first major address after his election, he apparently answered this question fully and unambiguously:

> We consider our *primary duty* to be that of promoting, with prudent but encouraging action, *the most exact fulfilment* of the norms and directives of the Council. *Above all* we must favour the development of *conciliar attitudes*. First one must be in harmony with the Council. One must put into effect what was stated in its documents; and what was 'implicit' should be made explicit in the light of *the experiments* that followed and in the light of *new and emerging* circumstances (17 October 1978 (italics added)).

The italics are added to bring out the remarkable degree of commitment to Vatican II this programmatic statement expresses. Conservatives heard these words with alarm. Away in his mountain fastness of Ecône, Switzerland,

447

dissident Archbishop Marcel Lefebvre must have thought he had waited in vain for the death of Paul VI.

However, more than ten years later, few could put their hands on their hearts and say that John Paul has done what he said he would do so soon after his election. The passage contains no hint of any of the 'dangers' or 'excesses' that were later alleged to be the fruit of the Council. Thus, according to Cardinal Joseph Ratzinger, named prefect of the Congregation for the Doctrine of the Faith on 21 November 1981, these 'dangers' and 'excesses' were the real reason why Vatican II was chosen as the subject of the 1985 Extraordinary Synod. The difference between Ratzinger and Lefebvre was this: Lefebvre said the Council was a bad thing with bad fruits; Ratzinger said that although it was a good thing 'in itself', it had alas been misinterpreted, manipulated, and thus had some distinctly rotten fruits.

Yet curiously enough, this was not a theme developed by the pope when he announced the Synod. On the contrary, he seemed to echo his 1978 sentiments when he declared:

> For me the Second Vatican Council has always been – in a particular fashion *during these years of my pontificate – the constant reference point of every pastoral action*, with *conscious commitment* to translate its directives into concrete, faithful action, at the level of *every* Church and of the *whole* Church (25 January 1985 (italics added)).

It would be harder to put the case more strongly – but now he is no longer talking about a future programme, but claiming to have realized one. Pope John Paul *thinks* his pontificate is the fulfilment of Vatican II. Here, it seems, we have a pope who can think of nothing else. Yet that is not what many observers see.

How can one explain this apparent optical illusion? Is John Paul insincere? Is he saying one thing and doing another? Such explanations are certainly to be rejected, for no one so exposed to the public gaze, however skilled an actor, could keep up this pretence for so long. And what motive would he have? The key to the mystery is rather to be provided by asking what content he puts into the 'Council' and 'Vatican II'. Utterly sincere when he declares his commitment to them, he nevertheless does not mean by 'Council' and 'Vatican II' what most people in the West mean by these terms.

The way to test this hypothesis is to read his book *Sources of Renewal* (Wojtyla, 1980). The Polish edition, published in Kraków in 1972, was and remains *the* introduction to the Council for Poles. Poland did not have the flood of books expounding the new insights of the Council that streamed from European and American (North and South) publishers in the heady few years just after the event. It took a long time even to translate the Council texts into Polish. The Poles did not have the review *Concilium* – their bishops rejected the idea of a translation on the grounds that all Polish theologians could read other languages; the same argument, however, was not used against the rival publication, *Communio*. What the Poles had was Karol Wojtyla's *U Podstaw Odnowy*.

He wrote the book, he explains, as an expression of his 'debt' to Vatican II:

> The Council had a unique and unrepeatable meaning for all who took part in it, and most particularly for the bishops who were Fathers of the Council. These men took

an active part for four years in the proceedings of the Council, drafting its documents, and at the same time deriving great *spiritual enrichment* from it. The experience of a world-wide community was to each of them a tremendous benefit of historic importance. The history of the Council, which will one day be written, was present in 1962–65 as an extraordinary event in the minds of all the bishops concerned; it absorbed all their thoughts and stimulated their sense of responsibility, as an exceptional and deeply felt experience (Wojtyla, 1980, p. 9 (italics added)).

This seemed a rather odd way to be talking about the Council. It is made to sound wholly content-less – as though its most remarkable feature was that it had happened at all. Again, it is presented as a private and largely incommunicable experience of *bishops*, as though it had not aroused expectations and enthusiasm among so many in the Church. And the remark about the as-yet unwritten 'history of the Council' shows scant respect for the work of Giovanni Caprile and Vorgrimler's five-volume commentary, not to mention more ephemeral works.

Another feature of Cardinal Wojtyla's account of the Council is that it appears as a wholly tranquil and harmonious event; one would never guess that there had been fierce rows at the time, and raging controversies afterwards. This is an imaginary picture of the Council, a pleasing and delightful fiction.

As his friend, Halina Bortnowska, pointed out in her introduction to the simplified Italian version, *L'Arrichimento della Fede*:

> *Sources of Renewal* was a first and provisional sketch. The author hides behind numerous quotations from the Council. Often he does not give his own thoughts . . . . The Council texts, and they alone, occupy the stage, and there is no reference to post-conciliar or even conciliar debates. One has a feeling of great abstractness and remoteness from the lives of people seeking some guidance for their lives (Bortnowska, 1981, p. 17).

This is a penetrating judgement, and it helps to explain why Pope John Paul devised a new kind of synod from which the press was excluded and where secrecy reigned: that is how the Council *would have been* had not the likes of Xavier Rynne and Henri Fesquet been muddying the waters.

John Paul's motive for calling an Extraordinary Synod on Vatican II in 1985 was not that of Ratzinger. He wanted to recapture the dream of sweetness and light that he remembered so well. Or, as he put it, 'to revive in some way the extraordinary atmosphere of ecclesial communion which characterized that ecumenical assembly through mutual participation in sufferings and joys, struggles and hopes, which pertain to the Body of Christ in the various parts of the world' (25 January 1985). Once again, the Council is, as it were, episcopally privatized.

So one can say in summary that the Council in Poland was differently perceived and differently 'received' (in the technical sense). Few Poles knew much about the Council or expected much from it. That included the cardinal primate, Stefan Wyszyński. This great hero of the faith told Pope Paul VI, as the Polish bishops said farewell to him:

> We are aware that it will be very difficult, but not impossible, to put the decisions of the Council into effect in our situation . . . .. Everything that occurs in our Church must be judged from the standpoint of our experience (Stehle, 1981, pp. 341–2).

449

In short, we know Poland better than you do.

Wyszyński was quite blunt about why he didn't like the Council. It had revealed a lack of enthusiasm for popular piety, processions and pilgrimages that were so important in Polish Catholic life. It had downgraded mariology. The 'kiss of peace', he averred, would 'turn the church into a salon'. Above all, the Council's eagerness to 'learn from the world' expressed in *Gaudium et Spes* and its lack of any direct condemnation of communism would sow confusion in his well-disciplined ranks. Paul VI equally bluntly told him that the Council would be implemented 'energetically and willingly' in Poland as elsewhere.

One can see why, therefore, Paul VI made Wojtyla a cardinal in 1967, when he was only 46, and pinned his hopes for the implementation of the Council in Poland on him. Wojtyla enjoyed the Council while Wyszyński bore it stoically, thinking of the Polish millennium due in 1966. Wojtyla was 'for' the Council in a way Wyszyński manifestly was not. Wojtyla appeared more 'to the left' or 'more liberal' than Wyszyński. And in Polish terms he was both. But the version of the Council he would make available for Poles would be adapted to their own special needs as an oppressed and staunchly Catholic people living under a regime they had not freely chosen, and from which, for geo-political reasons, they could not escape.

This explains why John Paul so regularly misquotes Pope John on the most fundamental question: What was the Council for? Here is John Paul II addressing the United States bishops in Chicago:

> On the opening day of the Council John XXIII made the following statement: 'The greatest concern of the ecumenical Council is this: that the sacred deposit of the Christian faith should be more effectively guarded and taught.' This explains Pope John's inspiration; this was what the new Pentecost was to be; this was why the Bishops of the Church – in the greatest manifestation of collegiality in the history of the world – were called together, 'so that the sacred deposit of faith should be more effectively guarded and taught' (5 October 1979).

So the purpose of the Council was essentially *defensive*. It was a matter of warding off errors, of *preserving* the deposit of faith.

But this was not what Pope John thought at all. 'Our duty,' he said 'is not only to guard this precious treasure as if we were concerned only with antiquity, but to dedicate ourselves . . . without fear to that work which our age demands of us' (Abbott, p. 715). That is clearly envisaged as a new task. As for 'defending the deposit of faith', Pope John explained that the purpose of the Council was not to 'restate the doctrine that has been repeatedly taught by the fathers and by ancient and modern theologians'. He added a remark that Pope John Paul blots out of his memory: 'For that [i.e. the restatement of familiar doctrine] *a Council was not necessary*' (Abbott, p. 715). So John Paul II attributes to the Council a defensive aim which John XXIII specifically repudiated.

Again one has to understand the psychology at work here. The anti-religious propaganda department of the Polish government (in which, sadly, many ex-priests found their only means of livelihood) presented in the mass media a Council that stressed only its 'progressive' aspects. They contrasted Pope John and the luminaries of the Council with the fuddy-duddy Polish bishops. The Polish bishops responded by saying that they were the only authorized interpreters of the Council.

It is also true that they consistently defended at home all the positions they had already put forward in Rome – whether this was the majority view of the Council or not. Karol Wojtyla was by far the sharpest-minded Polish bishop present, and usually acted as their spokesman. His interventions have been studied in detail by Jan Grootaers (1981, pp. 152–66). The following picture emerges.

On ecclesiology, he did not much like the term 'people of God' because for him it failed to reflect the Church's nature as a 'perfect society'. On the other hand, when it was accepted as the controlling concept, he agreed that it should come before the chapter on the hierarchical nature of the Church. He strongly defended the idea of the Church as 'communion', said he did not want a passive laity, and urged 'intra-ecclesial dialogue'. But he continued to hold that the Church was a 'perfect society', and therefore underplayed its pilgrim status and need for constant reformation.

Religious liberty was a cause close to his heart, not out of any special ecumenical concern (postwar Poland, with its frontiers shifted westwards, was much more homogeneously Catholic than ever prewar Poland had been), but as a claim made against the atheistic state. In talking about ecumenism, he warned, one should stress the links between liberty and truth, freedom and responsibility in order to guard against 'liberalism' or 'indifferentism'. On civil liberty, he echoed the thunderous speech of Wyszyński of 20 September 1965, on the folly of making 'public order in conformity with juridical norms' a limitation on freedom. His own government, he pointed out, could use that to suppress any expression of opinion it did not like. So the phrase became 'public order in conformity with the objective moral order' (*ordini morali objectivo conformes*). This eventually became 'the just requirements of public order' of *Dignitatis Humanae* (2,3). Grootaers concludes that Wojtyla's role was to mediate on this matter between Wyszyński and the Secretariat for Christian Unity (Grootaers, 1981, p. 167).

It is somewhat easier to pinpoint his contribution to *Gaudium et Spes*, because the Polish bishops were so disappointed with the draft at one stage that they proposed a 'Polish alternative' that had a certain, though limited, impact. We know that Wojtyla was its chief author. The Poles showed themselves deeply worried by 'secularization', which they thought of primarily as something from which they suffered at the hands of their atheistic government; but they also saw 'secularization' invading democratic societies as well. The different situations, and different questions involved, were not sufficiently distinguished.

Wojtyla personally stressed the perils of 'horizontalism'. The 'optimism' of some Western Europeans, notably the Dutch and the French, often attributed to the influence of Pierre Teilhard de Chardin, seemed to him to be highly dangerous. He shared the 'German' view that the ravages of sin should be more forcefully brought out. He was therefore inclined to a 'pessimistic' judgement on the world and unaided human society.

451

This recall of his role at the Council helps to explain most of his attitudes as pope. The Extraordinary Synod of 1985, seen in this light, was an attempt to put back in to the Council texts elements that the Council itself failed to emphasize. In this regard, *The Ratzinger Report* acted as a trial-balloon for the Synod, and if Ratzinger did not wholly get his way, the main theses he had been advocating were duly incorporated into the final report (including a deep scepticism about the theological status and authority to teach of episcopal conferences).

In this new ecclesiology, *Lumen Gentium* is modified by reducing chapter 2, on the people of God, to a metaphor that is dangerous because of its 'democratic' connotations (see on this, Ratzinger, 1988, pp. 3–28). Then chapter 1, on the Church as 'Mystery', is extolled as the antidote to a one-sidedly 'institutional' or merely 'sociological' view which is said to have prevailed in the last few years. Self-critically, the Synod asks, 'Have we not put this idea into [i.e. young people's] heads by talking too much about reforming external structures and too little about God and Christ?' (Synod Final Report, A,4). Finally, having substituted mystery for sociology, one can give the central place to chapter 3 of *Lumen Gentium*, on the hierarchical nature of the Church, drawing special attention to the *Nota Praevia* which tilts the balance of collegiality towards the primacy (Synod Final Report, C,4).

The personal stamp of John Paul II appears more clearly still in the Final Report's treatment of *Gaudium et Spes*, which harks back to the 'Polish alternative' rejected in 1965:

> The Church as communion is the sacrament of the world's salvation . . . .. In this context we assert the importance and the great relevance of the pastoral constitution *Gaudium et Spes*. At the same time we observe that the signs of the times differ to some extent from those which the Council discerned, for today anguish and suffering have increased. *All over the world today there is hunger, oppression, injustice, torture, war, terrorism, and other forms of violence of every kind.* This demands a new and deeper theological reflection to interpret such signs in the light of the Gospel (D,1).

So *Gaudium et Spes* represented an insufficiently deep level of theological thinking. (The italics here signify that the passage was added at the last moment.)

While accepting that the afflictions listed are very much part of the contemporary scene, one has to add that they subvert the meaning of 'signs of the times' as understood by John XXIII and *Gaudium et Spes*. In *Pacem in Terris* John found *positive* signs of the presence of the Holy Spirit in the emancipation of women, the growing prosperity of the workers, and the end of colonial rule.

Gaudium et Spes follows this same positive line, and speaking of the concern for human rights and where the impulse to defend them comes from, says:

> God's Spirit, who with a marvellous Providence directs the unfolding of time and renews the face of the earth, is present to this development. The ferment of the Gospel arouses in men's hearts a demand for dignity that cannot be stifled (*GS* 26).

Of course it is difficult to make this idea comprehensible to suffering people in Kampuchea, the Lebanon and South Africa. Their way is more obviously the way of the cross. But all Christians have to pass by the way of the cross with varying degrees of intensity. There are no short cuts to Easter Sunday.

That is not in question. What is questionable is to turn the 'signs of the times' theology into a banal synonym for 'whatever happens to be going on at the moment'. Yet that is what John Paul regularly seems to do. Here is an early example that set the tone. Addressing religious women in Washington on 7 October 1979, he said:

> As daughters of the Church . . . you are called to a generous and loving adherence to the authentic magisterium of the Church, which is a solid guarantee of the fruitfulness of all your apostolates and an indispensable condition of the discernment of the 'signs of the times'.

Additionally, we are no longer dealing here with optimistic versus pessimistic readings of 'the signs of the times', but with who is to discern them. *Gaudium et Spes* sees this as a task for the whole Church:

> With the help of the Holy Spirit, it is the task of the entire people of God, especially pastors and theologians, to hear, distinguish and interpret the many voices of our age, and to interpret them in the light of the divine word (*GS* 44).

It is a big jump from that to saying that adherence to the magisterium is the criterion of true discernment.

With the Dogmatic Constitution *Lumen Gentium* and the Pastoral Constitution *Gaudium et Spes* thus re-edited, how do other Council documents fare?

We have seen what Cardinal Wojtyla thought of *Dignitatis Humanae*, the declaration on religious liberty. If it has not been repudiated, neither has it been celebrated; and in one respect it has been systematically undermined. John Paul believes that in countries where Catholics can achieve this goal, legislation on moral issues such as divorce, contraception, abortion, IVF and even sexual orientation, should reflect official Catholic moral teaching. This is a frequent theme of his exhortations, especially during visits to traditionally 'Catholic' countries like France and Spain.

His remarks on this subject were most politically explosive when he visited Argentina in spring 1987. President Raúl Alfonsín, who had returned the country to democracy, not only sought to bring to justice the torturers and killers of the previous military regime, but also by introducing legislation on divorce and abortion, to reflect the fact that Argentina was by now a very mixed and pluralistic society.

John Paul thundered against this, showed little enthusiasm for the restoration of democracy, conspicuously failed to denounce the 'dirty war', and in the name of 'reconciliation' (his alternative to the semi-Marxist 'liberation') urged a *punto final*, an end to the pursuit of the guilty officers. Not surprisingly, there was a military revolt a week after he left, and Alfonsín's position was rendered deeply insecure. One might be tempted to conclude that John Paul's reading of *Dignitatis Humanae* does not allow for pluralism in a 'Catholic' society.

Argentina proved relatively fertile ground for Archbishop Marcel Lefebvre. John Paul's dealings with him illustrate his attitude to *Sacrosanctum Concilium* and the liturgy. Very early in his pontificate – indeed in November 1978 –

Pope John Paul gave Lefebvre the private and secret audience Paul VI had always refused. This was followed by three meetings with Cardinal Franjo Seper, the prefect of the Congregation for the Doctrine of the Faith. Clearly, a 'solution' was being urgently sought. But none was immediately forthcoming.

Then, on 3 October 1984, the Congregation for Divine Worship issued an indult which gave permission for the 1962 (i.e. Tridentine missal) to be used under certain conditions. This looked like a concession towards Lefebvre, and a pre-emptive strike against a gathering of 228 bishops and experts who met at the Congregation's invitation later that same October. The guests were angry because in 1981, polled by *Notitiae*, the Congregation's house-organ, their verdict was that the Tridentine Mass was now definitively and irrevocably superseded, and that its restoration would do nothing to bring back dissidents like Lefebvre – since the traditionalists' basic objection was not just to what they called 'the hybrid and democratic Mass of Paul VI', but to the Council as a whole.

There were further meetings, this time with Cardinal Joseph Ratzinger, Seper's successor, in the summer of 1987, and then, during the Synod on the role of the laity in the Church and the world, two rather stunning events occurred. The first was a passage in a homily by Pope John Paul on 11 October 1987, the 25th anniversary to the day of Pope John's address to the Council. The following paragraph was hastily added at a late stage:

> The Council was able to complete the enormous task of re-affirming the Church's doctrinal patrimony and building on it a contemporary, up-dated, programme for Christian life and behaviour at both the personal and community level. Hence, the teaching of the Council, in its entirety, rightly understood in the context of the previous *Magisterium*, can well be called a programme for action for the present-day Christian (I leave this in the translation provided by the Vatican Press Office).

Was this an olive branch held out to Lefebvre? He was, after all, prepared to accept the Council 'rightly understood in the context of the previous *Magisterium*' if by that one meant, for example, that *Dignitatis Humanae* should be read in conjunction with the nineteenth-century teaching that 'error has no rights', and *Gaudium et Spes*' optimism qualified by the 1864 Syllabus of Errors.

A week later, Ratzinger told the Synod that 'the hoped for definitive solution based on the presupposition that there exists the obedience due to the Supreme Pontiff and loyalty to the *Magisterium* of the Church' was at hand (17 October 1987). Once again, there was ambivalence about what precisely was meant by 'loyalty to the *Magisterium*'. The rest of the story is less relevant here. In May 1988 Lefebvre accepted, and then – the next day – rejected the generous conditions offered to his Society of St Pius. Despite Roman pleas he went ahead with four episcopal ordinations before the world's television cameras on 28 June, and was inevitably excommunicated. Much time and energy have since been devoted to 'recuperating' the traditionalists, and it has been noted that liberation theologians, for example, have not been given such gentle treatment.

This discrepancy can be explained if Pope John Paul, who has never willingly given Communion in the hand and appointed Georg Eder, who prefers to say Mass with his back to the people, as Archbishop of Salzburg, Austria, actually connives to some extent with Lefebvre. In December 1988 he announced a new document commemorating *Sacrosanctum Concilium* which said that the 'reform of the liturgy . . . must be continued, sustained, and, where necessary, purified' (*The Tablet*, 17 December 1988, p. 1469). However, he is a resolute supporter of the vernacular liturgy, in all the fifty-three languages he has used on various occasions.

This may seem a harsh judgement on a pope whom some ecumenical partners hail as a great communicator and a great leader. Within the Church, a right-wing magazine assured us that Pope John Paul's pontificate 'is leading to a certain euphoria about the "recovery" after the great post-conciliar recession' (*Thirty Days*, December 1988, p. 46). Readers may decide for themselves how much evidence there is for 'euphoria' and how it has been induced, if at all.

Two Polish judgements can help us conclude. Halina Bortnowska, already mentioned, holds that his most important magisterial document is the apostolic letter *Salvifici Doloris* (dated 11 February 1984). Why prefer this to great social encyclicals like *Laborem Exercens* (1981) with its support for co-partnership, and *Sollicitudo Rei Socialis* (1987) with its post-Chernobyl hints on the ecology crisis found in the telling phrase 'solidarity with the earth'? Because he speaks about suffering not as a philosopher nor even as a theologian discoursing on 'the problem of evil', but as a human being who has experienced collective suffering in Poland and personal suffering when Mehemet Ali Agca shot him. Watch how he lingers over the sick, demonstrating what ministry (in one form) means. The most moving moment on his visit to Britain in 1982 was in Southwark cathedral when the pope and seventy priests fanned out among the people lying on their mattresses and gave them the sacrament of the sick.

Kryzysztof Sliwiński, another Polish intellectual, has made the surprising (for foreigners) point that after more than ten years away from home, Pope John Paul has become less Polish and much more 'Western' in his thinking. He gave two examples. He alleged that John Paul 'shocked' some Polish priests during his 1987 visit home by the place he gave to the laity in the Church. A rather more serious example is the fact that *Mulieris Dignitatem*, read in the West merely for the paragraph that rejects women's ordination, in fact takes aboard much of the feminist agenda. It says, for example, that 'women symbolize the human' better than men; it rejects the Victorian idea that the sexual sins of men are the result of irresistible feminine provocation; it shows the compassion Jesus showed towards the woman taken in adultery.

One sees the point. But John Paul still has a long way to go. All this talk of 'feminine genius' recalls Goethe's *das Ewigweibliche* (the eternal feminine) which draws us upwards. But it is found in Mary, who stands for *agape*, rather than Eve, who represents *eros*. This is romantic poetry more than theology, and it fits in with Polish gallantry and the supremacy of Mariology. John Paul has spoken about sexuality, shame, *animus* and *anima* and related topics with greater frankness than any previous pope (see Durkin, 1983, for his originality; Ms Durkin is Fr Andrew Greeley's sister).

One would like to hope that John Paul continues to learn from his stay in the

West, not to mention from his world-wide journeys; and that he might spend as much time trying to understand the rest of us as we have spent trying to understand him. It may be that his providential role is to test the conservative hypothesis to breaking-point. At the conclave that elected him, it was possible to argue that the Church needed a strong hand on the tiller. At the next conclave, that argument will not wash: the conservative option will have been tried, and may well be found wanting. In the spiritual life, everyone fails. The seed falls into the ground and dies. But this will be a magnificent, heroic failure on a cosmic scale, with that special Polish dash.

16 John Paul II: Bibliography

Blazynski, G. (1979) *John Paul II: A Man from Kraków*. London, Weidenfeld & Nicolson.

Bortnowska, H. (1981) *L' Arrichimento della Fede*. Rome, Vatican Press.

Durkin M. G. (1983) *Feast of Love: John Paul II on Human Intimacy*. Chicago, Loyola University Press.

Frossard, A. (1984) *Be not Afraid!' André Frossard in Conversation with John Paul II*. London, Bodley Head.

Grootaers, J. (1981) *De Vatican II à Jean-Paul II, le Grand Tournant de L'Eglise Catholique*. Paris, Centurion.

Hebblethwaite, P. (1982) *Introducing John Paul II: The Populist Pope*. London, Collins.

Malinski, M. (1979) *Pope John Paul II: The Life of my Friend Karol Wojtyla*. London, Burns & Oates.

Ratzinger, J. (1988) *Church, Ecumenism and Politics*. Slough, St Paul Publications.

Stehle, H.-J. (1981) *Eastern Politics of the Vatican 1917–1979*. Athens, Ohio, Ohio University Press.

Whale, J., ed. (1980) *The Pope from Poland: An Assessment*. London, Collins.

Williams, Huntston G. (1981) *The Mind of John Paul II: Origins of his Thought and Action*. New York, Seabury Press.

Wojtyla, K. (1979) *The Acting Person* (originally Kraków, 1969), Analecta Husserliana, *The Yearbook of Phenomenological Research*. Dordrecht, The Netherlands, D. Reidel Publishers.

Wojtyla, K. (1980) *Sources of Renewal* (originally Kraków, 1972). London, Collins; New York, Harper & Row.

Wojtyla, K. (1981) *Love and Responsibility* (originally Kraków, 1960). London, Collins.

17

AN OUTSIDER'S EVALUATION

EDWARD NORMAN

For the Protestant observer – as doubtless also in reality for the Catholic – it is difficult now to distinguish the developments and changes that have taken place as a consequence of the Second Vatican Council, in the past two decades, from those that would anyway have occurred. The Council was summoned to take stock of the faith in a world of cultural and intellectual disorientation. Or so it seemed in 1962, when the sessions began. But the cultural and intellectual changes that were to take place in the years immediately following the closing sessions, in the later 1960s and in the 1970s, were much more fundamental – even if they have left no greater coherence as their legacy.

An extravagant crisis of values, associated in the popular mind with youth protests against the Vietnam war, descended upon the West amid an atmosphere of general cultural iconoclasm. There is a sense in which the Council was an attempt to restate the faith in categories more suited to the modern world than the patently discarded ones of the Thomists and the Schoolmen, but to the extent that that was intended in precise categories it was frustrated in large measure by the lack of an agreed replacement. No single dominant intellectual or theological mode emerged at the Council; the pluralism of the modern world seeped into the proceedings, yet the resulting reformulations of the faith were, in the event, surprisingly unitary and conservative. By the standards of criticism that came to prevail within the Western intelligentsia just a few years afterwards, the intellectual assumptions of the Council fathers may still be identified, despite occasional hints of things to come, as belonging to the old world. It was a Western world too. At the time, and as many subsequent commentators have contended, it seemed as if the Council was the first to be addressed to a global context. That was certainly the view of Karl Rahner. Yet there was no real sense in which either the proceedings themselves, or the cultural context in which they were received and interpreted, witnessed to the rise of 'third-world consciousness'. The numerical strength of bishops from the non-European world, and the repeated assertions that the experience of the developing world was seminal in the proceedings, ought not to obscure the fact that it was the cultural and intellectual adjustments of the European and North American intelligentsia that furnished the background to the Council, and that it was the Westernized leadership of the Church in the developing world which moulded its teaching in the years that followed. Little of the rhetoric of third-world Christianity has been much more than a loud echo of the European world declaiming its own loss of cultural certainty.

This will seem, to many, a contentious conclusion; it is introduced here, however, to illustrate a central Protestant interest in the Council's work: the

457

ecumenical dimension. Yet it is difficult to believe, again, that most of the developments of the ecumenical scene that have occurred in the last couple of decades derive from the Council. Most, surely, would anyway have taken place in some form or other as a response to the general cultural climate. In its partial removal of restrictions on joint worship with non-Catholic Christians, and in the escalating access given to observers at its sessions, in the various liaison commissions in several countries that have succeeded, and in the Declaration on Religious Freedom, the Council obviously stimulated ecumenical contacts. But the ecumenical dimension, so crucial to Protestant observers in their understanding of the Council's legacy, was not a priority – was not even a major preoccupation, except for the external observers themselves – of the Council fathers. Beneath the ecclesiastical courtesies – and the self-deception of those whose desire to move ahead of opinion on this issue was so great that it misinterpreted little gusts as great winds of change – there was a basically unchanged landscape. Protestants have tended to suppose that the Vatican Council signalled the 'Protestantization' of the Catholic Church. They saw the new services (bleak to some, and certainly more austere and less extravagant of ornament than the simulations of the old rite still performed in 'Anglo-Catholic' churches) as the herald of basic ecclesiastical change. They welcomed the place given to the laity in the Dogmatic Constitution on the Church (*Lumen Gentium*) as a step like that taken by Protestants some centuries before. They approved the definition of the Church, in the same document, as 'the people of God', and the emphasis on collegiality, and identified it as the shedding of Catholic hierarchical exclusivity.

They were mistaken in nearly all of these things. What in fact they were observing was the emergence of a universal Church from the transient clothing of ultramontanism; its Italianate devotional styles, its centralized bureaucracy, its sacerdotalism, were all providentially necessary for the nineteenth-century world – born after the pillage of Rome by the forces of French atheism, sustained in opposition to the secular liberalism of the emergent Italian state, used as the essential means of religious advance in the confused societies of the non-European world where missionary endeavour required convinced central direction. By the middle years of the succeeding century, that world had passed away, and with it the conditions in which ultramontanism flourished.

As the thick Italianate clouds dispersed, a familiar old terrain became visible again: the first priority of the external mission of the Catholic Church was not to the fringe Protestant phenomenon, whose own internal disintegration at times did not appear too far off, but to the historic Churches of the East. It is no coincidence that both John XXIII and John Paul II had seminal direct experience of the contemporary problems of Eastern Christianity: the one of the Church in contact with Orthodoxy, the other of the Catholic Church locked in contact with scientific materialism reared into a state system. For the Council fathers who gathered in 1962, as for their successors, the external priority was not a rapprochement with the Western Protestants, but the rediscovery of the universality of the Catholic Church itself, and the attempt to draw closer to Orthodoxy.

The Council sought to express the Christian faith in terms of existing world society; to accept legitimate local differences, to discern the temporary from the permanent in the affairs of men, of rescue true religiosity from absorption by the alluring moralism of secular culture, and to activate the apostolate of the laity in a world increasingly 'laicized' in its attitude to religious phenomena (or so it seemed until the unexpected emergence of Islamic fundamentalism).

If Protestants were mistaken in their wistful hopes of a radical shift in Catholic priorities, mistaking charity and love of brethren for organic restructuring, they were certainly equally mistaken in their own ecumenical presuppositions. Protestants and Catholics have fundamentally different doctrines of the Church. No matter how many accommodations may be made to derive formulae of agreement over the Eucharist or the nature of ministry, or whatever, the basic cause of organic division between Christians is still the doctrine of the Church itself. It is crucial because it is not about some obscure and dated obsession of the highly clericalized, but about the very means by which truth itself is known and authenticated.

The historic Churches believe that Christ delivered the truth about himself to a body, the Church, which was, under the immediate guidance of the Holy Spirit, protected in infallible understanding – when discerning the truth collectively. Protestants suppose that there is no infallibility in the Church, which is, indeed, conceived atomistically, so that the Holy Spirit is regarded as guaranteeing certainty to individuals in their construction of Holy Scripture. A religious body that claims to be part of the historic Church must show how it can discern truth: how it can take part in, or help to summon, a general Council. The Anglican Church, for example, is plainly Protestant by this definition, and in the twenty-first of its Thirty-Nine Articles of Religion, indeed, it does explicity declare that Councils, which may only be called with the authority of civil authority, 'may err, and sometimes have erred, even in things pertaining to God'.

The Second Vatican Council's Dogmatic Constitution, *Lumen Gentium*, in stark contrast, repeats the doctrine of an infallible Church: 'The universal body made up of the faithful, whom the Holy One has anointed, is incapable of being at fault in belief.' What is then declared is 'not the word of men but what really is the word of God' (*Lumen Gentium* 12). Protestants seeking an accommodation with the Catholic Church, and some German Catholic theologians, occasionally appear much exercised by the practice of *papal* infallibility. But the pope only speaks infallibly when he speaks collectively; he is inseparable, as *Lumen Gentium* makes plain, from the whole movement of the people of God and articulates the consensus of the faithful. As it happens, the Second Vatican Council did not declare any new teachings of the Church as dogma, and the issue of the infallibility of the Church did not, therefore, emerge in a way disturbing to those Protestants sufficiently well informed about such matters to have minded. It is not, however, the infallibility of the pope, but of the Church itself, which is the major difference between Catholics and Protestants, and the Council underlined and restated that difference, in *Lumen Gentium*, with great clarity and precision. It is difficult to see how it is possible, in view of this, to regard the Council as an ecumenical advance –

using 'ecumenical' to mean, as most Christians of all denominations now do (including apparently many Catholics), a movement towards organic unity.

What the Council did do, and it has been of inestimable benefit, was to enhance brotherhood between the Christian bodies. In subsequent experience of shared worship, in particular, the Christian world has been hugely enriched. If the findings of the sociology of religion are correct, the historic divisions of religion anyway tend to correspond to non-religious conditions of society: to social marginalization of given groups, perhaps, or to their social dis-orientation. So it may well be that whatever the declarations or intentions of Church bodies, the fissures and cracks will always reappear. A clear example is provided in contemporary England, where the poor urban black population, in conditions of considerable social disorientation, are forming their own black churches and sects rather than resort to the formalized white bourgeois worship of the mainstream Protestant churches.

The reforms consequent upon the Vatican Council have been of enormous advantage, in the countries of the developing world, in assisting the emergence of indigenized Catholic leadership. To what extent were these reforms, also, the effective result of the Council, and to what extent were they anyway inevitable as a result of the disintegration of the values of the old world? Were they a response, which the Council moulded dynamically, to the 'signs of the times' to which John XXIII alluded? In his official opening address to the Council, in October 1962, he said:

> It is one thing to have the substance of the ancient doctrine of the *depositum fidei* but quite another to formulate and reclothe it: and it is this that must – if need be with patience – be held of great importance, measuring everything according to the forms and proportions of a teaching of pre-eminently pastoral character.

This, he had said, must be done 'in accordance with the methods of research and literary formulation familiar to modern thought'.

The greatest problem for the Church in every age has always been the difficulty experienced by its contemporary luminaries in determining what things are of the essence of Christianity and what things are transient modes of interpretation. At times in the history of the Church, indeed, the problem of interpretation, in this sense, has been so radical as to make it seem as if Christianity has no stable content at all. Such an age may now be upon us, and the Council can in this perspective be regarded as a necessary stocktaking in order to jettison those accretions no longer helpful in the dissemination of the faith, so removing impediments to belief. Since the Council made no new dogmatic definitions, the new emphasis it gave to existing formulations – in the part of the laity, for example, or in the nature of worship, the relationship to separated brethren, and religious toleration – could anyway have occurred, and would inevitably have occurred, without it. But there would have been much greater disruption to the life of the Church in the adjustments that had to be made.

The advantage of a Council in circumstances of considerable change of emphasis and practice are obvious: no local areas can lag behind the others in the changes, on the grounds of peculiar circumstance, and none may go too fast in the direction of adjustment; the various national elements whose presence has throughout history given additional texture to the interpretation of Christianity could not impose themselves too greatly; the tensions between Roman authority and the priorities of particular groups and intellectual modes could be eased within an agreed framework of general interpretation. One of the greatest dangers for the Church in modern circumstances remains the resurgence of 'national' churches, in the developing world (through the competition, in secular terms, for national objectives against rival emergent nations), and in the European and North American theatre (because of the increasing approximation of the Catholic leadership in each place to the secular priorities of the intelligentsia). The Council, while not removing these dangers, which are implicit in so much contemporary culture, did provide the Church with a set of references within which adjustments can be made much more sympathetically and with much less risk of overall disruption.

For all that, however, it surely remains clear that the reforms of the last two decades, while stimulated and regulated by the atmosphere of the Vatican Council, were likely to have occurred even had it not been assembled. Local synods and the beginnings of the various processes whereby the laity are consulted would anyway have evolved, the liturgy would have been performed in the vernacular, relations with non-Catholic Christianity would have improved, the Italian domination of the curia would have lessened, and a general and pervasive sense in which the truths of the Church should be understood in the context of the needs of the contemporary world – the pastoral emphasis – were anyway going to happen.

Each has its counterpart in the Protestant churches; and all correspond to some crucial and widespread assumptions of modern liberalism. There is, in the mind of the contemporary secular intelligence, an impatience with 'dogma', a desire to seem open to variations of interpretation, an impulse to decentralize and to respect local opinion, a will to create occasions of wide participation in the structures of government, and an emphasis on humanity and its needs. All these classic characteristics of received liberalism found their expressions in the emphases of the documents of the Vatican Council. But they were *emphases* only, not radical restructuring – and certainly not root-and-branch departures from the preceding history of the Church.

The Council documents were actually rather conservative in the sense that the 'mystery' of the Church was never submerged beneath accommodations to the values of the secular culture. Those values were allowed to provide a structure of reinterpretation for the practice of modern men and women, as the Council fathers had intended, but were never to penetrate the essential title deeds of the Church which, Catholics believe, were laid down for all time by Christ. Hence the surviving decisive difference between the doctrine of the Church maintained by Catholics (and by the Orthodox), which rests, as ever, on the organic mystery protected by the consensus of the faithful, and the Protestants' contention – so much more readily accommodated to the shifting bases of the secular culture – that Christian truth finds its authority in the sovereignty of individual adhesion to Scripture.

The processes of the Second Vatican Council themselves demonstrated the differences of these two positions. As at the First Vatican Council, there were abundant evidences of fixing behind the scenes, especially in the earlier stages when a not-too-well-hidden campaign by reformers successfully sought to open up the proceedings to more generous acceptance of changes in the thought of the modern world. These manoeuvrings, however, occurred within a general framework still subscribed by all, except a very small fringe of theologians whose leading intellectual presuppositions were anyway, by surely any standards, Protestant. To behold a large conference of authentic Protestants – a World Council of Churches General Assembly, or an Anglican Lambeth Conference – is to observe a quite different gathering. In place of the Council fathers, with their sense of internal authority and organic responsibility, these Protestant gatherings are occasions of individual judgement by the collected assemblage of diverse moralists. The results are resolutions of majorities, not the discovery of the mind of an organic unity. There may, of course, be all kinds of good reasons why this is the case, and if Christ did not, after all, commit the knowledge of himself to an infallible institution, then a periodic demonstration of scarcely controlled ecclesiastical shambles might be an unavoidable accompaniment of the diversity of truth as perceived by fallible men. Or it could be too great an absorption into the world's own priorities.

The Second Vatican Council, at any rate, was an attempt to allow the Catholic Church to address itself to the world in terms the world could recognize, but not in worldly terms. It was virtually the only Council not to have produced a schism in the process. That is, in itself, an indication of its success; and however painful may have been the adjustments to the non-Tridentine Mass – and those other accidents of things which seem so pressing at the time, but in the perspective of centuries are not – they are as nothing compared to the maintenance of the unity of the faithful during a period of unprecedented change in the history of the world. Enormous difficulties in the continuation of that unity lie ahead, as education spreads and more and more Christians lay claim to express their beliefs, with individual emphases. The Council, however, has set an example of diversity within unity which it would be difficult, perhaps impossible, to better.

INDEX